Grace Abounds

Northwestern Publishing House
1250 N. 113th St., Milwaukee, WI 53226-3284
www.nph.net

Published 2015
Printed in the United States of America
ISBN 978-0-8100-2657-5
ISBN 978-0-8100-2658-2 (e-book)

26 27 28 29 30 31 32 33 34 35 13 12 11 10 9 8 7 6 5 4

GRACE ABOUNDS

The SPLENDOR of CHRISTIAN DOCTRINE

DANIEL M. DEUTSCHLANDER

NORTHWESTERN PUBLISHING HOUSE
Milwaukee, Wisconsin

Contents

Preface

This book is intended to serve a couple of rather different purposes. First of all, it is the author's hope that it might be used in doctrine courses in our Lutheran high schools or in such other courses as might be offered in churches or schools for the education of our laity in the chief doctrines of the Bible as taught by confessional Lutheran church bodies. As such, this book is a summary of what the Bible and our Lutheran Confessions teach.

Second, it is the author's hope that Lutherans may find this work useful as a reference. That is, someone may be wondering what the Bible teaches about one particular doctrine; a person may wonder, for example, what the Bible has to say about the sacraments or about faith or about the two natures of Christ. The chapter headings of this work could be consulted and answers could be found to that person's specific question, why the answer is important, and how that answer relates to other doctrines in the Bible.

Those very purposes may present the reader with a couple of problems with this book, which in this Preface we would like to anticipate.

First of all, the reader will find in this work that there is a good deal of repetition of certain central teachings. The second purpose of the book is one of the reasons for that repetition. Doctrine is, so to speak, whole cloth. There is no such thing as just one doctrine that can be considered in isolation from all other doctrines. Our German fathers recognized that when many of them declined to ever use the word *doctrine* in the plural; for them all doctrine was tied together in a harmonious whole. To deny anything that the Bible teaches was to harm either directly or indirectly everything else that the Bible teaches.

Thus especially four doctrines will appear in one way or another in just about every chapter. Those four doctrines are like gold and silver threads that make their way through the entire tapestry of God's Word. Those doctrines, which inform and affect all others, are

1. the doctrine of original sin together with its consequences
2. the doctrine of justification, that doctrine by which the church, as our fathers said, stands or falls
3. the doctrine of the means of grace
4. the doctrine of the theology of the cross

What ties these doctrines together and makes them each in their turn so vitally important is Christ. The doctrine of original sin shows us our total, our absolute, and our desperate need for him and for his work. The doctrine of justification shows us the triumphant and saving consequence of his work for us. The doctrine of the means of grace shows us how the great miracle of what he did for us is crowned with the great miracle that through the gospel we believe it. And the doctrine of the theology of the cross shows us how in life, as a consequence of his cross, we bear willingly the cross that Christ sends us; for he sends the cross to keep us close to him and to bring us finally to share in his glory in heaven.

Thus it is to Christ that this book returns again and again. It has been our aim that he should be its center, really its whole, just as he is the center of the Bible itself and its whole point. It is to the praise of his name that this work is dedicated. And it is without apology that this praise of him and thanksgiving for his work resounds through every chapter and in every doctrine.

At any rate, we hope that the person reading through the book will not find the repetition annoying. Those using this work as a reference book may, on the other hand, find it quite useful; to such the work will seem more unified by virtue of that very repetition which someone else might find a bit annoying.

The second problem that some may have with this work is that it is at times polemical. That is, in the consideration of individual doctrines, no attempt is made to hide the fact that many disagree with what the Bible teaches concerning the doctrine under consideration. It is popular in our day to imagine that all doctrines, all differences in what churches or religions teach, are just matters of personal opinion or interpretation. These bromides are very popular: "Well, it doesn't really matter what you believe, as long as you believe something" or "It doesn't matter what you believe, as long as you are sincere" or "Well, ultimately there is only one God and he loves everybody, so it doesn't matter what name you call him; we're all going to heaven anyway, because a God of love would never send anyone to hell." A poll taken on the street would without any doubt find any or all such utterances acceptable to the vast majority of those asked. We thoroughly reject such notions as blasphemous insults to God, the ultimate Author of the Holy Scriptures. For it is God who says, "This is the one I esteem: he who is humble and contrite in spirit, and trembles at my word" (Isaiah 66:2).

Accordingly, with the humble recognition that we know nothing of him with certainty and nothing at all of the way of salvation apart from his Word, in the contrite awareness that all of our life apart from Christ and his redeeming work is fit only for eternal wrath and punishment, and trembling in awe before the majesty of the God who has loved us and given himself for us in Christ, we believe, teach, and confess what is contained in the following chapters. And without apology we reject the errors of those who either out of ignorance or malice confound, deny, or attack anything that God teaches us in his holy, inerrant, and verbally inspired Word. We agree with our Lutheran Confessions that any teaching of the truth that does not expose and reject error is a failure to teach the whole truth of God's Word. The Formula of Concord, for example, declares:

> In order to preserve pure teaching and fundamental, lasting, God-pleasing unity in the church, it is necessary not only to present the pure, beneficial teaching correctly, but also to censure those who contradict it and teach other doctrines (1 Tim. 3[:9]; Titus 1[:9]). For, as Luther states, true shepherds are to do both: pasture or feed the sheep and ward off the wolves, so that they may flee from other voices (John 10[:4b-5,16b]) and "separate the precious from the vile." (Jer. 15[:19, Vulgate])
>
> [While shunning] unnecessary and useless quarrels . . . , false teaching, which is contrary to these articles, must be repudiated. (FC SD RN, 14,15 pp. 529,530)[1]

Often in the coming chapters when an error is being exposed and refuted, the reader will come across what are for us and our forefathers the three compelling and identifying marks of all heresy, of all false doctrine. We will take brief note of them now as our defense for the polemics, which the reader may find at times difficult. All false teaching has these three identifying characteristics; where one of them is found, the other two will rarely be far away. False doctrine

1. contradicts the clear teaching of the Scriptures
2. robs Christ of his glory
3. deprives the stubborn sinner of salutary warning and the penitent sinner of needed comfort

Any one of those reasons should be sufficient for all of us to be ever on our guard against false teaching. These reasons should as well make

---

[1]All quotations from the Lutheran Confessions are from *The Book of Concord: The Confessions of the Evangelical Lutheran Church,* edited by Robert Kolb and Timothy J. Wengert (Minneapolis: Augsburg Fortress Press, 2000).

us ever more eager to learn as much as we can of God's saving Word. And, all those reasons should bring us to an ever-growing gratitude for who our God is, for what he has done for us, especially in the person and work of Christ, and then for his amazing grace in giving it all to us freely by the faith created and sustained through his saving Word.

Finally, some may consider a book that attempts to present a summary of doctrine for laypeople unnecessary. After all, we have our pastors and the teachers of the church to take care of doctrine, to see that it is taught in its truth and purity, and to guard the faith of the church against error. Why bother laypeople with that sort of thing? The simple answer is that purity of doctrine is too important to be left to the "professionals." That certainly was Jesus' attitude as well when he instructed the sheep to be on guard against false teachers in Matthew 7:15. That likewise was the attitude of Peter, Paul, and John in their epistles; their letters are addressed not just to pastors and teachers but to all believers. For all of us share in the blessings of God's Word and sacraments, and all of us share as well in the obligation, yes, the high honor, of both defending his saving Word and sharing it. That too was the attitude of our Lutheran forefathers—it was at the request of laymen that *The Book of Concord* was assembled and presented to the church.

In the writing of this book we have tried to keep Greek, Latin, and German words to a minimum. But some words are either so much a part of a theological vocabulary or else so expressive of some point that to pass them by altogether was simply not possible. We beg the kind indulgence of those unfamiliar with these languages; we trust that there will be some using this work who are familiar with these languages of the church and who accordingly will find the terms employed of some benefit.

We commend the following pages with the prayer that the reader will find the work a clear and faithful exposition of the body of doctrine committed to us by our God and Savior in his Word. We pray as well that the reader may thereby be edified and encouraged in faith, in love, and in life that finds its source and center in Jesus Christ our Savior.

Abbreviations

Lutheran Confessions

AC Augsburg Confession
Ap Apology of the Augsburg Confession
SA Smalcald Articles
Tr Treatise on the Power and Primacy of the Pope
SC Small Catechism
LC Large Catechism
FC Formula of Concord
RN Rule and Norm
Ep Epitome
SD Solid Declaration

Other abbreviations

e.g. for example
et al. and others
i.e. that is

PART I

Prolegomena

Chapter 1
What Is Religion?

In every nation, language, and culture one will find religion. The religion may be a highly developed and formalized one. It may have doctrines and rituals, usually with a teaching or priestly group that watches over and transmits the teachings and performs the required rituals. It may have a complex set of rules or regulations dealing with diet, festivals, hours of prayer, positions for prayer, and the like. It probably will have a mechanism for dealing with either the possible evolution of teaching or of disciplining those who deviate from it.

On the other hand, there are religions that are very simple and devoid of almost all the elements of the more highly developed and formalized religions of the world. The spirit worshipers of tribal societies in Africa and Asia and in the Americas have little in the way of organization or set doctrines. But simple religion is not the exclusive domain of primitive societies. Highly sophisticated cultures in Asia, Europe, and North America also have a number of very simple religions, religions in which the only doctrine is the feeling of the moment and the only truth that which seems true to the individual at any given time. In between highly organized religions and very simple religions we will find just about every variation on the scale that can be imagined.

Definition of the term

What then is religion? The word itself knows of no easy definition. Each religion would probably define the word a little differently. But at the base of all the definitions we would find the following closely related characteristics:

1. A religion is a system of few or many beliefs dealing with dimly understood needs inherent in the human race.
2. A religion is a system of few or many ways and means of dealing with dimly understood forces beyond direct human observation or outside of human control.

The universal presence and existence of religions and religious life of one kind or another points to natural, inherent, deeply rooted, and almost irresistible longings inside of human beings. By nature we ask questions that have supernatural or religious significance. We yearn to know: *Why am I here? Where have I come from? Where has everything around me come from and why does it exist? Where am I going? What is the point and purpose of life, of joy, of suffering, of death? What happens after death? Is there a God out there? Am I accountable to him? If there is a God, does he control all of life, part of it, or none of it? How can I know that any of the answers to any of these questions are the right answers? Is there more than one right answer?* In religions from the simplest to the most complex these questions are of primary importance. Religions exist to deal with and provide answers to these questions.

The Bible speaks of these longings for answers to questions that are part and parcel of what it means to be a human being. It addresses the ways in which people may find at least partial answers to their questions about life and its meaning, about the existence of God and his relationship to the world and those who dwell in it. The doctrine that treats of the natural ways in which we can know about God and our relationship to God we call the doctrine of

The natural knowledge of God.

St. Paul made reference to the natural knowledge of God in his sermon in Athens. For generations Athens had been and still was in St. Paul's day the center of intellectual life in the Mediterranean world. Many of the most brilliant men who ever lived, men like Plato and Aristotle, taught there. St. Luke, in introducing Paul's sermon, tells us that the men of Athens and foreigners who came there were devoted to nothing else than discussing the latest ideas, ideas which often dealt with the nature of man, of life and death, of the existence and nature of God (Acts 17:21).

At the beginning of his sermon St. Paul recognized the desire of the Athenians to find and to know God. He said, "As I walked around and looked carefully at your objects of worship, I even found an altar with this inscription: TO AN UNKNOWN GOD" (Acts 17:23). That altar bore witness to two universal truths recognized by almost everyone. On the one hand, people have a sense that there is something outside of and above us to whom we owe worship. The Athenians did not want to fall short in their devotion to whomever that might be or to however many such beings there might be. On the other hand, the altar also bore witness to the uncertainty in our natural knowledge of God. The Athenians were sure that there was something "out there," but they did not know with any certainty what that something was. It was evident to the Athenians that by ourselves we may search for God, but we will never be certain that we have found him. We may make good or bad guesses about him, but we can of ourselves never be absolutely sure which guesses are good and which are not.

The best guesses people make about God are based on evidence that God himself has planted in nature. That evidence bears witness to God's existence and to at least some of his attributes or characteristics. That which we can discover about God from nature we call *the natural knowledge of God.*

The witness of nature and conclusions of reason

There are two basic sources for the natural knowledge of God. The first is observable or physical nature itself. Psalm 19:1-4 speaks eloquently of the witness of nature to the existence of God. The psalmist sings, "The heavens declare the glory of God; the skies proclaim the work of his hands. Day after day they pour forth speech; night after night they display knowledge. There is no speech or language where their voice is not heard. Their voice goes out into all the earth, their words to the ends of the world." Where is there a nation or race that has not pondered the witness of nature to the existence of God? The more we know of nature, the more beautiful its witness. Look at the sky with the naked eye, or examine it through a telescope or from a telescope on a space station. All that we see in space declares the glory, might, and majesty of God.

Whether considered in its greatness or in small details, the study of nature suggests much more than the mere existence of God. Nature, for example, tells us that he is powerful. It suggests that he must be even more powerful than nature or than all the power of nature combined. For a power less than that in nature could not have produced power greater than itself. The power of God must be a power above and beyond nature. The power evident in our sun alone is beyond calculation. The power needed to create the sun, the moon, and all the stars is beyond imagination. Nature declares the power of God.

Nature also tells us that God is wise—yes, wiser than anything in creation—with a wisdom above and beyond the created. What wisdom lies behind the relationship between the planets, between plants and animals, between the smallest parts of nature and the largest! The sun warms the earth and draws the waters to the sky. The waters fall again to thirsty fields and forests, to plants and animals. The plants produce food for the animals, and the animals produce nourishment for the plants. And it all happens, not in a gray and mechanical fashion, but with a profusion of color and variety. There is the delicacy of a rose throwing off its scent in a breeze as well as the strength of a whale splashing in the oceans. What wisdom, what genius! We can only but scratch the surface of the proclamation that day and night nature displays a wisdom unfathomable.

Nature also points to the truth that God is a God of order. All that we observe in nature follows certain predictable rules and laws. Gravity is reliable. The orderly rotation of the planets and the changing of the seasons are never in doubt. The orderly relationship of cause and effect is evident everywhere in nature, in what we call the natural order of things. Winds above the surface of the water or earthquakes below cause waves. Changes in the oceans cause changes in the weather on land. Planting, watering, and feeding cause growth. Even death and decay, destruction and renewal in nature have a kind of order in them. Order stretches over all things great and small, with all of nature working in a marvelous harmony. The order in the universe and in nature points to One who caused the order, One beyond and above nature and all things created.

The order that proclaims the glory of God in the skies and on earth happens in fulfillment of God's express promise to Noah. After the flood, God promised, "As long as the earth endures, seedtime and harvest, cold and heat, summer and winter, day and night will never cease" (Genesis 8:22). God has kept that promise so perfectly that the order he implanted in his creation testifies of his glory to people living in every corner of the earth, whether or not they know of that promise.

These attributes of God, his power and his wisdom and the order in him that is reflected in his creation, should be obvious to all. They so clearly point to a divine creator that the Bible sees no need to declare that God exists. The existence of all these things testifies to his existence. For all material things have a cause. That they would have no cause strikes a reasonable person as absurd. Thus, the Bible too declares that "the fool says in his heart, 'There is no God'" (Psalm 14:1; 53:1).

Nature reveals yet other attributes of God that to some are obvious but that to others are not so obvious. Some viewing nature may conclude, for example, that God is good. As we observe beauty in nature or experience good things in life or ponder the richness of variety and color and order in creation, we may conclude that God is good, especially to human beings. For God has designed all human beings in such a way that we may see and appreciate and enjoy nature like no other creature. From that perceived goodness some may even conclude that a God who is so good to humankind must be also a God who loves humankind. The perception of God's goodness, perhaps even of God's love, moves some to seek him or even to seek ways of pleasing him.

Still others may draw the conclusion from nature that God is capable of great anger. They see the struggle of some and the misery of others that come because of disasters in weather or plagues of sickness or personal tragedy. Instead of order, they see only chaos. They note that at the end of all struggle there is a final defeat: we die. Those especially who consider the evidence of God's anger in nature may turn to religion as a way of stilling or escaping the anger of God or of lessening it.

Finally, some, looking at the same evidence, may give up in confusion and come to the least rational conclusion of all. They may conclude that if there is a God, he is indifferent to all that he has made with such power, wisdom, and care. They despair of either finding him or pleasing him.

Natural law and the witness of conscience

That brings us to the second major source for the natural knowledge of God. The second source is locked deep inside of people, planted there by God himself. It consists of the *natural law* and the *conscience.* People know by nature that some things are right and some things are wrong. They have a standard implanted within them from conception and birth. To be sure, that standard of right and wrong will vary from individual to individual. It may to some extent be shaped, refined, or distorted by education, class prejudice, or cultural taboos of an unknown origin. But at bottom that standard contains some fairly universal elements. Everyone knows that stealing is wrong. Everyone knows that murder is wrong. Everyone knows that unfaithfulness to a spouse or to a friend is wrong. While everyone may agree that these things are wrong, there may be much less agreement on the exact definition of stealing, of murder, or of unfaithfulness. For example, is it stealing when a government redistributes wealth by means of a tax code? Or is it stealing when a starving person grabs a loaf of bread from the bakery? While all grant that stealing is wrong, there is no universally agreed upon definition of what constitutes stealing. Is the execution of a murderer itself murder? Is it unfaithfulness when one is unfaithful to an unfaithful spouse or friend? These questions too admit of no universally accepted answer, even though all agree that murder and unfaithfulness are wrong.

Thus it is difficult to define with precision all that belongs to natural law. In some people the standard is a highly developed one. In others it is but a dim reflection of the law that God wrote on the heart of the human race at the beginning. A sense of the natural law can be sharpened by reflection. It can be diminished by a conscious attempt to wipe it out. We see an example of the first in the great philosopher Aristotle (384–322 B.C.), especially in his masterpiece, *The Nicomachean Ethics.* Few if any in recorded history have written as brilliantly as he did on the subject of good and evil, right and wrong. The standard inherent in him was refined and developed by a keen intellect. Other philosophers have attempted as well to figure out how societies and cultures originally came up with their assorted legal codes. Montesquieu (1689–1755) in his *The Spirit of the Laws* sought logical explanations for assumed standards of right and wrong. So too did Rousseau (1712–1778) in his *Social Contract.* These and countless other thinkers have searched in history and in their own minds both for a standard of right and wrong and also for an explanation of how one should judge such standards. Though their answers vary considerably, the search itself bears witness to at least a dim original standard imprinted on or inherent in man.

On the other hand, many have used equally keen intellects to erase the natural law. Among the ancient Greek philosophers, the Sophists became very clever at defending any course of action as right. In more recent times existentialist philosophers like Kant (1724–1804) and Kierkegaard (1813–1855) have opposed vigorously any notion that there is such a thing as a moral absolute, or absolute truth, or an absolute standard of right and wrong written in the human heart by God. Since their day much of present-day psychological and educational theory likewise has opposed any notion of absolute right and wrong inherent in our nature.

In spite of all attempts, however, to wipe out the very idea of natural law written on the human heart, *conscience* still testifies to the presence of that natural law. The conscience sits in judgment over behavior according to the standard of right and wrong inside of a person. Just as that natural law standard may vary from person to person, so too may the judging voice of conscience. Some people have a sharp conscience and some have a dull one. But whether sharp or dull, all have by nature this implanted judge—the conscience. If one violates the standard of law in his own heart, his conscience accuses and we say that such a person has a guilty conscience. Technically, it is not the conscience that is guilty; it is the individual who is guilty.

His behavior has violated whatever code of law he accepts, and his conscience now condemns him as guilty. If one obeys the standard of law, the conscience applauds, and we say that such a person has a good conscience. Again, technically it is not the conscience that is good. Rather, the individual whose behavior has conformed to the standard of such law as his heart embraces is called good by the conscience. Some go to great pains to silence the conscience by ignoring it or simply by denying even that conscience exists. Nevertheless, it is virtually impossible to completely eliminate either the natural law or the conscience, so deeply are they embedded in our nature.

The presence of both the natural law and the conscience point to the existence of God who implanted them and to yet another of his attributes. Conscience especially points to God's attribute of justice. Even people who do not consider themselves "religious" may say things such as, "Well, George finally got what was coming to him." Then out comes the story of the evil that George did, along with the evil that he is now suffering. Behind the statement "got what was coming to him" lays the assumption that there is a judge of human actions. That judge weighs actions in a balance and sooner or later hands out to the evil that which they deserve. There are many similar expressions in English idiom that people use every day. For example, there is the old adage that says, "What goes around comes around" or "Sooner or later it had to happen." All such have behind them the assumption of a just judge out there somewhere. That judge who balances the scales is, of course, God.

As already noted, great philosophers have speculated for centuries about the origins of various law codes that have emerged from every culture and civilization. But the simple fact is that with all of their guessing they cannot account with any sense of certainty for the universal presence of laws in all societies. The laws emerge from an essentially interior process in human beings, a standard of right and wrong written on our hearts from the beginning.

Conscience, on the other hand, drives people to search for the God who stands behind conscience and to whom conscience and the natural law bear witness. Conscience at its best draws us to conclude that there is a God who is a just judge of all people and of all actions. When conscience drives people also to consider that God is powerful, they begin to fear him. In that fear they seek ways of dealing with him. All man-made religions are an attempt to deal with the God who is behind the natural law and the conscience.

St. Paul captures both the reality of the message about God taught by conscience and the interesting ways in which people try to deal with

God who confronts them in their conscience. He speaks eloquently about the conscience as a source of the natural knowledge of God in the first two chapters of his epistle to the Romans. He tells us:

> Indeed, when Gentiles, who do not have the law [i.e., the written law of God, given to Moses on Mount Sinai], do by nature things required by the law, they are a law for themselves, even though they do not have the law, since they show that the requirements of the law are written on their hearts, their consciences also bearing witness, and their thoughts now accusing, now even defending them. (Romans 2:14,15)

Sadly, the religions that are invented to deal with the God behind the conscience often end up teaching things that contradict both conscience and natural law. St. Paul describes such religions and the perversity of those who invent and follow them. He speaks of religions that turned the God of conscience and the God of power into created animals that were worshiped as a substitute for God. For example, the Egyptians found it easy to think of the cat as a god. After all, it was the cat that kept the population of mice in check so that grain could be stored in storehouses; without such storehouses, city life would have been impossible. So Egyptians worshiped the cat god. The Nile was the vital element for irrigation, which made Egypt the breadbasket of the ancient world. So the god of the river or the river itself was worshiped. The hope of the worshiper was that the respective gods would then be favorable to the land and the worshiper and that they would not punish the evil deeds of the nation but reward those that were good.

Worse still, in an attempt to quiet the voice of conscience when it condemned their evil deeds, people began inventing gods who favored what conscience called evil. The fertility cults of both the ancient world and the present-day world do exactly that. There have been religions devoted to the worship of sex, sexual acts, and sexual organs. With such worship people pervert both the natural law and conscience. The performance of evil becomes an act of worship. That is basically what Baal worship was in the Old Testament. Baal was worshiped by adultery, fornication, and self-mutilation. That is also what much of the worship in the Greek and Roman world of St. Paul's day amounted to. Everyone knows that Bacchus, for example, was supposed to be the god of wine—he was worshiped by drunkenness. Temples to various goddesses had temple prostitutes as part of the permanent staff. Today, the temples of such gods and goddesses still exist.

Even in societies that have no such temples, the attempts to deal with the God behind the conscience and the natural law are no more sophisticated than the worship of Baal or Bacchus. Instead of making gods out of vices, and thus stilling the condemning voice of conscience, people now simply deny that there is any such thing as conscience or natural law or a just God who stands behind that natural law and conscience. They make a religion out of the latest theories of philosophers and psychologists. If people can convince themselves that they are just animals on a slightly higher scale, then animal behavior—and worse—can easily be sanctioned. If people can convince themselves that the natural law and the voice of conscience are just conditioned societal reflexes, then too perhaps conscience can be stilled and any behavior rationalized. If people can persuade themselves that there really is no God, then they need not concern themselves with absolute standards of right and wrong taught by natural law and enforced by conscience. Then good becomes whatever the individual wants at the moment, and evil is whatever gets in the way. Power and sexual pleasure become gods that affirm or prove human existence just as in the ancient world. All of that is nothing but the religion of the Baal and Bacchus worshipers in a new but still very tattered and tacky dress.

That individuals, societies, and whole cultures could invent religions contrary to all natural law and conscience is itself a testimony to the power of conscience as well as to the power of evil. So great does the love of evil become that conscience must be overcome by the virtual worship of the evil. St. Paul in Romans 1 is speaking of just such things when he tells us:

> The wrath of God is being revealed from heaven against all the godlessness and wickedness of men who suppress the truth by their wickedness, since what may be known about God is plain to them, because God has made it plain to them. For since the creation of the world God's invisible qualities—his eternal power and divine nature—have been clearly seen, being understood from what has been made, so that men are without excuse.
>
> For although they knew God, they neither glorified him as God nor gave thanks to him, but their thinking became futile and their foolish hearts were darkened. Although they claimed to be wise, they became fools and exchanged the glory of the immortal God for images made to look like mortal men and birds and animals and reptiles.
>
> Therefore God gave them over in the sinful desires of their hearts to sexual impurity for the degrading of their bodies with

> one another. They exchanged the truth of God for a lie, and worshiped and served created things rather than the Creator. (Romans 1:18-25)

The apostle continues with a description of their further descent into evil. But the chief point we want to note here is that even the descent into the worst wickedness is part of an attempt to still the voice of conscience and the natural law either by denying their existence or by the worship of the vices condemned in the natural law and the voice of conscience.

To be sure, not all man-made religions or religious practices descend into the depths of depravity described in Romans 1. Some religions may enforce an outwardly rigorous moral standard. They may listen very carefully to the natural law and the voice of conscience. They may even go beyond the natural law and the voice of conscience in an attempt to appease the anger of God against violations of natural law. Thus, for example, if conscience condemns sexual immorality, they may prescribe celibate lives in the vain hope of eliminating sexual immorality. Monasticism and asceticism, both ancient and present-day, have something of that attitude in them. If drunkenness is a sin, make all drinking a sin, so that drunkenness will be impossible. If greed is evil, make poverty a virtue or make economic equality a religious goal so that the possibility of getting rich is eliminated (as though that would eliminate greed or the desire for wealth!).

Still other man-made religions seek to satisfy the God behind nature, the natural law, and the conscience with ritual. The Hindu washes in the Ganges River. The Muslim makes a pilgrimage to Mecca and prays toward the holy city at prescribed hours of the day. The Shinto person offers sacrifice to his ancestors.

Yet other religions seek unification with the invisible God whom they perceive in nature and in themselves by renunciation of the material world. The Buddhist shuns pleasure and the physical world as he searches for enlightenment. The Hindu hopes for unification with God after countless reincarnations. Pantheist and animist religions in Asia, Africa, and in tribal societies in the Americas make nature itself a god and thus worship the spirits of forests, rivers, and mountains; of fertility; and even of death.

The list could go on and on. But all of the religions and religious practices so far discussed have one fatal flaw: They all lack certainty. Some religions and religious practices turn vice into virtue, and others turn virtue into vice. Some acknowledge both virtue and vice and attempt to appease the God who judges both. Some in despair of ever knowing what is true deny that there is any such thing as truth. Some are satisfied that there is truth and a God out there, but they confess to ignorance of his ultimate essence or purpose—and hope that he is indifferent to their essence and purpose as well. Regardless of the almost infinite number of differences in the religions of the world, all man-made religions share this common trait: Not one of them can legitimately assure its followers that it is the one and only true religion. At best one can claim to be the most reasonable of all the alternatives and attempt to prove its case from reason, or even from natural law and conscience.

Anthropocentric religions

Observable nature on the outside, the natural law and conscience on the inside of man—all these point to the existence of God. They indicate various attributes of God—some clearly, some less clearly. But the natural knowledge of God in nature, the natural law, and conscience can never tell us who God is. Nor can they tell us with certainty what he wants of us, how he relates to us, or how we should relate to him. All man-made religions therefore are essentially *anthropocentric,* meaning they are human centered; they make man the ultimate measure of truth, even of the definition of God. They are not *theocentric,* meaning God centered; they cannot claim the voice of God himself for their origin or their definition of any proper relationship with God. They cannot trace their origin in history to the beginning of history. They cannot with the voice of the prophets show God's promises and their fulfillment. A truly theocentric religion has God at the center—God as the source of truth, the source of right and wrong, the source of life and death, the source of immortality, and all that belongs to these categories. Religion that is anthropocentric will reflect dimly at best what all should know of God from nature, natural law, and conscience. But their laws, their doctrines, and their rituals are of human invention. Ultimately, the decision of what to do, what to teach, and what to believe is found in human beings who are frail and uncertain at best and whose self-chosen doctrines, therefore, can never have any real or absolute certainty about them.

Because they are anthropocentric and not theocentric, man-made religions ultimately fail to satisfy the ultimate purposes and goals of religion. They cannot answer with certainty the questions: Why am I here? What purpose is there in all that exists? How can I have a sure and certain peace with God? What is the point of pain and suffering? What is the reason for death, and where do we go, if anywhere, after death? Their answers are merely guesses, even though the teachers of anthropocentric religions may be sincere and their followers may be satisfied with them and wholeheartedly trust in them.

Anthropocentric religions, to be sure, have an entire arsenal of weapons with which to do battle for the allegiance of their followers. A religion may appeal to reason in support of its answers to the basic questions of life and death. But reason is often self-contradictory. A reasonable argument can be made for opposite propositions. For example, a reasonable argument can be made for both of the following religious propositions: Since we cannot prove that there is life after death, it is reasonable to conclude that there is no life after death; or since no life and certainly no suffering make sense without life after death, there must be a life after death. Both arguments have a kind of rational appeal to them, but only one of the two conclusions can be correct. Reason alone cannot settle the argument. Something more is needed.

Perhaps the something beyond reason will be emotion. But emotions too, so long as they are merely and purely human emotions, are most unreliable guarantors of truth or certainty. Emotions are also contradictory. One person purely out of emotion declares confidently, "I just really feel that God wants me to live forever." Another can answer with equal confidence, "I just feel that God wants us all to find him now and never mind about hereafter." Both cannot be right. The religion that goes from an appeal to reason on to an appeal to emotion still lacks any real certainty.

In an attempt to provide some degree of certainty, many people will turn to science for answers to their religious longings. But science is not qualified to pass judgment on what it cannot observe or test. It cannot test for a purpose to all that exists. It cannot test for a reason to live. It cannot test for an ultimate source or first cause of things created. It cannot test for the wholly immaterial (e.g., the existence of the soul or even of reason itself) or answer any questions about the immaterial. Thus, answers to religious questions based on the scientific method alone are doomed from the start. For the scientific method does not deal with ultimate source and cause. It deals only with the observable results of some ultimate source and cause. It may point to the existence of such a source and cause, but it cannot identify it.

Thus, reason and emotion and science provide inadequate bases for religion. They are anthropocentric and therefore uncertain and contradictory. Though they point in one way or another to the existence of

God, they cannot tell us who he is, who we are, why we are here, or where we are going.

Perhaps the best that reason, emotion, and science could do with the matter of religion would be to conclude: If there is a God and if he wants something from us or a relationship with us, then he must reveal himself. For reason cannot find its own source, emotion is fickle, and science can only have any competence at all in things that it can observe or test. The author of reason, the one above all fickle emotion, and the creator of all that science can observe or investigate must be altogether above and beyond reason, emotion, and science.

Therefore all attempts at answering the great questions suggested by the natural knowledge of God in reason, emotion, and science are doomed to failure from the start. They can only witness to the truth that there must be a God. But they cannot reach him unaided. To think otherwise is both the height of folly and arrogance. And that's the great irony: even the best guesses of reason, emotion, and science are irrational, fickle, and unscientific. Reason, emotion, and science on their best day must confess that they are altogether incapable of answering with any degree of certainty the great questions of life—the very questions that religion proposes to answer.

St. Paul brilliantly captures that exact thought in one of the lines from his great doxology in Romans 11, when he exults in verse 34, "Who has known the mind of the Lord? Or who has been his counselor?" God speaks in a similar vein in the Old Testament when he addresses Job in chapters 38 and 39.

St. Paul goes on in his doxology with a verse that rejects yet another characteristic flaw of all anthropocentric religion. He sings, "'Who has ever given to God, that God should repay him?' For from him and through him and to him are all things" (Romans 11:35,36). What the apostle here declares to be an absolute truth flies in the face of another characteristic of all anthropocentric religion. Anthropocentric religion is always work-righteousness. It begins with the assumption that we by our behavior or works can satisfy God. Even the most decadent religious practices, practices that fly in the face of natural law and do violence to conscience, are performed as part of an effort to satisfy God. The adulterous worship of Baal was supposed to please him. Human sacrifice does violence to all natural law and conscience, but nevertheless it was performed as a supreme act to please the gods of the Moabites (2 Kings 3:27) and others. Even the religions of those who deny the existence of absolute truth or of divinely implanted natural law and conscience teach that human behavior will satisfy whatever there is of God out there somewhere. The teaching may be as simple as "Do no harm," "Do the best you can," or "Love!" Such is the religion of the Deists, Unitarians, and the like.

Religions that take conscience more seriously and do not attempt to deny its judgments place a greater emphasis on specific works designed to satisfy an angry God. Hindus and Muslims for example have prescribed ceremonies for removing guilt. Such ceremonies are over and above the expectation that the follower should lead a life according to the law prescribed by the religion.

Even Christian religions, to the extent that they depart from their source, Christ and his Word, end up sharing in this common characteristic of anthropocentric and humanly devised religion: They make man's efforts the key to pleasing God and removing guilt. But St. Paul shatters the vain imagination of all such anthropocentric efforts to merit God's favor with that one simple sentence: "Who has ever given to God, that God should repay him?"

Summary

In sum, human beings are by nature religious. That is, they seek answers to basic questions of their existence. The questions are religious in nature and the answers, no matter where they are sought and found, are thus also religious answers. That is so even when the answers are limited to answers from reason, emotion, and science. The questions and the answers are attempts to deal with the natural knowledge of God as it exists in nature, in natural law, and in the conscience. But as varied as the answers are, to the extent that they have only the natural knowledge of God as their starting point, they are inadequate answers. For the natural knowledge of God can tell us only that God exists and suggest some of his attributes. It can tell us neither who he is nor how we should relate to him. Such knowledge must have a source outside of nature, outside of the natural knowledge implanted in mankind at creation.

So desperate have some been to find that source outside of and above nature that they have resorted to extreme and bizarre measures. In both the ancient world and in the present-day there have often been cults that seek the divine by means of drug-induced trances. Hoping to go beyond the veil that separates life and death, the finite and the infinite, their followers see strange visions during their trances and trust that their visions are revelations from God. The visions however never make any real sense; they require someone to interpret them. The interpretation rarely has anything at all to do with the vision. Again, the religion that results, though it attempts to have a source outside of reason, emotion, and science, is still anthropocentric, totally lacking in certainty, with only illusions and delusions for content. The same conclusion applies to religious information sought from horoscopes, seances, and the like. While the purveyors and followers of such things seek answers from the God who is above nature by ignoring nature, they end up with empty shells that they insist still contain pearls of wisdom.

Any religion that deals only with the natural knowledge of God, whether to deny or affirm it, is anthropocentric. It lacks certainty. It is work-righteousness. Any religion that seeks answers to our basic human longings in opposition to the natural knowledge of God by drug-induced trances, by the reading of horoscopes, by séances, and the like is altogether folly, having no foundation at all in reality—much less in God.

Standing in sharp contrast to all such religions, their very antithesis, is biblical Christianity. It alone of all religions, while affirming the importance of the natural knowledge of God, is *theocentric;* that is, it is based on the *revealed knowledge of God.*

Chapter 2
The Bible: Its Inspiration and Use

The names

Of all the religions of the world, Christianity makes a unique claim. The claim is that it alone possesses the mind of God through his own revelation of himself in his written Word and in the incarnation of his Son. It is the first of these unique aspects of Christianity that we will examine in this chapter—God's unique revelation of himself in his written Word.

The uniqueness of the Christian claim is already evident in the name given to the object of our study. It is called *the Bible.* The term simply and most profoundly means "the Book." In reality it is a collection of 66 books. However, so united in ultimate authorship, in purpose, in message, and in combined effect is that collection that it has the single designation of *the Book.* It is not just a book, one among many, but *the Book.* If all the other books of the world would perish, this one will never perish. Had no other book ever been written, this one would have been. If we had access to no other book, just by having this one we would have access to the mind and heart of God and he to us, we would have purpose for this life, and we would have life eternal.

It is also called by another equally simple and profound designation: *the sacred Scriptures.* The phrase simply means "the holy writings." There are many writings in the world considered by millions to be holy writings. There are the writings of Muhammad—the Koran. There are the ancient books of the Hindus, the sayings of Confucius, the works of Mary Baker Eddy (who founded the Christian Science religion), and the writings that make up the *Book of Mormon.* All these claim to be sacred. But none of these works have God himself as their ultimate author. None of them can claim human instruments of divine authorship stretching over more than a thousand years, with but one and the same central message progressively unfolded through the ages. None of them can point to that special aspect of prophecies fulfilled, some near to the time of the prophecy itself, some hundreds of years later. None of them, in short, can demonstrate divine authorship the way the Bible does. The Bible is altogether unique in its aspects of prophecy and fulfillment. It is altogether unique, most important, in its faith-creating message of salvation by grace through faith in the work of its Author, who came down from heaven for us and for our salvation. Yes, the Bible is uniquely sacred because of its divine authorship; and it is sacred as well because of the holy work of God in Christ that he reveals and gives to us in it for our salvation.

There are still other books that we might consider holy. We think of the writings of the great church fathers, the works of St. Athanasius, St. Augustine, Martin Luther, and others. We think of the great written confessions of the faith—the three Ecumenical Creeds and the six Lutheran Confessions. These indeed have a certain holiness to them. But they are not the sacred Scriptures. Any merit or holiness that such works have is due only to their faithfulness to the sacred Scriptures. These are sacred, and uniquely so, both because of their cause in God and their saving effect in us. They are sacred because they come from the holy God himself and have him as their ultimate source and cause. They are also sacred because of their sacred and saving effect on us; they bring holiness to poor, lost sinners in their proclamation of forgiveness because of God's grace and Christ's merit.

Thus, the subject at hand is of the utmost importance. We are considering the Book that is a miracle in its origin, its preservation, its content, its value, and its effect. What could be more important than that?

The Canon

The term *canon* means "the rule." It is a term that is applied to the 66 books of the Old and New Testament. We use it to indicate first of all the *function of the Bible.* We use it to indicate that all doctrine must have its source in and be drawn from the Bible. The Bible is *the Canon, the rule,* the standard, and the norm by which all doctrine is to be judged. If a doctrine cannot be proven from the Scriptures, then it is a false doctrine, a heresy, mere human speculation, or superstition.

Thus, the 66 books of the Old and New Testament are referred to as *the canonical books of the Bible.* That distinguishes them from all other ancient writings, writings such as the Apocrypha, for example. The term *Apocrypha* itself means "hidden," because no one knows the origin or the authorship of the apocryphal books. The Apocrypha may still be found in between the Old and New Testaments in some old English and German Bibles; however, it is not part of the Bible, is not among the canonical books. The books of the Apocrypha were written some time during the InterTestamental Period, after the last Old Testament book and before the birth of Christ. They were never accepted by the Jewish church of Jesus' day as canonical nor did the early Christians ever consider them canonical. Jesus and the apostles never refer to them in the New Testament. Though there are some passages in the Bible that are similar to passages in the Apocrypha, these books were never accepted or recognized as part of the Bible. They were included in some editions of the Bible in between the canonical books simply because they had always been considered useful reading and because of their great age; however, they were never used in the church as a source of doctrine or to prove a doctrine. In point of fact, the books of the Apocrypha contain no passages that could be used to prove a doctrine that is not otherwise and much better proven from the canonical Scriptures.

The Roman Catholic Church during the Council of Trent (1545–1563) elevated the Apocrypha to the same status as the canonical Scriptures. Roman Catholics consider the apocryphal books a part of the Bible. The elevation of the Apocrypha by the Council of Trent, however, does nothing to help Roman Catholics prove doctrines not contained in the Canon. The decree of Trent and of the pope that all must accept these books as canonical, in spite of the lack of support from Christ and the apostles, or even from the early church fathers, is evidence of papal arrogance. How does one dare to decree that the Bible should contain books that were never in it before? How does one dare to decree that those who refuse to accept such sacrilege are to be condemned by God and the church? It is not too much to suggest that the elevation of the Apocrypha to a canonical status is just another way of lowering the Canon! For the papacy declares that the church comes before the Canon and that the pope, therefore, has the right to create doctrines, even if they are not found in the Bible.

The papacy even boldly declares that the church created the Canon and therefore comes before the Bible. That claim diminishes the role of the Canon and makes it subject to the will of the pope. In point of fact, of course, it is the Bible that created the church, not the other way around; for it is the Word of God—not the church apart from the Word of God—that creates and preserves faith and thus creates and preserves the church. The church recognizes the Canon; she does not create it. And when the church recognizes the Canon, she is recognizing her mother. Just as no one would be so insane as to claim that a child makes its own mother by recognizing her, so no one should be so blasphemous as to claim that they have created the Canon by recognizing it. But without blushing, the papacy makes itself the judge of the Bible and its content. It calls the Apocrypha canonical in spite of the fact that the Jewish church of Jesus' day did not consider it that, nor did Jesus, nor therefore did the apostles and the early church.

Other books that were written in the New Testament period that are not included in the canonical Scriptures are sometimes called the New Testament Apocrypha or Pseudopigrapha. These books likewise are largely of uncertain or unknown authorship. Many of them claimed to be written by an apostle, but the claim was easily proven false, hence the term *Pseudopigrapha,* that is, false writings. Often the purpose of the book is to advance some heretical point of view contrary to what is contained in the Scriptures.

Groups of the canonical books

The books of the Canon itself can be divided into various classes or categories of books. The most obvious of these is the division between the Old Testament and New Testament. The former refers to the 39 books beginning with the 5 books of Moses through the last book of the prophets, Malachi. The Old Testament Canon can be further subdivided into the heading of Moses (or the law) and the prophets, i.e., the five books of Moses, and then all the books written in the Old Testament after the time of Moses. It can be divided into the law (the five books of Moses), the historical books (Joshua through Esther), the poetical and wisdom books (Job through Song of Songs), the major prophets (Isaiah through Daniel), and the minor prophets (Hosea through Malachi). The distinction between "major" and "minor" in the writings of the prophets has to do chiefly with the length of the respective books.

The 27 books of the New Testament are likewise subdivided into the gospels of Matthew through John and the epistles, from Acts through Revelation.

The 39 books of the Old Testament belong without any doubt to the sacred Canon. For Christ himself witnessed to them when he referred to the Canon accepted by the Jewish church of his day. He spoke of that Canon in John 5:39 when he said to the leaders of his people: "You diligently study the Scriptures because you think that by them you possess eternal life. These are the Scriptures that testify about me." Jesus accepted that it was altogether appropriate to seek eternal life in the Old Testament Canon of the Jewish church. He accepted that Canon, and he saw himself as its center. Likewise in John 10:35, when refuting his enemies, he refers to the Old Testament Canon and declares, "The Scripture cannot be broken." His declaration is almost a parenthetical remark; that is, it is so obvious that the Scriptures cannot be broken that one hardly need mention it. He mentions it, however, because even among those who accepted the Canon, there was all too often a refusal to believe what it said. That was especially true of the Sadducees who accepted the Old Testament but only recognized the first five books as authoritative. As is the case today, so it was even in Jesus' day: People reject parts of the Bible because they don't like its message. The Sadducees, under the influence of Greek philosophy, didn't like the doctrine of the resurrection and therefore rejected the books in the Old Testament that most clearly teach it. Jesus, however, showed them that even the first five books teach the resurrection (Matthew 22:23-32). In the Sermon on the Mount Jesus again makes reference to the whole of the Old Testament Canon and its authority. He says, "Do not think that I have come to abolish the Law or the Prophets; I have not come to abolish them but to fulfill them" (Matthew 5:17).

It was self-evident to the apostles and to the early church, therefore, that the Old Testament Canon was the same as that used by the church of the Old Testament and by Jesus himself. Even before Pentecost, St. Peter referred to the Old Testament Canon when he addressed the others in the upper room about the need to replace Judas in the apostolic number. He quoted from the Old Testament Canon as he began his address: "Brothers, the Scripture had to be fulfilled which the Holy Spirit spoke long ago through the mouth of David concerning Judas" (Acts 1:16). Likewise, in the sermon that Peter preached on Pentecost (Acts 2), he made constant reference to the Canon of the Old Testament. St. Paul also made frequent reference to the Old Testament Canon and quoted extensively from it in his epistles (e.g., Romans 9–11; 1 Corinthians 1, 2, 10:1-11; the entire epistle to the Galatians). Thus, there can be no legitimate doubt as to the composition of the Old Testament Canon. It was the Bible used by Jesus and the apostles and the early church. Neither Jesus nor the apostles raised even the smallest question about which books belonged to the Canon or about the divine origin of the Canon.

The list of the books in the New Testament Canon is likewise assured beyond any legitimate doubt. The 4 gospels, Acts, the 13 epistles of St. Paul, and the first epistles of St. Peter and St. John were always recognized as the sacred Scriptures of the church from its earliest days. These works were either written by apostles or, in the case of the gospels of Mark and Luke, in connection with the apostles Peter and Paul. No one ever registered any doubt about the authorship or authenticity of these works. They are called the *homologoumena* (unanimously accepted works) of the New Testament because of their early and universal recognition by the church as canonical. These works appear on all the lists of canonical books that we have from the early church.

Hebrews, 2 Peter, 2 John, 3 John, James, Jude, and Revelation are also part of the Canon. But they are called *antilegomena* (questioned works); they do not all appear on all of the most ancient lists, and some had questions about the authorship of these works. Most writers in the ancient church recognized the authority of these works and considered them canonical, in spite of the questions that were raised about their authorship. However, even if someone were to have the most serious doubts about the books in the antilegomena, even if one were to question whether or not they should be used to prove doctrines since they lack a bit in standing in the early church compared to the *homologoumena,* no doctrine would change. There is no doctrine taught in the *antilegomena* that is not also taught in the *homologoumena.* Thus, there is no practical difference in their authority or acceptance by orthodox Lutherans.

In discussing the Canon and the books that belong to it, it is again important to emphasize that the church did not create the Canon. She received it. She recognized it. She understood from the beginning that God had spoken through these books—that they were ultimately God's books.

The books themselves speak the same way. St. Paul defends his apostolic works and words, whether spoken or written, when he declares in 1 Corinthians 2:7,10,13 that his words are not from men but from God: "We speak of God's secret wisdom. . . . God has revealed it to us by his Spirit. . . . This is what we speak, not in words taught us by human wisdom but in words taught by the Spirit." He repeats much the same thought in 1 Thessalonians 2:13. St. James is speaking of the New Testament Canon written and preached as God's Word and the source of spiritual life when he reminds his readers that God "chose to give us birth through the word of truth, that we might be a kind of firstfruits of all he created" (James 1:18). St. Peter speaks in the same way when he declares, "You have been born again, not of perishable seed, but of imperishable, through the living and enduring word of God" (1 Peter 1:23). That is exactly how the church from the beginning received these books of the New Testament Canon. The holy writers wrote them and sent them to the churches. The churches received what was sent to them, recognized the authority of the books, with greatest care copied them and preserved them, and then sent them on to others. The believers recognized and accepted as divinely revealed truth what St. Paul says in Ephesians 2:20, namely, that the church is "built on the foundation of the apostles and prophets, with Christ Jesus himself as the chief cornerstone."

Thus the Canon created the church, and not the church the Canon. The church has no authority to create the Canon or change it. She has the duty and the great joy to receive it and proclaim it for what it is—the Word of God.

Attacks on the Canon

Since the 18th century there have been countless scholars and theologians who have rejected both the authorship and the authority of much in both the Old Testament and the New. Their attacks on the doctrines taught in the Canon usually begin with attacks on the origin of the Canon. Many, for example, have rejected the Mosaic authorship of the first five books of the Bible. They have tried to assign different sections of the books to unknown authors, whose works were later sewn together by an editor. They have sought two authors for the book of the prophet Isaiah. They have rejected the apostolic authorship of much in Matthew and John and the apostolic authority behind Mark and Luke. They have spurned the Pauline authorship of some of his epistles. By the time these scholars and theologians are finished, there is nothing left of the authority of the Canon or any certainty as to the origins of any part of it.

Why? Why have so many in the last centuries spent so much time and effort trying to demolish the Canon? Is it because there is evidence for their conclusions within the Canon itself? Is it because some documents have been discovered from the ancient church or even from Old Testament times that casts doubt on the authenticity of part or the entire Canon? The answer is a resounding NO! There is not a scrap of evidence in the Canon itself, in the discoveries of present-day archaeology, or in the records of the ancient church that supports any of their conclusions. In point of fact, the more we learn from archaeology and from ancient records, the more ridiculous the attacks on the Canon appear.

Why then has there been such a concerted effort to overthrow the Canon? It is because those engaged in the effort do not like the message of the Canon. In ancient times it was the habit to persecute and kill the messengers of God, whether prophets in the Old Testament or apostles, pastors, and teachers in the New Testament. Killing the messengers has gone very much out of fashion, at least in the Western world. So instead unbelief seeks to kill the message and thus make the messengers irrelevant. Unbelieving scholars, for example, reject the very idea of miracles. Therefore, they dismiss the miracles of both the Old Testament and the New Testament. They seek some explanation outside of the Canon for the miracles recorded in it. They dismiss the creation account in favor of the theory of evolution. They dismiss the miracles of the exodus in favor of a completely unsubstantiated notion that the story was fabricated as part of a nationalist mythology. They dismiss the virgin birth and resurrection of Christ as the pious wish of the early church in an unscientific age and then make that wish the source of the biblical accounts.

The notion that the disciples and their hearers were so unsophisticated that they could be easily tricked by things that seemed to be miracles and by the resurrection itself is shown to be ridiculous by the gospel accounts themselves; Jesus often scolded the disciples for their slowness to believe—not for some imagined gullibility. Even on Easter Sunday they were still slow to believe the message of the Savior's resurrection. They were not easily persuaded or convinced. To claim that the disciples believed in the bodily resurrection of Christ because that's what they wished would have happened is accordingly contradicted by their own early doubts. Or to say that the resurrection really just takes place in human hearts is likewise ridiculous on the face of it: Why would anyone want a risen Christ in his heart if that Christ is in fact still dead and buried somewhere in Palestine? Yes, and why would anyone want a Christ who promised to rise and then didn't?

But again, there is not a shred or a scrap of evidence to support the theories of those who attack the Canon, neither inside of the Canon nor in sources outside of it. Indeed, no two of those attacking the Canon can be found who agree on what in the Canon is authentic and what is not. Were their methods as scientifically reliable as they claim, it should not be that difficult for them to reach agreement at least with one another. But consult their works: the works of Friedrich Schleiermacher, Harry Emerson Fosdick, Albert Schweitzer, Rudolph Bultmann, Karl Barth, and all the rest. Proofs for their assertions are altogether lacking. They start in their scholarship with their own conclusions as to what is true and what is false. Then they attack the text of the Canon, not on the basis of the evidence but solely on the basis of their own preconceived notions.

The reasoning largely goes like this: "Since miracles do not happen, Moses could not have written . . ." Or this: "Since the early church wanted to believe that Jesus was still alive, it put words into his mouth and into the mouths of the apostles that declare him to be risen from the dead."

For all of the attacks on the Canon, the Canon remains. It is utterly and absolutely reliable as to its origin and to the books that belong to it. No church and no individual has the right to change the Canon. For, again, the Canon creates the church and the church recognizes and receives the Canon as the source and the authority for all that she believes, teaches, and confesses.

However, someone may object because we do not have the original texts of the Canon. We will not find somewhere in a museum the *autographs,* i.e., the actual signed and certified manuscripts of the apostles and prophets. What we have are copies, and copies of copies. Could not mistakes have been made in the process of copying the writings in the Canon?

Indeed, mistakes were made in the process of copying. The Hebrew and Aramaic manuscripts of the Old Testament and the Greek manuscripts of the New Testament all contain what are known as *variata.* The variata are variations in the copying of the text. But the surprising thing about the variata is that they contain no surprises at all. Most of the variata are matters of spelling. Often manuscripts were read aloud while others copied down what they heard. Sometimes the copier did not hear exactly or did not spell a word correctly. The error got into his manuscript, and if someone else copied it, the error was repeated. But we need to remember that the copyists of the books in the Canon considered the works they were copying to be the very Word of God. Therefore they exercised an extraordinary degree of care in their work. The number of variata for the Bible is insignificant compared, for example, with the variata of manuscripts written by Homer or the other famous Greek and Latin authors who lived during Old or New Testament times. It is in fact impossible to put together an assured text of the works of Homer (d. ca. 850 B.C.). No such problem exists in constructing the texts of the Old Testament and the New Testament.

In point of fact, if we were all very poor scholars of the manuscripts and were wrong on all of our choices for the correct reading of a text, not one single doctrine would be affected! That is how insignificant the variata are in number and in kind. It is not because of the variata that attacks are made on the Canon. *No* case for any false doctrine can be based on the variata. Thus, the manuscripts we use in translating the Bible today are reliable to the very highest degree.

But does not the matter of translation itself create yet an additional problem for our use of the Canon? How can we be sure that the translation is accurate, that it does not mislead us? It is sad but true that there are translations of the Bible in which the translators have superimposed their own convictions on a passage, instead of allowing the passage to correct their convictions. Precisely because it is possible for translators, even with the best of convictions and intentions, to err, it is important that our pastors be trained in the use of the biblical languages. At least the pastors should be able to write, preach, and teach on the basis of texts in the original languages. They should know enough of those languages to be able also to check translations and to check assertions made by others about the meaning of the original text.

Having said that, 99.9 percent of what we have in the translations commonly in use among us reliably transmits the intention of the divine author behind the text. The message of the law and the gospel is clearly conveyed in those translations. The entire doctrine that God planted in the Scriptures is likewise clearly discernable. Therefore, we need not doubt that when we pick up our Bibles we have picked up the *Canon* of the Old Testament and the New Testament, *variata* and translation notwithstanding.

But is it not a true saying that most writings lose something in translation? That saying is almost always true. It is true as well with translations of the Bible. That again is why it is important that our pastors be familiar with the Bible in its original languages. It was no accident that God chose Hebrew and Greek for the writing of his Word. There is subtle beauty, especially in the Greek language of the New Testament, that cannot be conveyed by a simple word-for-word translation of the text. Nevertheless, the primary meaning and the most important truth taught by the text is clear also in translation. Even those who are limited to reading the Scriptures in translation will never exhaust its richness and depth; nor will they ever finish learning it or be able to say that they have finally mastered it.

The doctrine of inspiration

We have already noted that the Bible is unique among books and that it is one of the many important factors that make Christianity unique among religions. In discussing the Canon we have drawn attention to the importance that the church attaches to its composition and transmission down through the ages. Jesus himself attaches the greatest significance possible to the Bible when he declares, “Heaven and earth will pass away, but my words will never pass away” (Matthew 24:35), and again when he testifies, “The words I have spoken to you are spirit and they are life” (John 6:63).

In order to understand better the significance of this all-important Word, we search the Scriptures themselves for an explanation of the way in which this Word has come from God to us. That the Word of God is identified with the Bible no Christian should question. But how is it the Word of God? In what sense is it the Word of God? How much of it is the Word of God? Those are questions frequently asked and often wrongly answered.

When we look for an answer in the Scriptures, we are looking especially for a *sedes doctrinae,* that is, a *seat of the doctrine.* A *sedes doctrinae* is one especially potent passage that best sums up a doctrine. Any number of other passages may say part of the same thing or emphasize one particular aspect of a doctrine or deal with yet other aspects of the doctrine, but a *sedes doctrinae* says the most.

The *sedes doctrinae* for the doctrine that tells us most about the *how,* the *why,* and the *what for* of the Bible is 2 Timothy 3:15-17:

> From infancy you have known the holy Scriptures, which are able to make you wise for salvation through faith in Christ Jesus. All Scripture is God-breathed and is useful for teaching, rebuking, correcting and training in righteousness, so that the man of God may be thoroughly equipped for every good work.

We will have occasion to make frequent reference to this passage in our consideration of the doctrine of the Word. For the passage tells us not only how the Scriptures were written, but as well the purpose of their writing and the use that we should make of them.

The apostle tells us that "all Scripture is God-breathed," i.e., *inspired.* That is how the Bible came into being. God breathed it. How much of it? The apostle is quite clear: all of it. The little word *all* leaves nothing to doubt and nothing to chance and nothing to man's imagination or interpretive ability. There is nothing in the original Hebrew/Aramaic and Greek texts of the Bible that God did not breathe.

Thus we believe, teach, and confess the doctrine of the *plenary* and *verbal* inspiration of the Scriptures. The word *plenary* means "full" or "complete." It is used in contrast to any notion of an inspiration of the Bible that is somehow limited. Some, for example, want to limit the inspiration of the Bible to those matters in it that deal with faith and morals. They teach only a limited inspiration in the interest of denying the teaching of the Bible about creation or about other historical, geographical, or scientific matters recorded in the Bible that might in some way conflict with present-day opinions. Paul leaves no room for any notion of a limited inspiration when he tells us that *all* Scripture is God-breathed.

The emphasis on the *verbal,* or word-for-word, inspiration of the Scriptures is much the same as the emphasis contained in the word *plenary.* The Scriptures consist of words. To be sure, those words transmit concepts and ideas that perhaps could have been expressed in other words. But the Scriptures are God-breathed. The words are of God's own choosing. God did not merely give the ideas to the writers and leave it to them to find their own way of expressing those ideas. No, he breathed the words, and the writers wrote what he breathed. Why would they have wanted to pick words other than those breathed by God? Surely it would strike the apostles and prophets as the height of arrogance to hear God breathing words and then to decide on their own to pick words they deemed more appropriate than those breathed by the author of all language and all truth. No words could be more appropriate than those chosen by God himself. The notion that God breathed ideas but not words is absurd on the face of it. For ideas consist of words joined together in a certain grammatical and coherent order. Thus to assert that God breathed ideas but not the words that express those ideas is a contradiction in terms.

The emphasis on words in contrast to mere concepts or ideas is thoroughly biblical. God, for example, says through the prophet Isaiah, "This is the one I esteem: he who is humble and contrite in spirit, and trembles *at my word*" (Isaiah 66:2). In Romans 10, St. Paul repeatedly links faith and the words, not merely concepts or general ideas, and concludes his emphasis by saying, "Consequently, faith comes from hearing the message, and the message is heard through *the word* of Christ" (Romans 10:17). And our Lord Jesus solemnly closes the Bible in its last book with an emphasis not on general ideas or concepts but on words: "I warn everyone who hears *the words* of the prophecy of this book: If anyone adds anything to them, God will add to him the plagues described in this book. And if anyone takes words away from this book of prophecy, God will take away from him his share in the tree of life and in the holy city, which are described in this book" (Revelation 22:18,19). If the apostles and prophets, following the lead of our Lord Jesus himself, placed such an emphasis on words, may it be far from us to ignore any of them, much less presume to change them!

Once God had chosen the words, the writers had no reason to pick other ones. Unlike the unbelief that rejects the doctrine of the plenary and verbal inspiration of the Scriptures, the apostles and prophets were not in the habit of correcting God—not his works, not his grammar, not his words either.

But do not the writers of the Bible employ different, even unique, styles of writing? If God breathed each and every word of the Bible, should we not expect that the style would be the same throughout?

To be sure the styles of writing are many and varied in the Scriptures. Isaiah and many of the psalmists write the most sublime Hebrew poetry. It is worth learning Hebrew just to read it! The prophet Amos, on the other hand, writes in a much rougher style that reflects his rough background as a sheepherder and a tree trimmer. Likewise in the New Testament the Greek of St. John is sublime in content but very simple in its style, grammar, and vocabulary. St. Luke's gospel reflects his background as a physician; he records more of the miracles of healing than any of the other gospel writers and often does so with the language that a doctor of his day would have used. St. Paul's language reflects his education in the Greek and Jewish schools of the day.

The writers were not just stenographers or word processors to the breath of God. But that in no way militates against the doctrine of plenary and verbal inspiration. God made use of their varied backgrounds and education in the inspiration of the Scriptures. But that did not alter in the least the fact that the entire Bible, each and every word of it, was God-breathed, divinely and verbally inspired. If God sees fit to use a number of very different men to transcribe his Word, why should we object that he chose as well to use their different styles of writing and speaking in his inspiration of the Scriptures? There is no reason to complain about that. Nor is there any reason to assume that using different men with different levels of education and knowledge might leave room for mistakes in their writing. No one writer knew all of God's mind and will. But what God wanted revealed through that writer, the writer wrote. And he wrote the words that God gave him, regardless of his own personal level of understanding or knowledge. It may be that David did not fully grasp how his prophecy of Christ's suffering in Psalm 22 would be fulfilled. It may be that Isaiah did not fully understand how the prophecy that he wrote on the same subject in Isaiah 53 would be fulfilled. It would not have occurred to either David or Isaiah to say as God was breathing his Word through them: "I don't quite understand all of this, so I'd better change it." That a writer may not have fully understood everything that he was writing does not change the fact that each wrote by divine inspiration, divine in-breathing. That is the assurance we have in the *sedes doctrinae,* when St. Paul tells us that *God breathed all of the Scriptures.* It is an assurance repeated in almost all of the books of the Bible.

Thus, the Bible does not merely *contain* the Word of God. It *is* the Word of God. It makes no difference whether the subject matter is faith and morals, history, geography, or science. Jesus in his great High Priestly Prayer just before his suffering and death speaks of the entire Bible when he declares: "Your word is truth" (John 17:17). That declaration covers the Old Testament already written when Jesus spoke these words; and it applies as well to the New Testament yet to be inspired after his resurrection. It applies to all of it regardless of the specific subject matter.

In point of fact, it is not possible to separate what the Bible says about faith and morals from what it says about other matters that may seem to be only about history, geography, or science. St. Paul, for example, discusses a most important matter of faith and morals in Romans 5:12-19. He speaks of our salvation as a work accomplished by one man, namely, Jesus Christ. But he bases the legitimacy of one man saving so many on the historical record of the creation and fall accounts in Genesis 1–3. If the account in Genesis 1–3 is merely a myth or a fable, not true, not historically or scientifically correct, then the apostle's argument about faith is reduced to nonsense. Likewise, Jesus foretells his own resurrection by twice making reference to Jonah (Matthew 12:39,40; 16:4). On both occasions Jesus treats the story of Jonah as history, as a miraculous but actual event in history. He promises that his resurrection will be the same—an actual and miraculous event in history. The literal history of the story of Jonah cannot be separated from Jesus' use of that history as a sign pointing to his own bodily resurrection from the dead.

Even in matters that may at first glance seem minor, it is evident that what the Bible says about faith and morals cannot be separated from what it says about historical and other matters in the Scriptures. Jesus, for example, frequently refers to Moses when he is quoting from the first five books of the Bible. Those who deny that Moses wrote those books must account for Jesus' constant reference to Moses when he quotes from them. Was Jesus mistaken in thinking that Moses wrote the first five books of the Bible? If Jesus was mistaken, then he cannot be God. For God does not make mistakes. And if Jesus is not God, then the whole of the Bible, not just what it says about history or science or geography, is a fraud and not the Word of God. Or was Jesus merely accommodating himself to the common notion of the day, which considered Moses the author of those books? If that were the case, then Jesus was guilty of deceiving the people. That is a sin. If Jesus is a sinner, then he is not the Savior; he is not God and the Son of God.

Thus, there is no such thing as a small error when it comes to the matter of the plenary and verbal inspiration of the Scriptures. The Bible is either the Word of God, as Christ himself and all of the apostles and prophets testify, or the Bible is the most terrible fraud ever put over on the human race.

Are there not many things in the Bible that did not need divine inspiration in order to be written? Matthew and John, for example, were eyewitnesses of the three years of Jesus' earthly ministry and saw him after his resurrection and at his ascension. Luke accompanied the apostle Paul on some of his missionary journeys and did not need divine inspiration to write about many of them in the book of Acts; Luke even introduces his gospel account by telling us that he had investigated the things that he was about to record (Luke 1:1-4). Moses was the most active and perceptive participant in the events described in Exodus; he did not need divine inspiration to write about many of them.

It is true that active participants in at least some of those events wrote about things that they themselves saw and heard. Nevertheless, a selection had to be made of which events to include and which to leave out. God himself by inspiration, verbal inspiration, decided that matter. God chose what to include and what to leave out. Moreover, God saw to it that human memory did not err when the writer described an event that the writer himself knew about firsthand. In addition, God revealed what the writer did not know and could not know himself. And the two parts—one known by the writer, which did not need to be revealed, and the other unknown to the writer, which had to be revealed—are both inspired. They are both God-breathed. So even the matters of which the writers had firsthand knowledge were not selected by the writers for inclusion in the Bible. God selected them. St. Peter assures us: "Prophecy never had its origin in the will of man, but men spoke from God as they were carried along by the Holy Spirit" (2 Peter 1:21). Whatever was written was the result of a divine process, a miraculous process, which guarantees that the Bible is indeed in all of its parts the verbally inspired Word of God.

The Bible rarely tells exactly how that inspiration took place. Occasionally we know that the writer received God's Word by way of a vision (e.g., Isaiah 6, most of Ezekiel, much of Daniel, Revelation). Sometimes God spoke "face to face" with the author, as in the giving of the law to Moses on Mount Sinai in the book of Exodus. But most often we are not told the *how* of inspiration. St. Peter simply says that the writers were "carried along by the Holy Spirit." Their minds and pens became instruments in God's employ. The impulse to write as well as what was written came from God. Sometimes the writers describe that impulse; sometimes they do not. Sometimes the writers were assured of their authority as spokesmen of God through their ability at God's command to perform miracles. Ultimately it is enough for us to know that all of the Scriptures are inspired. The details in each case involving the *how* of inspiration we leave to God. If he had wanted us to know more about that, he would have told us.

The same is true of matters that may interest us but which are not discussed in the Bible. Some would like to know about dinosaurs. Others would like to know more about the angels. Others wish there was something else about the state of souls in heaven before the Last Day. Still countless additional questions arise that are not answered by the Bible. It is not our business to tell God what he should have recorded simply to satisfy our own curiosity. It is our business to occupy ourselves diligently with what he has inspired—that's what God considers important for us to know.

Fundamental and nonfundamental doctrines: the chief purposes of the Bible

Does the fact that the entire Bible is verbally inspired mean that all of it is of equal importance? All of it is the Word of God and therefore all of it is important. But it is also true that some of its parts are more important than others. The Scriptures themselves make that point when, for example, St. Paul tells us that the Old Testament ceremonial and dietary laws no longer apply in the New Testament church (Colossians 2:16,17). Additionally, when addressing the Corinthian Christians, Paul reminds them that as their missionary pastor he had started the work of their instruction; others had built with further instruction on the foundation that he had laid (1 Corinthians 3:1-11). This too suggests that some doctrines must be grasped of necessity and that some doctrines need more time and further instruction.

Thus we make a distinction between *fundamental doctrines* and *nonfundamental doctrines*. We discover which belong in each category by examining *the chief purpose* of the Scriptures. The Bible leaves us with no doubt about the reason why it was written. St. John, close to the end of his gospel account of our Lord's earthly life and work, speaks of the ultimate purpose of his gospel. What he says of his purpose, one can easily say of the entire Bible:

> Jesus did many other miraculous signs in the presence of his disciples, which are not recorded in this book. But these are written

that you may believe that Jesus is the Christ, the Son of God, and that by believing you may have life in his name. (John 20:30,31)

St. Paul says much the same thing in the *sedes doctrinae* for the doctrine of inspiration. At its very beginning he reminds Timothy and us of the most important purpose of the Bible when he says that Timothy has "known the holy Scriptures, which are able to make you wise for salvation through faith in Christ Jesus" (2 Timothy 3:15). That same point is made repeatedly in the New Testament, the most important purpose of the Bible is to show us our Savior and bring us to faith in him.

The second great purpose of the Bible, one closely related to the first, is to teach us how to lead a godly life in this world as a fruit and give proper thanksgiving to God for the gift of our salvation and saving faith. The Bible does that by showing us the will of God in the law and then by comforting and strengthening us through the gospel as we try to live according to his will. St. Paul tells us in Romans 12:1,2: "Therefore, I urge you, brothers, in view of God's mercy, to offer your bodies as living sacrifices, holy and pleasing to God—this is your spiritual act of worship. Do not conform any longer to the pattern of this world, but be transformed by the renewing of your mind." He goes on then to describe just what kind of a life it is that is holy and God-pleasing. Jesus also often refers to this purpose of his Word. For example, he tells us in the Sermon on the Mount, "Let your light shine before men, that they may see your good deeds and praise your Father in heaven" (Matthew 5:16). At the end of the same sermon he warns that the bearing of fruit in response to the gospel is not optional: "Every tree that does not bear good fruit is cut down and thrown into the fire" (Matthew 7:19). As Christians bear fruit they remain yet in the world, suffer temptations, opposition, frustration, sickness, and finally temporal death. But through it all the Word of the gospel, the good news of our salvation, keeps bringing forgiveness to heal the soul. It strengthens faith, comforts in sorrow and affliction, and finally brings us triumph over death in our last hour. By all of these God shows us and leads us to an ever more godly life.

These two purposes are accompanied by yet another, the ultimate purpose of all that God has said and done for us and for our salvation. That ultimate or final purpose is the glory of his own name and his great grace. St. Paul expresses that truth in the most sublime terms in Ephesians 1:9-14. He speaks of the work of God for our salvation, beginning before time began and extending all the way into eternity; he speaks of the revelation of all that God has done for us and our salvation and concludes with this ultimate purpose: "Having believed [the Word], you were marked in him with a seal, the promised Holy Spirit, who is a deposit guaranteeing our inheritance until the redemption of those who are God's possession—to the *praise of his glory*" (vv. 13,14). When we hear his Word of the gospel and by it are given faith and through it are preserved in that faith to eternal life, God's name and work and grace are praised and glorified. Our faith is the result of his Word and work, and so also is our Christian life as a fruit of faith. Thus, our Christian faith and life exalt God and his Word.

Our Lutheran Confessions give voice to these three great purposes of the Bible and adopt them as the purposes for all that we teach in our churches. They put it this way, as they answered the criticism that their teaching was destructive to the unity and harmony in the church:

> Rather we have a deep yearning and desire for true unity and on our part have set our hearts and desires on promoting this kind of unity to our utmost ability. This unity keeps God's honor intact, does not abandon the divine truth of the holy gospel, and concedes nothing to the slightest error. Instead, it leads poor sinners to true, proper repentance, raises them up through faith, strengthens them in new obedience, and thus justifies and saves them eternally, solely through the merit of Christ. (FC SD XI, 96 pp. 655,656)

These three great purposes of the Bible, namely, God's honor and glory, our salvation, and then our growth in obedience, suggest what we mean by the distinction between fundamental and nonfundamental doctrines. Those doctrines taught by the Scriptures that most directly advance these purposes are fundamental doctrines. Thus, the doctrine of the Trinity, the virgin birth of Christ and his bodily resurrection, his work for our salvation, and our need for that work are fundamental doctrines. The importance of these fundamental doctrines is already evident when a baptism is performed; for all these doctrines are confessed in the Apostles' Creed at the Sacrament that brings an infant into the Christian church by creating faith in the Word proclaimed. Without these doctrines faith is impossible. Where there is no faith, there are no fruits of faith. Where faith and its fruits are absent, God's name and his glorious grace cannot be glorified.[1]

---

[1]We will consider this point further, especially as it relates to infants, in chapter 14, "The Means of Grace," under the heading "The Sacrament of Baptism."

There are doctrines that are somewhat further removed from these purposes. Faith would be possible even if one were ignorant of them. Earlier it was noted that Moses wrote the Pentateuch, the first five books of the Bible. If someone did not know that, such a lack of knowledge would not make faith impossible. Someone might not know the doctrine of the sacraments. Faith would still be possible. Someone might be ignorant of the doctrine of the angels or the doctrine of creation. Such ignorance would not destroy faith or make it impossible. Therefore, such doctrines are called nonfundamental doctrines.

But does nonfundamental mean the same thing as unimportant or optional? Most definitely not! St. Paul tells us—and the truth is repeated constantly in the Scriptures—"All Scripture is God-breathed and is useful for teaching, rebuking, correcting and training in righteousness" (2 Timothy 3:16). Orthodox Lutherans are not, therefore, "fundamentalists." Fundamentalist church bodies decide that some doctrines are necessary and therefore fundamental and that the rest are open to question and not necessary. Most fundamentalist church bodies will pick five or six chief doctrines of the Bible, teach those, and ignore or leave as open questions all the rest. That is no different than what Roman Catholics do when they add to the Canon of the Bible and then make the whole of the Scriptures subject to the authority of the pope. In both cases people place themselves above the Word of God and consider themselves free to hold to and teach as much or as little as they please.

When we speak of nonfundamental doctrines, we refer only to the nearness or distance of a doctrine to the purposes that God gives in his Word for the inspiration of that Word. We do not at all count anything that God has said as unimportant or as something we may dispense with as we please. Earlier we noted that a unique aspect of Christianity is that it is and ought to be *theocentric,* God-centered. To dispense with any part of God's Word or to call it unimportant and not worth teaching is to give up the theocentricity of Christianity. It is to go back to religion that is *anthropocentric,* man-centered. For man makes the decision, sits in judgment on the Word of God, decides for himself what is worthy and what is not. Woe to all such! They lay violent hands on the Word of the living God. They forget what God said to Isaiah: "This is the one I esteem: he who is humble and contrite in spirit, and trembles at my word" (Isaiah 66:2).

Thus, to set aside nonfundamental doctrines or to declare any part of God's Word unimportant or optional for teaching and for faith is very dangerous. Not only does that insult God, whose Word is truth, but it also endangers faith in the fundamental doctrines. We may call to mind the examples of nonfundamental teachings mentioned earlier. That one does not know that Moses wrote the Pentateuch may not endanger faith. But to know that this is what the Bible teaches and to reject it is quite another matter. For, again, if Moses did not write it, Jesus must have been mistaken when he spoke of Moses as the author. Or, Jesus must have misled the people when he did not correct their conviction that Moses was the author. Thus, what starts out as a seemingly minor error can ultimately attack major, fundamental doctrines and finally destroy faith. Think again of the example of Jonah. Faith might not be harmed by ignorance of Jonah as an historical figure who actually was swallowed by a great fish. But to deny the truth of the story is to call into question Christ's use of that story and his acceptance of the book of Jonah as historical. That is a very serious matter indeed and seriously threatens faith in the essential deity of Christ. Likewise, the same can be said concerning the Bible's teaching of the sacraments—ignorance of that teaching might not destroy faith, but rejection of the Bible's teaching, however, is quite another matter. For the teachings of the Bible concerning the sacraments are gospel teachings. To reject them is to reject the gospel itself. It should be obvious that such a thing is most perilous indeed for faith and can eventually be fatal to it.

We might make the analogy of driving a car. There are some things that one must know in order to drive an automobile. One must know how to turn on the ignition, how to use the accelerator and brake pedals, and how to steer. Ignorance of the need for fuel or the need to check the radiator and oil levels might not keep one from driving a car. But eventually ignorance of these things will hinder, perhaps altogether prevent, effective use of the automobile.

Thus, while we distinguish between fundamental and nonfundamental doctrines, we in no way teach that some doctrines are not important. For the denial of any truth of the Scriptures is a coarse insult to God in and of itself. And the denial of any truth of the Scriptures may ultimately result in an attack on a fundamental doctrine and bring about the destruction of faith. Indeed, how could it be otherwise? The whole history of doctrine teaches us that false doctrines once accepted only multiply. As soon as one part of the Bible is called into question, there is nothing to prevent other parts from being called into question. As soon as one part is denied, other parts inevitably will be denied. Finally, in disgust, as history both in the Bible and since it was written amply demonstrates, God removes his

Word. That is exactly what God himself has promised through the prophet Amos. He warns:

> "The days are coming," declares the Sovereign LORD, "when I will send a famine through the land—not a famine of food or a thirst for water, but a famine of hearing the words of the LORD. Men will stagger from sea to sea and wander from north to east, searching for the word of the LORD, but they will not find it." (Amos 8:11,12)

That is a warning which all should take seriously. For "God is not a man, that he should lie, nor a son of man, that he should change his mind" (Numbers 23:19). (God spoke this last passage through the mouth of Balaam, who later abandoned God's Word and perished because of it. See Numbers 31:8.)

The miracle and the mystery of the Bible's inspiration

Finally, before we move on to a consideration of the attributes of the verbally inspired Canon, we should pause and stand in awe of the *miracle* and *mystery* of the doctrine of inspiration. A miracle is something that can only happen because of God's direct action or intervention in history. The word *miracle* certainly fits when we are discussing the inspiration of the Scriptures! A mystery, as the term is used in the Bible, is something that is hidden from human eyes, unless or until God reveals it. *Mystery* well describes the Bible and its doctrines, including the doctrine of inspiration. For, as noted in chapter 1, we may guess at some truths about God and ourselves, but it is in the divinely and verbally inspired Bible that God himself speaks and makes known to us the truth about himself and us, about his purposes and how he achieves them in history and through his Word.

We stand in wonder and awe before the miracle and the mystery of the inspired written Word of God. We marvel first of all that God even wants to speak to us. For God—who is above and beyond all creation, who stands in need of nothing and no one, who is absolutely independent, who knows all things past, present, and future in perfect detail—speaks in the Scriptures to man. But what is man? He is a creature, totally dependent and needy, limited in every way by time and space, frail and weak and subject to death, a sinner even in his best moment. We marvel that God would want to speak to human beings who can do him no ultimate good and who offend and insult him ceaselessly with their sins.

We marvel as well that God could find a way to speak to mortals and to sinners in a way that they would be able to understand. How would a master builder or a physician or a physicist explain their crafts to an infant who knows nothing of architecture, biology, or mathematics? It should be easier to do such a thing than for God to explain so much of himself in his Word to mortals and to sinners who grasp nothing by nature of immortality or perfection. Nevertheless, God does exactly that and so much more in his Word. He uses simple words, common grammar, the writing of ordinary men to set forth the glory that is his and to call us to share in it.

We marvel most of all at what it is that he has to say in the Scriptures. For the pre-eminent doctrine of all the doctrines contained in his Word is the doctrine of the gospel that "God so loved the world that he gave his one and only Son, that whoever believes in him shall not perish but have eternal life" (John 3:16). It is the doctrine "that God was reconciling the world to himself in Christ, not counting men's sins against them" (2 Corinthians 5:19). So intense was his desire for our salvation, and so earnest was his zeal for an eternal fellowship with us! Could there be better news than that? Could there be a better reason than that for us to stand forever in grateful awe before the miracle and mystery of his inspired Word and to be eager to know it ever better?

This miracle and mystery of inspiration is an article of faith; that is, we believe that the Scriptures are divinely and verbally inspired because God through the Scriptures themselves has convinced us of their inspiration. Thus, we say that the Scriptures are *self-authenticating.* They do not need some other authority or outside source to convince us of their inspiration. They are inherently capable of convincing us of their inspiration, since God is always with his Word and can never be separated from it. St. Paul speaks of the Word of God that he brought to the city of Thessalonica. People heard the Word. They trusted its saving content. They recognized the Word as God's Word. For faith in the content of the message goes hand in hand with faith in the source of the message. If the message is a message of law and gospel from God, then God is the giver of the message. And that message is communicated in words, words given by God himself. It cannot be otherwise. Thus, the apostle says of the Thessalonian Christians:

> For we know, brothers loved by God, that he has chosen you, because our gospel came to you not simply with words, but also with power, with the Holy Spirit and with deep conviction. . . . And we also thank God continually because, when you received the word of God, which you heard from us, you accepted it not as the word of men, but as it actually is, the word of God, which is at work in you who believe. (1 Thessalonians 1:4,5; 2:13)

That was how the ancient church came to recognize the inspiration of the Canon in the first place. And that is how we recognize it as well. The church heard the Word of God and was created by it. The church heard the Word of God and recognized it as such.

To be sure, the Bible gives us many reasons for trusting in its unique and divine origin. Our loyalty is by no means mindless. For example, and as already noted, we see the unity of its message, despite its variety of authors and the times of their writing. From age to age, authors separated by centuries proclaim the law and the gospel. The message becomes ever more complete, but all of it is already implicit in Genesis 3 (a point we shall consider in greater detail later). In the unity of the message and unlike any other writing that claims to be of divine origin, we observe in the Bible the unique characteristic of prophecy and fulfillment. From Genesis 3 all the way to the last chapter of Revelation the Bible contains one promise after another. Some of these are short-term promises fulfilled within a relatively short time span. Other promises wait for centuries to find their exact fulfillment. Still other promises have a short-term and a long-term fulfillment. The promises of God to David concerning his son and the building of the temple, for example, are only partially fulfilled in the reign of Solomon and in the construction of Solomon's temple. Their complete fulfillment did not take place until the coming of David's distant descendent, David's son and David's Lord, our Savior. And the promises regarding the temple were never fully kept until the birth of the New Testament church. Indeed some of the promises made to David and later to Isaiah concerning the church only reach their complete fulfillment in heaven.

The study of this one unique feature of the Bible, that of promise and fulfillment, cannot be fully carried out here. We will make mention of only a few of the specific promises and their fulfillment by way of example. God threatened the flood and carried out the threat exactly as he said he would. He promised Abraham a son and gave that son, contrary to all human expectations. In Genesis he promised to give the descendents of Abraham the land in which Abraham was a wanderer and a pilgrim. In Exodus—four hundred years later—he kept the promise. Through the prophets Isaiah and Jeremiah, God threatened the destruction of Jerusalem, and the threat was carried out just as he said it would be. He promised a restoration after 70 years of Babylonian captivity. He even gave the name of the ruler under whom the restoration would take place long before the ruler was born or his kingdom had come to preeminence (Isaiah 44:28). He carried out the promise to the letter.

Most important and precious of all, of course, are the promises of the Messiah. From age to age the promise unfolded, beginning with Genesis 3:15 and ending in Malachi 4, the last chapter of the Old Testament. In the New Testament the promises are fulfilled with the coming of Christ, his life, death, and resurrection. The promise of the virgin birth in Isaiah 7:14 had its exact and literal fulfillment in Matthew 1:22,23. The prophecies of his suffering and death in Psalm 22 and in Isaiah 53 were carried out to the letter on Good Friday. Repeatedly the gospels, especially St. Matthew's gospel, refer to promises made in the Old Testament, which are fulfilled by Jesus in the New Testament. Likewise, the book of Acts and the epistles of Peter and Paul are filled with a repetition of the promises made in the Old Testament and the promises carried out by the work of Christ in the New Testament. Christ himself prophesies events in his own life and carries them out completely. With ever-greater detail he foretold his death and resurrection, and not one word of promise fell in vain to the ground. He prophesied the destruction of Jerusalem, and the prophecy was fulfilled in A.D. 70. He prophesied about the work of the church, both its trials and its triumphs, and those prophecies are still being carried out. There is no end to this aspect of promise and fulfillment in the Bible. There are promises for history, promises for the work of salvation, promises that find their fulfillment every day in the life of the church and her members. No other book can make and sustain such a claim—or even a fraction of it.

To be sure, as noted earlier, scoffers try to rearrange the history of the Bible, so that the promises and their fulfillment will not appear miraculous. But their attempts are in vain. They offer no proof, no evidence. When their work is finished, the great promises regarding the life and work of the Savior and the promised results of that work stand unrefuted.

Thus, our trust in the unique origin and the divine and verbal inspiration of the Scriptures is not a mindless trust. We have ample reason for it in the Scriptures and especially in the record of promise and fulfillment. But, ultimately, we do not trust what the Bible says about the Bible simply because it makes more sense than anything else, nor because we just feel that way about it, nor because of any arguments that might be marshaled outside of the Scriptures in their defense. We believe, teach, and confess that the Bible is the verbally inspired Word of God because God has moved our hearts to trust what he says in the Bible about the Bible. So, again, the doctrine of inspiration, like all the great teachings of God's Word, is an article of faith. The best advice we can give to one who needs to be persuaded of the inspiration of the Bible and the absolute truthfulness of its message is this: Read it! All of the arguments that make it sensible to accept the Scriptures, their message and their authority, are useful; but, ultimately, the Holy Spirit working through his Book convinces us that it is his Book. That's what we mean when we say that the Scriptures are self-authenticating.

Chapter 3
The Attributes of the Bible

We have examined the Bible from the standpoint of its composition (the Canon), its divine origin (verbal inspiration), its divine purposes (the glory of God as it creates our faith and trains us in obedience), its doctrinal nature (fundamental and nonfundamental doctrines), and the reasons for receiving it as God's Word (the chief of which is found in its self-authenticating nature).

We turn now to a consideration of its characteristics or attributes. The attributes of the Bible are consistent with and follow from the fact of its divine inspiration. St. Paul directs us to the attributes of the Scriptures in the previously cited *sedes doctrinae* for the doctrine of inspiration itself. He tells Timothy:

> From infancy you have known the holy Scriptures, which are able to make you wise for salvation through faith in Christ Jesus. All Scripture is God-breathed and is useful for teaching, rebuking, correcting and training in righteousness, so that the man of God may be thoroughly equipped for every good work. (2 Timothy 3:15-17)

The Scriptures are inerrant

The first attribute to be noted in the *sedes doctrinae* is that the Scriptures are true. That is self-evident from the words, "All Scripture is God-breathed and is useful." God cannot lie. It is contrary to his very essence for him to sin in any way. Therefore, what God says is always the truth. Because God said it and because it is therefore the truth, the Bible is useful, profitable, and beneficial for the holy uses that God himself here has assigned to his Word. A lie can neither come from God nor be useful for accomplishing God's holy purposes, as those purposes are described by St. Paul.

When we say that the Bible is true, therefore, we mean that it is *inerrant*. It cannot and does not err or make a mistake in anything that it says, whether it is speaking of matters directly concerning faith and morals or speaking of matters in history, science, or geography. Although teaching us about secular history, science, or geography is not the ultimate purpose for which God gave the Bible, nevertheless, when the Bible speaks on these matters it is inerrant. "All Scripture is God-breathed" includes everything, excludes nothing.

The doctrine of the inerrancy of the Scriptures and their absolute truthfulness has come under increasing attack since the 18th century. Some of the attacks, as already noted in the last chapter, are crude and coarse. The scoffer simply dismisses the Book as a collection of myths or fables; perhaps he considers it interesting as literature and a history of some religious thought, but certainly not as the verbally inspired and inerrant Word of God.

Other attacks on the inerrancy of the Scriptures are more subtle. Some teach, for example, that the Bible is God's Word and it is therefore true. But by "true" they do not mean "factual," or "corresponding to history." What they mean is that underneath the history there is a sort of divine message that comes through, even though the events described may not actually have happened. For example, some would say that the creation account in Genesis 1,2 contains the truth that God somehow is responsible for our existence or is the originator of all that is, but they deny that Genesis 1,2 is a correct and truthful record of what actually happened. In the same vein some teach that the account of Christ's virgin birth and his resurrection are true, but they do not mean, thereby, that Christ was actually born of a virgin or that he physically, bodily rose from the dead. They mean rather that the account of the virgin birth points to the uniqueness of Christ. His resurrection, they assert, takes place when his message becomes alive in our hearts.

We condemn all such playing with words. When we teach that the Scriptures are true and inerrant, we are simply being faithful to what the Scriptures say of themselves, what Christ said of them, and what the apostles taught concerning them. They are the Word of the God who does not lie. What they say happened, actually did happen. What they report, actually occurred.

Sadly and tragically, most church bodies that call themselves Christian—and most Lutheran church bodies among them—have abandoned this basic truth that the Scriptures are inerrant. In varying degrees they teach that the Bible is truthful in its basic message, but that it nevertheless contains errors of fact. How a truthful message from God can be based on errors and still be reliable they cannot say. In point of fact, they end up not even sure of what the basic message of the Bible is. The Lutheran World Federation, to which most Lutheran church bodies belong, has given up even the crown jewel of biblical and Lutheran theology—the doctrine of justification. It cannot agree on that doctrine's content or on justification as the cardinal teaching of the Scriptures. We should expect nothing less once the doctrine of the verbal inspiration and the inerrancy of the Scriptures has been denied and lost. For, as noted earlier, false doctrine is never content to be alone; false doctrines always multiply until the heart and the core of the gospel is denied.

Lutheran churches that deny the inerrancy of the Scriptures do so contrary to the faith of the Lutheran church confessed in its historic doctrinal statements. The Lutheran Confessions from beginning to end assert the divine origin and the truthfulness of the Bible. Luther, for example, in his Large Catechism, under the heading of the Sacrament of Baptism, says repeatedly about the Bible: "[In the Bible God] will not lie or deceive me. . . . God does not lie. . . . God's Word cannot deceive" (LC IV, 56,57 p. 464). Under the heading of the Sacrament of the Altar, Luther declares his trust in the real presence of Christ in the Sacrament because of Christ's word and promise. He says, "For as Christ's lips speak and say, so it is; he cannot lie or deceive" (LC V, 14 p. 468). And under the same heading he repeats it over and over again: Why do we believe that Christ's true body and blood are in the Sacrament and there for our forgiveness? Because Jesus said so—because the Bible says so! And Jesus and his Word do not and cannot lie. The last great confession of the Lutheran church speaks of the Scriptures in exactly the same way. The Formula of Concord, in sorting through the difficulties surrounding the doctrine of election, exhorts us: "We should especially abide by the revealed Word that cannot and will not fail us" (FC Ep XI, 14 p. 519).

To depart from the doctrine of the inerrancy of the Bible is to depart from a basic and historic teaching of the Christian church and from an assumption and fundamental premise of genuine Lutheranism. To suggest to Luther or the writers of the Lutheran Confessions that the Bible is truthful in its underlying message but not true in the message itself would certainly have struck them as absurd and blasphemous.

The Scriptures are efficacious

The second attribute of the Bible that we note in the *sedes doctrinae* is that the Scriptures are *efficacious,* that is, capable of accomplishing their saving purpose. St. Paul says that they "make you wise for salvation through faith in Christ Jesus" (2 Timothy 3:15). That is one of the great purposes of the Bible. It makes us wise for salvation by means of its two greatest teachings, the law and the gospel.

The Holy Spirit uses the law to reveal our sins to us, to show us our guilt and what we deserve because of our sin. By the law he drives us to despair of ever gaining the favor of God, forgiveness, and eternal life through our own efforts. St. Peter uses the law for that purpose in his sermon on Pentecost, when he declares, "Let all Israel be assured of this: God has made this Jesus, whom you crucified, both Lord and Christ" (Acts 2:36). The Holy Spirit drives that terrifying message of the law like a stake through the heart, as we see in the very next verse: "When the people heard this, they were cut to the heart and said to Peter and the other apostles, 'Brothers, what shall we do?'" (v. 37). St. Paul sums up the righteous decree of the law over all men:

> Now we know that whatever the law says, it says to those who are under the law, so that every mouth may be silenced and the whole world held accountable to God. Therefore no one will be declared righteous in his sight by observing the law; rather, through the law we become conscious of sin. (Romans 3:19,20)

Jesus often used the law in the same way, i.e., to drive us to despair of ever saving ourselves or contributing somehow to our own salvation. This use of the law is what Isaiah (28:19-22) refers to as God's "strange work," his foreign work *(opus alienum, das fremde Werk Christi).* It is called that because of what Jesus ultimately wants to accomplish in us with his Word of the gospel; he wants to save us, to forgive us, and to bring us to heaven and life eternal. However, before he can do that he needs to bring us to a recognition and confession of our total helplessness, of our absolute need of his grace and mercy. This is known as his "proper work" *(opus proprium).* In sum, he needs to drive us to despair. And he does that with his strange work, his preaching of the law. That preaching of the law is so forceful that the only appropriate response to it is despair. Read the Sermon on the Mount (Matthew 5–7). Who qualifies for the favor of God on the basis of their own works? Not one! Read the parable of the good Samaritan (Luke 10:25-37). Where is there anyone who has always acted as the Samaritan did? There is none to be found, not one. The verdict of the Lord through the psalmist stands:

> The LORD looks down from heaven on the sons of men to see if there are any who understand, any who seek God. All have turned aside, they have together become corrupt; there is no one who does good, not even one. (Psalm 14:2,3)

Once the Holy Spirit, working through the law, has carried out this function of revealing sin and driving to despair, the Holy Spirit then uses the gospel message for the creation of faith. St. Peter in his Pentecost sermon waits until the Holy Spirit has done the work of the law. Then at once he proclaims the gospel: "Repent and be baptized, every one of you, in the name of Jesus Christ for the forgiveness of your sins" (Acts 2:38). That is exactly what St. Paul also does in Romans, after he has destroyed every basis in humankind for boasting before God. Once the law has made it clear that none is righteous, no not one, the apostle shows the only way of righteousness. That one and only way by which we can be righteous before God consists in this: God gives us righteousness, he justifies (i.e., forgives) us on the basis of Christ's work and not our own. And all of that is received by faith, by trusting that God is serious and really means me, even me, when he declares us righteous. Paul puts it this way:

> Now a righteousness from God, apart from law, has been made known, to which the Law and the Prophets testify. This righteousness from God comes through faith in Jesus Christ to all who believe. There is no difference, for all have sinned and fall short of the glory of God, and are justified freely by his grace through the redemption that came by Christ Jesus. God presented him as a sacrifice of atonement, through faith in his blood. (Romans 3:21-25)

The preaching of the gospel of forgiveness, life, and salvation is what our Lord Jesus came to do. That is his real work, as distinguished from his "strange work" of preaching the law. Notice how beautifully Jesus goes from his strange work to his real work in Mark 10:17-27. First he shows the rich young ruler and his disciples how impossible it is to earn heaven. For no one has perfectly kept the law, least of all the First and the greatest of the commandments. God's teaching and preaching of the law, especially of the First Commandment, is efficacious; that is, by that law the Holy Spirit works death and despair in us in a way that is beyond reason. For apart from the work of God in the preaching of the law, in this *foreign, strange work,* we would still cling to the notion, to the delusion, that at least in part we deserve heaven. After the law has done its work, the disciples in Mark 10 ask the appropriate despairing question, "Who then can be saved?" Jesus introduces the gospel: "With man this is impossible, but not with God."

Consider also Jesus' discourse with Nicodemus in John 3:1-21. First, Jesus does his strange work of showing that entrance into the kingdom of heaven is impossible for man. Then after Nicodemus is in despair over Jesus' words, Jesus shows himself as the Savior of the world, the One who as God's gift has come to give what man could never achieve for himself. The efficacy of that gospel message for the creation of faith showed itself in the faith of Nicodemus after Jesus' death (John 19:39) and arguably even sooner (John 7:50).

St. Paul said in the *sedes doctrinae* regarding the doctrine of inspiration that Scripture makes one wise to salvation. That is its efficacy: It works in accomplishing God's intended purpose. It has the ability in the law to bring us to despair because of our sin and guilt; and then in the gospel it brings us to faith, to trust in the forgiveness won for us by Christ. And that attribute or characteristic of efficacy is not a natural but, rather, a supernatural one. Someone may write a book on how to repair an automobile. If the book is well written and technically correct, we may say that the book is efficacious for teaching us how to repair an automobile; it can accomplish the purposes for which it was written. But the book's ability to do that is altogether a natural efficacy. It depends on nothing more than the natural intelligence and understanding of the writer and the reader to accomplish its aim. That is not at all, however, the nature of the Bible's efficacy. The efficacy of the Scriptures is supernatural. The writer to the Hebrews speaks of this supernatural characteristic of the Scriptures when he says that "the word of God is living and active. Sharper than any double-edged sword, it penetrates even to dividing soul and spirit, joints and marrow; it judges the thoughts and attitudes of the heart" (Hebrews 4:12). The Bible can truthfully make such a claim because the power of the Holy Spirit is inherently and inseparably connected to it.

Such a supernatural efficacy of the Bible is necessary because of the perversity of the fallen human race. We do not want to admit our ruin, nor do we want by nature to embrace a Savior who has entirely won righteousness for us in the way that St. Peter describes it in his Pentecost sermon or in the way that St. Paul teaches it in Romans 3. Both the law and the gospel would remain veiled messages to us, rejected in unbelief, were it not for the perpetual presence and power of the Holy Spirit with his Word. For "no one can say, 'Jesus is Lord,' except by the Holy Spirit" (1 Corinthians 12:3). He moves us to make this confession of faith by the gospel, as St. Paul testifies repeatedly. In the introduction to the epistle to the Romans he says, "I am not ashamed of the gospel, because it is the power of God for the salvation of everyone who believes" (1:16). In 1 Thessalonians 1:5 he again points out that the gospel is efficacious because it contains the power of the Holy Spirit who is always present with the gospel: "Our gospel came to you not simply with words, but also with power, with the Holy Spirit and with deep conviction."

This attribute of the efficacy of the Scriptures, therefore, is a most precious one. It is because the Bible is efficacious that we are convinced and convicted of our sin and guilt. It is because the Bible is efficacious that we believe the message of the gospel and are delivered from sin, death, and hell. It is because the Bible is efficacious that we accept all of its sacred teaching as teaching from God himself, the ultimate author of the Scriptures.

But could not a good sermon or a well-written book, even a pamphlet, likewise be efficacious for the creation of faith, for the strengthening and preservation of faith, for giving effective guidance in our Christian lives, or for proclaiming above all else the glory of God? In fact are not these the very purposes of sermons and other religious materials that we hear and read and ponder? Does not even a sacred picture or a crucifix inspire us with devotion to Jesus and thus prove itself also to be efficacious? Could not sacred music, let us say Bach's chorales or some other Bible-based hymn, also be efficacious for accomplishing the purposes that God has given in his Word? The answer to these questions is decided—Yes! However, these are efficacious only because and precisely because of the Word of God on which they are based and to which they direct us. The devout use of such things is beneficial because they help to surround us with the message of the gospel.

But what about a book or a sermon that at least in part contains false doctrine, a corruption of the truth taught in the Bible? The Holy Spirit is inseparably connected with his Word, not with perversions of it. If faith is created and preserved through a sermon, a book, or a work of art in which the gospel is presented in a corrupt form, it is only the presence of the gospel at all in such a work that can truly inspire or strengthen faith. In such, the gospel accomplishes its holy purposes in spite of the error that a false teacher may attach to it, but never because of the error. It is analogous to a person eating tainted food; the food may nourish in spite of some contamination, but never because of the contamination. Indeed the contamination may ultimately destroy what benefit there is or was in the food initially. If we shun contaminated food, which may ultimately hurt the body, how much more concerned we should be to shun all corrupt doctrine, which hurts and can ultimately destroy faith.

When we say that the Bible is efficacious, we are concentrating on its ability to overcome our inborn resistance to its message and to create faith. We are not, however, saying that its efficacy is irresistible. It is clear from the Scriptures and even from experience that the

Bible does not always accomplish its purpose of creating faith, in spite of the power of the Word and the intention of God in that Word to save the lost through its gospel message. When the Bible does not create faith, it is not because there is something wrong with the Word or with God's intention. The fault is in the one who rejects the Word, as the Scriptures repeatedly declare (Matthew 23:37; Acts 7:51-53; et al.). Thus, we are confronted with another of the great mysteries in God's Word: Anyone who believes the Word of God has only God to thank for it; for the Word was efficacious in spite of that person's inborn resistance to it. But anyone who rejects the gospel in unbelief has only himself to blame for it. Neither God's gracious intention (John 3:16; 1 Timothy 2:4; 2 Peter 3:9) nor the efficacy of the Scriptures can be blamed (Romans 10:17).[1]

The Scriptures are sufficient

The Bible is inerrant, it is efficacious, and it is *sufficient.* The sufficiency of the Scriptures is the third attribute we consider. The sufficiency of the Scriptures likewise has to do with its purposes. As already noted, the three main purposes of the Bible are to create faith in us, to guide us in a holy life, and to glorify God. St. Paul, again in the *sedes doctrinae,* tells us that the Bible is sufficient for accomplishing all of these purposes. The apostle declares that the Bible "is useful for teaching, rebuking, correcting and *training in righteousness,* so that the man of God *may be thoroughly equipped for every good work"* (2 Timothy 3:16,17). Do we want to know the way of righteousness through the righteousness of Christ given to us by faith? The Bible is sufficient for showing us and giving us that way of righteousness. Nothing else is necessary. Anything else that is not in the Bible or based on the Bible will just get in the way and take us off the path of righteousness. Do we want to know what a righteous or good work is in the eyes of God? The Bible is God's Word, and it tells us of those attitudes of the heart and works in our lives that are pleasing to him. We are not left to our own devices to figure it out. We do not wait for God to whisper in our ears a new word of right or wrong, or a word about what we should do or should not do. The Bible is sufficient. Do we want to know how his name is glorified in our lives and in his church? The Bible is sufficient, "so that the man of God may be thoroughly equipped for every good work."

---

[1]The power of the gospel to convert and man's ability to resist that power will be examined more thoroughly under the doctrines of justification and conversion and the means of grace in chapters 12-14.

Jesus tells us the same thing many times in the gospels. He says, for example, "If you hold to my teaching, you are really my disciples" (John 8:31). And where are his teachings? They are in the Scriptures! By those teachings in his Word we become disciples, learn how to live as disciples, and give glory to God by the faith he gives through the Word and the life that flows from faith in obedience to his Word. Indeed, Jesus sharply rebukes those who look for righteousness, a holy life, and the glory of God apart from his Word. In the account of the rich man and poor Lazarus, the rich man had not been content with the Word of God in his lifetime. In hell he still was not content with it. He pleads with Abraham to send Lazarus back from the dead to warn his brothers. And what is the reply? "If they do not listen to Moses and the Prophets, they will not be convinced even if someone rises from the dead" (Luke 16:31). The Word is sufficient to create and sustain faith.

Thus, to wait for God to prove himself in miracles the way the rich man did and so many others still do and to wait for miracles that he has not promised is contrary to his Word. Jesus warned and sternly rebuked his own generation for its refusal to listen to the all-sufficient Word when he said, "A wicked and adulterous generation looks for a miraculous sign, but none will be given it except the sign of Jonah"—by which sign Jesus was promising his own resurrection (Matthew 16:4). Indeed, the miracles of Jesus were intended as signs pointing to the Word; they were not substitutes for it. The Word is sufficient. Likewise, to seek Jesus or the will of God in one's own visions, dreams, and imagination or to hope to find him apart from or anywhere else than in the Scriptures (or in the "visible Word," the sacraments) is to deny the sufficiency of the Scriptures.

It is almost an understatement to say that the Scriptures are sufficient, so rich are they in their application. The Scriptures, the apostle declares, are useful for teaching. Any teaching that does not conform to the Bible or contradicts it is false teaching, is heresy. The Scriptures are useful for rebuking. If doctrine or life does not conform to the Scriptures, it is from the Scriptures that such a doctrine or such a life should be rebuked. The Scriptures are useful for correction. Once the false doctrine or the life that does not glorify God and that does not conform to his Word has been rebuked, it is to the Scriptures that we look for its correction. The Scriptures are useful for training in righteousness. What else is it that we want from God but to be righteous before him? The Scriptures give us righteousness in the gospel of forgiveness. And in the moral law they show us how to live in a way that is right before God. Then in the gospel they give us the proper motivation of love to God and zeal for his glory, so that we grow in such obedience. Yes, it is almost an understatement to say that the Scriptures are sufficient. So sufficient are they that with them we are *"thoroughly* equipped for *every good work"* (2 Timothy 3:16,17).

It is all too common that people are not content with the sufficiency of the Scriptures for finding and knowing the will of God. Like the rich man in Luke 16, they want to know the will of God from something other than the Scriptures.

In Roman Catholicism, for example, it is common to look to the church itself as the source of doctrine. "My church says . . ." or "The pope says . . ." becomes the answer to this question: What do you believe? In point of fact, in Roman Catholicism there are four sources of doctrine: the Bible, tradition, the decrees of church councils, and the pope. The Bible is considered insufficient in and of itself. Tradition, things taught or practiced in the past, is called the unwritten word of God. Councils of the church considered doctrinal problems and controversies and passed resolutions that attempted to solve the problems. Working with the assumption that God will not forsake his church (a promise that Christ surely makes, but only on the condition of faithfulness to his Word!), the decrees of the councils are accepted as sources of doctrine. But since there are so many traditions and so many decrees from so many councils, inevitably many of the traditions and decrees contradict one another—and contradict the Bible as well. Therefore, to serve as the ultimate authority over truth and doctrine, the pope has been elevated—and has elevated himself—to a position of infallibility. According to long-standing claims of the papacy and then also to the decree of both the First Vatican Council (1869–70) and its pope, Pius IX, when the pope speaks *ex cathedra* (i.e., from the chair or throne of Peter) on matters of faith and morals, he is infallible; he claims to be the vicar of Christ on earth and the successor of Peter. With such glorious and self-imputed titles and importance he gets away with what really is blasphemy. The papacy claims for itself a role that only the Scriptures truly have as God's own Word.

It is because of the denial of the sufficiency of the Scriptures that a whole host of false doctrines has arisen in Roman Catholicism. There is no scriptural proof for such things as purgatory, prayers to saints, masses for the dead, the requirement of priestly celibacy, the role of Mary as "mediatrix of all grace," or the position of the papacy itself. Indeed, all of these teachings and many others are directly contrary to the Scriptures. Nor is any but the most feeble attempt made to justify such teachings from the Bible. To Rome, convincing proof from the

Bible is not necessary. For the church itself, especially in its head, the pope is the ultimate source of doctrine. To such depths can a church fall when it rejects the sufficiency of the Scriptures that it can even condemn and curse the most precious and beautiful and comforting of all of the Bible's teaching. That is exactly what happened during the Reformation and at the Council of Trent after the Reformation when the popes and the council cursed the doctrine of justification, together with those who teach it and believe it![2]

Still others reject the Bible's own teaching that it alone is sufficient for the doctrine, faith, and life of the church. They look to human reason as a source of doctrine in addition to the Scriptures. Reason is one of God's greatest gifts to the human race; however, human reason was never assigned the task of sitting in judgment over the Scriptures or in adding to them. Nor does reason have permission to contradict or correct the words of the living God. Sadly, such a blasphemous use of reason is a cornerstone of much in Protestant theology (as distinguished from genuine Lutheran theology). To cite only the most obvious examples, Protestants deny that Christ is bodily present in the Sacrament of the Altar, deny that the Sacrament of Baptism creates faith, and deny even that the gospel itself creates faith. Why? Is it because these things are not clearly taught in the Bible? No! It is because they appear to Protestants as contrary to reason. It does not seem reasonable that Christ meant it when he said, "This is my body" and "This is my blood" (Matthew 26:26-28; Mark 14:22-24; Luke 22:19,20; 1 Corinthians 11:23-25). Therefore, Jesus must have meant something else. It does not seem reasonable that Baptism could create faith, forgive sins, and bring life and salvation. Therefore, St. Peter could not have meant that when he said Baptism saves us (1 Peter 3:21). Likewise, St. Paul could not have meant it when he said that Baptism with the Word makes us holy and cleanses us (Ephesians 5:26).

Once reason becomes a source of doctrine, the sufficiency of the Scriptures is set aside and there is little to limit the fall into all manner of false doctrine. While Protestants do not go so far as to curse the doctrine of justification, they nevertheless do not clearly teach it either. In fact, many Protestants very much cloud it and put it into doubt.

The point should be obvious: Whenever the sufficiency of the Scriptures is set aside, whenever anything else becomes a source of doctrine, the Scriptures end up being contradicted and the chief teach-

---

[2]H. J. Schroeder, *Canons and Decrees of the Council of Trent,* Fourth Printing (St. Louis: B. Herder Book Co., 1960), pp. 43-46.

ing of the Scriptures concerning our justification is threatened. In point of fact, two or more sources of doctrine always set up a competition between them for the dominant position. One of them will win out in the end. History amply demonstrates that when any source of doctrine is placed alongside of the Bible, it is the Bible that comes in second. The other supposed source always gains dominance at the expense of the Bible.

Increasingly common is yet another way of rejecting the sufficiency of the Scriptures. Many cast aside the sufficiency of the Scriptures in favor of their own emotions or will. Within every church body one will hear people who justify false doctrines and sins with sentences that start with the words, "Well, I just feel . . ." Fellowship principles and practices set forth in God's Word (Matthew 7:15; Romans 16:17) are set aside with words such as, "I just feel that God wants us all to get together." Homosexual practices and living together outside of marriage are justified with, "I just feel that God loves everybody and would have nothing against what we are doing." Many adopt such a position in spite of the stern warnings of the Scriptures (Galatians 5; Ephesians 5; et al.). The roles of men and women are turned upside down without regard for the clear words of the Scriptures (1 Corinthians 14:33-38; Ephesians 5:22-33; 1 Timothy 2:8-14; et al.). The only defense is this: "Those were different times; I just don't feel that God wants that these days." The most basic doctrines of all, the doctrine of the Trinity and the doctrine of salvation through faith in Christ alone, are cast aside with the simple assertion, "I just feel that God is whoever you think he is and that he would never send anyone to hell." Some may even declare that their conscience requires them to hold views that are unsupported by or contrary to the Scriptures. However, a conscience unsupported by the Word of God is no more reliable as a guide to God-pleasing doctrine and life than any other will or imagination separated from the Word of God.

What else is all of this than rejecting the sufficiency of the Scriptures for accomplishing the purposes that God himself has given to them? Opinion, sentiment, and emotions are no better complements to the Scriptures than reason or the papacy. As with reason and the papacy, once opinion, sentiment, or emotions are admitted into the church or into the individual's heart as an additional source of doctrine, the Scriptures are quickly set aside and contradicted on every hand. St. Paul sternly rejects all such in the clearest possible terms in 2 Corinthians 10:1-5, concluding with the words, "We demolish arguments and every pretension that sets itself up against the knowledge of God, and *we take captive every thought to make it obedient to Christ.*" When tempted to replace the Scriptures with our own opinions or feelings, we do well to remember the example of Samuel, who prayed, "Speak, for your servant is listening" (1 Samuel 3:10). We have the Scriptures, and that is where God has promised to speak to us. Woe to the one who arrogantly prays instead, "Listen, Lord, for your servant is speaking, and this is how I feel you *should* have spoken and what you *should* have said!"

There is yet one more way by which the sufficiency of the Scriptures is commonly set aside. People want to know what God would have them do and what choices he wants them to make in the everyday matters of their lives. What occupation should I pursue? Should I marry, and if so, whom should I marry? Should I change jobs, move from here to there, buy this house or that one?

The question may be serious or may be trivial. A Christian nevertheless wants to do the right thing. And we want to know what God wants us to do. But to seek God's mind apart from the Scriptures is to seek him where he has not promised to be. He has promised to reveal his will nowhere else than in the Scriptures, as our Lutheran Confessions also remind us. In the Apology of the Augsburg Confession, the Confession speaks of the problem of establishing ways of worshiping God that are not in accord with or prescribed by God's Word. In part of the discussion the Confession declares as part of a rhetorical question, "We can affirm nothing about the will of God without the Word of God" (Ap XV, 17 p. 225).

Essentially what people are looking for when they want answers to life's questions apart from the Word of God is a *hidden will of God.* God reveals his will in his written Word. But there are many things that God knows which are not in his written Word, things hidden in the mind of God. Perhaps, or so the reasoning goes, if I pray, God will tell me those things about my everyday life that are not in the Bible. That is very mistaken thinking. We cannot say it too often: God never promised to speak to us apart from his Word in the Bible. His Word is sufficient for all that we need to know from the will of God. Anything in his will that is not revealed in his Word is hidden. If God has hidden it, we should not try to pry it loose. The Formula of Concord speaks of the danger of trying to peer into those things that God has reserved for himself when it considers the doctrine of election. Instead of seeking God where he has not promised to reveal himself, instead of looking for his will apart from his Word, the Formula exhorts with respect to the doctrine of election:

> We must carefully distinguish between what is specifically revealed in God's Word concerning this article and what is not. For, beyond what has been said to this point (all of which is revealed in Christ), God has maintained silence and has hidden a great deal related to this mystery, reserving it for his wisdom and knowledge alone. We may not inquire into this or follow our own thoughts in this matter. We may not form conclusions or brood about this but must cling to the revealed Word. This reminder is most necessary. (FC SD XI, 52 p. 649)

What the writers of the Formula say here is a solid general principle and one that they emphasize throughout the Formula.

But is it wrong to seek the Lord's direction for the day-to-day questions of our lives? Is it wrong to seek his will on matters of vocation, marriage, and the like? Is it wrong to pray about these things and expect some kind of an answer? It is certainly not wrong to pray about the decisions that we have to make in life. The Scriptures everywhere encourage us to do that. Jesus invites us to do that with boldness and confidence, perhaps most beautifully when he teaches us his own prayer (Matthew 6:5-15; 7:7-12). St. Peter tells us, "Cast all your anxiety on him because he cares for you" (1 Peter 5:7).

But when we pray, we are not asking God to make his will known to us apart from the Scriptures. Instead, we are bringing our every concern to him in the confidence that he will hear us as he has promised. We give him thanks for the choices he has given us in our everyday lives, and we pray for his blessing as we strive to make those choices in the light of his Word and to the glory of his name. Thus, we pray for God's blessing on a decision about our vocation in life. We weigh our options. We consider what the Scriptures have to say about working as for the Lord. We weigh what the Scriptures say about the use of earthly wealth for the support of our family, for aiding the poor, and for supporting the work of spreading the gospel. We call to mind the Bible's warnings against greed, the love of money, and pride. We think about how we will balance work time, family time, and leisure time with time to help others and to serve the church. And then we make our decision. The decision often will not be one between good and evil, but between good and good. Whichever choice we make, we seek the honor of God and the well-being of those around us. We commend our choice to God and ask his blessing on it; but we do not torment ourselves trying to guess what lies hidden in the mind of God. God has revealed his mind in the Scriptures. The Scriptures are sufficient.

In the same way we pray for God's blessing on all our earthly choices. And we strive to live so that in our choices we follow the Word of the Lord through St. Paul: "Therefore, I urge you, brothers, in view of God's mercy, to offer your bodies as living sacrifices, holy and pleasing to God—this is your spiritual act of worship" (Romans 12:1). In the remainder of Romans 12 the apostle gives us an excellent summary description of just such a life of worship. St. John tells us, "This is love for God: to obey his commands" (1 John 5:3). That is exactly what Jesus himself tells us, "If you love me, you will obey what I command" (John 14:15). Our goal is to live in such a way that we glorify God in all the choices for which we seek his blessing. That is what St. Paul is speaking of when he says, "So whether you eat or drink or whatever you do, do it all for the glory of God" (1 Corinthians 10:31). Yes, even when we seek the counsel and advice of others, something altogether appropriate and proper, we weigh what they advise in the light of God's Word. Indeed, the best counsel that we can get from others is exactly that counsel which has its roots in God's Word. It is no small blessing from God when we have friends or family members, pastors or teachers who can help us make decisions with God's Word as the ultimate guide.

In sum and again—God's Word is sufficient. Those who seek some other guide for doctrine and life are looking for God where he has not promised to be. It makes no difference whether the something else is a church, human reason, emotions, will, or even a conscience uninformed by the Word of God. Anything that competes with the Scriptures ultimately replaces the Scriptures, which are "useful . . . so that the man of God may be thoroughly equipped for every good work" (2 Timothy 3:16,17).

The Scriptures are clear

The fourth important attribute of the Bible, one that is also evident in the *sedes doctrinae,* is the attribute or characteristic of *clarity.* If the Scriptures were not clear, then they would not be able to accomplish the work ascribed to them by St. Paul when he tells us that through them we become "wise for salvation through faith in Christ Jesus . . . and . . . thoroughly equipped for every good work." If they were not clear, they would not be "useful for teaching, rebuking, correcting and training in righteousness." If they were not clear, they would not be sufficient for any of the purposes that God has given for his Word.

But they are clear, so clear that anyone with a normal grasp of language, its vocabulary and grammar, can grasp the meaning and intention of the words of the Bible. Jesus tells us that through his

Word we will "know the truth" (John 8:31,32). If his Word were not clear, we could not know that it is the truth or what that truth is. There is nothing fuzzy or clouded in the words of the gospel as summarized by Jesus in John 3:16. Jesus is crystal clear: God loved the world. God gave his Son. All who trust in him have, even now, eternal life. In Romans 10:17, St. Paul is crystal clear when he tells us how that faith is created: It comes by the hearing of God's Word. There is nothing muddy or murky about Jesus' words when he instituted the Sacrament of the Altar: "This is my body; this is my blood, given and shed for you for the forgiveness of sins." There is likewise nothing unclear about St. Paul's words in Titus 3:4-7 with respect to the Sacrament of Baptism: It is a means by which God saves and gives us every heavenly blessing. The intention and object of God's love and grace in Christ as it is expressed in John 3:16 is likewise in need of no clever interpretation or giant intellect: The object of all his grace and blessing is the whole world, every one of us, each one of us, none excluded. How could anyone miss the point? St. John repeats it in 1 John 2:2, and St. Paul emphasizes it in 2 Corinthians 5:19.

Just as the doctrines mentioned are clearly taught in the clear words of the Scriptures, so too are all the other doctrines of the Bible clearly taught in the clear words of the Scriptures. That people reject some or all of the doctrines taught by the Scriptures cannot be blamed on the Scriptures or on some supposed lack of clarity in the Scriptures. That many reject its doctrines in part or completely is the fault of the devil and of those who reject those doctrines. St. Paul makes that point when he says, "Even if our gospel is veiled, it is veiled to those who are perishing. The god of this age has blinded the minds of unbelievers, so that they cannot see the light of the gospel of the glory of Christ, who is the image of God" (2 Corinthians 4:3,4).

As already noted, it is the work of the Holy Spirit, working through his Word, that one believes the doctrines taught in the Bible. But fallen mankind retains the ability to resist the operations of the Holy Spirit working in the Word. Thus, for example, St. Stephen (Acts 7) delivered a clear and convincing testimony to the truth of Christ's coming, his work, and its purpose before the Jewish Sanhedrin. The members of that council understood him; there was nothing unclear in his message. But they effectively resisted the message, became enraged, and murdered the messenger. In the book of Acts we have a number of the sermons of the apostles Peter and Paul. The sermons are clear. No one who rejected the message did so because he did not understand it. Quite to the contrary, the people understood the message very well.

However, they did not like the message heard, rejected it in unbelief, and persecuted the ones who proclaimed it. The same is true of Jesus' words. Often the leaders of the Jews understood his message even better than did his own disciples (e.g., John 11:45-53; Matthew 27:62-66; 28:11-15). But in stubborn and willful unbelief most of the leaders rejected that message, in spite of the clarity of the message and the power of its contents to create saving faith.

The same can be said of those in our day who corrupt some of the doctrines of the Bible. We note especially among Protestants the habit of denying the clarity of the Scriptures. Protestants deny the real presence of Christ's body and blood in the Sacrament of the Altar, but not because Christ's words are unclear. Rather, false teachers have decided that he could not have meant what he clearly said, because what he said appears to be contrary to reason. Among the Protestants many (e.g., Dutch Reformed and some Presbyterians) deny that Christ died for the sins of the whole world, teaching instead that he died only for the elect. They reject the clear message of John 3:16 and of 2 Corinthians 5:18-21, et al. Still other Protestants (e.g., Methodists, Baptists, and Pentecostalists) deny that faith is completely a gift of God, teaching instead that it is a decision made by us with perhaps some help from God. They do so in spite of the clear Word of God in Ephesians 2:8 and Romans 10:17. They argue that these passages are unclear. But they are unclear only to those who do not like what the passages say, unclear only to those who have decided that the Word of God must conform to the dictates of their own reason. As noted in the discussion of the sufficiency of the Scriptures, whenever another source of doctrine is allowed in addition to the Scriptures, it is always the Word of God that is discounted when a disagreement between sources occurs. Thus a denial of the sufficiency of the Scriptures often is accompanied by a denial of the clarity of the Scriptures.

Are not the Protestants and others correct when they say that doctrines clearly expressed in the Bible appear to be contrary to reason? We will not and do not argue that everything taught in the Bible can be easily harmonized with fallen human reason. The most precious doctrine of the Bible appears also to be the one most at odds with human reason. Human reason cannot fathom that the holy and almighty God would become man for us and for our salvation. Human reason cannot grasp of itself that the God-man would endure the torments of hell to save the lost and totally undeserving human race. Nevertheless, that is what the Scriptures clearly teach. So again, the accusation that the doctrines of the Bible do not appear reasonable does not mean that they are not clearly taught. In point of fact, as already noted above in the discussion of the efficacy of the Scriptures, it takes the power of the Holy Spirit, which cannot be separated from the Scriptures, to overcome the objections and the resistance of reason and the sinful human nature to its saving truths. But the Holy Spirit uses a clear Word, not an obscure one, to overcome that resistance.

Does that mean then that everything in the Scriptures will be equally clear to all or that at least some will understand everything contained in the Word of God? It does not mean that. Certainly some passages in the Bible are very difficult to understand as are, for example, some of the visions of Daniel and Ezekiel in the Old Testament and of St. John in the book of Revelation. St. Peter tells his readers that some things in the epistles of St. Paul are hard to understand (2 Peter 3:16). The difficulty is due to our own limitations and to the difficulty inherent in some of the passages themselves. We have a hard time understanding some of the biblical descriptions of heaven and hell, for example, because heaven and hell are in eternity, i.e., outside of time and space and the usual earthly relationships of cause and effect. It is hard for us to think through a time when there is no time and a place without the normal limits of space. It is difficult for us to imagine a life without any sin and without any of the sad consequences of sin. Nevertheless, in none of those places in the Bible that are difficult for us to understand is there any contradiction of passages that are not difficult for us to understand.

To put it another way, all of the doctrines taught in the Bible are clearly taught. The fundamental doctrines are the most clearly taught of all. The brightest and most beautiful clarity is evident throughout the Scriptures when they most directly aim at their great purposes, namely, showing us the way of salvation, how to live a godly life, and exalting the glory of God. Those who reject those teachings cannot do so on the grounds that the Scriptures are unclear. Nor can they successfully assert that the clear passages are contradicted by those which are more difficult for us to understand.

The mysteries of God's grace, of the Trinity, and of Christ's incarnation and saving work are all clearly presented in the Scriptures, even though these mysteries may well be impossible for us to harmonize with our limited reason. That God is three in one is clear; how that can be remains a mystery. That God became man is clear; how that can be remains a mystery. Nevertheless, the clear Word of God itself convinces us of the truthfulness of these mysteries of faith.

Thus it is that we bow low before God in wonder and awe, in the most hearty gratitude that God has deigned to speak to us as he does in his Word. Yes, in grateful adoration we delight to receive him and all his gifts as he comes to us there not just to reveal himself to us but to give himself to us and for us in Christ. Ultimately, and in point of fact, nothing that reason can present apart from his Word is more reasonable than to submit to what God has said and to what God gives by means of his Word. Nothing that emotions can offer can compare with the rock solid joy and confidence that is ours from Christ in his Word. Nothing that the world has to offer in wealth, in education, or in pleasure can compare with the riches and the wisdom and the sheer delight of forgiveness, of the constant presence of Christ for us, and of the assurance of eternal life that is ours through the message of the gospel. Therefore, let all who think themselves wiser than the Scriptures and the God who comes to us puff and prance and claim what they will. For those of us who believe may God's Word ever be our joy and our delight, our life and our salvation! For in it Christ finds us and makes us his own. In it he shows himself as our God and only Savior. What more could we possibly want?

Chapter 4
The Proper Use of the Bible

From all that has been said previously about the nature and the characteristics of the Bible, it should be self-evident that God wants us to use it. It should be equally self-evident that more than anything in the world we would want to use it. Were we to receive a letter from a loved one, it would not be necessary for anyone to tell us that we should read it, treasure it, remember it. Were we to receive a letter from the president, no one would have to tell us to read it, prize it, and share it. But look at how perverse our nature has become as the result of sin: Even those who know that the Bible is the Word of God often must be urged to hear, read, remember, and share it.

From the beginning to the end of the Bible, God bids us pay close attention to his Word. For by his Word he created all things (Genesis 1). By his Word he performs the miracle of bringing us doomed and damned sinners to saving faith in the Savior (Genesis 3:15; John 3:16; Romans 10:17). By his Word he preserves that faith in the midst of all the trials of this life and up to the gates of death itself (Romans 5:1-5; 8:31-39). And by his Word he will finally bring this world to an end, raise all the dead, judge all flesh, and take the church on earth to the full enjoyment of heaven (Matthew 24,25; 1 Thessalonians 4:13-18; Revelation 22:7-21). It is therefore fitting that we hear it, meditate on it, take it to heart, and live in the Word of our great God and gracious Savior, even though our sinful nature will always oppose it. May we grow in our eagerness to make use of God's Word in a way that is pleasing to the God who has given it to us!

The use of God's Word should correspond to the purposes for which God has given it. As we often have reason to note, God gave us his Word

1. to bring us to faith. Since nothing less than our salvation comes by means of his Word, we hear it, read it, meditate on it, cherish it, and share it in union with the church that teaches and preaches it in all of its truth and purity. For it is by the pure teaching of his Word that the Holy Spirit creates and preserves faith. Just as the Word is the source of faith, so it is also the content of faith. Anything that con-

tradicts that Word is error and delusion and superstition, the opposite and the opponent of faith. Error always harms faith and can destroy it. Therefore, we want and need to know the Bible well, so that our faith may have God's Word alone as its source and content, so that we may be able to defend our faith against all error that would potentially destroy our faith, and so that we may share his Word in its truth and purity (Matthew 7:15-27; 28:18-20; Luke 10:16; Romans 1:16,17; 16:17-20; Ephesians 6:10-17; Colossians 3:16; 4:16; Jude 3,4; Revelation 22:18-20).

2. to show us how to live in a manner that is pleasing to him. Therefore we strive to conform our lives as well as our doctrine to his Word. Christians strive to live in accord with the Word of God, not because they hope to earn heaven thereby, but as the reasonable and God-pleasing response to the salvation already earned for them by Christ. They use the Word both to show them what kind of a life is God-pleasing and to beat back their own sinful nature, which prefers to remain in its sin. Those who hear the Word but still coddle the sinful flesh will find to their eternal sorrow that God always takes his Word seriously, whether we do or not (Matthew 24,25; Romans 12,13; 1 Corinthians 5–7; Galatians 5:13–6:10; Ephesians 4:17–6:18; James 1:19-27). Our Lord often warns against the hypocrisy, which doesn't mind listening to the Word but refuses to take it to heart. Such hearers are even called worse than unbelievers (1 Timothy 5:8), because they know from his Word what is right but choose to live in and practice what is wrong. St. James even says that those who only hear the Word but neither trust it nor live it have a "faith" that is no better than that of the devil (James 1:19-27; 2:14-19)! They shame the gospel and disgrace the Savior who died to redeem them. They are mere mouth-Christians *(Maulchristen),* that is, not Christians at all. Their refusal to struggle against the sin from which Christ redeemed them at so great a price will come to light on the Last Day; they will be cast down with the unbelievers into eternal punishment.

To be sure even the greatest of the saints in this life never got to the point where they triumphed over all sin and temptation. We will never get to that point on this side of heaven either. That's why Jesus bids us pray constantly for his pardon and forgiveness—for we need that above all things every minute of our lives. But having said that, we should not conclude that since we will never be perfect this side of heaven, we now have an excuse for our sins, an excuse even to wallow in them. No, not at all. Those who use forgiveness as a license to sin will perish in their sins. Rather, the love of God so perfectly shown in

Jesus' great sacrifice to win our forgiveness spurs us on to show him love in return (1 John 3; 4:9,10,19).

We long to show that love by a struggle against all which displeases him—yes, against all of that from which he has redeemed us at so great a price. The one who uses God's love as an excuse to sin while claiming to love God is like the wicked husband. He says he loves his wife and is sure that she loves him; and since he can count on her love, he thinks he has a license to commit adultery or otherwise mistreat her. Such a husband clearly knows nothing about love, no matter what he says. And, likewise, a "Christian" who says he loves and believes in God but uses God's love for him as an excuse to live in sin knows nothing of faith and love as God defines faith and love in his own inspired Word. It is in the Bible that we learn what those works are that flow from faith and trust in Christ's work for our forgiveness. It is in the Bible as well that God gives us that love for him which wants to grow in the practice of those works pleasing to him.

To summarize, in his Word, God shows us how to live, warns us against despising his direction, and then gives us both the strength and the desire to follow his Word in the gospel of his love for us in Christ.

3. for the honor and glory of his own name and grace. While all of creation resounds with the echo of God's glory (Psalm 19:1-6), it is from his Word alone that his name and grace are revealed and given to us. From the Word we know his name as our Father, his name as the Son our Savior, and his name as the Holy Spirit, the One who makes us holy by means of his Word of forgiveness. Therefore we cling to the Word that from it we may learn best to sing the praises of our great God and Savior. That purpose of praise sounds forth everywhere in the Scriptures, as do the two purposes already considered. The psalms of the Old Testament dwell on the adoration of God because of his works in our creation, our salvation, and our sanctification (e.g., Psalms 65–68; 111–117; 134–139; 144–150). It was to the sound of angels praising God's name over the fields of Bethlehem that Jesus was born (Luke 2:14). Jesus himself sings the praises of the Father who desires our salvation and reveals himself in grace (Matthew 11:25-30; John 17). The apostle Paul in his letters breaks out into hymns of praise and adoration for the whole revelation of God's will toward us in Christ our Savior (Romans 11:33-36; Ephesians 1:3-14; 3:20,21; Colossians 1:3-23). It is not too much to hope that the Christian who grows from year to year in the knowledge of God's Word will likewise grow in eagerness to praise and adore God for his revelation of himself and his grace in that Word. We do that in private devotions, in public worship with those whose confes-

sion of faith we share, and in the sharing of the Bible's saving message with those who know it and with those who know it not.

Yes, and most and best of all we praise God and give him glory when we believe what he tells us and receive what he gives us in his Word. Is that not an amazing thing? People consider themselves best thanked when we do something for them that they want; but God considers himself best worshiped when we repeatedly and eagerly receive from him the forgiveness, life, and salvation that he pours forth for us day after day in his precious gospel! Surely it is a great joy for us to know that the best way we have of praising God is to make use of his Word, to hear it and read it, to treasure it, to believe it, and to share its saving truth. His praise resounds not by our climbing a high mountain or walking over burning coals or fasting day and night out in the cold or in a desert. No, his praise sounds best in God's ears when we show reverence and receive him in his Word and then share that Word whenever we can.

Misuses of God's Word

Any use of God's Word that does not correspond to the purposes for which God has given it is sinful and blasphemous. Those who make jokes about things revealed in the Bible or about doctrines drawn from the Word of God are guilty of breaking the Second Commandment: You shall not misuse the name of the Lord your God. For it is in his Word that God reveals and gives himself, his name, and his grace. To hold that Word up to any sort of ridicule is an insult to the glory and grace of God. God warns against all such when he declares that he will not hold those guiltless who take his name in vain (Deuteronomy 5:11). Would we read the letter of someone we love the most and make fun of it? If not, then how could we be anything but heartsick when someone makes fun of God's love letter to us, his Word of our salvation by which he gives us life and life eternal?

Likewise, the teaching of false doctrine with the claim that it is based on God's Word is a serious misuse of that Word and a violation of the Second and Third Commandments. The books of the prophets Jeremiah and Ezekiel are especially filled with warnings and woes against those who presume to say, "Thus says the Lord," when the Lord did not in fact send them or when they spoke not his Word but their own (e.g., Jeremiah 23; Ezekiel 13). Jesus also warns against such a misuse of his Word in the teaching of false doctrine (Matthew 7:15; Revelation 22:18-20). Most of the epistles of St. Paul were written, at least in part, because of a misuse of God's Word by teachers of false doctrine. St. Paul is not at all gentle in his rebuke of all such false teachers (Romans 16:17,18; Galatians 1:6-9). The teaching of false doctrine is not only an insult to God, it is as well most harmful to those who hear and accept the false teaching. For as already noted, false doctrine can never strengthen faith; it can only harm it and may ultimately destroy it. Ultimately false doctrine makes God out to be a liar. The false teacher, no matter how learned or pious he may be, whether he intends it or not, is really saying that he himself is right and God is wrong, that God has said something in his Word that is not true.

The interpretation of the Scriptures

Since the Scriptures are holy because of their ultimate Source, their divine characteristics, and their sacred and saving purposes, due diligence needs to be taken in their interpretation. In the interpretation of the Bible we need to have an important principle in the front of our minds. The purposes God has given to his Word suggest that principle. The principle is this: *Theology is a practical aptitude (Theologia est habitus practicus)!* The principle means simply that God did not give us his Word for the purpose of speculation; he gave it to us for the purpose of our salvation, to show us both what to believe and how to live, and for his own eternal glory. Notice, for example, how practical St. Paul is in the passage considered in the previous chapter, 2 Timothy 3:15-17, the great *sedes doctrinae* for the doctrine of inspiration. Look at it again and see how practical everything is in that passage. When we study the Scriptures, we are not looking for or expecting to find some strange or difficult vocabulary or some exalted, impossible-to-fathom philosophy.

The Bible is practical in its purposes and practical in its teaching. It answers questions that are basic, in words that are plain and clear. Those who use it for what they imagine to be clever speculation count letters in the Bible; they then give them strange meanings and end up missing the point and purpose of the Bible. Those who try to devise a detailed blueprint for current historical events from visions in Ezekiel or Revelation interpreted with a fertile imagination likewise miss the purposes that God has given for his Word. Those who use it to speculate about the exact time of Christ's return on the basis of biblical numbers or chronological flowcharts also fail to grasp the fundamental purposes that God has given to his Word.

Theology and the interpretation of the Scriptures are ultimately always a practical matter of showing us the way of salvation, the way we should live, and the glory of God in his revelation of himself from the beginning to the end of the Bible and especially in the person and work of Christ. Anything that deviates from those purposes turns theology into speculation or philosophy, or it turns the interpretation of the Bible into a mere intellectual or emotional exercise that ultimately misleads people and is damaging to faith, if not completely destructive of it.

Thus, when we have questions that we would like God's Word to answer, we need to see if God's Word provides an answer. If it does not, then the question is either improper or we will have to wait until we are in heaven for an answer. We may, for example, wish to know what exactly we will be doing in heaven. But the Bible does not tell us exactly what we will do in heaven. It tells us that we will be like Jesus and we will see him as he is. It tells us that we will enjoy his presence without sin or any of its consequences, in perfect harmony with God and with one another. The Bible tells us enough to make it clear to us that we will be perfectly happy there. It tells us enough to assure us that we will not wish we were somewhere else or doing something else. To speculate about things such as kitty cats and puppy dogs, organ music, and palm branches turns theology into an exercise in imagination. It then ceases to be a practical aptitude that has its whole delight in what *God* says, as distinguished from what mere mortals may imagine. We may wish to know how the true body and blood of Christ can be present in the Sacrament. The Scriptures tell us that Christ is present with his true body and blood, but they do not tell us how. Therefore we leave the question alone; we concentrate instead on what the Bible says for our rich comfort and for the building up of our faith through its teaching about the nature and use of the Sacrament.

Theology is a practical aptitude when our whole delight is to hear the Word of God and conform our mind and soul to it. That is exactly what St. Paul was doing when he said, "The weapons we fight with are not the weapons of the world. On the contrary, they have divine power to demolish strongholds. We demolish arguments and every pretension that sets itself up against the knowledge of God, and *we take captive every thought to make it obedient to Christ*" (2 Corinthians 10:4,5).

When theology is a practical aptitude that pursues the purposes that God has given to his Word, then the interpretation of the Scriptures becomes a practice that merely follows where the Scriptures themselves take us. A correct interpretation of the Scriptures takes the Scriptures on their own terms. Strictly speaking, therefore, it is inappropriate for anyone to ask, What is your interpretation of this or that passage? The correct question is this: What does this passage say? What do related passages say that shed light on this passage? One who wishes to interpret the Bible correctly is one who knows the Bible, cherishes it, and uses it within the framework of the purposes God has given for it. And one who practices theology properly is one who sits with Mary at Jesus' feet (Luke 10:38-42), hears his Word, applies it to himself, and then faithfully shares it with others. That's what we mean when we say that theology is a practical aptitude.

While certain intellectual gifts are necessary for such a study (e.g., a basic understanding of language, its vocabulary and rules of grammar, the various types of literature and how to recognize them), the most important gifts for the proper study of the Scriptures are spiritual. They are given by God through the Word itself and not apart from it. St. Paul describes those gifts and their proper use in 1 Corinthians 12–14. What unites all of the gifts of which the apostle speaks is love—love for God and therefore love for his Word, love for our own soul's salvation and edification, and love for our neighbor, who will be built up in faith through the faithful teaching and preaching of God's Word.

In studying the Scriptures with that basic principle in mind, we follow some basic rules of biblical interpretation that are drawn from the Scriptures themselves. We turn our attention now to consider the four most basic rules of interpretation. In each of them we will note that the rule is not concocted apart from the Bible and then imposed on the Bible. Rather, each of the rules is drawn from the Bible itself; the rule is set forth as a way of keeping the student's mind fixed on the Word of God and not on his own imagination or supposed cleverness when it comes to interpreting the Bible.

The text has a single simple sense

This rule is just another way of saying that we take the Scriptures on their own terms. We do not try to import our own opinions, reason, or feelings into the text. We want to read the biblical text and take it as it is.

Thus, for example, St. Matthew's gospel reports, "While they were eating, Jesus took bread, gave thanks and broke it, and gave it to his disciples, saying, 'Take and eat; this is my body.' Then he took the cup, gave thanks and offered it to them, saying, 'Drink from it, all of you. This is my blood of the covenant, which is poured out for many for the forgiveness of sins'" (Matthew 26:26-28). How does the rule of one single simple sense apply to this passage? We read the passage and take it as it stands. All the words in it mean exactly what they say. When Jesus said to his disciples, "This is my body," he meant exactly what he said. "This" was the bread he held in his hands; "is" means the same thing as "equals"; "my" refers to Jesus himself; and "body" is his own body as it was right there before their very eyes.

He adds that what he is giving is "for the forgiveness of sins." Again, we take him at his Word, that this is the benefit he wants to convey in the gift of his body and blood. He plainly states what he is giving and what it is for.

To object that the words could not mean what they say places man as a judge over God's Word. To say that the words must mean something else ultimately makes the reader the primary authority and the Scriptures merely a spark or a spur to his own imagination.

To ignore the rule of one simple single sense is to deny that the Scriptures are clear and sufficient and reliable as an expression of the mind of God and the only true source of doctrine. How arrogant for the creature to correct the Creator! How shameful for the one who must learn language and never fully masters even one language to correct the grammar and vocabulary of the One who created language! Jesus does not need our interpretation of the passage. The passage is clear as it stands. Jesus certainly does not need us to correct him when he speaks. Rather, we need to listen. That's what we do when we apply the rule of one single simple sense.

Thus in formulating the doctrine of the Sacrament of the Altar we do little more than repeat what Jesus has said and receive his gift with faith and thanksgiving. It is his true body and blood, given with the bread and wine for the forgiveness of our sins (1 Corinthians 10:16). We do not attempt to correct his words or deny them, as do the Protestants who insist that the words couldn't mean what they say because they conflict with the laws of reason and physics ("A body cannot occupy more than one place at one and the same time"). Nor do we add to his words and create all sorts of doctrines not found in the text (e.g., the Roman Catholic teaching of *transubstantiation,* that is, the notion that the priest magically transforms the bread and wine into Christ's body and blood by virtue of the power of his ordination or the teaching that the sacrament is a sacrifice for the souls of the dead or the teaching that the elements of bread and wine left on the altar should be objects of adoration). We simply take Jesus at his Word. The Sacrament is his gift to us, not our sacrifice or gift to him for purposes about which his Word says nothing. He gave it for us to eat and to drink, not to worship it on an altar or carry it about in a parade or use it to buy his favor for our "special intentions" or for the benefit of our dead relatives supposedly suffering in some imaginary purgatory.

In the reading of the Genesis account of creation (Genesis 1) we follow the same rule. The text speaks of six consecutive days. It gives us no reason to think that the term "day" means anything else than what it normally means, namely, a 24-hour period of time. Could "day" mean something else to God and therefore have a different meaning in this text? God gave us this text for *our* edification and understanding, not for his! He wanted us to know what happened at the beginning. We therefore take him at his Word. We do not allow any authority to tell the only One who was there at the beginning that he must be mistaken in his account of what happened. And so, in formulating the doctrine of creation, we believe, teach, and confess that God made all that is in six 24-hour days. If people are embarrassed by that teaching or don't like it, they will have to take the matter up with their Creator. The proper practice of theology is to listen, to receive with a believing heart and with gratitude what God has said, and then to faithfully teach the same. That is what we are doing when we follow the rule of one single simple sense. That is what Jesus has told us to do when he said, "If you hold to my teaching, you are really my disciples" (John 8:31).

The Scriptures interpret the Scriptures

Are there not passages in the Bible that have something other than a literal meaning? How do we deal with passages like Jesus' words in John 15:1 where he declares, "I am the true vine"?

First of all, it should be noted that even such passages have a single simple sense to them. We understand that single simple sense when we look at the context in which those words were spoken. We ask not our reason or our sentiments but the Scriptures themselves to explain what is meant by those words of Jesus. Jesus himself tells us what he means. He explains that he is using a metaphor to make a point when he adds, "I am the vine; you are the branches. If a man remains in me and I in him, he will bear much fruit; apart from me you can do nothing. If anyone does not remain in me, he is like a branch that is thrown away and withers" (John 15:5,6). Jesus himself in his Word provides the understanding he wants us to have of that picture of himself as the vine and believers as the branches. He is not talking about literal twigs and leaves and grapes. But we did not need to figure that out for ourselves. He tells us in his own words what he meant for us to grasp and understand.

That is what we mean by the second rule of interpretation, the rule that the Scriptures interpret the Scriptures. If the single simple sense of a passage is other than a literal one, then *the Bible itself must provide us with the correct understanding.* In the examples listed under the first rule, there is nothing at all in the text that tells us to understand the words in other than their literal sense. When Jesus instituted the Sacrament of the Altar, he did not say, "Here is a picture; this meal represents something beyond what is apparent." No, he said without any further qualification or interpretation, "This is my body. . . . This is my blood . . . for the forgiveness of sins." He gives us no reason, not in this passage nor anywhere else in the Bible, to look for some hidden meaning that will change the plain sense of the words. The creation account in Genesis 1 falls into this same category. The text is reporting history. There is not one word in the text or anywhere else in the Bible that would suggest anything other than a literal meaning for the chapter. Since that is the case, we take the words of the Scriptures as they stand. But in John 15 and elsewhere when Jesus is using a metaphor or figurative language, he himself tells us that. And then he explains how we should understand the metaphor or the figure.

There are any number of passages where the Bible itself will tell us how a given passage should be understood when the understanding is not a literal one. To take a very simple example: The Bible tells us that we should always pray (1 Thessalonians 5:17). St. Paul in all of his epistles tells us that he is always praying for those addressed in the epistle. Does that mean he did nothing else all day long but pray and that's all we should do too? Clearly it doesn't mean that. But how do we know? We look at the near and remote context of the passage. We find that Paul was very busy indeed, busy with travel, with writing, with preaching and teaching. How then should we understand it when we are told to pray always and that Paul was always praying? In light of the rest of what the Bible says we should be doing in life, we understand Paul to mean that we should live a life of prayer. Our prayers may occupy our attention fully at times; but at other times we are in an attitude that always looks to God for his help and grace and for the wisdom and strength to live a life that praises him. And so the Scriptures interpret the Scriptures; we do not take the passage literally, but understand it in the context of what the Bible says about prayer and about our lives lived in Christ and in submission to his Word.

At still other times we will have passages that are poetry or expressions that are proverbial. We see these most commonly in the psalms and in the wisdom books (Proverbs, Song of Songs, and Ecclesiastes). Just to mention one psalm by way of example: Read Psalm 46. In it we see a number of expressions that we do not take literally: the river in the city of God, God's help at break of day, God is a fortress, God breaking bows and burning shields. It is the very nature of poetry that it is to be understood in a figurative rather than a literal sense. As we read the psalm, its point is crystal clear; there is no need to force a literal meaning out of it. The psalm is praising God for the "river" of grace that flows from his Word, for his assured protection, and for the preservation of his church and his faithful people. How do we know that? That is what the Bible says expressly in so many other places—for the Scriptures interpret the Scripture. Again, we are not forcing a meaning on a text, nor are we subtracting anything from it; rather, we search the Scriptures for a clear understanding of the imagery in its poems and a clear understanding of its proverbial expressions. To put it another way, historical accounts we read as history; doctrinal pronouncements and formulas such as those we have so often in the epistles we take as doctrinal pronouncements, meaning exactly what they say; poetry and proverbs we read as poetry and proverbs. We take the Scriptures on their own terms and within their own frames of reference.

We also have in the Old Testament and in the New Testament a number of visions reported. Sometimes the vision is very simple and clear and the Lord himself very plainly explains its meaning. Thus, for example, we are left in no doubt about the meaning of the vision that St. Peter had, as it is recorded in Acts 10. The Lord provided the explanation of the vision in the same chapter, and the significance of the vision is further explained in Acts 11. The Scriptures interpret the Scriptures. But in Ezekiel and Daniel and in the book of Revelation numerous other visions are recorded. Sometimes the meaning is plainly provided by the text itself; sometimes it is not provided. Ezekiel's vision of the wheels within the wheels, for example, is difficult for us even to picture, much less to explain (1:15-21). Daniel's visions are sometimes provided with an explanation in the Scriptures and sometimes not.

What then should we do? When the explanation is provided, we have no difficulty. When the explanation is not provided, we listen to the Word of the Lord and marvel, as did the prophet. Then we may have to remain silent, sometimes with our questions unanswered, if the Scriptures themselves do not provide an explanation. The Scriptures are clear when they teach us those doctrines which create and preserve faith, which teach us how to live, and which promote the glory of God; but sometimes passages not so directly connected to those primary purposes of the Bible may be more difficult for us to understand. When that is the case, we bow humbly before the wisdom and majesty of God and wait, perhaps until heaven, for him to make those passages clear to us. We don't consult our imagination and weave convoluted interpretations out of a vision left uninterpreted by the text or by any other part of the Scriptures.

There are still other places in the Bible where the text by itself does not tell us everything that is intended by the passage. The passage is however explained in some other part of the Bible. We see that so often in Old Testament prophecies concerning Christ and the New Testament church. To note just a few examples of such texts, read Psalm 22 and Isaiah 53. How completely did David and Isaiah understand their prophecies of Christ's suffering and death for the sins of the world? Jesus' own words from the cross (Matthew 27:46) make so much of Psalm 22 spring to life for us. And Isaiah 53 comes to life as well on the lips of Philip in Acts 8. Clearly in the light of the New Testament fulfillment we understand David's and Isaiah's prophecies much better than they could have. Yes, and so often the New Testament makes explicit what is pictured in the Old Testament. Most of the epistle to the Hebrews in the New Testament, for example, is a "fleshing out" of the full significance of the Old Testament ceremonial law, of the laws concerning sacrifices for the forgiveness of sins.

As the Scriptures interpret the Scriptures, so we come to see more clearly in Hebrews and elsewhere that Christ is the center of the whole Bible, not just of the New Testament. Paul makes that point even for much of the history in the Old Testament when he tells us that what happened to the Israelites in the Old Testament was all intended for our learning as an example of the importance of faithfulness to Christ and his Word (1 Corinthians 10). Read Acts 1–3 and note how Old Testament passages are seen as clearly fulfilled in the New Testament with Christ always at the center. See in the gospels too how often Jesus himself takes Old Testament passages and gives them their fullest interpretation. He proves, for example, in Matthew 22:32, the doctrine of the resurrection with a simple reference to the tense of a verb in the Old Testament. All of the examples of that are simply too numerous to mention here.

So interconnected are the Old and New Testaments with prophecy in the Old and its explanation as well as its fulfillment in the New that one of the great early church fathers, St. Augustine, was moved to say that the New Testament lies hidden in the Old and the Old is unveiled in the New. Jesus himself gave St. Augustine reason to say that when Jesus told his hearers with regard to the Old Testament that it testifies about him (John 5:39). The point again is simply this: The Scriptures interpret the Scriptures; where a passage means more than we can see on the surface, the Scriptures themselves will tell us that. We are not left to weave spiderwebs of interpretation from our own imagination.

Difficult passages, where possible, should be explained in the light of easier passages

This rule flows from the second rule considered above. At the very beginning of our discussion of this rule, we need to repeat again that the Scriptures are clear. Nevertheless, some passages appear difficult to us at first glance. But further examination of the Scriptures may shed light on the difficult passages.

For example, Revelation 7:4-8 tells us that the number of those sealed for eternal life is 144,000 with 12,000 coming from each of the 12 tribes of Israel. Should these numbers be taken literally in the same way that we take the number of the days of creation in Genesis 1 literally? If we understand the numbers figuratively, are we not breaking the rule of one single simple sense? The very same chapter answers the question for us; it tells us that the numbers are to be understood figuratively. For in the very next verse (v. 9) St. John reports that the number of those in heaven was so great that no one could count all who were there. Twelve thousand from each tribe would be difficult to count, but it would not be impossible. Additionally, he tells us that those in heaven came from every nation and tribe and language. Thus we understand that the numbers and the identification with Israel in verses 5-8 are not to be taken in a literal sense. We conclude that those verses are designed to emphasize that God has chosen his believers and each one will be guarded and protected by him so that they reach the goal of eternal life. A difficult passage is made clear by one that is straightforward and plain.

The solution to the problem, however, is not to be found in our own imaginations. Nor should we expect that God will whisper in our ears some secret meaning for his Word. His Word explains his Word. He has not promised to tell us anything apart from that which is written in the Bible. That is where we look for him, because that is where he has promised to be found and to find us! Again, the simple single sense will be provided by the Scriptures themselves or not at all. And to find that sense we sometimes need to look at other passages in the Bible *that are speaking about the same thing,* whether close at hand or in the context of the whole Bible, to get the clear, single simple sense of a difficult passage.

The analogy of faith

This final rule is closely related to the previous ones. Most simply stated the rule of the analogy of faith is this: In order to find a doctrine in the Bible, we examine all of the passages that speak about the same thing, compare them in the light of one another, and then as the sum of them all state a doctrinal proposition. In the course of stating the doctrinal proposition, that proposition will and must always agree with the most fundamental of all doctrines—the doctrine of salvation by grace, solely on account of the merits of Christ and through faith in that gospel and faith-creating message. That gospel message is always reflected in one way or another in every doctrine. For Christ and his gospel are the heart and core, the beginning, the middle, and the end of God's revelation and gift of himself in the Scriptures.

Do we want to know who God is? Then we examine all of the passages that speak about God. We note that the Bible declares repeatedly that there is only one God. We note that he has different names. Sometimes he is addressed as Father, sometimes as Son, sometimes as Holy Spirit. And yet these three names are clearly not just different names for the same person. Rather, each is usually a name for a distinct person. We see that so clearly in Jesus' references to his Father and to the Holy Spirit in, for example, John 14, 16, and 17. After all the passages have been compared and examined, we are ready to come to a conclusion that is solidly based on and drawn from the Scriptures. Our conclusion is that God is three distinct persons, yet only one divine essence. We call him the Trinity.

The conclusion and the formula for the doctrine follow the rule of the analogy of faith. The doctrine of the Trinity does not come from our own reason or feelings. It is not the result of some clever interpretation dreamed up by learned theologians. It is rather the result of a humble and faithful examination of the Scriptures. Each of the passages considered is taken in its single simple sense. Each is examined in the light of other passages that speak about the same thing. If one seems difficult, the resolution for the difficulty is sought in the other passages speaking about the same thing. For example, Deuteronomy 6:4 means exactly what it says: "Hear, O Israel: The LORD our God, the LORD is one." Likewise, Matthew 28:18-20 and its reference to three persons means exactly what it says. So too does the word of St. Peter addressed to Ananias in Acts 5:3, where the apostle identifies the Holy

Spirit as God. So too do all of the countless other passages that describe the names and works of the persons of the Trinity and call each person the one true and only God. Not a single passage contradicts any of the others. Each of those passages helps us to understand all the others. And taken together all of the passages that teach us the doctrine of the Trinity show us the one God in three persons who was from the beginning devoted to our salvation.

But, some will ask, what about passages of the Scriptures that at first may seem to be contradictory? For example, the Old Testament law commanded Israel to follow this rule: "Show no pity: life for life, eye for eye, tooth for tooth, hand for hand, foot for foot" (Deuteronomy 19:21). But in the New Testament Jesus tells us, "You have heard that it was said, 'Eye for eye, and tooth for tooth.' But I tell you, Do not resist an evil person. If someone strikes you on the right cheek, turn to him the other also" (Matthew 5:38,39). Isn't that a contradiction?

If we examine the context of the passage in Deuteronomy, we will see that this passage is part of the civil law that God gave the nation of Israel. It was designed for use by the government in Israel as it set up its legal system for the punishment of evildoers and the protection of those who lived according to the law. But if we examine Jesus' words in Matthew 5, we will see that those words are part of the Sermon on the Mount. The sermon was addressed not to the government in its relations with evildoers but to Christians in their personal relations with their neighbor. St. Paul makes exactly the same point when he speaks about the individual Christian and how he should act toward those who hurt him (Romans 12:17-21). Neither Jesus nor Paul is contradicting Deuteronomy 19, and we understand that when we use one passage *in its context* to understand both it and a related passage. Only when the passages are taken out of their contexts does there appear to be a contradiction. Again, the Scriptures interpret the Scriptures.

Thus, it is important to keep in mind that the passages studied in formulating doctrine must all be about the same thing. That perhaps should be obvious. Sadly, it is not obvious at all to some who distort the Scriptures by taking passages out of their proper contexts to make a point that is contrary to the Scriptures themselves. For example, some point to 2 Peter 3:8 in an attempt to overthrow what the Bible says about creation in Genesis 1,2 and elsewhere. St. Peter says, "With the Lord a day is like a thousand years, and a thousand years are like a day." Is the apostle talking about the days of creation? He is not! He is talking about the patience of the Lord in seeking our repentance and our salvation. Even in this passage a day is still a 24-

hour period of time; the apostle's point is not that God is confused about how long a day lasts, but that God is not bound by time at all in his calculations for our salvation. To take these words of the apostle and use them to conclude that Genesis 1 is not talking about 24-hour days is contrary to the Scriptures. Genesis 1 is giving a historical account of what happened at the beginning, and it should be understood that way. Second Peter 3:8 is discussing something entirely different and it should be understood in its own context.

The anti-Christian religion of the Jehovah's Witnesses does much the same with almost the entire Bible. It takes passages out of their contexts and uses them to deny what the Bible clearly teaches. To mention but one example, they refer to Jesus' words in John 14:28 in an attempt to prove that Jesus is not true God and to attack the doctrine of the Trinity. There Jesus says, "If you loved me, you would be glad that I am going to the Father, for the Father is greater than I." But what is Jesus talking about in this discussion with his disciples? Is he talking about his person and the relationship of the persons Father, Son, and Holy Spirit? He is not! He is talking about the mission that he is about to complete in his human nature, his mission of suffering and dying. In the carrying out of that mission, in his human nature, in his time of humiliation before his resurrection, he declares his obedience to the will of the Father and his subjection to that will. In all of what he does in his human nature and in the time of his humiliation he declares that the Father is greater than he is. But when he speaks about the essence of his relationship with the Father he says something very different. In John 10:28-30 he says, "I give [my sheep] eternal life, and they shall never perish; no one can snatch them out of my hand. *My Father,* who has given them to me, *is greater than all;* no one can snatch them out of my Father's hand. *I and the Father are one.*" The Jews understood that Jesus here made himself and the Father not only equal but one in essence. Jesus' words were crystal clear to them, and they wanted to stone him to death because of what he had said. And what was Jesus' response to their anger? Did he say, "You've misunderstood me"? No, not at all. Quite the contrary; he went on to make it plain that they had understood him correctly. It is to this passage, one in which Jesus speaks of his relationship to the Father, that we look when we want to examine that relationship. This passage, of course, together with scores of others that speak of the divinity of Christ and of the Trinity, the Jehovah's Witnesses either ignore or twist.

Again, the point is that in the interpretation of the Scriptures we want to let the Scriptures speak. We do not want to draw out of them something that is not there; nor do we want to read into them something that we think they should say. Rather, in the formulation of a doctrine we want to examine all of the passages that speak about the same thing. Then, on the basis of those passages and what they say, each on its own and in its relationship with all the others, we formulate the doctrine. In coming chapters we will observe this rule of the analogy of faith as we draw from many places in the Bible summary statements of doctrines.

We also observe the rule of the analogy of faith in a very practical way when we apply the Scriptures to our everyday life. We do that when we read them on our own and when we hear a text explained and applied in a book or in a Bible class or in a sermon. The Bible says, for example, in the Seventh Commandment that we shouldn't steal. Does that have any application to the way I fill out my tax return or the way I work for an employer? Clearly it does, even though there is no passage that says, "Don't cheat on your tax return and don't rob your employer by wasting the time that he is paying for."[1] Likewise, there is no passage in the Bible that tells me I should marry Fritz/Gertrude instead of Hans/Hilda. But the Bible says a lot about marriage and family life; I consult what it says and apply what it says as best I can to the choices I make, whether for marriage, for the raising of children, for the choice of vocation, or for how I spend the time and the health and the wealth that God is pleased to give me. The application of the Bible to our lives, to what we think and feel and do, is rich and beautiful and a never-finished project.

Indeed, some passages in the Bible we could read every day and never finish their beautiful and practical application to our lives. John 3:16 is such a passage. It gives me new reasons every day for delight in God's Word, for gratitude to and adoration of the Savior. Today again my sins have given him new reasons not to love me and redeem me. But still today the passage is as true as it ever was and embraces me no less today than it did on the day of my baptism. I know that such an application of the passage is legitimate both because it is clear in itself and because so much of the rest of the Bible says "Amen" to such a use of the passage. That's a very simple and practical application of the rule of the analogy of faith.

Or consider the parables of our Lord. Each one finds the Christian at a moment in life and sums up his ever-changing life in that parable.

---

[1]There are, of course, some passages that come very close to saying exactly that, e.g., Matthew 22:15-22; Romans 13:6,7; Colossians 3:22,23.

Jesus, for example, tells the parable of the sower and the seed in Matthew 13:1-17, and then he explains it in verses 18-23. As we read the parable and his explanation we are moved to ask ourselves: Is my heart good soil? If so, how did it get that way? Are there days when my heart is a rocky road? Have I heard his Word today with a stony heart that rejoices in an instant and then goes away and forgets or ignores what was heard? Are parts of my heart still infested with thorns and thistles? What kind of fruit does his Word have in my life today? A lot? A little? None at all? And how is all of that different from the last time I heard the parable? Such considerations accord with what Paul tells us in Romans 12, for example. Or consider the little parable about the yeast in Matthew 13:33. Through how much of the dough of my life has that yeast spread? Is it in my heart, my hands, what I think, what I say, or how I behave towards friends, relatives, and enemies? And how is its spread through my life different from the last time I heard the parable? Is it not clear that the Word of God is always new and fresh? The understanding of the parable is neither fanciful nor allegorizing when it conforms to what the rest of the Scriptures say on the same subject, that is, when it does not contradict the analogy of faith.

The rule of the analogy of faith keeps us from going beyond the intention of the text; it helps us to "interpret" a particular passage only in such a way that the interpretation conforms with and does not contradict some clear passage of the Scriptures. Thus, for example, if someone would read the account of the disciples' rescue in the storm on the Sea of Galilee (Mark 4:35-41) and conclude, "See, as long as you believe, you will never drown," he would be violating the rule of the analogy of faith. For the Bible doesn't tell us that we will never drown. Or if someone would read any of the accounts of the miracles of healing that Jesus performed and then say, "See, all you have to do is have enough faith and you will be healed of every disease," that too would violate the rule of the analogy of faith; for God in his Word never promised us that we would never get sick. In applying the accounts of Jesus' miracles we follow the rule when we conclude that all things are in his hands; we follow the rule when we submit our lives into his care and keeping, even if he does not miraculously heal us of every sickness. Though he still may do that sometimes, he has not promised to do it always. To put it another way, we apply the miracle accounts to our own lives with the principle that the apostle Paul gives us in Romans 8:28-39.

It should be evident from the consideration of the rules of interpretation that we are to pay the highest respect to the Scriptures as the verbally inspired and inerrant Word of God. For the rules of interpretation take the Scriptures as they are. Each rule is just another way of saying exactly that. The rules do not read anything into the Scriptures. They wish only to draw out from the Scriptures what is actually there. To be sure, we are not mindless when we study the Word of God. As already noted, we pay attention to language, to vocabulary, to rules of grammar, to various and distinct types of literature in the Bible, to its use of analogy, metaphor, simile, and the like. In short, we make use of human reason as we study the Scriptures, interpret them, apply them to our every day lives, and formulate doctrines drawn from this Word of God. But it is important to remember that reason plays only a *servant role,* not a *teaching role,* in the interpretation of the Scriptures *(ministerial use of reason, not magisterial use).* That is, if reason contradicts the Bible, then reason is faulty and mistaken. Reason does not instruct or correct the Word of God; reason is instructed and corrected by the Word of God. Reason is a necessary and useful tool in the house of theology, but it is not the master of the house. When used properly, reason is a very useful tool; when allowed to contradict the clear Word of God, reason becomes what Luther called reason thus misused: the devil's whore.

The rules of interpretation accordingly are not the fruits of reason but reason paying the highest respect to the purposes that God himself has given to his Word. With these rules of interpretation, reason submits to the Word. God has given us his Word, as noted earlier, in order to show us the way of salvation, in order to show how we should live, and in order to glorify God. When we pay heed to those purposes given by God, when we take seriously the Word he has given, then theology and the interpretation of the Scriptures will be the practical aptitude that God intended and wills.

Thus all that we believe, teach, and confess should be grounded and rooted in God's own Word. *Sola Scriptura* (Scripture alone) was a motto of the Lutheran Reformation. It remains our aim to this day, that nothing taught in our churches be contrary or in addition to the Word of God. It remains our goal in this book to study the Scriptures and draw from them alone the doctrines that we, by God's grace, continue to believe, teach, and confess.

The creeds and confessions

Do we not also have other sources of doctrine? When we are confirmed, we take an oath of loyalty to the Bible but also to the creeds and what we have learned from, for example, Luther's Small Catechism. When pastors and teachers are installed, they are required to swear to teach the Word of God in harmony with the creeds and with the Lutheran Confessions. Does that not contradict our claim that all our teachings are drawn from the Scriptures alone?

It does not contradict the principle of *sola Scriptura* at all. Quite the contrary, the oath of loyalty to the creeds and the confessions supports the principle of Scripture alone as the one and only source of doctrine. For the creeds and confessions are drawn from the Scriptures; they are themselves an application of the rules of interpretation discussed above, and especially of the rule of the analogy of faith. It is their sole intent and purpose to confess faithfully and exactly what the Scriptures teach and to reject and warn against doctrines that are contrary to the Scriptures.

Thus, for example, the Formula of Concord, the last and most extensive of the Lutheran Confessions, begins with this solemn declaration: "We believe, teach, and confess that the only rule and guiding principle according to which all teachings and teachers are to be evaluated and judged are the prophetic and apostolic writings of the Old and New Testaments alone" (FC Ep, 1 p. 486).

If the creeds and confessions grant that the Scriptures alone are the source and judge of all doctrine, and if they themselves wish to teach nothing else than the Scriptures, why bother with creeds and confessions? Why not be content with saying, "We teach the Bible and nothing else"? The creeds and confessions were written and we still use them because they provide an excellent and correct summary of what we mean when we say that we believe, teach, and confess only what the Bible teaches. Thus, for example, should someone ask what we believe, the Apostles' Creed provides an excellent summary statement. Were we to answer, "We believe the Bible," we would not be telling the questioner anything at all, for he may not know anything about the Bible. But we can recite in about a minute the whole creed as a summary of the Bible's most important teachings.

If someone would ask, "What do you believe about the Sacrament of the Altar?" we could just quote the appropriate Bible passages; there would be nothing wrong with that. But the questioner might be left wondering if we understood those passages literally or figuratively. Luther's Small Catechism is one of our confessions. It provides a beautiful summary of exactly how we understand the words of the Bible and at the same time quotes them. So we might answer the question by saying, "We believe that it is the true body and blood of our Lord, along with the bread and wine, given for the forgiveness of sins." That all but quotes the summary statement in the catechism.

It tells anyone asking both what the Bible says and how we understand those words.

What if someone would ask, "What do you believe about Jesus?" We could begin with the quotation of passages in the Old Testament and the New Testament, which taken together answer the question. But the hearer really wants a summary statement. We could recite the Second Article of the Apostles' or the Nicene Creed. We could quote Luther's masterful explanation of the Second Article in the Small Catechism. There the one asking would hear a beautiful and correct summation of what the Scriptures say about Jesus and his work for our salvation. We would have added nothing to the Scriptures, nor would we have taken anything away from them.

Even for ourselves the creeds and confessions serve a useful purpose. When we are thinking about our faith, we may wish to concentrate on its most vital aspects. At such a time we will call to mind the summaries provided by the creeds and confessions. The familiar lines of the Apostles' Creed, as we call them to mind, hold before us great and grand chapters of the Bible and scenes from the story of our salvation. We remember Genesis 1,2 as we think about the First Article. The whole of Christ's life and work are vividly held before faith's eye as we rehearse in our mind the Second Article; the Christmas story is there, the suffering Savior is there, the triumph of Easter and the ascension is there, and the goal of history and of our faith in Christ's return on the Last Day is there. The brief words of the Third Article summarize for us what Christ's work has accomplished for us in crisp, short phrases; the words summarize the work of the Holy Spirit in the life of faith and in the history of the church. In mere moments, all the great themes of the Bible are brought to mind and again impressed upon our hearts.

Thus creeds and confessions are not additional sources of doctrine. They are the result of a correct interpretation of the Scriptures, following the principles drawn from the Scriptures themselves. That is already evident in the very word *creed.* The word comes from the first word of the Apostles' Creed in Latin, *credo.* It means "I believe." Thus, a creed or a confession is by definition "a statement of what we believe, teach, and confess" on the basis of the sacred Scriptures.

That's the first purpose of the creeds and confessions of our church: To summarize for ourselves *what we believe* as a result of the work of the Holy Spirit who creates that faith through his Word.

Their second purpose is closely related to the first. The creeds and confessions summarize *what we teach in our churches and schools.* We come together in church on the basis of what the Bible teaches; we share with one another our confession of that faith in its teachings. Because those worshiping with us hold to the same creeds and confessions as we do, we trust that we are one in that confession of faith. We encourage one another to continue in faithfulness to the teachings of the Scriptures as we share our confession of faith when we join in reciting the Apostles', the Nicene, or the Athanasian Creed. We are saying to those worshiping with us, "This is what I believe too! You are not alone! We are knit together in a fellowship with one another by our confession of the same faith, worked by what the Holy Spirit has taught us in his Word!"

The third purpose of creeds and confessions is connected to the first two. The creeds and confessions summarize for the world *what we confess.* Should someone from another church or someone from no church want to know the flag we fly, we answer boldly, "Ours is the faith of the prophets and the apostles; it is the faith drawn from and based on the Scriptures alone; it is the faith confessed by those loyal to the Scriptures always and everywhere; here you can see it; here are our creeds and confessions."

When we call and install pastors and teachers, we therefore require and expect them to be faithful to the creeds and confessions. They take an oath that all of their preaching and teaching will conform to the creeds and confessions. They swear that they will not depart from that teaching. That oath is not an oath of loyalty to something other than the Scriptures. It is an oath of loyalty to the Scriptures because the creeds and confessions are drawn from the Scriptures.

Thus, the creeds and confessions are called a normed, or guided, norm *(norma normata),* as a standard of pure doctrine. They do not create doctrine. Only the Scriptures do that. The Scriptures are called the norming, or guiding, norm *(norma normans).* It works something like this: In Greenwich, England, there is a clock by whose time every clock in the world is set. The time on that clock is called Greenwich Standard Time. That standard is the norm; all other clocks take their measure from that clock and are correct because they conform to the norm. Such other clocks we might call normed clocks, and Greenwich Standard Time we might call the norming clock. The Scriptures are the norm, the standard from which all doctrine comes and by which all doctrine is judged. The creeds and confessions, since they are drawn from the Scriptures, are the "normed norm." To depart, therefore, from the doctrinal content of the creeds and confessions is to depart from the doctrinal content of their source—the Bible.

Unfortunately, there are those who receive the creeds and confessions only for traditional or historical reasons, but they do not accept and teach according to them. There are doctrines in the creeds and confessions to which they object. Some do not like it that the creeds and confessions declare that one is saved alone by grace through faith. Some do not like it that the confessions in numerous places declare that doctrine can come only from the Scriptures. Some do not like it that the confessions take it as a given that man came into being as a result of the creation described and reported in Genesis 1,2. There may be many doctrines or just a few to which they take exception. Their real objection is to what the Bible teaches, as that teaching is reflected in the creeds and confessions.

Nevertheless, many of these will still take an oath of loyalty to the creeds and confessions. They will declare, and their church body has encouraged this declaration: "We subscribe to the creeds and confessions only *in so far as* (Latin: *quatenus*) they are drawn from the Word of God." That may sound very pious on the surface. But in fact a *quatenus* subscription, or oath, only sounds pious; it is really a fraudulent subscription, ultimately no subscription at all. For it tells us nothing. It would be like saying—to continue with our analogy about the clock—"My clock is correct only in so far as it agrees with Greenwich Standard Time." Now I know nothing about the accuracy of his clock; for I don't know to what extent it agrees with Greenwich Standard Time. And so it is with an "in so far as" adherence to the creeds and the confessions. What in the creeds and confessions does such a person think is contrary to the Word of God, or not drawn from the Word of God? What does such a person teach instead? We have no answer. We do not know what they believe, teach, and confess. The whole point of the creeds and confessions is lost.

Therefore we reject a *quatenus* subscription, or oath, and we reject fellowship with all who make it. For a refusal to teach in accord with the creeds and the confessions is essentially a refusal to teach in accord with the sacred Scriptures. Sadly, most Lutheran church bodies today require nothing more than a *quatenus* subscription. And many non-Lutheran Protestant churches, likewise, grant no more than a *quatenus* subscription even to the Apostles,' the Nicene, and the Athanasian Creeds—creeds which provide summaries of what the ancient church believed, taught, and confessed, especially about the person and work of Christ as God's Son in the flesh and our only Savior.

We require those who publicly preach and teach in our churches to give a *quia* subscription to the creeds and confessions. The Latin word *quia* means "because." We swear to teach in accord with the creeds and confessions *because* their doctrines are drawn from the Word of God. Only those willing to make a *quia* subscription are allowed to be pastors and teachers in our churches and schools. An honestly given *quia* oath of loyalty tells us that we can expect such a person to preach and teach the Scriptures faithfully, because he has sworn loyalty to the Bible as the sole source of doctrine and loyalty to the creeds and confessions as correct summaries of the doctrines taught by the Bible.

Of course, faithfulness to the creeds and the confessions is not an excuse for sloppiness or laziness with respect to the Bible. We do not study the creeds and confessions as a substitute for the Bible or as an excuse for not searching the Scriptures diligently for their teaching. Nor for that matter would we tolerate in our churches and schools someone who taught contrary to the Word and used the argument: "But the confessions don't talk about this particular thing, so I'm free to say whatever I want about it." Quite to the contrary! The confessions themselves would urge us to follow always the motto of Martin Chemnitz, who was an author of one of our greatest confessions, the Formula of Concord. His motto was *Ad fontes! (Back to the source, i.e., the Bible itself!).* Every generation must heed the inspired admonition of the Bible itself from beginning to end. From the Scriptures as the unique, sole, and all-sufficient source of Christian faith and life we draw all that we believe, teach, and confess. In the creeds and confessions before all else we bear witness to that one divinely inspired and infallible source.

The creeds and confessions to which we hold are the three ecumenical creeds and the six Lutheran Confessions.

The ecumenical creeds are so called because anyone who is a Christian accepts their doctrinal content. The ecumenical creeds are

the Apostles' Creed. It was not written by the apostles, but it is a summary of what they believed, taught, and confessed. It emerged in the ancient church, probably already beginning at the time of the apostles. It grew out of the formula for Baptism. It is easy to see how that would happen. The formula for Baptism is "I baptize you in the name of the Father and of the Son and of the Holy Spirit." Those baptized would confess their faith, identifying with a brief statement who each of these persons is. And thus was born the Apostles' Creed. It is called an *irenic* creed. The word *irenic* comes from a Greek word that means "peaceful." The Apostles' Creed is called an irenic creed because in a quiet and peaceful way it simply states and confesses the most basic doctrines of the Bible.

the Nicene Creed. Its initial author was St. Athanasius. He boldly confessed his faith in Christ at the Council of Nicea in the year A.D. 325 against the heretics who denied that Christ is true God, one in essence with the Father. This creed is called a *polemical creed,* from a Greek word that means "war," because it was written as a result of a great doctrinal battle against those who denied that Christ is true God. The creed underwent refinements required by the cleverness of heretics who kept finding new ways of subverting the doctrine subscribed at the Council of Nicea. It took until A.D. 451 for it to reach its all-but-final form as we have it today. Only one word was added after that, the word *filioque* in the Latin version of the Third Article, in which we confess that the Holy Spirit proceeds from the Father (and the Son) *filioque.*

the Athanasian Creed. It is named after St. Athanasius. Though he did not actually write it, this creed gives a full expression of what he believed, taught, and confessed. Its origins are lost in history, but it probably was written in Spain or in the south of France in the fifth century A.D. It is the most complete creedal statement of the doctrine of the Trinity. It shows the results of an extensive study of the doctrine of the Trinity on the basis of the Scriptures during the fourth century when so many attacks were made on this doctrine.

The six Lutheran Confessions are

the (Unaltered) Augsburg Confession of 1530. This is the central confession of the Lutheran church. It was written by Philip Melanchthon, one of Luther's coworkers during the German Reformation, and presented by the Lutheran princes and others to Emperor Charles V at the Diet (or Parliament) meeting in the city of Augsburg. The emperor had requested a written statement of faith from the "Lutherans," and this was the statement they presented. It is basically an irenic confession, simply stating in summary fashion what was believed, taught, and confessed in the churches of Germany that had returned to the pure teaching of the Scriptures. The date of its presentation (June 25, 1530) has sometimes been called the birthday of the Lutheran church. The word *unaltered* is sometimes added as a part of its name because later versions of the confession watered down some of the biblical teaching in the original. Many Lutheran church buildings have the letters UAC carved into their cornerstones to indicate that they are faithful to the Unaltered Augsburg Confession.

the Apology of the Augsburg Confession. The word *apology* is really a Greek word that means "defense." The Apology was written by Philip Melanchthon shortly after the presentation of the Augsburg

Confession. The emperor and the Catholic theologians at the Diet of Augsburg rejected and bitterly attacked the Augsburg Confession. Melanchthon wrote the Apology in its defense. In the Apology he gives a more detailed account of the doctrines presented in the Augsburg Confession. It is a polemical confession.

Luther's Small Catechism. It was written by Martin Luther in 1529 as a result of a visitation of the parishes in the German state of Saxony. The visitation revealed that even many of the priests knew little or nothing about doctrine. Their people were steeped in ignorance and superstition. Luther and his coworkers were so alarmed by these conditions that he set about writing the Small Catechism as a brief summary of Christian doctrine. It remains to this day an unequalled masterpiece of Christian literature and doctrine. It quickly became, along with the Bible and the hymns that Luther and others were writing, a standard textbook in parish schools. But it was especially written for parents, so that fathers and mothers would teach their children, whether their children could go to school or not. It is an irenic confession.

Luther's Large Catechism. It was written at the same time as the Small Catechism and is to a large extent an expansion of it. It is, however, more polemical in nature than the Small Catechism. It too is a literary and doctrinal masterpiece. Anyone who wants to taste the "flavor" of the Reformation and of Luther at his best can do no better than to take in hand this great confession of faith.

the Smalcald Articles of 1537. These were written by Martin Luther in response to a request from some of the princes. They had been commanded by the emperor to attend a proposed council of the church that the pope had promised to call. The purpose of the council was the destruction of Lutheran doctrine and Lutheran churches. The princes asked Luther to draft an answer to the summons for consideration at their meeting in the city of Smalcald. Luther responded with these articles in which he again summarizes Christian doctrine on the basis of the Scriptures and boldly declares that he cannot and will not depart from the Word of God. He notes, as does an article written by Melanchthon and attached later to the Smalcald Articles, that the pope has all the marks of the Antichrist spoken of by St. Paul in 2 Thessalonians 2:1-12. It is the most polemical of our confessions.

the Formula of Concord. It was written in 1577 by a number of Lutheran theologians in response to attacks on Lutheran doctrine. Many false teachers had invaded the Lutheran churches under a false subscription (much like the *quatenus* subscription referred to previously) to the Augsburg Confession in order to escape persecution by the emperor. (Lutheranism had become a legal religion in 1555, at least in those parts of the empire that had a Lutheran prince.) Other attacks came from inside of the Lutheran churches from those who wished to compromise the truth of God's Word either for the sake of harmony with Catholic teaching or for the sake of union with an assortment of non-Lutheran Protestants, or simply as a result of their own speculations. The doctrinal situation had become so clouded that many claimed they no longer knew what it meant to be a Lutheran. The Formula of Concord clearly and completely states the doctrine of the genuine Lutheran churches as it was drawn from the Bible, and it just as clearly rejects all of the errors that had arisen after Luther's death. It is the longest and most detailed of our confessions. Its two most important authors are Jakob Andreae and Martin Chemnitz. The work of Martin Chemnitz was so important to the preservation of pure Lutheranism that it is often said that were it not for the work of this second Martin, the work of the first Martin (i.e., Luther) would have perished.

Summary of what we believe, teach, and confess concerning the Word of God

The 66 books of the Old and New Testament Canon are the sacred Scriptures, the Bible. The Bible is verbally inspired and therefore does not merely *contain* the Word of God, as though something in it might not be the Word of God. It *is* the Word of God and is, therefore, inerrant, true, and corresponding to reality in all that it says, whether it is speaking of faith and morals or of other matters, such as science and history. Since it is the Word of God, it is the only source of doctrine. Through it God himself creates faith in the saving work of his Son, who is the center of all of sacred Scripture. Through it God preserves the faith thus created. Through it God shows us the life he wants us to live in response to his saving work in Christ and in Christ gives us the desire and ability to begin leading such a life to the glory of his name. We use the Word of God correctly, therefore, when we hear it, study it, meditate on it, believe it, live according to it, and share it in its truth and purity. When we summarize it in doctrinal formulae, or statements, these must be drawn, as are the creeds and the Lutheran Confessions, from the Scriptures alone, without the addition of mere human opinion or feeling, without subtracting anything from it that reason, emotion, or science falsely claim or that public opinion might find objectionable. Faithfulness to the Scriptures and to the purposes that God has given them is the mark of true theology. Such true theology sees Christ and his saving work as the center of all of God's Word and the source, content, and goal of Christian faith and life. Faithfulness to the Scriptures in faith and life seeks the glory of God, the true author of both the Scriptures and the faith born from the Scriptures.

PART II

THEOLOGY PROPER

Chapter 5
The Doctrine of God

The word *theology* is most often used in a broad sense to mean the study of things sacred or religious, or the study of the Bible and its teachings. However, the word actually comes from two Greek words that mean "the study of God." While we also use the term in its broad sense, in part 2, we turn to theology proper, or the study of theology in the narrow sense of the term; we turn to the study of God, his nature and essence, his works and attributes.

It should be self-evident that we would want to get to know as much as possible about God. Fear alone might drive that desire: If he exists and if I am accountable to him, I need to know how to please or at least how to satisfy him. Love instead of fear should impel each Christian even more to want to get to know as much as possible about God. For the Christian knows that God has created us. He preserves and keeps us. And wonder above all wonders, he has redeemed us; he wants to enter into a loving relationship with us that will last forever. Thus, he is both God and Savior. We love him because he has loved us and given himself for us. Where love rules in a relationship, there is a natural desire to want to grow in knowledge about and understanding of the one loved. We have more reasons to love God than we have to love anything else or anyone else. Therefore we desire to know and to understand him ever better.

But as soon as we begin to study God, we run into a problem. We might like to have a nice, simple, rational definition of God. But no matter how well we get to know and understand God on the basis of his Word, we can never fully grasp or define him. For God is above and beyond all possibility of human definition, as St. Paul reminds us:

> Oh, the depth of the riches of the wisdom and knowledge of God! How unsearchable his judgments, and his paths beyond tracing out! "Who has known the mind of the Lord? Or who has been his counselor?" "Who has ever given to God, that God should repay him?" For from him and through him and to him are all things. To him be the glory forever! Amen. (Romans 11:33-36)

The creature cannot suppose that it will ever fully grasp the essence of its Creator. The mortal should not suppose that he could fathom the One who is life itself. God is beyond time, beyond space, and unlimited by anything created. For little, limited, and dependent human beings to imagine that they could come up with a definition that would show complete knowledge or understanding of God would be the height of folly. It would be easier for an ant to understand us than for us ever fully to understand God.

Nevertheless, it is possible for us to get to know God, to get to know him well, even if not perfectly or completely. We have already noted in our consideration of the nature of religion (chapter 1) that God has left footprints, so to speak, of his nature and attributes in his creation. Nature proclaims the power of God and his wisdom. Natural law and conscience likewise drive people in every culture and in every age to the conclusion that there is a God to whom they are accountable. But for all that nature, natural law, and conscience may suggest about God and his attributes, they cannot tell us who he is. They cannot tell us with any degree of certainty what he thinks about us, his poor and dying creatures. They cannot give us any certain basis for a relationship with him or peace with him.

Because we cannot find out by ourselves with any certainty who God is, any sure and certain knowledge of God must come from God himself. Any relationship with God must have God as its driving force. Any peace with God must be peace that God himself establishes on his terms, not ours. For, again, we are the creatures. He is the Creator.

Happily, God has provided us with sure and certain knowledge about himself. God has willed to enter into a relationship with us. God has established that peace with us which the world cannot and could never give and was never intended to give. And all of that he makes known to us in his revealed will, the Bible. The Bible does not provide us with a complete definition of God, because we are incapable of grasping such a definition. But what the Bible tells us about God is sure and true, because it comes from God himself. It is what he wants us to know about him. It gives the basis of the relationship that he wants to establish with us. It is therefore with intense interest that we listen to God's own testimony about himself.

The doctrine of the Trinity

Following the rules of interpretation outlined in the previous chapter, we search the Scriptures for God's description of himself. From the first verses of the Bible to the last that description is awe-inspiring. It fills us with wonder and amazement that a God so great and glorious would want to reveal himself and would want to enter into a relationship with us and would be willing to give himself in order to establish it.

The first thing that the Scriptures teach us about God is the simple, basic truth that there is only one God. The great national anthem of the Old Testament declares, "Hear, O Israel: The LORD our God, the LORD is one" (Deuteronomy 6:4). The very first of the Ten Commandments and the sum of them all commands all people everywhere, "I am the LORD your God. . . . You shall have no other gods before me" (Deuteronomy 5:6,7). Jesus repeated these great passages of the Old Testament when he was asked which of the commandments was the greatest (Mark 12:29,30). St. Paul likewise declared that there is but one God when he preached in Athens to those who ignorantly worshiped many gods (Acts 17:22-31). He reminded the Corinthians of this basic truth when he wrote about the eating of foods sacrificed to idols. He said, "We know that an idol is nothing at all in the world and that there is no God but one" (1 Corinthians 8:4).

At the same time the Scriptures declare from beginning to end that this one God is three distinct persons. When we use the term *person* we mean that which exists fully and completely in itself. You are a person. You are not just another name for your father or mother. You are a person, unique and self-contained, not to be confused with any other person or persons, each of whom also is unique, self-contained, and not just another name for you. The persons in the Godhead likewise are not just names for one another. Each person exists.

The existence of more than one person in God is evident throughout the Old Testament. In the very first verse of the Bible, the noun that is used for God is a plural noun, but the verb is singular. If we were to translate literally, we might translate thus: "In the beginning Gods he created heaven and earth." In the second verse of the Bible, the Spirit of God is identified as moving in a creating way over the vast chaos that God was about to organize on the six days of creation. And when creation began, it began with the voice of God, the Word of God, which is so often and consistently identified as a person (John 1:1). Then, when God created man, he addressed himself in divine council: "Let us make man in our image, in our likeness" (Genesis 1:26).

Likewise, in the Old Testament there are a number of appearances of God in angelic or human form *(theophanies)*. In these appearances, God is worshiped and accepts the worship, even though a distinction is often made between the appearing form and God. Thus, in Genesis 18, when three visitors came to Abraham to warn of the destruction of Sodom and to promise the birth of Isaac, the one who spoke is identified as the Lord, and Abraham recognized him as such (Genesis 18:10-33). Jacob wrestled with God in human form (Genesis 32:24-30). Joshua worshiped the "commander of the army of the LORD" and that worship was both expected and accepted (Joshua 5:13-15). The Angel of the Lord is worshiped in Judges 2,6,13, et al. These and numerous similar incidents elsewhere in the Old Testament indicate a plurality of persons in God, without ever calling into question the basic truth that there is only one God.

The Old Testament prophecies concerning the coming of the Savior speak of him as God and man, and yet distinguish him as a person from the One from whom he comes and the Spirit who dwells in him (e.g., Isaiah 9,11,42). The promise of Pentecost likewise speaks of the Spirit of the Lord in terms of two distinct persons, not just a spiritual aspect of one person (Joel 2:28,29). The closing chapters of the Old Testament promise the appearance of the Messenger of the covenant who is sent by the Lord to carry out his will perfectly (Malachi 3,4). But the work of that Promised One is work that is called the Lord's own work. In sum, throughout the Old Testament, in passages too numerous to list here, the idea that God is one and that he is persons (always the Sending One, the Sent or Coming One, and the Spirit of the Lord) is evident.

It is interesting to note in this connection that in the New Testament record no one ever objected or expressed surprise when Jesus spoke of the plurality of persons in God and called them by name. Some to be sure violently objected to Jesus' identification of himself as one of the three, but they did not object to the idea of three in one itself. The disciples on their weakest day never asked, "What in the world are you talking about?" when Jesus taught the truth that God is three and nevertheless one. It was a truth already known to them to a certain extent from the Old Testament. God's identification of himself as one God in three persons is, of course, most clearly spelled out and expressed in the New Testament. The *sedes doctrinae* for the doctrine of the Trinity is Matthew 28:18-20:

> Then Jesus came to them and said, "All authority in heaven and on earth has been given to me. Therefore go and make disciples of all nations, baptizing them in the name of the Father and of the Son and of the Holy Spirit, and teaching them to obey everything I have commanded you. And surely I am with you always, to the very end of the age.

The passage is an altogether remarkable and magnificent one! Jesus clearly identifies himself as the one God. There is no authority in heaven or on earth that is not in his keeping. Who else can say that but the one, true, and only God? He tells the disciples to teach not what *God* has commanded, as though he were less than God, but to teach obedience to everything that *he* has commanded. No one has the right to do that except the one, true, and only God. Additionally, he promises that his presence will abide with them, no matter where they are and no matter how long the world stands. None but the one and only God could make such a promise and be expected to keep it. And yet, when he commands them to baptize, he does not tell them to baptize only in his name or in the name of God, as though God were somehow different from himself. Baptism is to take place in the name of the Father, Son, and Holy Spirit. But still there is no suggestion that there is more than one God. All three persons are linked inseparably together in the formula for Baptism. And yet each person is mentioned as distinct from the other two.

It is in exactly the same way that the persons are distinguished and yet always together in the rest of the New Testament. Jesus' own incarnation sets the pattern. All three persons are involved without any hint that there are three gods (Matthew 1:18-24; Luke 1:26-35). We see it again at Jesus' baptism, where all three persons are evident together and yet distinct (Matthew 3:16,17). We see it in the identification of Jesus with the prophecy of Isaiah 42:1-4, where the Father speaks, the Son is the chosen Servant of the Lord, and the Holy Spirit abides in him (Matthew 12:18-21).

It is in John's gospel that we see the relationship of Father, Son, and Holy Spirit most beautifully spelled out. Always the persons are distinct and yet always they are one, one in essence, united in will, one in a perfect loving harmony with one another, and one in the burning desire for our salvation. We cannot help but be struck by the beauty of the words that the members of the Trinity speak to and about one another. Read the gospel of John. You can almost see the glow on Jesus' face as he talks about his Father—everything he does, he does out of love for and in obedience to the Father who sent him (e.g., John 5:19-38; 8:27-29; 12:23-28,44-50). No less the Father, when he speaks; he points to the Son as the sole, great object of his delight, to whom all mankind should give heed (e.g., John 12:28; Luke 3:21,22; Mark 9:7). When Jesus speaks of the Holy Spirit, it is as though everything was for the glory of the Holy Spirit who comes forth from the Father and the Son (John 16:5-11). And then when the Holy Spirit speaks, who and what does he speak about? The Son! Everything is the Son! He speaks so that we remember and think always about Jesus (John 16:12-15). (Just imagine what life would be like if husbands and wives and friends spoke that way about one another!)

In Acts and in the epistles too we see the same thing. The Father, the Son, and the Holy Spirit are spoken of as clearly distinct, not just different names for different activities. Jesus makes a clear distinction between the persons at his ascension in Acts 1:7,8. The Holy Spirit comes as distinct from the Father and the Son at Pentecost in Acts 2:1-4. When St. Peter preached as a result of the activity of the Holy Spirit, what is the subject of his sermon? It is the work of all three persons for our salvation (Acts 2:17-39). The Holy Spirit is specifically called God in the story of Ananias and Sapphira (Acts 5:3,4). Typical of St. Paul is his opening address to the Romans in which he speaks of all three persons as distinct (Romans 1:1-7).

And yet with all of these references to the persons as distinct, there is no hint that they are three separate gods. Quite to the contrary, Jesus testifies to the unity of the Godhead in its essence when he declares, "I and the Father are one" (John 10:30). He tells Philip, "Anyone who has seen me has seen the Father. How can you say, 'Show us the Father'? Don't you believe that I am in the Father, and that the Father is in me? The words I say to you are not just my own. Rather, it is the Father, living in me, who is doing his work. Believe me when I say that I am in the Father and the Father is in me" (John 14:9-11). Thus, if we ask God who he is, the answer that he gives in his Word is that he is one God, in three distinct persons: Father, Son, and Holy Spirit. Anyone who worships a god other than this one God who is Father, Son, and Holy Spirit is worshiping a false god.

It has become common in our day for many to speak of "the three great monotheistic religions of Christianity, Judaism, and Islam." The assumption is that all three religions worship the same god, just calling him by different names. That is entirely contrary to the Holy Scriptures. It is amazing how many people who call themselves Christians imagine that the Father would not mind if people rejected his Son, that the Son would not mind if people cast him and his work aside, or that the Holy Spirit would not mind if he and the Son were for all practical purposes dismissed as irrelevant. No, there is only one God. A god minus Christ is not God. A god minus the Holy Spirit is not God. Jesus said it as clearly as it can be said: "He who does not honor the Son does not honor the Father, who sent him" (John 5:23). The writer of the epistle to the Hebrews is very emphatic on the same point when he warns the

Jewish Christians against going back to Judaism and thus forsaking Christ (Hebrews 3:7-16; 6:4-6). St. John, the great apostle of love, loves both Christ and the souls of his readers when he warns, "Who is the liar? It is the man who denies that Jesus is the Christ. Such a man is the antichrist—he denies the Father and the Son. No one who denies the Son has the Father; whoever acknowledges the Son has the Father also" (1 John 2:22,23).

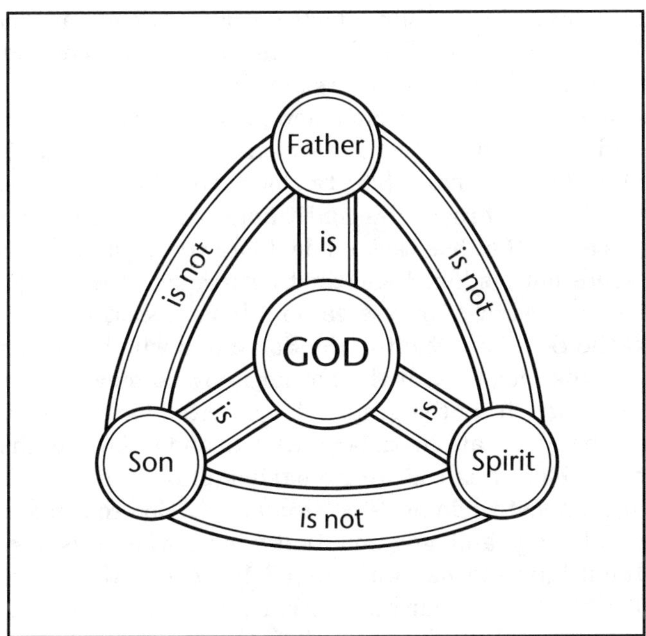

External and internal works of God

We get a still clearer picture of who God is when we note the works of God as they are described in the Bible. We can distinguish between two basic types of works that God does. The two types of works are God's external works and his internal works.

The external works of the Trinity

The external works of God are all those works that God does outside of himself. The Apostles' Creed summarizes them best in its three articles. The First Article speaks of creation, the Second of redemption, and the Third of sanctification. God does all of these outside of himself. They take place not in eternity, but in time, in history, in the universe. It is fairly easy for us to see that creation, redemption, and sanctification are not God; they are the results of God's activity, hence works that he does outside of himself.

Who does these works? Does each person of the Trinity have specific works? Or do the persons act together in all of the works? The answer will help us to see a bit more clearly into the profound mystery of the Trinity.

Who created us? In the Bible the work of creation is ascribed to all three persons of the Trinity. The Bible calls both the Father and the Son our Creator when St. Paul says, "Yet for us there is but one God, the Father, from whom all things came and for whom we live; and there is but one Lord, Jesus Christ, through whom all things came and through whom we live" (1 Corinthians 8:6). St. John identifies Christ as Creator when he tells us, "Through him all things were made; without him nothing was made that has been made" (John 1:3). Psalm 104:30 states that God sends out his Spirit and the Spirit renews the creation.

Who does the work of our salvation? It is easiest to identify that work with the Son, because it is the Son alone who became man and suffered and died for us. But the Father is by no means excluded. As all of the passages from the gospel of John cited earlier demonstrate, the work of the Son is also from beginning to end the will of the Father. Jesus himself identifies the work of redemption with the Father as well as with himself when he tells Nicodemus, "God so loved the world that he gave his one and only Son, that whoever believes in him shall not perish but have eternal life" (John 3:16). Nor is the Holy Spirit in any way less involved in our redemption. For "no one can say, 'Jesus is Lord,' except by the Holy Spirit" (1 Corinthians 12:3).

Who sanctifies us, that is, who brings us to faith and ultimately to heaven through the gospel? Who inspires and preserves the Bible? Who creates the church by it? Most often we identify that work with the Holy Spirit. For Jesus himself points to the Holy Spirit as the One who brings us to faith (John 16:12-15). The book of Acts, beginning with the account of Pentecost itself, points repeatedly to the Holy Spirit as the author of faith, who works through the preaching of the Word and the administration of the Sacrament of Baptism. And St. Peter tells us that the Holy Spirit inspired the writing of the Bible (2 Peter 1:21). But again calling the work of our sanctification the work of the Holy Spirit is never meant to exclude the Father and the

Son. Jesus, in the very chapters of John's gospel that most eloquently discuss the sanctifying work of the Holy Spirit, connects that work inseparably to the Father and to himself. For example, in John 14, just after promising the gift of the Holy Spirit, Jesus says, "If anyone loves me, he will obey my teaching. My Father will love him, and we will come to him and make our home with him" (John 14:23). Jesus joins himself and his Father to our sanctification through the Word.

So we see that in the external works of God, in those works that God does outside of himself, the three persons cannot be clearly distinguished; that is, we cannot say each person does a particular work to the exclusion of the other two. In the external works of the Trinity, the persons of the Trinity work in common, in complete harmony and cooperation.

An understanding of God's external works helps us to avoid any hint of *pantheism* in our thinking about God. Pantheism is the error common in both many ancient and present-day religions. Pantheists teach that God and nature are one, that God is nature or that nature is God. God however cannot in any way be equated with his creation or with nature. He is outside of nature, above and beyond it. All of nature is God's handiwork, not part of God. All that happens in nature is not God but God's activity outside of his essence. That is so clearly evident already in the creation account in Genesis 1: God *speaks* the universe into existence; he does not give birth to it from inside of his essence, as Hindu and other pantheist religions imagine.

The lack of a distinction between the persons of the Trinity in the external works of God also serves a good purpose for us as we try to understand as much as we can about the Trinity in the work of our salvation. The total and complete harmony and union of the persons in the external works helps us to see that each person in the Trinity is eager for and cooperates in our salvation. It is not as though the Father decided on our salvation and then left it to the Son to carry it out, sending him perhaps even unwillingly to suffer and die. No, all three persons were perfectly united in will and in the work for our salvation. It is not as though the Son, once he finished his labors in the Garden of Gethsemane and on the cross, left the world and us behind. Nor is it that after his ascension he sent, perhaps as his inferior, the Holy Spirit to do what he wished with the Word and the sacraments. No, all three persons are active together equally in complete harmony of will in the entire work of our salvation.

The total unity of the persons of the Trinity in the external works underscores their essential equality in power and glory. The Father is the all-powerful Creator, whose majesty we adore in all that exists, seen and unseen. So is the Son. So is the Holy Spirit. The Son is the merciful Redeemer whom we worship and adore for our salvation. Likewise the Father. Likewise the Holy Spirit. The Holy Spirit powerfully preserves the church through Word and sacraments and is therefore worthy of all thanks and praise. No less the Father. No less the Son.

But does not the Apostles' Creed seem to credit the Father with creation, the Son with redemption, the Holy Spirit with sanctification? If all three act equally in all of the works, why this apparent distinction in the creed? It is simply a matter of convenience. Most often, though not exclusively, when the Scriptures speak of creation, they speak of the Father. Most often when they speak of redemption, they speak of the Son, because he is the One who became man, who suffered and died and rose again for us. Most often when they speak of sanctification, they speak of the Holy Spirit because of the promises of Jesus in the gospel of John and because of the prominence of the Holy Spirit in the book of Acts.

The internal works of the Trinity

While the external works demonstrate the unity of the persons in the Trinity, the internal works of the Trinity show us their distinction from one another. The internal works of God are those works that God does inside of himself. In these works there is no possibility of confusing the persons with one another. There is no possibility of thinking of the persons as just different names for the same person.

The internal works of the Trinity are these: Inside of the Godhead, the Son is begotten of the Father. Already in the Old Testament this work of God is proclaimed. In Psalm 2:7 the Son quotes his Father's words in eternity as he tells the Son, "You are my Son; today I have become your Father" (literally: have begotten you). The word "today" in this passage, as we shall see also from the other passages that speak about the same thing, is a timeless "today"; it is the "today" that is often called the eternal now in which God lives without any limitations of time or space. Jesus refers to himself as the only begotten Son of God in John 3:16 and 18. Likewise, 1 John 4:9 refers to Jesus as the only begotten Son of God. (The NIV translation is unfortunate in these verses; it has the correct translation of "only begotten" in the footnotes.)

This mysterious begetting of the Son, as already noted above in considering Psalm 2:7, did not take place in time, but in eternity. It is a begetting for which there is no beginning. St. John tells us that at the beginning of time Jesus was already there (John 1:1). He is the eternal fulfillment of the promise made in Micah 5:2, where the coming of the Messiah is promised. But that coming is of one who has existed forever. The Son, eternally begotten of the Father, has no beginning and no end, just as the Father has no beginning and no end. That too is exactly what Jesus says when he tells the Jews, "Before Abraham was born, I am" (John 8:58). That phrase, "I am," is the name by which God had identified himself to Moses at the burning bush (Exodus 3:14). The Jewish leaders who hated Jesus understood his words exactly as he intended them to understand them. They took up stones to kill him, because he was with those words identifying himself with and as the eternal God. With his Father he enjoyed eternal glory before the world began (John 17:5).

We see then this strange work inside of God, that the Father begets the Son, but in such a way that the Son is not somehow less than or younger than the Father, but altogether his equal. For to honor him any less than the Father is an insult to God; the one who dishonors the Son loses the Father as well as the Son (John 5:23). So how does this begetting take place? We cannot know. What exactly do the words *beget* and *begotten* mean in this eternal mystery? We know only that these are the words that the Scriptures use, and therefore we use them too. They describe a profound mystery in which only this much is clear: The Son is eternal God and a person distinct from the Father. Nevertheless, since there is only one God, he is the same essence as the Father.

And what of the Holy Spirit? The Holy Spirit proceeds from the Father and the Son. The words *beget* and *begotten* are never used to describe this internal work of the Trinity. Instead, we are told that the Spirit is "sent" or "goes forth from" the Father and the Son. Jesus told his disciples, "When the Counselor comes, whom I will send to you from the Father, the Spirit of truth who goes out from the Father, he will testify about me" (John 15:26). St. Paul and St. Peter refer to the Holy Spirit as the "Spirit of Christ" (Romans 8:9; 1 Peter 1:11). St. Paul calls him the Spirit of God's Son, whom God has sent (Galatians 4:6). Just as the Son therefore is one in essence with the Father, so the Holy Spirit is one in essence with the Father and the Son. He proceeds from them in eternity; he comes out from them. He is distinct and yet shares with them in equal honor and power and glory. For he is called God (Acts 5:3,4), and he is united with the Father and the Son as the name in which we are baptized (Matthew 28:19).

Again, we stand in the presence of the most profound mystery. The word *proceeds* or the phrase "goes out from" or just the English preposition *of* (which in Greek is a preposition but also often just a genitive case and not a separate word) designates this internal proceeding of the Holy Spirit from the Father and the Son as unique. It is not the same as *beget* or *begotten*. Those words are never used of the Holy Spirit and his procession from the Father and the Son. But exactly what the difference is, we cannot say. All that we can say is that these are the words and phrases the Bible uses, and so we will use them too.

The point is that in these internal works of the Trinity we see a clear distinction made between the three persons. The Father is not the Son and the Son is not the Father or the Holy Spirit. Each person has a unique relation to the other two. Nevertheless, there is only one God. All three persons are that one God, coequal, coeternal, with none before or after the other.

What then should we conclude on the basis of God's own description of himself in his Word? The church from the second and third century has coined the word *Trinity* as the best summary for God's description of himself. *Trinity* is simply a two-word Latin compound that means "three in one." *The doctrine of the Trinity is that God is three distinct persons in one divine essence.* For the Scriptures everywhere declare that there is only one God. And they also declare that the one God is these three distinct persons. We do not imagine that we can grasp this truth with our reason. The Trinity, for example, cannot be reduced to a mathematical formula, as though each person were one-third of God. No, the Father is God totally; the Son is God completely; the Holy Spirit is God altogether. And yet the three distinct persons have but one divine essence.

The Christian does not presume to challenge God's description of himself. Nor does the Christian imagine that he could ever give a complete definition of God. Instead, we receive with humble reverence the mystery and leave it as a mystery. It may be that in heaven we will understand it better. It may well be that even in heaven the creature will never fully grasp the glory of the Creator, Redeemer, and Sanctifier—ever three distinct persons, yet ever one divine essence.

The best and most complete formulation of the doctrine of the Trinity is contained in the Athanasian Creed. On the basis of the Scriptures and in union with Christians in every age and place, we accept the creed and condemn as heresy and blasphemy any teaching that is not in harmony with the doctrine of the Holy Trinity. The worship of any god other than the Trinity is the worship of a false god, an idol, a god of man's own fabrication.

Among such false and non-gods in our day is the god of present-day Judaism. Tragically, Judaism has turned its back on the God of the prophets in the Old Testament. For it rejects Christ as the promised Savior, the second person of the Holy Trinity. Some Jewish sects still look for the coming of the Messiah and a few even consider the coming Messiah to be God. But they wait in vain. He has come, and he came also to save them. Their rejection is as sad and tragic as Jesus himself indicated in Matthew 23:37,38.

Likewise, the god of Islam is no god at all. For Islam recognizes Jesus only as a prophet, and one inferior to Muhammad.

Present-day American-born religions also have abandoned the Trinity in favor of a god of their own invention. Mormons and Jehovah's Witnesses and members of the Christian Science church often like to present themselves as Christian. They are not. They deny the doctrine of the Trinity. They see Jesus as less than the Father and not as the eternal God, one in essence with the Father. Unitarianism is an outgrowth of 18th century Deism. It holds that there is probably a god out there somewhere, but we cannot know who he is with any certainty. The doctrine of the Trinity has no place in Unitarianism. Numerous and ever-changing New Age cults likewise dismiss the doctrine of the Trinity in favor of the notion that we are all gods or potential gods.

Sadly, even much of present-day Christianity has ceased to preserve and faithfully teach the doctrine of the Trinity. Where the spirit of the age has been allowed to push out the Spirit of Christ, God has been demoted to whatever the individual thinks God is. Thus, for example, members and clergy of many Protestant and Roman Catholic churches have no problem worshiping and praying with those who have always rejected the Trinity. Common prayers and worship between Hindus, Muslims, Jews, Unitarians, assorted Protestants, and Catholics are not uncommon anymore. Where is the faithful confession of the Trinity in such worship? It is nowhere to be found. Where is the grateful song of thanksgiving and adoration to the God who loved us and gave himself for us in such worship? It is altogether absent, even carefully avoided, lest someone be offended. And isn't it remarkable how much more worried people are about offending their fellow mortals than they are about offending God? We need to remember Jesus' warning that those who refuse to confess him before men, he will not confess before his Father in heaven (Luke 12:9).

The attributes of God

Everything that exists has attributes or characteristics. Basically there are two kinds of attributes. The first kind is called *essential* or *substantial attributes.* Essential or substantial attributes are those that help to *define* a thing; they are necessary for that particular thing to exist. If something loses a substantial attribute, it ceases to exist.

For example, we may say that in this life a body and soul are essential or substantial attributes of a human being. If either is lost, the human being is no more, is dead, ceases to exist this side of eternity. We may say that wood is an essential attribute of a tree. If the wood rots or is burned, the tree has ceased to be a tree. A book has pages. No pages, no book. Pages are a substantial attribute of a book.

However, created things also have other attributes that *describe* them, rather than define them. Such attributes are called *accidental attributes.* The word *accidental* here does not mean that they are a mistake. It simply means that such attributes may be lost without the destruction of the thing they describe. A man in his youth had hair on his head. As he got older he lost it, but he did not thereby cease to be a man. His hair did not define him; it merely described him. The tree had leaves. During the fall of the year it lost the leaves, but it did not cease to be a tree. The pages of the book became brown with age, but though the color of the pages changed, the book was still a book. The color of the pages was part of the book's description, not part of its definition.

It is evident that most things have relatively few essential or substantial attributes and comparatively more accidental attributes. Few characteristics define; most characteristics describe.

But what about God? God too has attributes or characteristics. He tells us about many of them in his Word, and we are about to consider some of them. God's attributes however are unique in that they are all substantial or essential. God is his attributes! He will never lose any of them. He is never without any of them. Thus, as we consider his attributes, we are considering God's own essence. Again, we will be confronted by mysteries beyond our full comprehension. We can but listen to his Word and marvel. In what follows we will consider briefly some of the attributes of God as he reveals them in the Bible.

Let the reader bear in mind that each of the attributes considered below belongs equally to each member of the Holy Trinity, no more to one, no less to another. May the reader also note that the consideration of the attributes of God is not a philosophical exercise. As noted earlier, theology is a practical aptitude. God has revealed his attributes in his Word so that we might be edified, warned, and encouraged in our Christian faith and life by that knowledge and that we might better worship and adore our great God and only Savior. To put it another way, God's proclamation of his attributes is also a proclamation of the law and the gospel, as is the entire Bible.

God is spirit. Apart from and before the incarnation of the Son of God in the womb of the virgin Mary, God had no body. No one can see him in his spiritual essence full and complete. So great is he in his essence that, were anyone to look at it, that person would die (Exodus 33:18-23). St. John tells us that only the Son of God himself sees fully the essence of God, and that is because the Son and the Father are one in essence (John 1:1,18). As a spiritual essence, God is not in any way limited by time or space, a point that will be considered further under the attribute of God's transcendence.

Though God is a spirit, at times the Bible speaks of God *anthropomorphically.* That is, the Bible describes God as though he has a body or human organs. For example, in Exodus 6:6 God promises to deliver Israel from Egypt "with an outstretched arm and with mighty acts of judgment." The expression "outstretched arm" is intended to help the Israelites grasp what God is about to do for them. It is equally clear from the account of the exodus that no one saw a physical outstretched arm. Likewise, the great benediction of Numbers 6:24-26 makes reference to God's face. It is clear that this *anthropomorphism* has the aim and intent of making God easier for us to grasp and of emphasizing to us that God is a personal God. For it is God who gives the benediction through Aaron in these verses. Yet he does not suddenly appear with a human face.

The favorite New Testament anthropomorphism is one that has its roots in an Old Testament prophecy about Christ. St. Paul tells us that Christ is seated at the "right hand" of the Father. It used to be that the prime minister or most important official of the court stood at the right hand of the king. It was the position of honor and of power. St. Paul makes it clear that such is the position that Christ holds, the position of power and honor. But does he intend that we should think of a literal right hand of the Father? He explains what is meant by God's right hand. He tells us that Christ is seated at God's "right hand in the heavenly realms, far above all rule and authority, power and dominion, and every title that can be given, not only in the present age but also in the one to come. And God placed all things under his feet and appointed him to be head over everything for the church, which is his body, the fullness of him who fills everything in every way" (Ephesians 1:20-23;

cf. also passages such as Hebrews 10:12; 12:2). He wants to point to Christ as the fulfillment of the promise made by the Father to the Son in Psalm 110:1. "The LORD says to my Lord: 'Sit at my right hand until I make your enemies a footstool for your feet.'" Thus, the right hand of God describes, as St. Paul explains it, not a specific place but the position of power and honor and authority. The right hand of God is where his power and honor and authority are, that is, everywhere, and wherever he is pleased to have it.

At other times God is spoken of as though he has human mental faculties. It is interesting to note that when such language is used, it is invariably used to introduce action. For example, in Genesis 6:5 and in 11:5, God is described as "seeing" the evil that people did. Other times he is described as "hearing" a cry from his people, as in Exodus 3:7. It is not as though God had not seen or been aware of what was happening before. It is not as though the cries of the people only first came to his attention at one particular point in time. For, again, God is spirit. He fills all things, knows all things, and is present everywhere. Rather these terms are used to indicate that God is about to intervene in human affairs and history; he is about to act for the rescue of his people.

God is a personal God. He is not merely a magnetic field or a force in physics. He is not a nameless and aimless spirit that somehow is all of nature, as pantheists suppose. He is personal. He shows us that on every page of his Word. For words do not come from impersonal forces or wandering ether. He speaks with Adam and Eve in the Garden of Eden. He addresses them as one having a mind and a will (Genesis 3). He gives himself names, as he did when confronting Moses at the burning bush (Exodus 3). He bids us to call him by name and promises to hear (Psalm 145:18; Matthew 6:9-13; 7:9-11). In the institution of the Sacrament of Baptism he bids us be baptized in or into his name, that is, into a personal relationship with his revelation of himself in the Word; he makes promises to us there that stretch from time into eternity (Matthew 28:18-20). Indeed, almost all of his other attributes will also point back to this one—that he is a personal God.

God is absolutely independent. When he speaks with Moses at the burning bush in Exodus 3, he identifies himself with this name: I AM WHO I AM. No created thing can ever be absolutely independent and declare what God here declares. He alone is utterly free from need or limit. All created things are bound by numberless limits that make them dependent. Not one of us can do whatever he pleases. We are shackled to time, space, and the laws of cause and effect. We cannot escape the need for food, air, water, or human companionship. But God needs nothing and no one and is free to do whatever pleases him (Psalm 115:3). If he needs us, it is only because he has freely chosen to need us. Jesus made that very clear to the disciples. He told them that they had not chosen him nor had they chosen to be his disciples; he had chosen them (John 15:16). His works of creation, redemption, and sanctification are all done because he has chosen to do them, not because he needed or had to do them. In our redemption he loves the world because he has chosen to love it, not because it deserved love or he owed it love. The point is made so beautifully and completely in that jewel of the gospel, John 3:16. He chose to love the world and in that love he chose to give himself for our redemption!

When we consider all of the gospel promises and all that God did in Christ to fulfill them, it is absolutely mind-boggling to us that God made the promises and fulfilled them in total freedom. How strikingly different that is from the way people usually act. People act almost always on the basis of needs or selfish wants or compulsion. We seek out the companionship of family and friends because we need other people, are afraid to be alone, or want to feel loved and needed. God has no such motivations. He is complete in himself. He was complete and needed nothing or no one before creation. He is no less free and complete and absolutely independent now. People speak very foolishly as well as wickedly when they angrily raise their fists in the face of God and declare, "Because you did such and such to me, God, I am not going to believe in you any more!" as though God depended on them or their faith for his existence. In point of fact, the reverse is true. Our need for God is total and our dependence on him is absolute. God, on the other hand, was free and complete before we were born and will remain so after we have gone. When God seeks us and our salvation, he acts freely and not because of something that he needed or would lack without us. Jesus makes that point powerfully in the Garden of Gethsemane. God promised our salvation in his freedom, and in his freedom Jesus chose to suffer for us to obtain it (Matthew 26:53,54). Why would he redeem us at so great a cost when he never needed anything from us, when he was perfectly free to damn us for our sins?

God is gracious. That is the answer to the question that closed our consideration of God's absolute independence. Grace is a unique kind of love that God alone has. It is not a quantity to be measured; for nothing in God is capable of measure or limitation. It is rather an attitude, a disposition in God, by which he loves with no other reason for it than God himself. God loves because that is his nature, that is his essence. God loves, not because the object is loveable but because he is loving.

Human love is the opposite. We love because the object is loveable. What foods do you like? Those that taste good to you. The cause of the liking is in the object, the food. What people do you love? Those who are kind to you, those who have helped you, those to whom you may be attracted for any number of reasons. Again, the cause is in the object, the people; something *in them* prompts you to love them. But why does God love us? Not because of anything in us. For since the fall into sin there is nothing in us by nature that is loveable. He loves because of who and what he is, namely, gracious, not because of who and what we are, namely, sinners. St. Paul tells us that we are saved by grace through faith. He tells us that our salvation is not of ourselves (neither the grace nor the faith) but of God (Ephesians 2:8). Thus the whole of our salvation rests on this attribute of God. St. John reminds us that we love God because he first loved us (1 John 4:10,19). Even our love for God has its cause in God not in us. But God's love for us has its cause only in God.

The closest human beings get to having the attribute of grace is perhaps a parent's love for a child. The child, after all, is a lot of trouble, always hungry or dirty or noisy or in the way. But a parent loves the child nonetheless. Still, parents do not love all children in the same way; the love they have for their own is exclusive and unique. But God's grace is not that way. This attribute of God is especially awe and trust and love inspiring because of the fact that it embraces and includes the entire human race (John 3:16; 2 Corinthians 5:19; 1 Timothy 2:6). Therefore not a single person among us need ever torment himself with the thought, "Perhaps God's grace does not include me; perhaps Christ's sacrifice was not meant for my benefit." That can never be true. For God is gracious. That is his nature. That grace, so active in the work of Christ and in the preaching of the gospel, is offered to all with the intent that each and every one of us should trust it.

In our consideration of this attribute of God we have chosen to include the attributes of love and mercy, even though these two are slightly different in their definition. *Grace,* as already noted, is love that is undeserved and has its cause in the one who loves, not in the object loved. When, however, God is described by the word *love* in the Bible, the emphasis is slightly different from the emphasis in the word *grace. The emphasis in the word* love *is on a kind of love that seeks the ultimate good of the one who is loved.* And what is the ultimate good as God sees it? It is our salvation, consisting in a blessed fellowship with God that lasts through time and into all eternity. Thus in John 3:16, God loves the world, that is, he seeks its ultimate good in sending his

Son to save it. In Hebrews 12:5-7 the Lord is described as loving those he chastens, or disciplines. The discipline is aimed at the best interest of the one being disciplined, and so, even if we experience pain in that discipline, it is called an evidence of God's love. Thus the love of God is not an empty emotion, not just a feeling. It is rooted and grounded in his will, a will that yearns for and longs for our ultimate good: our salvation. Again, God's love longs for it so ardently that it is expressed in the life and death of Christ for us. God's love yearns for our salvation so perfectly that it is in love that God even permits and sends us a measure of sorrow and suffering in this life. He does it so that we will not perish in a love for the world and things in it. He does it so that we will be drawn to him as our only refuge and hope in life and our glorious goal in death.

Mercy is yet another type of love. Its closest synonym is *pity. Mercy is the kind of love that is provoked by the need and misery of someone.* Thus, the lepers and the blind man (Luke 17:13; 18:38) call out to Jesus for pity, for mercy. Their situation is wretched and miserable, and they hope that their misery will move Jesus to be merciful. We too in our private prayers as well as in the liturgy of the worship service frequently pray: Lord, have mercy on us. It is a prayer in which we recognize our total helplessness and absolute dependence on God; it is prayer in which we beg him to look not on our merit but on our need, and to take pity on us. (In church, in the liturgy, in our own reading of the Bible, it may be useful to keep these distinctions between grace and love and mercy in mind; the distinctions help deepen both our understanding of and our gratitude to God for who he is in his attributes, in his essence.)

All three of these words *(grace, love, mercy)* are action nouns when they are used to designate attributes of God. That simple fact, that they are action nouns and action attributes, is what elevates them so far above their pale imitations in us at our best. We, for example, may see a picture of a starving child in some far away country and feel a certain anxiety, a kind of love, some pity for the plight of that child. But at the same time we may feel the frustration that we can do nothing about that child's plight. That is not the way God is in his grace and love and mercy. He acts to carry out what his grace desires, namely, our salvation. He acts in time and in history to accomplish what his love desires for our ultimate good, namely, that we should hear the gospel and finally be saved. He acts in mercy to rescue us from our wretched plight as captives of sin, death, and hell; as well he acts day by day in the same mercy to preserve our life and rescue us from a thousand perils, even perils we are not aware of.

God is just and holy. The gods of the ancient Greeks and Romans, and today the gods of the Hindus and of some tribal religions, are not much different from people. The gods were described as sharing in human desires, human virtues, and most human vices. That should not surprise us, since they are gods invented by people. However, the true God, the God of the Bible, is not a human invention. His attributes of justice and holiness magnify God's complete "otherness" from all created things.

These attributes of God, like his grace, love, and mercy, are attributes that tell us both about God's essence and about God's activity. He is absolutely just inside of himself; justice is his very essence. He cannot, therefore, act unjustly. Abraham appeals to God's justice when he prays for the cities of Sodom and Gomorrah, and in so doing helps us define the term. He prays, "Far be it from you to do such a thing—to kill the righteous with the wicked, treating the righteous and the wicked alike. Far be it from you! Will not the Judge of all the earth do right?" (Genesis 18:25). To be just is to have an absolutely perfect standard of right and wrong, yes, to be the standard of right and wrong; to act justly is to judge perfectly according to that standard, to condemn and punish all sin and imperfection, and to praise and reward all perfection. God is just. The psalmist declares that his standard is sure and his judgments according to that standard are altogether reliable (Psalm 19:9). It is not, of course, that the standard exists outside of God, independent of him or coming before him; the standard is, we might say, of God's very DNA. The apostles Peter and Paul tell us that God exercises his justice without playing favorites (Romans 2:11; 1 Peter 1:17).

The word *holy* means "separate from sin." St. Paul helps us understand the term in 2 Corinthians 7:1 and in Ephesians 5:27, where he shows us that the opposite of holiness is any kind of moral uncleanness or imperfection. God is the very opposite of all that is evil or wrong, unclean or imperfect. He cannot tolerate evil or accept it either; to do so would be unholy as well as unjust. He revealed his holiness and his justice already in the Garden of Eden when he warned Adam and Eve against eating the forbidden fruit and then attached the penalty they should expect if they disobeyed (Genesis 2:17). So perfect is his holiness that death, i.e., total separation from him, is the consequence of imperfection, uncleanness, and sin. Such a judgment is also just; for with sin the creature has rebelled against the Creator and has lost the very purpose for which the creature was created, namely, to magnify the glory of God by perfect obedience to God. The just judgment of the holy God, the judgment of death, is a separation from God and at the same time a separation from all of his goodness and grace. That separation is the very essence of hell—it is eternal torment.

God's attributes of justice and holiness present us with a serious problem. It is not difficult at all for us to realize that at its best humankind is not just and is not holy, not in thoughts and actions, not in judgments either. Sometimes when we must judge, the justice is imperfect because we do not know all the facts. Sometimes our judgments are unjust because we are too impressed by outward appearance, be it good or evil. Sometimes justice is imperfect because we are imperfect, prone to good moods and bad, which may influence justice. What parent does not know these things? The parent warns the misbehaving child but does not follow through. So the child continues to misbehave. Finally, the parent has had enough and swoops down on the child with a vengeance. And there it is: Vengeance has taken the place of justice, and the punishment no longer fits the crime but exceeds it because of the parent's own failure to follow through on an earlier warning. And as to holiness, it is an absolute virtue; that is, it is either present or absent. Someone or something cannot be a little holy or a lot holy. Any fault, flaw, or error renders that person or thing unholy. But if God is just and holy, and if God therefore cannot accept anything less than justice and holiness, who can stand before him (Psalm 130:3)? It will not do for God simply to forgive. For that would be unjust. And it would render God unholy. And he can be neither unjust nor unholy.

The problem goes still deeper. If God does not forgive, then how can he be loving, gracious, and merciful? The attributes of God appear to lock him in an impossible conflict within himself! Even most man-made religions recognize the dilemma and struggle to resolve it. Some try to resolve the apparent tension between God's love and his justice by minimizing his justice and exaggerating human goodness. Their reasoning goes like this: "Just do the best you can; follow the rules and observe the rituals and God will be satisfied, will let it go at that." But then God is not just; he cannot be just and holy and just let evil pass, much less accept it.

God resolves the impossible! He does it in Christ. To satisfy his love and grace and mercy, to satisfy no less his justice and his holiness, God punishes and wipes out all injustice and unholiness through the substitutionary obedience and suffering of his Son (John 1:29; 2 Corinthians 5:18-21). And since the Son wills this task for himself, no injustice is done to him when he suffers in our place; that's what he chose to do, what he longed for and wanted to do! While this resolution of the dilemma will be considered more thoroughly under the doctrines of Christology and Soteriology, we need at least to take note of it here. For it is the heart and core of the gospel, our whole joy and delight!

The attributes, therefore, of justice, righteousness, and holiness are not only attributes that are essential and personal in God. They are also attributes that are *imputed.* That is, his righteousness and his holiness are credited to us because Christ has taken away all of our unrighteousness and forgiven all our unholiness. The point is as important as it is necessary: Since holiness and righteousness are absolutes (again, there is no such thing as a little or a lot holy; one is either holy or a sinner, either righteous or unrighteous; those are the only alternatives), God cannot accept us unless we are holy and righteous. And that's what we become when our sins have all been paid for and when Christ imputes to us (i.e., credits to our account) his own perfect holiness and absolute righteousness! That is how God's attributes of grace, love, and mercy are brought into perfect harmony with his attributes of justice and holiness. They have their harmony in Christ's redeeming work. That harmony is so perfect and complete that the psalms frequently praise God for his righteousness and justice. If he did not impute his holiness to us, we would have reason only to bewail his justice! Consider, for example, the joyful praise in Psalm 85:10, which sings of the harmony of God's attributes for our benefit: "Love and faithfulness meet together; righteousness and peace kiss each other." Likewise Psalm 101:1,2 delights in that harmony and expresses the Christian's eagerness to respond with a life of obedience and faithfulness: "I will sing of your love and justice; to you, O LORD, I will sing praise. I will be careful to lead a blameless life—when will you come to me?"

God is transcendent and immanent. Transcendent simply means that he is above and beyond all that is created. That is, God is not his creation, as the pantheists and nature worshipers imagine. He cannot be confused in any way with his creation. The psalms give us especially beautiful descriptions of God's transcendence. They speak of his existence before the mountains ever were created (Psalm 90:2). They extol him as the One who changes creation as one might change clothes, now letting one thing stand and then setting it aside and letting it perish (Psalm 102:25-27). But in it all God remains the same, forever above and beyond all time and space, so that even the heaven of heavens cannot contain him (2 Chronicles 2:6). Thus, if we were to launch a rocket from earth to the farthest planet it could reach, then another from there, and yet another and another, we would never get to the essence of God; he is beyond and above and separate from all that he has created. Time and even space have limits. There is a time where there is no time and a space where there is no longer space. God is above and beyond it all. Knowledge of the attribute of God's transcendence guards us against all forms of pantheism or nature worship.

But at the same time, God is also immanent. To be immanent is to be close at hand in time and space. He is so close that nothing is hidden from him, absolutely nothing. He tells Jeremiah, "'Can anyone hide in secret places so that I cannot see him?' declares the LORD. 'Do not I fill heaven and earth?' declares the LORD" (Jeremiah 23:24). Jesus spoke both of his own immanence and of his transcendence in the very moments when he was removing his visible presence from the disciples. In Matthew 28:18-20 he tells them that he has all power in heaven and earth; that means he is above and beyond heaven and earth, outside of their control or influence, in a word, *transcendent.* But immediately he adds that he will be with them always, that is, immanent, close at hand. Unlimited and unconfined by time and space, they should be sure of his constant presence. The Formula of Concord puts it very simply: "[Christ is] one person with God, far, far beyond things created, as far as God transcends them; and, on the other hand, . . . as deep in and as near to all created things as God is in them" (FC SD VII, 101 p. 610). As noted earlier, God's attribute of transcendence warns us against pantheism; his attribute of immanence warns us against the equal and opposite error, that of thinking that God is a mere philosophical abstraction or an indifferent and absentee landlord far removed from his creation.

These two attributes when taken together are not just mind-boggling. They are powerful proclamations of the law and the gospel. The one who fights against God cannot win. The evildoer and the hypocrite alike will not escape. For neither God's power nor his presence has any limit. His power is absolute in its transcendence. And he is present everywhere in his immanence. The puny little creature that sets himself against God acts the part of a fool; such a person will perish and apart from repentance be eternally punished for it. Ah, but those who trust in him on the basis of his Word, they will never be disappointed. For he who is beyond limit always has the ability to save; and he who is immanent always knows the best way to save. He who is transcendent can carry out his every promise; he who is immanent hears with complete attention the prayers and cries of each one who calls on him. Both when we listen to him in his Word and when we pray to him, we should not imagine that God is absent or only fractionally paying attention to us. Oh no, that could never be! When we hear him in his Word and when we speak to him in our prayers, we have the undivided attention of the God who is One, who cannot be divided from himself or separated into fractions. What a beautiful truth! These practical applications of God's attributes of transcendence and immanence are among those that God himself often invites us to make in his Word (Isaiah 57:15; Psalm 139:7-12; John 14:23).

We include in our consideration of God's transcendence and immanence his attributes of **omnipotence** (i.e., being all-powerful) and **omnipresence** (i.e., being present everywhere). He is beyond all that is created, and he is beyond all limitations of power or space or time. He acts according to his will as it pleases him. He is according to his promise where he is pleased to be. So complete is his transcendence and so perfect his immanence that it applies also to the human nature of the ascended Christ (Matthew 28:18-20; Ephesians 1:19-23; Colossians 2:9).

God is immutable. He does not change. He is who he is (Exodus 3:14). His essence, his attributes, and his will are changeless. He does not grow. He does not evolve. He does not reverse himself, so that grace would run out or the union of love and justice in Christ would cease to be valid (Psalm 33:11; 1 Samuel 15:29; Malachi 3:6; Matthew 24:35; James 1:17). Thus in whatever God does, his actions reflect his essence. That is, when God spares us the consequences of some of our sins in this life, he is acting in grace for the sake of the consequences that Christ suffered for our sins. On the other hand, when God chastens us and allows us to suffer in some measure the consequences of our sins, it is not because he has changed. It is not because he no longer is loving or gracious or merciful. Quite to the contrary, it is because he is still all of those things. The consequences of our sins, a measure of sorrow in this life, and even temporal death all come from the hand of the immutable God. They come to teach us to dread and shun sin, lest we fall completely away from him and his Word. They come to separate us from the love of the world that perishes and passes away, in order to draw us closer to himself and his Word that alone can satisfy (Psalm 73). The knowledge that God is immutable in his love and grace and mercy is especially comforting in times of sorrow, suffering, and death.

God is wise. Wisdom is the ability not just to know but to understand and to apply or use profitably what is known. God is **omniscient,** that is, he knows all things. But more than that, he understands all things and knows how best to use what he knows for his ultimate glory and our eternal good. It may well seem to us that the little word *wise* is just too small a word to apply to the One who is wisdom itself! He has, after all, shown his wisdom in such incomparable ways. The psalmist marvels at God's wisdom when considering the creation of the world and man's creation in particular (Psalm 104). People today may well marvel even more at that wisdom, given our ability to look into small things unimagined in the days of the psalmist and to examine things removed farther from the earth than was conceivable in his day. A microscope or telescope or a picture from a space ship should provoke the song of Psalm 19 in always fresh, new ways. A consideration of the unity of all living things and their interdependence should make us marvel again with the Old Testament hymn writer in Psalm 104. The intricate workings of the human eye or even the eye of a fly should leave us breathless with wonder at the wisdom of the Creator.

Even more we stand in awe before the wisdom of his plan of salvation. No mortal could devise such a plan that reconciles us to him by reconciling his justice and his grace through his sacrifice of himself on a cross. No god of human invention, nor all of them put together, could match for an instant the wisdom implanted in his Word, by which he saves us in time and for eternity (Isaiah 40:13; Ephesians 3:10,11; Romans 11:33-36).

Since God is wise, yes, is wisdom itself—a point made frequently in the book of Proverbs—how utterly foolish and trivial is all human thinking about God apart from his Word! Indeed how perverse and wicked! On any subject that God addresses in his Word, let all mankind be silent and listen. Woe to the one who answers the Lord with, "Well, I just feel . . ." or "But I think . . ." or "It seems to me . . ." It is folly on the face of it for the creature to contradict the Creator. It is wicked beyond understanding, especially when it comes to the truths of our salvation. God himself has told us that especially in the matter of our salvation his thoughts and ways are far beyond ours (Isaiah 55:8,9). Since those ways nevertheless end up in our salvation, why would anyone even want to contradict him? No, may ours ever be the mind of the apostle Paul who said, "We demolish arguments and every pretension that sets itself up against the knowledge of God, and we take captive every thought to make it obedient to Christ" (2 Corinthians 10:5).

It should be clear from this all too brief and incomplete consideration of the attributes of God that God is incapable of a complete definition. He defines himself in part when he reveals his attributes to us that we might know him, fear his wrath, and trust his promises. In the process he draws us to the totally appropriate conclusion that he is in his essence wondrous and beyond our understanding. For we must bear in mind that all of these attributes of God and such others as might be considered are not mere descriptions. God is these attributes. All of them are present in God always and perfectly.

We may appreciate the enormity of that truth if we set God and his attributes on one side and ourselves and our attributes on the other. Most of our attributes, such as knowledge or wisdom or mercy or love or justice, are not essential attributes in us; they merely describe us in part. Nor are they ever perfect or complete in us. Nor are they ever even present all the time to the limited degree that we have them. We are able to concentrate, for example, on relatively few things at one time. We may think about our plans for today or perhaps about our lives ten years ago; we may concentrate our attention on plans for tomorrow or perhaps even for ten years from now. But our grasp of any of these things is narrow and limited. We can never think of them always or all at once, much less understand them all. But in God everything is always in his perfect grasp all of the time. He knows everything and he knows every moment. The history of the world, your history and mine, the dawn of creation and the end of time, every moment and everything in between are always present in the mind of God in complete and perfect detail. Moreover, when we are just or kind, we are the one now and the other at some other time; today I am just in giving my children what they deserve; tomorrow I am merciful in giving them much more than they deserve. But God is always and at the same time both just and merciful. As already noted, and as we will note often, in Christ both justice and mercy always meet and are perfectly meted out.

Are there attributes in God that are not revealed in his Word? We need not speculate about that. He has revealed in his Word what he wants us to know. He has revealed in his Word what serves our everlasting good. He has revealed in his Word that which we may apply as proclamations of his law and gospel. If that is good enough for God, it should certainly be good enough for us.

God himself shows us the reverence with which we should consider him and his attributes in Exodus 33:12-23. Moses so loved God that he wanted to see God in all of his glory, know him in all that he is. But God is too great to be fully grasped even by so great a prophet as Moses. Even for Moses God remained a hidden God in his essence, but at the same time the God who reveals himself in his Word. With that Word Moses would have to be content. Much the same point is made to the prophet Elijah in 1 Kings 19.

Jesus rejoiced that God, whose essence is hidden, nevertheless reveals himself in his Word (Matthew 11:25-30). And he rejoiced in this most amazing truth of all: When God reveals himself in Christ and in his Word, he at the same time gives himself to us; he comes in his revelation of himself to dwell with and in us (2 Corinthians 6:16). Those who will not be satisfied with the hidden God made known in his Word end up fashioning a golden calf for a god (Exodus 32); it may be made of real gold, like Aaron's calf, or of the imagined gold of one's own feelings and imagination, human reason, or what is sometimes passed off as "science." Whatever its substance, it will be an idol that neither hears nor helps, that cannot act or save.

The will of God

Closely related to the subject of the attributes of God, but meriting separate attention, is the subject of God's will. The will in man is that function of the soul by which man is conscious of choices, of causes and effects, and by which he decides to act, prompted and influenced by any number of things inside or outside of himself. Thus, we decide in our will to buy a house; we consider with our reasoning ability that its price is appropriate and location is desirable. Our emotions may be attracted by its layout and its surroundings, but it is the will that finally makes the decision to buy it.

God has a will too by which he acts. Thus, when the creation of the universe took place, it did not happen spontaneously or by chance. It was the result of an act of the will of God, who then spoke and it was done. Likewise, when we on the basis of his gospel in Word and sacraments come to believe and trust in him, it does not just happen by accident; nor does it happen by our will, deciding to abandon sin and unbelief and make a decision for Christ. No, it is the result of God's will, effective and active in the Word and sacraments (Matthew 11:25-27; Romans 10:17; 1 Timothy 2:4; James 1:18).

In his Word God allows us to view his will from a number of different perspectives. Thus, for example, we see God's will in the Scriptures as a *revealed will.* God tells us about his will. If we want to know what God wills and for whom, we need only look at the Scriptures and at the Scriptures alone. He tells us, for example, through the prophet Ezekiel that he has no pleasure in anyone's death and damnation. It is his will that all repent and live (Ezekiel 33:11). Jesus says the same thing in John 6:38-40.

It was the will of God that the sins of the world be taken away through the work of Christ (John 1:29). The apostles Peter and Paul stress that truth, that it is the will of God that all be saved (2 Peter 3:9; 1 Timothy 2:4). It is the will of God that the salvation won for all by Christ become ours through faith alone (John 3:16; Romans 3, 4). Likewise, the revealed will of God makes it clear that our lives should reflect our love to him for his priceless gift of salvation. It is his will that we live in accord with the moral law summarized in the Ten Commandments, in humble obedience to his Word, in loving service to him and to our neighbor (1 Peter 2:15,16; Romans 12; Ephesians 5:17–6:18). Thus, God's law summarized in the Ten Commandments is an expression of God's will.

Again, if we want to know the will of God, we look to where he has told us what his will is. We look to his written Word; his written Word is his revealed will. But there are many more things in God's mind and will than he has revealed in his Word. As much as his essence is hidden, so too much in his will is hidden. Thus we say, as we noted also in the last chapter, that God has also a *hidden will.* The disciples wanted to know more than Jesus had revealed about the future. But Jesus told them that some of the things they wanted to know were hidden in the mind and will of God and there they would remain (John 21:20-22; Acts 1:6-8). In fact, he emphasized repeatedly after his resurrection that they should pay attention to the revealed will, to concentrate and focus on what was in the Word and not concern themselves with God's hidden will (Mark 16:7; Luke 24:25-32,44,45; John 20:30). When we want to know things hidden in the will of God, things not revealed in his Word, we do well to remember Jesus' warnings to his disciples. If you want to know about choices you have to make in this life, choices about marriage, about vocation, about buying this and selling that, don't go searching for the hidden will of God. Rather, pray for his blessing on your choices, and then let those choices be guided by what God says in his Word about marriage, about work and family, about the use he intends us to make of his spiritual and material blessings.

We make the choices between one good thing and another, and we do so praying chiefly that whatever choice we make will be to the glory of God and the benefit of our family and/or our neighbor. Thus, the apostle urged that a collection be taken for the poor in Jerusalem and Judea (1 Corinthians 16:1-4). But he did not tell anyone how much it should be or who should organize it or anything of that sort. That was all left to the choice of the children of God, with the urging that they be generous, as God had blessed them. Later on in the same chapter the apostle reports that he had encouraged Apollos to visit them. But Apollos decided not to do so at that time. The choice for Apollos was between two things; he decided what he considered best at the time, though to do the other would certainly not have been wrong.

The point is simply this: When the Scriptures do not decide something with a principle from God's revealed will, then we are free to decide. We ask God to lead and guide us by his Word. But we do not expect him to decide the matter for us, because he has nowhere promised to do that. He has entrusted us with his Word. He has not given us the unbearable burden of trying to guess his hidden will and climb into his mind for things hidden there. We leave it to him, once we have examined his Word, to work things out for our good and his glory in whichever choices we make that are not contrary to his revealed will. He has promised to do exactly that (Romans 8:28).

Much damage has been done by those who are not satisfied with God's revealed will and want somehow to get at his hidden mind and will. On the one hand, they place an enormous burden on themselves to get at the mind of God that he has not promised to open to them apart from his Word and sacraments. On the other hand, they presume and imagine that their own feelings and choices are God's feelings and choices. They confidently declare that they feel "led by the Lord" to do this or that which is not revealed in his Word. In their judgment, anyone who gets in the way is getting in the way of the will of the Lord.

Mentally deranged individuals have committed murder with that kind of thinking. But others pursue the same principle as the deranged when they look for the will of God inside of themselves instead of where he reveals it, namely, in his written Word. The sad fact of the matter is that those who imagine that God's will is revealed in their minds and in their feelings often move farther and farther away from the Word of God. For what need is there of his revealed and written Word if I imagine that he is speaking to me directly and apart from his Word. More and more of present-day religion is of just such a sort. No Bible is really necessary, nor any sacraments, nor the church, and certainly not a trained clergy—unless of course these agree with how I feel at the moment. All that is necessary is how I feel at the moment; that's my religion. The sad truth is that that's idolatry; it's no better than superstition.

So we need to find the narrow and biblical middle road between the two false alternatives. On the one side is the ditch into which those fall who think that God is the absentee landlord of life; they think that he has left us on our own once he took care of the matter of our creation and our redemption. On the other side is the swamp of thinking that God has decided everything for us and that he makes his choices known in our minds or in our emotions; whatever we feel and choose must be God's choice.

Between these two false alternatives is the narrow biblical and Lutheran middle road. We commend all of our life to God's care and direction. We search his Word for that guidance in the law and the gospel. We decide matters not decided by his Word, asking his blessing on our thinking and deciding. We neither act as though we are independent of God's help nor as though God has decided everything for us and that, therefore, whatever we do must be the will of God.

There is much more that needs to be considered under the heading of the will of God. This much will suffice as we consider the will of God from the standpoint of God's essence and attributes. We will revisit the subject in some of its other dimensions when we consider God's will under the heading of "The providence of God" in the next chapter.

Chapter 6
God's Creating Activity

The creation account (Genesis 1:1-25)

The creation account that God himself has provided through Moses in Genesis 1, 2 is at once profound and simple. From beginning to end it records the facts without elaborate explanation. It tells us what proceeded from the will and Word of God in such a way that God's rational creatures, i.e., human beings and angels, would never cease to be amazed by it. God the Holy Trinity spoke and it was done. He did not merely will all created things into existence. He spoke them into existence, a point that those made spiritually alive by the Word of God cannot fail to notice and appreciate.

Accordingly we have no obligation to prove the doctrine of creation apart from the Word of God itself. God alone was there. God alone was the cause of all that happened. God alone is fit to describe the events and their significance. As with all doctrine, our obligation is to listen to the Word of the Lord and to receive it with believing and thankful hearts. The doctrine of creation, like all true doctrine, is first and foremost an article of faith (Hebrews 11:3). We believe, teach, and confess the truthfulness and historicity of the creation account for no other reason than that it is what the Word of God teaches. Proofs and arguments from geology and archaeology may all be very interesting and sometimes worthwhile, but our faith does not rest on anything other than the clear Word of God.

And what does the Bible teach about that creation? First of all, it was a creation out of nothing *(creatio ex nihilo).* Before God began the work of creation there was neither time nor space, neither energy nor matter. God was sublimely independent and alone. As the account indicates, there was no compulsion and no need for God to create. He created because it pleased him to do so (Psalm 115:3).

The account begins with the solemn introduction, "In the beginning." That's when creation took place. The very first thing that God created was the beginning, time itself. Before the beginning there was nothing except God, the author of the beginning. He existed in the timeless time of eternity where there is neither beginning nor ending.

He declares of himself, "Before me no god was formed, nor will there be one after me" (Isaiah 43:10). Moses sings of him, "Before the mountains were born or you brought forth the earth and the world, from everlasting to everlasting you are God" (Psalm 90:2).

For ages the curious have wanted to know what was going on in eternity, what God was doing before he created this beginning. Luther perhaps answered the question best when a boy asked him about it. He said that God was busy making switches with which to spank little boys who ask such foolish questions. We cannot answer the unanswerable. It is highly doubtful that we would understand the answer if God gave us one. For action to us implies time and space. But before this "in the beginning" there was neither time nor space. There was only God. We have enough in his Word to keep us usefully occupied for a lifetime and beyond. We will not bother ourselves with questions whose answers we would not understand, even if we had them. It is enough to say what the Scriptures say about God's activity at the beginning. As to what God was doing before there was a "before," we will be content to delight in what St. Paul tells us; he says that even in eternity God was planning our salvation (Ephesians 1:4; 2 Timothy 1:9).

And what was it that God did in this beginning? He "created the heavens and the earth." Those words form a chapter heading and a summary for what is about to be described in Genesis 1. God created all that is in the sky above us and in or on the earth beneath our feet as described in this chapter. Nothing was left out. Everything that exists in time and space (God himself excepted) has its origins in this beginning.

The vast void was by definition "formless and empty." It contained neither order nor potential until God spoke. At this start, at this beginning of the beginning, God made a sort of primordial mass or soup of matter and energy *(Urstoff)*. But until God did more and spoke more that mass of matter and energy still lacked any organizing principle. But the "Spirit of God was hovering over the waters." Therein lay its potential, not in matter and energy itself but in the moving, creating Spirit of God. God does not move mindlessly or aimlessly. He moves with purpose and intent. He moves and there are always results or effects that follow from his moving.

But still nothing happens until he speaks. And speak he did! There began his mighty decrees of "Let there be . . . and there was." The living Word of God is exalted at the dawn of creation in this, that God did not merely move or will or think his creation into existence. He spoke it into existence. And that speaking is linked to the second person of the Trinity, the Son of God, who is called the Word of God (John 1:1).

We note that there is no long period of time between any of these divine decrees and their execution. He speaks and it is done in a day. Not millions of years intervene as one thing develops from another. There is room in the account neither for raw evolutionary theory nor for its pious sounding cousin, "theistic evolution." Raw evolutionary theory supposes that it all just happened over the course of billions of years, without reference to any ultimate cause. Theistic evolution imagines that God somehow got the process going and perhaps even directed it to a limited extent, but then, once begun, the universe and all that is in it unfolded over billions of years through a natural process of selection.

Those who hold to a theistic evolutionary theory are trying to find a way to accommodate what the Bible says with evolutionary theory. The attempt is futile on a number of levels. First of all, it will never really satisfy those who by way of their evolutionary theories want to remove God altogether from the explanation of life and its purpose. And, second, they must stumble over an inherent contradiction in their own theory, namely, if one considers God the miraculous source of all that is, it is no stretch to accept his own account of how all that is came into being; nothing is accomplished by accepting God as the miraculous Originator but removing his own description of the miraculous origin of all that is.

The creation to be sure does move from the basic to the complex. But it does so on consecutive days at the command of the Lord. Thus, light was created on the first day and separated from darkness. That day, like those that follow it, is designated as the "evening" and the "morning." From that description of the day, the Old Testament believers came to designate sunset as the beginning of the day and the dawn as the end of the first half of the day. (That designation has an interesting psychological twist to it. If sunset marks the first period of the day, then people are more likely to think of rest a bit differently than we do today; they are more likely to see themselves as resting not from their work but for it.)

On the second day the waters were separated with some above the earth and some on it. We have the impression of a vault in the skies that contained and held back the water above the earth. That impression is reinforced by the later description of the way in which God watered the surface of the earth. It was not by rain but by a mist and streams (Genesis 2:6). The first mention we have of rain is in the account of the flood in the days of Noah (Genesis 7:11,12). The wording of that account too is most interesting; Genesis tells us that "the floodgates of the heavens were opened," again suggesting the idea of the vault in the skies that held back the rain until that time. Even the formation of the rainbow after the flood (Genesis 9:13) points in the same direction; it points to the conclusion that it did not rain until the time of the flood. Whether there was rain or not before the flood, what a horror that first experience of rain on the scale described in Genesis 7 must have been for those who perished in the flood. The faith of Noah appears to us as all the more impressive with the thought that it had never rained until the time of the flood. How much more ridiculous must he have appeared to his neighbors as he built the ark. For his neighbors the very idea of a downpour and a flood might well have been inconceivable.

On the third day God began to organize the mass of energy and matter by separating the waters and the dry land. Was it all divided into the seas and continents, as we know them today? Perhaps not. The flood (Genesis 6–8) certainly had a profound effect on the topography and geography of the earth. The important point is that the separation prepared for the creation of plants and animals. Notice that the word *create* as it applies to the whole of the earth and the skies means "to make out of nothing." But with the third day the word *create* takes on a different shade of meaning. For with the things created on the third day and thereafter God makes use of what he had already created. He does what will become for God the usual way of dealing with creation. He uses means. He makes the plants out of the soil. He organizes matter and energy in the skies into planets.

Of the plants we are told that they are set into "kinds." The same will be said later of the animals, that they are established in "kinds." There is no room for one kind to develop or evolve out of another kind. The kind is set in the seed of plants and animals. While we may have some difficulty in establishing exactly a scientific definition of the term *kind,* for our purposes it is enough to know that the kinds were set and defined by God. With the kinds, God established a range beyond which one thing could not breed with another. Could there be development within a kind? Yes. But one kind cannot successfully interbreed with or become another kind. A bird cannot eventually evolve into a dog or a fungus into a man. If the DNA of one kind closely resembles that of another, it is a gigantic leap to say that therefore the one must have evolved from the other. It is much more reasonable to conclude that both have the same Creator and that their similarities rest in his arrangement, not in their own evolution.

On the fourth day God further organized the universe. Some have wondered how there could have been days of 24-hour duration on the first three days. For the sun and the moon and the stars were not yet set on their courses until the fourth day. And we know that the length of the day is determined by the rotation of the earth on its axis around the sun. Or is it? To be sure, that is how we observe it now. But on the first three days of creation it was God who determined the length of the day and the night. On the fourth day of creation he gives us no reason to think that he changed his mind about how long a day should be. Rather, he set the planets in their orbits to fit the pattern that he had already set for the length of the day and the night.

On the fifth day God again made use of the material he had already created. By his decree he brought forth the fish and the sea creatures and the birds from the sea and the sky. Again there is an emphasis on kind, on the range within which these creatures may reproduce. Some have imagined that the birds evolved out of the fish because of this or that similarity. The similarity results from their having the same Creator and their creation on the same day, as God moved from the basic to the ever more complex.

On the sixth day the land animals were created out of the earth at God's command. Their kinds too were set at their creation.

God looked with pleasure and satisfaction on all that he had made and declared that it was good. The word *good* can mean morally and ethically good. But God gave no commands to the visible creatures created before the creation of man except to reproduce after their respective kinds. There is no suggestion of a moral or ethical element in their nature.

But the term *good* can also mean useful, beautiful, and harmonious. Those meanings certainly apply to the creation even to this day, so long after sin has damaged so much of it. The planets are beautiful to behold whether from a far distance in the night sky or close-up with a telescope or from a rocket or a spaceship. They move in their orbits in a way that is predictable. But even with their predictability we cannot create a perfect timepiece to match that predictability; the best of calendars and clocks must be adjusted periodically. On earth, plants feed animals and animals feed plants. All are arranged in such a way that the loss of some causes damage to others and to the whole, unless there is some sort of compensation in nature to readjust the balance. How does the shark know that it should not eat the fish that clean its gills? The turtle hatches without the least care or concern or instruction from other turtles, but it knows instantly what it must do if the species is to have any chance of survival. How does it know that? The seabirds always swallow fish head first. Why? Who told them to do that? The seeds of the grasses and other plants freeze in the winter but emerge in the summer sun and flourish anew. The elephants know how to protect the delicate ears of their young from the sun. Who taught them that? The eyes, the noses, and the ears of countless species of animals are all wondrous in their detail and harmonious in their functions.

God saw that it was good! It was all beautiful to behold: its parts useful to the whole, its organization utterly rational, and its harmony a perfection of form and function. It was good! And it all came into being as the result of God's speaking. No great effort. No confused half starts. No failed experiments. Yes, it is all done with no pattern or plan existing before. Just think of that for a moment: Everything that man "creates" he creates on the basis of pre-existing material; he develops what others have begun. It is true what Ecclesiastes says: "There is nothing new under the sun" (Ecclesiastes 1:9). God at creation is the One who makes things genuinely new, without a pre-existing pattern or plan. And the result is "good"! As is so often in the Bible, the word *good* hardly seems adequate to describe the reality. But what other word could there be that would ever do justice to the magnificence of God's creating activity?

All of God's creative activity on the six days of creation had one sublime and ultimate purpose. That purpose is the glory of God himself. To be sure, nothing in creation can add to or subtract from the glory of God, since God is perfection in his essence, altogether apart from any created thing. Nevertheless, the creation reflects his glory and makes it known (Psalm 19:1). The whole of creation by its very existence testifies to the power and wisdom of God, the Holy Trinity (Romans 11:33-36).

For the attentive reader of the New Testament the creation reflects the glory of God in a very special way. Jesus uses the natural visible world to teach many divine and saving truths. By doing so he holds up the visible and natural world as a mirror of invisible spiritual truths. Thus, for example, in John 6 he calls himself the Bread of Life and the indispensable food that has come down from heaven. Every Christian, who according to the order of nature gets hungry each day for physical food, can call to mind the true hunger and the true food. The true hunger is the longing of the soul for the Savior himself, and he gives us himself to satisfy that hunger. Or consider the many parables about the kingdom of heaven. Jesus uses the picture of seeds that grow and mature and bring fruit. Christians may look at nature and be reminded of the seed of God's Word that brings and keeps them in the kingdom of God, which brings and keeps the kingdom of God in them. Or think of the Sacrament of Baptism and the Sacrament of the Altar. Jesus employs simple natural elements to satisfy deep spiritual needs. Again, as we daily wash outwardly, we are reminded of the true washing in the Sacrament of Baptism. As we daily satisfy earthly hunger, our souls are drawn to the contemplation of the sacred food offered in the Sacrament of the Altar and its much greater benefit.

In short, it may not be so much that Jesus used these pictures and tools from nature because they were readily at hand and easy to understand. It may rather be that nature was formed and fashioned in the first place in such a way that the believing child of God would be surrounded by reminders of the invisible spiritual truths mirrored in the visible natural world. What better way could there be than that for creation to reflect the glory of God? Everything in the visible world is a sort of tap on the shoulder to remind us of a deeper spiritual truth that is being reflected by the physical, the visible, phenomenon. The baby bird in the nest squawks frantically for the worm the robin brings in spring. Its eyes are closed. It sees nothing. It knows only its need and its total dependency. That's how I am both physically and spiritually before my God and Savior. The leaves on the tree are the most beautiful just before they die, but die they must. And so too I must die, and that day will be most glorious as I am through death ushered into heaven and life eternal. In the spring the tree and all the plants so dead all winter will rise. And so will I. There is no end to such happy reflections. And, of course, it is the Word of God itself in the Bible that moves us to such reflection.

The providence of God

The Word was perfect in its creating power from the beginning, and it did not lose that power once the Word was spoken. When God spoke his creating Word, he set for all time the natural order of things, the order of creation. God gave the command that plants and animals should reproduce after their kinds. The Word is still effective in each season, in every generation. By means of the Word the world was brought into being. By means of the Word the natural world is preserved and continues.

It is evident, therefore, that God has implanted in his creation what are generally called laws of nature. They are not laws that nature has produced but laws or principles that God established already at creation. He powerfully confirmed these after the flood when he promised the human race in the person of Noah, "As long as the earth endures, seedtime and harvest, cold and heat, summer and winter, day and night will never cease" (Genesis 8:22).

Mediate and immediate preservation

The care that God has taken in the preservation of his creation through the laws implanted in nature is a part of the doctrine of the providence of God. It is ultimately to God's providence, his active goodness in his rule over his creation, that we owe the dependability of the natural order of things. He sustains the planets in their orderly rotation so that the seasons are predictable. He continues to make his decree effective so that the plants and animals reproduce after their kinds and in their season. We cannot but call it to mind: The Word of God is indeed powerful. It not only brought all that is into existence, but by just one single command that each produce "according to its kind" he imbedded in plants and animals a durable ability to continue in existence to this day. This preservation of creation is called a *mediate preservation.* That is, God preserves *by means* of those laws and principles that he has implanted in nature. The laws are those that govern the rotation of the planets. They are those laws by which plants and animals reproduce after their kinds. They are the laws of biology and botany by which plants and animals are sustained by one another. They are all part of God's mediate preservation, his use of means for the fulfillment of his promise to Noah in Genesis 8:22.

We make a distinction between God's *mediate preservation* and his *immediate preservation.* The term *immediate* is defined as a preservation *without natural means.* God has not promised in his Word to preserve his creation *immediately,* that is, without means. In the covenant made with Noah, referred to earlier (Genesis 8:22), God promised to use means present in nature itself for nature's preservation. But occasionally God will preserve *immediately.* He will for his own purposes suspend the natural law and the normal means of preservation. Essentially that is what happens in a miracle. In a miracle God acts apart from or above the normal means. Thus Jesus fed the thousands with a few loaves of bread and a few fish (Mark 6:34-44; 8:1-9). That much bread and that amount of fish should be able to sustain only a few and that for a very short period of time. But Jesus caused it to multiply apart from natural law so that it sustained thousands. The same is true when he cleansed the lepers. According to the natural law the leprosy should have taken its normal medical course and resulted ultimately in death. But it did not. Jesus showed his mastery over nature by saving the lepers *immediately;* he cleansed them of their leprosy by, so to speak, speaking them clean (Mark 1:40,41) or just "willing" them clean (Luke 17:11-14). Even when he performed the miracle by speaking—by, we can say, means of his Word alone—we call it an *immediate* act because it came directly from Jesus without the ordinary means implanted in nature.

Those who expect miraculous preservation in times of need or illness or death are expecting something that God has not promised. If he chooses to, he certainly can and sometimes still does preserve *immediately,* but he has not promised to do so. God promised to provide for his creation and its preservation only *mediately.* Those who despise medicines and physicians while they await a miracle are not acting in a way that accords with the promises of God. Those who receive the tools of mediate preservation with thanksgiving to God for these means act according to his Word. Those who wallow in their problems and wait for solutions to drop down from heaven act contrary to the Word of God. Those who employ God-pleasing means and work to resolve problems act according to the Word of God. Again, that is not to say that God never acts *immediately* anymore. He certainly does at times dramatically and in most unexpected ways intervene in the normal course of things for the rescue of one who seems doomed to destruction. When that happens, we can but marvel and give thanks. But the point remains that that is not what we should expect, for that is not what he has promised. Normally, without himself being bound by natural means, he nevertheless has bound us to them.

The providence of God in the preservation of his creation embraces all that he has created. He did not merely wind up the universe he had made like some sort of great watchmaker in the sky and then indifferently leave it to wind down. He is always aware of everything that takes place in his creation. He even knows about the bird that falls from the sky (Matthew 10:29), though the bird may know nothing of God and his kindness in preserving it up to the moment of its fall. Over all creatures he keeps watch, and he provides for them through his orderly rule of the universe for as long as they live. Psalm 104:10-30 beautifully describes that care of God for his creation.

Of still greater concern to God than the animals is the whole human race. He looks down and considers all the plans of human hearts and weighs all of their actions (Psalm 33:13-17). He takes care to provide for the needs of the whole human race (Matthew 5:45; Acts 14:17). He even observes and controls the course of history and the movements of people acting in it; he governs it so that ultimately his purposes will be served (Acts 17:26,27).

His greatest concern, however, he reserves for his church, for those who worship him in spirit and in truth (Psalm 33:18,19; John 4:23,24). All those who worship the Holy Trinity by receiving from him forgiveness, life, and salvation are united to Christ as members of his spiritual body on earth (John 14:19-24; 1 Corinthians 12:27; Ephesians 4:15,16). It is for their sake and benefit that Christ rules all things in heaven and on earth (Ephesians 1:22,23). Even what seem to be disasters and tragedies, whether they appear as random acts in nature or the deliberate designs of evil spirits and people, even the results of our own sins and follies fall within and under the providence of God. In them all he rules and governs in such a way that they serve the ultimate best interests of the elect (Romans 5:5; 8:28-39).[1]

St. Paul knew that this teaching concerning the providence of God in misfortune and apparent disaster would not be an easy one for people to understand or accept. He experienced the difficulty firsthand. Already from the time of his conversion God told Paul that he would bring glory to God through much suffering (Acts 9:16). Nevertheless, the apostle faithfully confessed the truth of God's Word. He pointed even to his own imprisonment as a means that God was using to advance the cause of the gospel. Thus he concluded that his imprisonment was further evidence of God's providence, of his kindness and goodness (Philippians 1:12-26).

The providence of God in working through the natural order implanted at creation for the preservation of nature, the human race, and the church raises some difficult questions. Three such questions that fit under the heading of the providence of God are of special importance. The first question has to do with God's concurrence in evil. The second question has to do with the problem of necessity and contingency in history. The third question deals with the matter of the antecedent and the consequent will of God.

God's providence and concurrence in evil

The first question is this: If God stands behind the laws of nature that he established at creation, does that make God responsible for evil? For example, if someone takes a gun and shoots it and murder results, is God responsible for that death? God created the elements in the gun and the bullet. God gave the laws of physics and stood behind them as that bullet made its way to the victim. God gave the laws of

---

[1]For a further consideration of this topic, cf. chapter 11 under the heading "Christ is our great King."

biology and did not suspend them when the bullet hit a vital organ and caused that person's death.

So, then, is God responsible for the murder? The answer to the apparent problem lies in a distinction that we make on the basis of the Scriptures about God's concurrence. When natural laws or principles in nature are carried out, we say that God *concurs in them materially.* He concurs when the sun shines and the rain falls for the benefit of the good and the evil alike. Jesus tells us in Matthew 5:45 that God "causes his sun to rise on the evil and the good, and sends rain on the righteous and the unrighteous." He concurs materially as well when people use the rain and the sun, whether for good or evil. The murderer, the persecutor, and the wicked of every sort use the rain and the sun to raise their crops, to harvest them, and then to make their daily bread. That daily bread, according to principles established in nature, will feed and sustain them, even as they carry out their evil intentions. When they carry out their evil intentions, God will not normally suspend the laws of physics or the laws of natural cause and effect.

Thus the bullet of the murderer, if properly aimed, will reach its victim and have, in accordance with the laws implanted by God himself in nature, its deadly effect. That's what we mean when we say that God concurred materially. He did not suspend the laws of physics or biology or the laws of cause and effect to prevent the carrying out of the natural law. Indeed, nothing in the universe can occur without God's material concurrence, since nothing exists or continues in existence without God's permission (Acts 17:25-28).

But God does not concur in every intention behind every action. That is to say, God concurs materially in that he stands behind the laws of nature and does not normally suspend them, but *he does not necessarily concur morally.* He is not responsible for the evil intent of the murderer. God is holy and therefore totally separate from sin. The Ten Commandments and the very way in which they were given demonstrates God's loathing of evil (Exodus 20:1-18). In his very essence God is holy and righteous and his acts are thus holy and righteous as well (Psalm 145:17). He declares his intention to punish the wicked intentions and actions of unbelievers and devils, and he can be counted on to carry out that holy and just intention (Matthew 25; Revelation 20:11-15). But he does not promise to force the suspension of natural law always and everywhere in order to force people to do what is right and to prevent their evil intentions from being realized in fact. How do we account for so much evil in the world? Not by blaming God!

The fault lies in fallen humanity and in the will of the devil—about which we will have more to say in chapter 8.

While God does not suspend the laws of nature to prevent every evil deed, he nevertheless does give evidence that he does not concur morally in the evil that is in the world. Frequently he has threatened his wrath against the wickedness of individuals and nations. He has carried out his threats as part of his providential preservation of the church. Consider just a few examples from the book of Genesis alone: the expulsion of Adam and Eve from the garden (Genesis 3), Cain's mark (Genesis 4), the flood (Genesis 6–8), the aftermath of the building of the Tower of Babel (Genesis 11), the destruction of Sodom and Gomorrah (Genesis 19), to mention just a few. If God concurred morally in the wickedness punished in these incidents recorded in the Bible, that is, if he willed them to happen, then God would be unjust in punishing them. But he did not will them. He did not concur morally in the wickedness. Indeed, in the case of the flood, he had Noah warn his fellow people for years that they would perish if they did not turn away from their evil deeds. It is the will of the wicked that is the cause of evil, not the will of God.

God, however, does not only punish acts with which he does not concur morally. He at the same time limits the evil and keeps it within certain bounds in his providential rule over history. Even some of the divine visitations of wrath are part of that limiting activity by which God protects his church from destruction. The flood came at the time of Noah, lest the church perish; the church was saved by the flood that destroyed the wicked. St. Peter emphasizes that very point when he compares the waters of the flood to the waters of Baptism—both save (1 Peter 3:20,21). Joseph's brothers wanted to kill him, but God limited the damage they did. The evil intention of Joseph's brothers was eventually overturned for the good, even of the brothers (Genesis 50:19-21). That was a result of the providence of God, i.e., his gracious rule over all things for the benefit of the church.

At times God does not limit sin's outbreaks and then its dread consequences; he lets sin, so to speak, run its course in order to punish evil with evil. St. Paul summarizes that truth in Romans 1:18-32. There the apostle speaks of God turning people over to their own wickedness. He allows people to heap sin upon sin, until in their sins they devour one another and destroy themselves. In the Old Testament we often see examples of God permitting evil in order to punish evil. The violent and horrible destruction of Jerusalem is a case in point (2 Chronicles 36:15-21). The tragic story was repeated in the year A.D. 70 when

Jerusalem was again destroyed for its rejection of the Word of God. That destruction was in fulfillment of Jesus' prophecy against that city, which had spurned all of the Savior's blessings and offers of rescue and redemption (Matthew 23,24).

In the doctrine of the providence of God a distinction must therefore be made between those things that God wills and those things that God does not will but that happen nevertheless. Evil things happen only with God's material concurrence, never with his moral concurrence. That is so even when God permits evil in order to punish evil. That is a point that needs to be stressed with some urgency. Many seem to think that since God is omnipotent, nothing happens without his willing it. Some Calvinists even imagine that God willed the fall in the Garden of Eden. Otherwise, they argue, it could not have happened. That would make God a monster and a hypocrite when he threatens and punishes evil, if God himself is responsible for it. The thought itself is monstrous as well as contrary to God's description of himself in his Word.

It is true that God is omnipotent, all-powerful. But it is not true that therefore everything which happens must happen because God willed it. God does not will evil. As we have seen, God limits evil. He even allows evil to punish evil. He overturns the evil intentions of some for the benefit of his church, as in the case of Joseph and his brothers and in the case of the imprisoned apostle Paul, mentioned previously. But man remains responsible for choices that God permits him to make, choices between outwardly good acts and outwardly evil acts. God forces no one to sin or do violence and injustice. God does not turn man into some lockstep robot form, in which all people are forced to do God's will.

This distinction helps us to answer the lament one often hears: If God is so good and if God is so powerful, then how come such terrible things happen in the world? How come there are monsters who murder and cause wars and untold suffering? Again, the answer is not to be found in God's power or goodness. The answer is to be found in man and in his evil. That there is any good in the world at all, that is God's doing. That the wickedness of evil people is often limited and overturned, that is God's doing. That sometimes good is brought out of evil like a rose out of a dung heap, that is God's doing. All of these things are evidences of God's active goodness in his rule over creation; they are evidences of his providence. Yes, they are even evidences of his omnipotence. But in it all he still limits the exercise of his own will and his power, so that human beings can remain human beings with choices in this life between *good and evil outward actions.*

Consider for example the greatest evil ever committed. It was Judas' betrayal of Jesus and our Lord's trial and crucifixion. Jesus makes it very clear that the responsibility for the monstrous crime of betrayal rests with Judas (Matthew 26:23,24). Jesus goes to great lengths to call Judas back from the evil Judas planned (Matthew 26:21-24,50; Luke 22:48). The result of Judas' wickedness and that of the Jewish council and the Roman government was the crucifixion of the Son of God. Out of that most monstrous crime, however, came the redemption of the world. Nevertheless, that was not the intention of any of those who carried out these crimes. Not a single one of them was the least bit interested in bringing about our salvation. Each of them was intent only on evil. All of them, accordingly, are held responsible both for their own evil intentions and for the monstrous crime they committed. Even though all of these crimes were prophesied in great detail long before they took place (Psalm 22; Isaiah 53), those who committed them did so by their own choice and willingly (Acts 2:22-24; 3:13-15; 7:51-53).

To sum up the matter of God's concurrence: on the one hand, God limits the exercise of his own omnipotence in permitting human beings to be human beings, that is, possessed of a *free will in outward actions.* On the other hand, he exercises his providence, his good and gracious will, his wisdom, and his omnipotence by limiting evil and even forcing evil to serve his purposes (cf. again Acts 2,3; Romans 8:28). At the same time people remain responsible when they act wickedly. God does not normally suspend the laws of nature to stop their wicked acts; he allows them to take place, without concurring morally in the act. And so God does them no injustice when he holds them accountable and punishes their evil deeds.

Does this explanation answer all possible questions and difficulties on the subject of God's will and providence over or against evil in the world? No, it does not. But the simple fact is that any other answer runs contrary to the Scriptures. The ancient Manichean heresy sought to solve the problem by asserting that there is a good principle and a bad principle in the world; these two are in constant competition and sway back and forth in victory and defeat. However, that notion flatly contradicts what the Scriptures say about God's essential omnipotence, goodness, and grace.

Still others, as indicated earlier, try to solve the problems by concluding that everything that occurs must happen because God wills it. That too contradicts what the Scriptures teach about the nature of God and his providence, as well as what the Scriptures teach about man and human responsibility. Such an error ultimately makes God the author of sin and evil, which is as monstrous in thought as it is impossible in fact. And at the same time such an error allows people to imagine that they can do whatever they please without any regard for the will and Word of God, and to blame God for their evil deeds and the misery they themselves bring into the world and over their own heads.

While the Bible's answer to the problem may not satisfy all of our longings to know why bad things happen to good people, it should set those longings at least in part to rest. For we see in the examples in the Scriptures the many times when God overruled evil for the rescue of his church, even though it often took many years for that to become clear, as in the case of Joseph and his brothers in Genesis 37–47. We may see the same in our own lives and history often enough to learn to trust in the promises and providence of God. During those times when the mind is restless and the soul troubled, we wait. We know that God permits evil but that he also limits and can overrule it. We know that God concurs materially but not morally—he is not its author. Eventually it will become clear, if not in this life then in the next, how he preserved us graciously in the midst of suffering and of the evil in ourselves and others. Perhaps the clearest example of God's providential use of evil is in death itself. Death is the result of sin; but through the evil of our physical death God delivers us from all sin and pain and takes us into the greatest possible joy and blessedness, that which is reserved for the saints and angels in heaven.

Necessity and contingency

A second question that arises from the consideration of the providence of God is the question of the *necessary* versus the *contingent* in history. This problem is closely related to the problem of concurrence considered previously. The question is this: Does everything that happens in history have to happen? Does everything happen of necessity? Or, are some things contingent, that is, could they have happened differently? Napoleon marched across Europe and his army was destroyed in Russia. Did that have to happen? Could Napoleon have decided not to invade Russia? Aunt Tilly bought this house instead of that house. Did that have to happen? Henry was involved in a tragic and fatal car accident. Was that the unalterable will of God? Was it necessary? Or could things have happened differently? Again, the matter of God's concurrence and of his providence is involved in the question. So too is the matter of God's omnipotence and omniscience.

As we have already noted, some answer that everything that occurs happens of necessity. Their answer to every disaster and every good thing as well is, "It must be the will of God; otherwise, it wouldn't have happened." Such people are called fatalists or determinists. There is much in Islam that is fatalistic and much in Calvinism that is deterministic. Some find in their fatalism or determinism an easy escape from thinking, from reading the Bible, or from personal responsibility. They reason this way: If everything that happens must happen, then why bother studying the Scriptures so that I may decide things as best I can and in accord with the Word of God? Just let happen what is going to happen anyway.

Others go to the opposite extreme. They fall basically into old or present-day forms of Deism. A Deist thinks that God is out there somewhere. But the Deist imagines that God really is not much interested in the day-to-day running of the world. God got it started, and now it is up to us to do with it what we can or what we will. For the Deist just about everything that happens is contingent, that is, it could have happened differently than it did. The Deist has little use for the Bible. He may consider the Bible too restricting, or he may just dismiss it as largely irrelevant, except for some interesting stories and perhaps some lofty moral principles. Present-day Arminianism, the religion of most non-Calvinist Protestants, in its more extreme forms is not much different than Deism in the matter of necessity. Thus Deists and the most extreme Arminians conclude that ultimately very little in history happened of necessity; almost everything, including and especially faith, is the result of human choices and decisions. While the strict Calvinists make God's freedom so absolute that there is little room left for human freedom, even in outward acts or things subject to reason, many Arminians go to exactly the opposite extreme; they make man's freedom so absolute, even in spiritual matters, that God ends up with almost no freedom at all.[2]

What then in history, whether the history of the world or one's own history, is necessary and what is contingent? What is the connection between God's omniscience or foreknowledge and his will on the one hand and man's freedom in things subject to reason on the other hand? And how is God's providence a part of the picture?

---

[2]For a present-day presentation of the Calvinist view, cf. John Piper, *The Pleasures of God: Meditations on God's Delight in Being God* (Oregon: Multnomah Publishers, Sisters, 2000), note especially pp. 313-340. For a current presentation of the Arminian point of view, cf. *A Case for Arminianism* (Grand Rapids: Zondervan Publishing House, 1989).

First of all, the Scriptures teach clearly that God does indeed know everything, that he is omniscient. He knows all that will happen before it takes place. Through the prophet Isaiah he declares that he alone knows the end of things from their beginning (Isaiah 46:9,10). The psalmist worships the Lord who knows our thoughts before they have even come into our minds (Psalm 139:1-4). Jesus demonstrated repeatedly that he understood all that was to happen to him long before it took place (Mark 8:31,32; 9:31; 10:33,34). Yes, already in eternity he knew all of it (John 3:13-17; 12:23-32).

But to say that God knows all that will happen is not the same thing as saying that he willed all that happens and that everything that happens, therefore, must have happened exactly as it did. Only some of the things that God knows are both willed by him and decreed by him. He willed and decreed it for himself that he should suffer and die for the sins of the world and on the third day rise again. All of that had to take place in fulfillment of his promises (Isaiah 53; Psalm 22). He has willed and decreed it that the church shall not perish as long as the earth stands (Matthew 16:17,18; 24:35). And, therefore, it is necessary that no matter how many may persecute her, the church will endure until Christ returns.

But much of what happens in history is *contingent,* at least as far as we can see it. Thus, for example, God wills and decrees that the church must endure, and so it will endure. But where? The church perished in Israel when the people turned their backs on Jesus and his work for their salvation. Was that the will of God? Clearly it was not, as Jesus testifies (Matthew 23:37,38) and as St. Stephen declared shortly before his martyrdom (Acts 7:51-53). St. Paul on his missionary journeys recorded in the book of Acts usually started by preaching and teaching in the synagogue. God's intention and St. Paul's as well was that the Jews would hear the gospel and believe it. But most of them rejected it. The church endured. But it did not endure everywhere. It could have continued among the Jews who heard the gospel. That was certainly God's will. But for the most part it did not continue among them. That the church endures is necessary. Where it endures is contingent.

The same could be said of the gospel seed planted all around the world. It is God's will that all should hear and believe. And because the church will never perish, some do. But those who reject the gospel, or who receive it for a time and then spurn it, lose it contingently—not of necessity, not because God willed it.

The same point can be made about most of human history. Some things must happen because God has decreed that they must happen. Those decrees that he has revealed we will find in his Word and not apart from it. Other things happen that could have happened differently—they were contingent. God knew how they would happen and turn out, but God did not will it that they turn out as they did. To put it another way, God's omniscience does not cause everything to happen that God knows will happen. Jesus in Matthew 23 foresaw and prophesied the destruction of Jerusalem. Clearly he did not want it to happen, and clearly it did not have to happen. It happened, nevertheless, because of the stubborn rejection of the gospel. To use an example of limited value, a teacher may know in advance that Fritz will fail the course. The teacher knows it because Fritz is lazy and never does his work. The teacher's knowledge, however, is not the cause of Fritz' failure. For that Fritz has only himself to blame.

It is a mistake to take too much of history, whether the history of the world or our own personal history, and think of all of it as necessary rather than contingent. We know those things that are necessary only from the Word of God. St. Paul tells Christians in Ephesians 2:10 that "we are God's workmanship, created in Christ Jesus to do good works, that God prepared in advance for us to do." And what are the good works that God prepares for us to do? They are the works he gives us in the Ten Commandments. They are a thousand opportunities in a day to serve him by serving one another. They are works among which we must daily make choices. Should I spend this hour with the Bible and my devotions? Is this hour best given to God by working, by spending time with my family, by serving in the community or at church? All these and others are works that God has prepared for us and places before us each day. Each day we make choices among them and look for balance in our choices; we do not want to spend all of our time working or all of our time praying. We have to pick and choose. Some days more time is spent with the family, other days more time at work, while still other days more time in active worship. On any given day we might have decided and chosen differently, and we had the freedom to decide differently in those things that were subject to human choice and reason. The choices are contingent.

What we do each day in making choices, we do for our lifetime as well. God knows where and how long we will live. He knows what our vocations will be and what jobs we will have. Some of these things he may indeed set in place for us (Acts 17:26; Job 14:5). But how many of those things are irreversibly decreed in the mind of God we cannot know. Nor does God expect or ask us to guess what such things might be. They are reserved to his hidden will, and in his hidden will they shall remain. God gives us choices to make in our lives, and as far as we know or can know those choices are contingent. If God has among those choices some few that are necessary, he will work them out as he sees fit. It is not for us to worry or be concerned about. But as we live out our lives, as far as we can tell, most things are contingent—they depend on decisions that God has left us free to make. Thus, God knows how long he wants us to live, but that time can be shortened by us in any number of ways, chiefly by ignoring the discipline of God's own Word (Proverbs 3:1,2). God knows whether and whom we will marry. We do well to give thanks to God when we have a pious spouse and a happy marriage, but at the same time we go too far if we say that God has chosen our spouse for us. The Scriptures do not teach that. That is a choice that God has left to us and one that he bids us make in the light of what his Word tells us about marriage (Matthew 19:11,12; 1 Corinthians 7).

Even collectively we decide many things that are contingent. We elect government officials and pass laws. Were these all the will of God and necessary? No, they were contingent. They could have happened differently, as far as we know from the Scriptures. We decide as a church to put on a new roof or open a school. The decision may be reached only after long and intense debate on the course of action. Once the decision is made, should we declare that it is therefore the will of God? The Bible gives us no warrant for saying that. The decision was ours. It was contingent. The vote could have gone the other way. Either way could have been *according to the will of God,* that is, not contrary to his Word. But that does not mean that the way it came out was the same thing as the will of God. Again, it was contingent, free to choice, not divinely decreed. The Scriptures do not even guarantee that the choices we make will always or necessarily be the best ones or the wisest. The side that prevailed makes an arrogant mistake when it declares: We won! Therefore, it must be the will of God, and anyone who disagrees is arguing with God!

Consider the disagreement that arose between Paul and Barnabas in Acts 15:36-40. Paul wanted to pursue one course of action, and Barnabas favored another course. They came to no agreement, and they ended up each pursuing a different course. But neither declared that his own decision was the will of God and that the conclusion of the other was therefore a sin. God's Word did not decide it. They were free to decide, and their decisions were contingent—they could have decided differently.

Consider then the pattern that St. Paul left us when he tells us how he decided things left free to his decision (1 Corinthians 9). He does not declare that simply because he decided these things that they were therefore the will of God. He was free to decide them differently. Others faced with the same choices did decide them differently. The decisions and following actions were contingent.

In sum, we want to avoid a mindless determinism and fatalism. We do not want to say that something is the will of God simply because it happened. We strive to live out our lives in conscious harmony with the Word of God. We want to decide those things that God has left free for us to decide for the glory of his name and the well-being of those we can serve (1 Corinthians 10:31-33). But in doing so, we will not be so arrogant as to equate whatever we decide with God's will. The decision may be according to God's will, that is, not contrary to anything in his Word, but that doesn't make it God's will and therefore necessary.

How is all of this connected to the providence of God? In all of the decisions that God has left free to us and that are contingent, we have God's providence as our consolation. So great is his power that he rules over all of our history. He carries out that rule in grace and mercy, intervening for our protection, acting for our ultimate good, and, yes, even taking into account our contingent decisions and actions (Romans 8:31-39). Gladly we commend ourselves to his care. With thanksgiving we decide such things as he has left to our decision, confident of his grace and mercy. In our prayers we entrust our every care to him and ask his blessing on our decisions and choices, confident that he will answer in the way that best serves our eternal good (Matthew 7:7-11; James 1:2-8).

If we keep this distinction between contingency and necessity in mind, and if we examine the Scriptures in the light of the Scriptures, the meaning of some often misused passages will become clear. In Psalm 37:5,6 we read, "Commit your way to the LORD; trust in him and he will do this: He will make your righteousness shine like the dawn, the justice of your cause like the noonday sun." And in Proverbs 16:3 we are told, "Commit to the LORD whatever you do, and your plans will succeed." Do these and similar passages mean that whatever we decide to do is the will of God, as long as we prayed about it? They do not. Rather, they urge us to examine the Word of God in making decisions, so that we may be certain that we are not acting contrary to his Word. Then whatever we plan that is according to the Word of God will ultimately bring him glory and will be blessed by God for our good.

Consider in this connection also Psalm 91, especially verse 11: "He will command his angels concerning you to guard you in all your ways." That is the verse that Satan distorted when he tempted Jesus (Matthew 4:5-7). The promise is not a blanket promise that whatever ways we go must be part of God's eternal plan and that therefore it will succeed under angelic protection. Rather, the passage encourages us to see to it that our way is one of faith in Christ and obedience to his Word as we make the many choices that God places before us. For his Word of the law and the gospel is the path that the Christian wants to follow. So long as we are walking in the way of the Word of the Lord, we trust that God will bless those contingent choices and that we will enjoy the promised protection of the holy angels. Yes, even if disaster befalls us while walking in the ways of the Lord, we remain confident that God and the holy angels have not abandoned us; rather, God is using disaster for our ultimate good and his eternal glory, as we see from the example of Joseph mentioned earlier. Psalm 119 is an extended prayer asking for that knowledge which comes from the Word of God for our path. Again, only in the Word of God do we find God's will. Not in our dreams. Not in our reason. Not in our feelings.

Our Lutheran Confessions also warn against seeking God's will anywhere other than in his Word. The Formula of Concord urges us to rely on his written Word for his revealed will and to look for it nowhere else when we want to know what his will is for our lives. It declares,

> For this reason, too, believers require the teaching of the law: so that they do not fall back on their own holiness and piety and under the appearance of God's Spirit establish their own service to God on the basis of their own choice, without God's Word or command. As it is written in Deuteronomy 12[:8,28,32], "You shall not act . . . all of us according to our own desires," but "listen to the commands and laws which I command you," and "you shall not add to them nor take anything from them." (FC SD IV, 20 p. 590)

Also, in Article XI of the Solid Declaration, in its consideration of the doctrine of election, the Formula warns against trying to peer into God's hidden will in order to find there answers to questions that he has not provided in his Word. For what he does not reveal in his Word he does not want us to know, at least not in this lifetime. The warning of the Formula is concerned particularly with the doctrine of election, but the principle is a good principle in general:

> For our impertinence always desires to concern itself much more with those things we cannot make sense of than with what God has revealed to us in his Word. Moreover, we have no command from God to do so. . . . We should not pursue the matter with our own

> speculations. We should not make our own deductions, form conclusions, or brood about this matter, but instead we should cling to his revealed Word to which he directs us. (FC SD XI, 53,54 p. 649)

Luther sums up the matter very well in the Smalcald Articles where he writes:

> In these matters, which concern the spoken, external Word, it must be firmly maintained that God gives no one his Spirit or grace apart from the external Word which goes before. We say this to protect ourselves from the enthusiasts, that is, the "spirits," who boast that they have the Spirit apart from and before contact with the Word. . . . Therefore we should and must insist that God does not want to deal with us human beings, except by means of his external Word and sacrament. Everything that boasts of being from the Spirit apart from such a Word and sacrament is of the devil. (SA III VIII, 3,10 pp. 322,323)

God's antecedent and consequent will

We have one more distinction that we should make concerning the will of God and the providence of God. In the last chapter we noted that from the perspective of God's essence and nature, his will is both a *revealed will* and a *hidden will.* In this chapter we have noted that God's will can be considered under the heading of his providence as a will that concurs in evil materially but not morally. We have also noted that his will stands over all that happens in history, whether what happens is necessary or contingent.

The one remaining distinction that we want to consider then regarding the will of God under the general heading of God's providence is that God's will can be seen as *antecedent* or *consequent.* This final distinction also helps us to understand the connection between God's will on the one hand and his actions in time and history on the other.

God's will is called an *antecedent will* when it goes before some event or human action and is the primary cause of that event or action; the word *antecedent* describes "something that precedes or goes before." Thus God wills the redemption of the world and the ultimate salvation of the elect. He wills it altogether apart from and absent anything done by anyone in the world to deserve salvation. St. Paul declares that even before the foundation of the world God chose us in Christ to be the heirs of salvation (Ephesians 1:4-8). God willed already in eternity how the message of the gospel would come to us in such a way that we would believe it and finally die in saving faith (Ephesians 1:9-14). In these same passages the apostle makes it clear that this will of God had nothing whatever to do with anything good that we might do to cause this gracious choice. He willed our salvation before we believed. He willed it in eternity. He willed it before we had done anything good. Indeed it is because of this antecedent will of God that we have heard the gospel and believe it and then do good as a result of the faith created by him through the gospel.

Thus, God's grace and Christ's merits and God's choice get all the praise and glory for our salvation through faith in the gospel. The apostle emphasizes the same truth again in Ephesians 2:1-10, where again all the glory for our salvation goes to God. Our faith is the result of his saving work, of his grace, yes, and of his antecedent will. It is an amazing and beautiful and richly comforting truth of the gospel that we owe our salvation to God's antecedent will. For if God thought of us already in eternity and if he so ruled over history that this will would be carried out and if our salvation has no cause in us but only in God working faith through the gospel, then we are absolutely sure of God's love for us. Then we can still the accusing voice of the devil and of conscience with God's promises in Christ (Romans 8:1). Are we unworthy? Of course! The antecedent will of God assures us that our worthiness was and is not a factor in God's choice. Do we fear that we might still fall? Then we fly to the gospel for reassurance and strength in the struggle, assured that it is God's will to save us through that gospel and that it was his will to do so already in eternity.

There are other actions of God, however, that do not flow from his antecedent will. Luke 7:30 speaks of God's intentions towards the scribes and Pharisees in the work of John the Baptist and of Jesus himself. But the scribes and Pharisees through their own fault rejected God's intentions towards them. What happened because of and as a result of their stubborn and persistent rejection of God's Word and Christ's work? They perished in their sins. Why? Because that's what God wanted in eternity? No. It happened because of their stubborn rejection. God's will was *consequent.* It was a will that came after their actions and a will that was provoked and caused by their actions. That is why Jesus laments over Jerusalem (Matthew 23:37,38) and weeps over it (Luke 19:41,42).

So much Old Testament history witnesses to this distinction between the antecedent and the consequent will of God. God declares repeatedly that he did not choose the Israelites to be his people because they were deserving of his choice. He chose them because of his own purposes and grace; he laid his choice on them to magnify his power and his kindness totally apart from any worthiness or merit in Israel. In

Isaiah 65:2,3, for example, in a passage quoted also by St. Paul in Romans 10, God declares the history of his grace toward Israel in a beautiful picture. He says, "All day long I have held out my hands to an obstinate people, who walk in ways not good, pursuing their own imaginations—a people who continually provoke me to my very face." How unlike human behavior! We might extend our arms to a stubborn child for seconds, perhaps for a minute, certainly not for more than two minutes. But God? "All day long" he expresses his antecedent will for their salvation, in spite of obstinacy, rebellion, and stubborn rejection!

But when Israel persisted in rejecting his gracious call, then, as a result of that rejection, God acted in judgment and in anger. His action was consequent, not antecedent. His action was the result of evil and wickedness chosen by the people. His antecedent will never changed, that will which sought their salvation. But their rejection of that salvation had consequences, namely, his judgment.

Read the book of Judges. This distinction between God's antecedent and consequent will is an ever-recurring theme in that book. Psalm 78 too speaks eloquently of the antecedent and consequent will of God. Likewise, in reporting the destruction of the Northern Kingdom of Israel, the holy writer declares, "All this took place because the Israelites had sinned against the LORD their God" (2 Kings 17:7). The entire account places in sharp contrast God's antecedent will and his consequent will. The account of the destruction of the Southern Kingdom of Judah also speaks of the consequent will of God. "It was because of the LORD's anger that all this happened to Jerusalem and Judah, and in the end he thrust them from his presence" (2 Kings 24:20; cf. also 2 Chronicles 36:15-21; Nehemiah 1:4-9; Daniel 9:1-19).

Even in the exercise of his consequent will, God often has the intention of saving according to his antecedent will. Again, consider the book of Judges and the whole history of Israel to the time of Christ's ascension and even after that (Romans 11). When God exercises his judgment in consequence of sin, he longs for the repentant return of those thus judged. In pardoning their transgression he again acts according to his antecedent will. Daniel shows the correct and beautiful understanding of this distinction in his prayer for the restoration of the destroyed city of Jerusalem and the temple. He prays, "We do not make requests of you because we are righteous, but because of your great mercy. O Lord, listen! O Lord, forgive! O Lord, hear and act! For your sake, O my God, do not delay, because your city and your people bear your Name" (Daniel 9:18,19). Moses had prayed in much the same way (Exodus 32:9-14).

The point is that God's will is antecedent when God acts to save; for God's own grace is always antecedent to man's acts as the cause. He acts because he is gracious, so that no one may boast before him (Romans 11:33-36; Ephesians 2:8,9). When God judges, condemns, and damns, he does it because of sin and wickedness; he does it in consequence of the rejection of his goodness and grace. Although we are not able to cause God's goodness and grace, we are capable of causing his wrath and judgment by rejecting his Word and choosing evil.

We have considered God's will from a number of different perspectives. His will is revealed and hidden. His will concurs materially in all that happens but never concurs morally in evil. His will determines history that is necessary and controls history that is contingent. His will is seen in the Scriptures sometimes as antecedent and sometimes as consequent. All of these distinctions taken together help us to understand in part what ultimately is unfathomable, as St. Paul declares (Romans 11:33-36). We do not expect to be able to answer every question that might occur with respect to the will of God. But all the same it is important for us to see what we can of it from his revelation of himself in his Word. For without at least this much understanding of his will and the different ways in which we can perceive and trace his will in his Word, we easily fall into dangerous errors. We end up assuming that whatever we feel is what God wills and whatever we do is God's will. We may become ensnared in fatalism or determinism; these errors ultimately make God the cause of evil and give people an excuse for being irresponsible. Or we may go to the other extreme. We may become victims of Deist illusions and think that we alone are the masters of our own destinies and are alone the captains of our fates. The path of the Christian is to search the Scriptures for God's will; it is to trust what God has revealed there; it is to live with our will subject to his Word; it is to make choices as acts of worship by which we serve him and our neighbor in grateful response to the gospel and in harmony with the law.

The angels

There is no mention of the creation of the angels in Genesis 1. We do not know exactly on which day they were created. We only know that it was on one of the six days of creation. For the Scriptures clearly tell us that everything created came into being during these six days (Genesis 2:2; Exodus 20:11). The ancient church fathers guessed that the angels were created either on the first day together with the light or on the sixth day, the day of man's creation. The Bible does not answer the question.

The Bible does however tell us much about the angels. They are spirits (Psalm 104:4), and therefore they usually do not have bodies. Occasionally they appear in a physical form to carry out some specific assignment that God has given them—indeed the word *angel* means "messenger." Two of the three who appeared to Abraham were angels; the third was God himself in a temporarily assumed human form (Genesis 18:1–19:1). Sometimes the angels appear with wings, as in Isaiah 6. Sometimes they seem to take a glorified human form, as at the tomb of Jesus on Easter Sunday (Luke 24:4). But usually they are invisible to us.

The angels were created with a fixed number that neither increases nor decreases. The number is very great, thousands times thousands (Daniel 7:10). There is no command for them to reproduce (Matthew 22:30), perhaps because they never die (Luke 20:36).

The angels are personal beings. They are conscious of who they are and what they are doing (Luke 1:19). They have personalities that experience emotions like joy and pleasure (Luke 15:10; 1 Peter 1:12). They appear to have rank, though we do not understand what that means in heaven and in eternity (1 Peter 3:22; 1 Thessalonians 4:16). They are powerful (2 Kings 19:32-35; Psalm 103:20). Perhaps to us their strangest attribute is that they are *illocal,* that is, they are not subject to the limits of time and space in the same way that we are. They are not omnipresent as God is. Nevertheless, Jesus describes the angels as guarding little ones while at the same time always beholding the face of God in heaven (Matthew 18:10).

As noted earlier, we do not know on which of the six days God created the angels. We do know that shortly after their creation a disaster took place. At their creation all of the angels were holy and they fit the description that God gives to all of his creation: They were very good (Genesis 1:31). But a large number of the angels were not satisfied with their place with God in heaven. They rebelled. It is impossible for us to imagine what that must have been like. The Scriptures paint a horrible, if unimaginable, picture of the event in Revelation 12:7-9. Jesus tells us that he "saw Satan fall like lightning from heaven" (Luke 10:18). With Satan (elsewhere called Beelzebub), their leader, all the angels who joined in the rebellion were expelled from heaven and cast into hell. Hell for them is not just a place; it is a condition of unutterable misery from which there can be no escape, for which there can be no relief. No matter where the devil is with his hosts he is always in hell.

There is no salvation for the evil angels and no possibility of repentance for them (2 Peter 2:4; Jude 6). It was for them that hell was prepared (Matthew 25:41). We do not know why God did not give this fallen host an opportunity for repentance; it is part of his hidden will. The Scriptures simply state the fact without any discussion of the why.

Though cast out of heaven and eternally miserable, Satan and his hosts are still very powerful. They still have a limited amount of freedom, but they are none the happier for it. Indeed their whole aim in the use of their limited freedom is to increase misery in the world. St. Peter describes the devil and by implication his cohorts as a "roaring lion looking for someone to devour" (1 Peter 5:8). Satan is the author of evil in the world. He lies. He murders. He is capable of no good, but only of evil and destruction (John 8:44). He uses a perverted reason in his attempts to deceive people and drive them either to arrogance or to despair (Matthew 4:5,6; 27:3-5). Even so, he is himself ultimately irrational in all that he says and does. His legions ask permission, for example, to go into the swine, as though they will somehow be better off for it. Perhaps to show us the ultimate irrationality of the fallen angels and their capacity only for destruction, death, and evil, Jesus grants their request. And so, after they enter the swine, the swine simply plunge into the water and drown in a demon-induced frenzy (Luke 8:26-33). In his rage and misery Satan bends his every effort to destroy the church by sowing false doctrine and hypocrisy wherever and whenever people take their eyes off of Christ and their attention away from the Word of God (Matthew 13:1-43; John 13:2; Ephesians 2:2; 2 Thessalonians 2:9).

So powerful and clever is Satan that he is able to seduce and rule in the hearts of most people in spite of the always ruinous consequences of his influence and rule (Ephesians 2:2). The astonishing thing for Christians is that they know the wrath and rage of Satan; they know his cunning; they know his goal. And still too often in their own weakness Christians also toy with his temptations as though Satan were really their friend, or at least harmless. That is how Satan presented himself to Eve in the Garden of Eden, as a harmless advisor, even a friend. The truth however is that he is a liar, a murderer, a destroyer, one bent on dragging us into hell, and one tragically successful with many in the endeavor. That should serve as a warning to Christians who do not take him seriously and who accordingly play with his temptations—they act as though he were a pet kitten to be played with, instead of the roaring lion bent on their destruction.

We may wish that God would simply destroy Satan and his entire host now so that he would no longer tempt us. But God has not chosen to do that. Instead, God gives us in his Word the powerful defense against Satan's seduction attempts and the weapons necessary to defeat him (Romans 13:11-14; Ephesians 5:1-20; 1 Peter 5:6-11). God shows us his own superiority and power over Satan (Matthew 12:22-29). He limits Satan's sphere of action (Job 1:6-12). He even promises us that he will not allow Satan to tempt us beyond our ability to withstand him (1 Corinthians 10:11-13). That ability to withstand is linked inseparably to the Word of God. Jesus himself demonstrated that for us perfectly in his battle with Satan (Matthew 4:1-11). Those not content with these weapons have already lost the battle. Despising God's own armor, they invite the ultimate delusion of the devil and fall into the waiting arms of the Antichrist (2 Thessalonians 2:1-12) or into other great shame and vice (2 Peter 2; Jude 3-11).

Once again the Scriptures are not going to answer every question we might raise on the subject of the devil and his angels. The Bible tells us enough for our warning. It tells us enough for our encouragement so that we cling to the Word of God for our defense. It tells us enough! Those who want to know more should be warned solemnly against Satanism, witchcraft, fortune telling, horoscopes, and such other manifestations of the occult among those not satisfied with the Word of God. We should not be surprised at people's interest in such things—it is a mark of a society headed for destruction (Romans 1:18-32; 2 Timothy 3:1-9; 4:3,4). The Christian should shun all such things with a horror altogether appropriate for the hellish. It is quite bad enough that we must contend with the devil day and night without going out of our way to look for him, as though his misery could be our delight!

Originally all of the angels were created (and Adam and Eve as well) with the ability not to sin *(posse non peccare)*. But after their fall, the devil and his angels are so steeped in misery and so totally separated from the grace of God and any possibility of it that they are described as "not able not to sin" *(non posse non peccare);* their entire existence is nothing but sin and a punishment for sin. The angels, however, who remained faithful to God have been confirmed in their bliss so that they are "not able to sin" *(non posse peccare)*. Jesus says of them that they always behold the face of God in heaven (Matthew 18:10). That constant vision of God in his glory will last forever. These are the angels who will accompany Jesus on his return on the Last Day

(Matthew 25:31). We should not think that because the holy angels cannot sin, they somehow are limited or that they might even resent such a limitation. Quite the contrary is the case. They have been confirmed in their bliss in heaven. That is what they want with all their might and will, that they should never leave God's side or lose the blessed vision of God in his glory. And that is the ultimate freedom, to have one's will perfectly conformed to the will of God. Such is the will of the holy angels and they would not want it otherwise.

The occupation of the holy angels is a blessed one indeed. They constantly serve God and do so perfectly, willingly, and happily (Psalm 103:21). A particularly beautiful evidence of their perfect and happy submission to the will of God can be seen from their appearances in connection with the life of Christ. In those appearances to people they always fulfill wonderfully their very name *angel,* which means "messenger." But notice how they do it. On the fields outside of Bethlehem they announced the birth of the Savior with great joy (Luke 2:13,14). They surely knew that the Savior was coming to suffer and die for the sins of the world. Nevertheless, they were happy that he whom they love, worship, and adore was pleased to come down and die for the fallen human race. There is no hint of resentment that he did not rescue the fallen angels. There is no trace of anger at human beings that Christ would suffer so greatly on their behalf. Their will submitted perfectly and gladly to the will of God, and they rejoiced in the coming salvation of sinful human beings! At Easter they likewise rejoiced not only in the resurrection of Christ but in their service to the church, that they were chosen as the first messengers of the resurrection (Matthew 28:2-7). And at his ascension they again appeared as those sent to put a period on the work of Christ on earth and to repeat the promise of his return when the work of the church on earth is finished (Acts 1:9-11). In all of these appearances of the holy angels, we might have expected them to be angry with humankind; for he whom they love and worship suffered on account of our sins. But so perfect is their submission to the will of God, they even rejoice in his suffering because that is what God willed for himself, and that for our sake! What an amazing thing!

God sends these holy angels to protect and guard his own (Psalm 91:11; Matthew 18:10; Hebrews 1:14). That service to us, unseen though it is, lasts our whole life long (Luke 16:22). Even on the Last Day the angels will accompany Jesus when he raises all the dead (Matthew 13:39; 24:31). Thus we are always in the company of the holy angels and do well not to shame them by our behavior. Nevertheless, the Scriptures nowhere tell us to pray to them. Prayer is an act of worship and God alone should be the one who receives our worship (Colossians 2:18). Instead we give thanks to God for all things, including the company and the help and the protection of the holy angels. Perhaps when we get to heaven we will have the opportunity of talking to the holy angels who were our companions and protectors. For now they listen to God and gladly answer his commission that they protect us and the church; and for now we are content to thank and praise God alone for that.

Likewise we do not expect the angels to communicate with us. They do not act independently and apart from God's specific command, as we see in all the references to the angels in the Bible. When they spoke to human beings, they spoke God's Word, not their own. It is a sad feature of the present-day world that people are eager for angelic manifestations or communication. But they don't want the revealed, written Word of God! If angels would appear to them, it would be in terror to rebuke their unbelief. Those who imagine that the angels talk to them are not receiving revelations from the holy angels; they are receiving delusions from fallen angels or from their own imaginations.

Again, the curious have all manner of questions that the Scriptures do not answer, and the idle become busy with their own imaginations about the holy angels as well as about the evil angels. We can only respond: *Ad fontes!* To the source! The Scriptures tell us what we need to know. They do not encourage us to wander on our own into speculation. Quite the contrary—they warn constantly against it. Some want to know why God "needs" the angels to protect us, especially since the Scriptures say so often that he is always with us himself for our help and protection (Psalm 46; Matthew 28:18-20; John 14:15-24). The answer, of course, is that God does not "need" the angels. He has chosen to use them and make them our companions and protectors, and that without in any way denying that he himself is our companion and protector. Why he has chosen to act that way, we leave to him. It is enough to say that ever since creation God has chosen to act through means. He preserves our bodily lives by means of the seasons and the ability of food to nourish. He protects by means of the holy angels. He creates and sustains faith by means of the Word and sacraments. He likes to use means. We receive them with thanksgiving. We follow the example of the holy angels mentioned above and gladly submit our wills to his will as we have it in his Word.

PART III

ANTHROPOLOGY

Chapter 7
The Creation of Man

We come now to the high point of the creation account—the creation of Adam and Eve. That their creation was in fact the high point is evident from the words that God himself has chosen to describe it.

The creation of Adam began with a solemn introduction, marking this work as unique, as special in every way. "Then God said, 'Let us make man in our image, in our likeness'" (Genesis 1:26). The Trinity took solemn counsel within itself before beginning this work. For unlike the rest of the visible creation, Adam and Eve were to bear the very image of God and his likeness. How that image should manifest itself is clear from the works God intended to give them: "And let them rule over the fish of the sea and the birds of the air, over the livestock, over all the earth, and over all the creatures that move along the ground" (Genesis 1:26). Adam and Eve, together with their descendants, were to serve as God's agents, his regents on earth. All that he had made on earth he intended to press into their service. All that he had made should be for their good and benefit. After all, God didn't make the sky, the flowers, the sea, and the mountains so beautiful so that he could enjoy them; he made them for us to enjoy, to use, to preserve, yes, to study so that by it all we might have reasons heaped on reasons to marvel at him and worship him, to give him thanks and praise for his generosity to us.

"So God created man in his own image, in the image of God he created him; male and female he created them" (Genesis 1:27). The words read like a love poem, an ecstatic utterance of the Creator at the creation of his own image and likeness. Note how the same thought is repeated three times in but slightly altered form, as though God wished to linger and to have us tarry as well over the wonder of what he had just done.

As soon as they were created, God entered into a loving relationship with Adam and Eve. He had formed everything else in the visible world by simply speaking it into existence and then implanting in it the natural law or instinct by which it should continue to reproduce after its kind. But in the creation of Adam, God took a special care. He formed and fashioned him from the dust of the ground and breathed into him the breath of life (Genesis 2:7). Then he spoke to Adam and Eve. His words are filled with power but also with kindness, with love, and with generosity. And unlike his words to the plants and animals, his words to Adam and Eve expect a rational response, not just the response of instinct.

> God blessed them and said to them, "Be fruitful and increase in number; fill the earth and subdue it. Rule over the fish of the sea and the birds of the air and over every living creature that moves on the ground."
>
> Then God said, "I give you every seed-bearing plant on the face of the whole earth and every tree that has fruit with seed in it. They will be yours for food. And to all the beasts of the earth and all the birds of the air and all the creatures that move on the ground—everything that has the breath of life in it—I give every green plant for food." (Genesis 1:28-30)

Genesis 2 reinforces our impression that God wished to linger and wishes us to linger over this great moment in the creation account. The work of creation, summarized in Genesis 1, is retold with particular emphasis on the creation of Adam and Eve.

The details also emphasize the special love that God showed Adam and Eve as distinct from all of the rest of creation. We see that special care and love of God most notably in the way that he proceeded with the creation of Eve. "The LORD God said, 'It is not good for the man to be alone. I will make a helper suitable for him'" (Genesis 2:18). But he didn't create Eve right away; he waited a bit. Why? The other creatures of the earth were created in pairs at God's speaking. Not so Adam and Eve. Adam was created first. Eve was created on the same day, but only after some time had passed. For God wanted Adam to become aware of his need for a human companion and mate and to understand as well that God in love provided for that need.

And so God had all of the animals, perhaps representatives of each "kind," pass in review for Adam to name. The work was a high honor for Adam. In the process of naming the animals Adam exercised his unique reasoning powers and his speaking ability. He served as God's companion. He showed himself as "like God" in carrying out this work fit only for one who is godlike. Indeed, God allows Adam to become aware of his own unique relationship with God, for God was speaking with him and working with him. He let Adam delight in doing something important and worthwhile as God's own companion and coworker. At the same time Adam could easily draw the conclusion that his companionship with God, as close and as intimate as it was,

was not the same as having a companion like himself. Adam was made aware of a fact that might otherwise have escaped his immediate notice: All of the animals were in pairs; each had a mate both similar to and different from itself. "But for Adam no suitable helper was found" (Genesis 2:20). And then very quickly, before Adam's awareness could rise to the level of discontent—which would be a sin—God satisfied the need he had allowed Adam to realize.

And so God created Eve from Adam's rib. She was like him. She shared with him the image and likeness of God through her creation from Adam. She was created to be his suitable helper and companion, to be, as it were, by his side as she had come from his side. The order of her creation and Adam's understanding of that order is expressed by Adam in the first love poem. God brought Eve to Adam and he received her with thanksgiving and delight:

> The man said, "This is now bone of my bones and flesh of my flesh; she shall be called 'woman,' for she was taken out of man." (Genesis 2:23)

The words that follow may have been Moses' commentary on Adam's poem or part of the poem itself; that matter is debated. However, the point is clear. Whether Adam said it or Moses wrote it by way of commentary, Adam understood at once the significance of Eve's creation as the "suitable helper" for him. She was a gracious gift of God to fill a need of which Adam had just become aware. "For this reason a man will leave his father and mother and be united to his wife, and they will become one flesh" (Genesis 2:24).

With Eve's creation and presentation to Adam, God established marriage. The first two purposes for marriage were given already in the Garden of Eden. The first purpose of marriage is companionship. Adam needed a companion, and his wife was to be that companion. He was created first and was by divine arrangement to be the head in that union. In the course of carrying out his role as head with her as his companion, he would also be her companion. The second purpose of marriage is the bearing of children. It is included as a primary purpose of marriage in the summary account of Genesis 1:28. The husband who is too busy with his work or his friends to be a companion to his wife and the wife who is too busy with her own life and pursuits to be a companion to her husband miss a primary purpose and intention of God in the institution of marriage. Likewise, couples who do not want to be bothered with children because they will just get in the way of things the couple considers of greater importance miss the second major purpose of marriage. Those who recklessly ignore and frustrate God's intentions for marriage should not imagine that God is indifferent to their misplaced priorities. Nor should they think that God blesses their flaunting of his purposes of companionship and children for their marriage. To be sure, there are times when physical or mental or genetic problems may place limitations on the happy fulfillment of these purposes, but when there are no such limitations beyond the choice or control of the husband and wife, then the purposes of marriage that God gave already in the garden should be accepted with thanksgiving to God. God out of love gave husband and wife to each other with these purposes in mind. As with every institution that God has established (i.e., the family, the church, and the state), it is in the carrying out of God's intentions and purposes that those institutions are blessed and are a blessing.[1]

Yes, and in spite of the many and perverse notions to the contrary that are popular these days, marriage is a divine institution intended for a man and a woman. "Marriage" for members of the same sex is not only a contradiction in terms but an abomination in the eyes of God (Romans 1:24-29). Nor is God the least bit interested in any polls taken among us that contradict him. It is always the business of the creature to listen to the Creator, not to imagine that the Creator needs the advice, much less correction, from the creature.

There were still further evidences of God's special love and care for Adam and Eve. Even before the creation of Eve, God "planted a garden in the east, in Eden" (Genesis 2:8). He was not content with placing man in the world and letting him organize it. God did that for him. The Garden of Eden was the very antithesis of the formless void and the chaos from which God spoke the world into existence in Genesis 1:1,2. Though all that God had made was very good, as God himself declared, the Garden of Eden was special for its beauty, its diversity of plant life, and the usefulness of its plants for food. The garden was to serve as a paradise on earth. Adam and Eve would both live in it and work in it. By their lives and by their work they would serve the Lord by serving one another. For God did not intend that they should be idle. He gave them work to do that should be a joy, because it was work that their loving God gave; it was work that they therefore could be sure was pleasing to him, again especially because by it they would also show their love for and their service to one another.

Even more important, he gave them a special commandment to keep. Their obedience to that commandment would be their way of

---

[1]For a further consideration of the importance of the three estates (family, church, government) in the Christian's life, cf. chapter 16.

showing a special reverence and love to the God who had given them everything. The commandment was not burdensome in the least. There was a special tree in the garden called "the tree of the knowledge of good and evil" (Genesis 2:9). Many languages have one word for "knowledge" that means being told about something (knowledge from a secondary source). But there is a different word for "knowledge" gained directly from experience. You may know, for example, that it is cold outside because you heard the temperature over the radio; that's the first kind of knowledge. But then you step outside and are struck with a blast of -10 degree Fahrenheit air. Now you know it's cold in an altogether different way; you know it from experience. Adam and Eve knew that eating from the tree was evil; for God had said that they would die if they ate from it. But they as yet had no experience of death, nor any experience of the difference between good and evil. If they ate from the tree, however, they would have this second type of knowledge, knowledge from experience. Hence the name *the tree of the knowledge*—the knowledge that would come from experience—*of good and evil.*

The command was clear: From this tree they should not eat. Nor was there any reason for them to want to eat from that tree. In the very moment when God commanded them not to eat of that particular tree, he told them that every other tree was theirs. They did not need this tree for food or for any other reason. The only purpose that it served was that of giving Adam and Eve a special opportunity to show their loving obedience to the God who had so richly blessed them with every good thing and that in abundance.

So God finished his perfect work of a perfect creation. Having declared it all to be "very good," the sixth day ended and the seventh began. That seventh day was a day of rest and blessing. It is called a holy day because God rested from his creating work on that day. For the first six days we are told that each day began and ended. For this day there is no such designation of an ending. It was God's intention that this rest should continue and be a rest in which he enjoyed a blessed and holy fellowship with Adam and Eve forever. Thus God's rest was not the rest that comes from exhaustion or weariness; his was the rest of satisfaction in the now completed work of creation, a satisfaction that he wanted to share with Adam and Eve.

It should be noted again that in the entire account of the creation of Adam and Eve there is no room for evolutionary theory or "theistic" evolutionary delusion. The entire account of their creation, like that of the rest of creation described in Genesis 1,2, is a report of what happened. It is not a parable. It is not merely a creation myth of an ancient Hebrew tribe. It is history, the factual account of what happened. Adam and Eve did not become human as the end product of a long process of development from some other species. They were created human. They were not half beast, half human, with little intelligence and less wisdom. Quite to the contrary, Adam and Eve had native, natural endowments of intelligence unequalled by any other human being except Christ himself. For they were in full possession of the image and likeness of God. Adam moreover showed that God-given wisdom and intelligence when God honored him at creation with the assignment to name the animals. He likewise showed his God-given gifts in the poem with which he honored God and his wife at her creation.

We cannot pass by this simple and yet magnificent account of man's creation without at least noting in passing that already from the beginning God deals with Adam and Eve in the same way that he deals with us, namely, by means of his Word. One of the passages in the Bible that sums up so much of his way of dealing with us is 2 Corinthians 5:7: "We live by faith, not by sight." And that faith is created not by what we see but by what he says, by his working in us through his Word. We noted earlier that God in his work of creation begins with the basic and moves to the complex, ending with the most complex work of all, namely, the creation of Adam and Eve. But it didn't have to be that way. He could have begun with Adam and Eve. He could have held them, so to speak, in the palm of his hand and let them see his majesty and power as he flung the planets into place, as he swirled the seas and separated them from the land, and as he stirred the waters and the earth so that they brought forth their multitudes of plants and animals. How Adam and Eve would have looked on in wonder and awe at these sights of the majesty and the power of God! He then could have let them see how he planted the Garden of Eden and made it a paradise set apart from all the rest of his wondrous creation, and that just for their enjoyment, use, and benefit. Yes, he even could have let them see the horrors of death and hell when he told them not to eat of that one tree, lest they die. But he didn't do any of that. What did he do instead? He spoke to them. He told them about it all. He gave them his Word and made their whole relationship with him dependent not on what they saw but on what he said. And that's his arrangement with us to this day. He gives his Word; he gives his Word the power to convince and to persuade. He gives his Word power to create out of nothing a trust in him and in all that he has said and done for us, especially in what he has done for us and for our salvation in the work of

Christ. And so as at the beginning, thus it is now and until we get to heaven: "We live by faith, not by sight."

The attributes of Adam and Eve

As noted earlier, everything that exists has attributes or characteristics. Some attributes are *essential;* that is, they define or are part of a definition of the thing that exists. Should the attribute be lost, the thing defined by it would no longer exist as such. Some attributes are *accidental* attributes; that is, they describe something. Should that something lose an accidental attribute, it would continue to be what it was, just somewhat altered. In God there are no *accidental* attributes. All of his attributes are his essence; he can never lose any of them. However, everything else in the visible world has both types, *essential* and *accidental* attributes.

The essential attributes in Adam and Eve and in their descendents are few in number. We can see that from the creation account itself and from the ways in which the rest of the Bible considers human beings as distinct from other living things. Adam and Eve were created with two essential attributes: they were created with body and soul.[2]

We should note at the outset the close connection between the body and the soul. So close is the connection between the body and the soul that it sometimes can be difficult to fathom where the one begins and the other leaves off. The soul, for example, knows very little apart from the body. The soul is constantly being informed by the organs of the body, by the eyes, the ears, the nervous system, connections in the brain, and the like. And the body, on the other hand, does things that are good or evil, not of itself but at the impulse of the soul.

We need to be aware of how closely connected the body and the soul are, as much as we need to distinguish between them. We make a point of that because of the common misconception that God is concerned with the soul and not with the body. In all of the Scriptures God shows his concern for the total person, consisting of both body and soul. Thus Jesus performed miracles that benefited the body as well as the soul. On the Last Day the total person, consisting of body and soul, will stand before God for the judgment. While we need to distinguish between the two—and the distinction is very useful—we do not want to make it appear that only the soul is important or essential and the other unimportant and not the object of God's special concern.

---

[2]Some prefer the division of body, soul, and spirit. It is not a distinction that involves any doctrinal difference.

It is just as bad or worse when some teach that the material, the physical body, is everything and the soul merely a name that stands for nothing. Those holding to such a notion are called materialists. Many atheists and many of those who subscribe to evolutionary theory are materialists. Indeed, materialism would appear to be an unavoidable result of evolutionary theory or atheistic philosophy. A materialist denies the existence of the soul and assigns all of its functions to the brain. A materialist teaches that the brain functions on a purely physical level. It responds to stimuli and input from a variety of sources. If it makes what appears to be a moral or a spiritual judgment, it is really only acting out of an instinct for self-preservation—little different from the hiss of a threatened cat or snake, little different from the squirrel hiding nuts or a bee storing honey. The brain decides to do "good" because it is useful to the self, not because there really is any such thing as "good" in any absolute moral sense. It decides to help the infirm in the hope of someday being helped or because mutual assistance is the best buttress for an orderly society that benefits all. Such notions flatly contradict the creation account as well as everything that God's Word has to say about our nature and its attributes.

The definition of Adam and Eve as body and soul is made most simply in the creation account. God formed a body and breathed life into it. The result of the forming and the breathing and especially God's speaking as he did was a human being, Adam. When Eve was formed from Adam's rib, the same basic process took place. She became a human being with body and soul as a result of God's special creative act. In the rest of the Bible people are simply assumed to have these two essential components of body and soul. The separation of body and soul is the end of the person's earthly life. Thus, death is described from our vantage point in Ecclesiastes 12:7 as dust returning to the ground from whence it came and the spirit returning to God from whence it originally came at the time of Adam's creation.

It is this attribute of a soul that makes Adam and Eve different, essentially different, from everything else that God created in the visible world. While all of the plants have life and while all of the animals have breath in one way or another, none of them has a soul to which God speaks and from which he then expects to receive an answer. God does not seek a fellowship or a relationship with any of them, though he provides for them and preserves them as long as they live. They have no natural capacity for a relationship with God. They were not created for such a relationship. That capacity for a relationship with God and fellowship with him was a gift given only to Adam and Eve in the visible creation. And that capacity is first and foremost a spiritual one, a capacity in the soul.

Characteristics of body and soul

For the sake of convenience and simplicity we may say that the body is material, consisting of atoms and molecules arranged into physical organs, such as eyes and ears, hands and feet, heart and lungs, and brain tissue and so on. The soul, on the other hand, is immaterial; that is, it does not consist of strictly measurable matter that occupies a defined place within the body. It cannot be weighed or seen. It is like breath itself, illusive and easier to describe in its functions than to define in its essence. Again, for the sake of convenience and to help us understand it a little better, we could think of the soul as also having organs. Like the organs of the body, the organs of the soul may function sometimes well, sometimes poorly, and sometimes they may seem to be functioning not at all, even though the capacity for them to function is still there. Thus, for example, when we sleep or when we are very young or when we are unconscious, the organs of the soul may seem to be dormant. But they are still there and capable of functioning, even when we are not fully aware of it.

The organs of the soul (if, again, for the sake of convenience we want to remain with that terminology) in ascending order of importance would then be, first of all, the emotions. With our emotions we feel likes and dislikes, affection and aversion. We may instantly like a certain song or even a certain person. We cannot always explain why; we just do. Our response to that song or person initially is a purely emotional one. It is the emotions that are the most closely linked to the body—the emotions are the easiest to excite by the physical senses of sight, sound, taste, smell, and touch.

The second organ of the soul is what we could call our will. With the will we make choices. We decide that we want or do not want this and that. To the extent that the will makes choices, love and hate reside in the will more than in the emotions. Aversion and attraction are in the emotions and we feel little need to explain them or defend them; but we choose to love this and to hate that—we can give reasons for our choice and argue in defense of it. Faith and trust likewise reside in the will, in so far as they are decisions and choices. To be sure, since the fall into sin, we are incapable of "deciding to believe," of deciding to have faith. That decision is a gift of God through the gospel. Nevertheless, the supernatural gift of faith once created by the gospel resides chiefly in the will. Unbelief, the natural state since the fall, also resides in the will. Of course the will is often influenced and will be touched by the emotions, for example, in matters of love and hate and in matters of faith too. But primarily these things reside in the will.

The third function or organ of the soul is the ability to reason, to weigh out relationships of cause and effect, to ponder the questions of why and what for, to make judgments that claim to be rational or logical. Reason makes judgments about the value of one thing compared to another. We may consider reason the weightiest of the organs of the soul. Reason can be creative and inventive as it considers nature and ways in which to control or arrange things in it. It can exercise a valuable discipline over one's life as it ponders the effect now of this behavior or choice, now of that.

Clearly it is often difficult to draw sharp lines between these three functions. Sometimes, for example, the emotions take control and dominate reason and will. In the lives of people whose emotions always dominate we can expect to see a good deal of disorder, even chaos. One sees that in the lives of people who have fallen victim to addictive behavior. Their emotions have taken control of their reason and their will to such an extent that contrary to all reason they are destroying themselves. On the other hand, in some people reason takes such a dominant position that their lives become cold, barren, unfeeling, and uncaring. In most people, however, there is a delicate balance between the three. Consciously or unconsciously a discussion goes on inside of the soul between the three over just about every issue of life. Emotions tug in the direction of that expensive new car; reason urges restraint; the will finally makes a decision about how much influence emotions should have and how much influence reason should be given. Emotion says that I should take that last piece of cake; reason may object that I shouldn't have had the first one! The will finally decides. The little child falls out of the boat; reason argues that helping is too risky; affection in the emotions is ready to throw all reason aside. Love or its lack in the will settles the matter one way or the other.

Again we are calling these functions organs of the soul simply for the sake of convenience, in order to help us better understand ourselves and matters we have yet to consider. Just as there is a fine line between the body and the soul, so likewise there is a fine line between these three organs, and it is sometimes difficult to distinguish between them.

The reasoning, the will, and the emotions of the soul become evident through the actions of the body. The will inside of the soul may decide to be generous, but it takes the organs of the body for the act of generosity to be carried out. So close is the connection between body and the organs of the soul that the body can be called the instrument or tool of the soul. Jesus does just that in Matthew 15:17-19, where he equates the heart with the soul and then speaks of the outward acts of the body that proceed from it. St. Paul does much the same thing in Romans 6:19 and 12:1. So the soul acts through the body. Conversely, the actions of the body never leave the soul unaffected. If the soul, let us say, is dominated by greedy emotions, it may use the hands to steal. Once the hands have stolen, it is in the soul, not in the hands, that guilt may be experienced. If the soul was noble, it may have used the hands to help someone in need. It is the soul that feels good about the virtuous act of the hands, not the hands. On the other hand, if the organs of the body are sick, it is the soul that cries out, that seeks ways of relief, and that ponders the meaning of sickness and health and the like. Thus soul and body can be distinguished from each other, but they are always working through each other.

If a human being has as essential attributes the body and the soul joined intimately together, then what are the accidental attributes of a human being? Skin color, personal temperament, and individual natural abilities and inclinations are accidental attributes. The state of a person's physical and mental health are accidental attributes. They may and do change without the person ceasing to be a person. Clearly a person may be deprived of some of the organs of the body and still be a person. If one were to lose an eye or some hair or an arm, that individual would still be a person. Likewise, there are *accidental* variations in the soul. In the soul some may be very emotional, some less so; some may have a strong will, others not; some may have excellent reasoning ability, others very limited reasoning ability. Furthermore, these capacities and abilities can and do change over the course of the individual's life. Emotions usually play a larger role in the life of the child; as the child matures, reason may be given a larger role than emotion. As in the case of the body, so in the case of the soul: some parts of the body may be lost without destroying the essence of a person; some parts or functions or capacities of a soul may change, but they cannot all be entirely lost while the person is still alive. For if there is no longer the possibility of emotion or will or reason, the person is probably dead.[3]

---

[3]We say the soul has probably left the body, lest we say too much in the case of someone unconscious or in a coma; whether such a person can recover and regain these capacities is often a difficult medical and ethical conclusion that can only be reached on a case-by-case basis.

It is both the body and the soul that we inherit from our parents, for that is what our parents are, body and soul. Some have thought that God creates each soul new and separate from the soul of the parents and that God gives the soul to the body at birth. But that would make God the creator of something sinful after the fall of Adam and Eve into sin, since after the fall both body and soul in all born according to nature are corrupted by sin. God by definition is holy and cannot be the author or creator of sin or any evil. In point of fact, in the Scriptures that which is in the womb of the mother is always identified as a person, never just a body. Thus David confesses his sinfulness from his mother's womb (Psalm 51:5). It is a person, not just a body, that is either sinful or not sinful; and a person is body and soul. St. John the Baptist even before his birth rejoiced in Christ his Savior (Luke 1:44). Such rejoicing came not just from a body but from a person consisting of a soul acting through its as yet unborn body. The teaching that the soul as well as the body is inherited from parents is called *traducianism.* The simple fact of the matter is that we have our "personhood," our humanity, from our parents whole and complete from the moment of conception. Accordingly, abortion kills not a "thing," not just tissue, but a person. Only if the life of the mother is seriously threatened can abortion be justified; then it is justified only because a choice has to be made between one life and another—a tragic and most painful choice indeed!

The image of God

Adam and Eve had one additional and extremely important accidental attribute that they received at their creation. That attribute was the image of God. God makes a point of it in Genesis 1:26,27, as we have already noted. Since God is a spirit, the image of God was chiefly a spiritual gift. But it affected their entire being, body and soul.

The image of God—likeness to God—was certainly the greatest of blessings for the functions or organs of the soul. Since they were like God and in his image, emotion, will, and reason were in perfect harmony with God. The emotions were naturally drawn to God and his will. The will was perfectly free and able to love God and choose obedience to God's Word and will and to refuse sin and evil. Reason was able to ponder the goodness of God, weigh his commands, and plan a course of action that it knew would delight the Creator. Adam showed his reasoning ability in his naming of the animals. Both Adam and Eve would be expected to use those same reasoning abilities as they carried out the assignment of tending the garden God had given to them. As God's Word instructed their reason, their will would choose to follow and their emotions would delight in God, his Word, and in their own blessed opportunity to obey.

Thus with emotions, will, and reason in perfect harmony, Adam and Eve could love God perfectly, completely, and freely. That love of the soul and the consequent obedient acts of the body would not be robot-like. Adam and Eve were not on some sort of instinctive, divinely programmed automatic pilot. Their love and their obedience were conscious, free, and willing.

What a bright and happy prospect for them to be in such a condition. They were free from sin and all its consequences and perfectly equipped to stay that way forever *(posse non peccare—able not to sin).* They were aware of their blessed condition and determined to retain it. If they had continued in the full possession of the image and likeness of God, they would have passed the same on to their children. Indeed, together with their children they would live forever! For immortality too was a fruit of their creation in the image of God.

The most important component of the image of God, its very heart and core, was the holiness and righteousness. Their holiness was a total separation from sin. Their righteousness was a state of being right with God, with nothing in them for God to forgive. We might think of it this way: the living shell of the image of God in Adam and Eve consisted of emotion, will, and reason, the organs of the soul; it is in their emotions, will, and reason that they can most easily be seen as "like God." But the heart and core inside of that shell and indeed that which permeated the shell and made it so beautiful was God's gift of righteousness and holiness.

It was this holiness and righteousness that made their bodies and souls immortal. Only sin brings death to the relationship and fellowship with God. They had no sin and thus no need to fear death, neither the death that is the separation of their bodies from their souls nor the far worse death that is the separation of both body and soul from God.

We saw earlier that everything that God created was very good. In the plants and animals that goodness had no moral implications. For the plants and animals are without souls; they do not ponder God's command, listen intelligently to his Word, and then consciously respond to it. But when Adam and Eve are called "very good" as part of God's creation, there is a definite moral element to that goodness. They do not merely function well biologically or instinctively. They had reason, will, and emotions that were consciously in harmony with the Creator. They were good, very good, not by instinct but by nature and then by constant and conscious choice of good over evil and that with delight. Indeed it was this condition of holiness and perfect righteousness that made the reason, will, and emotions of Adam and Eve so godlike.

In sum, by virtue of their creation in the image and likeness of the perfect and holy God, Adam and Eve were perfect and holy. Like God they had reason, will, and emotions. But what made that likeness so glorious was the image of God, his holiness and righteousness in their souls; from deep within their nature that holiness and righteousness could shine forth and radiate through all the works carried out through the use of reason, will, and emotion. There was no flaw or fault that might predispose them to sin. There was no flaw or fault in them that might doom them to death in either body or soul. The image of God carried with it the capacity to remain sinless and to live forever.

Could there have been any greater way for God to show his love for Adam and Eve than this, that he gave them his own likeness and image? Could there have been a more sublime way of reflecting his own glory, which was the purpose of the whole creation, than this, that Adam and Eve were like God? They were free to live forever. They were free to serve as his regents on earth. They were free to enjoy a blessed and eternal fellowship with the One who thus loved them and showed his love with the gift of his own image and likeness from the moment of their creation. Adam could reflect that image of God in his rule over creation and in his headship over and love for his own family. Eve could reflect her bearing of that image by willingly accepting her role as the helper suitable for him. And both of them together could conform emotion, will, and reason to God's law with respect to the tree of the knowledge of good and evil. And thus they could retain that perfect holiness and righteousness, the essential element of the image of God. One could expect that they would also grow in their love and appreciation and understanding of God with the passing of time, as they exercised their emotions, will, and reason in their fellowship and communication with their Creator.

The fall, Genesis 3

Many of the church fathers have commented that all of theology is contained either expressly or by implication in the first three chapters of Genesis. It would be difficult to overemphasize the importance of these three chapters. We now consider the third chapter. It relates the saddest and most tragic story ever told.

The events that are described in chapter 3 occurred shortly after the creation of Adam and Eve. We know that it was not a long period of time from the simple fact that Adam and Eve conceived no children in the Garden of Eden. We get the impression from Genesis 4:1 that their first sexual union occurred after the fall. Since God at their creation had told them that one of the purposes of marriage was children, we would expect that, had they been in the garden for any length of time at all, they would have come together and Eve would have conceived a child in accord with God's command and promise. Since that did not happen, we conclude that the events here described took place very soon after their creation.

Because of the profound significance of this chapter, we will consider it verse by verse.

> Now the serpent was more crafty[4] than any of the wild animals the LORD God had made. He said to the woman, "Did God really say, 'You must not eat from any tree in the garden'?"
>
> The woman said to the serpent, "We may eat fruit from the trees in the garden, but God did say, 'You must not eat fruit from the tree that is in the middle of the garden, and you must not touch it, or you will die.' " (vv. 1-3)

The serpent, of course, under normal circumstances cannot speak. It is Satan himself who takes on the guise of the serpent and speaks through it. As a fallen angel, he can do nothing that is constructive. He cannot create. He can only destroy. That is his intent as he speaks to Eve in this chapter; his aim is to destroy, to bring about a fall that will make Eve and then Adam as miserable and wretched as he is.

We have already noted that not everything that happens does so because God wills it. God clearly did not will nor did he concur morally in what Satan set out to do through the serpent. But he did permit it. For in spite of Satan's intention, the temptation gave Adam and Eve an opportunity to show their love and faithfulness to their Creator and thus to reflect the image of God. Their will was entirely free and capable of doing exactly that.

Notice the way in which Satan frames the temptation. He still frames his temptations in exactly the same way. First, he calls into question both God's love and God's Word. He does that by twisting and distorting God's actions and words. Behind his distortion of what God had actually said we can already see Satan's thinly veiled and wicked

---

[4]"Crafty" in this verse is perhaps not the best translation, as it often implies something evil. But there was no evil in the serpent as such; he was part of the creation that God called "good." A better translation would be "clever."

agenda. He wants to picture God as arbitrary, as small minded and loveless. Then Satan wants to present himself as the friend of Adam and Eve.

Notice too that Satan does not address Adam. He approaches Eve. That is not because Adam was otherwise occupied or elsewhere. For we see in verse 6 that as soon as she had eaten from the fruit, she simply handed it to her husband. Even if Adam were not immediately at hand, Satan certainly would not have had any difficulty in finding him and in making Adam his first target. Why doesn't Satan approach Adam? After all, Adam was the head of the house and priest in his family. Why doesn't Eve even turn to her head and consult with him? Worst of all, why doesn't Adam at any point in this tragic story exercise his headship and do something to prevent the disaster that is unfolding in his presence? Satan is tempting Eve to take over the role of head, to act independently of her husband. He is tempting Adam not only to abandon his role as head but as well his responsibility to act in love towards his wife by helping her overcome the temptation.

Eve answers the tempter's question. But already, as indicated above, there are warning signs of danger in the beginning of the dialogue with Satan, even though the answer as such is not wrong. To be sure, she has added a few words to the command from Genesis 2:16,17. For God had said nothing about touching the tree. But it could be argued that Eve properly concluded that if they were not to eat from it, the best course for them to follow was to stay away from it altogether.

> "You will not surely die," the serpent said to the woman. "For God knows that when you eat of it your eyes will be opened, and you will be like God, knowing good and evil." (vv. 4,5)

Jesus reminds us that the devil is a liar from the beginning and the father of lies (John 8:44). There is nothing at all subtle about this first lie from the father of lies. It is blatant. It is blasphemous. It is outrageous. It is a vile contradiction of the Word of God. And still, the lie in its totality has a slight grain of truth in it. Almost all lies do. That's what makes them believable. False doctrine is usually a lie with some grain of truth that has been perverted and corrupted at its center. Here the small grain of truth is that they will know *from experience* the difference between good and evil, if they eat of the fruit. But notice the package for that grain of truth. It's poison through and through. Satan lies. He is telling Eve that God is petty, perhaps even jealous of them, and wants to withhold something good from them. He portrays the evil of death as nothing to worry about and the good of obedience as self-denial for no good reason. Indeed, he wants Eve to think that the temptation to sin will make her even more like God than she already was! What could be wrong with that?

Has anything changed in Satan's tactics? He still portrays sin as nothing to be concerned about. He still portrays evil as good and good as pointless self-denial. Ask the drunk, the thief, the drug addict, the adulterer if it is not so. Ask yourself! Yes, he still attempts to picture God and his pure Word as too limiting, petty, mean, and narrow-minded.

Now consider Eve's situation. She is confronted with a clear choice. She is perfectly capable of making the correct choice. On the one hand is her Creator, a God of love and kindness. She has experienced from him nothing but generosity and goodness. His command was clear. She understood it. She had no reason at all either inside of herself or in the garden to suspect that God had evil motives or intentions towards her and her husband. The temptation should have been an easy one to overcome. However . . .

> When the woman saw that the fruit of the tree was good for food and pleasing to the eye, and also desirable for gaining wisdom, she took some and ate it. She also gave some to her husband, who was with her, and he ate it. (v. 6)

What a disaster! Sin enters the world and death by sin (Romans 5:12). It is nothing less than a terrible death that we see taking place in these words. Eve died spiritually and so did Adam in this verse. The basic meaning of the word *death* is "separation." Here their life of blessed fellowship with God ended and they were fearfully separated from him.

Some trivialize the verse and complain, "What's so terrible about eating a piece of fruit?" That's not the major crime here. In fact, it is fairly far down on the list. The major crime is blatant unbelief. It's not doubt that wonders or questions or is tossed back and forth between two alternatives. No, it's unbelief! Adam and Eve threw away God's Word and embraced instead the devil's lie. For, again, God's Word was crystal clear, and they had no reason at all to doubt it. God had fully equipped them to resist the temptation successfully and thus to reflect his glory and image with a free, willing, and eager obedience. But that is not what happened. Instead, Eve lusted after the fruit on the tree; for *lust* by definition is "to desire what is forbidden." The lust is the evil fruit of her unbelief; before she lusted, she had to cast aside God's Word and all of her trust in his goodness and his love. Once faith and trust are gone, a whole host of sins quickly follows. For unbelief is the source, together with the devil, of every other sin. And thus unbelief, the rejection of God's Word, is the greatest sin of all.

Eve was dead spiritually. A moral freefall followed. She lusted. She became arrogant, imagining that disobedience to God could give her wisdom better than the wisdom in his Word. Then the lust brought forth disobedient outward acts, a theft and the actual eating of the forbidden fruit. Sin is never content to be alone. Where there is one sin, others are close behind. Nowhere is that more evident than in this chapter, where sins are piled on top of sins—all of them the result of the chief sin, that of unbelief, of the rejection of God's Word.

Do you notice the interplay between the organs of the soul and then between body and soul in this entire episode? The emotions, if we can put it that way, were the first to demonstrate the unbelief; lust is in the emotions. There quickly followed the fall of reason; she weighed her options in her reason and irrationally concluded that she would be better off with the wisdom promised by the devil. Then she made the choice in her will to act out the disobedience that had now taken place in the soul. Thus deceived by the devil's words and her own fault, she made her body the organ of her fallen soul; with her hands she stole the fruit and with her mouth she ate it.

Then with body and soul she became the devil's missionary. She sought to assure herself that she was not alone in her rebellion, in her unbelief. For just as one sin is never content to be alone but always wants the company of more sin, so too the sinner. Eve wants the company of another sinner, and she hands the fruit to Adam, who joins her in her unbelief and rebellion. Adam had heard the temptation and watched all that had happened in these dread moments. He had done nothing to prevent it, even though St. Paul tells us that he understood fully what was happening, that he was not deceived in the way that Eve was (1 Timothy 2:14). He bears responsibility for the entry of sin into the human race, even though Eve was the first to actually eat the fruit. Adam's fall did not begin with the eating. His death, like Eve's, had occurred before the actual eating; and so, when St. Paul declares that death came into the world by the action of one human being, he is blaming Adam no less than Eve for bringing death into the world (Romans 5:12-14).

> Then the eyes of both of them were opened, and they realized they were naked; so they sewed fig leaves together and made coverings for themselves. (v. 7)

Now the bitter results of sin begin to show themselves. To be sure, as Satan had said, they gained an understanding from experience about the difference between good and evil. But that understanding from experience was no blessing. Their relationship with each other before the fall had been without sin. It had been a relationship of peace and love and harmony, of complete openness to each other in every way. But now they begin to hide from each other. They do not want to be so well known to each other. They experience shame in the bodies created for them by God.

Moreover, they began to lose wisdom and intelligence. For their solution to the problem was a very short-term and impractical one, an utterly unreasonable one. Fig leaves sewn together would not provide the cover they were seeking, nor would it eliminate the shame they now were experiencing. They should have known that. They should have at the very least known that fig leaves were not durable or long lasting enough to solve any of their problems. So even their intelligence and ability to figure things out was marred by their sin; they quickly figured out how to sew but were blind to the futility of sewing fig leaves to hide shame and guilt. At their creation they were wise; now they were becoming foolish, even on the most basic, the most practical of levels.

> Then the man and his wife heard the sound of the LORD God as he was walking in the garden in the cool of the day, and they hid from the LORD God among the trees of the garden. (v. 8)

God is omnipresent, always present everywhere. But he is especially and graciously present in his Word. Somehow God let Adam and Eve know when he wanted to speak with them. He let them know by sound. Just what that sound was of the Lord "walking in the garden" we cannot say for certain; perhaps it was nothing more complicated than a special rustling of a breeze in the trees. Whatever it was, Adam and Eve recognized it. And what was their response? We would think that their beginning shame and their beginning folly with fig leaves—yes, the beginning of unhappiness—should have been enough to drive them towards the sound of God. We might expect that they would cry out at once for mercy, for pardon, for another chance, for forgiveness, for restoration. But that is not at all what they do. And why not? Because they are dead, spiritually dead, and thus incapable of any God-pleasing spiritual impulse or action. The dead can do nothing good; the dead can only stink both literally and figuratively. And Adam and Eve now prove it. They are in a free fall and cannot stop. They knew God before the fall. They knew that he was omnipresent. Nevertheless, they hide. Wisdom has been replaced with godless folly. Yes, and worse still, love that flows from faith has been replaced by fear that flows from unbelief.

> But the LORD God called to the man, "Where are you?" He answered, "I heard you in the garden, and I was afraid because I was naked; so I hid." (vv. 9,10)

Notice that God came to Adam first, not to Eve. For Adam is the first reflection of God's glory. He was the head, and therefore he had primary responsibility. God was not looking for information with his question. Nor was he merely interested in Adam's physical location. "Where are you?" is a call of the law to repentance. The only truthful, the only rational answer to the question is, "Here I am, a lost and condemned sinner!" But that is not the answer of Adam. He tried to avoid God, not only physically but also mentally and spiritually. Notice that he does not answer the question. Indeed, what he tried to pass off as an answer sounds like the answer of the little child in the kitchen whose thieving hand in the cookie jar brought the cookie jar down from the countertop to the floor with a crash. His mother calls, "Where are you? What are you doing?" He answers with fear—and with a lie from the father of lies: "I was just walking by. It fell. I don't know how. I didn't do it!" How evil the answer of Adam! His fear is not God's fault but his own. His shame is the result of his sin, and in his folly he imagined that he could hide that too from God.

> And he said, "Who told you that you were naked? Have you eaten from the tree that I commanded you not to eat from?" The man said, "The woman you put here with me—she gave me some fruit from the tree, and I ate it." (vv. 11,12)

God did not destroy Adam and Eve as they deserved, even though they were now spiritually dead and giving more and more proof of it by the minute. He asks and then asks again. Adam and Eve cannot complain that they had no opportunity to repent. They had ample opportunities. But with each of these questions, one after another, the totality of Adam's guilt became ever more evident—he is not just a little bit guilty, a little bit a sinner; he is from top to bottom, from inside out, totally and completely a sinner. "Who told you that you were naked?" Adam cannot think of an answer that will get him off of the hook of his sin. Anything he says in reply will condemn him. Adam was caught and he knew it. There was no escape. But what does he do? Does he at last cry out for mercy? Not a bit of it! Exactly the opposite! He, so to speak, raised his fist in the face of God and defied him. He blamed God for the whole thing. Had God not put the woman there, none of this would have ever happened!

So much for a blessed fellowship and communion with God. So much for a blessed fellowship and communion between man and wife. Gone is the beautiful and grateful love poem with which Adam had received his wife from the kind and generous hand of God. So much for happiness! The ultimate happiness of a blessed fellowship with God was destroyed by the unbelief that now degenerates into spite and hatred of God. The second happiness of a perfect union between husband and wife was destroyed by the accusation that Eve's presence was also a cause of the fall. What is all that but the loss of the image of God, that is, the loss of holiness and righteousness?

That loss is the source of all unhappiness and misery, contrary to the lie believed by mankind since the fall. Since the fall, one of Satan's favorite and most successful lies is that our happiness consists in a separation from God and the doing of our own will instead of his. Even a superficial examination of one's own life should convince us of the evil, the misery, and the unhappiness that comes from following that lie. As Satan's temptations have changed little since the fall, so the answers people give in their sin and guilt have likewise changed but little. Someone else is always to blame. Ultimately, it's all God's fault! Repentance? Return to the Word of God? Better to lie, to hide, and to die. No, this account of the fall into sin is not at all trivial!

> Then the LORD God said to the woman, "What is this you have done?" The woman said, "The serpent deceived me, and I ate." (v. 13)

Now God turned to Eve. Though Adam as head of his family bears a special responsibility in this whole tragic affair, Eve was obviously not without blame. As she shared in guilt with Adam, so God gave her also the opportunity to confess and to repent. The dialogue is very brief. It is as marked by the same total absence of remorse as the dialogue with Adam had been. The only difference is its subtlety. Unlike Adam she does not directly accuse God; she leaves it to God to figure out whose fault it is that the serpent was there in the first place. Clearly, in her view, it was not her fault. Whose fault then could it be? Only God's! Or perhaps she was criticizing her own creation, that she was capable of deception; that in her view was certainly not her fault. In any case her opportunity to repent was squandered as wickedly as her husband's opportunity had been. Both of them equally demonstrate that their blessed relationship with God had died. It had turned to anger, to hostility, and to hatred. The emotions, will, and reason of both of them were fully engaged in this rebellion and their hands and mouths became the busy instruments of lust and theft and spite and hatred. As holiness and righteousness were supposed to shine through the organs of the soul, so now with their loss it was sin and guilt that manifested themselves in the now thoroughly corrupted organs of the soul.

> So the LORD God said to the serpent, "Because you have done this, Cursed are you above all the livestock and all the wild animals! You will crawl on your belly and you will eat dust all the days of your life. And I will put enmity between you and the woman, and between your offspring and hers; he will crush your head, and you will strike his heel." (vv. 14,15)

There was no discussion with the serpent as such, because the serpent as such had no moral responsibility for what happened. Nevertheless, the serpent is cursed. All of creation was affected by the sin of Adam and Eve and made subject to death (Romans 8:20-22), but the serpent carries this special curse. Many people are afraid of snakes or consider them loathsome. Whether this is a taught fear or one inherited from Adam and Eve matters little; when we see a snake, we recall the disaster of the fall.

But in cursing the snake, God addressed Satan, whose instrument the snake had been. Notice that God asks Satan no questions, not because Satan bears no moral responsibility but because Satan's doom had already been sealed at the time of his own fall. But in addressing Satan in the snake, the most astonishing thing occurs. In the curse lies the greatest blessing possible, a blessing beyond human imagination or rational comprehension. It is the *Protevangelium,* the first gospel! In the midst of such misery and spite, such deliberate and inexcusable evil on the part of Adam and Eve, God promised the Savior! The address is primarily for Adam and Eve to hear, even though it is addressed to Satan in the form of the serpent.[5]

The words are in the form of a Hebrew poem. In Hebrew poetry the first line makes a statement and the second line explains or expands on the statement. Thus here God promises in the first line that there will be enmity, strife, warfare between the serpent/Satan and the woman. That promise of enmity already contains in it the promise of a restoration of Eve to a blessed fellowship with God. For if Eve would not be restored to such a blessed fellowship, there would be no strife at all between her and the devil; she would just continue to follow his promptings. Ah, but with a restored fellowship with God, there will be a ceaseless struggle against the devil and his death-dealing deception.

How that enmity will be fought out is explained in the second line; it will be first and foremost between the offspring or seed or followers of the serpent and the one Seed ("seed" is a better translation than

---

[5]Just as a side thought, we might guess that Satan was especially galled by this first gospel: It was addressed to him but not intended to include him.

"offspring") of the woman. That one Seed of the woman would crush the head and therefore destroy the serpent/Satan. It is the promised victory of the one Seed that will restore Eve and make possible the struggle between her and those descendents of Eve that follow her in faith. But the one Seed of the woman will not be left without suffering. The suffering of the one Seed however will be in the heel, not in the head, that is, not permanent.

Notice that the one Seed is of the woman. But seed is not a property of a woman; it comes from a man. Nevertheless, the words are plain and clear. The Father of this One will not be a mere man! A woman will be his only human parent! That's more than just a hint of the Savior's virgin birth!

So this first gospel has in it the promise of Eve's restoration—for without it she would never struggle against the devil. And it contains more than a hint of the promise that the Seed will come from a virgin birth. It also has implicit in it a promise of the resurrection for fallen man. For the devil will win if man is not restored. The devil will win if the restored still die and stay dead—both spiritually and physically.

This first gospel is rich indeed. To be sure, we may not see all of the promises in our first glance at the first gospel: the promise of a virgin-born and suffering Savior, the promise of restoration by faith in that promise, and the promise of an ultimate resurrection. But as we read the rest of the Bible and especially the New Testament, we see all of these promises spelled out in ever-greater detail and then fulfilled in the life and death and resurrection of Christ. Then looking back on this first gospel, we come to see that the fulfillment is already promised there at the beginning. Take a deep breath and try to take it all in!

What caused God to make such a promise? There certainly was no cause in Adam and Eve. They had through their own fault brought death into the world, the death of the image of God in their own souls, and death later on to their bodies and to those of all their descendants, except for Enoch and Elijah (Genesis 5:24; 2 Kings 2:11). They had corrupted and contaminated the entire visible creation. There was nothing, absolutely nothing good in Adam and Eve that could prompt the promise of the Savior. The cause of the promise must be and is in God alone. It is an entirely gracious, that is, undeserved, promise. Nor should we imagine that there would be anything that Adam and Eve could have done after the fall to make up for the damage they had done and thereby merit the promise. For in point of fact nothing merely human can undo that damage and restore immortality and holiness. Only God himself can do it.

The promise of the Savior was intended to restore the relationship between our fallen, spiritually dead parents and God. It was intended to bring them back from spiritual death to spiritual life. That restoration could only be accomplished by this life-giving Word of the gospel. Eve's words in Genesis 4:1 at the birth of Cain indicate that she once again, and Adam as well, came to trust in the love and mercy of God. It was a trust born of the promise in 3:15. It was a trust in God's forgiveness and his grace, his undeserved love.

But still:

> To the woman he said, "I will greatly increase your pains in childbearing; with pain you will give birth to children. Your desire will be for your husband, and he will rule over you." (v. 16)

Even though God had promised the Savior, even though that promise restored a relationship between God and our first parents, nevertheless sin has its consequences for the sinner. In Eve's case the consequences are twofold. First, she will suffer pain in childbirth. Her pain and that of her daughters will serve as a reminder that God takes sin seriously, whether we do or not. But even more so, that pain should serve as a reminder of the one Seed to come through the birth from a woman, the one Seed who would bear the ultimate pain of sin as he crushed the head of the serpent. As is always the case with the consequences for sin, the unbeliever only cries out in pain; however, the restored believing daughter of God could cry in the pain of repentance and also in joy over the one Seed who was to come and now has come.

The second word to Eve has to do with her relationship with her husband. Again, the unbeliever will experience this consequence in one way, those who strive to submit to the Word of God in quite another. Before the fall the relationship between husband and wife was perfect. Adam was head of the household and Eve was happy with his headship because God had established it. As long as their emotions, will, and reason were consciously and happily in harmony with God's will and Word, that relationship between Adam and Eve would have neither strain nor resentment in it. As a result of the fall, the relationship between husband and wife has been damaged. Now the headship of the husband will not always be so easily born and his rule will not always be either gentle or willingly accepted. To the extent that the household is a Christian household, the headship of the husband will be a loving and serving one and the submission of the wife will be willing and satisfying (Ephesians 5:22-33). Indeed, and ideally, husband and wife encourage each other in their respective roles when each carries out the role assigned respectively to husband and wife. Where one ignores that role, the other is hindered and discouraged, though not excused from the carrying out of the assignment God gives to each. All too often one sees husbands and wives to the great harm of marriage and the family throw away God's design and then justify the behavior by the imperfection of the partner. Little wonder that there are so few marriages that last or are patterns worthy to be followed by the next generation. Again, we cannot help but note it: God takes his Word seriously whether we do or not; where it is pushed aside, there will be unhappy consequences.

After God addressed Eve, he turns to Adam.

> To Adam he said, "Because you listened to your wife and ate from the tree about which I commanded you, 'You must not eat of it,' Cursed is the ground because of you; through painful toil you will eat of it all the days of your life. It will produce thorns and thistles for you, and you will eat the plants of the field. By the sweat of your brow you will eat your food until you return to the ground, since from it you were taken; for dust you are and to dust you will return. (vv. 17-19)

The very first rebuke of Adam has to do with his relationship to God and to his wife. He had turned his face away from God and allowed his wife to take his headship from him. He listened to her when he should have been listening to God and speaking to her on the basis of God's clear command. But now, because he turned his face away from God, he will turn his face downward to the soil from which he came and to which he must return. Frustration and hard work will replace the delight of tending the Garden of Eden, which had neither thorns nor thistles.

Again the consequences of sin are severe and painful. God has not repealed them. But also again the Christian bears those consequences differently than an unbeliever. To be sure, for the Christian as for the unbeliever, the pain, the sweat, the frustration, and finally the physical death are all very real. At times the pain and the frustration of his life will be so great a burden that he may wrestle with the still greater problem that comes from the question, How can God say he loves me when he lets me suffer thus? And that pain, that struggle, that cross will come again and again through all of the Christian's life. But for the Christian the pain will be eased and the cross carried with the balm that comes from the promise that follows the gospel; that promise is best summed up for the cross-carrying Christian by St. Paul in Romans 8. For the Christian, hard labor and frustration serve to remind him of his sin and of the promise of rest at the end of his days. That rest and the joy it will bring will far surpass the toil and the burdens of life lived now under a cross. Death will come also to the Christian. But as gruesome and terrible as it may be, death becomes the gate to eternal life.

The unbeliever has no such consolation. For him the toil and the frustration end in his final defeat in the hour of death. His face remains turned away from his Creator and Redeemer and ever turned down to the earth; if he thinks about it—and he tries hard not to—the grave is his only goal and ultimate destination. In spite of all his efforts, he must die and be separated not only from God in this life but also in the life to come, in an eternity of frustration and misery with the devil that he served by both nature and by choice. The dust and ashes in his grave are the final witness to the justice of God and the futility of the creature's battle against his Maker.

> Adam named his wife Eve, because she would become the mother of all the living. The LORD God made garments of skin for Adam and his wife and clothed them. And the LORD God said, "The man has now become like one of us, knowing good and evil. He must not be allowed to reach out his hand and take also from the tree of life and eat, and live forever." So the LORD God banished him from the Garden of Eden to work the ground from which he had been taken. After he drove the man out, he placed on the east side of the Garden of Eden cherubim and a flaming sword flashing back and forth to guard the way to the tree of life. (vv. 20-24)

As the relationship with God was restored by the gospel promise, so the relationship between husband and wife was likewise restored. In fact, by the very naming of his wife, Adam points us to a restoration of the relationship with his wife that doubtless flowed from a restored relationship with God. But neither relationship would ever be quite the same again as long as they lived. Adam's sons will often be confronted by the temptation to abandon the leadership role that God wants them to have; they will be tempted to prefer freedom to the satisfaction and the effort involved in faithful service as husband and father. Eve's daughters will have to wrestle with the tension inside of them to rebel as Eve did against the headship of their husbands and the desire implanted to have a reliable and faithful leader to follow and assist.

Every marriage has to work out these competing tensions that began already in the Garden of Eden. Where the effort is made by a Christian husband and wife devoted to following the perfect lead of God in his Word, that effort becomes an act of worship by which the husband and wife seek to mirror the marriage of Christ and the church. It should be the goal of the young to seek and to find a spouse who wants to do exactly that. Where only one partner to the marriage wants that kind of a marriage, the imitation of the union between Christ and the church will be frustrated if not impossible.

Let those who prefer a different model look around themselves and see the chaos in families and in society where God's arrangement has been scuttled. Daughters do not know what to look for in a husband and sons have no sense of the honor that God wants to give them as imitators of his own fatherhood. And so generations flounder. Women are left to raise children alone, and their children have no one to show them a better way. Men who find no respect at home, and often enough deserve none, leave and carry with them the guilt of having abandoned the most important work that God could ever give them, that of being a husband and father. And in it all, children, even in some families that stay together, have no idea what Luther is talking about in his explanation to the introduction of the Lord's Prayer in his Small Catechism. Luther says that the words "Our Father," which introduce the prayer, should remind us that we can approach God with all boldness and confidence even as dear children approach their dear earthly father. But what of children who have no such experience with an earthly father? How will they understand even the introduction to the Lord's Prayer? So, let young ladies look for husbands who can explain it and show it. And let young men have as their highest ambition in marriage to be that kind of father! Obviously the goal is never perfectly reached. But where it is not even attempted, there one should expect the unhappy consequences that we see in the fall at the dawn of time.

Back to Adam and Eve. Notice how far the kindness of the Lord extends. Adam and Eve had figured out how to make clothes out of fig leaves—how foolish, how silly. But God, in his grace and mercy, makes for them garments of animal skins. Those were obviously much more suitable and durable. His kindness to them extends even to this small detail, the protection of their bodies from the elements that now because of their sin would turn hostile. And notice too that it is with the skin of something dead that God clothes them; even in what they wear as a gift from God, they would have the reminder of how they had brought death into the world.

As for the tree of life, it is enough to observe that God acted again both in grace and justice when he blocked the path to the tree of life. God had attached to that tree the promise of eternal life. We can well imagine that someone in fear of death and in folly would try to eat from that tree in order to live on this earth forever—and God would be obliged to keep his promise of eternal life for the one who ate from it. That would be no blessing after the fall had taken place! Therefore, in grace God blocked the path. In justice the garden was closed. No further mention is made of the garden or of the cherubim that blocked the path to the tree of life. But for years to come, probably up to the time of the flood, the angels were frightening reminders of God's justice and warnings against sin. Likewise, they were reminders of the grace and mercy of God who did not destroy everything in hell but who instead promised the Savior to deliver from the misery of this life and the greater misery of the next.

It would be difficult indeed to imagine a greater contrast than that between the state of Adam and Eve before the fall and their condition after the fall. They went from being perfect bearers of the image of God to the condition of lost and condemned sinners. They went from immortal and wise reflections of God's glory to dead and foolish followers of the snake. They went from perfect harmony with God, with each other, and with all of nature to hatred of God, strife with each other, and a doomed nature that also doomed them to futility, frustration, and ultimately to dust and ashes. Yes, ponder the contrast just in the change in those three relationships:

Before the fall	**After the fall**
Perfect love and harmony with God	Rebellion and hatred against God
Perfect love and harmony with each other	Blame and hostility, shame and selfishness
Perfect submission of nature to man and wife	Pain in childbirth, thorns, thistles, sweat, death

We could even add a fourth, though that will take more time to become evident: the relationship of the person to self. Before the fall there was harmony, happiness, and contentment in the soul. After the fall there is strife inside, frustration, discontent, and all manner of lust and jealousy to guarantee that this dissatisfaction in the soul will continue and increase—and that to the harm of the individual and those around him as well. For how many people is the struggle to get along with self the chief problem they have in life, a problem that ultimately poisons all of their relationships with others? The loathing of self makes friendships all but impossible and marriage and family life more of a burden than a blessing.

Notice as we bring this chapter to a close the great contrast between God and his fallen creatures. He was good and gracious in their creation. They by their own choice and fault became wicked and ungrateful rebels. He was generous beyond measure. They became thieves who tried to rob him of his deserved glory. Nevertheless, after the fall he became the restorer of life through a gracious promise. He will become the virgin born and suffering Savior for those who deserved to suffer. And it is in the suffering of the Savior that God remains perfect in his grace and perfect in his justice, and all that for the benefit of the fallen, the evil, the ungrateful, and the spiritually dead!

From beginning to end, the third chapter of Genesis magnifies the glory and grace of God and puts into the sharpest possible focus the absolute and desperate need of mankind. It exalts too the power of his Word, by which he first created all things and by which after the fall he brings back to life those who trust his promise. No, this chapter is not a trivial myth about eating forbidden apples! It is one of the most profound and important chapters in all of God's Word! Clearly from it we see that death and damnation are entirely deserved. Clearly from it we see that our salvation must be entirely the work of God. Clearly we see that even faith, especially faith, must come alone from God working on us and in us through his promises in the gospel. The rest of the Bible and the rest of this book are devoted before all else to making exactly these points and, by them, to bringing us ever and again to a renewed love and longing for the glory of God through faith in the Savior. For he is the heart and core, the all in all, of that gospel message and of the life that reflects our love to him for it.

Chapter 8
The Doctrine of Original Sin

The effect of the fall into sin on our *attributes*

The fall of Adam and Eve into sin had profound and lasting consequences for the entire human race. Their fall was the fall of the human race, since they constituted the entire human race and all human beings are descended from them. Their fall brought sin into the world, not just to their own inestimable harm but to that of the whole race from their time to the end of time. We will consider what the Bible has to say about sin under several different headings and from a number of different vantage points. We begin with a consideration of the doctrine of original sin.

The fall of Adam and Eve was most devastating in the change that it worked in human nature. From the moment of their sin, Adam and Eve lost for themselves and for the whole human race that most beautiful and sublime attribute: the image of God. To be sure, there were still traces of God's likeness left, its shell, so to speak. Adam and Eve continued to have a soul. They still retained what we referred to earlier as the organs of the soul: their emotions, their will, and their reasoning capacity. But the heart and core of the image of God, his holiness and righteousness, those were totally and altogether lost. For there is no such thing as being a little bit sinful or a little bit holy or a little bit righteous or a little bit guilty. All of these terms—*sinful, holy, righteous,* and *guilty*—are exclusive terms. That is, they either are present or absent, present fully or absent altogether. Holiness is the absence of sin. Righteousness is a correct status or right relationship with God according to his standard. Any sin destroys holiness and renders the sinner unrighteous, a rebel against God and an enemy of God. Any sin makes one a sinner.

Since the image of God was an *accidental* attribute, its loss did not make Adam and Eve "unhuman." As noted in the last chapter, man's *essential attributes* are body and soul; Adam and Eve still had these. They were still human beings. But now they had this new *accidental attribute,*[1] that of sinfulness. Just as the attribute of the image of God had wonderful implications for body and soul, so the loss of that image and its replacement with the attribute of sinfulness had horrible implications for body and soul. We have already noted in the last chapter the initial results of that loss for Adam and Eve. They died spiritually. Death by definition is a separation. To be spiritually dead is to be separated from God. Genesis 3 details the dreadful nature of that spiritual death, that spiritual separation from God which Adam and Eve caused by their sin. Gone was the loving relationship of children to a kind and loving Father. In its place there was anger and hatred. Gone was the trusting relationship between children and an altogether reliable Father. In its place there was resentment. Gone was the cheerful and eager listening to the words of the Father who gave life and all that is good in it. In its place there was a fearful hiding, avoiding, and shunning. God had told them that they would die on the day they ate of that tree. And he kept his Word. The most important kind of death, spiritual death, a separation from that blessed fellowship with God and from his gift of righteousness and holiness, is the death they experienced at once. Along with that spiritual death so total and complete came the prospect of physical death, the separation of body and soul. Left to themselves, the still more horrible prospect of eternal death lay before them. Eternal death is the eternal separation of body and soul from God in the torments of hell.

This attribute of sinfulness and its instant companion of spiritual death left Adam and Eve in an absolutely hopeless and desperate condition. The physically dead cannot bring themselves back to life. Neither can the spiritually dead raise themselves to new spiritual life. Because they were dead in sin, there was absolutely nothing that they

---

[1]It may be necessary to repeat at this point that the term *accidental* does not mean unimportant. Rather, the term is used to refer to an attribute or characteristic that *describes* something, as distinguished from an *essential* attribute, which *defines* something (cf. ch. 5 on God's attributes and ch. 7 on Adam's and Eve's attributes at creation). We shall see shortly how significant sinfulness is as an attribute. It is important to maintain, however, that it is an *accidental*, not an *essential*, attribute. If it were an essential attribute, then Christ would not have been a human being since he had no sin, or he would have been a sinner; both notions contradict everything that the Bible has to say about Christ. Additionally, if sin were an essential attribute, then Adam and Eve would not have been human beings before the fall—again a notion altogether contrary to the Word of God in the creation account.

could do to help themselves. They could not even wish or will that they might have spiritual life again. Indeed, so complete is that spiritual death that Adam and Eve were not even aware of it, of its depth, or of its dreadful consequences. Instead of being aware of their miserable condition, their nature had so changed that they were aware only of their hatred and hostility toward God. Instead of seeking help or rescue, their changed nature expressed itself with a raised fist in God's face. While physical death and the trials and tribulations of life that were promised in Genesis 3 could point to their desperate condition, it could not reveal to them the total futility of their existence and the horror of physical and eternal death yet ahead of them if they were left to themselves.

It is this wretched and tragic condition that all born according to the laws of nature inherit from Adam and Eve. Since they had lost the attribute of holiness and righteousness, they could not pass it on to their children. Since they had become sinful instead, it is the attribute of sinfulness and of spiritual death that they pass on to all of their natural born descendents. Jesus sums up the matter and defines it with crystal and devastating clarity when he declares, "Flesh gives birth to flesh" (John 3:6). David spoke plainly when he confessed, "Surely I was sinful at birth, sinful from the time my mother conceived me" (Psalm 51:5).

St. Paul explains fully what that means when he tells us in Romans 5 that Adam brought sin into the world and, as a result, death and the wrath of God have come down to all from Adam. For God remains holy and righteous. He cannot be indifferent to the sin and certainly not to the rebellion that has robbed him of the honor due to him as Creator. St. Paul declares that "sin entered the world through one man, and death through sin, and in this way death came to all men" (v. 12). And "the result of one trespass was condemnation for all men" (v. 18). In sum, the sinful human race inherits not only the sinfulness itself but as well its dreaded consequences. What that death includes Paul spells out in Ephesians 2:1-3:

> As for you, you were dead in your transgressions and sins, in which you used to live when you followed the ways of this world and of the ruler of the kingdom of the air, the spirit who is now at work in those who are disobedient. All of us also lived among them at one time, gratifying the cravings of our sinful nature and following its desires and thoughts. *Like the rest, we were by nature objects of wrath.*

All of these passages make it clear that we are not born morally or spiritually neutral. We do not come into the world as blank pages on which good and bad experiences will be written, which experiences will make us good or bad. No, we come into the world already as children of wrath. From conception our nature is poisoned against God and hostile to him. By nature we are inclined to evil, before we have done good or evil, before we have experienced good or evil. The primary evil is unbelief, which by definition is the absence of trust in God and his Word. It is always accompanied by active rebellion against God. We see that already in Genesis 3; first, Adam and Eve reject trust in God and his Word; and then second, they actively rebel with their thoughts, words, and deeds.

That rebellion is at times subtle, not outwardly violent or vicious. In the newborn baby we may say that we see nothing but sweetness and light. But however sweet and lovable, beneath that surface is that corruption bequeathed to us by our first parents. Whether the rebellion is obvious and outward or not, there remains in us by nature the desire to do our own will instead of the will of God. But even when it is thus subtle, it remains rebellion, a refusal to submit to the will of the Creator. From that most basic rebellion, that idolatry of self and of one's own will, flows all the *cravings of our sinful nature,* whether we satisfy all those cravings or not. At the root of our nature is the desire to be God and to have all of creation serve the self. A child does not have to be taught that; it wants to be God by nature. It has to be taught to control that desire.

Who doesn't see that? A child before it can speak knows how to express selfishness. Early on its motto is: "What's mine is mine; what's yours is negotiable!" A child wants what it wants and wants it now! The child will learn to control its self-centeredness only to the extent that it is forced to control it. Even that lesson is learned only with great difficulty. And once it is learned, self-control is practiced only because it serves the individual's own best interest—the basic self-centeredness remains. And after we have grown up, think how many sins we could commit, might even want to commit; we might not commit them for no other reason than the fear of getting caught or the fear of the consequences that might come as a result of that sin. There is no merit or great virtue in sins grudgingly avoided. Thus the outward behavior may moderate and improve, but the basic desire to be God and to be served has not changed at all. St. Paul is speaking about himself and all of us in our fallen nature when he declares, "I know that nothing good lives in me, that is, in my sinful nature" (Romans 7:18).

This condition in which we are conceived and born is called *original sin* or *inherited sin.* Original sin is not a sin which we commit. It is not something that we do. It is rather something that we have, that we inherit. We are conceived and born in the image of Adam and Eve. We are conceived and born physically alive but spiritually dead. That is our nature with all that spiritual death implies and carries with it. The hatred of God, the inability to do anything about it, the inability to do anything at all that is God pleasing, even the ignorance of our condition and its dreadful consequences—all of that is part and parcel of original sin. As the previous passages make clear, our condition by nature is just as desperate and absolutely damning as was the nature of Adam and Eve after they fell into sin. We cannot do anything about it any more than Adam and Eve could change their nature back to a sinless one after the fall. By nature we do not want to do anything about it. We cannot change our nature as sinful, spiritually dead creatures any more than we can change the physical characteristics we inherited from our parents.

Thus, in sum and by definition, *original sin* is a deep-seated, thorough-going tendency to evil; it is an inherited *accidental* attribute which causes all of the naturally born descendents of Adam and Eve to be by nature spiritually dead, enemies of God, and deserving of eternal separation from him in hell.

Arminian and Pelagian attacks on the doctrine of original sin

Thus we reject as contrary to the clear Word of God all forms of *Arminianism.* Arminianism (named after the 16th and early 17th century Dutch theologian Jacob Harmensen, popularly referred to as Arminius) is the false teaching that people are born either spiritually neutral or basically good. It denies the doctrine of original sin and settles for what is referred to in theology as the *opinio legis*—literally, the opinion of the law. The *opinio legis* is itself the result of original sin. It is the result and proof of spiritual blindness. It is the notion or opinion that people want to have about themselves, the notion that we are all basically good (or at the very least, I am basically good!) and that it is only corrupt or evil influences and surroundings that make people bad. Improve their physical and psychological environment and people will become good and ever better. The *opinio legis,* to the extent that it considers God, holds that this supposed basic goodness in human nature is sufficient for man at least in part to earn God's favor and to deserve heaven, if not by perfect works, then at least by a decision to believe. The chief proponents of Arminianism are Methodists and Baptists and the daughter religions, e.g., Salvation Army, Pentecostal, and Holiness church bodies. All of these churches either deny the doctrine of original sin or deny its dread consequence of spiritual death in us by nature.

We likewise reject all forms of Pelagianism and semi-Pelagianism. Pelagianism (named after the fifth century British monk Pelagius) in its crudest form is the false teaching that even without God's help we can perform good works that are good and meritorious in the eyes of God. Pelagianism was condemned on the basis of the Scriptures in the ancient church most effectively in the writings of St. Augustine. So-called semi-Pelagianism, however, has never ceased to infect the church. In point of fact, it too has its roots in the *opinio legis,* in the blind zeal of fallen man to think himself worthy in God's eyes and, perhaps even more important, in his own eyes.

Those guilty of the error of semi-Pelagianism do not deny the doctrine of original sin entirely. Rather, they minimize its depth and the extent of its consequences. Semi-Pelagianism has its church home in Roman Catholicism and in Eastern Orthodox churches. The Roman Catholic Church teaches that even though we are born in sin, it is possible for us to do by nature works that are pleasing to God. Thus, even unbelievers, non-Christians—if they do the best they can according to the dictates of their own consciences *(facere quod in se est)*—will be saved without faith in Christ as the sole Redeemer, without repentance, without the Word, and without the sacraments. As for Christians, Roman Catholicism teaches that Baptism removes original sin in such a way that the Christian with the "initial grace" provided in Baptism can cooperate by his works in his own salvation. For Roman Catholics, therefore, original sin is but a blemish. It may be described as the "tinder" *(fomes)* for sinful acts; it may even be called the tendency toward sinful desires (concupiscence), but Roman Catholicism does not see the inclination or the desire to sin as damnable in itself. When all is said and done, the practical difference between Pelagianism and semi-Pelagianism is slight indeed.

The *opinio legis* is deeply rooted in us all. As already noted, it is part of our inherited spiritual blindness, part of original sin itself. Thus it is not surprising that the church always has to fight against it. Nor is it surprising that we ourselves find Arminianism and Pelagianism flattering and appealing also to our sinful nature. In our inherited spiritual blindness we want to hang on to an imagined self-worth apart from Christ and his redeeming love for us, even in the face of the whole of God's Word testifying to the contrary. Yes, we want to cling to such notions even when the voice of conscience, albeit at times weakly, condemns at least our sinful acts, if not our sinful desires and intentions. St. Paul explains our natural and stubborn clinging to Arminian and Pelagian notions contrary to the Word of God when he declares, "The sinful mind is hostile to God. It does not submit to God's law, nor can it do so" (Romans 8:7), and, "The man without the Spirit does not accept the things that come from the Spirit of God, for they are foolishness to him, and he cannot understand them, because they are spiritually discerned" (1 Corinthians 2:14).

As Christians restored and reborn through the work of Christ and the promises of the gospel, we want to submit to the Word of God also in its evaluation of our nature. That nature is steeped in original sin, so that by nature we cannot please God; by nature we are lost and condemned creatures; by nature we are totally depraved, so totally depraved that we cannot know the extent of our depravity apart from God's own revelation in his Word. In rejecting and condemning all forms of Arminianism and Pelagianism, we believe, teach, and confess what the Scriptures teach about our nature. In doing so we teach in harmony with our Lutheran Confessions. Clearly and unequivocally the Augsburg Confession declares:

> Furthermore, it is taught among us that since the fall of Adam, all human beings who are born in the natural way are conceived and born in sin. That means that from birth they are full of evil lust and inclination and cannot by nature possess true fear of God and true faith in God. Moreover, this same innate disease and original sin is truly sin and condemns to God's eternal wrath all who are not in turn born anew through baptism and the Holy Spirit.
>
> Rejected, then, are the Pelagians and others who do not regard original sin as sin in order to make human nature righteous through natural powers, thus insulting the suffering and merit of Christ. (AC II, 1-3 pp. 36,38)

Likewise, the Formula of Concord:

> We believe, teach, and confess that original sin is not a slight corruption of human nature, but rather a corruption so deep that

> there is nothing sound or uncorrupted left in the human body or soul, in its internal or external powers. Instead, as the church sings, "Through Adam's fall human nature and our essence are completely corrupted." The damage is so indescribable that it cannot be recognized by our reason but only from God's Word. (FC Ep I, 8,9 pp. 488,489)

And this:

> Holy Scripture alone provides a full understanding and explanation [of the nature of original sin]. It testifies that original sin is an indescribable impairment and corruption of human nature so deep that nothing pure and good remains in it or in any of its internal and external powers. Instead, all is so deeply corrupted because of this original sin that human beings are truly spiritually dead in God's sight, having died, with all their powers, to the good. (FC SD I, 60 p. 542)

As we noted earlier, in spite of the total devastation of the spiritual abilities that accompanied the image of God at creation, the shell or traces of God's image are still to be found in our nature. We are still human, endowed with a soul that has intellect and a reasoning ability, a will, and emotions. If the heart and core of God's image, his holiness and righteousness, are totally lost as a result of original sin, what about this shell of humanity? What effect has the fall and original sin had on the human intellect, will, and emotions?

These too have been thoroughly corrupted by the fall, though not entirely destroyed by it. Their corruption is so deep and so thorough that the emotions, the will, and the reason are by nature incapable of any spiritual good, that is, good in the eyes of God. St. Paul certainly makes that abundantly clear in the passages cited previously from Romans 5 and Ephesians 2.

Does original sin mean that we are incapable of doing good works?

Are we not capable of doing good deeds? Do we not see in atheists and other unbelievers many good works? They may serve their neighbor, help the poor, and even become great in the eyes of the world for their service to their nation and their fellow man. And does not even God bless such outwardly good works, even those of unbelievers?

To be sure, since the fall human beings are by nature capable of doing many *outwardly* good things. And in a certain *outward* sense

God prospers such outward goodness. We see that in all of recorded human history. Nations that follow laws intended to punish those guilty of crimes against their fellow man and to protect those who lead lives useful for society tend to prosper so long as and to the extent that they are well-ordered. Likewise, individuals who may care nothing for the Word of God but who nonetheless lead an outwardly decent life often prosper or are held in high regard by their fellow citizens, and deservedly so. But the good they do is only good *outwardly.*

However, such works are not good *spiritually,* that is, spiritually good and deserving of eternal reward in the eyes of God. For by nature all are spiritually dead. A non-Christian may object that he does not hate God, that he really wants to please God. He may even claim and think that he loves God. But his refusal to submit to God's Word, to recognize his sin and his desperate need of a Savior, and to see in Christ that one and only Savior—all of that amounts to a hatred of the only true God; the god he professes to love is one of his own invention. For to reject what God has said and what Christ has done in favor of one's own opinions is to reject the only true God. The unbeliever cannot and does not have the only motive that would make his works God-pleasing, the motive of loving and grateful service in obedience to God's Word and trusting in the work of his Son for salvation. For how can one truly please God when he rejects God's Word and the enormous sacrifice of his Son for our salvation?

Unbelievers may have any number of motives for doing outwardly good works. People might do good in the hope of reward, even reward from God, whose favor they hope to earn by their own efforts. But that is not a God-pleasing motive. They may do good in the hope of human rewards or fame or gratitude from men. They may do good motivated by the good feeling they get when they do good or by a noble love of humanity. But, and that is the point, they cannot do good as the result of a childlike relationship with God. For such a relationship was lost and replaced by original sin at the time of the fall.

We sometimes call the outwardly good works of the unbeliever *good works according to the order of Cain.* Cain brought a sacrifice to God (Genesis 4:1-7), but he did not sacrifice as the fruit of faith, out of love and trust in God's Word and promise. And so his sacrifice was not pleasing to God, nor accepted by him. In the gospels we hear of the outwardly good works and noble lives of the Pharisees. We note especially the outward goodness of the rich young man in Matthew 19:16-22. He wanted to live a God-pleasing life and outwardly he was indeed virtuous; any parent would be proud to have such a son. But inside of him there was neither a longing for the mercy of God nor a recognition that he needed it. Instead, he trusted in himself and in his wealth. When Jesus pointed out his idolatry, the young man went away sad instead of confessing his sin and looking to Jesus for his rescue.

The Apology of the Augsburg Confession sums up well what our fallen nature is capable of and what it is incapable of. It declares:

> The human will possesses freedom regarding works and matters that reason can comprehend by itself. It can to some extent produce civil righteousness or the righteousness of works. It can talk about God and offer God acts of worship with external works; it can obey rulers and parents. By choosing an external work it can keep back the hand from murder, adultery, and theft. Because human nature still retains reason and judgment concerning things subject to the senses, it also retains the ability to choose in such matters, as well as the freedom and ability to achieve civil righteousness. For Scripture calls this the righteousness of the flesh, which carnal nature (that is, reason) produces by itself apart from the Holy Spirit. (Ap XVIII, 4 pp. 233,234)

Then shortly thereafter:

> Therefore, even though we concede to free will the freedom and power to perform external works of the law, nevertheless we do not ascribe to free will those spiritual capacities, namely, true fear of God, true faith in God, the conviction and knowledge that God cares for us, hears us, and forgives us, etc. These are the real works of the first table [of the Ten Commandments, Commandments 1-3], which the human heart cannot produce without the Holy Spirit, just as Paul says [1 Cor. 2:14]: "Those who are natural," that is, those who use only their natural powers, "do not perceive the things which are of God." (Ap XVIII, 7 p. 234)

Thus good outwardly and good in the eyes of humanity and good by human standards is not the same thing as good in the eyes of God. That is God's own verdict in his Word. His Word declares:

> The LORD looks down from heaven on the sons of men to see if there are any who understand, any who seek God. All have turned aside, they have together become corrupt; there is no one who does good, not even one. (Psalm 14:2,3)

God speaks plainly of the total spiritual corruption of our reason, will, and emotions when he speaks to Noah after the flood about the natural human condition and declares of all men, "Every inclination of his heart is evil from childhood" (Genesis 8:21).

Therefore when we speak of original sin, we are speaking of that total destruction of the image of God in man at its heart and core, that is, the total destruction of the innate holiness and righteousness given to Adam and Eve at their creation. That holiness and righteousness has been replaced by sinfulness. We are not speaking of the destruction of humanity or of human nature, even though original sin also has thoroughly corrupted those traces of God's image that are left in man's humanity, in the "organs" of the soul: man's intellect, will, and emotions. These organs are still able to function. God has left fallen humanity with a certain *freedom in those things that are subject to reason.* Were it not for that remaining freedom in those things subject to reason, the human race would have perished long ago; it would have lacked the ability to think and thus to devise ways and means for its survival. Just as God in his mercy clothed fallen Adam and Eve in the skins of animals after their fall to protect them from physical harm in a hostile world, as well as to hide their shame, so he clothes the human soul with the capacity to reason and a freedom to act in those things subject to reason lest mankind perish altogether in the inability to do anything at all that would keep the race alive and functioning.

Thus even though sinful and bereft of innate holiness and righteousness, the shell of God's image remains. And that shell is no small blessing. We are still human, still have reason, will, and emotions, so that outwardly people are capable of producing works that are good in the eyes of humanity. Outwardly one can choose to steal or not to steal, to lie or not to lie, to commit adultery or to lead an outwardly chaste and decent life. With the remaining shell we can create works of art and beauty, useful medicines and machines, and the like. All of these abilities and their exercises imply a certain limited freedom even for fallen humanity, and that in spite of the fact that by nature we are enslaved by sin. Our remaining natural freedom is the freedom to make choices in *those things that are subject to reason.* That freedom and ability is evident and noted already in the book of Genesis shortly after the fall (4:20-22). The Formula of Concord distinguishes well between the natural ability of fallen humanity on the one hand and the inability to please God by that ability on the other hand:

> For works that belong to the maintenance of outward discipline are also demanded of the unbelievers and unconverted and are performed by them. Even though such works are praiseworthy in the world's sight and are rewarded by God in this world with temporal benefits, nonetheless, because they do not proceed from true faith, they are sin in God's sight. That is, they are tarnished with sins and are regarded by God as sin and impure because of the corrupted human nature and because the person who performs them is not reconciled with God. For "a bad tree cannot bear good fruit" [Matt. 7:18], as it is also written in Romans 14[:23], "Whatever does not proceed from faith is sin." For a person must be acceptable to God beforehand (and that alone because of Christ), before that person's works are at all pleasing to him. (FC SD IV, 8 p. 575)

In what sense are Christians free to choose what works they will do and which they will not do?

Christians also exercise this capacity to reason and this freedom to choose in those things subject to reason. The fall did not destroy it, and faith does not abolish it. Outwardly we have the freedom to choose whom we will marry, what vocation we will pursue, or whether to buy this and sell that. Even for the Christian, God does not normally make these choices for us. As the Formula of Concord teaches both with regard to Christians and to unbelievers:

> [We reject] the mad invention of the philosophers who are called Stoics, as well as the Manicheans, who taught that everything that happens has to happen just so and could not happen in any other way, and that people do everything that they do, even in external things, under coercion. (FC Ep II, 8 p. 492)

The Christian prays for God's guidance and seeks God's blessing in the choices left to reason. But the choices remain ours. God nowhere promises to whisper them in our ears in response to our prayers. Having sought his guidance, we choose those outward things left to reason. Then we trust that God will bless our choices (Romans 8:28). We give thanks to God for the gift of daily bread, but we choose whether to have chicken or pork. We give thanks to God for our spouse, but we choose the spouse. God has left us our humanity and has not turned us into robots or puppets as a result of the fall. Outwardly, in those things subject to reason, he has left us a great deal of freedom.

But again, by nature and apart from faith in Christ, we have these two elements in our nature: Spiritually we are dead and incapable of any good in the eyes of God, but still we have the shell of his image in our reason, will, and emotions. We are still human, even though that shell of reason, will, and emotion has been badly corrupted by original sin.

How the presence of the shell and the fact of its corruption work may be clearer to us if we consider a few examples. Someone's emotions, for example, incline him to drunkenness or drug addiction; initially he likes the feeling his intoxication gives. He chooses in his freedom to love his poisons. His intellect bends every effort to justify his behavior and to find ways and means of satisfying his depraved desires and choices. He has exercised his freedom in something that is subject to reason. He could have acted reasonably. But he chose not to. He has acted in an unreasonable, irrational way, even though his emotions, choices, and rationalizations unchecked can only lead to his destruction. The adulterer is attracted in his emotions to another. With his freedom his will chooses to cheat and to love another instead of remaining faithful to his spouse. He bends his reason to justify his behavior and to find ways and means of getting away with it. But again, his behavior is corrupt and irrational by most human standards because of the risks to his own health and welfare, not to mention those of his family.

The presence of the shell and how it functions are likewise evident in the collective actions of society. Civil society argues the pros and cons of this political party's platform and of that ideology. But it comes to no universally accepted understanding of what is right and wrong, or what is best under the given set of circumstances. The well-reasoning poor man marshals rational arguments in favor of the redistribution of other peoples' wealth. The well-reasoning rich man argues with his reason that such redistribution stifles initiative and ultimately diminishes the wealth-creating potential of the whole society. This group rationally defends the need for a strong defense. That group with the use of reason argues that weapons beget war not peace.

So God has indeed left us free to use our reason, will, and emotions in those things that are subject to reason. But even in those things subject to reason the corruption of our nature by original sin is such that in our choices we often are left with uncertainty and doubt as to what is best and what is right. And often, even when the choice between good and evil ought to be self-evident from natural law, conscience, experience, or observation, people in their freedom still choose evil to their own harm.

We may summarize the impact of original sin on human nature this way:

Before the fall	After the fall
Man = body (atoms, molecules, limbs, physical organs) soul (reason, will, emotions)	Man = body (atoms, molecules, limbs, physical organs) soul (reason, will, emotions)
Man with the image of God—holy and righteous in both body and soul: Body—perfect and immortal Soul—reason, will, and emotions in perfect harmony with God and capable of remaining sinless *(posse non peccare)*	Man without the image of God—sinful in both body and soul: Body—subject to sickness and death Soul—reason, will, and emotions spiritually dead and incapable of anything good in the eyes of God, by nature not able to stop sinning *(non posse non peccare);* in those things subject to reason, the reason, will, and emotions are free and capable of many *outwardly* good and constructive and useful works, but even with this freedom in outward works we remain corrupt and the works often openly demonstrate that corruption

Given our fallen nature, can we nevertheless "decide for Christ" (synergism)?

It should be evident from all of the above that by nature we cannot save ourselves. As already noted, all forms of Pelagianism and Arminianism are to be rejected. But so too are all forms of *synergism.* Like Pelagianism and Arminianism, synergism originates in the *opinio legis.* The word *synergism* comes from a verb that means "to cooperate." Synergism is the false teaching that even though we are conceived and born in sin—even though the Scriptures describe us as blind by nature, dead, and enemies of God—nevertheless, we can and must cooperate with God *in our conversion.* Synergism ascribes to the will of man a freedom in spiritual things as well as in those things subject to reason.

Synergists maintain that man is capable by his natural powers of "making a decision for Christ" and responding to the gospel. Synergism is an especially important element in Arminianism. Most Protestants today are synergists, devoted to "decision theology." The sermons and the music of synergist churches tend to be highly emotional. They seek to put people in the right frame of mind or mood to make their decision for Christ, to decide "to take Jesus into their heart." Synergism often is also part and parcel of the semi-Pelagianism so evident in much of Roman Catholic teaching. Protestant synergists would find no fault in the following citations from the *Catechism of the Catholic Church:*

> Adam and Eve transmitted to their descendants human nature wounded by their own first sin. (par. 417)[2]

And since human nature is only considered as wounded, synergists conclude that we have a natural ability to assist in our conversion and thus in our salvation. Again, quoting from the current Catholic catechism, words with which Protestant synergists would agree:

> Our justification comes from the grace of God. Grace is *favor,* the *free and undeserved help* that God gives us to respond to his call to become children of God, adoptive sons, partakers of the divine nature and of eternal life. (par. 1996)

> The *preparation of man* for the reception of grace is already a work of grace. This latter is needed to arouse and sustain *our collaboration in justification through faith,* and in sanctification through charity (second emphasis added, par. 2001)

> God's free initiative demands *man's free response,* for God has created man in his image by conferring on him, along with freedom, the power to know him and love him. (par. 2002)

But how can the dead make a "free response" and thus decide to be alive? How should the by-nature-hostile-enemy-of-God invite Jesus into his heart? The Scriptures tell us repeatedly that we have no spiritual ability of ourselves, as we have noted previously in Genesis 8:21; Romans 8:7; Ephesians 2:5; 1 Corinthians 2:14; et al. No, it can never be that the blind decide to see, the dead decide to live, and the enemies of God decide to trust in him! Rather, the Scriptures ascribe all the

---

[2]This and the following citations are from the *Catechism of the Catholic Church*, United States Catholic Conference, Inc.—Libreria Editrice Vaticana, Mahwah, New Jersey: Paulist Press, 1994. (The italics in these citations are in the original.)

glory to God when we come to know his Word and trust in him for our salvation. Faith is not a human rational choice; it is the gift of God from beginning to end, as is everything else that has to do with our salvation. St. Paul states it as clearly as it can be stated when he declares,

> But because of his great love for us, God, who is rich in mercy, made us alive with Christ even when we were dead in transgressions—it is by grace you have been saved. For it is by grace you have been saved, through faith—and this *[everything that has to do with salvation, including faith]* not from yourselves, it is the gift of God—not by works, so that no one can boast. (Ephesians 2:4,5,8,9)

The doctrine of salvation and faith will be considered again and in detail under the doctrine of soteriology (chapters 12,14). But in considering the doctrine of original sin it is important to take note of the consequences of original sin in the matter of coming to faith. It is important that we understand from the beginning that as a result of original sin we are not able to play an active role in our own salvation. We are entirely passive *(pure passive).* It is God who loved us in spite of our sinfulness (John 3:16). It is Christ who came into the world to redeem us by his blood, without any help or cooperation from any of us (Romans 5:6-8). It is the Holy Spirit who works to raise us spiritually from the dead by means of the gospel in Word and sacrament (Romans 1:16; 10:17; 1 Peter 3:21). While someone may for any number of reasons decide to read the Bible, he cannot decide to believe it. That conviction is worked by and is the gift of God alone through the gospel message itself.

Why opposing Arminianism, Pelagianism, and synergism is so important

Thus we must steadfastly resist and oppose the errors of Arminianism, Pelagianism, and synergism. They attack the heart and core of the gospel message. They rob God of his glory as author of truth in the sacred Scriptures. They rob Christ of his glory as the only Savior and transfer at least part of that glory to fallen man. They rob the Holy Spirit of his glory as the author of faith by making his Word and work through the Word purely informational in nature, when in fact that gospel is "the power of God for the salvation of everyone who believes" (Romans 1:16). Carried out to its logical conclusion, Pelagianism, Arminianism, and synergism may even end in unbelief. For the essence of faith is trust in the Word and promise of God, trust in that grace alone and in the merit of Christ alone for salvation. Pelagianism, Arminianism, and synergism cast aside that crucial word *alone* and credit man with a role, be it large or small, in his own salvation.

Indeed, these errors if carried out to their logical conclusion will drive those who hold them either to self-righteous Phariseeism or to despair. For those who think their own works or decisions have contributed to their salvation or caused their conversion are Pharisees—they may congratulate themselves on their good works or their decisions rather than giving God the praise he alone deserves for salvation. The pride of both the Pelagian Pharisee and the Arminian synergist is the opposite of faith. Faith listens to the Word of God. Faith despairs of its own merits. Faith trusts alone the promise of God to forgive out of grace and on account of the work of Christ. "For all have sinned and fall short of the glory of God, and are justified freely by his grace through the redemption that came by Christ Jesus" (Romans 3:23,24).

On the other hand, the law and conscience may drive the synergist, Pelagian, or Arminian to despair. Conscience may ask, "Have I really done enough? Have I really decided yet?" Conscience looks at the works done and the decision made. It weighs all that against the hammer blows of the law, which requires perfection in every moment, in every thought, word, and deed. It considers the good left undone, the good done grudgingly, and the good done imperfectly. Yes, conscience calls to mind the evil thoughts, words, and deeds and drives the sinner to cry out with St. Paul, "What a wretched man I am! Who will rescue me from this body of death?" (Romans 7:24).

Yes, left alone with the law, the conscience may well drive the Pelagian or the Arminian to despair. The cure for despair however should not be sought in one's own works or feelings. For because of original sin, all of our works are stained and all of our own feelings are suspect. It should be sought and found in the Word of God. The Word of God teaches us to confess with St. Paul, "I know that nothing good lives in me, that is, in my sinful nature" (Romans 7:18). It bids us cry out with him, "What a wretched man I am! Who will rescue me from this body of death?" (Romans 7:24). It is the power of God working through the gospel that brings us to join in St. Paul's divinely inspired answer: "Thanks be to God—through Jesus Christ our Lord!" (Romans 7:25). The cure for despair is the gospel. The Word of full forgiveness because of God's grace and Christ's redeeming work overcomes the despair worked by the law and conscience. That gospel replaces despair with the quiet confidence that Christ has done everything necessary for our salvation and the assurance that God will not lie to us in that gospel message. To put it another way and most simply: When it comes to the matter of our salvation, we look not inside of ourselves, neither to our works nor to our feelings; instead, we look outside of ourselves, to the cross of Christ and all he did for our salvation. All of that and its benefit come to us from and through the Word of the gospel.

How the image of God is restored in us

It is in the creation of faith by means of the gospel in Word and sacrament that the damage of original sin begins to be undone. For it is through that gospel message of Christ's work for our salvation that God forgives the guilt of all sin, including original sin. St. Paul tells us that in Baptism God has washed and cleansed the church (i.e., all who believe in Christ as their only Savior), so that the church might be "a radiant church, without stain or wrinkle or any other blemish, but holy and blameless" (Ephesians 5:27). In Acts 22:16 he tells us that Baptism is the washing away of sin. And in Galatians 3:26,27 he reminds us that our status as children of God has been restored to us by Baptism. With that gospel message God overcomes our spiritual deadness *and* the hostility of our fallen will.

Through that gospel message in the Word and in the Sacrament of Baptism God gives us a new will, one that sighs in God-created confidence, "The promise of God is meant for me! Christ died even for me! Even my sins are forgiven!" It is as St. Augustine says, "God makes willing people out of unwilling people and dwells in the willing ones" (FC, Ep II, 15 p. 493).

Thus, while original sin destroyed the holiness and righteousness that were the heart and core of the image of God in Adam and Eve, in the forgiveness of sins that holiness and righteousness are restored. There are, however, some differences in the image of God as it was in Adam and Eve and as it is now in believers.

First of all, the image of God in Adam and Eve was *innate.* That is, it was an attribute of their nature and something that they had from the moment of their creation. The image of God in the believer however is not innate. Rather, it is *imputed.* That is, righteousness and holiness are "credited to us, charged to our account" on account of the grace of God and the work of Christ for our redemption. As noted earlier, holiness and righteousness are absolute terms; that is, strictly speaking there is no such thing before God as a partial holiness or an in-process righteousness. The holiness and righteousness imputed to us through faith is Christ's own holiness and righteousness. It is therefore perfect and complete *in God's eyes.* It renders us holy and righteous in God's eyes without any works or merits in us when and for as long as we trust the gospel promise of full and free forgiveness on account of God's grace and Christ's merit.

Thus it is not our sinful nature that is changed through faith in the gospel. What has changed is our *status*. Since our sin has been forgiven through faith in the gospel, we are no longer children of wrath and heirs of damnation. Our status has changed; we have become dear children of God and joint heirs with Christ. God, who reconciled the whole world to himself by charging all of the sins of the world to Christ's account (2 Corinthians 5:21), now calls those who trust in Christ's saving work his own dear children (Romans 8:16; 1 Corinthians 6:11; 1 Peter 1:23).

St. Paul beautifully explains this chief truth of the Scriptures in Romans 1–5. We note here only a few excerpts from these chapters and refer the reader to a careful consideration of everything in those chapters.

> But now a righteousness from God, apart from law, has been made known, to which the Law and the Prophets testify. This righteousness from God comes through faith in Jesus Christ to all who believe. There is no difference, for all have sinned and fall short of the glory of God, and are justified freely by his grace through the redemption that came by Christ Jesus. (Romans 3:21-24)

> Where, then, is boasting? It is excluded. On what principle? On that of observing the law? No, but on that of faith. For we maintain that a man is justified by faith apart from observing the law. (Romans 3:27,28)

> Now when a man works, his wages are not credited to him as a gift, but as an obligation. However, to the man who does not work but trusts God who justifies the wicked, his faith is credited as righteousness. (Romans 4:4,5)

While the most important damage of original sin is entirely undone by this *imputed* restoration of holiness and righteousness through the forgiveness of sins, we still live in our sinful flesh. With St. Paul and all the saints on earth we daily stand in need of forgiveness. For our renewed nature, our Christian emotions, will, and reason must struggle against the old emotions, will, and reason inherited from Adam and Eve until we finally reach our goal in heaven. St. Paul tells us about that struggle:

> What I want to do I do not do, but what I hate I do. . . . For I have the desire to do what is good, but I cannot carry it out. For what

> I do is not the good I want to do; no, the evil I do not want to do—this I keep on doing. . . . So I find this law at work: When I want to do good, evil is right there with me. For in my inner being I delight in God's law; but I see another law at work in the members of my body, waging war against the law of my mind and making me a prisoner of the law of sin at work within my members. (Romans 7:15-23)

Thus the *imputed* righteousness of Christ, the holiness and righteousness that is ours by faith alone, is perfect and complete. But the Christian life is still weighed down by struggle and weakness, by temptation and doubt, and finally by physical death. All these remain the continuing consequences of original sin, which continues to infect our nature even though its guilt has been forgiven. It is the goal of the Christian's life to struggle against the sinful nature with the same Word that created faith in the first place. St. Paul urges us to enter the battle against the flesh with the sword of the Spirit, the Word of God (Ephesians 6:17). In that battle against our other nature, we strive more and more *to become what we are.* And what are we? In the eyes of God we are holy and righteous by faith, righteous because our sin has been forgiven. We want to live as holy and righteous ones, ever closer in life to the restored image of God that is ours by faith.

An understanding of the doctrine of original sin helps us to understand ourselves and others a lot better

We have spent a lot of time on this doctrine. It would be difficult to overestimate the importance of the doctrine of original sin. Most of the worst false doctrines begin with an attack on or a corruption of this doctrine. Moreover, it is impossible to understand human nature correctly without understanding original sin and its consequences. Who does not often ask himself, "How could I have done such a thing? How could I have thought such evil? How could I have wanted to do such a thing and refrain only out of fear that I might get caught?" But if we correctly understand the doctrine of original sin, then we will have gone a long way towards understanding how evil could lie so close to the heart of even the best of Christians. We will understand that within each of us there is the potential for all manner of wickedness because of the fallen nature that we have inherited from Adam and Eve. We will understand why our motives when we refrain from evil and do what is outwardly good are so often a mixture of God-pleasing motives inspired by the gospel and half-hearted, even grudging willingness caused by the sinful nature.

We will also have gone a long way towards understanding the weaknesses and struggles of those around us. Though the particular struggles and weaknesses of those around us may be different from those we feel and experience, their source is in the same fallen sinful nature that we have, in original sin. That should help us to be both more humble and more charitable. We have the same fallen nature, no matter how different the evidence of that fallen nature may appear on the outside.

Finally, we do well to marvel at the grace and mercy of God, especially as we contrast his grace and mercy to our unworthiness. Our need of grace and mercy is constant, total, and absolute. But the grace of God and his mercy in Christ Jesus are even greater than our sin, our guilt, or our need, as St. Paul joyfully confesses, "Where sin increased, grace increased all the more, so that, just as sin reigned in death, so also grace might reign through righteousness to bring eternal life through Jesus Christ our Lord" (Romans 5:20,21). As depressing as the doctrine of original sin is to the pride of our fallen nature, so much more heartening and cheering is the message of the gospel of imputed holiness and righteousness by faith in God's gracious promise and in Christ's perfect work for our salvation. The doctrines of original sin and of God's grace in Christ give all glory to God for our salvation. They as well give the ultimate comfort to the sinner. For if we cannot save ourselves and God does not expect us to contribute in any way to our salvation, then our salvation is secure—it rests entirely in the hands of God who promised it in Christ. And it rests entirely in the perfect work of Christ for us and his payment for the sins of the world on the cross. That's what God has promised. And God will not lie to us or deceive us.

Summary of what we have lost because of original sin and how God in grace restores what we lost

Since the fall of Adam and Eve, every human being born according to the natural law (that is, every human being except the virgin born Son of God) is conceived and born with original sin.

Original sin is not an act or a deed performed but a deep-seated, thorough-going tendency to evil; it consists of the total loss of innate holiness and righteousness; then the corruption of the remaining natural abilities of the soul in its emotions, will, and reason; and finally the loss of immortality.

Because of original sin we are born spiritually blind, dead, and enemies of God, with no ability to change our status before God; by nature we are children of wrath, and in our original guilt we merit nothing but eternal punishment.

Though by nature we may still perform outwardly good works, none of those works are God-pleasing in the sense that they could merit heaven or any part of it; for they do not flow from a heart that trusts Christ as the only Savior. Therefore, they are, even at their best, sins deserving only God's eternal wrath and punishment.

The lost image of God can only be restored by God himself. He restores it by imputation, that is, he gives us Christ's own perfect righteousness and holiness when he forgives all of our sins for Jesus' sake and then creates trust in our hearts by his Word of the gospel. With that forgiveness and by faith alone in his grace and in Christ's merit, the holiness and righteousness of Christ are imputed to us.

Christ's imputed holiness and righteousness do not erase or change the fact that we have a fallen nature; rather, the guilt of that fallen nature is forgiven. The gospel in fact creates in us a new, Christian nature. This new nature is not a change in man's essence or an addition to it; rather, it is a spiritual life and a renewed capacity in the intellect, will, and emotions that now struggle against the old nature. The Christian with this renewed intellect, will, and emotions tries to live a life of gratitude to God for salvation, a life of obedience to the Word of God. The struggle between the old nature and the new is never finished in this life. As we strive to become in life what we already are by faith (i.e., holy and righteous), we trust in the grace of God and the merits of Christ for our forgiveness and salvation. Our Christian good works are the result of that forgiveness, not the cause of it.[3]

---

[3]We will consider further the Christian life and good works in the next chapter and in chapter 16.

Chapter 9
Actual Sin and the Law

Unlike original sin, which is sin that we have rather than sin that we commit, actual sin is any breaking of God's law. It matters not, as far as the definition of actual sin is concerned, whether the breaking of the law was conscious or unconscious, intentional or unintentional, a failure to do what was commanded or a doing of what was forbidden. Every breaking of God's law is by definition sin, and to distinguish it from original sin, it is called actual sin.

The three sources of actual sin

The devil

There are three basic causes or sources of actual sin. The first is the devil, Satan himself, and his fellow fallen angels. We see that from the fall account in Genesis 3. We see it again in the account of Jesus' temptation in the wilderness. The devil came to him in order to seduce and trick him into setting aside his saving mission for us in favor of self-saving and self-serving (Luke 4:1-12).[1] Later, in rebuking the unbelief of the Jewish leaders, Jesus told them, "You belong to your father, the devil, and you want to carry out your father's desire. . . . When he lies, he speaks his native language, for he is a liar and the father of lies" (John 8:44).

In his blind, unreasoning rage against God, who has cast him out of heaven into eternal punishment and misery, the devil has a limited freedom to attack and tempt. God permits those attacks to test us. The test is not so much so that God can find out how much we love him and want to serve him; he already knows that. Rather, temptations permitted are for us to see how strong/weak we are, how ardent/dull our love and obedience. Such testing should always have the outcome that we more and more come to see that all of our strength to resist and

---

[1]Is it not an amazing thing? Luke tells us that Jesus was tempted during the entire 40 days. During that entire time he successfully resisted the assaults of the devil! When was the last time you resisted for one day? For even one hour? And Jesus did it all for us!

overcome rests in God alone. Yes, and even more important, as we view our life of stumbling struggles against the destroyer, we marvel all the more at the love and grace of God in Christ our Savior; for he wants nothing more than to call us to himself in Word and sacraments, to show us his grace and favor, and finally to bring us to himself forever in heaven at the end of this earthly time of testing.

As in the Garden of Eden, the devil presents himself as a friend who wants only to make our lives easier and free of the restraints so disagreeable to our sinful nature. But in reality he is a murderer of souls, who wants only that we share in his eternal misery. St. Peter warns us, "Be self-controlled and alert. Your enemy the devil prowls around like a roaring lion looking for someone to devour" (1 Peter 5:8). It is remarkable indeed that even though we know that what St. Peter says is true, know it both from the Word of God and from our own experience, we nevertheless so often play with the devil and his temptations. We treat him more like a gentle kitten to be petted than like a ferocious lion to be dreaded and shunned.

Though Satan wears a friendly disguise, the tactics he employs for our destruction have not changed since the time of the fall in the garden. First, he attacks or tries to undermine in some way the truth of God's Word and our trust in it. Just a little compromise on a little doctrine, that's all. Life for the Christian and for the church will be so much easier if we just stop insisting on every word. So much opposition could be avoided and so much ridicule prevented if we just dropped the doctrine of creation or the doctrine concerning the proper roles of men and women or the Bible's teaching about chastity before marriage. But his goal is destruction. His intention is to drive a wedge between the Christian and the Savior by causing us in effect to call God a liar; for that's what we do whenever we deny or contradict any part of his Word. If the devil succeeds in drawing us away from one doctrine, he will have an easier time of it in drawing us away from more and more of God's Word. Those who oppose sound doctrine, St. Paul says, have fallen into the snares of the devil (2 Timothy 2:25,26). Ultimately his goal is to tear us away from the heart and core of God's Word, the doctrine of the forgiveness of sins and eternal life that are ours through faith in the saving merit of Christ our Savior. When he has succeeded in his attacks on that most fundamental doctrine of the Scriptures, church for us will have degenerated into a social club with a cross on the roof. Only then will he be satisfied.

When the devil does not at once succeed in his attacks on doctrine, he may turn his attack to the Christian's life. If he can get pastors and teachers and laity to see their faith only in terms of memorized doctrinal formulae without any follow-through in their lives, then he will have an easy time of it later on in tearing them and others away from the pure doctrine they may have taught. The pure doctrine of the drunkard, the gossip, the gambler, the adulterer, the liar, or the cheat impresses no one; the life of the hypocrite drives away those who might otherwise have listened to the Word. Jesus connects our lives to our doctrine when he tells us, "Let your light shine before men, that they may see your good deeds and praise your Father in heaven" (Matthew 5:16). The life that is seen by others as flowing from the Word of God may well draw others to hear that Word. But the hypocrite's life may well become such a mess that he not only repels a potential hearer but he himself finally has no energy or time left for pure doctrine. St. Peter's warning referred to above (1 Peter 5:8) remains a very good one indeed. For if the devil can seduce us into ignoring Peter's warning, then the devil will have already won half the battle. Doctrine and life will be his easy targets, and Christians his easy prey.

Whether the temptation is to dilute sound doctrine or to compromise the Christian life, the devil likes to start out with a small temptation and work up to the bigger ones as one error begets another and one compromise makes another all the easier. How clear that is already in the Garden of Eden at the time of the fall of Adam and Eve!

This is how the devil so often proceeds: First, he minimizes the sin to which he tempts us, lest the conscience be shocked and resist. After he has succeeded in convincing us that sin is trivial and nothing to be concerned about, it is an easy matter for him to seduce into one sin after another, until our fall is complete. Then, after he has seduced us into sin by convincing us that sin doesn't really matter, he comes with his second favorite trick: He maximizes guilt. First, he says the sin is nothing to worry about. Then, after the sin has been committed, he bellows through the conscience: "You did what? And now you imagine that you will be forgiven? Never! Do you think that you can play God for a fool?" He tries to drive us to despair of the grace of God. In Satan's mind too doctrine and life are always connected. First, he lies to us about God's law and tries to get us to believe that God doesn't really mean it or take it all that seriously. When he succeeds with that lie, he follows up by lying about the gospel, insisting that God doesn't mean that either. Thus he seeks to deceive the careless, bring them to shame, and destroy their faith.

Consider the example of King David in 2 Samuel 11,12. First he was tempted to neglect his work, become lazy, and ignore his duty. That seemed like such an unimportant sin. But it provided the occasion for lust, then for adultery, then for murder. When his fall was complete, David was ready to despair. He turned his back on confession and repentance until God sent his pastor to him with the powerful message of the law and then with the life and faith-restoring message of the gospel.

The unbelieving world

The second cause or source of actual sin is the world itself. Created by God as good, it has become through its misuse by sinners a source of sin. The devil makes it a favorite weapon in his arsenal for attacking the Christian. So much are we surrounded by the world, by the visible and the enjoyment of the visible, that it is easy to be deceived into thinking that the world, with its wealth and pleasure, is what life is all about. How many Christians have let their faith starve to death while they have satisfied the desire for idleness or pleasure or a few extra dollars of overtime when the Word of God was being preached and the sacraments administered? How many children after confirmation have given up the faithful hearing of the Word in favor of hearing noise that appeals only to the flesh? Perhaps they listen to the appeal of poorly chosen friends. Such friends already have only the world as their god; they are enslaved to its fleeting promises of pleasure and heedless of the consequences of their behavior either for this life or the next.

Following faithless friends, so many turn their backs on the purity given in the gospel and called for in the Christian life. After a busy Saturday night with the world, they are just too tired—or perhaps feeling too ashamed—to spend time with Jesus on Sunday morning. They really meant it at confirmation when they pledged undying loyalty to Christ and his Word. But then as their connection to the Word became ever more distant, they were ever more easily seduced by the fleeting and imagined pleasures of the world. Then they were drawn away further still by the supposed wisdom of the world in natural science or the humanities. Finally, swallowed up by the world, they may turn away completely from the everlasting joy and the ultimate truth of the gospel.

The world seems so impressive, so really smart to them, and the gospel just too old-fashioned, too simple. How many, whether young or old, at some point in life stop looking at the cross because other sights seem for a moment more appealing? So seductive is the lure of pleasure or of worldly success or wisdom, so rich the promises of happiness or fulfillment if we just cast the Word of God aside and with it duty, honor, reverence, and obedience!

That the world and all things in it perish with their use does not occur to the one who has abandoned the Word for the pleasure of the moment. That even the promise of pleasure and satisfaction is a lie likewise escapes the notice of most. But think about it: Who in the worship of wealth ever was satisfied that he had enough of it and that it was safe and secure? And who in the worship of pleasure was not ultimately left alone with nothing to show for his worship but guilt or shame? Who in the service of this world's wisdom had real peace of conscience and the promise of eternal life? All these had only illusion and delusion, only the assurance of dust and ashes at the end, only a fearful waiting for the judgment of God in eternity for casting him, his Son, his Word, and sacraments aside in favor of the temporary, the shameful, or the pretend wisdom of the moment.

Jesus has warned us in advance: "No one can serve two masters. Either he will hate the one and love the other, or he will be devoted to the one and despise the other. You cannot serve both God and Money" (Matthew 6:24). He urges us to think carefully and seriously about the exchange we make when we trade in the treasures that are ours in following him and his Word for the tinsel that the world has to offer. In Mark 8 he puts it most succinctly: "What good is it for a man to gain the whole world, yet forfeit his soul? Or what can a man give in exchange for his soul?" (vv. 36,37).

Let us say, for the sake of argument, that it was possible to gain the whole world, all of its wealth and health, all of its wisdom and fame and popularity. Eventually, with the passing of time, each of them would fade away and disappear. When sickness comes or when one is all alone or in the hour of death and on the day of judgment, what does such a one have? How will he rescue himself from sickness and loneliness, from death and judgment? All the world's wealth and wisdom cannot save him. Of course, even the wealthiest, most popular, most healthy, or most wise never get the whole world; they forfeit their souls for much less than the whole world. If it's a fool's bargain to trade in the treasure of Christ and all that he is for us in the gospel for the whole world, how much more of a fool's bargain is it to settle for the baubles and the tinsel that would be ours on our best day apart from Christ? For baubles and tinsel are the best we can hope for in the exchange; such trinkets are a long way from the whole world that even a fool must know can never be his.

In the great parable of the sower and the seed Jesus warns us against being deceived by the promise of satisfaction in the wealth and pleasure of the world. Those thus deceived, he says, are choked by the deceitfulness of riches; they get the opposite of what riches promise when they turn their ears from the Word and their eyes from Jesus in favor of fleeting pleasure and perishing wealth (Matthew 13:22).

And St. John warns us as well:

> Do not love the world or anything in the world. If anyone loves the world, the love of the Father is not in him. For everything in the world—the cravings of sinful man, the lust of his eyes and the boasting of what he has and does—comes not from the Father but from the world. The world and its desires pass away, but the man who does the will of God lives forever. (1 John 2:15-17)

St. John, of course, is not telling us that we should despise God's creation. Not at all! Insofar as it is God's creation and used as he intended it, the world is good. It reminds us of our Creator and his glory (Psalms 19 and 33). Its wealth can and should be used and also enjoyed for our own maintenance, for the support of our families and the needy, and for the work of the church. There were people in both the Old and New Testaments who were wealthy and were not condemned for it. The patriarchs in Genesis were wealthy. David and Solomon were wealthy, as were a number of other heroes of faith. In the New Testament one of Paul's epistles is addressed to a wealthy man, his letter to Philemon. It is when the world, its wealth, and its pleasure become the goal of life and life's meaning for us that its use is perverted, faith is lost, and the sinner perishes with his false god. Given God's great generosity to us in his gifts from the world, the Christian is always well advised to watch out that he not fall for the temptation to worship the gifts instead of worshiping the Giver. With just such a caution in mind St. Paul urges us:

> Godliness with contentment is great gain. For we brought nothing into the world, and we can take nothing out of it. But if we have food and clothing, we will be content with that. People who want to get rich fall into temptation and a trap and into many foolish and harmful desires that plunge men into ruin and destruction. For the love of money is a root of all kinds of evil. Some people, eager for money, have wandered from the faith and pierced themselves with many griefs. (1 Timothy 6:6-10)

Our own sinful nature

The third source and cause of actual sin is our own sinful and fallen nature. When Jesus was tempted in the wilderness (Matthew 4:1-11), the temptations had to come to him from outside of himself. For he had no sinful nature from which temptations or sinful desires could arise. But since the fall, as we have already seen in our consideration of the doctrine of original sin, we are conceived and born in sin. The Bible often refers to that sinful nature with the term *flesh.* The sinful nature is called *flesh,* whether the appeal of temptation is to our body or our ego or our intellect or our emotions. It is our own sinful flesh that tempts us to envy, greed, desire for revenge, become addicted to pleasure, pride in our own supposed wisdom, and the like. To say that the devil uses our flesh as his platform or ally in tempting us is also certainly true. He doesn't have to work very hard to convince our flesh; our flesh is inclined to these things even apart from the devil's prompting. For our sinful flesh is deeply imbedded in our inmost being, in our soul no less than our body. As we noted earlier, the body is ultimately the tool and instrument of the soul. We are not followers of Plato or of the Manicheans. Platonists and Manicheans taught that the body is evil and the soul is good. That's not what the Bible means when it speaks of the sinful "flesh." The body does not sin by itself or apart from the soul. The soul is just as sinful as the body. For the whole of human nature is corrupted by original sin, with the soul using the body as the instrument for accomplishing its "fleshly" desires.

Thus our own nature, corrupted as it is by original sin, is a source and cause of actual sin, together with the devil and the world. They form an unholy alliance with one and the same goal: the destruction of faith. St. James puts it this way: "Each one is tempted when, by his own evil desire, he is dragged away and enticed. Then, after desire has conceived, it gives birth to sin; and sin, when it is full-grown, gives birth to death" (James 1:14,15). The flesh, our sinful human nature, in this life is so closely allied with the devil and the world that it is difficult for us to see where the temptation of one leaves off and the other begins. Each of us can testify to the closeness of that alliance and the way it works itself out in James' description of actual sin: An evil thought pops into the head—whether a lust for forbidden pleasure, a desire for revenge, a bit of envy or jealousy, a momentary delight in another's misfortune. And what happens? Is the desire immediately expelled by the cry to God for mercy and strength? Often the mind toys with the temptation of the devil or the lure of the world, plays a while with the idea. It doesn't take long before the sin in the mind (which because of original sin was prone to that sin anyway) is hard to expel or is turned into a sinful outward act. Only in heaven will we finally be free in both body and soul from the sinful flesh and its two prods, the devil and the world.

But how do we deal in the here and now with the problem of a sinful nature prodded by the devil and poked by the world? The Christian, though still weighed down by the sinful nature and plagued by temptations from the devil and the world, has received a renewed nature from the Holy Spirit working through the gospel in the Word and in his baptism. God adopts us to be his children. We have been redeemed. We are forgiven. That forgiveness and our salvation are perfect and complete. Now that new nature created by the gospel wants to struggle against the sinful flesh, the old nature. But the flesh in combination with the devil and the world continue to plague and tempt, to entice and seduce, with the goal of destroying faith and thus killing that new nature. St. Paul recognized the problem in his own life and in ours as well when he spoke of the constant struggle going on inside of him. On the one side is the Christian nature in us, which wants nothing but what God wants and which strives in all of life to carry out the will of God according to his Word. On the other side is the sinful flesh, which wants nothing but its own will and the fulfillment of self-serving desires. St. Paul says:

> I know that nothing good lives in me, that is, in my sinful nature. For I have the desire to do what is good, but I cannot carry it out. For what I do is not the good I want to do; no, the evil I do not want to do—this I keep on doing. Now if I do what I do not want to do, it is no longer I who do it, but it is sin living in me that does it. So I find this law [i.e., this principle] at work: When I want to do good, evil is right there with me. For in my inner being I delight in God's law. (Romans 7:18-22)

So persistent is that old nature, St. Paul is saying, that no matter what good my Christian self wants to do, the sinful flesh is always there to obstruct it, to prevent it, to corrupt it, and to spoil the good. This is what Jesus is talking about when he tells us in Mark 8 that we who follow him must bear the cross of self-denial. It is often a heavy cross and one that is difficult to carry; for it is the burden in the soul of warfare between the always sinful flesh and the Christian nature that really wants to follow Christ.

Who does not know that from daily experience? The Christian within wants to hear the Word of God; the flesh distracts us even when we do hear it, so that much of it is quickly forgotten. The Christian nature wants to pray; the flesh interrupts the prayer and turns our attention elsewhere. The Christian inside wants to help the poor and support the spreading of the gospel; the flesh complains over every penny thus "lost." The Christian nature gets up in the morning with the plan and the desire to be useful and to serve; the sinful flesh is quick to impatience, to annoyance at petty slights, to irritation when others get in the way or are unkind and ungrateful. And so on and on it goes. The struggle between the two is such that in this life we are able to produce not one single work that is perfect; all of our works, even the best of them, are stained by some fault attached to them by the sinful flesh and its unwillingness and hostility. It is correct to say that even in our best works we sin because not one of them is ever perfect.

But what is the point of struggling against these powerful foes, the devil, the world, and our own sinful flesh? Why try to avoid actual sin if at the end of the day we must still confess that we have failed even in our best efforts to offer up to God so much as a moment that was totally devoted to him? St. Paul gives us the answer. After wrestling with the same dilemma, he sums up both the problem and its solution: "What a wretched man I am! Who will rescue me from this body of death? Thanks be to God—through Jesus Christ our Lord!" (Romans 7:24,25). He then continues in chapter 8 to describe the Christian as triumphant over the sinful flesh, not because he has succeeded in destroying it but because Christ has forgiven all our sins, including the sins that stain our good works. Yes, so perfect is God's forgiveness, even of the stains on our best works, that God delights in our thus forgiven works and is pleased with them.

And so St. Paul encourages us to continue to strive after those works which please God—not because the works in themselves are perfect but because in Christ we together with the works are perfect! For we have been forgiven! He speaks of that never-finished struggle to serve God perfectly when he says, "Not that I have already obtained all this, or have already been made perfect, but I press on to take hold of that for which Christ Jesus took hold of me" (Philippians 3:12). That is just another way of saying that he is striving to become what he already is; he already is perfect and a saint by virtue of the full forgiveness of his sins. Now he presses on to become in his daily life what he already is by faith, even though he knows that he will not reach that holy goal of perfection until he gets to heaven.

So then we have here a great paradox: Even though the devil, the world, and the flesh seem to win at least part of every battle (since no work in this life is perfect), nevertheless the devil, the world, and our own sinful flesh have lost the war and are defeated! We are already victors! For Christ gives us his own victory by virtue of his death for us and his rising again. Even now the victory achieved for us by Christ is evident in the persistence of faith in spite of all its opponents and obstacles. In heaven that victory won for us will be fully realized also in us. For in heaven all temptations of the devil, the world, and our own flesh will cease; sin will be gone forever and so too its horrible consequences of shame and guilt, pain and loss. As Christ set aside the cross in his resurrection, so too the pain of our struggle will end when we join him in the eternal victory celebration in heaven.

Thus, in spite of the temptations of the devil and the world, in spite of the persistence of the flesh in staining even our best works, our Christian lives and our willingness to carry the cross of self-denial are pleasing to God. They are pleasing to him, not because they are perfect but because they are forgiven—covered with the blood of Christ our Savior, washed in the flood of Baptism, and fed by the living bread of heaven in the Word and the Sacrament.

Therefore we strive against the flesh out of love to him for our salvation, not in order to gain that salvation or contribute to it. We strive against the devil, the world, and our own sinful flesh lest we again become their captives and slaves. St. Paul puts it this way:

> Just as you used to offer the parts of your body in slavery to impurity and to ever-increasing wickedness, so now offer them in slavery to righteousness leading to holiness. When you were slaves to sin, you were free from the control of righteousness. What benefit did you reap at that time from the things you are now ashamed of? Those things result in death! But now that you have been set free from sin and have become slaves to God, the benefit you reap leads to holiness, and the result is eternal life. For the wages of sin is death, but the gift of God is eternal life in Christ Jesus our Lord. (Romans 6:19-23)

> We have an obligation—but it is not to the sinful nature, to live according to it. For if you live according to the sinful nature, you will die; but if by the Spirit you put to death the misdeeds of the body, you will live, because those who are led by the Spirit of God are the sons of God. (Romans 8:12-14)

So the life of the Christian is a sacrifice of thanksgiving to God for the salvation received. It is a life that grows in love for God and in service to those around us. That important work of thanksgiving shows itself best in this struggle against the devil and the world and our own sinful flesh. That struggle is real. But so too is our rejoicing in the Savior's gift of forgiveness, by which he renews both our strength and our desire to continue with that struggle. Yes, and it's important to remember that God is pleased, is delighted with our effort. He follows our progress with the greatest interest and with his blessing. He even saves up in his memory all that we have done in gratitude for our salvation. On the Last Day he will bring it all out for the whole world to see and marvel at (Psalm 33:18-22; 147:11; Matthew 25:34-40).

It is important to note in any consideration of the sources and causes of sin that God is not the source or cause of sin. Nor does he will or want us to sin. No one can say when he sins that it must have been the will of God or it would not have happened. Sin by its very definition is contrary to the will of God. St. John declares, "God is light; in him there is no darkness at all. If we claim to have fellowship with him yet walk in the darkness, we lie and do not live by the truth" (1 John 1:5,6). And St. James says, "When tempted, no one should say, 'God is tempting me.' For God cannot be tempted by evil, nor does he tempt anyone" (James 1:13). As noted in the consideration of the attributes of God, God is holy and righteous in his essence. He is totally separated from sin. The Formula of Concord emphasizes the truth that God is not the cause of sin in its consideration of the reason why some do not believe and ultimately are therefore damned. It says:

> For all preparation for condemnation stems from the devil and human beings, through sin, and in absolutely no way from God. . . . The only cause of condemnation is sin, for "the wages of sin is death" [Rom. 6:23]. Just as God does not will sin, and takes no pleasure in sin, so he does not will the death of the sinner and has no pleasure in his or her condemnation. (FC SD XI, 81 p. 653)

To be sure, God still permits the devil, the world, and our own sinful flesh to be active. His permission serves the useful purpose of giving us the opportunity to show him our love and gratitude for our salvation by resisting temptations and struggling against the rule of sin. That was true already in the Garden of Eden. God told Adam and Eve not to eat of the tree of the knowledge of good and evil. That command gave them the opportunity to show their love, their loyalty, and their trust and obedience. Their obedience would not earn them the status of God's beloved children; they already had that. Rather, obedience would give evidence of their delight in that status. That's the way it is with us too; obedience to God's Word both in doctrine and in life does not earn our status as forgiven children of God. We have that blessed condition by virtue of the forgiveness won for us by Christ and given to us by faith in his gospel promise. Obedience and the struggle against the devil, the world, and our flesh are fruits of faith, the results of faith, not its cause.

In sum, actual sin is distinguished from original sin. Actual sin is any failure in life or in doctrine; it is any thought, word, or deed that does not perfectly conform to the Word of God. Its cause is the devil, the world, and our own sinful flesh.

The three kinds of law in the Bible

The political law

Having considered the causes of actual sin, we turn next to a consideration of the law. For actual sin is the breaking of law. The Bible contains three different kinds of laws. In the Old Testament, God gave the people of Israel a *political law* that served as a constitution and legal framework for the governance of the nation of Israel. The political law assumed that the nation would have in it both believers and unbelievers. It assumed that even believers at times and in the weakness of their sinful nature might violate the person or property of a fellow citizen. The political law was intended to direct the government of Israel as it dealt with such outward violations of another's person or property. Because the Old Testament nation of Israel was to serve as the guardian and chief transmitter of God's promise of a Savior, church and state were tightly joined together. That's why idolatry and the teaching of false doctrine were also crimes against the nation and were to be punished.

The political law of the Old Testament is considered at length in the book of Deuteronomy. Deuteronomy is Moses' farewell address to the nation, delivered shortly before his death and Israel's crossing of the Jordan into the Promised Land. God through Moses gave instructions for the setting up of courts (17:8-13), provided for those guilty of accidental murder (19:1-13), set up a draft law for the army (20:1-9), forbade the charging of interest (23:19,20), dealt with marriage and divorce issues (24:1-5), and the like. All in all the political law of the Old Testament provided Israel with a fairly comprehensive legal code.

From their reading of the political law in the Old Testament some have come to the incorrect conclusion that the Bible contradicts itself. For the political law sums up the matter of punishment for crimes against persons and property by declaring, "Show no pity: life for life, eye for eye, tooth for tooth, hand for hand, foot for foot" (Deuteronomy 19:21). But Jesus in the Sermon on the Mount says, "You have heard that it was said, 'Eye for eye, and tooth for tooth.' But I tell you, Do not resist an evil person. If someone strikes you on the right cheek, turn to him the other also" (Matthew 5:38,39). Indeed, much of the Sermon on the Mount appears at first glance to contradict the political law in Deuteronomy.

In point of fact, there is no contradiction at all. In the Sermon on the Mount, Jesus is not speaking about legal relationships and legal rights in a nation. He is not addressing the government. He is speaking about the behavior of Christians as children of God striving against their own sinful flesh. He is speaking about behavior governed not by legal norms but by a heart in which he rules by his Word. St. Paul speaks the same way in Romans 12:9-21 and elsewhere. Jesus' words in the Sermon on the Mount are his own commentary on the Old Testament political law; it was designed for that particular government. It is not a blueprint of personal behavior for the New Testament Christian. Whether some of those laws might serve nations well today and others not so well is not a subject that is taken up in the New Testament. The New Testament does not as such contain or concern itself with setting up forms of government and political legislation. The teachings of Jesus and the apostles about the law are concerned with Christians as individuals in their relationships with God and with others; they deal with the way that Christians should reflect their love for Christ in those relationships.

The point is that the political law bound those to whom it was addressed. It was addressed to the Old Testament nation of Israel, not to the New Testament believer. Thus, we are not bound by it. Jesus makes that clear. The political law, for example, called for the execution of false teachers (Deuteronomy 13). But Jesus, by no means minimizing the seriousness of false doctrine, tells us to "watch out for false prophets" (Matthew 7:15). He doesn't tell us to put them to death. St. Paul also urges us to have nothing to do with false doctrine and false teachers (Romans 16:17). But the ultimate punishment of false teachers is left to God; for the Christian there is the warning to have nothing to do with them in our religious life. We heed Paul's injunction in Romans 16 and in the many other passages in God's Word that warn against false teaching and false teachers when we decline to worship with them or engage in church work with them. That refusal is a strong witness that we take all of God's Word seriously. However, nowhere are we urged to use political means to persecute or suppress false doctrine or false teachers. Our ultimate weapon against false doctrine and false teachers is the Word of God itself and a faithful teaching and preaching of that Word. Faith is created and error corrected, not by the sword of the state but by the pure preaching and teaching of the Word of God.

Ultimately the political law of the Old Testament dealt primarily with outward behavior. The law that applies to us however deals first and foremost with the attitude of the heart and then with the outward behavior that is to reflect that attitude of the heart (about which more will be said shortly in our consideration of the moral law).[2]

The ceremonial law

The second type of law in the Old Testament is called the *ceremonial law.* The ceremonial law governed the worship life of the nation of Israel. It prescribed the forms for public worship in the tabernacle and later in the temple. It governed the various types of sacrifices to be offered, the religious calendar, and the provision for priests and others who should fill the religious offices of the land. Exodus and Leviticus deal extensively with the ceremonial law of Israel. The chief function of the ceremonial law was to point the way to the Savior. By its many regulations for ceremonial cleanliness and sacrifices for various types of sins and offenses, the ceremonial law showed the need for a Savior. Even more it pointed to the Savior who would one day come and be both High Priest and sacrifice for the sins of the world.

The New Testament letter to the Hebrews speaks beautifully of Christ as the fulfillment of the Old Testament ceremonial law (cf. especially Hebrews 4–10). St. Paul tells us that the ceremonial law has served its purpose and that it no longer applies to us. He calls it a "shadow of the things that were to come; the reality, however, is found in Christ" (Colossians 2:17). One might understand what something is or looks like at least in part by looking at its shadow. But once the object itself becomes visible, there is no further need to look at the shadow. The Old Testament ceremonial law was such a shadow; it gave a partial picture of Christ and his work for the believers of the Old

---

[2]We may note in passing that the Ninth Commandment contains an element of political law in a moral law setting. It forbids coveting, i.e., desiring that which God clearly does not want us to have; that's the moral law in the Ninth Commandment. In Old Testament Israel it was a sin even to desire a neighbor's house, if it had been inherited, because the neighbor was not allowed by the law to sell it (cf. Numbers 27:8-11; 36; 1 Kings 21). We may desire to purchase our neighbor's house; in and of itself that wouldn't be a sin, even if the house had been inherited. But if we could not afford it or the neighbor refused to consider selling it and we continued to desire it, that would be an example of breaking the moral law in the Ninth Commandment.

Testament who longed for the Savior's coming. But now its only remaining purpose is to demonstrate that God has indeed fulfilled the shadow in Christ. Thus, the Old Testament ceremonial law does not bind the New Testament Christian or the New Testament church.[3]

The moral law

The third kind of law contained in the Bible is the *moral law.* The moral law was initially written in the hearts of Adam and Eve at creation. But since the fall it is only dimly and darkly present in the hearts of their descendants. To the extent that it is there at all, we call it the *natural law.* People know, for example, that stealing is wrong. They know that unfaithfulness to friends or to a spouse is wrong. They may know that drunkenness and pornography and murder are wrong. Most of the moral and legal codes devised by philosophers or nations are built to a greater or lesser extent on this natural law, this remnant of the law of God written in the hearts of men already at the time of creation. Law codes based on natural law are designed to keep the outward behavior of people in check and to punish those who trample on the lives and property of others. At the same time it is a testimony to the perversity of mankind in general that the laws of nations and states take up whole shelves, even whole libraries. That's necessary because for every law some will find ten ways around it, so that then ten new laws have to be written to cover the loopholes drilled into even the best designed legal codes.

Because no one possesses the natural law in all its original perfection on account of original sin, natural law is insufficient for knowing the will of God. The natural law is so blurred in the sinful flesh that it is impossible for people even to agree on much of it. Everyone, for example, may agree that murder and stealing are wrong, but finding two people who can completely agree on the definition of murder or stealing is quite another matter. Nevertheless, the more closely the natural law in people and in society corresponds to the moral law written in the Bible (in particular the Fourth through Tenth Commandments), the more orderly and peaceful that society is likely to be.

---

[3]The reference to the Sabbath in the Third Commandment is ceremonial law. Luther in his Small Catechism explanation for the Third Commandment captures well the moral law heart and core of the commandment when he tells us that we should not despise God's Word and its preaching but gladly hear and learn that Word. In the New Testament we are not bound by the ceremonial law of the Third Commandment, namely, worship on the Old Testament Sabbath, but the moral law behind that ceremonial regulation does still apply to us.

One of the greatest benefits of the natural law is that it serves as a springboard or a starting point for our hearing of the law revealed in the Bible. The natural law, for example, tells us that we should not murder. But it is in the moral law of God in the Bible that we hear from God himself what murder is and where it begins. It begins with hatred in the heart. And so the moral law in the Bible bids us to love God and in such love to serve our neighbor (Matthew 22:37-40; Romans 13:10). How we should serve our neighbor is summarized in the Fourth through Tenth Commandments. When the criteria of the moral law in the Bible are applied to the natural law, I learn that stealing is not just armed robbery, which the natural law could teach almost anyone. Stealing is also any act that takes from my neighbor what is rightfully his, even if I can find some technicality in the law to hide behind—one sees a lot of that sort of thing in contract disputes and in law suits over inheritances. Stealing is also a refusal to help my neighbor to keep and protect what is his. Stealing is taking an unfair advantage of him, cheating, unfaithfulness on the job, even cheating on my taxes (since it robs the state of what it is legally entitled to in the law); stealing is failing to help my neighbor when he needs my help in protecting his property. Murder in the light of the moral law in the Bible's commentary on the Fifth Commandment is not just shooting someone; it is the lack of love in the heart that prompts one to hurt or to fail to help a neighbor in his time of need (1 John 3:15; Romans 12:19; Isaiah 58:6,7).

In short, natural law is a beginning; it is unclear in many and to some extent blurred in all because of the devastation on the minds and hearts of people that comes from original sin. But because original sin has darkened the mind so that it can no longer fully grasp the will of God by nature, God gave the moral law in his Word. It is summarized in the Ten Commandments.

While there are numerous instances in the New Testament where God makes it clear that the political law and the ceremonial law were binding only on the Old Testament nation of Israel, the same is not true with respect to the moral law. The moral law is repeated again and again in the New Testament. It is an expression of the unchanging will of God for all people of all times.

Sin by definition is the breaking of the moral law. The breaking of the law is actual sin as distinguished from original sin. Jesus summed up the whole of the moral law when he answered the question of the scribe who asked him which commandment was the greatest.

> "The most important one," answered Jesus, "is this: 'Hear, O Israel, the Lord our God, the Lord is one. Love the Lord your

> God with all your heart and with all your soul and with all your mind and with all your strength.' The second is this: 'Love your neighbor as yourself.' There is no commandment greater than these." (Mark 12:29-31)

All of the rest of the commandments are contained by implication in these two. Any thought, word, or deed that does not reflect perfect love to God and obedience to his Word is a sin against the first great commandment. The first three of the Ten Commandments, which we refer to as the *First Table of the Law,* summarize how God himself wants to be served. The Fourth through Tenth Commandments comprise the *Second Table of the Law* and deal with how we should show our love to God by serving him in the service of our neighbor.

The First Table of the Law

Jesus spoke of the perfect love for God that is required in the First Table of the Law as a love like that which he himself had for his Father. His love for his Father was a love that was perfect in every respect. His Father sent him into the world to save sinners (John 3:16), and he came willingly to carry out his Father's will. He declared shortly before his suffering and death:

> "When you have lifted up the Son of Man, then you will know that I am the one I claim to be and that *I do nothing on my own but speak just what the Father has taught me.* The one who sent me is with me; he has not left me alone, *for I always do what pleases him."* (John 8:28,29)

That is the kind of love required of us all in the First Table of the Law, a love in which our entire life—our body and soul; our reason, will and emotions—conforms to the Word of God. It is the kind of love of which the psalmist sings when he writes, "Whom have I in heaven but you? And earth has nothing I desire besides you. My flesh and my heart fail, but God is the strength of my heart and my portion forever" (Psalm 73:25,26).[4] Jesus tells us plainly that such love is not optional but required:

> "If anyone would come after me, he must deny himself and take up his cross and follow me. For whoever wants to save his life will lose it, but whoever loses his life for me and for the gospel will save it. What good is it for a man to gain the whole world, yet for-

---

[4]Luther has noted well that "the whole Psalter [is] but meditations and exercises based on the First Commandment" (LC Preface, 18 p. 382).

> feit his soul? Or what can a man give in exchange for his soul?" (Mark 8:34-37)

And again:

> "Anyone who loves his father or mother more than me is not worthy of me; anyone who loves his son or daughter more than me is not worthy of me; and anyone who does not take his cross and follow me is not worthy of me." (Matthew 10:37,38)

Such a love to God must be rooted and grounded in the revealed Word of God, not in one's own thoughts, imagination, or feelings. That is the essence of both the Second and the Third Commandments. We love God when we know, love, and obey his Word, as Jesus said, "If you hold to my teaching, you are really my disciples" (John 8:31). It is a commonly accepted notion these days that any teaching about God or religion is as good as any other. That is clearly not what God has said in his Word. His Word alone: love for it and obedience to its every doctrine and command is the beginning of the law. No obedience to the law is possible, no matter how pious or noble that obedience may seem outwardly, without this very beginning, namely, love for God as he has revealed himself in his Word. How foolish it would be for a child to tell his or her mother, "I love you and want to prove it by breaking all of the dishes, instead of by washing them as you told me to do!" Just so foolish, indeed perverse, is the one who declares, "God, I will love you, not as you have told me to love you but as I see fit. And I expect you to be more pleased with my way than with yours, for I have concluded that my way is better and wiser than yours!"

It should be shocking to us that so many think just that way. They declare that they love God and then do exactly as they please. They announce to all that they have decided that all religions are basically alike and that, therefore, God should be satisfied with any and every one of them, whether they deny all or part of his Word, yes, even if they reject his Son. Outward acts of kindness to our fellow man, even heroic works for the benefit of humanity, cannot be pleasing to God where there is not first a reverence for God and his revelation of himself in Christ. That is why the First Commandment is first also in Jesus' summary of the law. All obedience to God begins with the First Table of the Law; no obedience to the Second Table of the Law (Fourth through Tenth Commandments) can be God-pleasing apart from love to God and the desire to submit to his Word.

Accordingly, the Second Commandment bids us to make good and proper use of God's name as he has revealed it in his Word. We honor his name by clinging to that Word. We honor his name when we pray to him and to him alone. We praise him for all that he is and for all that he does for us and for all that he gives us, especially in the Word and sacraments. A true God-pleasing use of God's name begins especially with a receiving in faith the gift of the Savior and of the salvation offered and sealed to us in his Word and sacraments. For that's God's favorite name: Savior! Any use of God's name apart from a delight in this his favorite name and all that that name gives is an abomination to God. Even fallen reason should be able to figure it out: Why would we expect God to be pleased with anything that we say or do if we reject his greatest gift, the gift of his Son for our salvation? It should come as a shock to no one when Jesus declares, "He who does not honor the Son does not honor the Father, who sent him" (John 5:23). St. John makes the same point: "No one who denies the Son has the Father; whoever acknowledges the Son has the Father also" (1 John 2:23).

Just as the best use of God's name is to receive from him the salvation that his favorite name promises, so also every other use of his name is worthy only when it agrees with his revelation of himself in his Word. So the keeping of the Second Commandment requires faith in his saving work; it bids us to cling to and teach his Word in all of its truth and purity, and it invites us to trust his name of Savior as we call to him for mercy, pray in every need, and give thanks for all that he is as our Savior.

It is easy to see that the Third Commandment is little more than a restatement of the First and Second Commandments. For when we worship the one true and only God, when we hold his name sacred and use it in accord with his Word, then it will be obvious that we gladly hear and learn that Word. Receiving what he offers impels us to respond with adoration and with a sharing of that Word and its saving benefit.

The Second Table of the Law

In the Second Table of the Law, any thought, word, or deed that does not reflect love to our neighbor, i.e., all our fellow human beings, is a sin against God. Jesus tells us, "Love your neighbor as yourself" (Mark 12:31). For so much does God love our neighbor that he counts anything a sin that does not serve our neighbor's best interest. He says, for example, in Proverbs 14:31, "He who oppresses the poor shows contempt for their Maker, but whoever is kind to the needy honors God."

The question arises then: Just what is love and what is my neighbor's best interest? *Situational ethics* and *moral relativism* declare that love is indeed the all-important essence of correct behavior toward our neighbor. However, the love in *situational ethics* is defined not by God in his Word but by the individual in a specific situation, even if the action planned contradicts the moral law in the Ten Commandments. Contrary to the love of situational ethics, the simple axiom remains true: We cannot defend sin by calling it love! The man who claims that he loves a woman and then behaves with her contrary to the Sixth Commandment defiles her and makes her an adulteress in the eyes of God. That's not love but lust, no matter what the man says. The woman who seduces a man into behavior that is contrary to the Sixth Commandment turns his face away from the face of God to vice and immorality. No matter how much she may insist that it is love, God's Word decrees otherwise. The abortion defender, unless the life of the mother is clearly in danger,[5] defends murder. The same is true of the one who supports assisted suicide or the use of active means for ending the life of the weak and terminally ill. These too conjure up some sort of meaning for love that will justify behavior contrary to the Word of God.

It is all too common these days to hear people, even those who consider themselves Christians, defending sins in the name of love. Love however does not rebel against the law; love submits to the will of God as he has expressed that will in his Word. Those who set love against the law need to think more seriously about the judgment that God pronounces on all such perversions of love in Romans 1:18-32. His conclusion and the divine verdict over all such still stands: "The wrath of God is being revealed from heaven against all the godlessness and wickedness of men who suppress the truth by their wickedness" (Romans 1:18).

Some even go so far as to maintain that love for our neighbor and the desire for his salvation justifies keeping quiet about teachings in God's Word that might offend people and keep them away from church. They remind us that Jesus has commanded us to go into all the world and make disciples of all nations. How, they object, can we do that if we insist on teaching what the Bible teaches about the six-day creation, the

---

[5]Abortion in cases where the life of the mother is at issue is still the taking of a human life, but in such instances a choice has to be made between two lives. Such a gruesome ethical dilemma and choice is painful indeed and in the extreme. When Christians have to make such a choice, they will bow low beneath what appears to be the heavy hand of God and cry to him for his mercy; they will wait as patiently as they can for the day when God will raise them up from beneath the pain of such a choice (1 Peter 5:6). That is advice easy to give, but difficult to bear. Only the power of God's promises in the gospel (again, especially those in Romans 8) makes it possible.

proper roles for men and women, the Bible's teaching about marriage and sexual relations outside of marriage, about homosexuality, and so on? They reason that teaching such doctrines only serves to drive people away from the gospel. What such objectors fail to notice or mention is that in the same verses that bid us make disciples of all nations, Jesus tells us how to do that; he tells us to do it by "teaching them to obey *everything* I have commanded you" (Matthew 28:18-20).

We reject, therefore, as altogether blasphemous and contrary also to both Tables of the Law the standards of moral relativism and of situational ethics. It is never an act of love to depart from the clear Word of God. God himself tells us how to show our love for our neighbor and defines our neighbor's best interest by what he commands and forbids in the Second Table of the Law, the Fourth through Tenth Commandments. He does not leave it up to us to figure out how our neighbor is to be served.

Love is, to be sure, the internal prerequisite of all God-pleasing obedience; a lack of love makes any and all thoughts, words, and deeds with respect to our neighbor actual sins, even if the outward behavior appears to be decent or helpful. That point needs to be emphasized because it is not at all self-evident to our fallen nature. Again, so great is God's love for all that he wants all to be served by all and counts anything less than loving service to all as a sin against himself. But it is God who defines what love is and who tells us how we should demonstrate that love in serving.

That service begins in the Fourth Commandment, in which God tells us that he wants us to respect and submit to those he has placed over us in positions of authority. This begins, of course, with parents. But included are those also who act in the interest of and for the preservation of order in government and in the church. Parents, officers of the government, pastors and teachers of the church—all these are his representatives. To despise them or to rebel against them is to despise the One who has sent them.[6]

The Fifth, Sixth, and Seventh Commandments tell us that it is love to God when we serve our neighbor by helping him to protect his life and family, his honor, and even his property.

Our neighbor's good name and its defense fall under the Eighth Commandment. Any use of our tongue that hurts his good name is an offense against God. The only exceptions to the rule occur when it is

---

[6]The Fourth Commandment will be considered more thoroughly in chapter 16 under the subheading of "The three estates."

necessary out of love for others that a public crime be reported to the police and when it is necessary to rebuke false doctrine. It would be loveless to our neighbors to know that Hans was the thief pillaging the neighborhood and then to keep quiet about it. It would likewise be loveless to keep silent in the presence of false doctrine that is spread as poison to the soul—that's certainly not what Jesus did and not what the apostles and prophets did either.

Someone might object: What should it matter to God that people kill one another, trash their marriages, or steal from one another? It hurts him in his essence not in the least. He is still God. Why should it bother him that children are disobedient and disrespectful or that spouses cheat on one another? What difference should it make to him that people lie, that they lie even under oath in court and on legal documents? Why should he care that they gossip either thoughtlessly or maliciously? Why should it matter to him that some people can't find enough ways of putting others down in order to exalt themselves?

To be sure, none of these crimes born in the heart and carried out in the body by word and deed directly touch God. So why should he care? It is as simple as this: God has given the law, not out of concern for himself but out of love for us and for all. Yes, he counts it a sin against himself chiefly in this, that we did not love him enough to love our neighbor; for he loves that neighbor just as much as he loves us. That shouldn't be so difficult to understand. If someone hurts one you love, will you not be angered and offended as much as if the harm had been aimed at you? So God takes our behavior towards our neighbor, whether helpful or hurtful, very personally! Luther reflects this thought well in his Small Catechism with his introduction to each of his explanations of the Second Table of the Law. He tells us that "we should fear and love *God*" that we do what the specific commandment requires of us in our behavior towards others.

Thus, while there is a distinction between sins committed against God (in the Ten Commandments, the First Table of the Law, the First through Third Commandments) and sins against our neighbor (the Second Table of the Law, the Fourth through Tenth Commandments), the two are really never separated. For any sin against another human being reflects a failure to love God with all our heart, soul, mind, and strength; if we loved him perfectly, we would love and serve our neighbor perfectly as well.

In short, all sins against the Second Table of the Law are also sins against the First Commandment. Indeed, that is the chief crime in any sin against the Second Table; a lack of love toward another betrays most of all a lack of love toward God. St. John makes the point with crystal clarity:

> We love because he first loved us. If anyone says, "I love God," yet hates his brother, he is a liar. For anyone who does not love his brother, whom he has seen, cannot love God, whom he has not seen. And he has given us this command: Whoever loves God must also love his brother. (1 John 4:19-21)

Jesus himself put it so simply when he said, "If anyone loves me, he will obey my teaching" (John 14:23), and again, "My command is this: Love each other as I have loved you" (John 15:12). Likewise, St. Paul sums up the whole of the Second Table when he tells us to serve one another in love: "The entire law is summed up in a single command: 'Love your neighbor as yourself'" (Galatians 5:14).

Thus, in the Second Table of the Ten Commandments, God himself spells out how we should show our love for our neighbor and how by loving service to our neighbor we show our love and obedience to God. Jesus repeats the essence of the Second Table in much of the Sermon on the Mount (Matthew 5–7). And the epistles of the apostles likewise reiterate the truth that the moral law in the Second Table is binding on all people of all times. Even on judgment day the importance of loving service to our neighbors as the visible reflection of our invisible love for God will be important. For Jesus will call to mind how we served him in serving them (Matthew 25:31-46).

It should be evident that the love required in the keeping of the law is something quite different from mere affection, from mere liking. Affection resides in the emotions. It is an attraction to someone. It may be prompted by very fleeting impressions or by surface appearance only. A person may feel a certain attraction to another because the other person is amusing or physically attractive. Affection, mere liking, is instantaneous or very close to it. It can change or leave just as fast as it came. I like my neighbor because he is agreeable, not a bother, helpful, friendly. If my neighbor changed and lost those qualities, my liking would change too. But the love that St. Paul is speaking about when he says, "Serve one another in love" (Galatians 5:13), is not merely affection, attraction, or preference that resides in the emotions.

The love of which the apostle is speaking dwells chiefly in the will. Such *love is the choice made by the will to seek the best interests of my neighbor, even if I cannot like him or feel any affection for him.* I may not like the grouch, the gossip, the predator, or the manipulator. I may be repulsed by the perverted, the cruel, the filthy, or the obscene person. However, I can still love people like that; that is, I can still choose in my will, inspired by the love of Christ for me, to do what I can to help such people in need, to pray for them, and to seek their ultimate and eternal good. So then, strange as it may sound, I can love them, even if I cannot really like them.

Notice how St. Paul describes the love called for in all of the Second Table of the Law; read carefully his masterful description of such love in 1 Corinthians 13. There you will see it clearly; St. Paul speaks of a love that is active in decisions and choices to behave toward my neighbor in a self-giving way, in a forgiving way, and in a serving way. He never says one word in that great chapter on love about mere sentiment, affection, or attraction. Consider as well what Jesus tells us in the Sermon on the Mount: "Love your enemies and pray for those who persecute you" (Matthew 5:44)—words which St. Paul echoes in Romans 12:9-21. Where such love is joined to affection, as in the love of friends and family, the practice of love will certainly be easier. Indeed, the joining of the two is a special blessing and gift of God. But at its heart and core the love Jesus inspires begins and has as its essence a decision in the will, not just in emotions, to serve the best interests of any and all as best I can.

Indeed, it is comforting to know that what God wants from us is not mere "liking" or feelings of affection. Surely we would all despair if he required of us feelings of fondness for the wicked, cruel, mean, and hateful people we often encounter and have to deal with in this world. However, it is not "liking" that he requires. It is love in the will that desires and seeks the best, not least of all the conversion, of those we may not be able to like. To be sure we all have a long way to go before we have such love for all; it comes alone through the message of Christ's love for us—and for them too! His love for us is always a love so busy, so zealous, so deep and profound that each of us has reason to ponder how far we have come in that virtue and how far we have yet to go.

The Ten Commandments show that such an attitude can arise only from a pure heart. The Ninth and Tenth Commandments forbid coveting. Coveting is a desire, not an outward act. It is the desire to have for myself that which God has given to another and has withheld from me. To want my neighbor's house or spouse, his lands or other possessions, his friends or other relationships that he may have in such a way as to win them away from him for myself is to covet. In the case of property, I may offer to purchase something from my neighbor, but if he declines the offer and I nurse a grudge or plot to gain what he has in a less than honorable manner, then I am coveting. Conversely, I show that I have a pure heart even towards a neighbor who has things that I might wish for myself when I think in my mind and heart what I might do to help him keep what is his. Again, that requires a pure heart, a heart that loves the neighbor and seeks his best, just as I love myself and seek what is godly and therefore best for me.[7]

It should occur to us that even in the law God shows us his love for us and for all. For to the extent that his law is kept, to that extent our lives on earth and the lives of our neighbors will enjoy peace and security. Yes, and with such peace and security it would be all the easier for us to love and serve God and then to grow in loving service to one another. Indeed, what a wonderful world that would be! To the extent that his law is ignored and broken, to that extent everyone's life is made the more painful and difficult; yes, to the extent that his law is despised, to that extent life becomes a misery and this world a veil of tears *(ein rechter Jammerthal).* How perverse mankind has become that most think just the reverse: the more liberated from the law the happier I will be. That both God's Word and all the experience and the history of mankind show the reverse to be true seems to give few people pause; most prefer to continue in their own rebellion and thus their own contribution to the chaos and the misery found in the world.

The uses of the law

The moral law as Jesus summed it up in Mark 12:29-31 and as it is summarized in the Ten Commandments has three basic uses.

Mirror

The first and most basic use of the law is its use as a *mirror.* God holds the law up in front of us so that we can see ourselves as we really are. Without the law as a mirror we would go on in the delusion that basically we are not all that bad. We would be in and remain in the religion of the *opinio legis,* that false dream that basically we are pretty good and that, therefore, we deserve heaven or at least somehow can contribute to our own salvation. The proper use of the law as a mirror should shatter that delusion. For when we look into it, the law shows us both our sinfulness and our sins. It shows us original sin. Without the testimony of the law throughout the Scriptures we would

[7]It is not possible here to give a complete consideration of all that is involved in the Ten Commandments. For a further and excellent treatise on the Ten Commandments, we can commend nothing better than Luther's commentary on the Ten Commandments in his Large Catechism. We will also return to the subject in chapter 16.

not know that we have been conceived and born in sin and that we are by nature blind, dead enemies of God. Then the law goes on to show us the dread consequences of original sin (that is, of our sinfulness) in actual sin. It reveals to us that we have failed to perfectly love God with all our heart, our soul, our mind, and our strength. It shows us as well how far we are from perfectly loving our neighbor as ourselves.

Jesus masterfully uses the law as a mirror in so many of his encounters with the self-righteous of his day and of our day as well. The story of the good Samaritan is a case in point (Luke 10:25-37). The expert in the law wanted to justify himself when he asked Jesus who his neighbor was. At the end of the story each one who heard it should have asked the obvious question: "If this is how the law must be obeyed, then what will become of me? For I have not acted the way the good Samaritan did!" The story as a mirror shows me that I am a sinner.

In Luke 18:18-27 Jesus gives us an especially brilliant example of his use of the law as a mirror. An honorable young man came to Jesus and asked what he must do to gain eternal life. Jesus told him to keep the commandments. For the one who keeps them perfectly merits eternal life. The young man honestly thought that he had done exactly that, but he still felt that something was missing. When Jesus told him to give all that he had to the poor, the rich young man went away sad. Why was he sad? He was sad and went away because he loved his wealth more than he loved God. In other words, he had not yet even begun to keep the law—he was breaking the first and most important commandment. Jesus' call to him to sell everything he had, to give to the poor, and then to follow Jesus revealed what the young man's feelings and even his conscience had not yet revealed to him, namely, that he was in desperate need of a Savior.

The disciples on that occasion gave Jesus the opportunity to drive home the point. Jesus told them how difficult it is for those who have wealth to be saved. The disciples recognized that not only the rich but also those who want to be rich (that is, almost everyone!) were included in Jesus' words; and so they answered, "Who then can be saved?" Hear Jesus' masterful reply: "What is impossible with men is possible with God." The law is an excellent mirror indeed when it shows us the impossibility of saving ourselves. It is an especially good mirror when it shows us that we have broken the First Commandment more than any other commandment. Yes, when the law has succeeded in showing us that all of our actual sins are ultimately a breaking of the First Commandment, then it has reached its goal and proper use as a mirror. For sin is always a failure to love God perfectly.

Thus the law as Jesus used it and as the Holy Spirit still uses it is a mirror to show us our inborn sinfulness and the actual sin that flows ceaselessly from our sinful nature. In so doing, the law makes us realize that we have an absolute and desperate need for a Savior. For anyone who looks into the mirror and hears the voice of the Holy Spirit speaking through the law must despair of ever saving himself by his own efforts and good works. The appropriate response to the law as it exposes our original sin and our actual sin is the response of the tax collector in the temple: "He would not even look up to heaven, but beat his breast and said, 'God, have mercy on me, a sinner'" (Luke 18:13).

The law, however, cannot convert us, cannot bring us to faith. The law commands perfection and shows that we are not perfect. It shows us that in our thoughts, words, and deeds we never will be perfect this side of heaven. But the law has no power to change us. It can only drive us to despair. That despair, however, is a very useful, even an indispensable, arrow in the quiver of the Holy Spirit. For those who do not see their desperate condition have no longing for the solution and the saving help that only the gospel can bring. Thus St. Paul concludes:

> Now we know that whatever the law says, it says to those who are under the law, so that every mouth may be silenced and the whole world held accountable to God. Therefore no one will be declared righteous in his sight by observing the law; rather, through the law we become conscious of sin. (Romans 3:19,20)

> Is the law, therefore, opposed to the promises of God? Absolutely not! For if a law had been given that could impart life, then righteousness would certainly have come by the law. But the Scripture declares that the whole world is the prisoner of sin, so that what was promised, being given through faith in Jesus Christ, might be given to those who believe. (Galatians 3:21,22)

This use of the law as a mirror is a very important use indeed. Clearly those who do not know the gospel need this mirror so that they will see their need for the Savior and his saving work. But those who are already Christians also have a continuing need for this use of the law. Without it we too easily lapse back into self-righteousness and lose our longing and love for the gospel. Our confessions recognize the ongoing importance of this first use of the law for Christians. The Formula of Concord declares:

> Furthermore, believers also require the teaching of the law regarding their good works, for otherwise people can easily imagine that their works and life are completely pure and per-

> fect. However, the law of God prescribes good works for believers, so that it may at the same time show and indicate, as if in a mirror, that they are still imperfect and impure in this life. (FC SD VI, 21 p. 590)

It is because of the importance of this use of the law as a mirror that the major liturgies of the church have a confession of sin at the beginning of the service. In that confession we do not merely acknowledge that we may have made a few insignificant mistakes during the past week. Rather, using the law as a mirror, we confess that we are sinners, by nature doomed and desperate. The recognition of that condition and its results in actual sin makes us long for the sweet voice of Jesus in the gospel of forgiveness by grace alone and on account of his merit alone and through faith alone. Without the law as a constant mirror we become self-righteous; without the gospel as the healing balm for the guilty soul we despair. Both self-righteousness and despair are the opposites of faith.

It would be a tragic mistake for the church to soft-peddle this use of the law for fear of hurting peoples' feelings. As Jesus pointed out so well, only the sick, yes, those who recognize how desperately sick they are, will pay heed to the Physician who heals with the gospel in Word and sacraments. What good does it do for people to feel good about themselves if their good feeling is nothing more than self-righteous self-deception? To paraphrase Jesus' words in a different context, they gain the world of good feeling and lose their souls in the process (Matthew 16:26). Woe to those who soft-peddle the law and thus prevent the Holy Spirit from accomplishing the work he wants to accomplish through the law, namely, the work of driving us to a despair that longs for the relief which Jesus longs to give us through the gospel.

Curb

The second use of the law is its use as a *curb*. Driving down a city street, we take careful note of where the curb is that separates the road from the sidewalk. The curb is there as something of a threat in order to save us from the consequences of carelessness. If we ignore the curb, we will endanger someone who may be walking on the sidewalk; we will also endanger and probably hurt ourselves in an accident. The law works that way too. It threatens consequences to those who ignore it. That is true of the natural law still remaining in fallen man, and it is true as well of the moral law in the Bible.

Like the first use of the law, this second use targets both unbelievers and believers. The unbeliever may be kept back from what are called coarse outbursts of sin by the threat of punishment, of painful consequences for gross outward sins. For example, someone may be tempted to steal but does not steal for fear of getting caught and suffering disgrace or even imprisonment for the crime. Another person may be tempted to drunkenness but resists the temptation for fear of losing health, wealth, and reputation. Yet another may be tempted to adultery or other vices but holds back for fear of disease or disgrace. Some unbelievers with a well-developed natural knowledge of God may hold themselves in check against many public sins or crimes because they fear the long-term consequences of vice more than they want sin's fleeting satisfactions.

It is this use of the law that helps to maintain order in a pagan world. St. Paul alludes to this use of the law in Ephesians 5:6, where he speaks of the wrath of God coming down on the children of disobedience. He also speaks of this use of the law in Romans 2:14,15, when he talks about unbelievers confirming that at least in part the moral law is written in their hearts (i.e., *the natural law*). With the conscience sitting as judge on their behavior, they may act in accord with the outward requirements of such law to the extent that they know and feel these requirements in their hearts. The tragic fact of present-day life is that so many of the consequences of public sin have been eliminated that public vice steadily increases to the detriment of all public decency and order. For to ignore even the natural law of God left in the human heart and to wipe the conscience of society clean by teaching that there is no such thing as evil can only lead to the progressive collapse of that society and nation. Again, the history of individuals as well as of nations should itself be sufficient to prove the point.

For the Christian, the function of the law as a curb works somewhat differently than it works in the unbeliever. In the first place, both the law itself and the warnings against ignoring it are much clearer to the Christian on the basis of the revealed Word of God than they are to the unbeliever using only his incomplete knowledge of the will of God in the natural law. The Christian has warnings that go way beyond the curbs in the natural law. The Christian hears and takes very seriously the warning of which the unbeliever is ignorant, the warning that if he neglects God's Word or compromises its truth, his faith may shrivel up and die (John 8:47; Luke 10:16; 11:28). The Christian has the warning against mortal sin (about which more follows), that if he would commit mortal sin, his faith would die and he would no longer be a Christian (Galatians 5:19-21; Ephesians 5:3-7; 2 Timothy 3:1-9).

But why should a Christian need these severe warnings, this use of the law as a curb, since out of love to God for the gift of salvation the Christian is striving to live a life of obedience to the law of God? The reason is quite simple: The Christian, as we noted earlier, still has his sinful flesh. To the extent that he is Christian, his renewed soul does not need the law as a curb. But the sinful flesh in alliance with the devil and the world keep trying to drag him back into sin and unbelief. For that reason the law as a curb is still necessary. For the Christian this use of the law may be its weakest use; but many a Christian will testify that in an hour of severe temptation, it was the threat of punishment, of painful consequences, that held him back from a fall into coarse outward sin. By the grace of God such a one will find a better reason to submit to the law; but in a moment of great weakness, the threat of punishment may be very useful for us. The curb might consist of nothing more than this: "If I do this, I won't be able to stand myself!" That might not be the best reason for virtue, but it beats the alternative, at least at that moment.

Thus the law used as a curb is like a club in the hands of the Christian side of me to beat the old pagan still left in me into submission. St. Paul speaks that way about himself and his need to struggle against the never-converted sinful flesh that remains even in the greatest of saints. He tells us, "I beat my body and make it my slave so that after I have preached to others, I myself will not be disqualified for the prize" (1 Corinthians 9:27). The beating of which Paul speaks is the discipline by which he was constantly striving to bring his whole life into conformity with God's Word as he carried out his apostolic office. Without such discipline, the sinful flesh, the sinful nature, would soon gain the upper hand, triumph over faith, and drag him into a life devoted to sin. For, as St. Paul tells us in Romans 7, the evil of his fallen nature is ever active in its effort to destroy Christian faith and life. The Formula of Concord also recognizes this second use of the law. It declares

> As far as the old creature, which still clings to [Christians], is concerned, it must be driven not only by the law but also by tribulations, because it does everything against its own will, under compulsion, no less than the godless are driven by the threats of the law and are thus kept obedient (1 Cor. 9[:27]; Rom. 7:[18,19]). (FC SD VI, 19 p. 590)

Ruler or guide

The third use of the law is its use as a *ruler* or *guide.* We use it to measure our lives. It shows us as a guide which works are pleasing to

God. For even though we are saved by grace alone through faith and our works can never earn or contribute to our salvation, the Christian earnestly desires to live in a way that pleases the God who has saved him. Without the law as a guide we would be left to guess which works are pleasing to God. Given our fallen nature, we would probably guess wrong, as indeed those do who set aside the written law in favor of works that they invent themselves. The mystic decides that God will be pleased if he walks on burning coals. The Hindu goes to wash in the Ganges River. The Muslim makes a pilgrimage to Mecca. The spirit worshipers make sacrifice to the rivers and forests. Roman Catholic priests, monks, and nuns take vows of celibacy, and their church prescribes fasts, penances, and pilgrimages in order to satisfy man-made rules and laws for pleasing God. None of these dreamed-up ways of pleasing him have even the least certainty that they please God. For none of these ways has God's own Word, his written and revealed law, as the source. Indeed, worse than the lack of certainty that such works please God is the certainty that they do not if they are intended as ways of setting aside the wrath of God—only the work of Christ can do that. To substitute our works for his is at the least the height of ingratitude.

Precisely so that we would not be confused or in doubt about the works that please God, God gave the law in his Word. The Formula of Concord states it well:

> For this reason, too, believers require the teaching of the law: so that they do not fall back on their own holiness and piety and under the appearance of God's Spirit establish their own service to God on the basis of their own choice, without God's Word or command. As it is written in Deuteronomy 12[:8,28,32], "You shall not act . . . all of us according to our own desires," but "listen to the commands and laws which I command you," and "you shall not add to them nor take anything from them." (FC SD VI, 20 p. 590)

The law tells us what works please God. And that law, summarized in Jesus' own summary of the law, covers all and every moment of our lives. Love God and serve your neighbor, and do that in accord with the Ten Commandments. Nothing in life is left out of the law as a guide.

God's Word also tells us what our motivation should be as we strive to keep the law. In Romans chapters 1–5 St. Paul beautifully teaches the doctrine of salvation by grace alone through faith in the merits of Christ. He follows the doctrine of salvation with a call to live as befits those who have been rescued from death and hell for eternal life and blessedness. He calls on us to struggle against the sinful flesh and to live a life of loving obedience to the Word of God. In the middle of his exhortations to godliness he says:

> Therefore, I urge you, brothers, in view of God's mercy, to offer your bodies as living sacrifices, holy and pleasing to God—this is your spiritual act of worship. Do not conform any longer to the pattern of this world, but be transformed by the renewing of your mind. (Romans 12:1,2)

St. Paul makes it very clear. The motivation for trying to live according to the law is a gospel motivation—in view of *God's mercy.* The life with that motivation does not consist merely in a few outward signs of decency and common morality. Rather, it is a life that is a *living sacrifice,* totally devoted to God whose mercy has rescued and continues to rescue us from our sins. Precisely because of the mercy of God, such a life of thankful sacrifice is pleasing to God. For in his mercy he forgives the sins that still stain even our best works. As St. Paul so joyfully declares, "Therefore, there is now no condemnation for those who are in Christ Jesus" (Romans 8:1).

The psalmist encourages us in much the same way. He sings, "The LORD delights in those who fear him, who put their hope in his unfailing love" (Psalm 147:11). The Christian knows that God is serious about all of his Word, including the law. Therefore he does not want to sin, to offend God by a life that ignores and casts aside God's Word. At the same time the Christian does not obey the law like a slave who lives in dread. Rather, he trusts in the mercy of God. And he has good reason to hope for God's mercy, since God in that same Word has promised it and in the sacrifice of Christ has already fully paid the penalty for our sins. The better we know our need for the Savior and the better we know the beauty of his grace and blessing in the gospel, so much the more will we be motivated to love the law of the Lord and so much the more will we strive to live according to it. For it is God's will that we follow and obey the moral law. He plainly declares it so often in his Word. One of the most beautiful passages teaching salvation by grace alone through faith has a call to live a life of good works attached immediately to it. St. Paul says,

> It is by grace you have been saved, through faith—and this not from yourselves, it is the gift of God—not by works, so that no one can boast. For we are God's workmanship, created in Christ Jesus to do good works, which God prepared in advance for us to do. (Ephesians 2:8-10)

The good works prepared for us are prepared and presented in the moral law. Those works and the life according to the law are not optional for the Christian. They are works that are fruits of faith, and they follow necessarily from faith. The sun shines because it is the sun; it doesn't have the option not to shine; it shows itself to be what it is—the sun—by what it does—it shines. The Christian does good works with the guidance of the law because he is a Christian. As shining does not make the sun but demonstrates that it is the sun, so good works: They do not make a Christian but demonstrate that we are Christians. As shining is not optional for the sun but a defining necessity, so too are good works for the Christian.

Therefore St. James declares that "faith without deeds is dead" (James 2:26). Jesus reminds us that a life of good works, which by definition is a life that conforms to the law, is even a tool by which he would draw others to hear the gospel. He tells us, "Let your light shine before men, that they may see your good deeds and praise your Father in heaven" (Matthew 5:16). It is as that common Lutheran axiom has it: We are saved by faith alone, but faith is never alone. Faith is always accompanied by consequent works. Those works are now this, now that, now many, now less; we remain works in progress—unlike Christ's work for us that is always perfect and complete.

We might note here again how different the attitude of the Christian with respect to the law and obedience is from the attitude of a person living only according to natural law. The Christian *wants* to keep the law. He is not looking for ways around it or for loopholes in it. In love for God he *wants* to please God. Those living only with human law codes or without a gospel motivation, on the other hand, are always looking for ways around it: The law says that the speed limit is 35 mph, but how fast can I go before I will be pulled over and get a ticket? The law says don't steal, but how much can I take from my employer before it is really considered stealing that will get me in trouble? The law says that I should lead a chaste and decent life, but how far can I go before I've really broken the commandment? To the extent that we are looking for loopholes in the law, looking for ways of getting around it, to that extent our old pagan nature is gaining the upper hand. Yes, and to that extent we see all the more our need for grace (the law as a mirror) and our need as well to club our old nature back into submission (the law as a curb).

In sum, the law serves as a mirror, curb, and guide. It does not serve as a way of gaining or contributing to our salvation (Romans 3:21-31). Nevertheless, without the Holy Spirit's use of the law to convict us of our sin and to show us our need for the Savior, we would not find the great joy and the healing balm of the gospel. Without the law as a curb we might more easily fall into great shame and vice. Without the law as a guide we would not know with any certainty those works that please God and serve our neighbor. Therefore we do well to imitate the apostles and prophets, to rejoice in our salvation, and still to meditate on the law day and night and make its works our delight (Joshua 1:8; Psalm 1,19,119; Romans 7:22; 1 Peter 4:1-11).

Actual sin by category

There are several ways of categorizing actual sins against the moral law as Jesus has summarized it and as it is summed up in the Ten Commandments. We will concern ourselves here with a few of the more commonly used categories or classifications. Actual sins may be defined as follows:

Sins of commission and omission

The former consist of an active breaking of the law, for example, murder; impure thoughts, words, or deeds; theft; or coveting (the desire for that which God clearly does not want me to have). The latter, sins of omission, are sins of failing to do what God has commanded, for example, failure to read and meditate on his Word, failure to pray and worship, failure to help our neighbor to preserve his life, property, and good name. Luther's explanation to most of the commandments in his Small Catechism makes this distinction by listing what should not be done and then what should be done. To do what is forbidden is a sin of commission; to fail to do what is commanded is a sin of omission. In point of fact, most sins are really both at the same time.

Internal and external sins

Actual sins are sins that are internal or sins that are external. Internal sins are committed in the mind and heart; external sins are committed in word or deed. People commonly assume that the internal sins do not matter and that only external sins need concern us. That is not, however, the way God sees it. Jesus declares, for example, that "anyone who is angry with his brother will be subject to judgment" (Matthew 5:22) and "anyone who looks at a woman lustfully has already committed adultery with her in his heart" (Matthew 5:28). St. John minces no words about internal sin when he declares, "Anyone who hates his brother is a murderer, and you know that no murderer has eternal life in him" (1 John 3:15). The Ninth and Tenth Commandments are directed chiefly against internal sins. Jesus warns against internal sin, evil in the heart, precisely because it is evil; he warns against it as well because of the external sins that it may produce. He says, "For out of the heart come evil thoughts, murder, adultery, sexual immorality, theft, false testimony, slander" (Matthew 15:19). Some perversely conclude that if the thought is already a sin, then I might just as well go ahead and commit the deed, since I am already guilty. Such a conclusion is indeed perverse; for to carry out the thought and act sinfully multiplies sin and guilt by the damage it does either to self or to my neighbor.

Mortal and venial sins

Actual sins are mortal sins or venial sins. This distinction is an especially important one. It is so important because of a common misconception that all sins are the same. It is true that all sins are the same in that they are offenses against God which merit eternal punishment. But not all sins have the same immediate and potentially eternal consequences. It is likewise an important distinction because of another even more dangerous misconception. Some imagine that because Christ died for the sins of the world and that because we are saved by faith alone, therefore Christians are now free to do whatever the sinful flesh wants; some seem to think that we have been saved so that we could sin freely, even boldly. Such notions are clever tricks of the devil to destroy Christians and drag them into hell. *Mortal sins, by definition, are sins that kill faith.* Those who die in mortal sin go to hell. Thus it is important to know what makes a sin a mortal sin.

1. A mortal sin is a sin that is committed consciously; that is, the one who commits it knows that what he is doing is a sin.
2. It is committed with premeditation; that is, it was planned out in advance.
3. It is committed without a struggle against it; that is, knowing the act to be sinful, the sinner did not care, did not worry about any offense to God or his neighbor, and cared only about whether he could get away with it.
4. It is a sin committed without repentance; that is, there is no sorrow or remorse for having sinned against God or no intention to amend or undo the damage done; given the opportunity to get away with it, the sin will most likely be repeated.

Where these conditions apply, the individual is no longer in a state of grace. And, again, should such a one die in mortal sin, he will go to hell. Let us say, for example, that someone plans to get drunk, to steal, or to commit adultery. He knows that what he plans is wrong and contrary to the law of God, but he doesn't care about that; all he cares about is getting away with it. And so he carefully plans how he will commit the sin in such a way that he will not get caught. Then he carries out the plan without a thought or care that he has offended God and harmed himself or his neighbor. Yes, he may even look forward to his next opportunity to commit the same sin. Such a person has no faith, no matter what he may think to the contrary. What anguish pastors and families have when, for example, a member dies in a drunken driving accident! Was the sin planned? Was it a mortal sin? How difficult it must be to comfort the grieving family when everything points in that direction! While we cannot judge what was in that individual's heart at the moment of death, the comfort for those left behind to grieve may indeed be threadbare if all the outward evidence points to mortal sin.

The Bible repeatedly warns against mortal sin in the strongest possible terms. St. Paul says, for example, when he lists the sins of the flesh, "I warn you, as I did before, that those who live like this will not inherit the kingdom of God" (Galatians 5:21).[8] He says the same thing with equal emphasis in Ephesians 5:5,6: "For of this you can be sure: No immoral, impure or greedy person—such a man is an idolater—has any inheritance in the kingdom of Christ and of God. Let no one deceive you with empty words, for because of such things God's wrath comes on those who are disobedient."[9] These are strong words of warning to which we do well to take heed! Christ did not pay so high a price for our redemption so that we could have a license to sin. The writers of our Lutheran Confessions were very sensitive to the accusation that the gospel of free forgiveness would be abused in just that way, would be seen as a license to sin. And therefore the confessions also warn

---

[8]The verb that is here translated "live like this" is the same verb that we find in John 5:29, where Jesus excludes from the kingdom of heaven those who have "done" evil; the verb carries with it the idea of *practicing* evil, of having a life devoted to the sins of one's choice. The verb is doubly interesting since it is in contrast to the verb that John uses at the beginning of the verse for those who are doing good things.

[9]Ephesians 5:6 is especially interesting in the original. Paul says literally that the wrath of God comes "on the *sons* of disobedience"; his emphasis is clear: such people claim disobedience as their inheritance and their right; disobedience is their accepted, even cherished, way of life. It would be hard to come up with a better definition of mortal sin!

often and in the strongest possible terms against such a godless and damning notion. The Formula of Concord, for example, declares:

> Therefore we must begin by diligently condemning and rejecting this false Epicurean delusion that some dream up, that faith and the righteousness and salvation we have received cannot be lost through any arrogant and intentional sin or evil work but rather that when Christians follow evil lusts without any fear and shame, resist the Holy Spirit, and intentionally proceed to sin against their consciences, they nonetheless at the same time retain faith, God's grace, righteousness, and salvation. (FC SD IV, 31 p. 579)

Sins that are not mortal sins are called venial sins. The distinction between mortal sin and venial sin is not a distinction between big sins and little sins or between sins that matter and sins that do not. The distinction is one that deals with the heart, with the attitude of the sinner, and with the consequences of the sin.

1. Thus venial sin may be a sin committed in ignorance. David prays, for example, "Who can discern his errors? Forgive my hidden faults" (Psalm 19:12). God himself informs us that we can never fully fathom all of our sin and guilt when he declares, "The heart is deceitful above all things and beyond cure. Who can understand it?" (Jeremiah 17:9).
2. A venial sin may have been committed in a moment of weakness, when one was overcome suddenly by a temptation. We walk down the street and see something better left unseen; in an instant there is lust. Or someone says something to us that is irritating, perhaps critical, whether rightly or wrongly; in a flash there is anger on the inside and perhaps an outburst of temper on the outside. The sin was not planned; there was no time even to consider it, so quickly did the temptation come and so quickly did we yield to it, whether in the heart alone or also in words coming from an angry heart. Clearly if the heart were always clean and the mind always intent on considering ways of serving God and our neighbor, there would be little room even for such quick temptations to find a place in our lives. But is there anyone that pure or devout?
3. When we are aware of sin, we try to recover our spiritual balance, so to speak, by repentance and by seeking refuge in the cross of Christ. St. Paul gives good advice from God himself on how to grow in the virtue of resisting sins of weakness that overwhelm

us. He says, "Whatever is true, whatever is noble, whatever is right, whatever is pure, whatever is lovely, whatever is admirable—if anything is excellent or praiseworthy—think about such things" (Philippians 4:8). Of course the one overcome by a sin in a moment of weakness will not want to dwell on the sin, lest it become a persistent sin or even a mortal sin.

4. Venial sins are also sins in which the Christian struggles against the temptation but loses the battle. He did not want to commit the sin, perhaps found no pleasure in it, but was overcome by it nonetheless. An abused child or spouse may have a great struggle to forgive, much less love, the abuser; he does not want to hate, struggles to forgive, but time and again must confess to God that he just cannot do it. A young person may more often be tempted by lust, a middle-aged adult by selfish ambition, an older person by bitterness or envy or fear. Each in turn struggles with the temptation but finds that it returns again and again. The worst mistake such can make is to conclude: There is no point in continuing the struggle; I am going to lose anyway. Struggle is a permanent part of the Christian's life. It is part and parcel of the cross that the Christian willingly bears as he struggles out of love for Christ against the devil, the world, and his own sinful flesh. Only the nature of the struggle changes. St. Paul encourages us in our struggle against our weakness: "No temptation has seized you except what is common to man. And God is faithful; he will not let you be tempted beyond what you can bear. But when you are tempted, he will also provide a way out so that you can stand up under it" (1 Corinthians 10:13). The way out is the gospel in Word and sacraments. The way to "stand up under it" is through constant cries to God for forgiveness and then constant recourse to God's answer to our cries in the Word and the sacraments. Through the gospel God gives strength to resist, strength to carry on in the struggle, and, most important of all, pardon for the penitent. For sins of weakness, repentance may be present even as we struggle against the sin. The one who gives up the struggle, however, will find to his sorrow that the sin only increases and that it may easily turn into a mortal sin to the ruin of his faith. Therefore the remedy of the gospel is absolutely indispensable.

5. Where there is the possibility of making restitution for a venial sin, restitution must be made. The thief who repents but does not return what he has stolen is not a penitent but a hypocrite. No one can say that he is genuinely sorry for his sin while he fully

intends to continue in it. Such an attitude makes the sin a mortal sin, not a venial one, even if it may have started out as a venial sin. Couples, for example, who are contemplating an unscriptural divorce need to give this point some careful thought. So too do couples who "live together" before marriage or who think it no sin to engage in sexual relations before marriage.

Again, the distinction between mortal and venial sin is not a distinction between big sins and little sins, sins that matter and sins that do not. All sin is serious. All sin breaks the law of God and merits eternal punishment. And all sins have consequences. In the case of mortal sin, the most serious consequence is the death of faith, and without subsequent repentance—really a reconversion—the one who dies in mortal sin will suffer its eternal consequence in hell. The consequences for venial sin are sometimes more difficult to discern, but there are nevertheless consequences. The one who struggles against the sin of drunkenness and sometimes loses in the struggle may face the consequence of shame, of guilt, of poverty, or of a broken family. The one who struggles against the sin of gossip and sometimes loses may endure the pain of loneliness because no one trusts that person. The one who has stolen something in a moment of weakness may lose his reputation. For some the worst consequence of a lost struggle is the memory of it; the conscience continues to condemn, even after there has been repentance and the assurance of God's forgiveness. The struggle continues as a struggle against despair.

We do not want to go so far as to say that every separate bit of misery in a person's life can be traced to some sin. We have the example of Job in the Old Testament and of the man born blind in the New (John 9:1-3); these and other such examples tell us that some pain or suffering comes from the hand of God by way of a test or for reasons of God's own glory without there being any specific sin at the root of the misery or the test. The test is useful for us as by it God brings us to see flaws in our trust and moves us to look to him and his Word for grace and correction. Nevertheless, we also need to remember that much of human misery can indeed be traced to sin.

The point is that sin has consequences because God takes his law seriously. If there were no consequences for sin, then we would be so foolish and perverse as to continue our mad plunge into an abyss of wickedness and shame. When we suffer as a result of our sin, whether the suffering is obvious to all or the silent suffering of an accusing conscience, we learn to struggle more diligently against temptation. The consequences of sin come from God's loving chastening hand. They come from his rule over history with the intent that ultimately we reach the goal of eternal blessedness that Christ has purchased for us at so great a price. Without any consequences for sin few indeed would ever reach that blessed destination where sin and all of its consequence are gone forever.

Parents and teachers, therefore, make a big mistake when they assume that forgiveness means no consequences. Sometimes those consequences can be very painful. Adam and Eve repented, but they never got back into the Garden of Eden. David repented too and was likewise forgiven, but the consequence promised through the prophet Nathan came to pass (2 Samuel 12:13,14). The undisciplined little child who never experiences the consequences of his bad behavior will grow up to be an unruly teenager and a lawless adult to his ruin both in this life and the next. The Bible tells us plainly that discipline is part of the office of the parent standing in God's stead. Much of the book of Proverbs is devoted to instruction for life given by a loving father to his son. And it is in Proverbs that we read, "He who spares the rod hates his son, but he who loves him is careful to discipline him" (Proverbs 13:24). Clearly the passage is not calling for violent or angry beating of children; notice the second half of the passage—it expects the physical discipline to be done in love, not in rage and over every little thing.

Sometimes then we may see that God disciplines us by sending suffering into our lives. When we see suffering in our own lives that can easily be traced back to some specific sin, we need to remember that the suffering comes from the hand of a loving Father, not from the rod of a vengeful judge. The suffering is not a payment for our sin—Christ has paid the full price of our sin with his suffering. Rather, our suffering helps us to remember the mercy of God in removing the eternal suffering that we deserve because of our sin. Additionally, it serves as a warning not to repeat the sin or otherwise treat sin lightly, lest still worse befall us as a further consequence of sin. Read the psalms of David, especially Psalms 6, 32, 38, 51, and 139 to see how he learned to be humble in the presence of both God and man as his suffering reminded him both of his sin and of God's mercy.

Persistent sins and hardening

There are still other categories of actual sins. We speak of persistent sins and the sin of hardening. They are closely related. Persistent sins are sins that one commits over and over again, perhaps by habit. The drunkard or the alcoholic or the drug addict lets himself get caught in a sin from which he now finds it almost impossible to escape. Try as he may, he falls into the sin again and again. The gambler, the thief, the one lured by pornography, all these and others find themselves enmeshed in a sin that may have become a sickness but that is still a sin. Certainly such a one has the responsibility to seek and receive as much help from others as he can obtain in dealing with the particular temptation. Certainly such an individual may need the wise counsel of a good pastor as part of the solution to the problem. But with all the help in the world, and with the best counsel from God's Word, a person may still have to struggle with the persistent sin.

If, however, someone knows that his persistent sin is indeed sin and against his own conscience gives up the struggle against it, that person is on the way to having a hardened heart. A hardened heart comes to those who sin so persistently against conscience and better knowledge that they block out the help of God in their need. The pharaoh of Moses' day is an example of one who hardened his heart. Pharaoh knew that Moses spoke the Word of the Lord. But against better knowledge he refused to listen and repeatedly changed his mind and broke his promises. Finally, so persistent was his sin and so stubborn his clinging to it that the Lord himself hardened Pharaoh's heart (Exodus 7–11). When God hardens a heart, he is concurring in what that individual has already done to himself. As a judgment on the individual's persistent and stubborn sin against his own conscience, God joins in the hardening and no longer sends his grace along with his Word. The prospect of such a judgment should send a shiver down the spine of the most callous sinner. Sadly, the fact that it does not suggests that the callous sinner probably has a hardened heart already, a tragic judgment of a just God who always takes his Word seriously and will not have it mocked (Galatians 6:7,8).

We should never accuse someone of having a hardened heart or of having a heart that God has hardened. Only God can read hearts and only God can know such a thing with certainty. But it is altogether proper to warn someone who is living in his or her sin about the danger he or she faces of becoming hardened in it.

The sin against the Holy Spirit

The final category of sin that we consider is the sin against the Holy Spirit, the unforgivable sin. We cannot know with certainty if another person has committed the unforgivable sin. The individual who commits it may know it, but does not care. Jesus speaks of this sin in Mark 3:29,30. The leaders of the Jews were telling people that Jesus could cast out the devil from the demon possessed because he himself was possessed by and in league with the devil. Jesus warns and Mark explains: "'Whoever blasphemes against the Holy Spirit will never be forgiven; he is guilty of an eternal sin.' He said this because they were saying, 'He has an evil spirit.'" The sin is unforgivable precisely because the sinner has thrown up a wall against the Holy Spirit who creates faith through the gospel. If a person decides that Jesus is a devil, the Holy Spirit has no opportunity at all to create faith because that individual will not allow the gospel even to be heard in his heart.

So also the one who has heard the gospel, knows that it is the truth, but still refuses to embrace it; such a one acts like these leaders of Jesus' day. Even after Jesus rose from the dead, they refused to acknowledge him as God and Savior, even though they knew that he had risen (Matthew 28:11-14)! No gospel = no Holy Spirit = no faith possible. That's the equation. The warning to pay attention to the Word of God and to heed it is again in place. But morbid worries about the possibility that I may have committed such a sin are out of place. For the one who commits it hates Christ and the gospel and calls the only Savior a demon, even though he knows that the gospel message is true.

Summary

It has not been possible in this chapter to dot every *i* or to cross every *t* with respect to the law of God. Even the Bible does not give us a codebook of rules that neatly covers every possible situation or condition of life. Rather, in the Bible we have summary statements of the will of God in the law, principles, and some applications of those principles that we should apply to our lives. The principles themselves are clear. But our own dullness—yes, and sometimes our desire to escape the implications of those principles when properly applied—can sometimes make their application difficult. In such difficulty we can but urge that the child of God pray for wisdom and for the strength to take God's Word seriously and for a growing desire to submit in love to all that God has said in his Word.

We can grow in that ability to apply the Word of God correctly by steeping ourselves in it. Read especially the epistles and see how clearly principles are stated and how the apostles applied them to specific situations in life. And then follow their example. One might well be advised in addition to read and ponder Luther's Small Catechism and then his Large Catechism. There too one will see the principles as drawn from the Word of God stated with crystal clarity. How Luther applied them in very practical and everyday situations will also give the reader a good model for imitation.

When all is said and done, we cannot help but again marvel at the grace and mercy of God in Christ and of the power of that grace in the gospel: The more we know of the law, the more we marvel that God yearns for our salvation and wants us to spend eternity with him in heaven. So much does he long for fellowship with us that even the sacrifice of his Son he did not consider too great a price for him to pay in order to create the saving gospel for us—and yes, any less a price would have been insufficient, given the greatness of our need.

PART IV

CHRISTOLOGY

Chapter 10
The Person of Christ

We have considered the glory of God in his essence and in his attributes. We have pondered his might and wisdom in creation. It should be evident from God's description of himself as well as from our creation at his hand that he has a right to demand and expect perfect love and obedience from us. He is the Creator—we are his creatures. He is almighty and independent; we are frail and utterly dependent. All that we are and have that is good comes from him, whether we are speaking of our bodies and souls, of our time and treasure, or of our abilities and possibilities. It is however equally clear that since the fall God has not received anything from us in our fallen nature that he had a right to expect. The fall has left us ruined in spiritual things and corrupt from head to toe, even in those things he has left subject to our reason.

As a result, our condition by nature is hopeless and absolutely desperate. We have by nature, from the moment of conception and in every moment since then, deserved his wrath and eternal punishment. We are absolutely helpless and can do nothing to prevent our doom. There is not even the will to prevent it, much less the ability.

What then is to become of fallen humanity? We noted in our consideration of God's attributes that he is just. A price must be paid for the sin of the world. It must be a full price. Sin must be punished, punished as it deserves to be punished, as an offense and a rebellion against the holy, just, and all-powerful God. God cannot suffer injury to his justice and still be God. God, however, also is gracious, loving, and merciful. Those are his attributes as much as justice is. In his grace, love, and mercy he longs for our rescue. But how can his justice be satisfied if he shows mercy and rescues us? And how can grace and love and mercy be satisfied if he treats us as we deserve and as justice therefore demands?

All man-made religions look to man for a solution to the problem. The offered solutions however are nothing but vain self-delusion that only makes the problem worse by keeping people away from the only real solution. Man-made and man-centered solutions offer the false hope that sinful human beings can perform for God some extraordinary work that will satisfy his justice and cancel out sin. Or, they imagine that if we just do the best we can (ignoring the all too obvious fact that there isn't anyone who always or probably ever does the best he can!), God should be satisfied with us and reward us with heaven. Even if a perfect work were possible for us or if we really did the best we could, such works would be less than the bare minimum demanded by God in the first place; perfection is what he is, and constant perfection is the minimum that he can accept. Not even a perfect work from us, therefore, could cancel out other imperfect works, much less blatant and deliberate sins.

Even conscience rejects and condemns such a one-sided and self-justifying delusion, especially in the day of tribulation or in the hour of death. At such times conscience cries out loudly and will not be silenced easily: "God is just and I am getting what I deserve!" The answers of human reason and emotion will give no assurance to an accusing conscience or certainty to the doubting soul when it feels the sting of adversity or ponders the hour of death and considers what it deserves for its sins.

Thus, if there is a solution for the problem of sin and sinfulness that is sure and certain, it must come from God himself. He is the judge of all the earth. He alone must find the way to solve the desperate problem that we cannot solve. He alone must show the solution to the dilemma of an apparent irreconcilable opposition in his own attributes of justice on the one hand and love on the other.

To God be eternal thanks and praise and adoration! He did find a solution for our desperate and hopeless condition. He did find a resolution that satisfies perfectly both his own justice and his grace, love, and mercy. The solution and the resolution revealed and given to us in his Word is summed up in one sublime name: JESUS CHRIST! To satisfy divine justice, he as the holy and spotless Lamb of God endured fully the punishment for the sin of the whole world (John 1:29). The punishment of death and the torments of the damned meted out to him on the cross have a weight and a value, have merit that exceeds the weight and guilt of the sin of the whole world! In him—and in him alone—divine justice was satisfied. At the same time divine love and grace and mercy toward us have reached their sublime peak and are satisfied as well by that one supreme and all-sufficient sacrifice.

God's solution in Christ is a solution that is ultimately and divinely rational. And at the same time God's solution remains forever the ultimate divine mystery. For as rational as it is that the sacrifice of God himself would be sufficient punishment and payment for the sins of the world, it is still a mystery; for no human being could have ever come up with this solution for our otherwise hopeless condition. The mystery has to be unraveled and revealed by God himself. Who could imagine that the holy God in order to save his sinful and rebellious creatures would himself become man and endure the torments of the damned in the place of the guilty? Who could conceive that he would do it all without any help from us, without our even willing it? It is simply inconceivable to human reason and our own imagined wisdom, so inconceivable that it takes a miracle to believe it, the miracle of faith created and sustained by God alone through the gospel in Word and sacraments. Thus, this sublime and divine wisdom remains foolishness to human reason, even though it is ultimate wisdom and perfect reason (1 Corinthians 1:18–2:16).

It is to this glorious gospel in Christ that we now turn our attention. In this chapter and in the next chapter we will consider first of all the person of Christ, then the work and the offices of Christ. God's Word fills us with joy and gladness in the person, work, and offices of Christ. For Christ is our life and our salvation. Even the angels in heaven delight to ponder the mystery of all that he did for our salvation (1 Peter 1:12). If they delight in it, how much more reason do we have for whose sake the work of redemption was so perfectly accomplished by God himself in Christ!

The two natures in Christ

Consider what God's Word has to say about our Savior. It tells us first of all that Jesus Christ is both the Son of God—the second person of the Holy Trinity—and the son of the virgin Mary. As such he has two distinct natures, a divine nature and a human nature.

The divine nature

His divine nature was his from all eternity. In his divine nature Jesus has *divine attributes* and *divine names.* He is eternal. His divine nature has no beginning and no end. In eternity, before and outside of time, he was begotten of the Father in such a way that his essence is the same as the Father's essence. Thus he is and always has been God in every respect. The Scriptures leave us in no doubt on this point and proclaim it repeatedly in both the promises of the Old Testament and in the descriptions of Christ in the New Testament. Isaiah's prophecy of Christ's birth gives him the divine names "Mighty God, Everlasting Father" (Isaiah 9:6). Psalm 2 speaks of him as the eternally begotten Son in a passage quoted also in the New Testament (Hebrews 1:5). In the psalm the Father himself speaks to his Son in eternity and declares, "You are my Son; today I have become your Father" [better translation: "today I have begotten you"] (Psalm 2:7). The "today" of the passage is not like the "days" considered in Genesis 1. This "today" is timeless; it is the eternal "today" in which God has always existed without the limitations of past, present, or future—the eternal now. To put it most simply: What is begotten of God is God, and God is eternal.

The Father has in Christ begotten the mirror image of himself. He is the Son who is one with the Father in essence, in eternity, in power, might, majesty, and glory. At his birth the angels spoke of the one who is already "the Lord" (Luke 2:11). And before that, when the angel Gabriel came to Mary to announce that she would become the mother of the Savior, Gabriel declared that her Son would be the Holy One, the Son of God (Luke 1:35). Jesus says as much of himself when he tells Philip, "Anyone who has seen me has seen the Father" (John 14:9). In his great High Priestly Prayer Jesus looks forward to his return to the full enjoyment of his glory, a "glory I had with you [i.e., the Father] before the world began" (John 17:5). St. Paul calls him God (Romans 9:5).

He has therefore divine names because those divine names express the reality: Jesus Christ is the eternally begotten Son of the Father, fully God, God in every respect, God no less than the Father is God and the Holy Spirit is God, God with all of the divine attributes. The Nicene Creed expresses and summarizes that truth powerfully in the second article: "God from God, Light from Light, true God from true God, begotten, not made, of one being with the Father."

His works also are the works that only God could do. His *divine works* match his divine attributes and divine names. His personal name is Jesus, which means "Savior," because that will be his crowning divine work. It is as the angel said to Joseph, "He will save his people from their sins" (Matthew 1:21). No sinful human being could ever save himself, much less anyone else; only God could "save his people from their sins." His title is Christ, that is, "the Anointed One." Anointing with oil was the Old Testament way of crowning kings and commissioning priests and prophets. Jesus is the Christ, the One anointed by the Father and the Holy Spirit for the offices—the works—of prophet, priest, and king (Psalm 2:2; 84:9; Luke 4:18; Acts 4:27; Hebrews 1:9).[1] These are works that only God himself could perfectly and fully carry out; and these are preeminent works of Christ.

---

[1]We will consider the works of Christ as prophet, priest, and king in detail in the next chapter.

Besides his works for our salvation, the Bible also tells us that he is the Creator. In John 1 we are told that as God he is the Creator of all things. If he created all things, then he cannot himself be created. Only God is uncreated and the Creator of all (John 1:1-3; Colossians 1:16; Hebrews 1:2,10-12). All that is owes its existence to him[2] who with the Father and the Holy Spirit is Creator and ruler over all.

During his earthly ministry Jesus demonstrated his power as God over the created world in his miracles. To be sure, in the Bible we have a record of miracles that were performed by prophets in the Old Testament and apostles in the New Testament. But their miracles had one significant difference when compared with the miracles of Christ. All of their miracles were derivative in nature; that is, they were performed by the prophets and apostles as representatives of God, either by some specific command or impulse from God or in response to their prayers or in the name of Jesus (e.g., the miracles recorded throughout the book of Exodus, as well as those recorded in 1 Kings 17; 2 Kings 4–7; Luke 10:17; Acts 3:1-16; 5:1-16; 14:8-18). But Jesus' miracles were all performed at his own will and under his own authority. Notice, for example, the prayer of the leper in Mark 1. The leper acknowledges that Jesus has the power to take away the leprosy, if only Jesus wills it. Jesus responds, "I am willing. . . . Be clean!" (Mark 1:40-42). Only God has such authority and the power to perform such works on his own authority.

Exactly the authority of Jesus as God was at issue when Jesus forgave the sins of the paralytic (Mark 2:1-12). The authority to forgive sin ultimately belongs only to God. For sin is first and foremost an offense, a rebellion, against God. But Jesus forgave the man's sin and did so on his own authority. Precisely to prove that he is God and thus has the authority to forgive sin, Jesus healed the paralytic, likewise on his own authority.

Even in the matter of his own earthly life and death Jesus demonstrated his divine power. He declared that he would lay down his life of his own free will and then take it up again of his own volition (John 10:14-18). It might be easy enough for someone to make such a claim. Jesus however proved that this was no idle boast. When the officers came to arrest him, it was not their power that prevailed but his (John 18:3-9). When he died on the cross, the moment of his death

---

[2]We do not speak of evil or sin as something created; rather, sin and evil are a lack, an absence, a loss of something, namely, the loss of the holy and gracious and beneficent presence and intention of God in creation.

was of his own choosing (John 19:30). His rising from the dead proved that he had the power over life and death, that he was telling the truth when he said that he had power to lay down his life and then to take it up again. Most important, only God could claim that this work was sufficient to pay for the whole world's sin and guilt. He is the world's Savior and he its final judge. And by it all he does what only God could do; as the Author of life he gives us eternal life (John 3:16; 5:19-30). In short, he is God—true, eternal, everlasting God—as his divine names declare and as his divine works demonstrate.

Because he has divine names, divine attributes, and divine works, he is entitled to the worship that is reserved for God alone. Those who do not worship him do not worship God. In his earthly ministry he claimed such worship for himself (John 5:23; 8:58) and demonstrated that he was entitled to it (Luke 9:18-36); both before and after his resurrection he accepted such worship (Matthew 14:33; 16:16; John 20:28). The mission of the church has been from the beginning a mission of proclaiming Christ as God and Savior who is worthy of worship because of who he is and most blessedly because of what he has done for us and for our salvation. The very first sermon preached after the birth of the church on Pentecost was filled with references to Christ as God and Savior (Acts 2:14-36). And the last book of the Bible proclaims that truth from beginning to end (Revelation 1:5-19; 22:7-21). Because he is God and Savior, all owe him worship. All of the epistles call us to the confession of the same truth, a truth so beautifully summed up by St. Paul in Philippians 2:10,11, when he tells us that "at the name of Jesus every knee should bow, in heaven and on earth and under the earth, and every tongue confess that Jesus Christ is Lord, to the glory of God the Father" (cf. also especially Ephesians 1:20-23; 1 Peter 3:22; Hebrews 1:8; 2:8).

Since he has divine names and attributes and works, and since the Scriptures repeatedly praise him as worthy of the worship due to God alone, we therefore most gladly worship him as the one, true, and only God, in union with the Father and the Holy Spirit in the blessed Trinity. Anyone who claims to worship God but does not worship Christ is an idolater. It is to faith in Christ as true God and the only Savior that the Holy Spirit points and to Christ that he directs us in the Word (Matthew 11:28; John 16:14,15). He is Savior and there is none other (John 10:9; 14:6). The Father has acknowledged him as his own beloved Son and plainly instructs us to listen to him (Luke 3:22). To reject the witness of the Spirit in the Scriptures and the voice of the Father from heaven and in his Word is to reject all three persons of the

Holy Trinity. That shouldn't be so hard to understand. For if the Father loves us so much that he did not spare his Son but sent him to suffer death and the torments of hell for us, how could we possibly imagine that the Father would be pleased with us if we rejected his Son and his sacrifice for us? To treat the Son of the Father with either indifference or contempt cannot accomplish anything but the eternal wrath of God for such arrogant and ungrateful unbelief!

Accordingly, we reject as idolatrous not only those religions which openly and admittedly refuse to worship Christ as the only true God (e.g., Islam, Buddhism, Hinduism, Judaism, et al.) but also those religions which present themselves as Christian but deny that Christ is the essential, true, and the only God with the Father and the Holy Spirit. The Church of Jesus Christ of Latter Day Saints (Mormons), for example, denies that Jesus is uniquely one in essence with the Father. They make of him a second Adam in such a way that even we ultimately can become his equal. That makes of Jesus far too little and of us way too much. Likewise the teaching of the Jehovah's Witnesses must be rejected and condemned. They too teach that Jesus is less than God, as did the ancient Arian heretics whose teaching they follow—teaching condemned so emphatically in the Nicene Creed and again in the Athanasian Creed. The religion of Christian Science also pretends at Christianity but denies the doctrine of the Trinity (as do the Mormons and the Jehovah's Witnesses) and the essential deity of Christ. Such religions are dangerous precisely because they ensnare the unwary with words and phrases that sound vaguely biblical, while at the same time rejecting this most basic teaching of the Bible, that Jesus Christ is God.

In the same category belong many organizations and movements, for example, most lodges and even the scout movement. While they may have a largely secular emphasis in their programs and activities, many of them at the same time have a religious element that is essential to the organization. In their charters and constitutions they claim that the members are all brothers or sisters doing works that please and are acceptable to God. Some have argued that this religious element, especially in the scout movement, isn't really all that important to the movement. Why is it in there then? Why is one required to take an oath that supports that supposedly unimportant aspect of the movement? Scouts promise to do their duty to God. What duty? The duty outlined in the scout law and/or the duty prescribed by whatever religion the scout belongs to. So then, each scout should recognize in every other scout the ability to do one's duty to God and do that by nature, even apart from Christ? Some argue: "Well, that oath isn't really all that important." Then why make it? Why insist on it as a condition of membership? In any case, even if it is unimportant to others, it is certainly not unimportant to those who claim a loyalty to Christ alone as God and Savior.

In short, membership in a brotherhood or sisterhood claiming to serve God but without Christ is clearly impossible for us. If these organizations would be content with calling themselves organizations devoted to benefiting one another and society, we would have no objection. But as soon as they claim that their works are done to make the membership acceptable to God even without faith in Christ as the true and only God and without trust in his redeeming work, they place themselves alongside the work-righteous Pharisees condemned by Christ so often in the gospels. Not only is it idolatry but also the height of ingratitude on our part if we claim allegiance to Christ as God and Savior on Sunday, but then go off on Monday to join an organization that flatly rejects him as the only true God and Savior. The claim that those who reject the Savior are pleasing to God with their works is an insult to the Savior; to be members of such organizations should therefore be unthinkable for us.

Even more dangerous than the religions pretending to be Christian are the teachers and theologians who claim to be Christian but who have abandoned Christ. Among Protestants of every label, among some Roman Catholics and some claiming to be Lutherans as well, there have been teachers who deny that Jesus Christ is true God, while still claiming to be members of their respective churches. It is scandalous and blasphemous and shameful in the highest degree; theologians write and religious publishing houses publish their works in which they claim that Jesus really did not know who he was. They teach that the church fathers invented much of what is written about Jesus in the gospels. They deny his essential deity, his virgin birth, his resurrection from the dead, his miracles, and some more, some less of the words of Jesus recorded in the gospels.

It is important to note that for their theories and assertions that Jesus is not God, they have not one shred of evidence from the Scriptures, nor one hint of proof that such was the view of the ancient church fathers. Rather, they start with the assumption that the Scriptures are of human invention and not the result of verbal and divine inspiration. They go on to assume that miracles recorded in the Bible are the products only of prescientific human imagination (as if "prescientific people" were incapable of recognizing the natural impossibility of walking on water, of feeding thousands with a few loaves and fishes, of being born of a virgin and rising from the dead!). They finally conclude with the verdict that much or most or all that the Bible says about Jesus was written by and for people who needed some consolation in a harsh and cruel world. They would have us believe that the apostles and early Christians were willing to suffer persecution, torture, and death for the sake of a feel-good self-inflicted delusion! It should shock us that even the previously cited *Catechism of the Catholic Church* without shame declares that those who deny the deity of Christ in non-Christian religions will be saved in spite of it as long as they follow their conscience (cf. par. 839-856). That is not what the Scriptures teach. That is not what God has said (Mark 16:15,16; John 3:18). It is God who does not lie and will not deceive us.

Such teachers, whether teachers in openly non-Christian religions or false teachers in churches that are Christian, are what St. John called them so long ago—antichrists, because they deny that Jesus Christ is God and Lord (1 John 4:1-3). St. Paul also warned against those who would come in the name of the Lord but without him (2 Timothy 3). St. Jude warned against the same thing (Jude 4). It is the responsibility of every Christian to see to it that doctrine in his church remains pure, the doctrine of the Holy Scriptures. Woe to those who ignore that responsibility! As history amply demonstrates, eventually they will get the teachers that their careless ingratitude for the pure gospel deserves, teachers such as those just described. When such teachers come, the doctrinally careless will be too ignorant of the truth or too indifferent to it to know the difference between truth and error.

Mere mortals can ill afford to contradict any of the truths that God has revealed in his Word. Least of all can they afford to turn their backs on the truth revealed about Christ, his person, and his work for our salvation. Our whole faith depends on it. Therefore with thanksgiving to God and without apology we join with the Lutheran Confessions in faith, doctrine, and confession: "We reject and condemn it when the new Arians teach that Christ is not true, essential God by nature, of one eternal divine essence with God the Father" (FC SD XII, 36 p. 659).

The human nature

This true and eternal God, the second person of the Holy Trinity, also has a human nature. His human nature is not eternal. He took on a human nature in time, when he was conceived in the womb of the virgin Mary. Thus the human nature has a beginning, although it has no end. The conception in the womb of the virgin Mary marks what we refer to as the *incarnation* of the Son of God. To become *incarnate* means *to take on flesh.* The doctrine of the incarnation is simply this: At the moment that the eternal Son of God entered into the womb of the virgin Mary, he took on a human nature, that is, a human body and soul. The Bible describes the incarnation in words of sublime simplicity:

> The angel said to her, "Do not be afraid, Mary, you have found favor with God. You will be with child and give birth to a son, and you are to give him the name Jesus. He will be great and will be called the Son of the Most High. The Lord God will give him the throne of his father David, and he will reign over the house of Jacob forever; his kingdom will never end. . . . The Holy Spirit will come upon you, and the power of the Most High will overshadow you. So the holy one to be born will be called the Son of God." (Luke 1:30-35)

The incarnation is a profound mystery and a glorious miracle. In fulfillment of the promise made at the time of the fall, a woman gave birth to the only One who could crush the head of the serpent; she gave birth to the man who is God! The child Jesus was, as promised (Genesis 3:15), from the seed of the woman alone, not the man. He was born, as promised, to a virgin (Isaiah 7:14). He had no human father (Matthew 1:18-25; Galatians 4:4).

Thus Jesus does not merely *become* God as a result of an especially holy life (the Adoptionist heresy of the second and third centuries). He *is* God from eternity in his divine nature; and he is God who takes on a human nature from the moment of his conception in the womb of the virgin Mary. As the angel Gabriel promised, he is miraculously conceived and he is called the Son of God because that's who he is. Thus, shortly after his conception in Mary's womb, when Mary went to visit her cousin Elizabeth, the mother of John the Baptist, "Elizabeth was filled with the Holy Spirit. . . . 'Why am I so favored, that the mother of my Lord should come to me?' " (Luke 1:41,43). Elizabeth, under the inspiration of the Holy Spirit, acknowledged that Mary was already carrying within her the *Lord;* that was not something merely potential but something already real.

Accordingly, the ancient church and we in union with it call Mary the mother of God, or literally, "the God-bearer" *(theotokos).* We do so in order to defend this truth that already from the moment of his conception the divine nature was joined to and took to itself a human nature. The title is not intended to make of Mary some sort of co-redeemer along with her Son, as many in the Roman Catholic Church teach. Rather, the title is intended to defend against the error that Christ only *became* the Son of God at some time after his birth.

The doctrine of the incarnation and the virgin birth of Christ is rightly called one of the great pillars of the Christian faith. If one could remove it, the Christian religion would collapse. For if Jesus were not born of a virgin, without a human father, then he would not really be the Son of God. Then he would have been conceived and born with original sin, just like the rest of us. He would have needed a savior himself. He could not have saved even himself, much less the rest of us. Yes, were he not born of a virgin, then all of the Scriptures would be a lie and Jesus would be the greatest fraud ever perpetrated on the human race.

But because God alone is his Father, he was not born sinful and a sinner like the rest of us. Original sin was not passed on to him in the course of a natural conception. For though natural and lawful conception in and of itself is not sinful, it is the means by which all human attributes are passed on to the parents' offspring, including original sin. Without a human father, Jesus received a human nature and all that is *essential* to a human nature (i.e., a human body and soul from his virgin mother). But by virtue of his miraculous conception and the union of the divine nature with the human nature, he did not receive the *accidental attribute*[3] of original sin and the other attributes that flow from or are the consequences of original sin. He is the Holy One of God, promised by the angel Gabriel, the Savior promised throughout the Old Testament and proclaimed throughout the New.

Thus with a human body and soul from his mother he was not, as the ancient Gnostic heresy taught, merely a phantom that looked like a human being. Nor was he God with a body but not a true human nature, as the Eutychian and Monophysite heretics of the fifth century claimed. No, Jesus, the virgin born Son of God, had a human nature, with a human body and a human soul.

Just as we know of his divine nature from the divine names, attributes, and works that the Bible ascribes to him, so also we know of his human nature from the same infallible source. The Bible calls him by *human names,* ascribes to him *human attributes* and *human works.* Jesus commonly referred to himself as "the Son of Man" (e.g., Matthew 16:13; Mark 2:10,28; Luke 9:58).[4] Jesus speaks of himself as

---

[3]Cf. p. 108 for the definitions of *accidental* and *essential attributes.*

[4]Greek has two words that are commonly translated "man." One of them is the word for a "human being," without reference to gender; the other is the word that we would translate as "man," meaning "male." The word that Jesus uses when he calls himself

having both body and soul (Luke 24:39; Matthew 26:38). The rest of the New Testament leaves us in no doubt—Jesus was true man; he had a human nature consisting of a human body and a human soul. It is not as though his body was his human nature but his soul was his divine nature; no, that's not it. For then he would not be a real human being. A real human being has to have all that is essential to being a human being: a body and a soul. And that's what Jesus' human nature was, a human body and a human soul.

That he has a true human nature is what made it possible for him to be under the law (Galatians 4:4); for the law was given to man. And man must obey it. Jesus as man takes on himself that task of keeping the law as the representative and substitute for all mankind. As the perfect keeper of the law, he can act before the perfect and holy God as our mediator. A sinful human being couldn't do that; every sinful human being needs someone—someone perfect—to act as go-between with God. Nor could God alone be the mediator; he would be talking to himself. And so Jesus as a human being submits to the law and keeps it perfectly; he does it for us; he does it so that he can be our mediator in God's court of justice. St. Paul has that point in mind when he calls Jesus the "man" who is the great mediator between God and man (1 Timothy 2:5). If he were not a true human being, St. Paul could not call him that. This is a point that especially the epistle to the Hebrews dwells on. The writer to the Hebrews, after teaching the doctrine of Christ's essential deity, goes on to explain the beauty of the doctrine that God became and is man in the person of Christ, the sacrifice for sin and our great mediating High Priest (Hebrews 4:14–5:10; 7:23-28; 9:11–10:23). For all of these names and titles can only belong to a human being: Son of Man, subject to the law, mediator, priest, sacrifice.

As clearly as the Bible gives him human names, so clearly it describes his human attributes and human works. He was born, he suffered, and he died. These are human events. He got hungry (Matthew 4:2; 21:18). He got tired and slept (Mark 4:38). He experienced human emotions in a very human way (Mark 3:5; 14:34; Luke 10:21). All of these are characteristics of a human being consisting of a human body and soul.

---

the Son of Man is the first of these two words. We mention it lest someone wrongly conclude that Jesus was referring to himself as having a male human being for a father. Notice too that he calls himself "*the* Son of Man"; he is unique, like no other son of man. What makes him unique? He is also the Son of God!

Could there be a more consoling doctrine than this, that our God is true man by virtue of his taking on a human nature at his incarnation? As the writer to the Hebrews emphasizes in the passages cited above, we are assured that he knows us well, for he is one of us, our brother. Our pain and sorrow he experienced, just as it was promised (Isaiah 53). The joys of human relationships with family and friends were his. He had a mother and a foster father who loved him. He had friends in his disciples who cherished their time with him and were willing to give up all in order to follow him. Likewise he had the experience of disappointment in family and friends as well. His relatives, including his mother, came to take him away on one occasion because they dared to think that he was perhaps suffering from a nervous breakdown (Mark 3:31-35). On still another occasion his mother was a bit more persistent than she had a right to be (John 2:4). And at the end of his life all of his disciples abandoned him (Matthew 26:31,56). Still, even on the cross he showed his love for his mother and his beloved disciple by giving each to the other as he died (John 19:26,27). Yes, it is a blessed comfort indeed: In our human condition, he, the God who is man, knows by experience exactly what we experience.

To be sure, God is omniscient, that is, he *knows* all things, and therefore he knows everything there is to know about each one of us. But that God in Christ also *experienced* what we experience in a body and in a soul like ours—that is a highly comforting truth indeed. It makes the words of St. Peter all the more consoling: "Cast all your anxiety on him because he cares for you" (1 Peter 5:7). It warms our struggling souls to hear the writer to the Hebrews describe the God who in Christ is man:

> Since the children have flesh and blood, he too shared in their humanity so that by his death he might destroy him who holds the power of death—that is, the devil—and free those who all their lives were held in slavery by their fear of death. . . . For this reason he had to be made like his brothers in every way, in order that he might become a merciful and faithful high priest in service to God, and that he might make atonement for the sins of the people. Because he himself suffered when he was tempted, he is able to help those who are being tempted. (Hebrews 2:14-18)

> We do not have a high priest who is unable to sympathize with our weaknesses, but we have one who has been tempted in every way, just as we are—yet was without sin. Let us then approach the throne of grace with confidence, so that we may receive mercy and find grace to help us in our time of need. (Hebrews 4:15,16)

While Christ is true man in every essential respect, there are some ways in which his human nature was unique. We have already alluded to some of them. He was unique in that he was born of a virgin. He was unique therefore in that he had no original sin. Thus, when Jesus was tempted, the temptation always had to come from outside of himself; unlike us, he could not be tempted by a sinful human nature, because his human nature was without sin.

He was also unique in that he had no actual sin. The union of his divine nature with his human nature made it impossible that he would ever sin. Nevertheless, we should not conclude that the impossibility of sin made the temptations brought to him mere playacting or shadow-boxing. The temptations were real and serious struggles, even though he could not fall into sin, and the temptations were in essence very much like those to which we are subject every day.

That the temptations were real and very much like those to which we fall prey is clear from the account of the temptations that concluded Jesus' 40 days of temptation in the wilderness in Matthew 4:1-11. Satan came with the first temptation to one who had had nothing to eat for 40 days. Jesus was hungry. The temptation at its core was a temptation not to trust God, to doubt God's promises and presence. While under normal circumstances there is nothing wrong with eating a meal, this was not the time for it for Jesus. This was his time for testing, for fasting. But still the temptation that Satan brought was very much like the temptations that we are subject to all the time. It is the temptation to think that maybe God doesn't really care about us and want what is best for us. This temptation is at the heart of these such thoughts: *You won't really be satisfied in life unless you steal pleasure from things that God has forbidden. Cheat or you will fail. Break the Sixth Commandment or you will be frustrated. God will not help you, so you have to help yourself, even if your self-help breaks the law!*

The second temptation is to put God to the test: *If God really does keep his Word, really does love me, then I can do as I please, be reckless and even bold contrary to God's own Word; God will still be obligated to take care of me. He promised to forgive me; good, then I can sin and not worry about it!* Sound familiar? While the first temptation is a temptation to doubt God's Word, the second is the opposite, a temptation to trust it as a license for sin—clearly not God's intention. Indeed such a trust in God's Word is not trust at all; it is base defiance, an attempt to play God for a fool. St. Paul warns us sternly against falling for that temptation in Galatians 6:7 "Do not be deceived: God cannot be mocked."

And what of the third temptation? It really is a summary and a restatement of the first two with its own little extra edge. It is the temptation to take a shortcut to success and happiness. *No need,* says the devil, *for struggle, for the cross, for death; take the shortcut and sin instead by casting aside childlike obedience to the Word of God, to duty and responsibility. If you really want to be happy, just sin! It's all so easy!* But just as in the Garden of Eden in Genesis 3, so in this third temptation as it comes to us each day, the devil leaves out the detail that sin never gives what he promises; it always and ultimately has consequences more painful than the pleasure promised. Who couldn't write his own book about that? Just examine the temptations that you most commonly face in your life. You will find that they are all variations on these three faced by Jesus in the wilderness.

But, to return to the main point here, the temptations in the wilderness were real and so was Jesus' struggle, even though he was incapable of sin. For St. Matthew reports that at the end of the temptations the angels came and served Jesus. If his struggle had not been serious and severe, there would have been no purpose in the coming of the angels to serve him. And just so, our temptations are real and severe; in those temptations and afterwards no less God gives his Word and sacraments to comfort and strengthen us.

Likewise, consider Jesus in the Garden of Gethsemane (Luke 22:39-46). So great was his anguish in the face of his coming suffering that "his sweat was like drops of blood falling to the ground." And again, in the face of such anguish, an angel came and served him. Indeed his temptations and tests were very real and intense, even though he did not fall and could not fall. If there is another difference between his temptations and ours, then surely it would be this: His were infinitely greater than ours! For he could not fail, no not even once, not even a little, and still be our Savior. Let no one conclude when tempted: Jesus does not understand what I am going through.

There were yet other differences between Jesus' human nature and ours. Because he had no sin, his body and soul are immortal. "The wages of sin is death" (Romans 6:23). He had no sin, and therefore sin's wages could not be paid to him without his consent. He could not be put to death without his consent, and he could not die without choosing to die. Someone might object that choosing to die is suicide and that's a sin. But Jesus' choice was made not in order to escape this world and its pain but rather to embrace punishment and suffering for our sake and as our substitute. His was not a selfish choice of death in order to escape the pain of the moment; his was the choice of death as a sacrifice for our sake, for the sins of the world, a choice that he had made in eternity, long before his incarnation, long before the moment of his death (Matthew 26:52-54; John 12:23-32).

Among other unique characteristics or attributes that Jesus had along with the immortality of his human nature is this: Jesus' body was incorruptible, that is, it did not decay after his death and while it rested in the grave. That was a promise that was made already in the Old Testament concerning the body of Jesus (Psalm 16:8-10) and a promise fulfilled and referred to by St. Peter in his Pentecost sermon (Acts 2:27).

One final unique aspect of Christ's human nature merits mention. We speak of the impersonality of his human nature. That is, of course, not to say that Jesus had no personality. Even the most superficial reading of the gospels should put such a notion to rest. Rather, the point is that the eternal Son of God already had a personality before he took on a human nature. At his incarnation his personality did not change. He always knew who he was and why he came and how he would carry out his saving mission. The personality of the divine nature was the personality of the whole person.

The hypostatic union and the communication of attributes

The characteristics of Christ's human and divine natures suggest an age-old question: How could two such different natures be joined together in one person? After all, the divine nature is God, perfect and complete in and of itself. It needs nothing to complete it. Since it is already perfect, nothing can be added to it. Nor can anything be taken away from it without a destruction of its perfection. A human nature, on the other hand, in its definition *(essential attributes)* and its description *(accidental attributes)* is limited, confined, needing space and time, food to eat, air to breath, work to fulfill it, and companionship to make it complete. It would seem on the face of it that the mere presence of the divine nature would destroy the human nature altogether and make it but an empty shell at best or, alternatively, the human nature would destroy the divine nature—something as unthinkable as it is impossible.

The Scriptures address the question and the manner of the union of the two natures in Christ in many places. But one passage shines forth with special brilliance and is the *sedes doctrinae* for the *doctrine of the communication of attributes.* The passage is Colossians 2:9, which states, *"In Christ all the fullness of the Deity lives in bodily form."* Though we will shortly make reference to many other passages that spell out to one extent or another how the two natures are joined in one person, this passage in particular is one to which we will constantly return. It tells us that the two natures are joined in a *personal (hypostatic) union. The divine nature, full and complete in itself, dwells fully and completely in the body and soul of the human nature; and it takes the human nature to itself.* That bodily form of Jesus is not an illusion, nor is it a form taken and then discarded as happened in the appearances of Christ in the Old Testament (the *theophanies*). On those occasions Jesus took on a human appearance and form for a limited time and purpose (e.g., Genesis 18; 32:22-32; Joshua 5:13-15; Judges 13). Once the purpose of his appearance was accomplished, we hear no more of the human form—it disappears. That is not the case, however, with the *hypostatic union* of the two natures after the incarnation. St. Paul tells us plainly that the fullness of God *lives* (not *lived* at some past time but no longer) in the bodily form of Jesus.

The term *hypostatic,* or *personal,* describes the union of the two natures; it is used to distinguish the union between the two natures in Christ on the one hand from the union of God with his church and the saints on the other hand. God's union with the church and with each believer is not a personal, hypostatic union in the sense that all the fullness of God dwells bodily with each believer. His union with believers is a spiritual union of grace, as Jesus describes it so beautifully in Matthew 28:20; John 6,14,15, and elsewhere. It is a union that assures us of the perpetual presence of God wherever his Word and sacraments are; it is a union that comforts us in all trials and temptations and that ultimately brings us in the hour of death to life eternal. But, again, it is not a personal union; that is, it is not a union that gives believers divine titles and attributes of omnipotence, omniscience, omnipresence, and the like.

To help us understand a little better, without presuming to understand completely so great and profound a mystery, the doctrine of the *hypostatic union* is explained by the doctrine of the *communication of attributes.* (The word *communication* here means "giving" or "sharing.") This doctrine seeks to answer the questions: How do the attributes of the divine nature and the human nature come together in such a way that the human nature is not destroyed by the splendor of the divine? And how do they come together in such a way that the divine nature is not destroyed by limitations when it joins together with the human nature?

There are three kinds of communication, or giving, of attributes that take place in the hypostatic union.

The majestic genus

The first kind *(genus)* of communication that we consider is called the *majestic genus (genus majestaticum).* Most simply stated, the majestic genus is this: *The divine nature gave all of its attributes (except eternity, since the human nature has a beginning) to the human nature in such a way that what can be said of the divine nature can also be said of the human nature.* This communication, or giving, of divine attributes did not destroy the human nature. The divine attributes do not become part of the essence of the human nature—they remain gifts to it. Nevertheless, by virtue of these gifts what can be said of the divine nature can also be said of the human nature, not of the human nature essentially but of the human nature by communication, or gift, from the divine nature. Is the divine nature all-powerful, present everywhere, and all-knowing? So too is the human nature because of the gift of these attributes to it from the divine nature.

If the divine nature did not give these gifts to the human nature, then we would end up having two Christs, one human and one divine. One nature would be all-powerful, the other would not. But Christ is not divided; he is one person. Thus, Jesus says, "I am with you always, to the very end of the age" (Matthew 28:20). He does not say that he is with us only with his divine nature. He says that *he* is with us. And who is he? He is true God *and* true man, the one person in two natures. A human nature would be unequal to the task by itself, but in Jesus the human nature is not by itself. It is united with the divine nature and has from the divine nature the gifts of divine attributes. Thus Jesus can be and is where he pleases to be in both natures by virtue of the majestic genus, by virtue of the gift of the divine attributes to the human nature. He said as much even before his resurrection in Matthew 18:20 where he promised to be wherever his church is. Again, he did not say that his divine nature would be present but that *he* would be present, the God-man, whose human nature shares in the attributes of the divine nature by gift from the divine nature.

In John 3:13 Jesus speaks of this great mystery when he tells Nicodemus that even while speaking with Nicodemus on earth, he is at the same time *as the Son of Man* also in heaven. In John 21:17 and in Colossians 2:3 all knowledge and wisdom are said to dwell in Christ. Again, the texts do not say that the knowledge and wisdom merely dwell in his divine nature; that's so obvious that it is trite. Rather, the Bible says that all wisdom and knowledge dwell *in him.* And once more, who is he? He is God and man in one person; thus, what is described belongs to the human nature by gift as well as to the divine nature by definition (i.e., essentially). "In Christ all the fullness of the Deity lives in bodily form" (Colossians 2:9).

While it is difficult to find anything that we might use by way of comparison, the church fathers have often compared the majestic genus to the union of fire and iron. If iron is put into the fire, it receives the attributes of the fire without any confusion of fire and iron. The fire remains fire; the iron remains iron. But the iron is so permeated with the heat of the fire that we say, "The iron is hot." Just so the majestic genus: The human nature remains in its essence a human nature of body and soul, but it is so completely permeated by the divine nature that what can be said of the divine nature can be said also of the human nature. The divine nature shares its attributes so fully with the human nature—like the fire giving its attributes to the iron. The other analogy that the fathers have used in attempting to describe the majestic genus is that of the union of a human body and soul. The soul so completely permeates the body that the actions of the body are at once also actions of the soul—the body is the instrument of the soul. Nevertheless, it is clear that the soul is not the body and that the body does not become the soul. That's the way it is with the union of the two natures in Christ. Each nature is distinct and neither nature loses its essential characteristics. Nevertheless, again, the divine nature so completely gives its attributes to the human nature that what can be said of the divine nature can be said of the human nature.

We readily grant that these analogies are not perfect. We would not expect them to be, given the sublime and unique nature of the hypostatic union, which even the Scriptures call a mystery (1 Timothy 3:16). Still these two analogies may be at least moderately useful in helping us to penetrate just a little that sublime mystery of the personal (hypostatic) union of the two natures in Christ.

We have spent a good deal of time on the majestic genus, especially because all non-Lutheran Protestants since the time of the Reformation have denied and attacked this beautiful truth of the Scriptures. They have rejected it because they do not want to grant that Christ's true body and blood are present in the Sacrament of the Altar. Some have said that his body or human nature only shared in the divine titles and names, but that it did not really possess the attributes themselves. Others have argued that the human nature received only created and thus limited power and glory but did not enjoy a real receiving of the divine attributes. Thus, they end up with two Christs: one divine, all-powerful, and present everywhere and the other a human body that was deposited somewhere in heaven after the ascension. They turn the two natures into two boards that are glued together at the incarnation and then torn apart at the ascension of Christ into heaven. However, that is not the Christ of the Scriptures. He and he alone knows who he is. And he has told us who he is in his Word. With our confessions (cf. especially Article VIII of the Formula of Concord) we will be content and rejoice to accept his own description of the blessed union of the two natures in his one person.

To be sure, we no longer can see the body of Christ. It is everywhere and is wherever he wants it to be, not because we see it but because he said so! His Word and promise remain forever sure and on them we rely and depend. Although invisibly, nevertheless, really and truly, Christ is present where he has promised to be, and that according to both natures by virtue of the majestic genus. He is present everywhere with his power and might. He is present with his grace wherever his Word is proclaimed. And he is present in the Sacrament of the Altar with his body and blood because that is what he has promised us. The grave could not hold either nature; neither can time nor space confine or limit either nature. He, as God, created time and space. He as the God-man now rules all time and space without any limitations on either nature (Ephesians 1:18-23). How this can be we leave to him. It is the very essence of faith in the biblical sense of the word that we trust him and what he says, whether we can perfectly grasp what he tells us or not.[5]

It was in and with this human nature that our salvation was accomplished, accomplished in a human nature invested with divine attributes by virtue of its union with the divine nature. For St. John tells us that "*the blood of Jesus,* his Son, purifies us from all sin" (1 John 1:7). The blood of a mere man could never accomplish such a thing. Ah, but the blood with which God himself is personally united, the blood therefore which has divine worth and holiness and merit, that blood and none other is sufficient to purify us from all sin. Indeed it is that flesh and blood and none other that gives us the life that is in fellowship with God and lasts forever, as Jesus tells us so beautifully in John 6. Even in that chapter, in which Jesus speaks so eloquently of the life and salvation that comes through him, he adds with seeming irony, "The Spirit gives life; the flesh counts for nothing. The words I have spoken to you are spirit and they are life"

---

[5]Those who wish to pursue this particular point further can do no better than to read Martin Luther's *Brief Confession Concerning the Holy Sacrament,* in which he considers in some detail how the body of Christ can be truly present even though it is invisible (cf. *Luther's Works*, Vol. 38, pp. 279-319).

(John 6:63). To be sure, flesh by itself counts for nothing. But as the rest of his discourse and even this verse makes clear, *his* flesh is not by itself but in an inseparable union with the divine nature. There is spirit and life everlasting given by him through his Word. There is forgiveness and salvation. And it is all from the God-man, the one person in two natures.

The idiomatic genus

The second genus in the communication of attributes is called the *idiomatic genus (genus idiomaticum).* Most simply stated, the idiomatic genus is this: *All of the attributes of the divine nature and of the human nature are given to the person of Christ in such a way that what can be said of each nature can also be said of the person.* While there is some overlap between the majestic genus and the idiomatic genus, they are not the same and must be carefully distinguished. The overlap is this: What can be said of the divine nature can be said of the human nature by communication, as a gift from the divine nature, and also can be said of the whole person. The difference is this: What can be said of the human nature can be said of the person—but not of the divine nature. Thus, in the idiomatic genus we say: The human nature was born, got hungry, became tired, suffered, and died; therefore, the person, Christ, was born, got hungry, became tired, suffered, and died. However, strictly speaking we cannot say that the divine nature was born, got hungry, became tired, suffered, and died. For to say that would limit God, would subtract from the perfection that is the divine nature, which is complete in itself, to which nothing can be added and from which nothing can be subtracted. The divine nature experienced birth, hunger, weariness, suffering, and death in the *hypostatic union, the personal union* of the two natures in the one person. But birth, hunger, weariness, suffering, and death never become attributes of the divine nature in the way that by communication omnipotence, omnipresence, and all wisdom and knowledge become gifts to the human nature. The divine nature gives attributes to the human nature (the majestic genus), but the human nature cannot give attributes to the divine nature, since the divine nature is perfect and complete in itself. Again, nothing can be added to perfection nor subtracted from it. Instead, the human nature and the divine nature give their attributes to the total person of Christ. That's what we mean by the idiomatic genus.

The distinction is an important one. Without a discussion of the idiomatic genus we could fall into one of two errors. On the one hand, we could end up denying the existence of the human nature. For if the human attributes did not really belong to the person, to Jesus, then he would not be true man. A true human being has to have human attributes and works. A human being is really born and eats and sleeps and suffers and is capable of death. Jesus had the *human attributes* of body and soul; he had the *human activities* of a real birth, of hunger and thirst, and of suffering and dying. He was a real human being. These attributes and works were those of the one person, Jesus Christ.

On the other hand, we must not say that the human attributes or works were given to the divine nature; for again, that would destroy the divine nature. The human nature has nothing that it can give to the divine. Being born, getting hungry, dying, having a body and a soul—all these are limitations, are things that distinguish man from God. If they were given to the divine nature, the divine nature would be limited and wouldn't be divine anymore.

Thus the human attributes and the divine attributes are given to the person, but the human attributes are not given to the divine nature. As we have seen in what the Bible says about Christ, he is truly man, with human names, attributes, and works. And he is truly God, with divine names, attributes, and works. As such he is one person with two distinct natures, wondrously joined without confusion of the natures or the destruction of either nature. In sum, Jesus Christ is and remains true God and true man in one person.

That is how the Scriptures consistently speak of him. We refer again to the great *sedes doctrinae* in Colossians 2:9: "In Christ all the fullness of the Deity lives in bodily form." Is there anything of God that does not live in him, that is separate from this *bodily form?* No! Is there any essential attribute or defining activity of a human being that is missing or excluded from that *bodily form*? No!

Someone will object: Sin and sinfulness are such a part of a human being that they would also have to be an aspect of Christ's human nature, if he is truly and fully human. Answer: Absolutely not! For sin and sinfulness, deeply rooted as they are in all the rest of us since the fall of Adam and Eve, are not *essential attributes* or defining activities of our nature. Sin and sinfulness were not in Adam and Eve at creation, and yet Adam and Eve were fully human. Sin and sinfulness will not be in us in heaven either; yet we will still be human. Christ, therefore, is no less human for his lack of sinfulness and sin. In fact, that lack makes him human as God intended humans to be at creation—he is, we might say, the most human of all, since in his human nature he is what God intended humanity to be in the first place. Sinfulness and sin subtract from our humanity; they do not add to it!

Already the great prophecies of the Old Testament concerning Christ foretell this wondrous unity of the divine and the human in his person. Isaiah 53, for example, speaks of the One who will come and suffer as a man suffers; but in his suffering, divine works will be accomplished that only God could accomplish, namely, the offering of a body and a soul as a perfect sacrifice to satisfy divine justice and then to live forever! Psalm 110 speaks of the One who will be both David's son and David's Lord. At one and the same time he will be a human being, descended physically from David's line, and yet the eternal God whom David worshiped a thousand years before Christ was born. Jeremiah speaks of that physical descendent of David who will be called "The LORD Our Righteousness" (Jeremiah 23:5,6; 33:16). Could it be said more clearly? The physical descendent of David, a human being, is the one and only Lord who is our righteousness and who gives us his own righteousness by taking away our sin through his sacrifice for us on the cross (2 Corinthians 5:21). He does all that as God with divine attributes in his person and as man with human attributes in his person.

In the New Testament as well the Scriptures speak of Christ as to his deity and his humanity in one breath. St. Paul in a single line joins together the human and divine attributes in the one person when he writes, "God sent his Son, born of a woman, born under law, to redeem those under law, that we might receive the full rights of sons" (Galatians 4:4,5). "God sent his Son"—the one who is God's Son from eternity; "born of a woman"—the one who has therefore a human nature, received in time from his mother; "born under law"—thus one who now obligates himself as man to keep the law; "to redeem those under law, that we might receive the full rights of sons"—a work accomplished by suffering and death, of which only a human being is capable, but at the same time a work accomplishing something that no mere man could ever accomplish—our redemption. In short, he is true man with human attributes and he is true God with divine attributes. Yet, he is not two persons but one person with two distinct natures. In 1 Corinthians 2:8 St. Paul declares that the one crucified was the "Lord of glory." Again, he has joined together in a single phrase a description of a unique person, both divine and human. He was crucified—something that could happen only to a human being; he was at the same time the "Lord of glory"—something that essentially can be said only of God. But the apostle is not describing two persons; he is describing one person with two distinct natures, one person to whom are ascribed both human and divine attributes. St. Peter in his temple sermon joins the two natures in the same way that the apostle Paul does when Peter declares that the leaders of the Jews had "killed the author of life" (Acts 3:15). The one person, Jesus Christ, true man, was killed. That one person is at the same time the author of life, true God.

Jesus himself is not silent on the union of the attributes of the two natures in his person. In John 6:62 he calls himself "the Son of Man" and declares that he will ascend again to where he was before, that is, to heaven, to the right hand of the Father. As the God-man he will ascend to where he as God lived in eternity with the Father. In seeking to lead the Jews to an understanding of the Messiah as both God and man, he quotes from Psalm 110, cited earlier. He speaks about himself to Nicodemus in John 3:13. Again referring to himself as the Son of Man, a human being, he declares that he both came down from heaven and even at that moment was still in heaven!

All of these and numerous other passages in the Scriptures compel the conclusion: Jesus Christ is the Son of God and Mary's son. He has two distinct natures and the attributes of both natures belong to that one unique person who is both God and man, without the confusion or the destruction of either nature. Thus what can be said of one nature can also be said of the person. That is what we mean by the idiomatic genus of the communication of attributes in the hypostatic union. While this last sentence sounds complicated, it is merely shorthand for a simple and yet sublime truth about our Savior. The doctrine does not eliminate the profound mystery of the union of the two natures, but it does help us to know him better and to avoid errors that contradict the Scriptures and therefore threaten damage to our faith.

The apotelesmatic genus

The third genus or type of communication of attributes is called the *apotelesmatic genus (genus apotelesmaticum).* The word *apotelesmatic* literally means "from an end." The apotelesmatic genus looks at the union of the two natures from the perspective of the end or goal accomplished through that union of the two natures in the one person. The majestic genus and the idiomatic genus describe *how* the two natures in Christ are united. The apotelesmatic genus tells us *why* the two natures were united in Christ. Indeed this genus tells us why it was necessary for him to have these two natures united in the way described above, namely, in order to accomplish the work of our salvation. Briefly stated, the apotelesmatic genus is simply this: *In Christ the two natures work together to accomplish our salvation, each nature contributing what was necessary in the hypostatic union for the reaching of that goal.*

Both natures were necessary if the goal of our salvation was to be reached. Christ made use of the particular attributes of each of his two natures *in the personal union.* Each nature in cooperation and union with the other nature carried out its necessary role to perfection. Thus, the human nature was necessary for his work of saving us because:

- In the Garden of Eden human beings received the Word of God and fell when they rejected it in unbelief. Their state of innocence could not be restored without a human being who could serve as their champion and defeat as a human being the foe who had seduced them. Thus God promised a Savior who would do just that, a Savior who would be the seed of the woman and whose heel would be bruised when he crushed the head of Satan (Genesis 3:15). Having crushed Satan, that one man could act as the mediator or go-between for us with God (1 Timothy 2:5), as one who in our stead did what none of us was able to do, that is, as a man he perfectly loved God and showed it by perfectly keeping his Word. Only such a man would be fit to enter into the presence of God on our behalf (Hebrews 2:14,15). In sum, the Savior would have to be man because it was man who broke the law and man who would have to suffer the punishment and pay the penalty.
- Such a Savior would have to be a human being so that he could be subject to the law and keep it perfectly. God is beyond the law and totally above it. How, for example, can God steal or covet when all things are his? How can he love another more than he loves himself, which the law can require only of human beings? The law was given for us to obey, not for God to obey. Thus, the Savior would need to be human to be subject to the law and to keep it. When he became man, he made himself obedient to the law and then kept it perfectly as our substitute (Galatians 4:4,5; 1 John 3:5; Hebrews 4:15).
- The penalty decreed for sin was death (Genesis 2:17). That penalty of death was not merely the cessation of life, a falling into non-existence. Death is separation, and the separation decreed as the penalty for sin was a separation from God in the torments of hell (Isaiah 66:24; Daniel 12:2; Matthew 10:28; 25:41; Revelation 14:10,11). Only a human being can suffer physical death, and only a human being or a fallen angel can suffer the torment of separation from God's grace and goodness that is the essence of hell. If we are to have a Savior, then he must be a human being

in order to suffer in our place that physical death and that separation from God's grace and goodness that is the penalty for sin. He must be one who has kept the law and is therefore himself innocent and then one who offers himself freely and willingly to endure the penalty of sin as the substitute for another.

Clearly a human nature was necessary if we were to have a savior. Our Savior had to be man so that he could be mediator for us with God, so that he could keep the law for us, and so that he could suffer the torments of hell and die in our place. Without the human nature none of those things would have been possible.

However, no mere man could accomplish such things. In order for a man to carry out this great work of our salvation, the divine nature was also necessary. Our Savior had to have a divine nature because:

- All human beings born according to the laws of nature are sinful from the moment of their conception. If Jesus would not have had the divine nature, if his conception would have been according to nature, then he too would have shared in our fallen state—he would have been born with original sin. Without the holiness that is the essence of the image of God, he would have been under the wrath of God and doomed together with all the rest of humanity (Genesis 5:3; Psalm 14:2,3; 51:5; John 3:6; Romans 3:9-23; Ephesians 2:1-3). He would have needed a savior too! He could have saved no one, not even himself, because of the curse that has fallen over all of humanity born according to nature, born with original sin. But he was not born according to the laws of nature! He was conceived and born without the stain and consequent curse of original sin (Matthew 1:18-23; Luke 1:26-36; Colossians 2:9). He came into the world needing no savior for himself. Then in his entire earthly life he perfectly kept the law, perfectly loved God and all humanity. Never once in thought, word, or deed did he falter in the least (John 8:46; Hebrews 4:15; 1 John 3:5). No mere mortal has ever done that. No fallen mortal could ever have done that. But Jesus, the man in whom the fullness of the Deity lives in bodily form, could do it and did do it. Thus, he needed no savior for himself because he had no sin—no original sin and no actual sin either.
- Since he was sinless he could offer himself as a substitute for a sinner. He could suffer the penalty of separation from God's grace and goodness in the stead of another. But he was not only a sinless man. He was God in man! Therefore the substitution that he was capable of as the God-man was of far greater value than the

> substitution of a perfect man would have been. For in the person of Christ it is the God-man (the idiomatic genus) who suffers, who endures the incomprehensible and inestimable torments of the damned on the cross! It is the divine nature in union with the human nature that gives his sacrifice such weight and such merit that it outweighs the sin and guilt of the whole world. Thus, St. John the Baptist can say of him, "Look, the Lamb of God, who takes away the sin of the world!" (John 1:29). St. John declares, "He is the atoning sacrifice for our sins, and not only for ours but also for the sins of the whole world" (1 John 2:2). If there could have been one perfect man in the world, he could have substituted for one guilty man. Ah, but the man who is God, he has made a sacrifice of inestimable value and merit, a sacrifice so great that it outweighs and pays for the guilt of every sin and every sinner.

Clearly a divine nature was necessary if we were to have a savior. For the savior would have to be without sin from the moment of his conception. He would have to be able to offer a sacrifice of greater value than any single human sacrifice could ever be worth, a sacrifice sufficient to pay for the sins of the whole world. Just such a savior we have in Jesus. He is the perfect Savior, the eternal Son of God in his divine nature and Mary's son in his human nature. And each nature in union with the other accomplished the work of our salvation. That is what the Scriptures teach us about the apotelesmatic genus.

Summary

It should be evident from all of the above that our Savior is great and glorious, worthy of praise and adoration. Already in eternity he worked out this plan for the accomplishment of our redemption. How great the love of the Father who sent his Son! How inestimable the love of the Son who willingly became man for us, suffered the torments of hell for us, and died for us and for our salvation! How beyond measure the love of the Holy Spirit who faithfully bears witness to the work of our salvation in the Word and sacraments and by that gospel brings us to saving faith, to trust in him and in him alone for our salvation!

We might note in bringing this chapter on the person of Christ to a close that all of these beautiful and intricate doctrines concerning the person of Christ demonstrate well for us what was discussed in earlier chapters concerning the proper use and interpretation of the Bible. We have taken God at his Word. We have let the Scriptures answer the question: Who is Christ? We have examined passages that speak to the question and formulated doctrine on the basis of the sum of those passages understood in their own simple and single sense. Have we used reason in the process? Certainly, but not as a source of the doctrine. With reason we assemble the passages that answer our questions; with reason we pay close attention to their wording; with reason we sort out specific answers to specific questions. But reason is not allowed to challenge the Word of God. Reason does not become a source of doctrine. Reason must sit as a schoolboy and listen to the Word of the Lord. Reason in any other role ends up denying the Scriptures and assuming the role of teacher. And reason thus rebellious and undisciplined would rob us of the beauty of the Savior, true God and true man. It would steal away the rich comfort contained in these doctrines of the Scriptures. The role of teacher belongs alone to the Holy Spirit in his revealed and written Word.

Likewise, our feelings and emotions do not determine or form our doctrine. To be sure, our feelings and emotions are not left untouched by the doctrine concerning the person of Christ. How could they be? We would be worse than stones if left unmoved by the enormity and beauty and the consequences of the love of God for us in the incarnation. For us and for our salvation the eternal Son of God left the glory he had with his Father and the Holy Spirit before the world began in order to share our poverty. For us and for our salvation he left the constant praises of the angels for the shrill cries of "Away with him, we don't want him, crucify him!" For us and for our salvation he who needed nothing became a needy infant. For us and for our salvation the king of heaven suffered the torments of hell. For us and for our salvation the Lord of life died. Adam and Eve fell when they wanted to grab equality with God that no created being could have. But God saved us by giving up the exercise of his unique position to become one of us. Whose feelings could be left untouched by such undeserved and expensive love? But it is not our feelings and emotions that form the doctrine. They might like the doctrine today, be repulsed by it tomorrow, and they would in any case always be fickle, unsure, and uncertain. Rather, our feelings and emotions receive the Word of the Lord and the person of the Lord through that Word. And then, together with our reason and our will, they delight and gladly submit to the Savior who comes to us in his Word.

Let us therefore rejoice and give thanks to God for his gift of the Savior. Let us rejoice and give thanks to God for the gift of his Word through which the Savior reveals himself and gives himself to us. Let us rejoice and give thanks to God for the opportunities that are ours to get to know him ever better on the basis of that same Word!

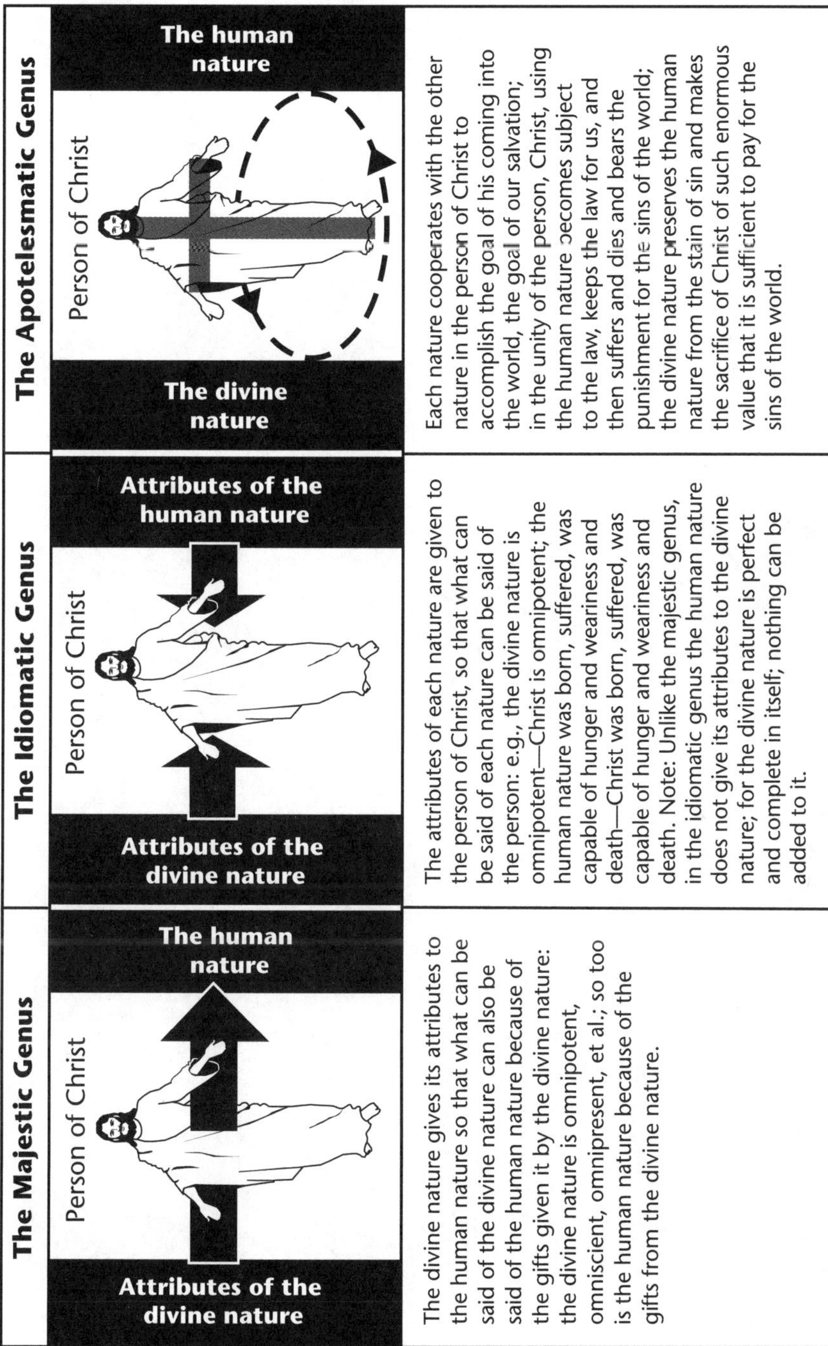
The Majestic Genus
Attributes of the divine nature
Person of Christ
The human nature
The divine nature gives its attributes to the human nature so that what can be said of the divine nature can also be said of the human nature because of the gifts given it by the divine nature: the divine nature is omnipotent, omniscient, omnipresent, et al.; so too is the human nature because of the gifts from the divine nature.
The Idiomatic Genus
Attributes of the divine nature
Person of Christ
Attributes of the human nature
The attributes of each nature are given to the person of Christ, so that what can be said of each nature can be said of the person: e.g., the divine nature is omnipotent—Christ is omnipotent; the human nature was born, suffered, was capable of hunger and weariness and death—Christ was born, suffered, was capable of hunger and weariness and death. Note: Unlike the majestic genus, in the idiomatic genus the human nature does not give its attributes to the divine nature; for the divine nature is perfect and complete in itself; nothing can be added to it.
The Apotelesmatic Genus
The divine nature
Person of Christ
The human nature
Each nature cooperates with the other nature in the person of Christ to accomplish the goal of his coming into the world, the goal of our salvation; in the unity of the person, Christ, using the human nature becomes subject to the law, keeps the law for us, and then suffers and dies and bears the punishment for the sins of the world; the divine nature preserves the human nature from the stain of sin and makes the sacrifice of Christ of such enormous value that it is sufficient to pay for the sins of the world.

Chapter 11
The Work and Offices of Christ

Now that we have examined the Scriptures to discover as clearly as we may who Christ is, it is time to consider his work. His work matches his person; that is, it is unique and a profound mystery. It is a work above all others in its importance to us. His work may be summarized in one glorious word: *redemption.* The word comes from the verb *to redeem,* which means "to buy back." His is the work of buying us back from the terrible consequences of our sin, namely, from slavery to sin, death, the devil, and hell. That work is so important, so beautiful for contemplation, and so beneficial to us that the Lord in his Word has found a number of ways of presenting it to us. In this chapter we will consider—but never exhaust—some of the ways in which the Bible presents this amazing work of the Savior.

That we need to be redeemed should be evident to all. We are creatures. God made us. He made us to reflect his glory with lives that happily submit to him in every thought, word, and deed. That's what we owe him just by virtue of the fact that he made us. That's what we owe him as well because of the incomparable generosity of his gifts to us our whole life long. He gives us not only life but also a measure of health and wealth. He gives us time and the energy to fill the time with the pleasures of a beautiful world, the satisfaction of work and play, and the enjoyment of family and friends. Luther summarizes it so well in his explanation to the First Article in the Small Catechism. All that we are and have are his. All that we are and have comes from him because he loves us and wants us to enjoy serving him. All that we have is altogether from his goodness apart from any merit or worthiness in us. So, yes, we owe him. We owe him a willing, eager, and happy submission to his Word and will. We owe him perfect obedience—nothing less.

However, as we have noted so often already, we have not paid that debt, no, not even for a minute. He has yet to receive from any of us a single moment of what we owe him, of perfect love and obedience, an obedience by which we "fear, love, and trust in him above all things"—as the Small Catechism sums it up in the explanation to the First

Commandment. As a result then of a debt we can never even begin to pay, we merit nothing but his wrath and punishment.

But can't we do something to redeem ourselves? Can't we pay the price of past guilt by being perfect from now on? Even if that were possible, we still would not redeem ourselves. For the minimum required by the law of God and by his justice is perfection in every moment of our existence. Even if we were perfect from now on (a laughable impossibility!), that would pay nothing on the debt owed; it would merely keep the debt from growing.

What then should the price be for our redemption, the price of our purchase from the punishment we deserve not only in this life but for all eternity? No matter what the price, some might think that it would be nothing for Jesus, the God-man, to pay it. After all, there is nothing created that he does not own, rule, and control. Nothing and no one, not all the evil in the world combined, can overpower him. Death could not hold on to him. The devil himself is under his heel, and hell has no power over him. The work of redemption therefore should not be difficult for so mighty and rich a Prince as he.

And exactly therein lays the profound mystery. Not all the wealth and power of the world, all of which he possesses, could redeem us. The price was too great for mere created things to be of any use at all in paying it. The Bible tells us plainly, "No man can redeem the life of another or give to God a ransom for him" (Psalm 49:7). The price of redemption was so great that only the God-man himself could pay it, and that not with things created but only with and in his own person. The price would not be bargain basement cheap or easy, no, not even for him. It was most costly. St. Peter sums it up when he tells us that "it was not with perishable things such as silver or gold that you were redeemed from the empty way of life handed down to you from your forefathers, but with the precious blood of Christ, a lamb without blemish or defect" (1 Peter 1:18,19). Jesus himself reveals the price when he tells us, "For even the Son of Man did not come to be served, but to serve, and to give his life as a ransom for many" (Mark 10:45).

Thus, the price would not be a price of things. It would be the price of a person, the person of the God who became man precisely so that he could pay the price of our redemption with his own blood, his own suffering, and his own death. Outside of the Bible itself, perhaps no one has summed up the work of Christ more beautifully and exactly than Martin Luther in his explanation to the Second Article of the Apostles' Creed:

> I believe that Jesus Christ, true God, begotten of the Father from eternity, and also true man, born of the virgin Mary, is my Lord.

> He has redeemed me, a lost and condemned creature, purchased and won me from all sins, from death, and from the power of the devil, not with gold or silver but with his holy, precious blood and with his innocent suffering and death. All this he did that I should be his own, and live under him in his kingdom, and serve him in everlasting righteousness, innocence, and blessedness, just as he has risen from death and lives and rules eternally.

Would not a person have to be colder than a stone and as perverse as the devil himself to remain unmoved by such a work or wish to be excluded from its benefits? In this chapter we want to examine this work of Christ our Redeemer on the basis of the Scriptures. It is not as though we have ignored the work of Christ to this point. Our redemption, the work of the Redeemer, is after all the heart and core of the Bible. Every doctrine in one way or another is related to the doctrine of our redemption or finds its ultimate significance in this doctrine. Accordingly, we consider the work of Christ in every chapter and in every doctrine. But in this chapter we seek to hold the diamond up to the light and examine its brilliant facets still more closely, still more carefully. We will consider the work of Christ under these headings:

- The causes of Christ's work of redemption
- The states of Christ in carrying out the work of redemption
- The offices of Christ the Redeemer

The causes of redemption

We encounter causes every day. The ball rolls down the hill because someone has put it on the slope and gravity pulls it downward. It rains because of moisture in an atmosphere that can no longer hold the water. The student fails because he thought himself so clever that he did not need to study. We pay the bank because we owe it money. The work of Christ also has causes. The first is called the *prompting cause* and the second is called the *meritorious cause.*

The prompting cause (the WHY of redemption)

The prompting cause for the work of redemption answers the question *why.* Why did Christ undertake the difficult, painful work of our redemption? He did not redeem us because he needed us or was forced to do it. As God he needed nothing and no one. As God he cannot be compelled by anyone or anything outside of himself to do anything. It is likewise clear that Christ did not carry out the work of redemption because he owed us that work. He owed us nothing, except wrath and punishment on account of our sinfulness.

Why then did he undertake this most costly work, the work of redemption? There is but one prompting cause, one reason why. It is *grace.* We have already considered that word under the heading of the attributes of God. God is in his very nature, in his essence, gracious. The words *grace* and *gracious* denote a special kind of love, a love that is ultimately unique, found purely in God alone. *Grace is that love which is caused by the one who loves, not by the person or thing loved.* Human love is usually caused by its object. We like a certain kind of food because it tastes good. The taste is the cause of our liking it. We love certain people because they love us, are good to us, or have certain traits that make them loveable to us. The cause of the love is in the ones we love; that is, it is caused by the object of our love. However, God's love is gracious; that is, *God loves not because we, the object, are loveable but because he is loving.* When the Scriptures speak of *grace* in the matter of our redemption, the word is most simply defined as "the undeserved love of God" *(favor Dei).* He loves us, not because we deserve it; he loves us freely because he chooses to.

St. Paul gives us this definition of *grace* in Romans where he speaks of it so often as a cause of salvation in contrast to works, that is, in contrast to anything in us or anything that we do, could do, or even might do in the future. Paul says, for example, in Romans 5:8 that God showed us his love (this unique love which we call *grace*) by dying for us while we were still sinners. Thus, the cause of his love is and must be outside of us and in him alone.

Paul puts God's grace in the sharpest contrast with our works in the matter of redemption when he says in Romans 3:22-24: "There is no difference, for all have sinned and fall short of the glory of God, and are justified freely by his grace through the redemption that came by Christ Jesus." That all have sinned is the constant in our condition; there is never a time this side of eternity when that is not the case. The cause, therefore, of God's love for us and our redemption must be in God, since on account of our sinful nature and condition the cause of our redemption can never be in us. It is alone in the grace of God in Christ Jesus.

Some have foolishly said, "Well then, sin causes him to love us; therefore, let us sin all the more that he may love us all the more." Paul says that those who reason this way truly deserve God's wrath and judgment (Romans 3:5-8) and can count on receiving it because of their blasphemy, a blasphemy which is itself a rejection of the redeeming work of Christ for them! Sin and sinfulness could never cause the sinless and holy God to love us, any more than sickness is the cause of a cure. Sickness shows the *need* for a cure; it doesn't cause the cure. Just so, our sin shows how desperately we need the grace of God and the redeeming work of Christ.

In Ephesians 1,2 Paul extols the grace of God most beautifully, especially in a magnificent summary statement of the matter in 2:8,9: "It is by grace you have been saved, through faith—and this not from yourselves, it is the gift of God—not by works, so that no one can boast." The phrase "this not from yourselves" refers to the whole matter of salvation, including faith. It is all caused by grace; it is all the gift of God. Grace, then, is not something that we cause *either* by anything in us by nature or by anything that we have done or might do at some future time.

Grace then is an *attitude* as well as an attribute in God, not a quantity that he doles out gradually. It is important to note carefully the definition of the term *grace* precisely because some end up denying the essence of the term by thinking of it as a quantity of something that God has, rather than as well and at least as importantly an attitude of undeserved love in God's own essence. Roman Catholicism, for example, treats God's grace in our redemption more as a quantity to be doled out than as an attitude in God. It teaches that through the sacraments correctly administered by a priest God gives a certain amount of grace; the purpose of that donation of grace poured into us in the sacraments *(gratia infusa)* is to enable the receiver to do works that will advance him towards the goal of salvation. The *Catechism of the Catholic Church* has many good things to say about grace, but it spoils them all when it ends with these comments:

> Since the initiative belongs to God in the order of grace, *no one can merit the initial grace* of forgiveness and justification, at the beginning of conversion. Moved by the Holy Spirit and by charity, *we can then merit* for ourselves and for others the graces needed for our sanctification, for the increase of grace and charity, and for the attainment of eternal life. (par. 2010)
>
> Grace is the help God gives us to respond to our vocation of becoming his adopted sons. (par. 2021)
>
> Moved by the Holy Spirit, we can merit for ourselves and for others all the graces needed to obtain eternal life, as well as necessary temporal goods. (par. 2027)[1]

---

[1]*Catechism of the Catholic Church,* United States Catholic Conference, Inc.—Libreria Editrice Vaticana (Mahwah, New Jersey: Paulist Press, 1994). (The italics in these citations are in the original.)

In Roman Catholic theology each sacrament gives another deposit of grace to advance one closer to that goal of salvation in heaven, a goal that will not be reached until the believer is holy enough to enter heaven. Even after death the believer will need to suffer in purgatory for the failure in this life to gain enough grace and works to merit entry into heaven. With this false understanding of grace, a Roman Catholic theologian may say that we are saved by grace alone, but he does not mean what St. Paul means. He means that grace *has made salvation possible.* Such a definition of grace is a denial of grace. Such a definition makes the cause of Christ's redemptive work a mixture of God's grace and our own efforts. And the tragedy of that mixture is that it takes hearts and minds off of Christ and the gospel and fixes them on oneself or on the saints or on the institution of the church itself in the effort to finish what Christ and grace have only started. In sum, such an attitude robs God of his glory as the sole source of our salvation.

Indeed, to the extent that one focuses on self, or even on the saints and on the church for the hope of salvation, that salvation will be unsure and uncertain. For any hope not given by the Word of God or depending on works other than Christ's work must forever be not only uncertain but an illusion. But grace, as St. Paul defines it in the passages cited earlier, has nothing unsure about it. It is perfect. It is complete. It is sure and certain. For it is founded on the promise of God in his Word. Thus, grace depends solely on God. If it depended on us in the least part, then it would be forever unsure, uncertain. For we would never know if we had done our part sufficiently to deserve forgiveness, peace with God, and eternal life. But the Bible's definition of grace as the sole prompting cause of our redemption moves us to joy and thanksgiving to God alone that we do not have to cause our redemption. His grace alone, his undeserved love, was the prompting cause of Christ's redeeming work.

Thus, grace, understood as the undeserved love of God, is the *sufficient* prompting cause for Christ's work of redemption. No other cause is needed; none other is possible. When it comes to the work of redemption, it is vitally important that we understand this definition of grace. For again St. Paul reminds us, "It is by grace you have been saved, through faith—and this not from yourselves, it is the gift of God—not by works, so that no one can boast" (Ephesians 2:8,9). We cannot repeat it too often or emphasize it too emphatically: The whole of our salvation, including faith, has grace as its all-sufficient and sole-prompting cause, a cause that is in God alone. Grace, the undeserved love of God, is a theme that St. Paul too never tires of repeating and emphasizing in the epistle to the Romans, especially in Romans 3–5, and elsewhere. Again and again the apostle emphasizes this meaning of grace as undeserved love, love whose only and sufficient cause is in God alone.

Grace is not only sufficient as the prompting cause of the work of redemption but it is also *universal.* Its universality is another most comforting characteristic of grace. Jesus said it so perfectly in the passage that sums up the whole of the gospel: "For God so loved *the world* that he gave his one and only Son, that whoever believes in him shall not perish but have eternal life" (John 3:16). Who is left out as an object of God's gracious love? No one! His grace, his undeserved love, has the whole world as its object. That world in its entirety is fallen and corrupt. That world deserves nothing but wrath and punishment. But God so loved the world, loved it so much that he sent his Son to redeem it.

The universality of grace likewise is a constantly recurring theme in the Bible. St. Paul, for example, tells us that God "wants all men to be saved and to come to a knowledge of the truth" (1 Timothy 2:4). And St. Peter urges us to repentance by telling us that God "is patient with you, not wanting anyone to perish, but everyone to come to repentance" (2 Peter 3:9). Who has not thought on his darkest day that perhaps the grace of God was meant only for others? Who has not at some point feared that perhaps God loved almost everyone but certainly or probably or maybe not me? How comforting to hear this truth from God, who does not lie, that grace is universal. How consoling to know it for sure, because God said so, that grace must apply to me. Grace is universal.

The sad truth is, however, that many deny that grace is universal. Calvinist church bodies (chiefly the Dutch Reformed and some Presbyterian churches) deny the universality of grace. They teach that God never really intended the grace-caused work of redemption to apply to all. They teach a "limited atonement," that is, that Christ died only for the elect. And he died only for the elect because God wills the salvation of some and the damnation of the rest in order to display his power and his justice. Thus, for the Calvinist, God's grace is not intended for all, is not universal. How sad! For if grace is not universal, then each may legitimately ask: "How can I know that grace is intended for me if it is not intended for all?" The Calvinist's answer: "You cannot know that with any certainty; either God has chosen to save you, or he has chosen to damn you." A Calvinist who is looking for some certainty of his salvation is left ultimately to look at his own works or even his worldly success; if he thinks himself pious enough or successful enough, he may conclude that he must be an object of grace or he would not be so blessed. On the other hand, if his conscience torments him or if his life is very painful and difficult, he may conclude the opposite: I must not be an object of God's grace, since he does not bless me and I have such a guilty conscience.

Such conclusions turn us away from Christ and his work and toward our own work. The result of such a turning away can only be either pride or despair, both of which are the opposites of faith. Both rob Christ of his glory as Redeemer. Both rob the Christian of the consolation that should be his because of God's grace. Yes, and both, though they may each in turn appeal to fallen reason, flatly contradict the definition that God gives us of his grace in his inspired and unerring Word.

The Scriptures are plain and clear. They mean what they say. God does not lie. "God so loved *the world,*" Jesus said. The apostles said it too: God desires the salvation of all; all are objects of his grace. Grace is universal. Its universality is a source of rich comfort to us. The fact of its universality is reason *for all* to thank and praise God unceasingly.

God's grace is sufficient and universal. It is also *active.* We might see or hear of someone who has suffered a terrible loss or endured an unspeakable tragedy. Perhaps we see pictures of starving children or of families whose lives have been destroyed by war or abuse of some sort. Our hearts may well be moved. We may wish that we could do something to help, to save, or to rescue. But we cannot. The problems are so enormous and require resources far beyond our capability. Our compassion is real—but inactive. God's grace is not like that; God's grace is both real and active. He saw our plight already in eternity. He felt our wretchedness, our poverty, and our misery. He knew the torments that, left to ourselves, we would suffer for all eternity. And so in grace he devised a plan for our redemption. And then, prompted alone by his own grace, he was active; he carried the plan out to perfection, even though that plan would cost the suffering and death of the Son of God and Mary's son. Hear again how Jesus himself sums up that active grace of God: "God so loved the world that *he gave his one and only Son*" (John 3:16).

Jesus was not merely a great man and martyr to a cause. He was not just someone misunderstood who ended up dying because people didn't like him or understand his message. No, Jesus came because God's grace was active in striving for and in working out our redemption. He came knowing full well what would happen to him, even willing it. The great prophecies of Christ's redeeming work in the Old Testament (e.g., Genesis 3:15; Psalm 22; Isaiah 53) all bear witness to God's grace as active in seeking and planning and then carrying out the work of redemption. He declared of himself: "I am the living bread that came down from heaven. If anyone eats of this bread, he will live forever. This bread is my flesh, which I will give for the life of the world" (John 6:51) and "I am the good shepherd. The good shepherd lays down his life for the sheep. No one takes it from me, but I lay it down of my own accord. I have authority to lay it down and authority to take it up again" (John 10:11,18).

Finally, grace is *efficacious.* That is, grace works and accomplishes something not only for us but also in us. We have already considered this characteristic of grace in our study of the doctrine of the Word in chapter 3 under the heading "The Scriptures are efficacious." We will consider it again when we take up the doctrine of faith and the means of grace in greater detail. For the present we note that *efficacious* means that grace is powerful in the message of the gospel at work inside of us. Grace is efficacious, that is, in the message of the gospel it can and does accomplish a miracle inside of us, namely, the miracle of bringing us to trust that Christ's work of redemption applies to us as individuals. For that is what the gospel is all about. When we say that the message of the gospel, the message of God's grace, is efficacious, we mean what St. Paul means in Romans 1:16,17: "I am not ashamed of the gospel, *because it is the power of God for the salvation of everyone who believes:* first for the Jew, then for the Gentile. For *in the gospel a righteousness from God is revealed,* a righteousness that is by faith from first to last, just as it is written: 'The righteous will live by faith.'"

Thus, God's grace does not only prompt the work of Christ from his incarnation to his ascension but also reaches down through the ages in the proclamation of the work of redemption. Yes, there is power dwelling in that message of grace. It is the power of God himself. That should not surprise us, since grace is not just something God owns but rather is an attribute in God's own essence. So, of course, God's grace is powerful when God reveals it in the message of the gospel.

The grace of God in the message of the gospel needs to be efficacious. That is, it must have a power from God in it to accomplish its purpose of creating this saving faith of which the apostle is speaking. For by nature we would not and could not believe it. Who would believe that God wanted to become man to rescue fallen creatures who have rebelled against him and do not want him? Who would believe that God in human form would suffer innocently the torments of hell itself in order to accomplish the work of our redemption? It sounds like foolishness to our corrupt and spiritually dead nature, just as St. Paul says in 1 Corinthians 1:18-21. After all, not a one of us would volunteer to suffer hell for another. Why then would God? Again, grace is the answer. And it is that same grace in the gospel message that brings us to faith and to trust in the saving message. That trust—God's gift from beginning to end—is then credited to us for righteousness. Yes, grace is and must be efficacious or we would never believe the message of our redemption.

Jesus tells us of the inherent efficacy of God's grace, of God's own presence and power, in his gospel message: "The words I have spoken to you are spirit and they are life" (John 6:63). Jesus said this at the close of his magnificent discourse on the Bread of Life; he declared himself to be that Bread of Life. He promised that whoever would eat his flesh, which he was giving for the world, would have life. He was speaking about the effect that is produced by the gospel. In the gospel he gives himself to us. To receive the gospel is to receive him; to receive him is to receive life and life eternal. Later he would institute the Sacrament of the Altar in which he would give his body and blood in still another way, through the joining of his promised presence with the elements of bread and wine. But in John 6 he is speaking of the efficacy of the gospel proclamation itself. St. Paul speaks of that efficacy as well when he tells us that "faith comes from hearing the message, and the message is heard through the word of Christ" (Romans 10:17).

We note that in these and in all of the passages of the Bible that speak of the efficacy of grace the emphasis is placed on the efficacy of grace *alone*. That is, the gospel message of God's grace needs nothing from us to complete it or to make it effective. The power is in the gospel of grace itself to raise us from spiritual death to spiritual life. That emphasis brings us the greatest comfort and gives to God all of the glory for our salvation. Sadly, most Protestants deny the truth that the message of grace alone is effective for the creation and preservation of faith. Most Protestant churches (Methodist, Baptist, Pentecostal, et al.) are Arminian; that is, they teach that we have the ability in ourselves to come to faith, "to make a decision for Christ," as they so often put it. They teach that the message of grace is not efficacious in itself, that we must make it so by our decision for Christ, by our faith.

That error gets everything backwards. It ends up making our decision and our faith the cause of God's grace. In truth it is the other way around, as the passages considered previously make clear (cf. also

Romans 8:7; 1 Corinthians 2:14; 12:3; Ephesians 2:1-9). It is God's grace in the gospel that causes faith, not faith that causes grace. God announces in the gospel that he is gracious to sinners, that he forgives sin because of Christ's redeeming sacrifice for us. That announcement, that gracious and grace-filled message, creates faith; that is, the message of grace causes us to trust that God is telling the truth, that our forgiveness has already been won for us. To put it another way, God is not gracious to us because we believe; rather, we believe because God is gracious and gives us the grace to believe in his gospel. We have not been redeemed because we believe; we believe because we have been redeemed. If the jailer announces to the prisoner that he has been pardoned, does the prisoner's believing the message cause his pardon? No. It's the other way around. The prisoner's faith doesn't cause the message; rather, the message causes the prisoner to trust and believe that he has truly been pardoned. St. Paul makes that point so often. Consider, for example, 2 Corinthians 5:18–6:1. He declares:

> All this is from God, who reconciled us to himself through Christ and gave us the ministry of reconciliation: that God was reconciling the world to himself in Christ, not counting men's sins against them. And he has committed to us the message of reconciliation. We are therefore Christ's ambassadors, as though God were making his appeal through us. We implore you on Christ's behalf: Be reconciled to God. God made him who had no sin to be sin for us, so that in him we might become the righteousness of God. As God's fellow workers we urge you not to receive God's grace in vain.

It is plain from this passage that we believe the message because the message is efficacious, powerful, and from God and is therefore utterly true, reliable, and, yes, believable. The power of God in the gospel has convinced us of that. St. Paul and his coworkers came to the Corinthians to announce as ambassadors the message of God, the great King of the universe. They did not come to announce a message that might be true or would become true only if the hearers believed it. No, they proclaimed the facts. The facts have God behind them and in their proclamation. We believe the message because it has the power within it to cause us to believe, to create faith that trusts the truth of the gospel of grace. "Be reconciled to God." On God's part that reconciliation has already been accomplished for you by the work of Christ. Why would you want to insist still either that God is angry with you or that you are angry with God? Receive the reconciliation that God has already accomplished!

The apostle warns us not to receive the message of grace in vain, not to turn away from it and reject it and thus lose its saving benefit. But the message of grace will remain true no matter how many turn their backs on it. Grace is still grace, still powerful and efficacious, even though we have the ability to reject its saving and faith-producing benefit. To return to the analogy of the prisoner who has been told that he is pardoned: What if the prisoner would stubbornly refuse to believe the message and cling to the bars of his cell? Would that make the message a lie? No, not at all! But the prisoner because of his unbelief would lose all the benefit of the message. Thus, if we reject the message of our redemption, we lose its saving benefit and we have no one to blame for that loss but ourselves (Matthew 23:37; Acts 7:51). If, on the other hand, we believe the message of grace, we have only the efficacious power of the message, that is, God's presence in and with the message, to thank for that faith. Again, faith is the result of the message; it doesn't cause the message (Romans 10:17).

Like the Calvinist, the Arminian may well be tempted either to pride or to despair as a result of his error. The Arminian who imagines that he has contributed to his own salvation by his own ability to believe the gospel may give himself credit that belongs only to the grace of God in the gospel message itself. Or, on the other hand, an Arminian may be tempted to despair when he considers the weakness of his faith; he may wonder if he really believes or believes enough to cause God to be gracious to him. In either case the attention of the Arminian is turned away from God's grace and Christ's work to self, to one's own feelings, decisions, or reason. That robs God of his glory as well as the Arminian of the true consolation intended by God's sufficient, universal, active, and efficacious grace. The simple fact is that for consolation in weakness and doubt we look not inward to our faith but upward to its source; we look to the sufficient, the universal, the active, and the efficacious grace of God in the gospel. For it was by the working of the Holy Spirit through that gospel that faith was created. It is likewise through the same working of the Holy Spirit through the gospel that faith is sustained amidst all doubt and weakness and affliction.

Grace is a most beautiful attribute in God. It is the attribute that served as the prompting cause for our redemption. To God be all glory for his amazing, sufficient, universal, active, and efficacious grace by which we are sure that we are objects of Jesus' redeeming work. Eternity will not be too long a time for us to marvel at his grace and to worship and praise and thank him for it.

The meritorious cause (the HOW of redemption)

The second cause of our redemption is called the *meritorious cause.* As the prompting cause answers the question of the *why* of our redemption, so the meritorious cause answers the question *how.*

Grace as the *prompting cause* works itself out in the *meritorious cause.* For God is not only gracious, he is also just. Given our lost and condemned state because of original sin and actual sin, on the one hand, and God's justice, on the other hand, how can anyone ever get to heaven? Justice demanded payment from each and every sinner for each and every sin. For sin always makes the sinner a debtor to God. As already noted, we owed perfect obedience but failed to pay what we owed and could never pay what we owed. Original sin makes it impossible for us to give to God even for a single moment the perfect obedience that is his due. We have nothing with which to pay the debt. The result is that at our best we must confess with David, "Surely I was sinful at birth, sinful from the time my mother conceived me" (Psalm 51:5); with Isaiah, "How then can we be saved? All of us have become like one who is unclean, and all our righteous acts are like filthy rags" (Isaiah 64:5,6); and with the greatest of the saints, "I know that nothing good lives in me, that is, in my sinful nature" (Romans 7:18). *Sin and sinfulness* in us, in our very nature, *create a debt that we cannot pay.*

Sin likewise is rebellion that must be put down and crime that must be punished. The punishment for rebellion and crimes against God is death and then eternal punishment in hell. Already in the Garden of Eden God said it: "You will surely die" (Genesis 2:17). He repeated it with emphasis when he gave the law through Moses: "Cursed is the man who does not uphold the words of this law by carrying them out" (Deuteronomy 27:26). Nor did the New Testament change the dread reality that we are by nature under God's wrath and deserve nothing but punishment and that we are totally incapable of doing anything about it. We don't even want to do something about it. It is as Jesus said: "Flesh gives birth to flesh" (John 3:6). The result is that "there is no one righteous, not even one" (Romans 3:10). Paul sums it up so well when he says that "the sinful mind is hostile to God. It does not submit to God's law, nor can it do so" (Romans 8:7). All of these passages have the same bottom line: Punishment dreadful and eternal is what we deserve!

Given the clear Word of God concerning our fallen nature and its inability to produce a single perfect moment—much less an entire life—that might merit God's favor, how shall we be saved? Given our desperate and by nature hopeless condition, what possible merit could we bring to God individually or collectively that might gain for us his favor? How could we ever pay the debt we owe and escape the punishment we deserve both because of our fallen nature and because of our fallen actions?

It should be obvious that any merit in us as a cause for our entrance into God's favor and ultimately into paradise is excluded and out of the question. It should therefore be shocking to us that not only non-Christian religions seek a way to earn God's favor but also many Christian church bodies do the same. The Roman Catholic Church teaches that even non-Christians can merit God's favor if they just follow their consciences *(Facere quod in te est)*. As if that were not bad enough, it goes on to teach that the works of others—e.g., saints, monks, martyrs, and especially the virgin Mary—are so great that they can be applied to our debt before God and help to free us from punishment and gain his favor.[2] In it all they teach that we fallen children of Adam and Eve become meritorious causes of salvation at least in part. Many Protestants are guilty of this same terrible error. Many Arminians make faith itself a *meritorious cause* of salvation, just as they make faith a *prompting cause* of salvation; they teach that one is saved because he believes, because he has made his decision for Christ.

In point of fact there is but one meritorious cause of our salvation and redemption. There is but one answer to *how* our redemption was accomplished: Christ! He is the Lamb of God who takes away the sin of the world (John 1:29). He is the one whom God gave for our salvation (John 3:16). He is the one who alone took our place under the wrath of God (Psalm 22; Isaiah 53). He is the one who traded places with us, taking all our sin and guilt on himself as our substitute (2 Corinthians 5:18-21). He is the one who purchased our forgiveness at the cost of his own blood (Ephesians 1:7; 1 Peter 1:18,19). In sum, Christ alone has merited salvation for us. He alone bought it and alone paid for it fully; he alone suffered the punishment that was our due.

To God be eternal thanks and praise that no other merit was necessary for our redemption than the merit of Christ. For no other merit could ever be enough to redeem, to buy back, and to pay for even one single soul. Not the merit of a single saint, not the merit of all the saints put together would ever be enough to pay the price of even one sin. St. John states the case plainly: "The blood of Jesus, his Son, purifies us from all sin. He is the atoning sacrifice for our sins, and not

---

[2]Cf. *Catechism of the Catholic Church,* par. 1030-32, 1054-55, 1173, 1471-1479, et al.

only for ours but also for the sins of the whole world" (1 John 1:7; 2:2). As the sinless Son of God, he had no sins of his own, no debt that needed to be paid, no rebellion or crime that demanded punishment. Innocent of original sin and of all actual sin, *he offered himself as a perfect payment for every sin* ever committed by our fallen human race from the time of the fall in the Garden of Eden down to the last sin that will be committed before the end of time. *He was punished for our every crime and crushed for our every act of rebellion* (Isaiah 53). St. Paul goes so far as to declare that "God made him who had no sin to be sin for us, so that in him we might become the righteousness of God" (2 Corinthians 5:21). That is to say, when God sees his Son on the cross he sees all of the sins and all of the sinners of the world, and Christ pays for and is punished for each sin, for all sinners.

That payment and punishment were horrible indeed for him. Even in purely human terms, the horror of it is impossible for us to grasp fully. Think of the one thing that you could not endure. Could you bear to be covered with snakes, let us say? Could you endure that? Would that experience or something like it simply be too much for you? Would you endure such a thing for the sake of anyone else? For Jesus sin was the one thing that he could not, so to speak, endure. He spent his entire earthly life in the effort to be free from sin, from the least hint of disobedience to his Father. But behold him covered with the sin and guilt of the whole world, every bit of it, in his suffering and death. Do you then perhaps begin to grasp the horror hidden in Paul's words cited above: "God made him who had no sin to be sin for us?" See how he sweats as it were great drops of blood in the Garden of Gethsemane. See how he endured betrayal and denial, ridicule and beating, shame and crucifixion.

Yes, and see most of all how he suffered in his crucifixion, suffered in both body and soul, the torment of hell itself, especially in his anguished cry: "My God, my God, why have you forsaken me?" (Matthew 27:46). To be deprived of the enjoyment of God's mercy and love is the very essence of hell. For the holy Son of God, whose divine nature was one in essence with the Father, that must have been a horrible suffering indeed! So great was the price! So great the punishment! But in it and through it Christ the God-man, redeemed us; that is, his merit was sufficient to pay for the sin of the whole world forever. His sacrifice, his punishment for us, was the ultimate act of selflessness: God turned his back on God. God who needed nothing punished the God-man whose perfection merited every good thing. And the God-man did it. He did it willingly. He did it with each one of us in his mind and on his heart. He did it thinking of you. He did it for you. That's how rich his grace is and how perfect and complete his merit, merit which in the message of forgiveness he transfers to our account before God.

It should be folly for anyone to imagine that any merely human works could be placed somehow alongside of the work of Christ as a meritorious cause of salvation. It should as well be seen as blasphemous ingratitude that someone would even want to merit what Christ has already merited fully and completely and at so great a cost to himself. Christ and Christ alone by his perfect life and death and resurrection is the Redeemer. None other is needed. None other is possible. Can you imagine how insulted and hurt a friend or loved one would be if he or she gave you an expensive present, purchased at great sacrifice, and you responded by saying, "Oh, how nice! But, here, I have ten cents. Let me give you that to match your generosity!" So the gift of redemption was purchased prompted by the grace of God alone; it was earned most expensively by the life and death of God's Son alone. Far be it from us to insult the heart of God so gracious or the price of redemption so expensive by imagining that we could ever pay for it or even contribute something to deserve or earn it even in the smallest part!

The teaching of the Scriptures, therefore, that Christ is the sole meritorious cause of our redemption, gives to Christ all the glory for our redemption. For that is his due. As well it gives us maximum comfort and assurance that the work of redemption has really been fully accomplished. For if we, even in the smallest way, had to be the meritorious cause of redemption, then we should despair. Indeed, in every moment of our existence the cry of the publican in the temple is appropriate for each of us: "God, have mercy on me, a sinner." It is in the message of redemption, with grace as its sole *prompting cause* and the work of Christ as the sole *meritorious cause,* that we hear God's own answer: Christ has died and paid full price for the sins of the world. That means for your sins too, for every one of them. When on the cross he cried, "It is finished!" he was speaking of the work he came to do, the work of your redemption. So then, as St. Paul said, "Be reconciled to God."

Therefore, in complete harmony with the Lutheran Confessions, we declare:

> Regarding the righteousness of faith before God, we unanimously believe, teach, and confess on the basis of the general summary of our Christian faith and confession expressed above that poor sinful people are justified before God, that is, absolved—pronounced

> free of all sins and of the judgment of the damnation that they deserved and accepted as children and heirs of eternal life—without the least bit of our own merit or worthiness [SC, "Creed," 4], apart from all preceding, present, or subsequent works. We are justified on the basis of sheer grace, because of the sole merit, the entire obedience, and the bitter suffering, death, and the resurrection of our Lord Christ alone, whose obedience is reckoned to us as righteousness. [FC SD III, 9 p. 563]

Not even our faith can be placed alongside of Christ's work as a meritorious cause of our redemption. For, as we must emphasize repeatedly in opposition to all forms of Arminianism, it is the message of redemption that causes and creates faith, not faith that causes or merits redemption. The Formula of Concord emphasizes that same point:

> Faith itself is a gift of God, through which we acknowledge Christ our redeemer in the Word of the gospel and trust in him. . . .
>
> For faith does not make people righteous because it is such a good work or such a fine virtue, but because it lays hold of and accepts the merit of Christ in the promise of the holy gospel. . . . Thus, the righteousness that out of sheer grace is reckoned before God to faith or to the believer consists of the obedience, suffering, and resurrection of Christ because he has satisfied the law for us and paid for our sins. (FC SD III, 11,13,14 pp. 563,564]

The states of Christ

As we continue to search the Scriptures so that we may learn as much as possible about the work of Christ our Redeemer, we note that the Bible makes a clear distinction between the way that Christ worked before his resurrection and then after his resurrection. We take note of that distinction by speaking of the two states in the work of Christ. The *sedes doctrinae* for the doctrine of the two states of Christ is Philippians 2:5-11. St. Paul tells us:

> Your attitude should be the same as that of Christ Jesus: Who, being in very nature God, did not consider equality with God something to be grasped, but made himself nothing, taking the very nature of a servant, being made in human likeness. And being found in appearance as a man, he humbled himself and became obedient to death—even death on a cross! Therefore God exalted him to the highest place and gave him the name that is above every name, that at the name of Jesus every knee

should bow, in heaven and on earth and under the earth, and every tongue confess that Jesus Christ is Lord, to the glory of God the Father.

The state of humiliation

The first state described in these verses is called the *state of humiliation.* The state of humiliation considers the work of Christ from the moment of his conception in the womb of the virgin Mary up until the moment he became alive in the grave on Easter Sunday morning. The state of humiliation applies only to the human nature of Christ. For the divine nature remains in every way the divine nature even after it takes to itself the human nature (cf. chapter 10, the *idiomatic genus*). What happened at that moment when the divine nature took on the human nature in the womb of Mary and gave to it its own attributes? The human nature was immediately humbled. St. Paul says that Christ in his human nature "did not consider equality with God something to be grasped" (Philippians 2:6). He did not consider that equality, the equality that the human nature had by virtue of its union with and gifts from the divine nature, something to be paraded about or put on display (cf. chapter 10, the *majestic genus*). And so he uses conception in the womb of a lowly virgin. There were no flashing lights, no parades, not even a halo around the head of the virgin mother of God. She was just as poor after his conception as before; even worse, she was likely to be scorned as a "fallen woman" if people found out about her "condition."

The lowliness of the God-man contained in the womb of his mother continued until the moment of his resurrection, and even deepened throughout his earthly life. Though Jesus in his human nature had all of the divine attributes (again: the *majestic genus*), he declined to make full and complete use of them. Instead, as we read in Matthew 1–2 and in Luke 1–2, the divine attributes were hidden and veiled. God in human form was hidden for nine months in the womb of a woman. He was born like any other human being, and even then under the most humble of circumstances. Who knew he was God? Only Mary and Joseph. Only Zechariah the priest and his wife, Elizabeth. Only the shepherds and the wise men. Only Anna and Simeon. And they knew that he was God, not because it was obvious, not because he looked like God, but because the Word of God had told them. Otherwise he looked like any other infant. He took on the form of a servant. Then as a servant he lowered himself still further and further, until he suffered the death of the worst of criminals, death cursed in the law, death on a cross.

We usually praise people who start out their lives on the bottom rung of the ladder, so to speak, and then rise to the top by the force of their will, determination, and hard work. Jesus, however, began his human existence on the very top. He possessed all of the attributes of God given by the divine nature to the human nature, but he concealed his glory. And then "being in very nature God" (Philippians 2:6) he worked his way down, so to speak, until he "was despised and rejected by men, a man of sorrows, and familiar with suffering" (Isaiah 53:3). And then, to make his humiliation complete, he endured even this, that "it was the LORD's will to crush him and cause him to suffer" (Isaiah 53:10) until in his anguish he cried out, "My God, my God, why have you forsaken me?" (Matthew 27:46) and, "It is finished" (John 19:30). Between the time of his birth and his burial few saw behind the veil of his self-chosen humility. When he went from one place to another, he usually walked. God in the flesh got hungry and tired (Matthew 4:2; Mark 4:38). At the grave of Lazarus, God clothed with a human body and soul wept (John 11:35).

During the state of humiliation, however, Jesus did at times pull back the veil that hid his divine nature and attributes. At times he made a limited use of the divine attributes. He performed numerous miracles, and always by his own authority. He did not need some direct command or impetus from his Father to perform the miracles. In Luke 7:1-10, when the centurion recognized the power of Jesus and his ability to do whatever he wished, Jesus did not at all contradict the centurion. Instead, he praised his faith and healed the centurion's servant without even seeing him. Then there were Jesus' miracles over the raw forces of nature; they certainly showed that he possessed the divine attributes. He stilled a storm with only a word (Mark 4:39), so that even the disciples were astonished at his power. He walked on water (Mark 6:45-52). He fed thousands with only a few small loaves of bread and a few fish (Mark 6:35-44; 8:1-9). These and all of his other miracles demonstrated his almighty power and bore witness to the truth that Jesus was indeed God. He told the unbelieving Jews exactly that. If they didn't believe what he said, they should at least believe the witness of the works he had done; for the works proved that he was in fact the Son of God, the promised Messiah (John 10:19-38).

Among the most impressive evidences of that power, that hidden but real glory, was the miracle of the transfiguration. St. Matthew reports that "his face shone like the sun, and his clothes became as white as the light" (Matthew 17:2). At his transfiguration Jesus pulled away the veil more than he had ever done before. Peter, James, and

John were permitted to see him as he spoke with the prophets Moses and Elijah of his coming suffering and death in as much of his glory as anyone on earth could (Luke 9:31). What a magnificent proof of his deity! What a powerful encouragement for these disciples to hang on to their trust and not despair when they would see him shortly thereafter on the cross, in the depths of his humiliation! That was the chief purpose of the transfiguration—it was for their benefit, not for his. But as so often happens also with us in days of sorrow or suffering, the disciples forgot the event that testified to their Savior's love for them and focused instead on the tragedy of the moment, only on what they could see on Good Friday.

All of his miracles and his transfiguration proved beyond any shadow of doubt that Jesus was indeed the Son of God, God in human form. No one but God could do what Jesus did. The disciples recognized that indisputable fact (Matthew 16:16). Others either recognized it or came very close to recognizing it (e.g., John 3:2; 4:29-42; 7:25-46; 11:21-32; Mark 1:40-45). Even his enemies could not escape the evidence that Jesus was the Son of God; it was hardness of heart, perverse and persistent unbelief that was at the bottom of their rejection of him, not lack of evidence (John 10:22-39; 11:45-53).

It is worth noting in all of his miracles that Jesus did nothing merely for his own benefit. He never used his almighty power to help himself or to relieve himself of any inconvenience, trouble, or suffering. Even on those occasions when he escaped from attempts to kill him, the escape was not because he feared death or wanted to avoid it; it was rather because the time that he had chosen for his death had not yet come (Luke 4:28-30; John 8:59; 10:31-39). His very escape on those occasions was further evidence of his deity. Always he acted in his miracles for the benefit of those around him, even while proving by the miracles that he was indeed the Son of God. His selflessness, his total devotion to his Father, and his love for us was perfect, even in the miracles. What mere man would ever behave like that, would never use his power for his own benefit but only for the benefit of others? So while pointing to his deity, the miracles at the same time point to his mercy, his grace; for they are done only in service to others, never in service to himself.

The first reason for Christ's humiliation

But though the miracles give evidence of his deity, the entire period from his conception to his coming back to life on Easter Sunday is marked by humiliation; it is marked by a hiding of his deity and giving only fleeting glances of it. But why did he endure the state of humiliation? Why did he veil his divine nature and make only limited use of the divine attributes? There were two very important reasons. The first is mentioned by St. Paul in the *sedes doctrinae* cited earlier from Philippians 2. "Your attitude should be the same as that of Christ Jesus," the apostle declares (v. 5). Jesus' humility remains down through the ages as a pattern for all children of God. He possessed all things and remained all powerful, even in the state of humiliation. But he told the disciples that "the Son of Man did not come to be served, but to serve, and to give his life as a ransom for many" (Matthew 20:28). He told them that his serving was to set the example for them. Realizing how unwilling their sinful flesh (and ours too!) would be to see service as the highest honor and a goal of life, he repeated the instruction on the night of his betrayal and arrest. He said, "The greatest among you should be like the youngest, and the one who rules like the one who serves" (Luke 22:26). Indeed he provided even on that fateful night a most striking example of such service: He washed their feet—the job of the lowliest house servant, a job that the disciples had never performed for their Savior. Lest they miss the point, he spelled out its significance:

> "You call me 'Teacher' and 'Lord,' and rightly so, for that is what I am. Now that I, your Lord and Teacher, have washed your feet, you also should wash one another's feet. I have set you an example that you should do as I have done for you. I tell you the truth, no servant is greater than his master, nor is a messenger greater than the one who sent him. Now that you know these things, you will be blessed if you do them." (John 13:13-17)

Could there be a more dramatic example of humility and of selfless service than Jesus' during all of his earthly life, but especially on that night? He was only hours away from his betrayal, his arrest, Peter's denial, and the flight of the rest of the disciples. And Jesus knew all of that in detail before it happened. But Jesus entered into the hours of suffering and death to serve. And nothing could keep him even from the lowliest form of service, even on that night before his greatest service.

The significance of his example in the state of humiliation is further underscored by some of the rest of the dialogue that night in the upper room. The disciples were squabbling, as they had before, over which of them was the most important. It is interesting to note that Jesus did not deny that they were important as he set about instructing them on the subject of humility and service. Quite to the contrary, he made it clear to them that they were in fact far more important than even they had imagined. He told them, "I confer on you a kingdom, just as my Father conferred one on me, so that you may eat and drink at my table in my kingdom and sit on thrones, judging the twelve tribes of Israel" (Luke 22:29,30). Precisely because they were so important, they needed emphatic instruction on the subject of humility, a humility like his own. Such glory as they had in this life as his apostles was to remain as hidden as Jesus' own glory was, and just as real. The glory that Jesus had he hid for our sake and for our salvation; so, likewise, the glorious status of his apostles was to remain hidden until they entered heaven, so that they could use all that he had given them in service.

Even in this whole upper room discourse, one cannot help but be struck by the humility of Jesus, by his total devotion to service. For if ever there was a time when Jesus should have been served, should have at least expected a little bit of sympathy and support from his disciples, surely it was that night. But what do we see? He received not the least bit of encouragement. Instead, he gave it. He received not one word of support. Instead, he gave it. He received not the least bit of sympathy. Instead, he gave it. No one washed his feet. He washed theirs. No one fed him. He fed them, and that with his very body and blood.

The New Testament frequently strikes that theme of humility for us. And just as with the disciples, so often God's Word calls us to humility at the same time that it speaks to us of the believers' greatness, of the believers' importance. Christians are heirs with Christ. They are citizens with the saints. They are children of God. God controls the whole world in their interest and for their benefit. They have everything. And precisely because they have everything, they are called to imitate Christ in his humility. After all, those who have everything as an undeserved gift have no reason or excuse for pride and arrogance toward anyone. As possessors of all things in Christ, even heaven itself (Romans 8:14-39; Ephesians 2:6,7), Christians should consider greed, selfishness, and envy as foolishness. What then is left for the Christian? There remains for them the call to imitate Christ in his humility. Lords over all by faith, they are to be servants of all for the sake of Christ who served them with his all (Romans 12; 1 Peter 1:3-9; and all of chapters 4–5).[3]

So then, Christ entered into the state of humiliation to set for us the perfect example of what our lives with one another should be like. In

---

[3]Cf. Martin Luther's famous treatise "The Freedom of a Christian," *Luther's Works* (American Edition), Vol. 31, pp. 327-377.

an age when people go to great lengths to demand their rights to the service of others, the call of Christ to imitate his humility by free and happy service to others, to all, is certainly timely. He was not ashamed to serve us with his all. Will we be ashamed to serve him in imitation of his lowliness? May it be the goal set before us by St. Paul in the great *sedes* cited above, that we make it our greatest ambition to outdo one another in service!

The second reason for Christ's humiliation

The second reason for the state of humiliation should be obvious. If Jesus were going to succeed in his plan for our redemption, then he would have to conceal his majesty and glory and power as the Son of God. He would need to veil the divine attributes and not make complete use of them. For how could he be arrested, mocked, spit upon, beaten, abandoned by all, and crucified if he always looked the way he did on the Mount of Transfiguration? Both in the Old Testament and in the New the appearances of God in his glory evoked dread, even as it did on the Mount of the Transfiguration. How could it be otherwise—the appearance of the Almighty to the impotent, of the only Holy One to sinners, of Life to the mortal—how could that help but inspire at first dread? Only by hiding his deity under the veil of lowliness and weakness would it be possible for him to do what he came to do, to redeem the world by his cross and passion.

By humbling himself he made it possible for people to inflict such suffering and pain on him; they did it only by his permission. Jesus made it clear more than once that he had the power to prevent any harm from coming to himself. He told his enemies plainly: "No one takes [my life] from me, but I lay it down of my own accord. I have authority to lay it down and authority to take it up again" (John 10:18). Even then, when the time had come, at the beginning of his suffering he demonstrated that his coming agony was not because he was unable to prevent it. In the Garden of Gethsemane at the time of his arrest he demonstrated his might; the soldiers who came to arrest him fell powerless to the ground when Jesus declared that he was the one they were looking for (John 18:6). He even commanded the soldiers, as they were about to take him away, to let his disciples go. They obeyed the one they had come to arrest! Who ever heard of such a thing, that the prisoner commands his captors and they obey? What an amazing union of both power and humility! They obeyed in spite of the fact that Peter had taken out his sword and cut off the ear of the high priest's servant. We would have expected the prompt arrest, if not the death, of Peter on the spot! But, no, they let him go and that at Jesus' bidding! Then, removing all possibility of doubt concerning his willingness to suffer and concerning both his grace and his power in the midst of hatred, Jesus restored the ear of the servant (Luke 22:51). Yes, he was led to the slaughter like a sheep and endured like a lamb before those who shear it (Isaiah 53:7; 1 Peter 2:21-24). But every step of the way, every blow, every injustice, every abuse, every nail, every moment of his passion happened because he permitted it to happen, not because he could not prevent it.

Was there ever love like this? Was ever grace so amazing? Many people devote their entire lives to avoiding any kind of pain, be it mental, emotional, spiritual, or physical. But Jesus entered into the state of humiliation at the moment of his conception. In the human nature, which possessed all divine power and might by gift of the divine nature, Jesus did not make full or complete use of his divine attributes. In the process he has left us a most powerful example of humility that seeks only to serve. In the process he has demonstrated the greatness of his grace and love for us, that he willingly suffered as no man has ever suffered or ever could suffer. For his was the suffering of the punishment that all the rest of us deserve on account of sin. His was a suffering so great that it paid for all sin. What suffering of anyone else could compare with that? What work of anyone else could compare with that? What great virtue or merit in anyone else could possibly be set next to his as a cause for redemption? It should be obvious that the work of redemption is his alone. It should be obvious that the credit for it is his alone. It should be obvious that the consolation for us could not be greater; for if he did it all, then all is done! Having finished his suffering on the cross, his humiliation was almost over, but not quite. Even in his burial his humiliation continued; for his grave was not his own but belonged to another.

Again, and we cannot emphasize it too strongly, all of his humiliation he endured willingly. He planned on it already in eternity. He knew exactly what he was facing before he was born and every moment of his earthly life. And still—willingly—he entered on the pathway to the cross; willingly for you he humbled himself; willingly for you he suffered and died. That's love, is it not? That's pure grace!

In sum, the state of humiliation is that state or condition in which Christ's human nature did not make full and complete use of the divine attributes that it had by virtue of the majestic genus; he made only limited use of the divine attributes to prove his deity and to demonstrate his love for those in need. The state of humiliation lasted from the moment of his conception in the womb of the virgin Mary until the moment that his body again became alive in the grave on Easter Sunday morning.

The state of exaltation

> Let us fix our eyes on Jesus, the author and perfecter of our faith, who for the joy set before him endured the cross, scorning its shame, and sat down at the right hand of the throne of God. Consider him who endured such opposition from sinful men, so that you will not grow weary and lose heart. (Hebrews 12:2,3)

What a beautiful parallel these verses are to the *sedes doctrinae* for the two states of Christ! As St. Paul urges us to share the attitude of Christ's humility when he begins his description of Christ's state of humiliation, so the writer of Hebrews encourages us to remember the ultimate triumph. The state of humiliation came to an end. In point of fact, Christ always knew both that it would end and the result of its ending. The ultimate result of Christ's humiliation is his exaltation. Each believer and the whole Christian church on earth imitates Christ in his state of humiliation so long as we are in this world. But the prospect is held before us: One day, in heaven, we shall be exalted as he was exalted—first the cross, then the crown. His cross won our crown. Our cross ends with the crown that he alone deserves, but which he nevertheless won for us. And so great and glorious is the crown that the cross is more than just bearable. That's what St. Paul teaches us when he declares, "I consider that our present sufferings are not worth comparing with the glory that will be revealed in us" (Romans 8:18).

It is therefore with such a joyous prospect before us, that of sharing in Christ's exaltation, that we turn our attention now to this second state of Christ. The *sedes doctrinae* for his state of exaltation is the second half of the passage cited at the beginning of our consideration of the two states of Christ, namely, Philippians 2:9-11:

> Therefore God exalted him to the highest place and gave him the name that is above every name, that at the name of Jesus every knee should bow, in heaven and on earth and under the earth, and every tongue confess that Jesus Christ is Lord, to the glory of God the Father.

The apostle's words are a summary statement of the glorious result of Christ's work of redemption. As with the state of humiliation, so in the state of exaltation the words apply to the human nature of Christ. God exalted him in his human nature far above all earthly, all created positions. He exalted him in his human nature to his own right hand (Hebrews 1:3; 8:1; 10:12; 12:2; 1 Peter 3:22). The right hand of God is not so much a place as it is a position. For God is spirit and does not therefore have a literal right hand. The right hand of the king was where the prime minister sat. The right hand is the position of preeminence. The nature of that preeminence is expressed by the names that he receives. He receives the names Jesus and Christ. Jesus was the name that was given to him already at the annunciation (Luke 1:31). It was the name that announced the very reason for his coming, namely, to save us. The name Jesus means "Savior."

The name *Christ* is really a title. It means the "Anointed One." Jesus describes himself as the One anointed by the Spirit of God to preach the gospel (Luke 4:18) in fulfillment of God's promise through Isaiah (Isaiah 61:1). The prayer of the believers in Acts 4:26 refers to him as the Anointed One spoken of in Psalm 2:1,2. St. Peter in his sermon at the house of Cornelius likewise refers to Jesus as the One whom God anointed with the Holy Spirit and with power (Acts 10:38).

Thus the glory of Christ's exaltation is this, that he has now fully earned the names given to him by promise in the Old Testament and at the annunciation in the New Testament. That is his glory, that he truly is *Jesus,* the Savior of the world. He truly is the *Christ*, the One anointed by God both to be and to preach the gospel. For he is the gospel, the Word made flesh (John 1:14), who alone has carried the sin and guilt of the whole world. Let every knee bow to him in thankful adoration because of who he is and what he has done in the work of the world's redemption! Those who will not bow in thankful adoration will nevertheless bow; they will bow in terror at the hour of death and on the day of judgment when they see and must confess that he is God and Lord.

Jesus rejoiced in his coming exaltation even as the hour of his suffering drew near and spoke of it eloquently in his great High Priestly Prayer (John 17). All that he did had this glory in mind and in view, that at the conclusion of his work he would have earned the name *Savior.* Thus even in his exaltation he thinks of us. That is the glory he sought by becoming man, the glory that he wanted for himself and worked so hard to achieve, that by his humiliation he would become and in his exaltation forever remain our Savior, yours and mine. He did everything in his humiliation so that he might share his exaltation with us in heaven forever, and so forever merit and be worthy of the name *Savior.* Even in his exaltation grace shines through in all its splendor, beauty, and glory. Can you imagine that anyone with perfect foreknowledge would come into the world just to suffer ridicule, the torments of the damned, and death so that you and I—sinners that we are—could be exalted with him in heavenly bliss and glory? Obviously, no one would do that for us, even if he could—except for the Son of God, Jesus the Savior!

The state of exaltation began the moment that Jesus became alive in the grave on Easter Sunday morning. In that connection it is important to emphasize that he was up to that point truly dead. Those who deny the possibility of miracles deny also the reality of Christ's literal and physical resurrection from the dead. Some allege that he never really died on the cross but merely fainted. Then, in the cool and damp of the tomb, he recovered (the so-called Swoon Theory). Others maintain that he did indeed die, but they claim that the grief stricken disciples only imagined that they saw him alive later on (the so-called Hallucination Theory). Still others assert that the leaders of the early church came up with the story of Jesus' resurrection in order to encourage persecuted believers. A variation on that theme is that the resurrection of Christ only takes place spiritually in the hearts of those who believe in him.

All of these theories fly in the face of the clear teaching of the Scriptures. Jesus died on the cross. That was the testimony of soldiers who were authorities on death and dying (John 19:33). That was the conviction of those who buried him (John 19:38-41); they loved him and certainly would not have buried him if they had any thought that he might still be alive. And that is the testimony of the prophecies in the Old Testament (Isaiah 53:8,9) and of countless references in the New. The Swoon and Hallucination Theories have no support in the Scriptures and none in the witnesses of the early church. They are unbelieving fantasies from beginning to end.

The idea that Jesus' resurrection is only a spiritual resurrection in the hearts of believers has an outward veneer of piety. But it too flatly contradicts the Scriptures. The sad fact is that many who claim to be Christians teach just such a phony resurrection. That teaching should strike one as absurd on the face of it: If Christ were still dead, why should believers find any comfort in just pretending that he is alive, when they really think him to be dead? In fact, if he were still dead, what point would there be in believing in him at all? A dead Christ is no redeemer. A dead Christ is a fraud. That is exactly St. Paul's point in his great resurrection chapter, 1 Corinthians 15. St. Paul answers completely the fabrications of present-day teachers of a mere spiritual resurrection of Christ in the hearts of believers when he says, "If

Christ has not been raised, your faith is futile; you are still in your sins. If only for this life we have hope in Christ, we are to be pitied more than all men" (1 Corinthians 15:17,19). As surely as Christ was truly dead when his body was placed in the tomb, just so surely he rose again from the dead on Easter Sunday morning. He rose, not allegorically, not metaphorically, but literally and physically.

The doctrine of Christ's physical resurrection from the dead, like the doctrine of the incarnation, is one of the great pillars of the Christian faith. For, as already indicated, if Christ did not literally rise from the dead, then we are not literally redeemed. His resurrection was God's own seal on the work of redemption. It established once and for all that God was satisfied with Christ's sacrifice for us and for our salvation (1 Peter 1:3; 3:21). Had he remained in the tomb we would have no reason at all to trust that he is the Savior of the world. Yes, had he remained in the tomb, he would not have earned the "name that is above every name" (Philippians 2:9).

Moreover, had he remained in the tomb he would have broken his Word. He promised to rise from the dead (Matthew 16:21-26; 20:17-19). He even called himself "the resurrection and the life" (John 11:25). And his promises were very exact: He said that he would rise on the third day. And he kept his promise. Buried before sunset on Friday (the first day), his body remained undisturbed all day Saturday (the second day). Then at the close of the first part of Sunday (the third day: according to the Jewish way of reckoning time, Sunday began at sunset on the previous evening), early in the morning (Mark 16:2), he rose from the dead. In keeping with the promise of Psalm 16:10, his body did not decay. His soul entered the uncorrupted body, and he was again alive. He kept his Word in every detail.

Thus he proved himself to be the Son of God. For who could promise his own resurrection and then so exactly keep the promise other than God and God's own Son (Romans 1:4)? Since he is the Son of God, since he has kept his Word, since God has shown himself satisfied with Christ's work of redemption by his resurrection from the dead, every knee should bow and every tongue confess that Jesus Christ is Lord to the glory of God the Father.

Finally, had Christ not risen from the dead, then the promise that we too will one day rise would likewise be a fiction and a fraud. Jesus promised that he would rise. Our expectation of our own resurrection is based on that promise. He promised our resurrection frequently and eloquently, especially in John 14: "I will come back and take you to be with me that you also may be where I am" (v. 3) and "Because I live, you also will live" (v. 19). St. Paul rejoiced in Christ's resurrection because it held the guarantee of our resurrection: "But Christ has indeed been raised from the dead, the firstfruits of those who have fallen asleep. . . . For as in Adam all die, so in Christ all will be made alive. But each in his own turn: Christ, the firstfruits; then, when he comes, those who belong to him" (1 Corinthians 15:20-23).

It is impossible to exaggerate the importance of Jesus' resurrection from the dead. It proves that his sacrifice for us was accepted. It proves that he is God. It proves that we too will rise, just as he promised. A rejection of the doctrine of Christ's resurrection is a rejection of the whole point of his coming and the whole goal of the Christian faith. It is just as St. Paul said, "If Christ has not been raised, our preaching is useless and so is your faith" (1 Corinthians 15:14). Yes, if Christ did not rise and if we do not rise, then the devil has won. That such will not happen God promised already in Genesis 3:15. The devil is crushed! Death is defeated! He is risen, is risen indeed! And so too will we rise, just as he has promised.

Again we note that the state of exaltation applies to Christ's human nature as does the state of humiliation. It is as impossible to exalt the divine nature as it is to humble it. On Easter Sunday life returned to the lifeless body in the grave. Human soul and human body were again complete and again completely infused with all of the attributes of the divine nature. But with the resurrection there was a change, so to speak, in the way the human nature worked in its union with the divine. Where the divine attributes were veiled during the state of humiliation, they were not veiled in the state of exaltation. Where the human nature did not make full and complete use of the divine attributes during the humiliation, it did make full use of them during the state of exaltation. Consider the sequence of events in the state of exaltation:[4]

First, Jesus became alive in the grave. No human eye witnessed this miraculous event. (What a wondrous thing. His total shame and humiliation he let everyone see, but his ultimate triumph took place without any human eyes to behold it and wonder at it!) And his resurrection happened without any outside means or help. He was dead. Now he became alive.

Second, immediately the risen Christ descended into hell with both natures intact. We confess that truth in the Apostles' Creed on the basis

---

[4]We will be considering here steps as sequences of time, not degrees of exaltation. His exaltation was complete from the moment that he became alive in the tomb.

of 1 Peter 3:18,19: "He was put to death in the body but made alive by the Spirit, through whom also he went and preached to the spirits in prison." His descent into hell therefore was not part of his humiliation. It was part of his exaltation after he became alive in the grave. He did not go to hell to suffer. He went there to proclaim himself the victor over hell and all those in it who opposed him when they were alive on earth. He went to hell to proclaim himself the victor over their captor, the devil. More than that we cannot say about this strange and mysterious descent into hell, because more than that the Scriptures do not say. And no wonder. What could even the Bible tell us about such a strange and wondrous event that we would be able to understand?

We reject the Roman Catholic notion that Jesus descended in order to deliver the Old Testament believers and take them to heaven.[5] According to this false teaching, all the believers of the Old Testament were waiting for Jesus to die and then come down and take them up to heaven after his work was finished. But the Old Testament believers were in heaven already and did not need to be delivered from anything or any place. Jesus spoke of Lazarus in Abraham's bosom (Luke 16:19-31). Abraham was already in heaven. He was not still waiting to get there. The Old Testament believers were not waiting for redemption. They were saved by grace through faith just as New Testament believers are (Romans 4), and that salvation was as complete for them as it is for us. The only difference is that their faith was in the coming Messiah and ours is in the Messiah who has come. Theirs was a faith in God's promise, a faith that expected God to keep his Word; our faith looks back on the fulfilled promise. The Messiah in whom they trusted did not disappoint them or leave them at their death to wait for anything. There is not a word in the Bible to suggest such a thing.

Nor did Jesus go into hell to preach the gospel in order to create faith in the damned and save them after their death. It is clear from everything that the Scriptures say about death and judgment that once we die the possibility of coming to faith is gone. Those who despise the gospel in this life will suffer eternally in the next because of their unbelief (Luke 16:19-31; Matthew 25). Since Jesus did not descend in order to rescue Old Testament believers, nor to do mission work among the damned, all that is left that fits St. Peter's word for "preach" is a proclamation of victory. Why Jesus wanted to make such a proclamation in hell the Bible does not tell us. We may guess at reasons, but our guesses will have no clear foundation in the Word of God. It is there-

---

[5]Cf. *Catechism of the Catholic Church,* par. 632-635.

fore best to leave that as a question that will have to wait for an answer until we get to heaven.

The sequence of events then is this: (1) Jesus became alive in the grave, (2) he descended into hell, and then (3) he came victoriously out of the grave. The events are covered by the Apostles' Creed with these words: "He descended into hell, the third day he rose again from the dead." The words "the third day he rose again from the dead" refer to his coming out of the grave after he became alive and had descended into hell to proclaim his victory.

It is worth noting that Jesus did not come out of the grave after the angel rolled away the stone but before. The gospel writers leave us very much with the impression that when the stone was rolled away, Jesus was already gone (Matthew 28:1-6; Mark 16:1-6). He did not need the help of the angels in coming out of the tomb. They rolled away the stone so that the women and the disciples could go into the tomb and see that he was not there, not so that Jesus could get out.

That Jesus simply left the tomb without bothering with the stone is another indication of the change that took place in the state of exaltation. From the time of the resurrection, Jesus no longer accepted the limitations of time and space the way that he usually did during the state of humiliation. Then, he walked from place to place. He occupied space, and he limited himself to time. But after his resurrection he does not regularly do that. So he came out of the grave without anyone seeing him and without any need to have the stone rolled away for him. So he appeared and disappeared in the upper room on Easter Sunday without going through the door; he did the same again the following week (John 20:19-31). So he hid his identity from the Emmaus disciples, then revealed it, then disappeared (Luke 24:13-31).

Nevertheless, he was not a ghost, not a phantom, and certainly not a hallucination. His body was real and his human nature consisting of the union of body and soul was intact. He still walked when he chose to, as with the disciples on the road to Emmaus. He let the disciples touch him and he ate with them (Luke 24:37-43; John 20:27).

That then is the next step in his exaltation. He appeared physically for 40 days after his resurrection when and where he wished to appear. He no longer walked regularly with the disciples, lived with them, or regularly ate and drank with them. Nevertheless, his appearances were such that there could be no doubt that he was indeed alive, that he had indeed risen from the dead. The closing chapters of the four gospels, the sermons in the book of Acts, and the epistles all rejoice in the reality of Christ's resurrection from the dead. St. Paul summarizes the resurrection appearances in 1 Corinthians 15:3-8. All of these appearances mentioned by Paul were appearances of the whole Christ—not just of his human nature, not just of his divine nature, but of the one Lord Jesus Christ, true God and true man in one person. For there are not two Christs, one divine and one human; there is but one Christ, the Son of God and Mary's son, true God and true man, one person. Whenever he appeared, whether to the women outside of the tomb (Matthew 28:9,10) or to the disciples in the upper room (John 20), it is the total, the whole, and the complete person who appears, now with his exalted human nature showing divine attributes that he had hidden during the state of humiliation.

At the end of the 40 days the next stage or step in the state of exaltation took place. Jesus ascended into heaven and sat down at the right hand of the Father. His ascension was his great coronation day on which all the angels and the believers already in heaven began the worship and adoration that will never end. They sing the song that we will one day join them in singing:

> Worthy is the Lamb, who was slain, to receive power and wealth and wisdom and strength and honor and glory and praise! . . . To him who sits on the throne and to the Lamb be praise and honor and glory and power, for ever and ever! . . . Salvation belongs to our God, who sits on the throne, and to the Lamb. (Revelation 5:12,13; 7:10)

Again, it is important to note that the ascension of Christ is with both natures inseparably united. The whole person ascended, as we see from the accounts of his ascension (Mark 16:19; Luke 24:50,51; Acts 1:1-9). And the whole person, the divine nature and the exalted human nature, *sat at the right hand of God* (Mark 16:19). It is not as though the human nature was deposited somewhere in heaven while the divine nature somehow resumed its place in the Trinity. No, it is rather just as St. Paul said in the *sedes doctrinae* for the doctrine of the personal union of the two natures considered in chapter 10: "In Christ all the fullness of the Deity lives in bodily form" (Colossians 2:9). Protestant church bodies generally deny this truth. They maintain that according to the laws of physics, a body cannot occupy more than one space at a time; therefore, Christ's body must somehow be limited after his ascension. But where do the Scriptures teach that? One nature may be humbled, as is the human nature at the incarnation so that its power and glory are hidden for a time. One nature may be exalted, as is the human nature from the moment of Christ's coming alive in the grave and forever thereafter. But the two natures remain undivided in eternity. Christ is not bound by the laws of physics. He transcends them as far as heaven transcends the earth. He is limited by nothing and by no one.

So, why all the fuss about the union of the two natures in eternity? What difference does it make? It makes a difference most simply because the Scriptures do not tell us to worship two Christs or imagine that there are somehow two Christs, one human and one divine. It makes a difference as well because Protestant churches add yet another and related error to this one. They teach that since the body of Christ can only be in one place at a time, then his body and blood cannot be truly present in the Sacrament of the Altar, even though Christ plainly says, "This is my body" and "This is my blood." We will not presume to tell the risen Christ where he can and cannot be. If he says that he is in the Sacrament with his body and blood, then he is in the Sacrament with his body and blood! Finally, it is a great comfort to us that the One who has become our brother has been exalted in his human nature to the right hand of the Father. That's the consolation that the writer to the Hebrews encourages us to take when he tells us:

> Therefore, since we have a great high priest who has gone through the heavens, Jesus the Son of God, let us hold firmly to the faith we profess. For we do not have a high priest who is unable to sympathize with our weaknesses, but we have one who has been tempted in every way, just as we are—yet was without sin. Let us then approach the throne of grace with confidence, so that we may receive mercy and find grace to help us in our time of need. (Hebrews 4:14-16)

Once again it is worth noting that the truth of the Scriptures always resounds to the glory of Christ and the consolation of the believer. This truth of the Scriptures is no different. Our Savior, who became our brother by taking on a human nature, with that human nature sits now at the right hand of the Father; that truth assures us that he knows our needs and understands us perfectly. What great glory is his and what great consolation is ours that as Savior in both natures he is unlimited in power and majesty and worthy of all worship and praise now and forever. On the other hand, the error that denies the abiding union of the two natures contradicts all that the Scriptures say of him, robs him of his glory by limiting him, and robs us of the consoling assurance of his abiding presence for us according to both natures at God's right hand and with us in his Word and sacrament. Before he ascended into heaven he assured us that all power was his and that he promised to be with us always (Matthew 28:18-20). We take him at his Word. He would not lie to us. Thus, on the basis of the Scriptures we believe, teach, and confess in harmony with the Lutheran Confessions:

> Therefore, he did not reveal his majesty at all times but only when it pleased him, until he completely laid aside the form of a servant [Phil. 2:7] (but not his human nature) after his resurrection. Then he was again invested with the full use, revelation, and demonstration of his divine majesty and entered into his glory, in such a way that he knows everything, is able to do everything, is present for all his creatures, and has under his feet and in his hands all that is in heaven, on earth, and under the earth, not only as God but also as human creature, as he himself testifies, "All authority in heaven and on earth has been given to me" [Matt. 28:18], and St. Paul writes: he ascended "above all the heavens, so that he might fill all things" [Eph. 4:10]. As present everywhere he can exercise this power of his, he can do everything, and he knows all things. (FC Ep VIII, 16 p. 511)

Christ is and remains for all eternity God and human being in one inseparable person, which is the highest mystery after the mystery of the Holy Trinity, as the apostle testifies (1 Timothy 3:16). In this mystery lie our only comfort, life, and salvation (FC Ep VIII, 18 p. 512).

It is in this exalted state that Christ now fills all things and rules over all things for the benefit of his church (cf. the subheading "Christ is our great King"). Ultimately the final step in Christ's exaltation will arrive on the Last Day.[6] Then Jesus will return as he promised (Acts 1:11). Then he will bring all earthly history to a close and take his church on earth to be forever with his church in heaven. And so all things finally will be brought together under his feet, to the glory of his name and the eternal bliss of those who trust in him and in his redeeming work (Ephesians 1:10-23).

In sum, the state of exaltation has reference to the human nature. It began at the moment that Christ's body became alive in the grave and it continues through all eternity. In the state of exaltation Christ's human nature in its inseparable union with the divine nature makes full and complete use of all of the divine attributes given to it by the divine nature *(majestic genus),* attributes which the human nature

---

[6]The German expression for the Last Day is *Der Jüngste Tag*—the Youngest Day; it places the emphasis where it belongs, on the joyous new beginning.

had from the moment of conception in the womb of the virgin Mary but which Christ concealed or veiled during the state of humiliation.

The three offices of Christ

Christ has redeemed us by the work he did for our salvation in his two natures perfectly and inseparably joined. Christ redeemed us by his work in the state of humiliation and entered into his glory in the state of exaltation. Christ however has not become idle since his ascension. Quite to the contrary, he who was our Savior by his work of redemption on earth continues as our Savior at the right hand of the Father in eternity. He assures believers of every time and age, "Surely I am with you always, to the very end of the age" (Matthew 28:20). At the right hand of the Father, exalted to that position of power and authority by which he is wherever he chooses to be, he chooses to be with us. He did not ascend in order to get away from us. That too is such a remarkable evidence of his love and grace. Anyone who had suffered as he did at the hands of humankind might well be expected to get rid of us. But not Jesus! He ascended so that he would always be with us, invisibly but truly, and that according to both natures. The work of the ascended Christ, always at the Father's right hand and always with us, is described in the Scriptures as the work of his three offices. Jesus entered into his work in these three offices during his earthly ministry and he continues in them still. He is the great Prophet, our Great High Priest, and our King.

Christ is our great Prophet

The biblical definition of a prophet is this: a prophet is one who is commissioned by God to proclaim the Word of God. God himself trained some of the prophets and some were directly inspired by God to write the books of the Bible. Moses was called by God directly at the burning bush (Exodus 3) and was the greatest of the Old Testament prophets (Deuteronomy 34:10-12). Other prophets were trained in the school of the prophets, the Old Testament equivalent of a seminary. The prophets Elijah and Elisha conducted such a school (2 Kings 2). But whether called by God directly or indirectly after their training in the school of the prophets, their work was one and the same: to proclaim the Word of God. That Word was law and gospel. That Word was sometimes prophecy of future events in Israel's history. Sometimes it dealt with future events of the New Testament church and of heaven itself. Most important, it was an unfolding of promises concerning the coming Messiah and his work. In point of fact, all of their work, the proclamation of the law and the gospel as well as their work of foretelling events yet to come, had Christ as its center.

Once Christ came, he revealed and still reveals himself as the great Prophet, the Prophet in a class by himself. To be sure, he proclaimed the Word of God, as did all the faithful prophets of the Old Testament. That's why he came, as he told the people of Nazareth (Luke 4:16-21). However, when he proclaimed the Word of God, he did it not with authority that came from outside of himself but with the authority of God, since that is who he is. He proclaimed the Word of God as the one who is himself the Word of God made man, as St. John so beautifully sets forth in John 1.

As the Word of God who had come down from heaven and had taken on a human nature, he proclaimed the law of God. His preaching of the law was unique. For he not only taught it but kept it, yes, kept it perfectly and fulfilled in heart and life its every precept. He showed that the law required far more than mere outward performance of rituals or moral decency. What the law required was a perfect love for God and for one's neighbor in every thought, word, and work (e.g., Matthew 22:34-40; Luke 10:30-37). And it is that perfection that his every thought, word, and deed offered to God. No other prophet was ever able to do that.

Having kept it perfectly, he showed in a way that no one else ever could how serious God is about the law. For he suffered all of the anger of God against sin, against every breaking of the law (Romans 3:25; 5:12-19; 2 Corinthians 5:21). When we see him on the cross, we see the suffering that every other human being has deserved. No one else could ever proclaim the law the way that his suffering does. That is the most fearsome proclamation of the law that could ever be preached. If you want to know how serious sin is and how serious God is about the law, look at Jesus on the cross! If you want to know how desperate your condition is as a lost and condemned sinner, look at Jesus on the cross! If you want to know what your fate would be for all eternity apart from the redeeming work of Christ, look at Jesus on the cross!

Jesus' preaching of the law from the cross is called his *strange work,* or his *foreign work (opus alienum),* the work spoken of by Isaiah (28:21). That is, his preaching of the law is most of all a preparation for his true and proper work *(opus proprium)* as the great Prophet, namely, the preaching of the gospel. The prophets of the Old Testament also preached the gospel. But as with Jesus' preaching of the law, so also his preaching of the gospel was unique. For Jesus is himself that gospel, the one who stood behind it and then fulfilled its promises of salvation. He is the one who gave those promises of forgiveness and eternal life their value and validity by his words and work. The word *gospel* means "good news." It is the good news that he has come to proclaim, the good news that he has fulfilled the law for us and brought life and salvation to light through his teaching and his work (John 1:17). Yes, he proclaims the message and he is that message; he is the good news; he is its heart and core, its very embodiment. He proclaims a forgiveness and salvation that he has won for us. To call him "the great Prophet" is an understatement if ever there was one! Again, he not only proclaims the Word of God, he is the Word of God incarnate.

Is it not an amazing thing? We look at the cross of Christ and there we see God's rage and wrath against sin and sinners. There we see the most severe preaching of the law. We look at the cross of Christ and there we see love incomparable and unequaled. There we see God so filled with longing for our redemption that he himself pays for it fully in the willing sacrifice of his Son; that is indeed the most wondrous preaching of the gospel! Again, Christ is the great Prophet because he is the Word of law and gospel that he preaches!

We need to express one word of caution when we speak of Christ as the Word of God. Some false teachers, in order to confuse and deceive their hearers, say, "We believe and teach that the Word of God is inspired and without error!" The hearer may assume that the speaker was referring to the Bible. In point of fact, the false teacher may have been referring only to Christ and not to the written Word of God, the Bible, whose teaching the false teacher does not accept or teach. He speaks as he does to lull the hearer into a false sense of security, of thinking that the false teacher is really faithful to the written Word of God, the Bible. Of course Christ is inspired and without error. He is God and the Son of God. But the Bible is also inspired and without error, precisely because God is its source and Christ the Word of God incarnate is its center, its heart and core. In point of fact, we know nothing of Christ, the Word of God incarnate, apart from the written Word of God in the Bible. It is in the written Word that the incarnate Word reveals and gives himself to us. The deceiver and false prophet who rejects the written Word also has rejected the incarnate Word; the two go together. We can never have the one without the other.

When, therefore, we say that Christ not only teaches the Word of God but also is the Word of God incarnate, we do not mean to detract at all from the written Word of God, the Bible. Nor do we detract from the unique glory of Christ as the Word incarnate when we speak of the Bible as the verbally inspired Word of God. We do well to ask, when someone declares his loyalty to the Word, whether he is talking about the incarnate Word or the written Word or both. If not both, then the speaker is a deceiver and a false prophet who is loyal to neither the incarnate Word nor the written Word.

The prophetic work of Christ continues to this day. Shortly before his ascension, he gave his Great Commission to the church to "go and make disciples of all nations, baptizing them in the name of the Father and of the Son and of the Holy Spirit, and teaching them to obey everything I have commanded you" (Matthew 28:19,20). On the basis of that commission, the church continues as the means through which Christ continues his prophetic work. The church proclaims the law and the gospel from his Word. It tells of things to come that are revealed in his Word, namely, those things pertaining to the work of the church and the coming of Christ again at the end of time to raise the dead and judge all according to his Word. The church proclaims the law and the gospel. But the chief focus and center is always on the gospel of forgiveness through faith in Christ's redeeming work. Jesus underscored that emphasis in his solemn and majestic commission to the apostles on Easter Sunday:

> Again Jesus said, "Peace be with you! As the Father has sent me, I am sending you." And with that he breathed on them and said, "Receive the Holy Spirit. If you forgive anyone his sins, they are forgiven; if you do not forgive them, they are not forgiven." (John 20:21-23)

Thus, the work of the church is not the work of establishing a visible kingdom of God on earth ruled over by the pope or dictated to by Protestant self-appointed clergy-guardians of society. The work of the church is the work of Christ's prophetic office. It is the work of proclaiming the law as Jesus did, so that people will see from it how serious God is about sin and therefore how desperately they need the Savior. It is the work of proclaiming the gospel with the goal of forgiving the sins of the repentant. It is the work of pronouncing God's judgment on those who do not repent (John 3:16-18). It is the work of showing believers those works which please God and those which call down his wrath (e.g., Romans 12; Galatians 5,6; Ephesians 4,6). In sum, it is the work of bringing the gospel to the lost and strengthening those who already believe it, so that their lives may more and more reflect their faith.

In order to carry forward his office as the great Prophet, Christ has especially established the office of the public ministry. He calls pastors and teachers of his Word through the church to exercise publicly and in his name what Luther's Small Catechism refers to as the ministry of the keys. Christ calls these public servants of the gospel through the church. They are Christ's servants in the midst of the people of God, his gifts for building up the people of God through the faithful proclamation of his Word (Ephesians 4:7-16). They are not rulers over God's flock, for Christ alone is King (1 Peter 5:2-4). Nor are they hirelings who merely follow the whims and fancies of those they serve (1 Timothy 4). As servants of Christ in the midst of the people of God, they serve his people best by faithfulness to his Word in their preaching and teaching as well as in their lives (1 Timothy 3).[7]

Christ is our Great High Priest

The high priests of the Old Testament had two major assignments: They offered sacrifices for the people and they interceded with God for the people as they offered those sacrifices. The high priest was set apart from the people and anointed for this special work. He was to be physically flawless; any physical defect would exclude him from so sacred an office and work. His vestments were of the finest linen, so that he would not sweat in them when he offered his sacrifices. He was in many respects removed from the common life of his countrymen to symbolize that in his person and work he was separate as the special and holy intermediary between God and his people. He wore a breastplate with the names of the tribes of Israel inscribed on it in precious stones, so that he would always know and remember that his function was to intercede with God for the people (Exodus 28,29; Leviticus 8,9).

The outward purity and holiness of the Old Testament high priests was to serve as a shadow and a picture of the one Great High Priest to come: Jesus Christ. He was the fulfillment of the purity and holiness that the Old Testament high priests could only picture. Thus, Christ is unique. He is the Great High Priest because he comes into the presence of his Father not just with an appearance of holiness like the high priests in the Old Testament but with real, actual, perfect holiness. There is no stain of sin in him. There is nothing that he needs to repent of and nothing for which he needs forgiveness.

Of all the sacrifices that the high priest offered, the most important was that offered on the great Day of Atonement (Leviticus 16). On that day the high priest would enter God's throne room on earth: the Most Holy Place in the tabernacle and, after the time of Solomon, in the temple. He entered it twice on that day and on no other. Each time he

---

[7]We will consider the subject of the church, its mission and ministry, more fully in chapter 15.

brought blood with him, the blood of a bull for his own sins and the blood of a goat for the sins of the people. The blood was sprinkled over the top of the ark of the covenant, called the mercy seat. The sprinkling of the blood covered up the stone tablets of the law, which were inside the ark. With the law covered up, so too then were the sins against it likewise covered by that blood. The high priest then took a second goat, called the scapegoat, and confessed the sins of the people over the goat. The goat, bearing the sins confessed over him, was then driven out of the camp and into the wilderness to die.

Christ, the Great High Priest, fulfilled all of those pictures. He offered a sacrifice, but his was not the sacrifice of bulls and goats or sheep. His was the sacrifice of himself as the perfect Lamb of God, who takes away the sin of the world (John 1:29,36). He endured the cross and the shame, suffering, and death. He, the almighty Son of God, at whose command the legions of angels stand at the ready (Matthew 26:53,54), refused to lift a finger of his own or a feather of any angel's wing to prevent or even lesson his torment. His is a perfect sacrifice on so many different counts. It is perfect because the One suffering is perfect; it is not for himself that he endures suffering but for us, for all mankind. It is perfect because he endures it willingly and freely just as Isaiah prophesied about him in Isaiah 53; as we have already noted, no one takes his life from him. It is the perfect sacrifice at the time of his own choosing. It is perfect in that it cannot be matched by any other sacrifice and because it need not be matched by any other sacrifice. His is the all-sufficient sacrifice, active as he wills it and passive as he permits and endures it, for the sins of the world. It is perfect because it covers the punishment due to all mankind and the debt owed to God for the sin of the whole world. From eternity to eternity the perfect sacrifice of the Great High Priest avails before the throne of God as the one, the only, the all-sufficient sacrifice for sin.

With the blood of his sacrifice he enters into the Holy of Holies in heaven as the Great High Priest for all mankind. He presents himself as the perfect Priest with the perfect sacrifice. He has once and for all poured out his own blood most holy to cover all the unholiness of sinful, fallen humankind. To this day and into eternity he continues as our Great High Priest, successfully interceding for us by virtue of his perfect sacrifice for us. St. John beautifully describes that work of intercession so inseparably linked to Christ's sacrifice for us. He tells us, "If anybody does sin, we have one who speaks to the Father in our defense—Jesus Christ, the Righteous One. He is the atoning sacrifice for our sins, and not only for ours but also for the sins of the whole world" (1 John 2:1,2).

What a perfect description of Christ's high priestly work! To this day, in this very hour, when we pray for forgiveness, there is our Great High Priest, the Holy One, acting on our behalf, interceding for us. In an eternal procession before the Most Holy Place in heaven he carries the blood of his own sacrifice that has once and for all won our pardon. His sacrifice, his blood, has washed away all our sins. Think of that grand and glorious, that saving procession of Christ behind the veil in the Most Holy Place in heaven—it's going on even as you pray. It continues at every cry of the penitent: "God, be merciful to me, a sinner!"

Again, we cannot help but note that it is biblical understatement to call him who serves us thus *Great!* While there is no other word that will do, that one word just seems too small for him as our Great High Priest in his high priestly office.

Again we refer to the epistle to the Hebrews in the New Testament, especially chapters 4–10, for a masterful outline of Christ's work as the fulfillment of the work of the Old Testament high priests. The universal benefit and eternal value of his unique sacrifice came from the fact that he himself, the God-man, was the sacrifice.

This work of Christ as the Great High Priest is summarized in the *doctrine of the vicarious atonement.* The *sedes doctrinae* for this doctrine is the passage just cited above, 1 John 2:1,2. This passage is a masterful summary of Christ's work as our Great High Priest. *"If anybody does sin," the apostle says. And there has never been anyone in the world except Christ who does not sin.* For all such sinners there is only one *Righteous One,* one perfectly Holy One, One who can stand before the Father as the defense attorney. He can stand before the Father precisely because he is the *Righteous One,* the One who has no sin to separate him from the Father. He is the One who perfectly kept his Father's law. He stands before the Father for us. Apart from him we would cower in dread before the Father's judgment seat. But Jesus stands there, full of confidence, devoid of the least fear. And he stands there for us. *"He is the atoning sacrifice for our sins."* The word *atone* means "to make a payment for, to make right again, to restore." An atoning sacrifice is one that makes payment or reparation for the damage done to God's justice and holiness. An atoning sacrifice is one that makes good what was ruined and made vile by sin. An atoning sacrifice is one that restores the damned to God's grace and favor by the payment of the price demanded for such a restoration.

The word *atonement* in this doctrine is modified by the adjective *vicarious*. That word means "substitutionary." Christ's sacrifice on the cross is not for himself; it is for our sins, and not only for ours but also for the sins of the whole world. On Good Friday he hangs on the cross as the substitute under the wrath of God to make atonement for the whole world.

This great work of Christ, the work of the vicarious atonement, as it is considered in the *sedes* in 1 John 2, also holds before us and summarizes the two kinds of obedience that Christ rendered as he redeemed us. The first type of obedience is called his *active obedience.* St. John sums it up nicely when he calls Jesus the *Righteous One.* Who is righteous, completely right with God by virtue of perfect obedience to the law of God? Only one! Only Jesus Christ! He "actively" obeyed the law and did so perfectly. He was never just a robot or, so to speak, on automatic pilot. With every thought, word, and work he consciously kept the law of God. That is, in everything he ever thought, said, or did in his nature he perfectly loved God and perfectly served him by loving and serving all around him. All that he thought and did was always by conscious choice and with loving intent. Try to find a moment in life when you can say that of yourself, and you will soon see how great a feat it is that Jesus Christ is by his active obedience rightly called and the only one who can be called the *Righteous One.*

The second kind of obedience is called his *passive obedience,* by which he permitted himself to be reviled, scourged, spit upon, and then crucified. He could have acted to prevent it. The legions of angels were at his command. He possessed all power in heaven and on earth. But as already noted, he did not lift a finger or stir an angel's feather to prevent his most gruesome suffering and deepest agony. He endured it and endured it willingly. Again, look for times in life when you were willing to suffer as an innocent one for someone truly and horribly guilty. What is the favorite and early cry of the child when it thinks it is being punished for the crime of another? "It's not fair!" The child cries that even when guilty. Again, when we think of how unwilling we are to suffer the least inconvenience "unfairly," we begin to get just the smallest inkling of what it means, this passive obedience of Christ, the suffering of the only innocent One for all the guilty, for *me,* the guilty!

Both the active and the passive obedience were accomplished for us. He obeyed the law as our substitute. He suffered his passion as our substitute. That's what St. John is telling us when he tells us that Jesus is the Righteous One who has made a perfect payment for the sins of the world.

Because of that substitutionary obedience, both active and passive, no one need fear that perhaps he has been left out, that perhaps the sacrifice was only for other people. When he hung on the cross, he bore the punishment for every sin and was the substitute under the wrath of God for every sinner. Who on days of guilt and shame, from the pit of despair, would not be moved to tears of joy to hear this? *For the whole world! Therefore for me, even for me, he, the one Great High Priest, is the vicarious atonement!*

Thus the doctrine of the vicarious atonement, briefly stated, is this: *Christ, as the substitute for all of humanity, paid the price and suffered the penalty for every sin and for every sinner by his perfect sacrifice on the cross.*

By virtue of the vicarious atonement Christ continues to make intercession for us at God's right hand. That's the second work of a priest, first to sacrifice and then to make intercession. St. Paul assures us of that continuing work of Christ, our Great High Priest, and of its importance for us: "Who will bring any charge against those whom God has chosen? It is God who justifies. Who is he that condemns? Christ Jesus, who died—more than that, who was raised to life—is at the right hand of God and is also interceding for us" (Romans 8:33,34).

We commonly end many of our prayers with a phrase something like this: "This we ask through Jesus Christ our Lord" or "This we ask alone through the merits and intercession of Jesus Christ, our Lord." That and similar conclusions to our prayers are our way of expressing our trust in Christ's high priestly office, in his vicarious atonement and in his continuing intercession for us as our Great High Priest. We have every confidence that his prayers, his intercessions, for us are heard by the Father, because he has merited and deserved an answer to his prayers for us by virtue of his perfect life and his substitutionary sacrifice. He himself declares in anticipation of his continuing high priestly work, "I lay down my life for the sheep. The reason my Father loves me is that I lay down my life—only to take it up again" (John 10:15,17). And he assures us that in him and because of him our prayers too are pleasing to his Father (John 14; 16:23-28).

Therefore when we pray for forgiveness, it is on the basis of Christ's high priestly vicarious atonement and his consequent and constant intercession for us that we pray. When we hear the proclamation of the gospel of forgiveness, we trust it because of Christ's vicarious atonement and his successful intercession for us. When we bring any prayer for spiritual blessings to God, we can be sure that Christ himself joins us in our prayer and grants it in his Word and sacraments, just as he has promised. When we bring prayers for temporal blessings to God, we bring those too on the basis of Christ's vicarious atonement, trusting that he will grant whatever best serves our eternal interests (Romans 8:28).

By his work as our Great High Priest, by the work done in the union of the two natures in one person, by his active and passive obedience, by the vicarious atonement, Christ accomplished fully the work of our redemption, i.e., the work of buying us back. He bought us back from the rule of sin, death, hell, and the power of the devil. The rule of sin was that power that sin had over us that was so complete that we could do nothing but sin. Conceived and born in sin, we were so chained by it that it controlled our every impulse, spoiled and stained our every thought, word, and work, whether we recognized that or not. For what is the ruling principle by which we live by nature? It is self-service and self-preservation. It certainly is not perfect love for God in every thought, word, and deed, or perfect love that wants only to serve our fellow man. And everything that does not spring from such a perfect love for God or does not flow from such a perfect love for those we can serve is sin. But Christ has redeemed us from the rule of sin. By faith in his redeeming work, sin does not control our every thought and action.

When we say that Christ has redeemed us from sin, we do not mean that we are now perfect in our nature or that we expect to become perfect in this life. Redemption from sin is complete on God's side. That is, no other price can be paid for sin than the one paid by Christ in his vicarious atonement. We have been completely cleansed of the guilt of sin by the blood of Christ (1 John 1:7). We have been liberated from the curse that the law pronounces over every sinner (Galatians 3:13). But on our side, in our Christian lives, in our daily experience, this freedom from sin's rule remains a work in progress. Neither our love for God inspired by his love for us nor our zeal to serve our neighbor inspired by his service to us is ever perfect this side of heaven. It is our *status*—not our nature—that has been changed so that we are now dear children of God, brothers and sisters of Christ, instead of children of wrath. But our sinful nature has not yet been completely destroyed, so that we must wrestle against sin and temptation as long as we live. Nevertheless, we show our freedom from sin's rule by the struggle against sin, as St. Paul tells us in Romans 7. Though the struggle is imperfect and incomplete, nevertheless now we actually do strive to live in love to God, in loyalty to his Word, and in service to one another. We still have our inherited sinful nature, but the fact and proclamation of our redemption, of our forgiveness, gives us a new will that hates sin.

The struggle of our new will against our inherited sinful nature is itself evidence of Christian faith and life. Where there is no struggle, sin has regained the mastery and re-enslaved us. Where there is no struggle, faith has died. The nature of the struggle changes during the various stages of life. But struggle there always will be. The great marvel and miracle is that though in our lives we never completely win a battle, the victory over sin is nevertheless total and complete. For the victory has been won by Christ for us in his perfect work of redemption; in his Word and sacraments he gives that victory to us in the message of forgiveness full and free (Romans 7:24,25).

In this connection it is important to remember that Christ has redeemed us *from* sin, not *for* sin. Some perversely imagine that since Christ's work of redemption is complete and that since Christ has paid for the sins of the whole world, it now no longer matters what we do; we can sin as much as we want, as long as we just believe or as long as we get around to repenting some time later. Such people know nothing of faith or repentance. Such people remain spiritually blind, dead, and enemies of God. Such people have turned Christ's incomparable love and his enormous sacrifice for them into a license to sin. St. Paul sternly warns against the notion that the work of redemption was accomplished so that we could wallow in the sin from which Christ has redeemed us at so great a price. He solemnly declares, "I warn you, as I did before, that those who live like this will not inherit the kingdom of God" (Galatians 5:21). He pleads with us, "I urge you, brothers, in view of God's mercy, to offer your bodies as living sacrifices, holy and pleasing to God—this is your spiritual act of worship" (Romans 12:1).

When Jesus speaks of our freedom from sin, he speaks of it as a freedom that we have as members of his holy family. He points out that a freedom *for* sin would be no freedom at all; it is in fact the worst form of slavery (John 8:31-47). St. Paul makes the same point (Romans 7:4-6). Thus while our struggle against sin and temptation does not save us and does not contribute in the least to our salvation, nevertheless the struggle against sin and temptation is necessary, not optional. It is the necessary result of our redemption, not its cause. (For a further consideration of this point, cf. chapter 9, under "Mortal and venial sins.") In point of fact, our struggle is a joyful struggle because of that assured victory. For by the struggle we have the honor of reflecting the love of Christ for those around us. By it we have the honor of being useful in imitation of him. By it we have the happy anticipation that in heaven we will see that, just as he said, our labor was not in vain (1 Corinthians 15:58).

Christ has also redeemed us from death by his vicarious atonement. Death is a consequence of sin. We all still die, because we still have sin in our nature and sin in our lives. But nevertheless it remains true: Christ has redeemed us from death. For though we die, our death has been turned into the ultimate triumph over sin, not the ultimate disaster in consequence of sin. Recall that the basic meaning of the word *death* is "separation." But what is there of separation in the death of the Christian? There is no separation from God, that dread death introduced by Adam and Eve in the garden. For the Christian at his earthly death continues to live with God—but now in heaven. Even the death defined as a separation of body and soul is only temporary as we await the experience of their reunification on the Last Day. And what of eternal death, that most horrible of separations, a separation from God's grace in the torments of hell forever? That death has been conquered and abolished altogether for those who trust in Christ's redeeming work. Death has become the gateway to heaven and the beginning of the enjoyment of eternal life with God and all the angels and saints. St. Paul sings a hymn of triumph as he contemplates death, which has been swallowed up in victory because of Christ's triumph (1 Corinthians 15:54-57). Death has become so insignificant that Jesus even tells us that in him we really will never die (John 11:25,26). It has in effect become a nothing *(ein Unding—* an *unthing).*

Christ has also redeemed us from hell and the power of the devil. Jesus showed his power over the devil when he drove the devils out of the possessed during his earthly ministry (Luke 11:14-22). He showed his power over hell in his triumphant resurrection from the dead and his descent into hell on Easter Sunday as the victor (1 Peter 3:19). That triumph and victory was accomplished for our sake, not for his own. As our original sin made us slaves to sin, so by our actual sins we voluntarily gave ourselves over in slavery to the devil (Romans 6, 7). Thus we became slaves to death and hell, the consequence and penalty for sin. But by his redeeming work Jesus has shattered the chains that bound us and has crushed the head of the serpent, just as God promised in the Garden of Eden (Genesis 3:15; 1 John 3:8). The devil may well accuse us of sin and claim us for his own; he may demand that we join him in his eternal torment. But Christ has redeemed us! That ends the matter. The devil may rage all he wants. Hell may claim us as its rightful prey. But over against the rage of the devil and the gaping jaws of hell stands the perfect obedience of Christ for us; over against the devil and hell is the entire high priestly work of Christ and his glorious resurrection. In the balance his vicarious atonement redeems us and sets us free (Romans 3:23,24).

Is it possible to overestimate the beauty and depth of the redemption wrought by Christ in his high priestly office? Could one ever exhaust the praise due to Christ or the consolation now belonging to each believer as a result of the vicarious atonement? We can but join in St. Paul's great hymn of praise as he comes to the close of the great doctrinal chapters in the epistle to the Romans that focus on the work of redemption:

> Oh, the depth of the riches of the wisdom and knowledge of God! How unsearchable his judgments, and his paths beyond tracing out! "Who has known the mind of the Lord? Or who has been his counselor?" "Who has ever given to God, that God should repay him?" For from him and through him and to him are all things. To him be the glory forever! (Romans 11:33-36)

The reader may note that there is a good deal of repetition in the setting forth of these doctrines concerning our redemption. That's because God himself in his Word never tires of finding ways of setting forth this central doctrine of the Bible. And the church has never tired of finding ways of restating and repeating this saving truth about our redemption as the be all and end all of what matters to us for time and for eternity! May the reader not find it tiresome but join with the church in unending delight over this cardinal truth from the heart of God to our hearts!

Christ is our great King

As we have noted so often, finding words to describe Christ leaves one a language beggar. For our Redeemer is unique in every way. Finding words that fit him would be impossible for us, if the Scriptures themselves did not provide the words. Even then, so many of the terms seem to us to be a gross understatement of the reality. So it is with this term: *King.* That is his name, "KING OF KINGS AND LORD OF LORDS," and there is none other (Revelation 19:16). Christ is all in all (Ephesians 1:20-23). Christ fills all things in his state of exaltation, and that according to both natures. Christ rules over all things in heaven and on earth and under the earth. Christ knows and controls all things so that even though his Word and his church always appear on the brink of destruction, they nevertheless continue from age to age, just as he has promised (Matthew 16:18; 24:35). Though the word may be inadequate to express the profound reality, we have no other word for this office of Christ: Christ is King.

In an attempt to appreciate the richness of the title King as it applies to Christ, we speak of him as King over three kingdoms. It is not as though they are separate, the way that kingdoms on earth are separate. They are perfectly united under his rule and control. The distinction between the three kingdoms is a distinction of convenience that helps us to understand the nature of his rule and his purposes in that rule as they are described for us in the Bible.

Christ's kingdom of nature/the world/power

The first kingdom of Christ is the *kingdom of nature* or the *kingdom of the world,* sometimes simply called the *kingdom of power.* Included in the first kingdom are all the forces of nature and all of human history. Even during the state of humiliation Christ showed himself as the ultimate King over nature and over history. He stilled the raging storm with only a simple rebuke, so that even the disciples marveled and exclaimed, "Even the wind and the waves obey him!" (Mark 4:41). With only a word or a touch and sometimes with nothing more than his will he demonstrated his rule over nature when he healed the sick, drove out demons, and raised the dead. His own arrest and crucifixion demonstrated his control over history, as we have noted earlier—his arrest and crucifixion could not take place until he permitted it.

He continues as King of the universe, ruler over time and tide, and over the history of individuals and nations. How he exercises that rule often remains a mystery to us. He does it in such a way that he does not destroy human freedom of will and action in those things subject to reason (cf. chapter 6, under "The providence of God"). But, nevertheless, when all is said and done that man can say and do, Christ remains in control. Without destroying the human will, he limits the damage that the wicked intend to do to harm his own and to destroy the church. And even when he permits their partial or seeming success, he still overturns their intention for the benefit of his own and for the church.

As King he advances and prospers the good works of those who serve him. He brings it about that their works are more beneficial than they had imagined and that the flaws and failings in those works are minimized. That is a most comforting aspect of his rule as King, not least for parents, pastors, and teachers. They are painfully aware of at least some of their weaknesses and limitations. Nevertheless, God blesses their work with his Word and in Jesus' name. Ask an aged pastor and he will tell you, "When I look back on my life, I marvel that the church was blessed through my efforts, and that in spite of all my mistakes and, yes, my sins too!"

Christ's kingdom of grace

The second kingdom is called the *kingdom of grace.* The kingdom of grace is not a place. The kingdom of grace is an activity. It is Christ's ruling activity in the heart and mind and life of each Christian. Collectively the kingdom of grace is his ruling activity in the church that hears his Word and teaches it. The church in its best definition consists of all those who trust in Christ as their only Redeemer (a point we will consider further in chapter 15).

The ruling activity of Christ in his second kingdom, the kingdom of grace, does not take place with a sword or a gun. It is not carried out through force and threats from earthly governments. It happens quietly in the souls of one Christian after another by means of the gospel in Word and sacraments. Almost all of the parables of Jesus speak of this second kingdom using analogies from nature to make the point. The kingdom of God is, Jesus said, like seed that is sown or like a tiny mustard seed in the garden (Mark 4:1-34). The seed of God's Word is sown in hearts that by nature are dead. That seed of the gospel of forgiveness, the good news of Christ's vicarious atonement, has within it the power to spring and sprout, to grow and bring forth fruit that is appropriate to and comes from the seed.

That is how the second kingdom is created, through the preaching of the gospel. By the gospel message of the forgiveness won for us by the Savior's work of redemption, Christ comes to the human heart and establishes his throne there. By that gospel message he creates trust in his work for us and for our salvation. By the seed of the gospel he turns our cold and dead hearts to hearts that are alive, yes, hearts in which he dwells together with his Father (John 14:23). He converts us from willing slaves of Satan to children of God. He gives us the new birth. He raises us up from spiritual death to spiritual life. By the gospel he produces the fruit of love and other good works, using the law to show us what good works are and how they should be done; he shows us that they should be done out of gratitude for the gift of salvation, not in order to earn or deserve it. He shows us that they should be done to his praise and for the benefit of our neighbor. That is how he creates and preserves the second kingdom. That is how he enthrones himself as King in our hearts and lives.

We see evidence in this second kingdom that his control and rule over the first, the kingdom of his power in nature and in history, is chiefly for benefit of the church. We see it in every age of history. For in every age there have been those who bent every effort to destroy the second kingdom. At the dawn of history Cain killed his believing brother Abel (Genesis 4). Saul persecuted the believers in Israel and tried to kill David (1 Samuel 18–24,26). Ahab and Jezebel persecuted Elijah (1 Kings 18,19). In the New Testament, the book of Acts is filled with examples of efforts to destroy the second kingdom. Saul (Paul's name before his conversion) and the leaders of the Jews tried to wipe out the early church. Efforts to destroy the church did not cease with the conversion of the rulers of the Roman world to Christianity. When in history were there not governments who either suppressed Christianity altogether or supported those who wanted to corrupt it from within by false doctrine? When have there not been heretics who wanted to replace the rule of Christ through his Word with the rule of reason or emotion? In our day a number of "isms"—e.g., humanism, fascism, communism, and materialism—threaten every day to destroy the second kingdom.

It is not too much to say that in each and every age of history one should have expected the final extermination of the gospel and its daughter, the church. And yet the church endures. Persecuted and hounded from forces outside of the church, corrupted by false teachers within, discredited because of the lives of hypocrites or weak members, the message of the gospel continues to be proclaimed. Christ rules in the first kingdom, the kingdom of nature and history, in such a way that nothing can destroy his second kingdom. He rules in such a way that even the attempts of his enemies only serve ultimately the purposes that he has for the preservation of the church and of believers through the power of the gospel.

In the Old Testament, God promised that such would always be the case; people would do their best to do the worst, to destroy the gospel and faith. But God would only laugh at them and their puny and futile efforts against him (Psalm 2). In the New Testament, St. Paul warned his young pastor protégé Timothy that false teachers would never go away but only get worse from age to age (1 Timothy 4). Heaven already has in it a host of saints and martyrs of every age who suffered or died at the hands of those who hated Christ and his gospel and who took it out on those who believed the gospel (Revelation 7:9-17).[8] But through it all the promise of Christ remains, that even

---

[8]For a relatively brief and very readable account of the persecutions that took place during the life of the early church, cf. Eusebius (d. 339) *Ecclesiastical History.*

the gates of hell cannot destroy his church or wipe out the gospel by which his second kingdom is created and extended and preserved (Matthew 16:18; 24:35).

The fact that the gospel has never been destroyed, the fact that therefore the kingdom of Christ in the hearts of believers has continued to this day and will continue to the end of time, is thus proof of Christ's rule over the first kingdom in the interest of the second kingdom.

To be sure a profound mystery yet remains. The questions are asked: If Christ rules and controls the first kingdom, why then does the second kingdom have to suffer at all? Why does Christ the King permit persecution and heresy to come within a hair's breathe of destroying faith and the faithful? Why does he even allow the Antichrist to emerge within the visible church to deceive so many and draw them away from heaven to their destruction (2 Thessalonians 2:1-12)?

The Bible draws back the veil and reveals in faith the useful, even indispensable service done to and for believers and the church by suffering. While those who cause suffering and those who damage the church by false teaching remain responsible and accountable before God for the harm they do, Christ the King nevertheless turns their intended harm to good for the believer and for the church. He limits the damage, so that the evil is never fully triumphant and so that the elect ultimately reach the goal of heaven. And in the process he uses the suffering of the church and of each individual believer to draw them closer to himself. For the greatest temptation of all, the one almost impossible to resist both for the church and for the individual Christian, is unhindered or unlimited success! So perverse are we that as soon as everything becomes easy for us, we forget the Giver, we forget our constant need for his intercession, and we forget that on our best day our greatest need is for the forgiveness won by his work of redemption. In a word, we quickly plunge towards or into the abyss of self-righteous unbelief. And so in love for the second kingdom, for his own ruling activity in our hearts and lives, Christ permits suffering to come to us from the first kingdom to draw us always back again to his waiting arms, to his pardon, to his rescue, and to his redeeming work.

In its suffering his kingdom of grace imitates the King himself. As Jesus suffered first and then entered into glory, so those in whom he lives and rules by his Word also suffer. He told his disciples in advance what they could expect for following him: "A student is not above his teacher, nor a servant above his master. It is enough for the student to be like his teacher, and the servant like his master. If the head of the house has been called Beelzebub, how much more the members of his household!" (Matthew 10:24,25).

In the same chapter Jesus promised his followers that they would be persecuted because of him, even by members of their own families. In some of the last words that he spoke before his ascension, he foretold the martyrdom of St. Peter. After his ascension when he spoke to Ananias in a vision about the future of the apostle Paul, Jesus declared, "I will show him how much he must suffer for my name" (Acts 9:16). The apostles recognized the necessity of such suffering in imitation of Christ's state of humiliation. They did not promise the early converts to Christianity a life of ease and glory in this world. Rather, St. Paul assured his hearers, "We must go through many hardships to enter the kingdom of God" (Acts 14:22).

As all of God's Word is true and as Jesus keeps all of his promises, so certainly he has kept his Word in this matter. It is the universal experience of the kingdom of grace that where the gospel is proclaimed in its truth and purity, and where there are those who believe it, there is always suffering because of it. The suffering takes many forms. It may be outward persecution by the enemies of the gospel. It may be ridicule from friends, family members, coworkers, or neighbors for faithfulness to the Word of God.

To be sure, attacks by false teachers and false doctrine inside of a church or congregation can be very painful. They can separate families and wreck long-cherished associations. But the attacks on the truth of God's Word also have a useful purpose; they can bring to light the faithful, those who love Christ and his Word above all else. That's the kind of love and loyalty that Christ the King has called us to; he warned against loving anyone, even relatives, more than we love him (Matthew 10:37-39). Attacks on the truth of Christ's Word give us the opportunity to show our love for him by remaining faithful to that Word and by standing up for it, an opportunity which we would not wish for all the world to pass up. That was the attitude of the early Christians. The apostles were flogged at the order of the Sanhedrin because of their faithful witness to the gospel. Did they complain that Christ the King had not protected them? On the contrary, "the apostles left the Sanhedrin, rejoicing because they had been counted worthy of suffering disgrace for the Name [of Jesus]" (Acts 5:41).

There are of course many other ways in which the subjects of Christ the King suffer in this life. Tragedy comes into the private life of an individual. A storm destroys the house. Devastating sickness brings terrible pain to a family member and wipes out the family's wealth.

Through no apparent fault of the individual, unemployment brings hardship to a home and strife to a marriage. A faithful spouse suffers the hurt and the shame of an unfaithful spouse. For believers the real suffering of these losses may consist in the doubt and fear that such suffering brings with it, the doubt and fear hidden in the question: How could God love me and let this happen to me? The loss becomes a challenge and a test to their trust in the providence of God and the loving rule of Christ the King.

And so the question persists and sometimes plagues us: Why? Why is suffering necessary for forgiven sinners, for believing children of God? Since Christ is King over the whole world and over all history, why does he not simply remove from his kingdom of grace all pain and sadness? St. Paul deepens our understanding of the importance of suffering in Romans 5. In addition to the reason already mentioned, that we imitate Christ's state of humiliation, the apostle tells us:

> Therefore, since we have been justified through faith, we have peace with God through our Lord Jesus Christ, through whom we have gained access by faith into this grace in which we now stand. And we rejoice in the hope of the glory of God. Not only so, but we also rejoice in our sufferings, because we know that suffering produces perseverance; perseverance, character; and character, hope. And hope does not disappoint us, because God has poured out his love into our hearts by the Holy Spirit, whom he has given us. (Romans 5:1-5)

To put it briefly, by suffering we and the rest of the church with us learn to despair of our own strength and wisdom, to let go of false pride and self-righteousness. We learn to abandon ourselves, to cling alone to the promises of Christ in his Word, by which the Holy Spirit comes to strengthen and keep us close and then bring us still closer to Christ. As gold needs to be refined by fire, so Christians need to be refined by suffering. St. John gives us an answer for the troubled soul in such perplexity. He tells us:

> Do not love the world or anything in the world. If anyone loves the world, the love of the Father is not in him. For everything in the world—the cravings of sinful man, the lust of his eyes and the boasting of what he has and does—comes not from the Father but from the world. The world and its desires pass away, but the man who does the will of God lives forever. (1 John 2:15-17)

So suffering and loss drive us back to the fundamental truth that the one who has Christ has everything. The one who does not have Christ has nothing, even if he seems to have everything. Health and wealth, house and home, all these are gifts of a most generous God. But they are like frosting on the cake—they are not the cake. Their loss may demonstrate to us that such things were becoming too important to us at the expense of what is really important. Job learned that lesson in most painful ways. Jesus taught it gently to Mary and Martha in the New Testament (Luke 10:38-42). Christ the King teaches most Christians the same lesson many times during their lives. The individual Christian and Christians collectively as the church may often have occasion to pray with the psalmist whose plaintive cry closes with the heartrending words: "Awake, O Lord! Why do you sleep? Rouse yourself! Do not reject us forever. Why do you hide your face and forget our misery and oppression?" (Psalm 44:23,24).

The lesson can be so hard to learn, and some problems in this life last a long time. Some problems, even those that do not appear to be the result of an exaggerated love for the world, have no solution or adequate explanation this side of eternity. They can only be endured. Not until heaven will they be resolved and all of the questions surrounding those problems answered. But, nevertheless, in it all, whether a problem/loss is slight or severe, of short duration or lasting for years, with no apparent cause in our own misplaced love or no apparent cause at all, Christ is still King. He still strives by his Word as it is applied to our lives to teach us perseverance, patience, and hope, which in the end will not be disappointed.

Last but not least, suffering makes it easier for us to console and help others who suffer. The one who never experiences pain or even doubt will have difficulty understanding the suffering and the doubts of others or will have little inclination to sympathize and help others in pain. The very words *sympathy* and *compassion* come respectively from Greek and Latin words that mean "to suffer along with." St. Paul understood the value of his own suffering as a help to him in helping others. He spoke eloquently about it in the introduction to his second letter to the Corinthians (1:3-11), which reads in part:

> Praise be to the God and Father of our Lord Jesus Christ, the Father of compassion and the God of all comfort, who comforts us in all our troubles, so that we can comfort those in any trouble with the comfort we ourselves have received from God. (vv. 3,4)

What better use could there be for suffering? Once it has begun to purify us of the inordinate love of the world, it fixes our attention on those missing the consolation that comes from the gospel when they suffer pain or loss. We might not even notice them, much less be moved to hasten to their help, if we ourselves had suffered nothing in life and had not found our hope together with lasting joy and peace in Christ and in his Word. Thus our suffering and times of loss can end up serving very useful purposes for those around us, both those who share our hope and those who may be brought to share it through our example. That's a beautiful and most useful way that Christ the King has of exercising his rule in us and through us in the kingdom of grace, as he uses us and our suffering to lessen the suffering of others.

Christ is King. Whether the suffering is obvious or subtle, known to all or known only to the sufferer and the Savior, Christ is still King. He seeks by that suffering to draw the Christian ever closer to himself and to assure God's child of God's abiding grace and mercy. It was with that conviction that the Holy Spirit moved St. Paul through many kinds of suffering to exclaim:

> I consider that our present sufferings are not worth comparing with the glory that will be revealed in us. . . . We ourselves, who have the firstfruits of the Spirit, groan inwardly as we wait eagerly for our adoption as sons, the redemption of our bodies. For in this hope we were saved. But hope that is seen is no hope at all. Who hopes for what he already has? But if we hope for what we do not yet have, we wait for it patiently. . . . And we know that in all things God works for the good of those who love him, who have been called according to his purpose. . . . If God is for us, who can be against us? He who did not spare his own Son, but gave him up for us all—how will he not also, along with him, graciously give us all things? . . . Who shall separate us from the love of Christ? Shall trouble or hardship or persecution or famine or nakedness or danger or sword? As it is written: "For your sake we face death all day long; we are considered as sheep to be slaughtered." No, in all these things we are more than conquerors through him who loved us. (Romans 8:18-37)

The rule of Christ the King over nature and history is therefore always in the best interests of his rule over the kingdom of grace, whether we consider that kingdom as the church consisting of all believers or whether we view it from the standpoint of his rule in the heart and life of an individual believer. Even the psalm of anguish referred to above (Psalm 44) closes with an expression of trust in the mercy of God, whether it is seen or not. The psalmist ends his cry with the words: "We are brought down to the dust; our bodies cling to the ground. Rise up and help us; redeem us because of your unfailing love" (vv. 25,26).

Unfailing love is the promise of Christ the King, who proved that love in his work of redemption. *Unfailing love* is what surrounds us whether we feel and immediately experience it or not. Because the promise of Christ the King is so solid and sure, St. Paul can urge us on with these words: "Rejoice in the Lord always. I will say it again: Rejoice!" (Philippians 4:4). He wrote those words from prison to a church that knew well what suffering is. Nevertheless, because Christ is King he can say *"Rejoice!"* He says it twice in the same verse to emphasize the fact that the joy has good and sure reasons behind it, even though the outward suffering would seem to remove all reason for joy. The joy is in the assurance of salvation, of *unfailing love,* no matter what the outward circumstance. The source of the joy is Christ's work and Christ's promise. They are always sure and certain. They never disappoint, for Christ is King.

All that the Scriptures have to say about the importance, the necessity, and the benefit of suffering in this life should put out of our minds and hearts certain cherished illusions that have become popular in our day. There are those who imagine and expect that because Christ is King the individual Christian and the church should triumph in this world. Completely contrary to what Christ has promised us in this life, they dream of an earthly rule of Christ and his church before the end of the world (millennialism). Or they expect as individuals that if they just have a strong enough faith, all of their own personal problems will be solved and every sickness healed. They may well drive themselves into a frenzy looking for such a faith and then fall into despair when they do not find it: "If I really believed, then this problem and sickness would go away. It is not going away. Therefore, I guess I don't really believe and am lost forever!" How tragic such thinking is! Those who follow such delusions do not grasp that *faith by definition is based on the promises of God.* Since God has never promised us a paradise in this life, the "faith" they seek does not exist. If they think they have found such a faith, it is in fact not faith at all—it is self-deception.

We call the above error *triumphalism* or a *theology of glory.* Pastors and congregations also need to beware of such triumphalism. A pastor or a congregation may imagine that because it has and proclaims faithfully the Word of God in all its truth and purity, it therefore should grow and prosper. Sometimes that may very well happen. But the church in this world nevertheless is always the little flock, beset and besieged on every side, plagued by opposition from the outside and problems of doctrine and life on the inside. The early church appeared to be prospering well in the first chapters of the book of Acts. But then a violent persecution broke out and Christians were scattered from Jerusalem and Judea. Surely at the time the persecution must have seemed a total disaster to almost everyone. Nevertheless, it was not the disaster that it seemed. In fact, even though the suffering was no doubt great, the blessed result of the persecution was even greater: The gospel spread far and wide. As persecuted Christians fled, they took the Word of God with them and shared it wherever they went (Acts 11:19-21). As a result of the persecution, the church actually grew in ways that only Christ the King could have fully foreseen—and caused.

When the church prospers and is at peace while faithfully doing the work of the Lord, it is enjoying a special blessing of the Lord. But to assume that such a condition is permanent flies in the face of both Christ's promise and all of church history. The norm is struggle. When the church struggles, it is too easy for some to assume that there must be something wrong with the message or the messenger. If the message is true but unpopular, changing it may bring outward growth. The new message may be glitzy with methods that appeal to pride and vanity, to the lust for the trivial and for entertainment. With such a changed message the church may appear to prosper outwardly. But changing the truth for the sake of apparent outward growth is to ensure inward rot. Unfaithfulness to the Scriptures is unfaithfulness to Christ the King. No outward growth is worth the loss of Christ and his Word! Consider carefully what Jesus has to say in Matthew 10:32-39 and 16:24-27 about those who deny him. Jesus even warns us that when everyone speaks well of us and there is no opposition to the message or the messenger, then we should remember that it was the same way with the false prophets. They were always popular, offended no one, and were spared persecution; however, in the end they perished under the wrath of God together with those who followed them (Matthew 5:11,12; Luke 6:26; and especially Matthew 7:21-23).

That the church will always be the little flock is not an excuse for laziness in our efforts to share the gospel. That we will always have and even benefit from problems in this life is likewise not an excuse to avoid working at solutions with the gifts that God has given to us in the people around us. The point is rather that our goal is first and foremost faithfulness to Christ and to his Word as we share the gospel and as we deal with the problems of life in this world. For Christ is King. He promises to speak in his Word and promises nowhere that he will deal with us apart from it. Therefore the church, whether it prospers or struggles, will be judged not by its outward success but by its faithfulness to Christ the King. No less so with the individual Christian. The measure of his Christianity in good days and in bad is his faithfulness to the Word of his God and Savior.

Thus, Christ is King over the life of the church and in the lives of each individual Christian. He is not far off, distant, removed, or unconcerned. He is a personal God who rules in love and grace, just as he promised. His goal in all that he does for us in his rule over the church and in our lives on earth is to bring us to the point where we can say with St. Paul, "I have learned to be content whatever the circumstances. . . . I have learned the secret of being content in any and every situation" (Philippians 4:11,12). What is the secret? It is an ever-growing trust that Christ always keeps his Word and provides what is best for us. It is a lifelong learning process that takes place only in those who keep their eyes and ears open to that Word through which Christ gives us joy and confidence in his abiding presence. By his presence in Word and sacraments, through days of godly pleasure and days of earthly suffering, the Christian learns to pray with ever-greater satisfaction and joy:

> Yet I am always with you; you hold me by my right hand. You guide me with your counsel, and afterward you will take me into glory. Whom have I in heaven but you? And earth has nothing I desire besides you. My flesh and my heart may fail, but God is the strength of my heart and my portion forever. (Psalm 73:23-26)

Not to be forgotten in all this talk of the presence and blessing of Christ the King in the midst of suffering and loss is the presence of Christ the King in the midst of life's many joys. The psalmist sees the goodness of God in all the pleasures of life, not his own merit or worthiness (Psalm 104). How quickly people blame God when things go badly—a destructive storm or flood is called an act of God and so it is. But so too is a good harvest, a raise in salary or rank, a successful year at school, a year of prosperity, or the morning when I get out of bed, nothing hurts, and I feel healthy and ready to take on the world! Too quickly we assume that all these are ours by right. Yes, and sadly we may loose them piece by piece and bit by bit just because of such arrogance or ingratitude. So let us look also on good days first and foremost to the kindness and generosity of Christ the King. There are few better ways of starting the day than with the prayer that Luther learned to pray when as a monk he was barely given so much as a crust of bread. It is the prayer *Benedictus sit Deus in omnibus donis suis!* ("Blessed be God in all of his gifts!").

Christ's kingdom of glory

As the rule of Christ over the kingdom of power in nature and history is in the interest of the kingdom of grace, so ultimately his rule over the kingdom of grace is in the interest of the third kingdom, the *kingdom of glory*. The kingdom of glory is in heaven. Its essence is the perfect enjoyment of being with Jesus without anything to diminish or ever hinder that enjoyment.

Though the Bible's descriptions of heaven, of the kingdom of glory, are not as complete as we might wish them to be, they are nevertheless breathtakingly beautiful for all their simplicity and lack of detail. Consider for example the description of our lives in heaven from Revelation 7:14-17:

> "These are they who have come out of the great tribulation; they have washed their robes and made them white in the blood of the Lamb. Therefore, they are before the throne of God and serve him day and night in his temple; and he who sits on the throne will spread his tent over them. Never again will they hunger; never again will they thirst. The sun will not beat upon them, nor any scorching heat. For the Lamb at the center of the throne will be their shepherd; he will lead them to springs of living water. And God will wipe away every tear from their eyes."

What more could we want? We will be with Christ. He will finally be the full focus of our lives. He will care for us and provide for us fully and freely. He did that while we were in this life too. But here we did not always see it or understand it, much less fully appreciate it. But there we will see and understand it and fully appreciate it. And we on our part will worship and serve him perfectly, without fears and doubts, without the interruption of temptation and sin. There Christ will finally be all in all to us and for us. Notice the balance that is struck in the above passage: Christ is always at the center, always on the throne; we on our part will always be provided for by him and perfectly led by him. Notice too how intimate, how very personal, the relationship will be between God and each individual believer. It always was just that personal; but in the here and now we did not always realize it. Oh, but there we will finally see it and experience it fully. Not one of us will be overlooked, unimportant, insignificant, or forgotten!

St. John expresses that truth with utter simplicity when he says of heaven, "We shall see him as he is" (1 John 3:2). How is he? He is Christ the King. He is our God and Savior. He is always merciful and gracious to us. He rules all things in heaven and on earth for our good and our eternal benefit. But in this life we do not always see that. We, as St. Paul says, "see but a poor reflection as in a mirror; then we shall see face to face. Now I know in part; then I shall know fully, even as I am fully known" (1 Corinthians 13:12). A mirror in St. Paul's day was not the shiny glass we use as a mirror today. It was often a polished piece of metal, in which the reflection was always a bit dim or blurred. Thus, we often see Christ now only dimly. Our ignorance of his Word, our difficulty in applying it, or the pain of the moment may obscure our vision of him as our always kind and gracious King. While we may come to understand much that is painful in our lives, in all likelihood we will never understand all of it in the here and now. But in heaven "we shall see face to face," and "we shall see him as he is." Our first utterance there may well be "Oh!" rather than "Why?" as all becomes instantly clear to us in the full enjoyment of his presence.

The final manifestation of Christ's office as King will come on the Last Day. Jesus promised that one day he will return visibly just as he departed visibly (Luke 21:27). On that day all earthly history will come to an end. Those living at that time will see the dead raised to life. Then Jesus will hold court and conduct the final judgment (Acts 17:31). No one can escape that resurrection and that judgment. But for the believers no escape is necessary and none is desired. For the believers will not be condemned (Matthew 24,25; John 3:16-18). In fact, when the signs of Christ's coming are clear, believers will rejoice to see them, for they are signs of their own ultimate rescue from this world for the kingdom of glory in heaven (Luke 21:27,28). At Christ's return for the judgment, the earth as we know it now will disappear, either totally destroyed or so renovated as to be unrecognizable by any current standard. In the last judgment the believers will be forever with the Lord in heaven. The unbelievers will be cast down to suffer eternal punishment with the devil and all his angels. The believers will be in heaven because of God's grace and Christ's merit, which they received in faith created and preserved by the gospel. They will forever sing the praises of Christ the Savior and claim no credit for their own salvation or for their faith; it was all God's gift in Christ, God's gift in the Word and sacraments (Matthew 24; Ephesians 2:8,9). The unbelievers, on the other hand, who go into hell to suffer eternally, will not be able to blame God for their torment; they will have an eternity to regret and lament their own shame and guilt. Those therefore who look forward to Christ's return in glory can do no better in the present than to cling to Christ in his Word and sacraments. For that is where Christ finds them and saves them. (For a further consideration of the last judgment and the doctrines of heaven and hell, cf. chapter 17.)

It should be evident from this chapter that there is really no end to our consideration of Christ and his redeeming work. Every doctrine brings us back to this one. Nothing in life or death or even in eternity is more precious to us than the doctrine of our redemption. And no one is more deserving of our entire devotion and attention than the one who is its source, its center, its beginning, and its end—Jesus Christ our Savior, our Redeemer, our Lord in time and in eternity, our All in all.

PART V

SOTERIOLOGY—
The DOCTRINE of SALVATION

Chapter 12
Justification

We have now examined in some detail what the mind and heart of God reveal to us in the Bible about his earnest desire for our salvation. Already in eternity he willed our salvation. Already in eternity the Holy Trinity devised a way of satisfying his attributes of grace and justice. Already in eternity God determined with a resolve that nothing in heaven or earth could shake that the tragedy of man's doom as a result of sin would be reversed. That reversal would be accomplished not by anything that fallen man would do or attempt or even will. It would be accomplished through the work of the second person of the Trinity. He would become man, born of the virgin. He would be free from the damning poison of original sin and live a life altogether separate from any actual sin. And then as the spotless Lamb of God, true God and true man in one person, he would offer himself as the sacrifice for the sins of the world upon the altar of the cross. Thereby he would become the High Priest and the sacrifice that takes away the sin of the world.

We have considered that central truth of the Bible within the framework of the doctrines of the person and work of Christ, especially in the great summation of it all in the doctrine of the vicarious atonement. We now turn our attention to a further and closer examination of the consequences of that work of Christ for us. In large measure the doctrines that we are about to consider are but beautiful restatements of the doctrine of the vicarious atonement. So sublime is that doctrine and so vital for our Christian faith and life that God has chosen to describe it in his Word from a number of different vantage points. He does that to help us better understand and glorify his grace and the work of Christ. He does it to help keep us from dread errors and sins that destroy Christian faith and life, especially the error of self-righteousness and the equally fatal sin of despair. The self-righteous imagine that they can save themselves or at least contribute to their salvation. The despairing imagine that their sin is too great for God to forgive. Both overestimate man's powers and underestimate in unbelief the grace of God and the work of Christ. Both the self-righteous and the despairing, left to themselves, perish in their unbelief. To turn us from these damning errors to saving faith God reveals the doctrines we are about to consider.

The first doctrine that we consider which discusses the result of Christ's work for us is the great doctrine of justification. The doctrine of justification, along with the doctrine of the vicarious atonement, can rightly be called the brightest jewel in the crown of biblical theology and therefore as well the brightest jewel in the crown of Lutheran orthodoxy. The doctrine is one doctrine with two sides to it: we consider it first as *objective* or *universal justification;* after that we will turn to the doctrine's other side and consider it under the heading of *individual* or *personal (subjective) justification.* It is not two different doctrines but one doctrine viewed from two standpoints.

Objective/universal justification

The doctrine of justification is a judicial doctrine. It looks at the work of Christ from the standpoint of a courtroom. In a criminal proceeding the accused is brought before the judge. At the end of the proceeding the judge issues a verdict. In the doctrine of justification it is the whole world that is brought into God's courtroom. The verdict pronounced therefore is a *universal* one; every mortal from the time of Adam and Eve down to the last individual to be born before the Last Day is there. The verdict pronounced is called *objective* because the entire world and each individual is the object of the verdict to be pronounced, whether any of them like it or not, believe it or not, or even know about it or not. God is the only one in the courtroom who acts, and his actions are not affected in the least by what any mere mortal thinks or does or might say. The accused is either declared guilty and condemned or pardoned and thus in effect pronounced innocent, not guilty. The *sedes doctrinae* for the doctrine of *objective (universal) justification* is 2 Corinthians 5:19,21:

> God was reconciling the world to himself in Christ, not counting men's sins against them. . . . God made him who had no sin to be sin for us, so that in him we might become the righteousness of God.

A closely related passage that considers this matter in much the same way is Romans 5:18,19:

> Consequently, just as the result of one trespass was condemnation for all men, so also the result of one act of righteousness was justification that brings life for all men. For just as through the disobedience of the one man the many were made sinners, so

> also through the obedience of the one man the many will be made righteous.

In both of these passages God and man are in court. They are on opposite sides of the bench. God is the judge and all of humanity is lumped together with the one word: *sinner.* How will the two be reconciled? It seems impossible. For God is just and man is unjust; God is holy and all mankind sinful. Man can do nothing to alter the horrible status he has before God. He is doomed. He appears damned.

Then God acts. God alone, without man's help or merit or will or request or works. He brings about reconciliation, and that without any violation of his justice. He reconciles *the whole world* to himself.

And how does that happen? Christ the holy, the innocent, the sinless, and the perfect is "made . . . to be sin" for all mankind. Mankind, doomed already by the trespass of Adam, has in Christ a substitute under the just wrath of God. "Made . . . to be sin"—God in effect declares Christ guilty of every sin that had ever been committed or ever would be committed, from the first sin of Adam until the last sin at the moment of Christ's second coming on the Last Day. When the Father sees his Son on the cross, he sees sin, guilt, and shame. The mind boggles! Who can wrap his senses around it? God sees God as guilty. God looks on his perfect, beloved Son and sees only disgrace, filth, sin, and shame. And he punishes him accordingly. With the supreme act of Christ on the cross, enduring the punishment and the wrath of God against the sin of the whole world, Christ trades places with all mankind. Christ is declared guilty and punished; the whole world is acquitted, is declared forgiven.

Thus, as St. Paul declares, one man, namely, Adam, brought sin into the world and in Christ one man takes it away and restores innocence and righteousness. Adam's sin brought sin and guilt on all mankind; Christ's work as the sin bearer and substitute under the wrath of God takes away sin for as many as had inherited sin and guilt from Adam; that is, Christ is the substitute and sin bearer for all, since all inherit Adam's sinful condition.

Thus *objective* or *universal justification,* briefly stated, is this: God *has declared* the whole world forgiven; he has declared that every sin has been paid for and punished in Christ. That's what the verb *to justify* means: "to declare 'not guilty' or 'forgiven' "! The world does not become justified by some change in man. Justification is *forensic,* that is, it's decreed; it's declared. Nor is this justification merely potential, a justification that might happen someday if people believe it or accept it or improve and somehow become worthy of it. No, it is *forensic;* the whole world has already been declared forgiven! Justification has already happened. Nor is justification a process by which mankind or individuals are changed in their nature from sinners to saints, from corrupt to virtuous. It's *forensic,* meaning it's decreed as something already complete, accomplished, perfect. That is exactly what Christ said on the cross: "It is finished" (John 19:30). He was referring not merely to his life but to the work of our redemption and justification.

As we noted in the last chapter, the completed work of redemption does not change man's nature; it changes his status. Formerly all were doomed and damned. Now all have been reconciled, justified. St. Paul underscores the already-accomplished, completed nature of justification when he continues the *sedes doctrinae* in 2 Corinthians 5 with these words: "And he has committed to us the message of reconciliation" (v. 19).

The message that the apostle brings comes from the palace of the King and judge of all the earth. Paul and all who are called to proclaim the gospel serve as ambassadors from that palace. They come not with a message of peace and reconciliation that is merely potential—if only the hearer will believe it or improve or somehow become at least a little bit worthy. Nor do they come with a message that is merely their own opinion or best guess. No, they come with a message of the one who sent them, a message of a peace and reconciliation already accomplished. Precisely because the reconciliation has already been accomplished, the ambassador calls and invites:

> We are therefore Christ's ambassadors, as though God were making his appeal through us. We implore you on Christ's behalf: Be reconciled to God. (v. 20)

In short, receive it, believe it, and you can trust that it is well and truly done. For it is God who was offended and angry and God who had the right to punish, but now God is satisfied. God is reconciled. Christ, his own Son, has stepped into the place of the whole world. Christ has removed the offense, has paid the debt, and has borne the punishment for all.

Again it must be emphasized that justification applies to and is for the whole world, no one excepted. The same point was made in the last chapter in discussing the doctrine of the vicarious atonement on the basis of its great *sedes doctrinae* in 1 John 2:2. Again we note that God has found a number of ways in which to describe the same thing, so that we will not miss the point. *Justification, vicarious atonement,* and *reconciliation*—each describes really the same thing, each from a slightly different perspective. Each describes the fully accomplished work of Christ for the world and therefore for each of us for our redemption.

In order to underscore still more the certainty and the universality of justification, we note its two causes. They are the same causes as those considered in the last chapter under the heading "The causes of redemption." By way of review, the two causes of the vicarious atonement, and hence also of objective justification, are the grace of God and the merit of Christ.

The grace of God is the prompting cause. It answers the question *why.* Why did God justify the world? What prompted God to justify the world? There is a one-word answer to the question. That word is *grace.* Bear in mind earlier discussions of that word; it means "undeserved love," love which has its cause only in the one loving, not in the one loved. "God is gracious" means that he loves the world not because the world or any of us in it is loveable but because he is loving. He loves, not because of the way the world is but because of the way he is. Every description of mankind since the fall makes it abundantly clear that justification could never have any of us as its cause. For we all are by nature dead in sin and children of wrath (Psalm 143:2; Isaiah 59:2; Romans 3:9-20; Ephesians 2:1-3). It was in spite of our sin and because of his grace alone that God loved the world (John 3:16), devised a plan for its justification, and carried out that plan completely.

The silly and the superficial may feel hurt that they are not the cause of justification, at least for a little or small part of it. But any serious reflection on the matter makes us jump for joy that we have no part at all, not the least fraction of part as a cause of justification. For precisely because grace is the only and all-sufficient prompting cause, our justification is sure and certain; we didn't cause it, so we can't make a mess of it. It is caused by God's grace, and therefore the cause is complete and perfect in God himself!

That brings us to the second cause of justification, the *meritorious cause.* It was not enough that God *wanted* our justification because of his grace. It was also necessary, since God is just, that justification be *merited, that it be deserved.* It would not be fair, it would not be just, if God simply ignored sin as though it didn't really matter. Sin put the sinner in debt to God and the debt must be paid; sin is an offense against God and the offense must be punished. Justification cannot be unjust! Justice must be satisfied. God's grace desires and yearns for our justification. His justice demands payment and punishment in full for every sin. The one-word meritorious cause of our justification is

CHRIST. He satisfies the divine yearning to be gracious and the equally divine demand for justice.

Jesus himself puts together both the prompting and the meritorious cause in John 3:16: God *loved* the world; God *gave his Son*. God's gracious love prompted the world's justification. Christ's work—his entire life, death, and resurrection—merited justification for the whole world.

So again, in everything that has to do with our salvation, our focus is on Christ, on God's grace, on the Savior's work for us and for our salvation. To his perfect obedience we make our appeal when the devil and conscience condemn us on account of our disobedience. We cry out: "I know I have not kept the law, but someone else has kept it and he kept it for me, kept it perfectly. His obedience I hold before the just Judge of all the earth. Christ's obedience I claim for my own!" That's exactly what St. Paul is urging us to do when he tells us to be reconciled to God (2 Corinthians 5:20). And that reconciliation takes place on the basis of the one who became sin for us—for us Christ kept the law, and God credits his Son's perfect obedience to our account. The struggles against the devil and sin carried out in his human nature were very real struggles, and they were struggles for us. The agony of Gethsemane and Calvary were real and greater than any suffering ever endured in the whole history of the world. And it was all for us, as our substitute, in our place under the judgment of God.

However, in it all he was victorious. He could throw out the challenge to his enemies: "Can any of you prove me guilty of sin?" (John 8:46). No one could legitimately charge him with any breaking of God's law, even in the way he suffered during the unjust courtroom proceedings of the high priest and then of Pontius Pilate and Herod. Unjustly accused and beaten within an inch of his life, he who had all power in heaven and earth utters no curse, vents no hatred, and doesn't even complain! He submits as a lamb led to slaughter (Isaiah 53:7). And—can you bear to hear it—he prays for his tormenters one and all (Luke 23:34)! Even on the cross he remained spotless, free from personal sin or guilt.

No one could point to a single sin, and not just because he had been careful so that no sin was seen. They could point to no sin because he was guilty of no sin (1 John 3:5; Hebrews 4:15). In every work that could be seen by men, in his human nature perfectly united with his divine nature, in every thought, in every moment of his life unseen by human eyes, he consciously kept the law. He perfectly loved his Father and did his will. He never for a moment failed to love all mankind perfectly and to show that love in perfect and willing service. He neither stole anything nor did he ever want to steal anything. He never committed adultery nor did he ever want to commit adultery. He was never mean and he never wanted to be mean. And again, he did it all as the substitute for all mankind. For he himself did not need the law because of the perfect union of his human and divine natures, as he testifies in Matthew 12:8. Only for us did he subject himself to the law and perfectly keep it in the stead of all mankind. And this, his perfect active obedience is for the whole world and credited to its account; on account of it the world is declared justified, as if all had kept the law perfectly.

If he had ever committed even one sin in thought, word, or deed, he could not have served as a substitute for anyone. He would have needed a savior himself. For the minimum standard demanded by the law of God is perfection (James 2:10). In his *active obedience* he was perfect in every respect from the moment of his conception to the moment of his death. As the *sedes doctrinae* (2 Corinthians 5:21) declares, he had no sin!

In his *passive obedience* he did not resist or rebel but willingly submitted even to abandonment by his Father on the cross. It is as the sinless Son of God and Mary's son that Jesus permits himself to be arrested, abused, tortured, and crucified. He submits to suffering and death voluntarily, again, not for himself but for the world, for all humanity. He had the power to prevent his suffering, as he tells us in Matthew 26:53. And none could kill him without his willing submission to death, as he declares in John 10:18. It is the very essence of his state of humiliation (Philippians 2:6-8) that he veiled his divine majesty and glory so that he could humble himself all the way to death on the cross. St. Paul sums it up succinctly in Galatians 3:13: "Christ redeemed us from the curse of the law by becoming a curse for us," and likewise in 2 Corinthians 5:14: "One died for all, and therefore all died."

As his active obedience was accomplished for and in the stead of all, so also his *passive obedience*—his suffering and death, the just punishment for sin—was endured in the stead of all and for the sake of all. For he is the perfect, sinless Lamb of God, who by his sacrifice has taken away the sin of the world (John 1:29).

We cannot help but note how closely connected the doctrine of justification is with the doctrine of the vicarious atonement considered in the last chapter. The essential points concerning our redemption are stated in a number of ways in the Bible so that we will not miss those points and, as previously noted, fall victim to faith-destroying self-righteousness or despair. We note again how fully our salvation rests in the hands of God. The justification of the world is the result of God's decree, not man's choice, will, or work. The justification of the world is prompted by God's grace alone and merited by Christ's work alone. The justification of the world would be a fact whether anyone believed it or not; it has been accomplished entirely and completely, from beginning to end, by God in Christ. God reconciled the world to himself! We need to keep repeating it because the pride of man wants to pervert it, the hatred of the devil wants nothing more than to destroy that message, and the wickedness of the world, obsessed only with things, wants to suffocate it with things that only perish in the using.

Attacks against the doctrine of justification

It is a tragedy of the first order that within the visible church so few teach or treasure this most precious of all of the truths of the Bible, the doctrine of justification. We need to be on guard against any perversion or the slightest weakening of this sacred truth, precisely because it is the heart and core of the gospel. Because it is the heart and core of the gospel, the devil together with the world and human pride persistently and unceasingly attack this doctrine. Some of the attacks are obvious and some very subtle. To resist and struggle against them we need to be familiar with at least those attacks that we are likely to encounter. Among these are theological relativism, Arminianism, synergism, Pelagianism, and Calvinism.[1]

Theological relativism is perhaps the most common of the ways in which the doctrine of justification (and most other doctrines as well) is set aside. Theological relativism is not so much a teaching as an indifference to teaching. We can find it in most church bodies today. Among Roman Catholics, most Protestant church bodies, and most Lutheran synods, theological relativism is an important component of the religious mind-set. Basically, theological relativism holds that there is no such thing as *one* truth, or absolute truth. What there is instead are various *traditions*—the Catholic tradition, the Baptist tradition, the Lutheran tradition, etc. Each of these has its own way of looking at the matter of redemption and salvation. No one of them is right and none of them is wrong; they share in the idea that God is love and man is the object of God's love, and that's all that really matters. So if one tradition holds that man is saved by his own works, that Christ merely set the example, that's fine. If another tradition says that man needs the help of grace and that Christ made salvation possible for all, that

---

[1]For a further discussion of Arminianism, synergism, and Pelagianism, cf. chapter 8, "The Doctrine of Original Sin."

too is just fine. If yet another holds that Christ is the fullest revelation of God and we really should listen to him, but that in the end God will accept all people who have a good will, that also is just fine.

Without much effort we will find such notions rampant in most denominations today. Teaching that Christ alone is the way to heaven (John 14:6) and the one who has won it by his perfect life and death for us and for our salvation, that teaching is sadly smothered by relativism. The teaching of the Bible that there is salvation in no other name under heaven but the name of Christ (Acts 4:12) is the only teaching that a theological relativist cannot tolerate. Most theological relativists will even go so far as to say that those who worship a god other than the Holy Trinity will also ultimately get to heaven, as long as they are sincere. It would appear, if the relativist is right, that Christ went to a great deal of trouble for nothing. After all, if salvation were possible without Christ's work, why would he do it, especially given how difficult that work was for him? Of course, if the relativist is right, then all of God's Word is wrong.

May God graciously preserve us through the pure proclamation of the Word from theological relativism! It is the devil's tool for the destruction of faith and the church from within the church itself. The only cure for relativism is the grace of God and the merit of Christ as these come to us in the Word of God. But relativism is not the only threat to the doctrine of justification.

Arminianism is the false teaching common to Methodist, Baptist, Pentecostal, and most other Protestant churches. They teach that man's redemption is possible, rather than already fully accomplished, and that man must therefore make it actual by inviting Jesus into his heart. Only then is there any justification for fallen man. This teaching is also called *synergism,* a word that means "to work with" or "to cooperate." Arminian synergists deny the doctrine of objective or universal justification. According to them we must ourselves finish the work, must cooperate and make it actual, by our own decision for Christ and by our own faith. They teach a justification that is only made possible by grace and by Christ's merit.

The passages considered above and in the last chapter on the doctrine of the vicarious atonement all reject Arminianism. The dread error of Arminianism or synergism, so popular especially in English speaking Christianity, robs Christ of his honor and glory as the only Savior. It is to Christ that the Father gave the name that is above every other name (Philippians 2:9-11), the name *Jesus.* That name means "Savior." It belongs to him and to none other. He does not share it with anyone (Acts 4:11,12). Even our faith has no claim to a place next to Jesus as though our faith were also our savior or the cause of our salvation. The grace of God in Christ prompts our salvation, not our decision for Christ. The active and passive obedience of Christ merit our salvation, not our invitation to Christ to come into our hearts. There is but one prompting cause and one meritorious cause. None other is needed. None other is possible.

But not only does synergism rob Christ of the honor that belongs to him alone as Savior, it also can drive the synergist either to self-righteousness or despair. The synergist may say to himself, "At least I made my decision for Christ, unlike those who have not; I have that to my credit." The synergist may end up putting his trust not in Christ but in himself and his decision—he may end up having faith in faith, more than faith in Christ. That isn't faith at all, but can easily become a subtle form of unbelief. Or the synergist may end up in despair. He sees the weakness that still plagues him, the temptations that will not leave him alone. He sees the troubles in his life—health problems, family problems, and work problems. On the basis of what he sees and feels, he begins to doubt whether God really loves him, really wants to forgive and save him. He doubts whether he really believes or believes enough. Instead of looking to the Word and promise of the gospel, instead of looking for his salvation in the grace of God and in the merit of Christ, he looks for it in his own feelings. When he doesn't feel saved, he concludes that he is not saved and falls into despair. Despair, like self-righteousness, is the opposite of faith. But the cure for despair is not found in naval-gazing. It is found in looking up to the cross of Christ, in his vicarious atonement, and in God's decree of objective and universal justification!

The heresy of *Pelagianism* or *semi-Pelagianism* is just as bad and just as common as synergism. Pelagianism is the false teaching that man by his own works can merit his salvation. In its crudest form Pelagianism is the religion of most non-Christians. To the extent that they think about God and life after death, they think that those who have done good or at least have tried or whose good deeds in general outnumber the evil deeds will end up in heaven. Such people ultimately expect just about everybody to end up in heaven on the basis of their good works and merits in this life. Pelagianism is the religion of the lodges and of the Scout movement (alongside of theological relativism). For those who have fallen into the Pelagian error, Jesus was a good man, a good teacher (whose teaching they would rather not be bothered with), a social reformer, or a martyr to his own private convictions.

More common inside of Christianity is what has come to be called semi-Pelagianism. Semi-Pelagianism has its home especially in the Roman Catholic and Eastern Orthodox churches. These teach that while it is true that Christ died for the sins of the world, nevertheless our salvation really is not complete until we on our part become holy. By our works we must complete what Christ by his work began, namely, our own salvation. For Roman Catholicism the work of salvation will not be finished until that process of holiness is finished. If we fail to become holy enough in this life, then we will have to finish becoming holy in purgatory after we die. Purgatory, about which the Bible speaks not one word, is the invention of Roman Catholic theologians, made popular especially by the Crusades of the 11th through the 13th centuries and by Dante (1265–1321) in his famous work, *The Divine Comedy*. According to Roman Catholic teaching, purgatory is a place where the sinner is purged by suffering for his remaining sins. The sins remaining are those mortal sins that he failed to confess to a priest during his lifetime; he should have confessed them and then done the work that the priest would have given him to do (called a *penance* or *a work of satisfaction*) to undo the suffering that the sin merited. What was not confessed and not undone by penance in this life must be made good by suffering in purgatory.

It is clear that both the notion of performing penance in this life to undo the penalty of sin as well as the whole wicked notion of purgatory flys in the face of the beautiful and thoroughly biblical doctrines of the vicarious atonement and justification. Where is the glory of Christ as the only and all-sufficient Savior in such wicked notions? It must be shared with the church imposing penance and providing ways of escaping suffering in purgatory. It must be shared with the sinner struggling to finish what Christ merely began. It must be shared with the saints, and especially the virgin Mary, for whose help both in this life and in purgatory the sinner constantly must pray.

Just as Arminianism and synergism rob the sinner of comfort, so too does semi-Pelagianism. For the treasure of sin forgiven and heaven secured must ever be mixed with the lead and the dross of human efforts, both works in this life and suffering in the next. Those who imagine that they have done their part, or at least will do it after they die, are self-righteous. Those who fear that they will never be holy enough, not even in purgatory, despair. For their despair the church points them not to Christ alone but to the saints; they point not to Jesus' blood and righteousness alone but to the masses and prayers for the dead that should somehow help after the poor despairing soul is in purgatory.

Yet another dread error that attacks the doctrine of universal justification is *Calvinism.* Calvinism is the dominant theology of the Dutch Reformed churches. The Presbyterian church was originally a Calvinist church, but many Presbyterians are now Arminians. Among the more distinctive doctrines of the Calvinist churches is that God has predestined some to go to heaven and the rest to go to hell. This, according to strict Calvinism, is how one should answer the age-old question: Why are some saved and not others? The Calvinists' answer: Because God only wanted to save some; the rest, in order to praise his own justice, he predestined to go to hell. Thus, if one goes to heaven, he indeed has only God to thank for it. But if one goes to hell, God must share the blame for it; for although all sinners deserve to go to hell, God never wanted to save those he predestined to hell and prevented such from believing the gospel, even if they did hear it. This is called the doctrine of *double predestination* or the doctrine of *limited atonement* (i.e., the atonement was limited to those predestined to heaven).

Clearly the false teaching of limited atonement robs Christ of his glory as the Savior of the world. It even makes the grace of God appear somewhat arbitrary and mean-spirited. Like every other error or attack on the doctrine of justification, Calvinism can drive people either to self-righteousness or despair. That was not Calvin's intention with this doctrine, but it is nevertheless the logical consequence of it. The follower of Calvin's teaching may well ask: "How can I know which side of the atonement I am on? For if God has predestined me to hell, it makes no difference whether I hear the Word or not; ultimately, I will go to hell!" The only comfort for such a fear, since the doctrine of universal justification has been rejected, is to look to one's own works for some consolation: "If my works are good and righteous, then I must be good and righteous and must be among those predestined to salvation!"

Indeed many Calvinist societies operated with just such an attitude. Many of the Puritan colonists, French Huguenots, and early Calvinists in Geneva, Switzerland, tried to establish "godly societies" that would be worthy of the "elect;" their godliness would indeed be evidence that they were the elect to salvation. They set up rules and codes of conduct enforced by church and state; they even made heresy a civil crime worthy of capital punishment. They wanted a society that would be a "Christian commonwealth," the home of the elect. The whole society had its focus on its own works as proof of salvation. That all led easily, if not inevitably, to self-righteousness for those who fit in and to despair for those who did not.[2]

It should be evident that the devil and human pride have been very busy indeed in devising ways of robbing Christ of his glory and the Christian of the comfort offered in the doctrine of justification. All false doctrines invented by the devil and adopted by the proud who are not content with the clear Word of God ultimately have this goal: to undermine and then destroy the doctrine of justification. For this doctrine gives all glory to Christ and maximum comfort to the poor sinner—the exact opposite of what the devil, the world, and the sinful human nature want!

It should likewise be clear that these errors—relativism, Arminianism, synergism, Pelagianism, semi-Pelagianism, and Calvinism—are not just theologians' squabbles or mere matters of opinion. They are able to destroy faith. To be sure, there are still people with saving faith who belong to churches that teach these errors. But their faith will be in spite of what their churches teach. And that faith will be under constant attack from the very ones who should strengthen and nourish faith with the pure proclamation of the gospel. We want nothing to do with these dread errors or with the churches that teach them, lest we end up encouraging them in their error or even embracing their faith-destroying errors ourselves! Our refusal to worship with or do church work with such churches does not stem from malice or hatred. It arises from hearts that love the gospel and the salvation that it brings. It stems from a Bible-based dread of all that contradicts the Word of God (Matthew 7:15; Romans 16:17,18), deprives Christ of his glory as Savior, and robs souls of the peace and joy in Christ as the only Savior. We refuse to become theological relativists by pretending that there is no such thing as false doctrine or that false doctrine doesn't really matter. It matters to God. It had better matter to us!

Let us never cease giving all thanks and praise to God, that in spite of all the attacks launched against this precious doctrine, God has preserved it in his true and faithful Word: God has justified the whole world, not because of the world's goodness or merit or even because of

---

[2]It may be interesting to note at least in passing that much of the political activism of Protestant churches and clergy is still rooted either in Arminianism or Calvinism. Arminians are trying to create a society in which it will be easier for people to make their decision for Christ; Calvinists are still trying to build the city of God on earth, a Christian commonwealth. Both often seek to use civil governments for their ends, whether they are on the political left or the political right. We will have more to consider on this point in chapter 16 on the three estates.

faith. He has declared the whole world justified and forgiven, and that prompted by his grace alone and merited by Christ alone! Therefore I need not doubt or fear that I somehow might be excluded from God's love and grace, from the merit of Christ, or from justification. For it applies to all.

Our Lutheran Confessions have such a beautiful and succinct summary of the whole matter under the heading of the doctrine of election:

> This teaching states that in his intention and counsel God had preordained the following:
>
> 1. That the human race has been truly redeemed and reconciled with God through Christ, who has merited with his innocent obedience, suffering, and death both the righteousness that avails before God and eternal life. (FC SD XI, 15 p. 643)

Subjective/personal justification

We next turn over the golden coin of the doctrine of justification and give our attention to its other side. As already noted, when we consider subjective or personal justification, we are not considering a new doctrine. We are simply looking at the doctrine from another standpoint, this time from the standpoint of the individual. In objective justification we considered the justification of the entire world, of the whole human race. Subjective justification focuses on the question: How do *I* come to enjoy this reconciliation that has been won for the whole world?

Our Lutheran Confessions take note of both the close connection between universal justification on the one hand and the need to apply justification to the individual on the other hand. Luther, for example, in the Large Catechism, beautifully observes the connection and the distinction between the two:

> There is great need to call upon God and pray, "Dear Father, forgive us our debts." Not that he does not forgive sin even without and before our prayer; and he gave us the Gospel, in which there is nothing but forgiveness, before we prayed or even thought of it. But the point here is for us to recognize and accept this forgiveness. For the flesh in which we daily live is of such a nature that it does not trust and believe God and is constantly aroused by evil desires and devices, so that we sin daily in word and deed, in acts of commission and omission. Thus our conscience becomes restless; it fears God's wrath and displeasure, and so it loses the comfort and confidence of the Gospel. Therefore it is necessary

constantly to turn to this petition for the comfort that will restore our conscience. (LC, The Fifth Petition, 88,89 p. 452)

Clearly the prompting cause for *my* justification cannot be any different from the prompting cause for the justification of the whole world. The *prompting cause* is still *grace* and grace alone. God's grace extends to the whole world (John 3:16) and therefore it extends also to me. It is out of his grace that God devised the plan for the redemption of the world; therefore, it is likewise out of grace alone that he devised the plan for *my* redemption. Likewise, the *meritorious cause* for *my* justification cannot be any different than the meritorious cause for the justification of the whole world. It is *Christ;* the merit of his active and passive obedience is credited to me, just as to the whole world.[3]

Nevertheless we reject the error of *universalism,* the false doctrine that eventually everybody will go to heaven. Not all go to heaven. While God is gracious and his grace extends to the whole world and Christ's merit has paid for the sin of the whole world, only those who believe, only those who have what we call saving faith, end up in heaven. It is by faith alone that the justification won by Christ for the world becomes my own. Look at it this way: A rich man tells the little boy that he has bought a beautiful new bicycle for the boy. The little boy may rejoice in the generosity of the rich man and claim the bicycle as his own, which in fact it is. When the boy does that, he first *believes, has faith* in the word of the rich man. Only when he believes the word of the rich man will the little boy enjoy the benefit of the bicycle. The word of the rich man caused the boy to believe him and then to claim the bicycle as his own. Should the boy brag, "I deserve the bike, because I did my part by believing and by having faith in the word of the rich man." Certainly not! It was the generosity *(grace)* of the rich man that caused him to buy the bicycle for the boy; it was the money *(merit)* of the rich man that actually procured the bicycle. *And* it was the word of the rich man that prompted the boy both to know and to believe that the bicycle was his.

That is close to how individual or subjective justification works. Faith is necessary *not* as a prompting or meritorious cause of salvation but as the *receiving organ* of salvation. Only in that sense can

---

[3]For an excellent and arguably unsurpassed consideration of both the essential unity of the two sides of the doctrine of justification and their proper distinction, the reader is encouraged to consult Prof. Joh. P. Meyer's masterpiece commentary on 2 Corinthians: *Ministers of Christ* (Milwaukee: Northwestern Publishing House, 1963), pp. 98-119.

faith be spoken of as a cause—as an *instrumental cause,* that is, the instrument *created and given by God in the gospel.* Through such a faith the individual receives the benefit of Christ's already accomplished work of redemption. Thc cause of faith is the gospel in the Word and the sacraments. Through the Word in the Bible and in the sacraments God comes to you and declares: "*You* have been redeemed! I reconciled *you* to myself! *You* are forgiven! I claim *you* as my own dear child! All this I do for *you* prompted by my grace alone, merited for *you* by Christ alone!" The cold and dead heart of one conceived and born in sin is acted on by the power within God's Word (Romans 1:16); it hears the Word (Romans 10:17) or receives that same message in Baptism (Acts 2:38,39; Romans 6:3,4; 1 Peter 3:21). The message brings the dead heart to life, causing it to sigh: "The Word of God is true! He means *me*! Christ is *my* Savior! He lived and died and rose again for *me* too, even for *me*!" So closely, so inseparably are faith and the gospel connected to each other that it is altogether appropriate to call the gospel itself the *instrumental cause* of our salvation—the gospel is the instrument used by God to create the instrument of faith by which we are saved.

Luther captures the connection between justification (both objective and subjective) and the Word as the vital *effecting* (i.e., creating) *cause* of faith in his comments on the Third Article in the Large Catechism:

> Neither you nor I could ever know anything of Christ, or believe in him and take him as our Lord, unless these were first offered to us and bestowed on our hearts through the preaching of the Gospel by the Holy Spirit. The work is finished and completed, Christ has acquired and won the treasure for us by his sufferings, death, and resurrection, etc. But if the work remained hidden and no one knew of it, it would have been all in vain, all lost. In order that this treasure might not be buried but put to use and enjoyed, God has caused the Word to be published and proclaimed, in which he has given the Holy Spirit to offer and apply to us this treasure of salvation. (LC, The Third Article, 38 p. 436)

Does the one who believes the message, who has faith, have a right to congratulate himself and claim some merit for himself because he believes, because he has faith? Certainly not! The grace of God, the merit of Christ, *and* the power of the gospel to create faith get all the credit. Thus, grace remains the prompting cause and Christ's work the meritorious cause. The gospel in the Word and sacrament is the effecting cause, because it is the means or tool that God uses to create saving faith. Thus *all* the causes of salvation are outside of man. That is so even when we call faith the instrumental cause, since faith is altogether the gift of God through the gospel. *All* the causes of salvation rest with God alone. God gets all the glory for our salvation. Faith receives the gift; it does not cause the gift, lest Christ be robbed of his glory and the poor sinner turn again to the self-righteousness of his works or to despair in his works.

To return to the analogy of the little boy and the bicycle: The little boy could insist on clinging to his own opinion and thus reject the good word of the rich man. The little boy could say to himself: "What I get I earn; nobody gives me anything" (self-righteousness). Or he could say to himself: "No! It cannot be! I do not deserve it. Therefore it is not true, and there is no bicycle for me!" (despair). The bicycle is his, although he rejects the word of the rich man. But because of his unbelief, he will never claim the bicycle as his own and will never enjoy the benefit of the bicycle. Whose fault is that? The rich man was sincere. The bicycle was for the little boy whether he believed it or not, whether he got the benefit of it or not. The fault for the little boy's loss of the bicycle's benefit rests with the boy himself, not with the man or with the bicycle.[4]

So also when the Bible speaks about saving faith and about those who trust the promise of grace and Christ's merit, all the credit then goes to God and the gospel. Those, however, who reject the promise and Christ's merit have only themselves to blame for it. God's grace was for them; Christ died for them. But they spurned grace, rejected Christ's merit, and preferred to call God a liar. But of those who have saving faith, St. Paul says:

> Like the rest, we were by nature objects of wrath. But because of his great love for us, God, who is rich in mercy, made us alive with Christ even when we were dead in transgressions—it is by grace you have been saved. For it is by grace you have been saved, through faith—and this not from yourselves, it is the gift of God—not by works, so that no one can boast. (Ephesians 2:3-5,8,9)

Could it be more clearly stated? Everything that has to do with our salvation, including faith, is God's gift of grace earned by Christ's merit,

---

[4]The analogy of the boy and bicycle is useful, though not a perfect analogy; the little boy believes the word of the rich man by an ability in his own will. That is not the case with the believer, who has no *natural* ability to believe the gospel; that ability comes from God through the gospel, is supernatural and always a miracle. We will have more to say about this point in the next two chapters but make mention of it here to avoid misunderstanding.

made our own through the message of the gospel. No credit is given to man's decision, none to his works, either his works preceding or those following faith. All glory goes to God in his grace, all praise to Christ our Savior, all credit to the message of the gospel!

On the other hand, what do the Scriptures say of those who reject the gospel in unbelief? Do they reproach God for not wanting the salvation of the unbeliever? Listen to Jesus' words on his way to his suffering and death for the sins of the world and therefore also for the sins of the people of Jerusalem:

> "O Jerusalem, Jerusalem, you who kill the prophets and stone those sent to you, how often *I have longed* to gather your children together, as a hen gathers her chicks under her wings, but *you were not willing.*" (Matthew 23:37)

Consider also these words of St. Stephen before the Jewish high court, the Sanhedrin, shortly before he was stoned to death for his faith: "You stiff-necked people, with uncircumcised hearts and ears! You are just like your fathers: You always resist the Holy Spirit!" (Acts 7:51). St. Paul in Romans 10 devotes an entire chapter to this same point, that God was willing and eager for the salvation of those Jews who rejected the gospel; God did everything to bring it about, but they of their own accord rejected his grace, Christ's saving work, and the constantly repeated call of the gospel.

The Old Testament makes the same point over and over again. Why did the Northern Kingdom perish and disappear? Was it because God wanted it that way from the start? Not at all! It was the stubborn refusal of the people to listen to his Word (2 Kings 17:7-23). Why did the Southern Kingdom of Judah likewise fall with its remnant carted off into the 70-year-long Babylonian captivity? For the same reason (2 Chronicles 36:11-17). In Psalm 78 the holy writer gives a detailed description of the whole history of the Old Testament. It is the history of God's grace on the one hand and man's rejection of his Word on the other. The point of the entire narrative is that man's salvation is always God's doing; man's ruin is always his own doing. Daniel makes the same point eloquently in his prayer for God to restore the nation and save his people, not because they deserve it but because of his glory and grace (Daniel 9:1-19).

In sum, the doctrine of subjective or individual justification is the application of the doctrine of justification to the individual. Prompted by God's own grace alone *(prompting cause)* and on account of the substitutionary life and death of Christ alone *(meritorious cause),* I too was justified; that is, I was forgiven. It is because of the power of the gospel in Word and sacrament *(effecting cause)* to create saving faith *(instrumental cause)* that I know and trust that I am justified; that is, I too have been declared forgiven and redeemed.

The Formula of Concord beautifully sums up the matter of our justification and the three causes in God that bring about the faith that is the instrument by which we lay hold of the divinely accomplished work of our salvation:

> In order that the troubled heart may have a reliable and certain comfort and that Christ's merit and God's grace may be given the honor due them, Scripture teaches that the righteousness of faith before God consists only in the gracious reconciliation or forgiveness of sins [Rom. 4:6-8; 2 Cor. 5:19-21]. This he bestowed upon us out of sheer grace solely because of the merits of Christ our mediator, and it is received only by faith in the promise of the gospel. Therefore, in the justification of the sinner before God, faith relies neither on contrition nor on love or other virtues, but only on Christ and (in him) on his perfect obedience, with which he fulfilled the law for us and which is reckoned to believers as righteousness.
>
> Thus . . . faith alone, is the sole means and instrument with which and through which we may receive and accept God's grace, the merit of Christ, and the forgiveness of sins, which are delivered to us in the promise of the gospel. (FC SD III, 30,31 p. 567)[5]

The doctrine of election (predestination)

Certain questions, however, persist and have been asked through the ages: Why is it that some believe the gospel and not others? How come some hear the gospel and rejoice in it, while others either reject it outright or receive it for a time and then fall away? Jesus himself draws our attention to the phenomenon that some hear and immediately reject the gospel; others hear and receive it gladly for a time, but then fall away; and still others hear and cling to the Word and bear abundant fruit (Matthew 13:1-23).

In dealing with all questions of doctrine, but especially with these, it is necessary that we remember that the Bible alone is our source

---

[5]The attentive reader cannot fail to note in this citation that also the three tests of sound doctrine to which we so often refer are plainly evident: Sound doctrine must be derived from the Scriptures, give maximum glory to Christ, and be of greatest consolation to the penitent sinner.

of doctrine. It is crucial that we follow the example of St. Paul and "take captive every thought to make it obedient to Christ," that is, to his Word (2 Corinthians 10:5). For many have gone astray by attempting to answer these questions not with the clear Word of God but with their own reason.

As already noted, the Calvinists have answered these questions by teaching that the reason some believe and others do not is to be found in God. They teach that God has a different attitude toward some than he has toward others. And, therefore, he elected or predestined some to believe and go to heaven, and he predestined the rest not to believe and to go to hell. Calvin and his followers to this day insist that that is the only *rational* conclusion that we can come to, since the Bible clearly teaches that God has predestined some to salvation. But to argue that God therefore *must* predestine everyone else to hell is completely contrary to the Scriptures. Reason may be satisfied with the Calvinist answer, but God is not. His Word plainly and repeatedly declares that his grace is universal and not limited (John 3:16). His Word plainly and repeatedly declares that Christ died for all (2 Corinthians 5:14,15,19; 1 John 2:2). God declares repeatedly and clearly in his Word that he fervently desires the salvation of all, that all should come to faith and be saved (1 Timothy 2:4-6; 2 Peter 3:9). All of these and countless related passages will have to be erased from the Word of God if the Calvinist teaching is accepted.

Nor will it help the Calvinist error to say, as many Calvinists do, that these passages are true, but they only apply to those whom God elected to salvation; that is, God loves all those elected to salvation, and Christ died for all of them. Such an assertion makes a mockery of the clarity of the Scriptures; if God says "all," he means all, unless there is something in the passages themselves that compel a different understanding. That, in the passages cited above, is simply not the case. We are not and do not want to be free to rewrite the Bible just to make it rhyme with our fallen reason.

Still others in the Calvinist camp argue that while it is true that God wants the salvation of all, he wants something else even more, namely, to demonstrate his justice. Such an argument, likewise, makes a mockery of the clarity of the Scriptures. Additionally, it fails to note that both God's justice and his grace have been fully satisfied in the obedience and the sacrifice of Christ.

The Calvinist answer to the question of why some believe and not others, therefore, fails all of the necessary tests for true doctrine: (1) It has no basis in the Bible and seeks one in reason alone. (2) It robs

Christ of his glory as the Savior of the world. (3) It can drive Christians to the self-righteous notion that there must have been something in them that caused God to pick them over others. And (4) it can drive other Christians to the opposite form of unbelief, namely, to despair when they conclude for whatever reason that they must have been predestined to hell.[6]

The Arminians were originally Calvinists, but they were very disturbed by the incorrect notion that God willed the damnation of those who go to hell. Rejecting the Calvinist double predestination, the Arminians set about finding a different answer to the question of why some believe and not others. Unfortunately, just like the Calvinists, they looked for an answer not in the Word of God alone but in fallen human reason. With reason as the source they came up with an equally wrong answer to the question. They concluded that the difference is not in God but in man; some people choose to believe, to have faith, and others do not. Therefore, it is the business of the church to do everything that it can to help people make the right choice, to decide for Christ. Church services and religious music should set the right mood, should appeal especially to the emotions, so that people will be in the right frame of mind to invite Jesus into their hearts and believe. Certainly emotion has a place in a worship service and in religious music, but if the assumption accompanying the use of emotion is wrong, then the service and the music too will be wrong. And the assumption underlying the use of emotion in Arminian worship services and religious music is called decision theology. Decision theology argues that the individual has the *natural ability* to believe and to make a decision for Christ in spite of the fall and all of its dread consequences in original sin.

Inherent in decision theology, therefore, is an effective denial of the doctrine of original sin. The Arminian sees natural man as religiously neutral, with the natural ability to believe the gospel. It considers the will of man capable by its own natural powers of considering the alternatives of faith and unbelief and, again with its own natural powers, of choosing to believe.

But that is not at all what the Bible teaches. Jesus says it very plainly: "Flesh gives birth to flesh" (John 3:6). St. Paul denies any natural ability in man to come to faith and, in fact, declares the opposite,

---

[6]For a more detailed consideration of both Calvinism and Arminianism as it relates to the will of God in the history of the world and also of individuals, cf. chapter 6 under the heading "The providence of God".

that "the sinful mind is hostile to God. It does not submit to God's law, *nor can it do so*" (Romans 8:7). He tells us that such a hostile sinful mind by nature is the object of God's wrath and that it is neither willing nor able by nature to do anything about it (Ephesians 2:1-9). If one therefore believes the gospel and is saved, he can only thank God for it (Ephesians 2:8,9).[7] Salvation from beginning to end, including the faith that believes the gospel, is God's gift.

Thus, Arminianism, like Calvinism, fails the tests necessary for sound doctrine: It contradicts the clear Word of God, and it makes Christ share that glory with man, since it is man's decision that saves and accomplishes the salvation that Christ's work only made possible. It likewise can drive the Christian away from faith into self-righteousness; for some may boast that at least they made the right decision—they end up with faith in faith rather than faith in Christ. Still others may despair; as they consider their weakness and remaining sin, they may conclude that they really haven't decided for Christ yet. Indeed, the very appeal of the "altar call" common in many Arminian church services pushes people in one of these two directions so opposite to faith. For the emphasis in the altar call is on the individual, how the person feels and what he should do, not on Christ and what he has done. The one who cannot yet "decide" is urged to continue to read the Bible and pray until he feels saved; when he feels saved, he is saved. That turns faith into nothing more than a feeling. It asks someone who considers himself an unbeliever to pray. Should he pray to someone in whom he does not believe, to someone he still considers his enemy? Such a prayer is not only unscriptural but is even unreasonable.

Yet one more error should be mentioned from the long list of efforts to find an answer to the question of why some believe and not others. Sadly this error comes from within the Lutheran camp itself. From the middle of the 19th century and stretching into the 20th century, a controversy raged inside of Lutheran churches in the United States known as the "in view of faith" *(intuitu fidei)* controversy. In attempting to answer the question of why some are saved and not others, a number of Lutheran theologians made poor use of a phrase that occurred in the writings of some of the orthodox Lutheran theologians of the 17th century. These American theologians concluded that God foresaw who would believe, and he predestined those whom he fore-

---

[7]For a more detailed consideration of the consequence of original sin in human nature and its significance for the matter of coming to faith, cf. chapter 8.

saw; he elected them "in view of faith" that he foresaw in them. Unfortunately this error gets everything just as backwards as does Arminianism. It makes faith the cause of God's choice and hence of our salvation. It is just the other way around. It is God's choice made known in the gospel that causes faith, which is completely the gift of God and the effect of the gospel's power to create faith. It leads to a denial of objective justification. Once more, Dame Reason is invited into a discussion where she does not belong.

"In view of faith" is an attempt to answer a question with reason apart from the Bible. Most of the Lutheran synods in the United States and Canada accepted the "in view of faith" error. Only the synods that made up the old Synodical Conference (the present-day Lutheran Church—Missouri Synod, the Wisconsin Ev. Lutheran Synod, the old Norwegian Synod—now the Evangelical Lutheran Synod, and the Synod of Evangelical Lutheran Churches—commonly referred to as the Slovak Synod) reject the "in view of faith" error.

If Calvinism, Arminianism, and the "in view of faith" error do not correctly answer the question of why some believe and others do not, what then is the correct answer of the Scriptures and therefore of the Lutheran Confessions? And how should we answer the question: What is the biblical doctrine of election or predestination?

It should already be clear from our consideration of the doctrine of justification that according to the Word of God plainly and clearly expressed in so many places, there is no cause of justification or of our salvation in us, not in our works and not even in our faith. Our salvation from beginning to end has its causes with God, that is, in his grace *(prompting cause),* in Christ's merit *(meritorious cause),* and in the power of the gospel *(effecting cause)* to create the faith that trusts that gospel *(instrumental cause).* Those who believe the gospel are not by nature better than those who do not believe. And God on his part did not choose some rather than others because he loved some more than others.

Thus, those who believe and are saved have only God to thank for it; those who do not believe and are damned have only themselves to blame for it. This is the clear teaching of the Bible. To it, and not to reason or human opinions and preferences, we bow in humble submission. As two poles on a magnet, both of these truths must stand, and they cannot be reconciled simply because reason is not satisfied with their distance. God has not asked us to reconcile these two truths any more than he has asked us to reconcile the two opposite poles of a magnet.

What then is the doctrine of election? We need to bear in mind throughout our discussion of this doctrine:

**THE DOCTRINE OF ELECTION:
FOR CHRISTIANS ONLY!**

If we keep this central point in mind, we will not so easily be led astray by any of the above-mentioned errors. When the Bible teaches us about the doctrine of election, it is *not* attempting to tell us anything at all about unbelievers. The purpose of the biblical doctrine of election is the same as the purpose of all biblical doctrine: the glory of Christ and the consolation of penitent sinners.

Briefly stated, the doctrine of election is this: In eternity, before the world began, God elected (predestined) those who would believe the gospel for salvation; he so ruled over all of history that they would hear the gospel, believe it, die in saving faith, and enter into heaven.

All questions that start out with, "Yes, but what about the unbelievers?" are improper because the doctrine of election does not deal with unbelievers. *It deals with believers.* While our reason wants to ask such questions, we must examine the Scriptures not only to look for an answer but also to see if the question is proper. To put it simply: If the Bible does not answer the question, then the question is not proper. We then must leave it alone and make use of the biblical teaching *on God's terms* rather than on our own. The refusal of so many to do that has been the cause of endless controversy and confusion on many doctrinal matters and especially on this one.

Therefore, let us get it clear in our heads and hearts: When the Bible speaks of unbelief and damnation, it speaks of man's fault; when it speaks of faith and the ultimate enjoyment of heaven, it speaks about God's doing and man's receiving, yes, God's election to salvation and all that he has done and does to gather all of the elect into heaven.

When the Bible speaks about predestination, it proclaims to the Christian a beautiful doctrine intended not for speculation and for reason's objections but for our joy and consolation. For what could be more comforting? *Already in eternity, God thought of me, loved me, determined to rule all of history so that I would hear his Word, believe it, and die in the possession of saving faith!*

Because there has been so much controversy in the history of doctrine about this particular doctrine, and perhaps because reason objects to this doctrine so strongly, we rarely speak or even think about the doctrine of election. Therefore it may be surprising to some to discover how often it is spoken of in the Bible. Of course, when the Bible speaks of it, reason is expected to remain silent, while faith, which trusts the Word of God, trusts that God would not lie to us. Faith created, rooted, and grounded in the gospel eagerly drinks in the rich comfort in those passages that teach us about predestination.

Consider, for example, this simple and clear passage from Jeremiah 31:3: "I have loved you with an everlasting love; I have drawn you with loving-kindness." The love of God for his people preceded their very existence: it was an "everlasting love." It was that loving-kindness that prompted God to draw his people to himself and to save them. In the context of Jeremiah, a book addressed to a stubborn and rebellious people, the loving-kindness is grace, i.e., undeserved loving-kindness. No merit in Israel prompted God's favor; no decision for him caused it either—certainly no work merited it. Again, the context of Jeremiah rules out anything but purest grace.

Consider some of the many passages in the New Testament that teach the doctrine of election. The reader will notice that none of the passages attempts to explain the doctrine or argue about it on the terms of human reason. The passages simply state what God has willed in eternity and done in time to accomplish our salvation. St. Paul declares, for example:

> But join with me in suffering for the gospel, by the power of God, who has saved us and called us to a holy life—not because of anything we have done but because of his own purpose and grace. This grace was *given us in Christ Jesus before the beginning of time,* but it has now been revealed through the appearing of our Savior, Christ Jesus, who has destroyed death and has brought life and immortality to light through the gospel. (2 Timothy 1:8-10)

Notice the simplicity and clarity of the passage. All of the causes of salvation are there. God's grace, not our merit, caused it; Christ's work, not ours, merited it; the gospel proclamation, not our choice, brought that salvation to us. All glory goes to God. Our salvation is assured because of grace, Christ's merit, and the promise revealed in the gospel. It was determined by God in eternity, accomplished in time by Christ Jesus, and brought to us in due course through the gospel.

Or consider the following verses from the first chapter of Ephesians:

> [God] chose us in him [i.e., Christ] before the creation of the world to be holy and blameless in his sight. In love he predestined us to be adopted as his sons through Jesus Christ, in accordance with

> his pleasure and will—to the praise of his glorious grace, which he has freely given us in the One he loves. In him we were also chosen, having been predestined according to the plan of him who works out everything in conformity with the purpose of his will, in order that we, who were the first to hope in Christ, might be for the praise of his glory. (Ephesians 1:4-6,11,12)

Once more we catch the beauty as well as the simplicity and the clarity with which the Bible presents this doctrine to us. Our certainty and consolation are grounded in God's grace and Christ's merit. There is not a word about our "decision for Christ"; in fact, in the following chapter our faith as part of our salvation is called God's gift, not our decision. And it all was predestined in eternity! In eternity God thought of his elect, planned for their adoption, and brought it about in time because of his own grace in Christ Jesus.

Then there are these words from the book of Acts: "When the Gentiles heard this [i.e., the gospel message preached by Paul and Barnabas], they were glad and honored the word of the Lord; and all who were appointed for eternal life believed" (Acts 13:48). Again it is clear that God's choice causes faith, not the other way around, as the "in view of faith" error has it.

Jesus speaks in the same way about predestination. He speaks of it only in connection with those predestined and elected to eternal life. He never talks about an election to damnation. The Last Day, for example, will come soon for the sake of his elect; and because they are the elect, even the worst heretics and seducers of souls will not be able to deceive them (Mark 13:20-22).

Romans 8, 9, and 10 give us the Bible's most extensive treatment of the doctrine of predestination. These chapters need to be read carefully and in context; piecemeal reading and passages taken out of the context of the chapters and the entire letter to the Romans will do injustice to these chapters and to the doctrine they contain. In the first part of chapter 8, St. Paul contrasts the mind and life of the Christian and the unbeliever. And what is the mind and life of the Christian? It is a mind and life in which the Spirit of God lives and rules. The mind and life of the unbeliever however is dominated by the unbeliever's own sinful nature. Already as the apostle sets the stage for the discussion of predestination, the emphasis is on the grace of God and the work of the Spirit in the believer; on the other hand, God is not blamed for the mind and life of the unbeliever—the unbeliever's own sinful nature is blamed. To emphasize the grace of God and the effective rule and consolation of the Spirit for the believer, St. Paul continues with the doctrine of election. So effective is that grace in election that nothing can separate us from the love of God in Christ (8:31-39). For God has called the elect out of grace, predestined and justified them, and glorified them with the assurance of the glory yet to come in heaven (8:29,30).

In chapters 9 and 10 the apostle continues the discussion of election and its cause in grace and grace alone. When he speaks of the election of Abraham, Isaac, and Jacob, his entire emphasis is on God's right to elect whom he pleases and to base that election on nothing but his own good pleasure, that is, on grace. Thus even when someone like Pharaoh rises up and rejects the Word of God through Moses, God ultimately hardens Pharaoh's heart and uses Pharaoh's wicked intentions and works to show his own grace and power in rescuing his children. Was Pharaoh's heart hardened in eternity because God hated him? Certainly not! But after Pharaoh repeatedly rejected God's Word, God used his very rejection to show the love he had for the elect. Then the apostle continues by noting that God is obliged to elect no one and that therefore any election can only be one of grace, whether it be the election of some in Israel or in the New Testament era and the election of Gentiles. Man's rejection of God's Word, be it that of Pharaoh or that of so many in Israel, is the cause of damnation. God's election is for salvation. And that election is carried out through the preaching of the gospel.

It is clear in Romans 9–11 that the apostle does not intend the doctrine of election to be used for idle speculation about who is elect and who isn't. Rather, as with all doctrine, it has the very practical purpose of magnifying God's grace and increasing our joy and consolation in Christ. The believer should consider himself among the elect and draw the intended comfort from this doctrine. The doctrine of election is especially comforting to the suffering Christian. The suffering may be physical or mental. Family life may be a shambles, finances in ruins, or the body plagued by sickness and pain. Perhaps the suffering is spiritual. The Christian is tempted by the devil, the world, and his own sinful flesh so severely that he wonders if he is a Christian at all or if he will be able to endure to the end. The suffering could be the result of his own sins or the sins of others; it could be persecution on account of his faith or the trauma of a church torn by strife, divisions, even heresies. Whatever the suffering may be, the devil and the world and his own sinful flesh press the question to his heart and soul: "Do you really think that God cares about you? If he did, then why are you in such torment? Listen to the counsel of Job's wife: 'Curse God and die'" (cf. Job 2:9).

In just such circumstances the believer calls to mind the beautiful promises of God in Romans 8. He consoles himself with the assurance that God is faithful to his Word. For just as God has promised that we will suffer in this life, so he has also promised strength to endure and has promised rescue and finally triumph in heaven. And these assurances of grace and strength stretch all the way back into eternity! There already God loved me, God chose me, and God determined to rule everything in time to bring about my salvation—and his purpose will not fail! That message of the gospel in the doctrine of election is powerful indeed. It brings joy and consolation and strength to those who simply listen to the Word as St. Paul proclaims it in these chapters.

Can those who today trust the Word fall tomorrow? Yes, they can, if they reject the gospel that today they trust. For the doctrine of election is not intended to bring us into what is called carnal security. Carnal security is the fleshly notion that I am elect and therefore can sin boldly, even separate myself from the Word, without a care. That's not the purpose of this doctrine. Those tempted to such a misuse of the doctrine of election should read carefully Paul's words about the life controlled by the sinful nature in Romans 6 and 8; Galatians 5:13-21; and Ephesians 5:1-20. The doctrine of justification and its expansion in the doctrine of election are not intended to serve as a license for sin, least of all for the sin of despising God's Word through which our salvation comes to us!

Again, the doctrine of predestination is intended not for speculation about who is in and who is out, not for the exercise of reason ("If some are elected, then . . ."), and not for carnal security, but for the praise and glory of God and for the consolation of the believer. What then should those do who worry about election? Those who want the consolation intended in this doctrine should fasten their attention on the gospel and on Christ in the gospel; then and only then will they be protected from a misuse of the doctrine; then and only then will they enjoy the sweet comfort it intends.[8]

The doctrine of justification, then, in summary form is this: God has declared the whole world justified, that is, forgiven. He made this declaration prompted by grace alone *(prompting cause)* and alone because of the work of Christ in his active and passive obedience as our substitute *(meritorious cause).* The personal benefit of this universal justification becomes our own through faith alone; God gives this faith

---

[8]For a beautiful exposition and summary of the doctrine of election, we refer the reader to Article XI of the Formula of Concord, both in the Epitome and in the Solid Declaration.

or trust in the promise of the gospel through the proclamation of the gospel in Word and sacraments *(effecting cause)*. Those who believe the gospel and who die in saving faith *(instrumental cause)* believe it not by accident or coincidence, not by some decision that they made of themselves or by some natural ability in themselves, but because already in eternity God in his free grace elected them and then in time ruled over all of history so that they would hear the gospel, believe it, and die in saving faith and so enter heaven.

Chapter 13
Faith

Faith is an indispensable element in our salvation. The sentence *"We are saved by faith alone"* is familiar to every Lutheran from childhood on. We have already considered the vital role of faith in subjective justification. However, we have yet to carefully define it and see how the Bible uses the words *faith* and *believe*. It is time now to examine the whole subject of faith in somewhat greater detail. Just exactly what is faith and what is its role in our salvation and Christian life? Perhaps no one outside of the Bible summarized the importance of faith and, yes, its miraculous nature, better than St. Bernard (1091–1153). He noted that there are three great miracles or unities recorded in the Bible. The first is the union of the two natures in the one person, Christ; the second is that this union takes place in the womb of a woman who is both mother and virgin at the same time; and the third is the wonder that the heart of man is both corrupted by sin but nevertheless grasps in faith those first two wonders!

Saving faith

The noun *faith* and its verb *to believe* have fallen on hard times in the present-day world. Many use those words as synonyms for an emotion or a feeling that has no necessary basis in fact. *Faith* for many is merely an unsubstantiated opinion. Thus, we may hear people say things like this: "Well, there are some things that we know and some things that we just believe," as though faith and fact or faith and history were opposites. Or a mother may say of her son convicted by overwhelming evidence of a monstrous crime: "I still believe that he is really a good boy," as though faith were legitimate even when opposed to facts. Or we have the words of a popular song: "I believe that for every drop of rain that falls a flower grows," in which faith is nothing more than a mindless sentiment.

Still others use the words *faith* and *believe* as though those words by themselves cause truth; something is true simply because they believe it. The theological relativists spoken of in the last chapter have such a view: What you believe or have faith in is true for you, though not necessarily true for everyone else; and you are free to believe whatever you want and to change what you believe whenever you want. For such people the word *faith* and the word *truth* as well have really lost all meaning. A pastor may run into such empty notions about faith and truth when dealing with an unbeliever who may say to him, "Pastor, I can't go to hell because I don't believe in hell." Such an individual imagines that anything he believes is true simply because he believes it and only as long as he believes it. All too common today is the experience of pastors who rebuke a sinful lifestyle and get this response: "Well, Pastor, I just don't believe that what I am doing is a sin," as though we have the freedom to create sin and destroy sin simply by deciding for ourselves what sin is and is not. All of these false uses of the terms *faith* and *believe* have reduced faith to an opinion, an emotion, or a mindless sentiment. That is not at all what the Bible means by those terms, and it is certainly not what we mean by the phrase *saving faith.*

What then is *faith* as the Bible uses the term? Jesus gives us a beautiful summary of what faith is in his great High Priestly Prayer in John 17. He shows us in that prayer that faith consists of three basic elements; without them there is no such thing as faith in the biblical sense of the term. We commend the entire chapter to the reader's careful consideration. For now we will give special attention to the following excerpts:

> "Now this is eternal life: that they may *know* you, the only true God, and Jesus Christ, whom you have sent. I have revealed you to those whom you gave me out of the world. They were yours; you gave them to me and *they have obeyed your word.* Now they know that everything you have given me comes from you. For I gave them the words you gave me and *they accepted* them. *They knew with certainty* that I came from you, and *they believed* that you sent me. Sanctify them by the truth; your word is truth. My prayer is not for them alone. I pray also for those who will *believe in me through their message,* that all of them may be one. . . . Righteous Father, though the world does not know you, I know you, and they know that you have sent me. *I have made you known to them, and will continue to make you known in order that the love you have for me may be in them and that I myself may be in them.*" (vv. 3,6-8,17,20,21,25,26)

What a magnificent prayer this is that Jesus prays shortly before he completed the work of our redemption on Good Friday! And how clearly and simply he defines faith for us in his prayer. The three elements that are essential to faith, as Jesus uses the term, are:

1. Knowledge *(notitia)*—There is no such thing as faith without knowledge. Jesus tells us in his prayer that he has made certain things known to his disciples. What he has made known to them is truth. That truth consists of certain facts. Notice how different Jesus' definition of truth is from the one so common today; for Jesus truth is not just opinion or feeling. Truth is not something that depends on the individual's acceptance before it can be true. Rather, *truth is factual and historical; truth agrees with and corresponds to reality.* He has come from the Father—that's a fact. He has come into the world to redeem it—that's a fact. He has come to show the love of the Father by all that he did for our salvation—that's a fact. The knowledge that Jesus gave his disciples doesn't become true if or when someone believes it; nor is it true for the individual only so long as he believes it. The knowledge he gave the disciples is true, factual, and historical, whether anyone believes it or not. Faith, then, is based on knowledge and must have knowledge of the truth as its foundation. Where there is no knowledge, there is no faith in the biblical sense of the word *faith.* For faith to be present, the individual must at least know who Jesus is and thus have some basic knowledge of the doctrine of the Trinity. For faith to be present, one must at least know why Jesus came and thus have some basic knowledge of the doctrine of salvation. St. Paul tells us the same thing when he says, "I know whom I have believed" (2 Timothy 1:12). He does not say, "I feel this way about him" or "This is my personal opinion." And he tells us as well where the knowledge comes from: It comes from hearing the Word of God (Romans 10:17). That is exactly the point Jesus is making in his High Priestly Prayer, as he thanks his Father both for the Word and his work for us revealed in the Word. The disciples believe on the basis of the knowledge that he has given them of himself and his mission—knowledge that is true, knowledge that is based on fact, and knowledge that he has made known to us through his Word.

People immediately raise all kinds of objections in the interest of hanging on to the notion that faith is just a feeling or an opinion. *But then an infant cannot have faith, since an infant cannot process knowledge!* How do you know a child cannot process knowledge? In point of fact, the evidence indicates the contrary. A child somehow "knows" its mother very early on. An infant easily figures out how to gain attention for the satisfaction of its needs. Fairly soon the child learns that talking is a quicker way to get what it wants than crying, and so it learns how to speak. How does a child "know" these things? How does it figure them out? We cannot say. We have long ago forgotten how we learned to think and speak, how words became the tools used for thinking. However, what we do know is that Jesus tells us that little ones believe in him (Mark 9:42; 10:13,14). We will let God worry about how they process the knowledge given in the gospel and conveyed in the Sacrament of Baptism. We will trust that Jesus is not mistaken when he tells us that they do in fact believe and have faith. How that exactly works we will leave to him. He after all is not only the source of faith but is as well the author of language and the giver of the mind that receives and considers knowledge. He will not prove inadequate, therefore, for the task of giving faith to the little ones who cannot tell us themselves just exactly how they believe. Jesus has told us that they do believe. That's good enough for us!

Still someone else may object: *But what about people who are sleeping or unconscious? Do they still know the truths of the gospel?* Just as in the case of infants and little children, so it is in the case of the sleeping or the unconscious. We should not assume that because one cannot express knowledge that that person has no knowledge. Does a person's knowledge of his family or vocation or life's story disappear because he is taking a nap? Certainly not; it is still there, even though it cannot be expressed at that point in time. Why should it be any different with the knowledge of the most important truth of all, the truth that Jesus is the Son of God and Mary's son, the Savior of the world? Yes, even in cases of intellectual disability or in cases of intellectual decline due to illness or old age, we will not limit or deny the power of the gospel to impart knowledge and to create faith when and where the Spirit wills (John 3:6-8). Ask those who work with the intellectually disabled or with people who are suffering from Alzheimer's disease; they will tell you story after story of people who folded their hands to pray the Lord's Prayer when those same people could not count to ten or recognize any longer their closest family members! No, we will not limit the ability of the Holy Spirit working through the gospel to give and preserve faith—faith rooted and grounded in truth revealed in the Word and work of the Savior.

2. Assent *(assentia)*—We "know" that Rome was founded by twins who were suckled by a wolf; we "know" that Atlas carries the world on his shoulders. But these are myths. We do not assent to them, do not accept that they are true, corresponding to history and reality. We do, however, assent to the truths of the gospel. That's what Jesus says of the disciples in his High Priestly Prayer. He has made known to them the truth of who he is and why he has come, and they have received his revelation. They have assented that it is not myth or fairy tale but

actual and factual. Again, we must note that today there are many who would say that they "know" the Christmas story and the Easter story. But they do not accept or assent that these stories are true; they treat them like the story about the founding of Rome or the story of Atlas. There is no faith in the biblical sense of the term without assent to the truthfulness, the historical validity of the gospel message. Where there is no knowledge, there is no faith; likewise, where there is no assent, there is no faith. St. Paul underscores the same point when speaking about the resurrection of Christ from the dead. He tells the Corinthian congregation that if Christ was not raised from the dead, if that is not a fact, if we treat it as just myth or a wish or an illusion, then faith is empty and we are still in our sins (1 Corinthians 15:12-20). As the knowledge comes from the Word of God, so too does the assent. It is worked or created in us by the gospel (Romans 1:16,17; 10:17). By now it should almost be obvious that there is an unbreakable, indispensable link between the gospel and faith; it is the link of cause and effect. The gospel is the cause, faith, the effect. The gospel is the link between the heart of God and the soul of man. It is the link or the bridge between the spiritual death caused by original sin and spiritual life created by the Holy Spirit through this same gospel message. It is, as St. Bernard put it so colorfully, the kiss of the Holy Spirit on the lips of the soul. We see this especially when we consider the third essential component of faith.

3. Confidence or Trust *(fiducia)*—This is the third indispensable element in faith. As vital as the first two elements are, it is this third element of confidence or trust that is the very center of faith. For as St. James reminds us, even the devil has knowledge of God (James 2:19). Indeed, he knows the history of salvation better than any of us—he was after all a witness to everything that happened. But the devil does not have faith, and the devil can never have faith. For he lacks the confidence and trust that is the center of faith, the confidence that the message of forgiveness applies to him. He lacks such a trust for the most obvious of reasons: It doesn't apply to him! For faith to be present it is not enough that we know the facts and even that we assent that those facts are really true; there must also be the confidence, the trust that those facts apply to me. We may think, for example, of the soldiers who stood guard at Jesus' tomb and of the members of the Jewish Sanhedrin who received the soldiers' report of Jesus' resurrection (Matthew 28:11-15). Both the soldiers and the priests knew that Jesus had risen from the dead; neither the soldiers nor the priests argued that the story was myth or fairy tale—they had

the necessary assent. But they nevertheless did not have faith; they did not trust that the resurrection of Jesus was God's gift of salvation for them, that by his death and resurrection Jesus had won their forgiveness and eternal life. Saving faith has knowledge as its basis, assent as a necessary prerequisite, but then it goes the vital third step further. Saving faith declares: I *know* that Jesus is the virgin-born Son of God who died for the sins of the world and rose again; I *agree (assent)* that this knowledge is true, that it is historical, factual, and corresponding to reality; and I *trust,* I have *confidence* that this knowledge applies to me; I trust that he came down from heaven *for me,* that he died and rose again for me, that my sins therefore are forgiven and *I* am justified.

It is just such a faith that Jesus speaks of in his great High Priestly Prayer, a faith that consists of all three elements: *knowledge, assent,* and *confidence.* That is as well how the rest of the Bible speaks of faith. Consider, for example, St. Paul's great discourse on saving faith in Romans 3,4. The apostle declares that our salvation comes through a faith that knows the promises of God in Christ Jesus. It is a faith that knows man's fallen, sinful, and desperate condition and knows as well the Savior's work. It is a faith that does not treat such knowledge as though it were a fairy tale but accepts that the Word is factual and historically correct. And, finally, it is a faith that trusts that God is true and that therefore God's promises apply even to me.

Of those who have such faith St. Paul says that God credits righteousness to that faith! "This righteousness from God comes through faith in Jesus Christ to all who believe. There is no difference, for all have sinned and fall short of the glory of God, and are justified freely by his grace through the redemption that came by Jesus Christ. God presented him as a sacrifice of atonement, through faith in his blood" (Romans 3:22-25). He goes on to show us Abraham as the Old Testament pattern for such believers and for such saving faith. God gave Abraham the promise of the Savior who was to come through Abraham's son. In spite of his and his wife's advanced age, Abraham trusted the promise of God. Abraham *knew* the promise. He did not dismiss the promise as a myth but accepted it, *gave assent and trusted* (often *assent* and *trust* can be virtually the same thing) that God would keep his Word. "Abraham believed God, and it was credited to him as righteousness" (4:3). The rest of the chapter, indeed much of the rest of the epistle to the Romans, considers the matter of saving faith in careful detail, from a number of different vantage points. However, the bottom line is always this: Saving faith consists of knowledge of God's promises in Christ; assent that these promises and Christ's work to carry them out are all true, historical, and corresponding to reality; and confidence that those promises and Christ's work apply therefore to me.

Is faith then a work that I do instead of the works of the Ten Commandments in order to earn God's favor? Is it my part in accomplishing my salvation, as though God did all the things spoken of in the gospel and now it's my turn—I must believe it?

It is true that *we* believe. God doesn't believe for us, but the fact that we believe is entirely the gift of God through the gospel. We can put it this way: Faith is an act of man but a gift of God. And just how is it a gift? The knowledge comes from God in the gospel; the assent is created by the gospel; the trust or confidence that the gospel message applies to me is the work of the Holy Spirit through and never apart from the gospel. That's why we call faith an activity, rather than a work; we do not want by calling faith a work to give the impression that faith itself is what merits salvation. In fact, in Romans 4 and often elsewhere (especially in Galatians), St. Paul contrasts faith and works with each other and deals with them as opposites. To put it another way: Faith is always a miracle performed by the Holy Spirit through the message of the gospel.

Especially illuminating in this regard is a consideration of Acts 16:30,31 in the light of what St. Paul says in Romans 4. The jailer at Philippi had just experienced the earthquake, and he was terrified that his prisoners (Paul and Silas) might have escaped. He was about to commit suicide in order to avoid the disgrace of being executed (execution was the punishment that the jailer could expect for letting his prisoners escape). But Paul shouted out and told him that they were all still there in the prison, that there was no need for the jailer to fear. The jailer, overwhelmed by this entire situation in which he himself came so close to death either by the earthquake or by his own hands, cried out, "Sirs, what must I do to be saved?" The jailer assumed that salvation is by works. But what did the apostle answer? Does he say, "This is what *you must do*"? No, he and Silas replied, "Believe in the Lord Jesus, and you will be saved—you and your household." Believing, having faith, in this passage as in Romans 4 and elsewhere is not a doing but a *receiving*! The apostle is telling the jailer in effect: "There is nothing for you to do; it has all been done by another, namely, the One we were preaching about in the city, the One we were singing about in the jail before the earthquake. He did it all. He did it for the world. He did it for you! Believe it! That is, trust that God would not lie to you, that he really means you!" For we are saved by grace through faith, and this whole salvation from grace through faith is the gift of God, not a work of man (Ephesians 2:8,9).

What a wonderful thing that is, this faith that is knowledge, assent, and confidence, this faith that is a receiving activity of man but entirely a gift of God through the gospel! Thus, even when we call faith an activity of man, the emphasis remains that man is passive and that God is active through the gospel. Thus no one need think that he is excluded, since the gospel message is addressed to all. Nor need anyone fear that perhaps he does not believe the gospel enough; for saving faith is not a work weighed on a scale that needs to reach a certain level before it is saving faith. Indeed, it can sometimes be misleading to speak of saving faith as being weak or strong, big or small, if that moves people to focus on whether they feel faith strongly enough to really have it; it is not the nature of faith to focus on itself, to navel gaze, so to speak. It is the nature of faith to look outside of self, to focus on Christ, his work for us, and his promise to us in his Word. The Bible speaks of weak and strong faith, but not when it is talking about saving faith. When talking about saving faith, it is either there or it isn't there. Either we know who Jesus is and what he did and trust that his promise and his work apply to us or we don't know and don't trust! There is no third alternative. Our knowledge may be limited; our trust may be battered by all kinds of storms, even fears and doubts, but at bottom we either know and trust Jesus as Savior or we do not. To speak too much of saving faith as weak or strong, big or little, may drive people again either to despair or to self-righteousness. It can push people in the direction of looking too much inside of themselves to see if their faith is enough to save them. Again, faith does best when it is focused outside of self, focused on Christ and the gospel. For Christ in the gospel is the content of saving faith; Christ in the gospel is the source of saving faith; Christ in the gospel is the goal of saving faith. The one who is worried about whether his faith is big enough or strong enough should focus attention on Jesus' beautiful assurance in John 6:37: "Whoever comes to me I will never drive away."

To return to his beautiful High Priestly Prayer, Jesus says that the knowledge given by him in his Word and the trust of the disciples worked by that same Word has this goal: "In order that the love you have for me may be in them and that I myself may be in them" (John 17:26). That is how Jesus brings us all he is and the benefit of all that he did for us and for our salvation. He saves us by the gospel message;

he saves us by bringing us to assent to the gospel message; he saves us by creating in us a trust that the gospel message applies to us. All of that is summed up when we say that we are saved by faith. By faith God's love and favor are ours, and by faith God dwells in us, forgives us, and gives us eternal life and salvation.

Our Lutheran Confessions speak in much the same way of saving or justifying faith. The Apology of the Augsburg Confession, for example, states the matter very simply and clearly. In the following citation, note the emphasis on "receiving" as contrasted with "doing." When we receive a gift from someone, we do not think that we are doing something thereby or meriting somehow the gift because we receive it. Just so with faith: We receive it and its benefit—we don't "do" faith, as though it were a work. Again, faith is an activity worked by the Holy Spirit through the gospel.

> The faith that justifies is not only a knowledge of history; it is to assent to the promise of God, in which forgiveness of sins and justification are bestowed freely on account of Christ. To avoid the suspicion that it is merely knowledge, we will add further that to have faith is to desire and to receive the offered promise of the forgiveness of sins and justification.
>
> Faith is that worship which receives the benefits that God offers; the righteousness of the law is that worship which offers God our own merits. God wants to be honored by faith so that we receive from him those things that he promises and offers. (Art. IV, 48,49 p. 128)
>
> Therefore, whenever we speak about justifying faith, we must understand that these three elements belong together: the promise itself; the fact that the promise is free; and the merits of Christ as the payment and atoning sacrifice. . . . Every time we speak about faith, we want the object [of faith] to be understood as well, namely, the promised mercy. For faith does not justify or save because it is a worthy work in and of itself, but only because it receives the promised mercy. (Art. IV, 53-55 pp. 128,129)

Thus, we often call faith *the receiving organ* of the gospel of salvation. It is the golden chalice created in us by the gospel, into which God pours forgiveness full and free, eternal life, and salvation. There is no salvation without that chalice. But all the credit for it and its contents goes to the God who created it, who preserves it, and who fills it with the precious gospel message.

God's work of bringing an unbeliever to faith—conversion

In order to emphasize and press this understanding of the nature of faith into our minds and hearts still more deeply, still more clearly, the Scriptures speak of *the process of coming to faith.* The Bible calls the process *conversion.* That word as it describes this process means "to be turned around." When we come to faith, we are turned around. We were heading straight for hell. We could not turn ourselves around and we did not even want to be turned around. God puts a prayer in the mouth of the prophet Jeremiah who had already been thus turned that expresses the matter of conversion, of being turned around, very well: "Restore me, and I will return, because you are the LORD my God" (Jeremiah 31:18). The return of the rebel is not the result of the rebel's effort or will or self-improvement. He was plunging headlong into destruction. Only one thing could change his fate: God's own intervention, God's restoring of his rebel child so that he would be turned around and return.

So it is with us. By nature we are headed straight for hell, without the ability or even the will to do anything about it. But God has intervened. The Holy Spirit came to us in the message of the gospel, picked us up, and turned us around to head in the opposite direction, in the direction of heaven. Perhaps the most dramatic example of what the word *conversion* means is the example of St. Paul himself (Acts 9:1-19). He was on the road to Damascus physically and on the road to hell spiritually. Did he ask to be converted? Clearly he did not. Did he cooperate somehow in the coming of Jesus to him on the road or in the message of Ananias to him in Damascus? He did not. Did he deserve conversion more than others? Obviously he did not. He was turned around nonetheless. He did not turn himself around. It all happened as a result of God's activity through the gospel message on the road and especially in the message of Ananias.

The same is clear at the beginning of the book of Acts in St. Peter's sermon on the day of Pentecost. People were converted, were turned around from unbelief to faith (Acts 2:14-41). Those who were converted confessed that they were not worthy, that they were guilty of crucifying the Lord of life. But the promise of the gospel in St. Peter's sermon picked them up and turned them around, so that they repented of their sins and trusted the promise of forgiveness and were baptized.

Jesus speaks of this process of coming to faith, of this matter of conversion, in John 6:44,45: "No one can come to me unless the Father who sent me draws him. . . . Everyone who listens to the Father and learns from him comes to me." How does one come to Jesus? Is it by one's own choice? Is it by a cooperation between God and man? Is it because that appears to a person as the most rational thing to do? No! It is all the gift of God! The Father draws us to Jesus. He does it through the gospel message of who Jesus is and what Jesus came to do. Jesus demonstrated the process often, as, for example, in the case of the Samaritan woman at the well (John 4:7-42). She was an unbeliever. She was steeped in a life of adultery. She was clearly headed straight for hell. But Jesus spoke with her. He showed himself as the Savior long promised and long awaited. By the message of the Savior about the Savior she was turned around; she believed his word about himself and even became an instant missionary.

In sum, the word *conversion*—"to be turned around"—describes the process of coming to saving faith; it is a process in which God interrupts the sinner headed for hell. He interrupts the sinner with the gospel proclamation of forgiveness, life, and salvation by grace on account of the work of Christ, through faith alone. The Holy Spirit uses that message to convert, to turn the sinner around and head him toward the goal of heaven. In that process God is active and doing; man is passive and receiving.

We might note as well that the process is instantaneous; one is either converted or not converted, either has saving faith or does not have saving faith. There is no such thing as half-converted or partly converted. To be sure, there may be a long or short period of time during which God himself is preparing a person for conversion—which is why we use the word *process* when speaking of conversion. Perhaps God sends or permits either a tragedy or a great blessing to come into a person's life, and that turns the individual's attention to God and to his Word. Then God uses the Word to accomplish the conversion. Perhaps the individual is in a Bible instruction course or attending services with friends or relatives or just out of curiosity. Choosing to attend the service or the class is a matter that the individual has within his own power and choice, something subject to reason. But believing what is heard or taught there, that's entirely God's work through the gospel.

Or, perhaps one is hearing the gospel once or often from friends or family members. At first he may have resisted what was being taught, may even have scoffed at what he heard. But then there comes a time when he no longer scoffs. There comes a time when the heart sighs: "God loves even me! Even for me Christ died and rose again! My sins too have been forgiven and washed away in the blood of Christ!" That person has been converted. He might not know at exactly what moment that change took place. The conversion could be quiet and subtle; it could be dramatic and obvious. The point is that there was a time when he was an unbeliever and then there was a time when he became a believer; there never was a time when he was neither.

Indeed, for many the instant of conversion cannot be identified. For many it was at their baptisms. Many Christians will say that they do not remember that there was ever a time when they did not believe that Jesus was their Savior. Nevertheless, there was such a time, even if it was only the matter of hours, days, or weeks before their baptisms. No one is by nature a Christian; we all are conceived and born in sin and therefore are unbelievers, heathens, and as such in need of conversion.

We should note at this juncture that conversion, being turned around from unbelief to faith, is always a miracle. That is to say, conversion is not the result of a natural process but of a supernatural process. In a natural process one may read a book about, let us say, engine repair or gardening. If the book is well written and if the reader has a knack for understanding such things, the reader will accept what he has read and be able to put what he has accepted to good use. But the process by which he turned from ignorance about the subject to knowledge about and application of the subject matter was entirely natural; it depended on abilities in the writer and the reader that were in no way miraculous or outside of the normal realm of natural abilities.

Not so conversion! The message of the gospel is addressed primarily to the will of man. But man's will, as we have already seen, is by nature dead in trespasses and sin. It is hostile to God and God's will. To the extent that it is active at all, it actively resists the message of the gospel and conversion. It has no natural ability to turn around, and it does not want to turn around.

Thus when conversion takes place, it takes place because of the power and activity of the Holy Spirit through the gospel, not because of a purely rational or active choice to believe on the part of the converted. It is not as though the gospel presents us with two alternatives and then God says to us, "Now you pick one!" No, that can never be the way it works, precisely because we are by nature dead and hostile and resist even and especially the salvation won for us by Christ alone (Ephesians 2:1-3). The spiritually dead cannot choose to live; it is the nature of the dead that they stay dead. As Lazarus and the young man of Nain did not actively decide to come back from the dead but needed the life-giving Word of Christ to act on them and give them life, so too the spiritually dead. They also need the life-giving Word of Christ to overcome their nature, their dead spiritual state.

Does God then convert us against our will? Is the Holy Spirit's activity irresistible or a function of God's omnipotence, as it was in the case of the raising of Lazarus and the young man of Nain? No, God does not convert us against a will that, so to speak, chooses to remain dead—the spiritually dead still have that capacity of refusing. The Holy Spirit's activity is not irresistible. Rather, the Holy Spirit uses the gospel. He uses it not as a hammer to bludgeon us into submission but uses it to draw, to entice, and to invite. In the gospel he shows us God's yearning, his longing, his earnest intent to convert by means of that gospel, as we clearly see in the Bible in so many places (e.g., 2 Corinthians 5:19-21; 1 John 2:1,2; 1 Timothy 2:4; 2 Peter 3:9). But in the process God retains a certain respect, so to speak, even for his fallen creatures and does not turn us into robots or puppets. While we have no natural ability to convert ourselves, we do retain the ability to reject his gracious call in the gospel. Many do exactly that and have no one to blame for it but themselves. We see that so clearly in Jesus' tears over Jerusalem and in St. Stephen's rebuke of the Jewish Sanhedrin (Matthew 23:37; Acts 7:51).

So, God does not convert us by force. It is rather this way: as St. Augustine in his famous work *The Enchiridion* (ch. 32) puts it fairly well when he tells us that God's mercy goes before the unwilling to make him willing and dwells with those thus made willing. God by the sweet message of the gospel knocks on the door of the soul and bids us invite him in. He lures us by that message. He draws us with it. He pursues us as a lover his beloved—a picture used so often in the Old Testament. Not with a club beating us over the head, but with words of love, of grace, and of mercy he comes to us and into us. At creation God breathed into man the breath of life and he became alive; so in the gospel he breathes into a spiritually dead soul and hostile will and gives the soul life and a new, changed will.

That's how Jesus pictures himself to us in the last book of the Bible: He stands at the door and knocks, waiting, longing to be invited in (Revelation 3:19,20). What lowliness, what humility on the part of God! How shocking his longing! How warm and inviting his call to the fallen, the doomed, the rebel, the lost and condemned! When conversion takes place as a result of his call and never apart from it (Luke 14:16-24; 1 Peter 1:3,23), the soul springs from spiritual death to life. It sighs its Spirit-worked response: "Yes! He means me, even me! I too am redeemed, justified, and forgiven!" With the precious gospel God woos and wins us, not against our will but by changing our will.

Are perhaps some converted then because they resisted less? No. There is no difference in our spiritually dead nature: dead is dead; one is not more or less dead than another. As we have noted so often before and need to note yet again, those who are converted have only God to thank for it and those who are not have only themselves to blame for it. That the miracle takes place in some is God's grace; that it does not take place in others is their own fault. The Bible does not attempt to address the problem that our reason has with this answer. It does, however, make it very clear that any other answer robs Christ of his glory as Savior, is contrary to the clear Word of God, and deprives the Christian of needed comfort by driving him either in the direction of self-righteousness or of despair.[1] We will therefore rest content with God's Word!

Our Lutheran Confessions echo the teaching of the Bible that conversion is entirely the work of the Holy Spirit through the gospel. We refer the reader especially to Article II of the Formula of Concord. The following brief citation from the Formula should serve to illustrate the point that the confessions are clear and emphatic in their presentation of the Bible's teaching on conversion:

> [It is our teaching, faith, and confession] that in spiritual and divine matters, the mind, heart, and will of the unreborn human being can in absolutely no way, on the basis of its own natural powers, understand, believe, accept, consider, will, begin, accomplish, do, effect, or cooperate. Instead, it is completely dead to the good—completely corrupted. This means that in this human nature, after the fall and before rebirth, there is not a spark of spiritual power left or present with which human beings can prepare themselves for the grace of God or accept grace as it is offered. . . . Rather they are "the slave of sin" (John 8[:34]) and prisoners of the devil, by whom they are driven (Eph. 2[:2]; 2 Tim. 2[:26]). Therefore, according to its own perverted character and nature, the natural free will has only the power and ability to do whatever is displeasing and hostile to God. (FC SD II, 7 p. 544)
>
> Holy Scripture ascribes conversion, faith in Christ, rebirth, renewal, and everything that belongs to the actual beginning and

---

[1]For a further consideration of this point, the reader may refer especially to the consideration of the doctrine of predestination in chapter 12.

> completion of these things, not to the human powers of the natural free will—neither totally, halfway, somewhat, nor in the slightest and smallest bit—but rather ascribes all this *in solidum* (that is, completely and totally) to divine activity and to the Holy Spirit alone, as the Apology says [XVIII, 7,8]. (FC SD II, 25 p. 549)

The articles continue then with an entire catalogue of examples from the Bible in which faith always finds its source in God's work through the gospel.

There are yet two other words that can be used to describe the process of coming to faith. These words underscore what has already been said of that process in the word *conversion.*[2]

Two other biblical synonyms for conversion

Regeneration—"to be born again." As already noted, no one is by nature a Christian, a believer. By nature we are all born sinners, condemned to hell, without any true spiritual life (John 3:6; Psalm 14:3; Romans 3:9,23; Ephesians 2:3). We have a birth from our parents, Adam and Eve. From them we have inherited this nature that is totally devoted to the worship of self. What can we do about it? Nothing by nature! We cannot change our parents and what we have inherited from them. If our parents were Chinese, we cannot decide to be ethnic Norwegians; no amount of wishing or effort will turn us into Norwegians.

We were born sinners, born blind, and born hostile to God in our nature. We had no sense that we should be otherwise. The solution to the problem of our birth, therefore, could not rest with us. We had to be born again, as Jesus said (John 3:3-7), born of water and of the Spirit, especially as that takes place in Baptism. Do we cooperate in that second birth? No more than we cooperated in our first birth, namely, not at all. Birth, be it our natural first birth or the spiritual second birth of coming to faith, is a process in which the one born is purely passive. In our spiritual birth, God becomes our Father through the gospel, as St. Peter puts it: "For you have been born again, not of perishable seed, but of imperishable, through the living and enduring

---

[2]We should note that the two words about to be considered are also used in the Bible and in the Confessions to describe the Christian's life of sanctification. When these words are used to describe the Christian's life, we say that the words are joining together cause and effect: the cause of the Christian's life is inseparably connected to the activity of God in creating faith in the first place; the Christian life is the effect, the result of the conversion that we have been considering here. We will pursue this matter further in chapter 16.

word of God" (1 Peter 1:23). Now with a new nature from a new Parent we have new characteristics. St. Peter tells us that the seed of God's Word is imperishable, that it lives and endures forever (v. 25). That is what we inherit as a result of this new birth. From Adam and Eve we inherited death. In the new birth, in regeneration, in coming to faith, we inherit life and life eternal through the message of the gospel. For in coming to faith we become God's children (Galatians 3:26), born anew of God (1 John 5:1). And all of this is from the will of God accomplished through the gospel (John 1:12,13). In it all we are passive receivers of God's grace and Christ's merit. As with conversion, so with regeneration: It is instantaneous. There is no such thing as sort of born, not quite born, or half born. One is either born or not yet born.

It is unfortunate that many churches expect the believer to be able to identify the moment of conversion, of regeneration. There is no scriptural need for us to do that. Indeed, we cannot recall the moment of our first birth either, but that does not mean that we were not born. The fact of conversion and regeneration, evidenced by a trust in the promise of forgiveness, life, and salvation on account of grace and Christ's merit, is what is important. The *what* of conversion and regeneration matters; the *when* does not. For some the moment may indeed be one that they remember very well and thankfully. But even for such, their trust and joy is in the fact, not in the recollection of the moment. To put the emphasis on the memory of moment is to take the emphasis off of Christ and his promise; it is to turn to faith inward instead of outward, to Christ and the gospel promise.

Quickening—"being brought from death to life." That is the third word that the Bible sometimes uses to describe the process of coming to faith. Much of what has already been said about regeneration can be said about quickening. The difference is that in the word *regeneration,* the individual is viewed as never having had life until God became a Father through the seed of the Word (1 Peter 1:23). In the word *quickening,* the individual is seen as dead, dead in trespasses and sins, as St. Paul puts it (Ephesians 2:1,5). When the gospel comes to the spiritually dead, they do not will their faith into existence nor do they cooperate in its coming into existence. Their faith, their new spiritual life, is entirely the gift of God through the gospel, as we have already noted in our consideration of conversion. And again, as we noted with conversion and regeneration, this quickening is instantaneous. There was not some magic period of in-between time for Lazarus in his grave when he was neither dead nor yet alive. There is no such in-between for us either. We are either spiritually alive or spiritually dead; there is no third possibility. It is either one or the other.[3] To tell someone that he should pray for his own conversion, for new birth, or for quickening is accordingly nonsense: the dead do not pray for life and the unborn do not pray for birth. Someone who prays for his own conversion is doubtless already converted; he already believes that God hears his prayer and therefore that God loves him and wants his forgiveness and salvation. In short, he already believes, has faith. On the other hand, one who does not believe that God hears or loves him and wants to forgive him would be a fool to pray to a God he does not believe in.

To sum it all up, what then can we say of saving faith on the basis of what the Bible says in describing the process of coming to faith? Saving faith has

1. *knowledge* of the basic truths of the gospel as its foundation.
2. *assent* that the message of the gospel, of the person and work of Christ for the salvation of the world, is not just myth or fairy tale but factual, historical, and true.
3. *confidence, trust* that the message of the gospel is not just for other people but also and even for me. Christ did not just die for the world in general; he was born for me, lived a sinless life for me, suffered and died on the cross for me, and rose again from the dead for me, so that I too have been justified, declared forgiven, and made an heir of heaven with Jesus my Savior!

And all of this—our faith, our coming to faith—described as *conversion, regeneration,* or *quickening* has these characteristics:

1. God is active; man is purely passive. God gives faith to the sinner entirely out of grace alone.
2. God is active through the gospel, through which God creates and preserves faith; apart from the gospel there is no such thing as faith in the biblical sense of the word.
3. The process is instantaneous. One is either converted, regenerated, quickened, or not; there is no third possibility.

---

[3]Some may wish to argue that to illustrate the process of coming to faith with the example of Jesus' raising Lazarus from the dead is inappropriate, since coming to faith takes place through the operation of God's attribute of grace, while the raising of Lazarus happened through the operation of the attribute of omnipotence. While it is true that regeneration takes place by grace and not by an omnipotent irresistible decree, we need to point out that Jesus himself in his parables used examples from the kingdom of power to illustrate the activity of grace; he did it without any confusion of grace and omnipotence.

Various questions related to the doctrine of conversion

All of what has been said may still leave us with a number of questions. An important question that arises on the subject of coming to faith is this: *What is the role of the law in the process of coming to faith?* We have noted repeatedly that it is the gospel, the good news of redemption and justification, that brings us to faith and preserves faith in us. But the law has a role to play as well. The Holy Spirit uses the law and works through the law to crush and to kill the self-righteousness in us. For the law of God shows us our sins. It shows us that our situation and condition is hopeless and that we are helpless before the judgment seat of God. It shows us that no matter how good we may think we are, we are nevertheless doomed, condemned sinners in the eyes of God. It shows us that we cannot by any means save ourselves, but that we are in desperate need of a Savior. St. Paul declares that the law condemns us all and leaves us all without any excuse before God (Romans 1–3).

Jesus often illustrated this use of the law as a tool to crush and destroy our pride and self-righteousness in his parables. The parable of the good Samaritan (Luke 10:25-37), for example, is directed at those who imagine that they could deserve heaven. The proper response of those who heard the parable would have been: "Ah, Lord Jesus, look on me with pity, and help! For I have not always and gladly acted as did the Samaritan! Must I then perish eternally?" Such a cry of despair would have shown that the law had hit its target in the human heart, killed and crushed its pride and self-righteousness. Then such a heart would have been ready to hear the glad tidings of the gospel of free forgiveness, of grace, of salvation.

Thus it is through the law that the Holy Spirit works to convict and condemn us. We would never come to faith, however, if the Holy Spirit only worked through the law. The law converts no one—it only convicts and condemns. It is the gospel message that converts, regenerates, and quickens. Still it would be a big mistake for us to underestimate or disregard the work of the Holy Spirit through the law. If the law is not used or is soft-pedaled, so as not to hurt anyone's feelings, people will not see their desperate need for the Savior. They will not appreciate the message of the gospel and they will continue to be self-righteous. The Holy Spirit wants to destroy and crush us with the damning message of the law so that the life-giving message of the gospel will be received with joy unbounded. It is the starving one who appreciates a banquet and the condemned one who treasures the message of pardon.

Jesus demonstrated that point marvelously in Mark 2:16,17. The Pharisees criticized him for eating with sinners. Jesus answered their criticism in such a way that, had they listened to him, they would have seen that they were the real sinners, even more than those with whom Jesus was eating. Jesus said, "It is not the healthy who need a doctor, but the sick. I have not come to call the righteous, but sinners." The Pharisees should have said to themselves: "Who is more sick and a sinner than the one who withholds the healing and the healer from those obviously sick? We then have sinned even more than these with whom Jesus eats; for we did not want them to receive his help and healing!" Jesus makes the same point in the home of Simon the Pharisee (Luke 7:36-50). It is those whom the law has crushed who are most ready to hear the saving message of the gospel. The Holy Spirit prepares us for the gospel by his use of the law.[4]

We do well to notice that Jesus' use of the law and St. Paul's use of it in Romans 1–3 concentrate on the First Commandment. It is important for us to realize that our greatest crime is this that we do not love God with our whole heart and soul, or our mind and strength. But if we do not love God above all things, then we love something/someone else more—namely, and especially, ourselves. That is the essence of idolatry. All of our other sins against all of the other commandments prove the point that we have not kept even for a moment the first and greatest commandment. For if we loved God with all of our heart, soul, mind, and strength, then we would not have broken any of the other commandments.

Luther recognized that basic truth about the law and taught it in his Small Catechism. His explanation of each of the commandments after the First Commandment begins with the words *"We should fear and love God."* With those words he takes us back to the First Commandment as the heart and core of the entire law. This one disobeys the speed laws and shows disrespect towards those in authority (Fourth Commandment); that one hates someone and holds a grudge, helps people only when there is something in it for him (Fifth Commandment); this one lusts in his heart and would break his marriage vows if he thought he could get away with it (Sixth Commandment); that one cheats on his taxes and takes things home from work that don't belong to him (Seventh Commandment); this one gossips and lies about his neighbor (Eighth Commandment); that one's heart is singed

---

[4]For a more complete consideration of the law and its uses, cf. chapter 9 under the heading "The uses of the law."

with envy and jealousy (Ninth, Tenth Commandments). What do all of these—all of us!—have in common? We neither loved nor feared God enough to shun and win the victory over these sins! It is not too much to say that any teaching or preaching of the law without this First Commandment at its heart and core is little more than moralizing; it will not bring us to see how great our sin is.

Great indeed is this crime of idolatry—it is monstrous in fact. For we were created with this one purpose, that we should love and serve God. What would you do with a washing machine that refused to wash anything but only tore up the clothes and made them useless? Eventually you would throw it out. Our crime is so much worse; for we fail to serve the purpose for which we were created, intentionally and persistently. Only when we grasp that fundamental truth will we come to appreciate and rejoice all the more in the glad tidings of salvation by grace alone through faith alone.

Thus, it is the business of the law to bring us to the first part of repentance. The word *repentance* is used in the Bible to mean "sorrow for sin." Sometimes the term includes trust in the message of forgiveness from the gospel. But that element of sorrow for sin is always present in repentance; at least initially it is the law that works the sorrow for sin, yes, the despair of ever finding salvation in the least part in ourselves. The gospel must work trust in forgiveness, the saving faith that embraces the message of the gospel. Jesus gives the basic assignment to the church that both repentance and the forgiveness of sins should be proclaimed in all the world (Luke 24:47).

St. Peter demonstrated just what such a preaching of repentance and forgiveness was on the day of Pentecost. How devastating was his message of the law: "God has made this Jesus, *whom you crucified,* both Lord and Christ."[5] And that message of the law, the murder of God's own Son, hit its mark. St. Luke reports: "When the people heard this, they were cut to the heart and said to Peter and the other apostles, 'Brothers, what shall we do?' Peter replied, 'Repent and be baptized, every one of you, in the name of Jesus Christ for the forgiveness of your sins' " (Acts 2:36-38). The law worked repentance, that is, sorrow for sin and even despair of any earthly help. The gospel mes-

---

[5]Those who insist on soft-pedaling the law for fear of hurting peoples' feelings and driving people away should notice that they are not following the example of Peter's Pentecost sermon, nor for that matter the example of any of the apostles or prophets or of Jesus himself in the preaching of the law. The law is intended to crush; to put some sort of feel-good, public-relations spin on it does more harm than good and flies in the face of God's own intent.

sage announcing salvation and forgiveness by faith alone worked faith. St. Peter uses the same order—first repentance, then the promise of pardon—in Acts 3:19,20; 4:8-12; and 5:29-32.

Repentance remains a part of the Christian's life as long as we are on earth. Daily the law shows us our sin and moves us to sorrow and to despair of our own righteousness. Daily we call to mind the message of the gospel and the gospel promise of forgiveness in the Word and in Baptism. Yes, daily in repentance we repeat the prayer that Jesus himself has taught us: "Forgive us our sins." Thus it is that Luther in the first of his famous Ninety-five Theses declares: "When our Lord Jesus Christ says 'Repent!' he means that the entire life of the Christian should be one of repentance," that is, of both sorrow for sin and trust in the Savior's work for our redemption.[6]

Indeed, it is not too much to say that among the Christian's greatest sorrows is that he has not yet nor can he offer up to God a perfect work that needs no repentance. If only just once I could look into the face of God and say, "Here is something that *I* have done out of perfect love for you, my Savior, and that I offer up to you in perfect thanksgiving for all that you have done for me." And while it may be one of our greatest sorrows that we cannot do that, at the same time it is our greatest joy that Christ has done exactly that for us and that it is in his perfect work, not our own, that our salvation and our certainty rest. And precisely because Christ has done it all, we strive all the more earnestly after the goal of humble and obedient submission to his Word in the law and the gospel. There's the great paradox: the deeper our repentance, our sorrow over our sins, the greater our joy in the gospel; the greater our joy in the gospel of forgiveness full and free, the greater our zeal for works that reflect our gratitude for the gospel. That's what Paul experienced too when towards the end of his life he confessed it all so well in Philippians 3:12-14. Immediately after a beautiful confession of faith in the salvation won for him entirely by Christ's work and not his own, Paul tells us that he is still striving after the perfection in life that he already has by faith in Christ. Again, a beautiful paradox!

Given the deep and profound nature of repentance and faith, one might ask or wonder: *Does the gospel change our nature, our essence, when it creates faith?* No, it does not materially or essentially change our nature, the nature we have inherited from Adam and Eve. We still

---

[6]For a further consideration of the three uses of the law (as mirror, curb, and guide), cf. chapter 9.

have body and soul as we had them before; we have the organs of the soul, so to speak, the capacity to reason, a will, and emotions. And our capacity to reason, our will, and our emotions are still subject to temporal death, still poisoned by original sin, and still have a deeply rooted tendency to sin. However, with the creation of faith God gives us also another will, a new or renewed will that struggles against the old will. The old will, variously called the old man, the sinful nature, or the flesh, does not completely die until we die and go to heaven. But the new man, the new or Christian nature, the spirit given to us by faith, does battle against the flesh.

Saving faith and this new will have a whole host of results in every aspect of the Christian's life. Before faith he was a child of wrath; after faith he is an adopted child of God and joint heir with Christ. Before faith his whole existence was devoted to self-will, which is self-idolatry; after coming to faith, devotion to Christ and his Word does battle with that old self-idolatry and refuses to surrender to it. Before faith the organ of emotion was devoted to joy in the pleasures of this world and often in the coarse sins of the flesh; after faith the emotions look for joy in the gospel and find sorrow in all that contradicts God's Word in either faith or life. Before faith the organ of reason was devoted to rationalizing whatever my own will chose and my emotions desired, but as a result of faith reason now fights against all of that and seeks to submit to the Word of God, to find ways in his Word and in life of pleasing him and serving my neighbor. So man's nature is not *essentially* changed, but clearly faith makes an enormous difference in the way man's nature works. Thus, St. Paul urges Christians to live as Christians by entering into that struggle against the flesh and living in the victory that Christ gives through faith (cf. especially Romans 5, 7, 8, 12; Jesus' parables likewise often illustrate the Christian life, e.g., Mark 4:1-32).

Another question frequently asked is, *Can a person fall from faith? What about the phrase heard in some circles—"Once saved, always saved"?* We have the examples of Saul in the Old Testament and Judas in the New Testament. Some claim that since both died in unbelief, they never really believed in the first place. But the Bible never says that. It gives us no reason at all to assume that God chose an unbeliever as Israel's first king and that Jesus chose an unbeliever as one of his disciples. When we read of the life of Saul, we see a young man who sought out the prophet Samuel and on whom the Spirit of God rested (1 Samuel 9–12). It was after he became king that he turned his back on the Word of the Lord and on his messenger and ended his life with suicide. Judas was so trusted by the other disciples that they made him their treasurer. Nowhere do the gospel accounts tell us that the disciples' trust at that time was misplaced. It was later that he became a thief (John 12:6) and was so overwhelmed by greed that he sold his Savior and then in despair hanged himself (Matthew 27:1-5). We have as well the example of the man who was guilty of incest (1 Corinthians 5:1-5). St. Paul doesn't say that the man was never a believer, that from the start he was a hypocrite. He tells the members of the congregation that by living in this sin, that is, by his impenitence and consequent refusal to amend his life, the man had become an unbeliever who should be removed, excommunicated from the congregation. In 2 Corinthians we learn that the man repented, that basically he was converted again. St. Paul tells the members to receive him again (2:5-11).

The "once saved, always saved" idea stems from the false notion that God's grace is irresistible and that therefore a *real* believer can never fall away. But God's grace is not irresistible, as we have already noted. Just as it can be and is resisted by those who hear the gospel but never believe, so also those who once believed may turn back again to unbelief and perish. It is exactly for that reason that the Bible urges us constantly to be on guard, to stay close to the Word of God, to arm ourselves with it, to struggle against the enemies of faith outside and inside of ourselves (Romans 13:8-14; 1 Corinthians 15:58; 2 Corinthians 13:5; Ephesians 5,6; et al.). If it were true that one cannot fall from faith, then all of these pleas from the Bible would be pointless.

Indeed, the "once saved, always saved" error pushes people in the direction of what is called *carnal security,* that is, the evil notion that it makes no difference what they do—they are still saved. That is a self-righteousness of a particularly vile sort. Another person, plagued by temptations that require constant struggle, may be driven to despair; he concludes that if he were *really saved, really believed,* he wouldn't have all these difficulties, and so he gives up. The above-cited passage and so many related ones make it clear that Jesus does not want us to use his grace and forgiveness as a license to sin. Nor does he want us to despair because of the struggle that he promised we would have as part of the Christian life (Mark 8:34-38). Rather, he calls us to faith by the gospel, and through the gospel gives us the strength to remain in saving faith, faith which will be lost if we depart from the gospel. It is like the man who wants to stay healthy and live; if the man refuses to use the means at hand for staying healthy, he will get sick and die. So too the Christian; the gospel brought him to faith and only the gospel can keep him in faith. If he spurns the gospel, the faith that he once had will die. Jesus says as much in the great parable of the sower and the seed. Many receive the Word with joy but then allow the plant of faith to shrivel, wither, be choked, and die (Mark 4:3-20). Only the renewed message of the gospel can bring such a person back to faith again, that is, convert him again with a renewed sowing of the seed of the Word.

Thus, all three happen: Some never believe the gospel because of their own rejection of it; some believe it for a time and then fall from faith; some fall from faith and then are converted again. Indeed, many will attest that this last, this reconversion, has happened to them many times as they struggled and fell, rose again to the struggle, fell again and were again revived by the gospel. We want neither the false security that leads to lazy Christianity nor the despair that gives up in the struggle.

So while faith is altogether the gift of God in the gospel and remains always and alone his gift, the Christian with that gift applies himself to the spiritual food God gives in Word and sacrament. By that food the Christian received spiritual life in the first place. And by the continual use of that same food God preserves the spiritual life, the faith that he created. We see then how the organs of the soul in the Christian function: The emotions are as the psalmist says, glad to go into the house of the Lord to hear his Word. Reason grasps from that Word that it is by the nourishment of the gospel that faith is preserved. The will responds with the choice of hearing God's Word faithfully. Consequently, there is this constant interplay between the old will, reason, and emotions and the new, as the old frustrates and hinders the new and as the new does battle against the old. In heaven that battle will end with the permanent death and defeat of the old and the gift of eternal victory from Christ for the new.

Outwardly then, with the continued hearing of the Word, the Christian cooperates with God; inwardly God does all the work of preserving with his Word and sacraments what he created in the first place with that same Word. So the Christian delights in this, that he can eat and drink the goodness and grace of God; however, all glory he gives to God for what God continuously and miraculously accomplishes through such eating and drinking, namely, the preservation of his faith.

Another use of the word *faith* in the Bible

To this point we have been considering *saving faith.* It is called *saving* not because it is a work we do to save ourselves or cooperate in our salvation but because of its content, namely, Christ and the gospel. It saves and is necessary for salvation in this sense that by the power of the gospel, faith lays hold of the promise of forgiveness, life, and salvation solely on the basis of God's grace and Christ's merit, to the exclusion of any and all merit in us. Thus saving faith *receives* the salvation won for us by Christ; it is not the prompting or meritorious cause of salvation. Indeed, it is the message of salvation that causes faith. Faith is, as noted earlier, *the receiving organ* of our salvation.

The Bible sometimes uses the term *faith* to describe something other than saving faith, strictly speaking. Consider, for example, Mark 4:35-41. Jesus has had a very long day, and in his state of humiliation has become tired. He falls asleep in the boat. So soundly does he sleep that even a storm does not awaken him. The disciples struggle with all their might against the storm, and when their efforts all seem in vain, they wake Jesus from his sleep with the anguished plea: "Teacher, don't you care if we drown?" Their cry shows that they knew Jesus could save them; their anguish and fear in the situation of that moment brought them to fear that he might not want to rescue them in this particular situation. After Jesus stills the storm, he turns to the disciples and asks them: "Why are you so afraid? Do you still have no faith?"

How does Jesus use the word *faith* in this context? Is he talking about that faith which knows that he is the Son of God and the Savior of the world and therefore their Savior? No, he is not. For the very prayer of the disciples indicates that they knew he was the Son of God with power to save them even in this particular situation. Their whole relationship with him was a confession of faith in him as the promised Messiah. That is why they were with him in the first place (John 1:40,41). What then does the word *faith* mean in this context? Faith in this context is still knowledge, assent, and confidence. However, it is knowledge of specific promises that Jesus had made to them, assent to those specific promises, and confidence that what Jesus had promised would come to pass. Jesus had promised that he would make them fishers of men (Mark 1:17). That promise could not be fulfilled if they were to perish in this storm. But at that particular moment in time they did not remember the promise, nor did they apply it to this circumstance. Therefore they had no faith in this sense that they did not apply a specific promise to a particular circumstance in their lives. That does not mean that they did not have saving faith. It does not mean that they had rejected Jesus as the Son of God and the promised Messiah.

Another example of the many times when the term *faith* means something other than saving faith is Jesus' use of the word in Mark 11:22-24. Jesus tells his disciples:

> "Have faith in God," Jesus answered. "I tell you the truth, if anyone says to this mountain, 'Go, throw yourself into the sea,' and does not doubt in his heart but believes that what he says will happen, it will be done for him. Therefore I tell you, whatever you ask for in prayer, believe that you have received it, and it will be yours."

It is vital in reading this passage to remember the basic meaning of the word *faith.* It always means knowledge of a promise, assent that the promise is true, and confidence that the promise applies to me. When Jesus speaks of faith in this passage, is he talking about saving faith, faith in his person and work as the Savior of the world and therefore as my Savior? Is he saying that as long as we believe that he is our Savior we will be able to throw mountains into the sea? He is not. He is talking about commands and promises that have to do with our Christian life from day to day. Thus, if he were to tell us that we should throw a mountain into the sea, we should believe that he would keep his implied promise and the mountain would go into the sea at our command. A proper use of the passage is to consider the commands and promises that Jesus has made to us and remember that, impossible as those promises may seem, Jesus will always keep his Word. He promises to be with us all our days. He promises at the end of our days to take us to himself in heaven. All of that and so much more may seem impossible to us, but we trust him and his Word, as impossible as its fulfillment may seem to us at some moment in time.

A beautiful passage that makes something of the same point but that is often misused by people is Philippians 4:13. There Paul declares, "I can do everything through him who gives me strength." People misuse the passage when they undertake something clearly beyond them that has neither a command nor a promise in God's Word. Paul is not encouraging us in this passage to act as though we were invincible and almighty. He is not telling us, "Do whatever you want and God will back you up as long as you believe he will back you up!" Quite to the contrary! He is urging us to be bold in living a life in accord with God's commands and promises in his Word. Then, no matter how impossible it may seem that we will survive, God will be with us and bring us to the goal of heaven, which Jesus has won for us.

The promise of God for Paul in his imprisonment was that even in such a situation, God was in control and would give him strength of faith to endure and even be useful. We share in Paul's confidence when we are thrust into painful situations or must struggle with seemingly overwhelming obstacles to our faith and Christian life. We remain confident that God will give us grace and strength sufficient for the day; and yes, we strive to stay in such circumstances all the more closer to him in his Word so that strengthened by it we endure and grow ever stronger. The critical thing is to trust his promise in the face of the seeming impossibility. In Paul's circumstance and in Jesus' mention of faith, the matter of weak and strong faith comes into consideration: Weak faith is that faith which does not see how the promises of God apply to my specific situation, so that I am cast on the shoals of fear and doubt. Strong faith, on the other hand, perhaps contrary to human reason or evidence that I can see, simply clings to the promises of God and applies them appropriately. To the extent that faith is thus strong, joy and confidence remain even under severe straining and testing.

Again, we need to remember that faith is not just something we wish for or want; it is always defined by the promises of God in his Word—not by our own emotions or imagination. Jesus' own example of refusing to follow Satan's temptation that he jump from the highest point of the temple illustrates the point well (Matthew 4:5-7): Faith is not brash and does not run after the desires, arbitrary or otherwise, of the flesh; rather, it clings to the Word and cannot exist without it.

Accordingly, what St. Paul says in Philippians 4:13 and what Jesus is talking about in Mark 11:20-24 is misused when someone makes a vow and enters on a course of action that has no command from God's Word and thus no promise that God will bless it. The one who contrary to his own nature takes a vow of celibacy and trusts that he will be able to keep it because he thinks he can do anything with Christ is misusing these passages. For Christ never commanded anyone to take such a vow and never promised that he would bless such a vow. In fact, his Word everywhere praises and promises blessing to those who follow the natural ordinance of marriage. Or, if someone would have the pious intent of giving everything that he had to the poor, trusting that God would somehow provide for him, that person is casting aside God's promise that he would bless our labors as we earn our daily bread and that we should then give according to how God has prospered our labors. He never told us that we should place ourselves in poverty or danger and that he would then be obliged to bless our self-chosen course of action.

People with the best of intentions get themselves into all kinds of needless difficulty when they embark on courses of action devoid of reason or sense apart from any requirement in the Word of God and then justify their folly with the misuse of these passages. "Let's build a house/a church/a school completely beyond our ability to pay for it; we just *really believe* that God will provide and that we can do anything we want if we just have enough faith." Sometimes there can be a fine line between a proper and humble trust in God's promises to provide for our needs and a folly that expects him to satisfy all of our *wants* if we "just pray and believe hard enough." Jesus didn't jump off the temple peak to prove that he was the Son of God; and he doesn't ask us to jump off of literal or metaphorical cliffs either to prove that we trust him.

Again, the point remains that faith, even when we are not considering *saving faith,* relies on the promises of God in his Word. The point is made with crystal clarity in Matthew 14:25-31. In the midst of a storm on the Sea of Galilee Jesus comes to the disciples, walking on the water. At first they are filled with terror that they are seeing a ghost. But Jesus stills their fears, both the fear of the still raging storm and the fear that a ghost has come to them, by telling them, "Take courage! It is I. Don't be afraid." The ever-impetuous Peter calls out, "Lord, if it's you, tell me to come to you on the water." Jesus responds, "Come." Now we have a clear command of Christ and the implied promise that Peter will not drown when he trusts the command of Jesus and steps out onto the raging water. And everything goes exactly according to plan. Peter walks on the water, trusting in the clear command and the implied promise of Jesus. He has knowledge, here in the form of a specific call from Jesus; he has given assent; he has confidence that all will be well. But then what happens? Peter looks around and sees the raging sea; he sets aside the clear words of Jesus and trusts instead in his senses, in what he sees and in what he feels. The result: he begins to sink into the waves. He would have perished had Jesus not rescued him. Listen to Jesus' words of rebuke to Peter: "You of little faith, why did you doubt?" When Peter gave up confidence based on the specific command and promise of Jesus, he had "little faith" and began to sink.

Again, the faith we are speaking of here is not saving faith; again, it is faith that knows, assents to, and trusts a specific promise relating to some aspect of the Christian's life. When speaking of the kind of faith we have been considering here, one may well say that such a faith is little or weak or strong. It all depends on how well the individual knows the promise and how well he applies it to his situation in life. Consider, for example, the promise implied in Romans 8:28,31-33. What if I am very sick or in great financial difficulty? I may know and trust that Jesus is my Savior and that at last he will deliver me from these problems and take me to heaven. But what if I do not remember the promise of Romans 8 and elsewhere that God governs all things for my good and that even suffering is intended for my benefit? If I do not remember the promise or apply it in my current difficulty, I may cry out just like the disciples in Mark 4: "Don't you care that I am perishing?" My faith in that circumstance may be very weak as I struggle to apply his promises to a specific problem. It may even be no faith at all *as far as that specific promise is concerned* if I have forgotten the promise or am ignorant of it. I may be like Peter walking on the water, confident at first in the promise of God, but then looking around and considering only what I can see and feel, I waver and begin to flounder in fear of some specific set of problems. But that does not necessarily mean that I no longer have saving faith. I have, with reference to the promises of God to help and bless me in every need, a weak faith—perhaps for a time little or no faith. That would be a horrible condition indeed, even if I still trust that Jesus is my Savior from sin and that he has forgiven me.

St. Paul (Romans 14,15; 1 Corinthians 8) also makes the distinction between the weak and the strong in faith when he speaks about *adiaphora,* that is, things neither commanded nor forbidden by the Word of God. Some people were weak in faith about adiaphora; they thought, for example, that they should not eat meat because in the Greek world most meat in the city came from a pagan sacrifice in a heathen temple. It bothered them to eat meat from such a source. Others, converts from Judaism, were bothered about eating meat that did not fulfill Jewish butchering requirements or that fell outside of the permitted meats from the Old Testament dietary laws.

Each of these was weak in faith. It was not that they did not have saving faith. Rather, it was that they did not understand the nature of God's Word about Christian freedom or did not see how it applied to this particular situation. St. Paul urges those strong in faith, that is, those who do understand the principle of Christian freedom and how it applies, to receive the weak in faith. The weak should not be rejected as unbelievers but led into a better understanding of God's Word so that they would not continue to bother their own consciences needlessly in matters of *adiaphora.* Such instruction may take some considerable time.

On the other hand, if those with a weak faith would become arrogant and insist that everyone else shares in their weakness, then the strong in faith would have to resist. Such was the situation that Paul addressed especially in the epistle to the Galatians. There some of the

Jews who had become Christian began to demand that Gentile converts be circumcised in accord with the Old Testament law. In effect they were making that law a condition of salvation, thus denying the very essence even of saving faith. Read Galatians 1 and you will see that Paul would not tolerate even for a moment such a denial of the gospel with the excuse that those denying it were merely weak.

To be sure, weak faith and no faith with respect to any promise that God gives is dangerous. For it may go so far as to threaten saving faith as it did in the situation that is such a prominent feature of Galatians. Weak faith can and should be strengthened through constant use of the Word of God and the Sacrament, lest we suffer needlessly from weak faith by not exposing it to the medicine of the gospel and lest we let weak faith infect and destroy saving faith. But as important as it is to deal with weak faith through the application of the Word of God to enlighten or strengthen it, we should not equate this kind of faith with saving faith. If we do, we will drive the weak to despair as they begin to doubt whether their faith is "strong enough" to be saving faith.

So then, *saving faith* is that knowledge, assent, and confidence which embraces Jesus, the Son of God and Mary's son, as my only Savior. Such a faith may be battered and storm tossed, but at bottom I either trust Jesus or I do not. Such faith is not a quantity to be measured, as though I had to have a certain amount of it before it could be called *saving faith.*

Weak/strong faith in the Scripture usually refers to a knowledge, assent, and confidence in some promise of God that pertains to my Christian life. It may be a weak faith if I have forgotten the promise or do not know how it applies to my specific situation in life, or it may be described as strong when I do know and understand the promise and am able to apply it correctly.

Chapter 14
The Means of Grace

We come now to a doctrine that is of particular beauty to Lutherans. We noted already in the Preface to this work that some doctrines are woven like golden threads throughout the whole of the Bible and find their way into just about every other doctrine. Such is the doctrine of the means of grace. We have assumed it in every chapter. Just as we would be lost without the doctrine of our redemption through the work of Jesus our Savior, so we would as well be lost without the means of grace. Though assumed in every other doctrine, and though often taken for granted and left undefined, the doctrine of the means of grace has a profound influence on the way we worship and with whom we worship; it informs the way we share the gospel in our families and throughout the world; it even shapes our attitude toward civil society and the state, as we shall note in due course.

What then is the means of grace and why is it called that? Most simply stated: ***The means of grace is the gospel message*** *that Jesus Christ, the Son of God and Mary's son, has redeemed the world and therefore me also by his perfect obedience and by his sacrifice on the cross in payment for our sins and the sins of all humankind.* In a word, the means of grace is the gospel. *It is that means by which God shows us that he is gracious and by which he gives himself to us by grace through faith for our salvation. The means of grace is God's own pipeline from his heart to our souls. He promises to come to us and to bring us to himself in no other way than through the means of grace, this gospel message.* As God saves and preserves our physical life through the means of water and air, food and sometimes medicine, so he saves us spiritually by the means of grace. As we cannot have a physical life without the physical means he has given for its preservation, so we cannot have spiritual life apart from the means of grace.

As brief and as simple as the summary definition is, it is at the same time of the greatest weight and importance. It is self-evident that without the gospel message we would know nothing of Christ and his work for our salvation. Thus without the gospel message faith in his work for us would clearly be impossible. However, just as important is the fact that left to ourselves we could hear the message, but we would not believe it. For who could imagine this to be true, that God, who needs nothing and no one, who lives in unapproachable light, and who is perfection and holiness in his essence and is justly angered by anything lacking that holiness and perfect righteousness, would become man? He was born of a lowly virgin in a stable so that he could suffer the torments of the damned on the cross and thereby redeem those who don't want him and want instead to be gods themselves. Who could believe that the holy and almighty God yearns for us to spend eternity with him in heaven and that he was willing to suffer hell just so that we would become his dear children and that by faith alone? Into whose mind would it ever enter that God has ruled over all of history to give and preserve for me, even for me, this holy, this mighty, this saving message and its benefit? Who could imagine or believe such things? No one!

Thus, the means of grace has to be more than just a message. Original sin makes it impossible for us to believe on our own or even to cooperate in coming to faith. Actual sin deepens in us the habit of resistance to God's goodness and grace. And so God in his inestimable mercy and grace has attached his own power to the gospel message, so that lost and condemned creatures born as blind, dead, enemies of God embrace the message with joy. Through the power attached to the message, God not only shows himself to be gracious but also becomes gracious for and to each of us as individuals. By his presence in and with the message God creates saving faith in us and preserves us in faith. So full and rich is God in his grace and so powerful is his gracious presence with the gospel that by means of the gospel the Holy Spirit brings us from spiritual death to life, from blindness to sight. Yes, so powerful is that gospel that it brings me from hatred and hostility towards God to the status of a beloved child of God, whose goal it is now to struggle against the remaining vile and vicious sinful nature in me and instead to love and serve him who loved us first and gave himself for us. Thus, faith, which believes the gospel, is always a miracle from its first inception to our last breath when God takes us through temporal death to eternal life. And that miracle is created and preserved by the means of grace.

But wait a minute! Are we saying that God's power is limited when we say that our faith depends on the means of grace? Not at all! Rather, God, who cannot be bound and who knows no limits in his grace and mercy, has chosen to bind us to the saving gospel. And we delight to be thus bound because of what God gives and does for us in this saving message of the gospel. Indeed no sinful mortal should wish to experience God in his unveiled essence apart from the gospel. He is a consuming fire in his holiness. In the Bible those who wished to experience him unveiled were spared when instead he came to them concealed in a cloud.

Consider Moses, for example. He was so close to God that God himself said that he was pleased with Moses. But when Moses wanted to see God in all of his glory, God showed himself not in his essence but in his Word of the gospel, so that Moses would not die (Exodus 33:15-23). Likewise, the great prophet Elijah needed the assurance of God's presence with him in the face of persecution and total frustration. But how did God show himself and reassure the prophet? Not by revealing his unveiled essence but by a still, small voice (1 Kings 19:9-18). Even the apostle who was always called the beloved apostle in the New Testament could not endure the presence of the ascended Christ unveiled. When Jesus appeared to him on the island of Patmos, St. John fell down as a dead man. Only when Jesus spoke, spoke a summary word of the gospel, did John revive and rejoice to meet again his Savior (Revelation 1:9-18).

And so God comes to us in the means of his own choosing, at the manger, at the cross, at the empty tomb, and all of it—all of himself and his grace and mercy, with forgiveness, life, and salvation—wrapped in the beautiful and powerful gospel.

Our confessions make this same point repeatedly. The Apology, for example, puts the matter so simply and succinctly: "The proclamation of the gospel produces faith in those who receive the gospel" (Ap XXIV, 32 p. 264). Luther emphasized this doctrine in almost all of his writings. He was especially concerned with its pure presentation because of the host of false doctrines and practices that brought chaos and even bloodshed to Europe when this doctrine was denied. In the Smalcald Articles he declared:

> In these matters, which concern the spoken, external Word, it must be firmly maintained that God gives no one his Spirit or grace apart from the external Word which goes before. We say this to protect ourselves from the enthusiasts, that is, the "spirits," who boast that they have the Spirit apart from and before contact with the Word. (SA, III, VIII, 3 p. 322)

He goes on to describe the great damage done to souls and to the church by a refusal of this so clearly taught doctrine of the Scriptures and then continues by saying:

> Therefore we should and must insist that God does not want to deal with us human beings, except by means of his external Word and sacrament. Everything that boasts of being from the Spirit apart from such a Word and sacrament is of the devil. (10 p. 323)

The sad fact is that a rejection of this teaching that God has promised to deal with us only in his means of grace still has a home in most church bodies. To be sure, most churches have a sort of doctrine of a means of grace; that is, they teach that there is a way by which God comes to us, but they deny that he comes to us as he promised, that is, exclusively by means of the gospel.

For Roman Catholics, for example, it is not the gospel that is the means by which God assures us of our salvation—it is the church itself, namely, that church which has the pope as its head. It is the church that guarantees salvation, not the gospel. It is fellowship with priests whose ordination is authorized by the pope through his bishops that give the sacraments their ultimate validity. Thus, ultimately, it is the church that is the means of grace, in keeping with the famous formula *Extra Ecclesiam nulla salus* (Outside of the Church no salvation). And the church by definition is the Roman Catholic Church. Though many Catholics hedge and dispute the meaning of the formula, it remains for the official church a primary teaching and emphasis. Those who place their hope of salvation in the institution of the church instead of in the promises of the gospel may delude themselves with a faith that is really no faith at all; that happens among those who care little or nothing for the teachings of the Bible but are content merely to call themselves "Catholics" and trust that for that reason alone their place in heaven is secure.

Among Protestants the doctrine of the means of grace as presented in the Bible is universally rejected. They argue that the doctrine of the means of grace limits God, who because he is all-powerful cannot be limited in any way. But as already noted, the doctrine of the means of grace does not bind God; he could if he wished create or preserve faith apart from the gospel. It's just that he never promises to do that apart from his promises in the gospel.

For most Protestants, faith itself, faith defined either as merely feeling saved or making a decision for Christ, is their means of grace. The certainty of salvation rests then not in the Word but in one's own feeling about the Word and work of Christ or even what they imagine God to be saying to them apart from the Word and work of Christ. Faith in faith is a weak reed indeed for certainty—it is altogether subjective. If in the anguish of temptation or under the afflictions of life I do not feel saved, then I'm not saved. That's a recipe for despair, the very opposite of faith. But certainty, faith, that rests in the promises of God in his Word and on the work of Christ for us all, brings peace even in the hour of death. The true means of grace, the gospel, is always certain and sure and a solid foundation precisely because God himself gave the gospel and is ever present with it.

It is interesting to note that those who imagine apart from the written Word of God that God has spoken to them invariably end up denying much of what God has said in his Word, the Bible. They end up making their own words and imagination a means of grace. Or, they turn their prayers into the means that God uses for speaking to us. But prayer is our speaking to God; he speaks to us where he has promised to speak to us—in his Word and sacraments. What we imagine to be a speaking that conflicts with what he clearly has said to us in the Word and the sacraments does not come from God but from the devil.

Certainly not all Roman Catholics or Protestants fall into blatant unbelief because of their rejection of the biblical doctrine of the means of grace. Nevertheless, that rejection has caused no end of mischief in church history and has done damage, sometimes fatal damage, to faith in many. For that reason alone we want to listen attentively to what God says about his gospel message, both as to its content and its saving effect in us. Nor in our faith and life do we ever want to depart even so much as a hair's breadth from that beautiful, comforting, life-giving, and saving gospel.

There is but one means of grace and that is the gospel. But this one means of grace wears, so to speak, three dresses. The gospel is received by us in the Word and in the Sacrament of Baptism and the Sacrament of the Altar. In what follows we will consider each of these three dresses separately. But in so doing we note that we are always dealing with one and the same means of grace: the gospel. For the gospel in the sacraments is in its essence no different than the gospel in the Word. The comfort and encouragement given by each may be more specific or less, but the essence of that comfort and encouragement is one and the same, the gospel. Only the outward form is different; the message, the essence, is the same.

The Word

When we speak of the gospel in the Word, we are speaking of the gospel as we find it in the Bible. Whether we are reading the message or hearing it read, whether we are meditating on it privately or sharing it publicly, whether it is the proclamation of forgiveness in the liturgy and the sermon or the content of a devotion or a book that we are reading, when the content is this, that Christ is our Savior, then we are receiving the Word as the gospel means of grace. Written or heard, spoken or sung, remembered in an instant or pondered in an hour, so long as the message is rooted, grounded, and in accord with the Scriptures, it is the same gospel. And by that gospel the Holy Spirit works in the heart and on the mind to create and preserve faith, as we noted at length in the last chapter.

So then, when we are speaking of the gospel in the Word, we are including also the application of that gospel to our specific circumstances and situations in life. A pastor or a Christian friend hears my anguished confession. The pastor or friend does not respond only with a list of passages. He will apply the passages. So in answer to a despairing confession, he may say, "Look, Jesus said that he loves the whole world and therefore he loves you too; besides that, look at all the people he received and blessed, like Peter, who denied him, and Paul, who persecuted the church; maybe you're not any better than they, but you couldn't be any worse or less deserving than they were! On the cross he thought of you no less than he thought of them. And willingly he died, eager to redeem you no less than to redeem them." Or, someone in sickness or in any of a thousand other reverses in life may hear his friend say to him, "God never abandons us; he promises to use even disaster, sickness, and death to bring us to himself in heaven. And God never lies. This too he will use to show you his gracious love and rule over all things for your good. After all, Jesus suffered and died for you. He will not forsake you now, after having loved you that much!" All such encouragement and that offered otherwise in Christian mutual comforting and strengthening may not have a specific passage of the gospel for quotation; nevertheless, it accords with the gospel in the Word, is based on that gospel. It is an application of the means of grace to a specific circumstance.

The point is that Christians should not be shy or reluctant to encourage one another just because they cannot remember a definite chapter and verse from the Bible to quote; they are sharing and applying the means of grace through which God himself is active and powerful, so long as the comfort and encouragement is based on the truths of the gospel. Obviously the better one knows that message in the Bible, the easier it may become to share and apply it. But the young in knowledge shouldn't hide what light they have under a bushel just because their light is a candle and not the sun at noonday. A candle for the darkness of a troubled brother or sister in faith may serve very well indeed!

It would be difficult indeed to list all of the passages of the Bible that urge this truth on us, that the gospel message in the Bible is God's own power-filled means for coming to us and bringing us to him. St. Paul says it in every one of his letters, says it in one way or another in almost every chapter of every letter. Consider his introduction to his great doctrinal epistle, the letter to the Romans. He declares, "I am not ashamed of the gospel, because it is the power of God for the salvation of everyone who believes" (1:16). The passage is so complete all by itself that nothing further should have to be said. Paul doesn't say that the gospel is a message that presents the possibility of salvation. He doesn't say that the gospel is the message that offers us a rational choice to make with our own native intelligence or natural reasoning capacity. No, none of that! The gospel brings with it its own power from God for salvation. The message is far too important to be left merely to the feeble minds of fallen, indeed hostile, creatures. So the gospel carries with it the power of salvation, a salvation that comes from the faith-creating message itself.

Paul emphasizes the same truth when he says that "faith comes from hearing the message, and the message is heard through the word of Christ" (Romans 10:17). And that message is never separated from the power of God's own presence in it. Paul reminded the Thessalonian Christians that when he brought the gospel to them, it had the effect of convincing them that God had chosen them for himself; that conviction was worked by the power that accompanied the message. He said, "For we know, brothers loved by God, that he has chosen you, because our gospel came to you not simply with words, but also with power, with the Holy Spirit and with deep conviction" (1 Thessalonians 1:4,5).

In 1 Corinthians, especially in the first three chapters, Paul gives us a beautiful and powerful essay, as it were, on the gospel message as the necessary and saving means of grace. He reminded the Corinthians that everything they had and were as Christians was a gift of God through the Word of the gospel. He reminded them that neither the wise of the world, nor they themselves, nor even Paul himself could come up with the message or convince anyone of its truthfulness; that would take the power of God's own Spirit in the message, a message so powerful that it causes those who believe to become God's own temple and dwelling place! To those merely wise with natural wisdom, all that seems to be foolishness. But with the power of God in the message, the message becomes life and salvation for those brought by the message to trust the message.

To be sure, the message is not irresistible. We noted that in the last chapter when talking about faith and have noted it frequently in other chapters as well. Because it is such an important point, we need to briefly repeat the point: Whenever we believe the gospel, we have only the grace of God and the power of the gospel message to thank for it. Those, on the other hand, who reject the message do so of themselves and have only themselves to blame for their ruin. So often the Bible makes that distinction. Faith in the Word comes from God in and with the Word; unbelief, rejection of the Word comes from the perversity of those who reject it. Paul on the missionary journeys recorded for us in the book of Acts always went first to the Jewish synagogue with the message of the Savior, but most there rejected the message. And Paul laid the blame for that rejection squarely on those who despised the Word, whether Jews or Gentiles (e.g., Acts 13:46; 2 Thessalonians 2:10). Just as emphatically he proclaims the truth that it is the power of God in the gospel message that accomplishes the salvation of those who believe it (1 Thessalonians 2:13; 1 Corinthians 12:3).

So the gospel message is, again, not just words but a message that is alive and life-giving because of the Holy Spirit's powerful presence in and with the Word. It was the Holy Spirit who inspired the message in the first place and who does not wish to be separated from his Word. Jesus demonstrated that same truth so often in the parables that dealt with his Word. The Word, Jesus says, is seed (Mark 4:3-8,14-20,30-32), and it is like yeast (Luke 13:20,21). The seed is what brings life to the soil. The soil is necessary as the receptacle for the seed but has no life of itself apart from the life-giving seed. The yeast is alive and the dough comes to life, as it were, when the yeast is brought to it. In his great High Priestly Prayer on the night before his death, Jesus praises the Word that he is leaving behind and in the mouths of his apostles; for by it and by their preaching of that Word, faith will be created for years and generations to come (John 17:20). Again, that faith is never separated from God, its source, or from the Word of God, the means of grace.

Thus, the creation of faith by means of the gospel in the Word is not something either automatic or mechanical or the result of our own natural powers. Rather, the creation of faith by God through the means of grace is always something that God intends and wills for that individual. God is pictured as a loving father who brings us to birth spiritually through living seed, the seed of his Word (1 Peter 1:23; James 1:18). The gospel means of grace as seed from God gives what God intends and wills as by it he gives us the status of his blood-bought children. Let the one who feels alone and unloved in the world ponder that blessed truth! Let the one who imagines that he is too insignificant or even too sinful for God to notice him dwell on that peace and joy-producing fact! The seed, the faith-creating Word, restores what was lost in the fall of Adam and Eve in the Garden of Eden. It gives us forgiveness. It gives us back innocence and righteousness in God's eyes, because that's what we have when sin is forgiven. It gives us eternal life now and in the hour of our death. And it does all that one by one, in each individual who hears the message and by its saving power believes it.

So attached is God to his Word, especially that Word of the gospel, that he by his rule over history has seen to it that the Word has endured indifference, corruption, persecution, and perversion of every sort down through the ages. Jesus promised exactly that. He expected his Word to be attacked. But he would not let his Word perish; even when heaven and earth perish, the Word will endure (Matthew 24:35). And he did even that just for me! Just for you! God's love for his Word is God's love for us. Little wonder that we cherish that Word, that saints down through the ages have been willing to suffer persecution and death rather than be separated from it!

Some have mocked confessional Lutherans for this emphasis on the Bible and have accused us of worshiping a book instead of worshiping God. The accusation is absurd on the face of it. We do not worship the Book. We treasure it so highly precisely because by it God comes to us and through it we come to know and to trust in Jesus and all that he has done for us and for our salvation. We cling to it because in it God gives us forgiveness of sins, life, and salvation by his grace and by Jesus' merit. Indeed, how could one treasure too highly that book which is God's very own Word? To treasure the Word is to treasure the One who gave it. To depart even a hair's breadth from it is to depart just so much and more from the One who said, "This is the one I esteem: he who is humble and contrite in spirit, and trembles at my word" (Isaiah 66:2).

Think of it this way: The gospel is the pipeline in its outward forms of Word and sacraments, as noted earlier, a pipeline from the heart of God to our souls. Flowing through that pipeline is the water of God's grace and mercy, his forgiveness, and its results for us of life and salvation. Who would be so foolish as to say that it doesn't really matter if the pipeline itself is bent and twisted or how pure the water in that pipeline is, so long as at least some water can get through and reach us? Would we not want the pipeline to be straight and unobstructed and the water in it to flow as a gusher purely and freely down to us, in us, through us? Indeed, that is just what Jesus promised (John 4:14). Could we be indifferent if someone twisted and bent the pipeline or inserted in it pollutants of one sort or another? Surely we would be angry at the effort and do everything we could to prevent that from happening. Or, what if we went to the store and looked for a can of peas on the shelf? Then we found a can that said on the label: "This is mostly good but contains some poison. It probably won't hurt you, but it might. Don't worry about it." Who would be so foolish as to buy such a product?

Just so foolish, indeed perverse, is the one who underestimates the importance of the Word of God and that Word taught in all of its truth and purity. Just so perverse is the one who says that it doesn't matter all that much what we believe, teach, or confess, so long as there is some of God's Word in it. No, never! The Bible is the Word of God and it contains the saving means of grace; we cannot tolerate in our teaching and preaching anything that strays in the least from that Word in the Bible. For to the extent that we depart from the Bible, to that extent we corrupt and pollute the means of grace and place obstacles in the path of God's saving intent in his Word. For to reject any part of that Word is to cast doubt on its core, the saving gospel message. So both out of love to God and gratitude to him for his Word and as well out of dread of insulting him and damaging our own souls through a corruption of his Word, we will cling to that Reformation watchword: *Sola Scriptura—Scripture alone!*

The sacraments

Before we begin our consideration of each of the sacraments, we should consider briefly the term itself. The word *sacraments* simply means "a sacred act." The word does not occur in the Bible. It is a word that the church has chosen to identify some very specific and special sacred acts. There are many acts that we may count as sacred. Helping one another, prayer, suffering for the sake of the gospel, all these and many others are sacred acts, but they are not sacraments. We restrict the term *sacrament* to designate those sacred acts that are pure gospel, as distinguished from all others, that are essentially consequences of the gospel—good works performed as a result of faith and the forgiveness of sins.

Sacraments as distinguished from good works that result from faith are those sacred acts that cause or confirm faith, sacred acts that convey God's grace and the forgiveness of sins just like the gospel proclamation in the Word. They are sacred acts in which God is active and we are passive recipients of his actions. For our purposes we define a sacrament as a sacred act (1) when instituted by Christ himself; (2) in which Christ has promised the forgiveness of sins, life, and salvation, and which therefore either creates or confirms faith; and (3) which has an outward visible element attached to it. Using this definition, there are but two sacraments, namely, the Sacrament of Baptism and the Sacrament of the Altar.

Roman Catholics operate with a somewhat different definition of the term, and they end up with seven sacraments (Baptism, Confirmation, Penance, the Mass, Marriage, Holy Orders, and Anointing of the Sick). According to the Roman Catholic Church, each of these offers some grace (never all of God's grace!) that the one receiving the sacrament can use to cooperate in gaining more grace and his ultimate salvation. Thus, the whole of the gospel is twisted into a confusion of law and gospel. But the gospel by definition gives everything, and our salvation is entirely God's gift in and through it. When it comes to our salvation, grace is never half done or done a little bit. Grace is God's attitude and attribute of undeserved love, full and free, by which the Holy Spirit in the gospel offers and gives us everything that Christ has earned for our salvation.

Protestants, on the other hand, deny entirely the doctrine of the means of grace, especially the sacramental means of grace. Though they regard Baptism and the Sacrament of the Altar as sacraments, they turn the sacraments into works that man does instead of saving gifts that God gives. They deny that there is any gospel in them. After all, they would insist, Baptism is something that we do in obedience to Christ's command, as is the receiving of Holy Communion; Jesus said, "Do it!" and so in obedience to this new law, we obey.

To be sure, outwardly the sacraments are acts performed by us—though in Baptism of course it is a work performed for us by another and even in the Sacrament of the Altar the chief aspect is receiving it and its benefit from another. To the extent that it is a human work, it is so only outwardly. In its essence it is the work of God by which he gives the gifts attached to that work. We can think of it this way: The outward work of baptizing and receiving the Sacrament of the Altar is like the shell of a nut. The shell is necessary but of itself does nothing; it is the content of the nut that feeds, nourishes, and delights us. So it is also with the sacraments. Their content is pure gospel; only the outward shell has the appearance of a work.

It is one of the saddest things in the whole of Christian history that the beautiful, comforting, and clear teaching of the Scriptures about the sacraments has been so corrupted by so many! It is always true, as we have often observed, that false doctrine contradicts the Scriptures, robs Christ of his glory, and deprives the penitent sinner of rich comfort. That is most especially true with respect to the false doctrines that have attacked the sacraments. We shall have more to note on this matter as we consider the sacraments individually.

The Sacrament of Baptism

Some have argued that if God gives us everything in the Word, what further need is there of sacraments that can only offer what we already have in the Word. The argument betrays an ignorance of the way God is and an ungrateful arrogance in the face of his generosity. God is rich in grace and mercy. If he chooses—and he does—to offer us the same rich blessings of forgiveness, life, and salvation in more than one form, who are we to object? Who would want to? Indeed, even in close human relationships do we not seek a number of ways of expressing love? The husband tells his wife that he loves her. He did that on his wedding day. But what a sad marriage that would be in which the husband never repeats the words and never finds ways of showing his wife that he means them. On the other hand, when husband and wife, even into old age, look for and find ways of expressing their devotion to one another, how blessed that marriage will be! So it should not surprise us, indeed it should delight us, that our gracious Savior who delights to call the church his bride has found more than one way of showing and showering us with his love and grace.

What happens in Baptism?

That's exactly what happens in Baptism. It is as though there were a great well and fountain of God's love and grace in heaven—love and grace that is of his very essence. Then in the Sacrament of Baptism God takes all of his love and mercy and pours it into a funnel. It gushes down from heaven through the funnel of Baptism and covers us as the spigot is opened fully in the simple baptismal act. The pastor acts as Christ's stand-in, in the name and in the stead of Christ. He repeats the Word of the gospel that gives the Sacrament such power. He says, "I baptize you in the name of the Father and of the Son and of the Holy Spirit." And it is as though Christ has taken the one being baptized in his arms and placed that one in the lap of his Father, declaring, "See! Here is one for whom I lived on earth, shed my blood, suffered the torments of the damned, and died! For my sake adopt also this one as your own dear child for time and for eternity.

Forgive all sin and conquer death so that also this one may live and reign with me forever in heaven."

And the Father delights to answer the prayer of his Son and to make us his own dear children. If there were a newspaper in heaven, surely the angels and the saints already there would cry out: "Stop the presses! Look what has just happened on earth! Another one has been washed of all sin and guilt! Another one has been born again! Another one has become an heir of eternal life through faith in the Savior's work and by his Word of the gospel!" For no matter what is happening on earth at the moment that may seem so important to people, nothing matches the beauty, wonder, awe, and power of what takes place in a baptism.

Does all of this sound like hyperbole? It is not! Listen to St. Paul's description of Baptism and its effect:

> When the kindness and love of God our Savior appeared, he saved us, not because of righteous things we had done, but because of his mercy. He saved us through the washing of rebirth and renewal by the Holy Spirit, whom he poured out on us generously through Jesus Christ our Savior, so that, having been justified by his grace, we might become heirs having the hope of eternal life. (Titus 3:4-7)

Or this:

> Christ loved the church and gave himself up for her to make her holy, cleansing her by the washing with water through the word, and to present her to himself as a radiant church, without stain or wrinkle or any other blemish, but holy and blameless. (Ephesians 5:25-27)

Could it be said any more eloquently? Could Paul's praise of the love and grace of God in Baptism be any more lavish? Everything that Christ is for us as Savior comes down to us from heaven through the "washing of rebirth." There is "renewal," the granting of the new birth and rescue from the consequences of original sin and guilt inherited from Adam and Eve. There is adoption as we become in Baptism heirs with the sure and certain hope of eternal life that comes only by virtue of Christ's work and only through faith. There is the gift of perfect holiness, the very righteousness of Christ, granted in the Sacrament. And all that is just another beautiful way of saying that Baptism gives forgiveness, life, and salvation. For where sin is removed, there its dread consequences of eternal death and hell are removed. There is life. There is salvation.

Paul made the point more than once and each time made it emphatically that in Baptism we receive grace heaped upon grace, forgiveness of all sin, life, and salvation. Everything in short that the gospel of salvation in the Word of God in the Bible offers and gives to us God gives as well in the Sacrament of Baptism. For the Sacrament is that selfsame gospel; it is the gospel wearing, as we put it earlier, another dress. It is just with such imagery that Paul tells the Galatian Christians, "You are all sons[1] of God through faith in Christ Jesus, for all of you who were baptized into Christ have clothed yourselves with Christ" (Galatians 3:26,27). In wearing Christ, we wear all that he is for us as Savior: his innocence, his righteousness, his life, his death, and his resurrection for us; thus, when God sees us, he sees Jesus. With this verse in mind Lutherans may well think of their baptisms when they recall that famous hymn verse: *"Christi Blut und Gerechtigkeit, das ist mein Schmuck und Ehrenkleid"* (Christ's blood and righteousness, that is [all] my adornment and [only] robe of honor).

St. Peter likewise sums up the matter so clearly and succinctly when he compares Baptism to the water of the flood at Noah's time. The water that destroyed the unbelieving world saved those held up by it in the ark. Peter says, "This water symbolizes baptism that now saves you also—not the removal of dirt from the body but the pledge of a good conscience toward God. It saves you by the resurrection of Jesus Christ" (1 Peter 3:21). If Baptism saves us, then it is certainly a means of grace, a means whereby God shows us his grace and brings us into possession of grace, the forgiveness of sins, life, and salvation. Yes, in it God is active, and man is passive; God gives everything and we receive his gift without our works, without our righteousness.

Peter had said exactly that in his great Pentecost sermon when his hearers were struck to the core by their need of God's mercy and forgiveness for the monstrous crime they had committed in the murder of God's Son. They wanted to know what they could or should do in the face of such monstrous sin and guilt—as though any work they might have done could ever atone for such an unspeakable crime! Peter told them:

---

[1]The word *sons* of course is not intended to exclude women. The word emphasizes a relationship that carried with it rights of inheritance. Thus all who are baptized, women as well as men, are sons in the sense that they all receive an adoption that includes with it the promise of inheritance at the death of the one who adopts: Christ made us such adopted sons and won for us the inheritance of sons by his death.

> "Repent and be baptized, every one of you, in the name of Jesus Christ for the forgiveness of your sins. And you will receive the gift of the Holy Spirit. The promise is for you and your children and for all who are far off—for all whom the Lord our God will call." (Acts 2:38,39)

There is nothing for them to do. Repentance, as noted in the last chapter, is sorrow and dread because of sin and is then trust in the promise contained in the gospel message. And as the Holy Spirit works dread and sorrow to the point of despair through the law, so he works trust in the gospel promise through the gospel. And that promise is there full and free, perfect and complete in the gift of Baptism.

All of that is exactly what Jesus promised when he spoke of and then instituted this Sacrament. He spoke to Nicodemus of its importance and necessity when he promised that regeneration, the new birth of spiritual life, would come through Baptism: "I tell you the truth, no one can enter the kingdom of God unless he is born of water and the Spirit" (John 3:5). And in his final and Great Commission to the church of every age Jesus linked salvation to the preaching of his Word and the administration of the Sacrament of Baptism. The preaching of the Word and the Sacrament are not an either/or proposition. They are a both/and, each in its turn bringing all that we mean by the word *salvation.* Jesus said,

> "All authority in heaven and on earth has been given to me. Therefore go and make disciples of all nations, baptizing them in the name of the Father and of the Son and of the Holy Spirit, and teaching them to obey everything I have commanded you. And surely I am with you always, to the very end of the age." (Matthew 28:18-20)

It is all so simple, so clear, and so direct. Disciples (i.e., those who learn his Word and believe it) are made through the teaching of the gospel and through Baptism. And indeed it is by that teaching and by that baptizing that Jesus promises to be present with us until the end of time and his return in glory. He can make such a promise precisely because he has all authority in heaven and on earth. The miracle of saving faith comes then through the means of grace, through his Word and Baptism by virtue of his power attached to his promise in Word and sacrament.

Objections raised against Baptism

As plain and clear as the Bible is in its teaching about the Sacrament of Baptism as an effective means of grace, one finds nevertheless no end of objections raised against it, objections that we have to at least address in brief.

1. *But wait a minute,* someone will object: *What about faith? I thought that faith saves. Is Baptism a substitute for faith?* No, Baptism is not a substitute for faith any more than the gospel message in the Word is a substitute for faith. Rather, just like the gospel in the Word, Baptism is a cause of faith. For Baptism is not a mere or empty ceremony. Baptism proclaims the gospel and applies it to us individually. The gospel in the Sacrament creates or confirms faith. For in Baptism God makes promises to us, promises that awaken faith, promises that faith then embraces. Just as with the promises in the gospel that we have in the Bible, if someone rejects those promises in stubborn unbelief, then that person rejects as well the saving benefit offered and conveyed in the Sacrament. Again, the Sacrament is not a different gospel; it is the same gospel that we have in the Word but in another form, another dress.
2. *What then is the difference between the baptism of an infant and the baptism of an adult who already believes the gospel promises in the Bible?* It is true that Baptism does not create faith in an adult who already has faith. But look at the examples in the New Testament (e.g., Acts 8:28-38; 9:17-19; 10:27-48). Adults who had already heard the gospel message and by it had come to faith were eager to be baptized. And why? Because of the promises that God has attached to Baptism, promises that in Baptism are applied to the individual. That is the special comfort that God gives in the sacraments: What he announces to the world in his Word and lets us apply to ourselves he gives to us individually, one at a time, in the sacraments. The adult looks back on his baptism and with great joy and with thanksgiving declares, "Look at the redemption Christ won on the cross for the world; and now look at how much he has loved me, even me, that he declares to me as an individual that the redemption is indeed meant for me!" So an adult brought to faith already by the proclamation of the gospel will eagerly ask for the Sacrament and most gratefully receive it. In fact, to refuse Baptism or to despise it is the same thing as despising the gospel; for that's what Baptism is, the gospel.
3. *But what about an infant? An infant doesn't ask for the gospel in either Word or Sacrament. In fact, how can an infant even believe and have faith if faith is what we said it is in the last chapter, namely, knowledge of, assent to, and confidence in the gospel mes-*

sage? It is exactly because we cannot sit down and teach an infant the gospel that the Sacrament of Baptism is so precious to us as a means of grace for little children. To understand that though, we have to sweep away some false assumptions both about children and about faith. First of all, who said that infants can't believe? Jesus certainly did not say that. In fact, he said the opposite: "If anyone causes one of *these little ones who believe in me* to sin, it would be better for him to have a large millstone hung around his neck and to be drowned in the depths of the sea" (Matthew 18:6). In Luke 18:15 Jesus took up little children, infants, in his arms and blessed them. Would someone want to say that his blessing was for nothing, just empty words, words without effect? Far be it from us to say such a thing! They received his blessing, a blessing that was gospel from beginning to end, and they received its benefit. Moreover, we have the many examples in the book of Acts (cf. for example, again, Acts 10 where the entire household of Cornelius together with the households of his relatives and friends were baptized). Are we to imagine that in all of these instances there were never any children? But even more than that we have the command of Christ in the institution of Baptism itself (Matthew 28:18-20), where Jesus commanded that "all nations" should be taught and be baptized. Children, even newborn infants, are part of nations; they receive the legal and other benefits of their nations even in infancy when they are unable to express their understanding of those benefits or an appreciation for them. Thus, while there is not a specific command to baptize children, children are included with all the rest of us as those who need it and those for whom its gospel blessings are intended. Finally, what about the assumption that children cannot believe because they cannot express their faith? The assumption is, even on the basis of observation, an empty one. Does an infant know its mother? Does it trust its father? Does it grasp that there is a difference between these two and all others? Who would doubt that? Yet the child cannot tell us such a thing or explain to us why or how it recognizes and trusts its parents. Indeed the simple fact of the matter is that we cannot analyze what an infant knows or doesn't know. For we have long since passed the day when our thinking was without words that we could express. We just do not remember how we went from the one stage to the other. All we know is that the child learns to express thoughts in words with the passing of time when it somehow figures out that it is easier to get what it wants with words than without them. So we will leave to God how he gives faith to the child in the gospel promises so abundant in Baptism. Yes, it is always far better to trust his promises and their power than to rely on our own feeble senses and fallen reason. Jesus says that infants believe. That's good enough for us! The "how" we will leave to him. We will most gladly apply those promises to our children and take great comfort in the love of God for us and for them as he pours it out in the Sacrament of Baptism. Indeed, while a child because of original sin needs Baptism's blessings as much as an adult and while faith, whether in a child or an adult, is always and alone a miracle worked by God through the gospel, one might dare to think that the miracle is easier for God to perform in a child than in an adult. Though the child's need is no different, at least the child has not yet acquired the bad habits of years of actual sin accompanied by perverse and fallen reason that throw additional obstacles in the path of the Holy Spirit's work through the gospel.

4. *Is Baptism then necessary for salvation? What if a believer for some reason dies without Baptism?* Jesus has given us the Sacrament for our comfort and encouragement. The one who knows that the Sacrament is a means of grace intended by Jesus to show us his love and grace for us as individuals but who despises and refuses the Sacrament has despised God's Word and grace. Such a one will surely perish. On the other hand, there may be times where it was not possible for a person to be baptized. Such was the case with the thief on the cross next to Jesus on Good Friday. But Jesus promised the thief that he would enter paradise that very day (Luke 23:43). Clearly there was no chance for the thief to be baptized first. So what do we find in the Scriptures? We find that where Baptism was possible, it was eagerly desired and administered. Faith that trusts the promises of God's grace and Christ's merit for our salvation will cling to those promises both in the Word and in the Sacrament. Where the Sacrament is not despised but cannot for whatever reason be administered, there we trust that faith saves in accord with God's promises. It might happen, for example, that a child past infancy wants to be baptized but his or her parents forbid and even prevent it. Such a child is surely in a state of grace, a dear child of God, a believer. As soon as it is possible, of course, the child will seek the Sacrament.

5. *But what about the child of Christian parents who tragically dies before it can receive the Sacrament?* Such cases are tragic indeed. In such cases the parents should draw comfort from the fact that it is a God of love and grace who has taken their child from them, that he as such did not will the damnation of their child; for that child, even for such a short time, was a gift of his love to them. As the Sacrament creates faith, so too does the Word that the mother heard while she was pregnant; it may be that the Lord was pleased to save their child through that Word heard in a case where the Sacrament itself could not be administered. We do have the case of St. John the Baptist who before his birth and inspired by the Holy Spirit praised the coming Savior (Luke 1:39-45), but the circumstances of St. John's birth and his wondrous joy before his birth are so exceptional that we would not want to make his faith something common, much less universal; all we can say is that St. John shows that such a faith is not impossible. So we commend the child to the mercy of God and trust that he can never be indifferent to our pain and anguish in such a tragic circumstance.[2] Yes, and we urge parents to arrange for the Baptism in advance of the child's birth in case there is some need to perform the Sacrament in an emergency. And as well we urge the parents to hear faithfully the Word of God also before the child is born.

These and other questions that cast doubt on the benefit of the Sacrament come primarily from Protestant church bodies. As Protestants generally deny the entire biblical doctrine of the means of grace, we can expect that they will deny the saving benefit of the sacraments. Their denials fall into two distinct camps.

Some (Baptists and most Pentecostal churches) deny that a child can believe. They therefore refuse to baptize infants. At the bottom of that refusal is also the error that Baptism is not a means of grace but a work of the law, a work of obedience. For such churches Baptism is a confession of faith, not a means whereby faith is either created or con-

---

[2]We can perhaps better understand why God has given us no clear word that will fully answer the questions posed by this tragedy. On the one hand, if God told us that all such children certainly go to heaven, we could expect that (given the perversity of human nature) people would neglect or despise the beautiful Sacrament of Baptism. On the other hand, if God slammed the door shut on any possibility of the salvation of such children, his own attribute of grace and love would be put in such doubt for the parents that they might be driven to bitter despair. Both such alternatives are averted by God's own silence.

firmed. Once someone has denied that Baptism is a means of grace and teaches instead that it is a work of obedience we render to God, then it is easy to see why he or she would reject infant Baptism. But it is a sad thing indeed to deprive children and their parents of the rich consolation that God promises in the Sacrament because of a rejection of God's power and the promise he has attached to this means of grace.

Most other Protestant churches (Methodists, Presbyterians, Congregationalists, et al.) do however "baptize" infants; nevertheless, they really prefer to call the ceremony a christening or a dedication. The child later on, when it can make a confession of faith for him or herself, may choose to count this "christening" as Baptism; or if not, the child/adult may choose to be baptized. Some of these churches deny both that the child can believe and often that the child even needs the forgiveness offered in Baptism. For just as they deny the possibility of faith to an infant, so also many deny that the child has any sin or guilt that needs to be forgiven. They too see the Sacrament as law-obedience, not gospel-promise. For they deny the devastating consequences of original sin. But whatever they choose to call the ceremony, so long as it is the application of water in the name of the Father and of the Son and of the Holy Spirit, it is a Baptism; for God's promises are extended in his Word to that child whether those presenting the child and those performing the ceremony believe it or not. The validity of God's promises depends on God, not on the unbelief of bystanders!

Roman Catholics do not deny that children need forgiveness. Nor do they deny that Baptism gives the forgiveness that they need. Rather, they limit the grace of the Sacrament. They teach that it forgives the guilt only of original sin and that in the process it gives the child some initial grace. As with all Catholic teaching about the sacraments, there is an unfortunate mixing of law and gospel. For, as already noted, grace is seen as a quantity; God doles it out in the sacraments so that by grace the individual may cooperate with God in gaining still more grace on the way to salvation. Thus, while there is comfort for their members in Baptism, the comfort is limited, as grace is limited.

In point of fact, none of the passages listed above limit to original sin the forgiveness offered and given in Baptism. The forgiveness held out in Baptism is for a lifetime! It is only lost when the one thus forgiven in Baptism turns his back on the blessing and becomes an unbeliever—that's the same way that the benefits of forgiveness in the Word are lost. The point is that Baptism is a means of grace—no more, no less than the gospel in the Word; the benefit comes to faith created by the gospel and the loss of the benefit to unbelief in the rejection of the gospel. The promise of God remains the same and is always reliable. Even those who have fallen away, if they hear the Word of God, repent, and return by the power of that Word, will have again all the promises of God in their baptisms.

In spite of the errors that surround the Sacrament of Baptism among Protestants and Roman Catholics, the Sacrament is valid, so long as Christ's institution of it is retained. That is, God gives the benefit of the Sacrament so long as Baptism is performed with the application of water in the name of the Father and of the Son and of the Holy Spirit. For that is the essence of the Sacrament—God's Word of promise joined to the ceremony. The gospel essence of that simple formula is that God becomes our Father in Baptism; the Son becomes for us what he came to be—our Savior; and the Holy Spirit does his special work of breathing into us the promise of forgiveness and salvation, which as promised is designed and intended to create faith or to confirm it in those who already possess saving faith.

We should add one word of caution: If either the Word or the water is absent, then there is no Baptism. In some Protestant churches the "christening" is performed with rose petals instead of with water! What a shocking abuse of God's Word and of this Sacrament! Where the essence of the Sacrament is absent, namely, the Word with the water, there is no Sacrament.

The point is that when someone joins one of our churches, there is no need to baptize them if they were baptized in a Christian church and their baptisms had the essentials of God's Word and the water. But we need to ask and be assured that such was indeed the case. If the Word was absent or the water was omitted, then there was no Baptism.

Practices and customs relating to Baptism

There are a few loose ends that deserve comment before we move on to the Sacrament of the Altar. It is our practice to have our pastors administer the Sacrament. That is what we have called them to do: to publicly proclaim the gospel in all its forms, in the preaching of the Word and in the administration of the sacraments. For an individual to take that responsibility on himself apart from the church would be at the very least disrespectful of the holy office of the ministry. It would violate good order and introduce confusion about the call of Christ and his commission to those in the pastoral office. And so we are happy to call on our pastors to administer the Sacrament in union with the church, so that the church can rejoice with us in this sacred act. In cases of emergency, where it is just not possible to reach a pastor and the child's life is in danger, any Christian can perform the Sacrament. All that is necessary is, again, water and the Word: "I baptize you in the name of the Father and of the Son and of the Holy Spirit." Many Christian parents will advise their (Christian) doctor and the hospital that in case of such an emergency, they should baptize their baby in just this way.

It is wise for parents to arrange for the Baptism of their children as soon as practical after their births. To delay it for weeks on end without some compelling reason is to delay the child's joy and ours too in the benefit afforded by this Sacrament. In many Lutheran parishes it was the custom that after the child came home from the hospital, it did not leave home again until it went to church to be baptized.

It has long been the custom that children have sponsors, or Godparents, when they are baptized. The custom goes all the way back to the early church when sponsors were required even for adults. Someone had to vouch for the sincerity of an adult seeking Baptism. Christianity was an illegal religion, and some would ask for Baptism so that they could get the names of Christians, in order to turn them in to the government. If a Christian was arrested and convicted of the crime of being a Christian, his property was confiscated by the state and a share of it was turned over to the one who handed in the Christian for arrest. Seeking out Christians became a profitable business. So having someone vouch for the sincerity of an adult seeking Baptism was a safety measure. Sponsors were also sought for infants. The sponsors promised that in the event that the parents died, the sponsors would take the child and raise it themselves and see to it that it was raised as a Christian.

While these functions of sponsors have long since ceased to be important at most baptisms, the custom of having them remains, though sponsors are no longer required. These days there are basically two kinds of sponsors. There are sponsors who make certain, very specific promises, chiefly the promise to do all that they can to encourage and assist the parents in raising their child in accord with the Word of God. When parents want the sponsors to make those kinds of promises, the sponsors must be from their own church fellowship; it should be obvious that one who does not accept the religion into which the child is baptized should not be expected to assist in raising the child in that religion. It would be unfair to ask for such a promise. Indeed, those outside of that church might not even know what it is that they are promising to do.

Where parents are not seeking sponsors who could assist and encourage them in this way, another type of sponsor is the sponsor who just serves as a witness. Such a sponsor promises nothing. Such a sponsor is asked only to note that the child is being baptized with water in the name of the Trinity. For sponsor-witnesses it is only required that they be Christians.

Very often pastors will encourage children in a confirmation class to ask their sponsors to tell them about their baptisms. It is a beautiful thing when someone in addition to the parents can sit down with a child and say, "Yes, I was there. I held you in my arms while the pastor poured the water over you and said those beautiful words." Especially if the sponsors were of the first type, children should know as they grow that their sponsors pray for them and are interested in their Christian training. It is a good thing when such sponsors take the time to take their God-children aside occasionally to tell them/ask them about their growth in the truths of the gospel.

Summary

So then, in sum, Baptism is a means of grace by which God shows us his grace and gives us all that his grace and the merits of Christ intend for us: adoption into God's family, forgiveness, life, and salvation. All of this comes as the gospel, the Word of promise in the sacramental act, creates faith or confirms it in those who already have faith. All of our lives we do well to remember our baptism as the gospel source of our life with Christ. In times of joy the sight of the baptismal font in church points us to our greatest joy, that of being a child of God by faith in Christ Jesus, no matter how old we are. In times of trouble and sorrow, calling to mind our baptism cheers and encourages us: No, God has not forgotten me, nor can he. He made me his own dear child in Baptism and never will he forsake me. Though deep the waters of trouble, though the shadow of death itself will threaten and finally overtake me, he is still my dear Father for Jesus' sake, and at the end he will take me to himself in heaven. In times of temptation, we remember what we have become in Baptism and struggle to live as God's own children, as a member of his household; we do not want to shame ourselves or disgrace his name by living in sin. In times when we nevertheless stumble and fall in the battle, we cling to the promises of forgiveness in the gospel, as those promises were made our very own in the Sacrament of Baptism. For the forgiveness offered and given in Baptism never runs out. It is always there in the gospel promises God made when he adopted us in the Sacrament.

The Sacrament of Baptism is indeed a beautiful means of grace, is it not?!

The Sacrament of the Altar

More ink has been spilled in attacking the Bible's teaching about the Sacrament of the Altar than perhaps any other doctrine of God's Word. Satan must really despise this powerful and beautiful expression from the heart of God to our hearts to have made it such a special object of his scorn and venomous hatred.

That the doctrine of this Sacrament has been so much the subject of abuse and error is all the more surprising to us when we consider from the words of Jesus how simple, plain, and clear his words are in his gift of this Sacrament. Matthew, Mark, Luke, and Paul give us Jesus' words of institution for the Sacrament. Matthew tells us:

> While they were eating, Jesus took bread, gave thanks and broke it, and gave it to his disciples, saying, "Take and eat; this is my body." Then he took the cup, gave thanks and offered it to them, saying, "Drink from it, all of you. This is my blood of the covenant, which is poured out for many for the forgiveness of sins." (Matthew 26:26-28)

Jesus' words are indeed plain and clear. It is the night before his death. His words come at the close of the Passover meal, that great sacrament of the Old Testament which called to mind the rescue of the people of Israel from death when the angel of the Lord passed over the houses on whose doorpost was painted the blood of a lamb. By the blood of that lamb—a picture of the blood to be shed by *the* Lamb of God who delivers from eternal death—they were spared. Now in this most solemn moment at the close of the Passover meal, Jesus makes his last will and testament. What on this most solemn night before his death will he bequeath to his beloved disciples? He has no earthly wealth or land. He has no palaces, no coffers filled with gold and silver. He has no earthly realms to bequeath for them to rule. And so, having nothing, he who had humbled himself so fully, so completely in his lowly birth and trouble-filled life and who would in the next day humble himself yet more in his death on the cross of a criminal, what would he leave for them? Having nothing, he left them—himself!

How sublime! How rich his grace and mercy! His words need no interpretation. They are utterly self-explanatory. What is in the Sacrament is exactly what he said and what he gave in his words of institution. His true body and his true blood are there. And in the giving of himself, he gives what he came to gain for us by the sacrifice of himself on the cross—the forgiveness of sins. The whole of the gospel is wrapped up there in those simple words, in the simple act of receiving him in the Sacrament.

Lest there be any doubt about it, years later the Holy Spirit inspired St. Paul to write the same thing with an added emphasis that was needed because already in his day people had started to corrupt the Sacrament. St. Paul writes:

> Is not the cup of thanksgiving for which we give thanks a participation in the blood of Christ? And is not the bread that we break a participation in the body of Christ? (1 Corinthians 10:16)

And then:

> I received from the Lord what I also passed on to you: The Lord Jesus, on the night he was betrayed, took bread, and when he had given thanks, he broke it and said, "This is my body, which is for you; do this in remembrance of me." In the same way, after supper he took the cup, saying, "This cup is the new covenant in my blood; do this, whenever you drink it, in remembrance of me." For whenever you eat this bread and drink this cup, you proclaim the Lord's death until he comes. Therefore, whoever eats the bread or drinks the cup of the Lord in an unworthy manner will be guilty of sinning against the body and blood of the Lord. A man ought to examine himself before he eats of the bread and drinks of the cup. For anyone who eats and drinks without recognizing the body of the Lord eats and drinks judgment on himself. (1 Corinthians 11:23-29)

What then do we have in the Sacrament? We have two earthly elements: bread and wine ("whenever you eat this bread and drink this cup," "whoever eats the bread and drinks the cup"). The bread remains bread, and the wine in the cup remains wine. But at the same time, as we receive the two earthly elements, we receive as well two divine elements, namely, Jesus' true body and true blood. Are the earthly and the divine mixed together? That's not what the text says. Do the earthly change into the divine? The text doesn't say that either. Are then the divine elements really there or are the bread and wine just symbols that represent Jesus' body and blood? The text certainly doesn't say that either. In fact, St. Paul is very emphatic that an irreverent careless receiving of the bread and wine is a terrible sin not against bread and wine but against the body and blood of Christ! What then is in the Sacrament? Bread and wine, and Jesus' true body and blood—and that because of his promise to be there, because he says so!

But doesn't Jesus sometimes speak in picture language, in metaphors, that are not to be taken literally, as, for example, when he tells us that he is the gate and the vine (John 10:7; 15:5)? Yes, Jesus often used metaphors and picture language. But when he did, he always explained what he was saying, always made it clear that he was using a metaphor and speaking in picture language. But he most emphatically does not do that in the words of institution for the Sacrament. He gives not the slightest hint that he might be speaking figuratively or that we shouldn't take him literally. Again, St. Paul emphasizes that in his words about the Sacrament.

So we take Jesus at his word. If he says that his body and blood are really and truly present in the Sacrament, then they are truly present. If he tells us that he thus gives us himself in the receiving of the earthly elements, we believe him. It is so odd that the very people who object to the doctrine of the means of grace because they think that that doctrine limits God who cannot be limited nevertheless maintain that it is impossible for him to do what he plainly tells us he is doing in the Sacrament.

How it is possible for us to receive Jesus himself, his true body and blood, when we receive the bread and the wine we will leave to him. He hasn't asked us to turn the Sacrament into a physics lesson. All he asks us to do is to receive it with humble and believing hearts. Unseen and miraculously he keeps his word.

Once we accept the simple truth about the essence of the Sacrament, it is easy for us to see its benefit. If Jesus gives us himself in the Sacrament, then, of course, there is the forgiveness of sins there! For when God looks at us, what does he see? He sees Jesus who is ours by faith and who is now ours also in this special way with the gift of himself, the gift of his true body and blood in the Sacrament. Yes, he sees in us the very price of our salvation! For it was with his true body and blood that he paid the price for our forgiveness. If we have in the Sacrament the price of our salvation, then surely we have the salvation that price paid for!

None of this contradicts in any way the necessity of faith. Again, the Sacrament is not a substitute for faith; rather, it confirms faith by giving us in yet another form what the gospel gives when it declares that Christ is the Lamb of God who takes away the sin of the world and who therefore has taken away also my sin and yours. And just as with the gospel, so with the Sacrament—for it is the gospel—the one who rejects the message in unbelief rejects also its saving benefit. That's exactly what St. Paul said in the passage cited previously: Woe to the one who receives it in the unworthiness of unbelief! Such a one sins against the body and blood of Christ! Could there be a greater crime?

But for those who hear the gospel, who hear the gospel in this Sacrament, and who by its power believe what Jesus said, for them the Sacrament is filled with blessing as a means of grace. Jesus has told them in their baptisms: "I have adopted you and washed away all your sins and you are now a dear child of God." Jesus has told them again and again in his Word as they have read it, remembered it, and heard it proclaimed in church: "My perfect life and innocent death on the cross has paid for all of your sins and won for you an eternal inheritance in heaven." And now in the Sacrament he tells them: "Here I am for you, with you, in you, by the power of the gospel with my true body and true blood. Now surely you will not doubt it that in days of joy and sorrow, in life and in death, I am closer to you than any human being could ever be. I know all that you are, all that you have done and will do, all of your good works and all of your sins, and I do not despise you; no, I want to be with you and live in you forever and ever!"

Could there be a greater incentive for Christian peace and joy? Could there be a stronger motivation for the Christian to strive to live a Christian life than his knowing this, that Christ is always in him, with him, for him? Little wonder that we love this Sacrament! Little wonder that the sick and the shut-ins and those near death look forward to and long for the Sacrament! Little wonder that we want to receive it often! For it is a means of grace. The promise of Christ in the words of institution are powerful; they move us to trust that he gives us what the Sacrament promises. Those words and the reality of Christ's presence give us the enjoyment of the Sacrament's blessed benefit. For just as we believe the gospel message because of the power in the message, so we trust that Christ is present in the Sacrament and gives us what he promises there. His Word moves us to believe it.

Because the Sacrament is such a precious means of grace, we do not approach it mindlessly or casually. St. Paul tells us that we should examine ourselves before we receive the Sacrament and warns against any careless use of this precious means of grace. And so we prepare ourselves to receive so great a blessing and benefit. Just as we listen attentively to the Word as it is preached or meditate on it devoutly as we read it, so no less we approach the gifts of God in the Sacrament with reverent attention and devotion. In times past it was the custom that people would not eat a meal before they went to Communion. There was nothing wrong with that custom when it focused the attention of God's guests more intently on the sacred meal that

God provides in the Sacrament. But whether one fasts before going to Communion or not, the true preparation for its reception is in the heart; it consists of penitently calling to mind my sins and hence my need of the forgiveness given in the gospel and in this sacramental means of grace; it consists of faith in the promise of forgiveness that comes from Christ's true body and blood offered on the cross and given in the Sacrament.

Some have mistakenly stayed away from the Sacrament with the thought: "I will wait until I am a better Christian, until I have overcome this and that sin first; then I will be fit to receive him in Holy Communion." Big mistake! It is not our worthiness that makes us fit to receive him; it is the promise of his forgiveness that makes us worthy—his worthiness given in the gospel makes us fit. Besides that, the one struggling against his own unworthiness is precisely the one who needs and should long for the Sacrament; for by it Jesus comes to pardon sin and to strengthen us with his forgiving presence for the continuing struggle. The one who stays away because he doesn't think himself holy enough to receive is like the starving man who says that he is too hungry to eat or the sick man who wants to wait until he is well again before taking his medicine.

Given the wealth of comfort offered in the Sacrament, it should not surprise us that the devil throws so much dust in the eyes of so many to keep them away from the Sacrament and its faith-confirming benefit! In the guise of "Professor Ja-but," the devil or his ally, fallen reason, objects: *Ja, but if you have received it once, does Christ's body and blood go away, so that you have to receive it again?* As noted before with the gospel as a means of grace in general, so we note with this form of the means of grace. If he wants to tell us again and again that he loves us and forgives us, we most gladly will receive him and his forgiveness as often as we can.

Ja, but what about the elements of bread and wine? When does Christ come to them and when does he leave them? Christ is present with the elements in their use, in their reception. Jesus said, "Take and eat . . . take and drink." As we receive the Sacrament, Jesus is there as he promised with his true body and blood. His presence is not a mixing in with the elements but a supernatural presence—a sacramental presence—as the bread and wine are received. So we consecrate the bread and the wine with the words of institution; that is, we set them aside for the sacred use intended. But we do not venerate them or worry about when Christ comes and goes. He is there with his true body and blood in the receiving of the Sacrament and not apart from it. To say anything more about it is to engage in useless speculation that can only distract from the blessed benefit promised in the words of institution.

Ja, but if his body and blood are really present in the Sacrament, do we chew him and digest him? Jesus never asked us to bother ourselves with such blasphemous considerations. He bids us eat and drink and promises to give himself to us as we do. We will be content with what he says and what he promises and what he gives us thereby.

Ja, but if we are already forgiven because all sin has been forgiven by his sacrifice on Good Friday, why do we need to look to the Sacrament for forgiveness? Does it mean that we are not forgiven when we are away from it? Again, the doctrines of objective justification and subjective justification (cf. chapter 12) are not two separate doctrines but two aspects of the same doctrine. The gospel of objective justification creates the faith that trusts that I too have been redeemed, justified, and forgiven. The sacraments apply that doctrine to me as an individual. The gospel says, Christ died for all! The sacraments say, Christ died for you! It's the same message, the same gospel, the same forgiveness, and the same peace and consolation. But who would say that it is useless redundancy? Indeed, it is difficult to understand why it is that so many Christians have to be urged to receive the Sacrament often, given the wealth of blessing offered to us in it. Each day we have reason to rejoice in the sum of the gospel that Jesus died for the sins of the world and therefore also for my sins. Each day we have reason to rejoice that he has assured me of that individually in the Sacrament of Baptism; its promises and benefits cover all of life, not just original sin. Each day we have reason to rejoice that he promised it all to me by grace and has given and pledged to give me again the price of my salvation in this Sacrament. Therefore, we delight to receive him in this Sacrament often!

We might note at this point if only in passing how especially kind Jesus is in his choice of earthly elements as the external vehicles of his grace in the sacraments. He bids us use water in the Sacrament of Baptism, water that with the Word washes away our sins. We instinctively like to be clean. We automatically wash when we are dirty. Each time we do so, we have a gentle reminder of the real dirt of our sinful nature and our actual sins; and in washing we have the gentle reminder of the real washing away of all of the filth of sin in the water with the Word in the Sacrament of Baptism. Likewise, we have in nature constant pointers to the Sacrament of the Altar. Every time we are hungry in body, we may call to mind the longing and the hunger of the soul for peace with God. And each time we eat and drink to satisfy physical longing, we may call to mind Jesus, the living bread from heaven, who always satisfies by giving us himself with all his grace and mercy, with forgiveness and eternal life, not only in the gospel in his Word but also in the gospel in the Sacrament.

Errors concerning the Sacrament of the Altar

It is sad that with such beauty and so many rich promises in this Sacrament we also have to note the many terrible errors by which the Sacrament is attacked. As already noted, Protestants deny the doctrine of the means of grace. And so they deny that this Sacrament is a means of grace too. Indeed, it is difficult to think that they even have this Sacrament at all. For a sacrament requires both the Word and the prescribed elements. But the Protestants have removed the Word from the Sacrament by denying everything that the words say. Jesus says, "This is my body . . . and this is my blood." The Protestants say, "No it isn't." Jesus says, "It is given and shed for you for the forgiveness of sins." The Protestants say, "No, not in the Sacrament!" What's left then is a shell without any content. What's left is not faith but a rejection of the Word that creates and confirms faith. As with the Sacrament of Baptism, so with the Sacrament of the Altar, Protestants turn it from a form of the gospel into a work of the law. If asked why they bother at all with this ceremony, about all they can answer is: "Jesus said, 'This do!' and so we do it in obedience to his command." Again, as with all false doctrine and with this one so obviously and so blatantly, Christ is robbed of his honor, his Word is contradicted, and the Christian is left without a rich consolation from the gospel in this Sacrament.

Roman Catholic errors are more numerous and more complicated than those of the Protestants. Roman Catholics do not deny that Christ is truly present with his body and blood, nor do they deny that God gives his grace in the Sacrament. But they are not content to leave it at that. Rather, they add a host of errors that turn the Mass into an abomination.

1. They teach that it is not only a sacrament but, even more important, a sacrifice. That in fact is the name they give to it: The holy sacrifice of the Mass. In it the priest is said to offer in an unbloody manner the body and blood of Christ to God in payment for the sins of the living and even of the dead. Thus, law and gospel are horribly mixed with the law receiving the emphasis. But where in the words of institution did Jesus command that his gift to us be turned into our sacrifice to him? He already made that sacrifice once and for all. And his once-and-for-all sacrifice was perfect and

complete; no repetition of it is either needed or possible. Nevertheless, the priest prays at Mass and asks those present to pray that his sacrifice may be acceptable to God. Moreover, he calls on the saints, the apostles, the martyrs, and especially the virgin Mary to assist him in making so great a sacrifice acceptable to God. If we think about it, Christ must share his work with the priest! The glory that belongs alone to Christ is transferred to a mere mortal, and the faith of the faithful is to rest in the value of this mortal's work as necessary for their faith.

2. Inseparably connected with the first error is the Roman Catholic doctrine of *transubstantiation.* According to that doctrine, the priest by the special power given to him from the pope through the bishop who ordained him changes the bread and wine into Christ's body and blood; no longer are bread and wine on the altar after the priest has spoken the words of institution to them but only the appearance (the *accidents*[3]) of bread and wine. Once this *transubstantiation* has occurred through the priest's power, they are fit to be offered to God as a sacrifice. Indeed, they are fit to be adored wherever the elements are kept. So the faithful are encouraged to come and pray before them even apart from the use commanded by Christ, when he said, "Take and eat . . . take and drink." People kneel before them in adoration. On special occasions the consecrated bread turned into the body of Christ is even put on parade around the church and through the streets of the city in the *Corpus Christi* (Body of Christ) festival. But again, where did Jesus ever ask for or command such a thing? He invites us to receive the Sacrament, not to venerate its elements or to separate them from the use he intended for them. Hence we follow the principle of *Extra usum, nullum Sacramentum* (Apart from the use, there is no Sacrament). All of this too, the adoration of the elements, the parades, put emphasis on man's works, not on Christ's gift.
3. As bad as all of the above is, perhaps worst of all is the teaching that the Sacrament can be bought and sold as an indulgence. That is, those seeking God's favor for some special need (a marriage problem, unemployment, a sickness, alcoholism, et al.) are

---

[3]As noted so often elsewhere, the term *accident* in theology means "that which describes something, rather than that which defines it." The term *essence* defines, e.g., man's essence is body and soul; the term *accident* describes, e.g., man has the accidents of hair, skin color, height, etc.

encouraged to purchase a Mass in order to seek God's help for their special need. These are called *votive masses.* Indeed one can even become part of a "mass union" for a price; for a one-time gift, usually to a monastery, the donor and their wish/intention will be remembered at Mass every day until the end of time. Nor are the benefits thus purchased only for this life; Catholics are encouraged to buy masses for the dead, to shorten the stay of their loved ones or their own stay in purgatory.[4]

4. Added to all of this is the withholding of the cup from the laity. Often only the priest drinks from the Sacrament. The practice of withholding the cup came from the error of transubstantiation. There was a fear that the wine in the chalice might be spilled and then trampled underfoot. So from a pious wish that such would not happen, the priest alone drank from the chalice and the theory evolved that if the laity were receiving Christ's body, they were also at the same time receiving his blood—for where is there a body without blood? But, again, the words of Christ have been set aside. He said both, "Take eat" and "Drink from it all of you." To be sure, these days in some instances and in some Roman Catholic parishes the cup has been restored to the laity. But the restoration is not because of Christ's command but only because of the permission granted by the church—so that the will of the church is more important than the command of Christ!

There are other errors that are somewhat more subtle than those listed above. But just from the ones listed it should be easy to understand why the Lutheran Confessions charged that all of the abuses introduced apart from and contrary to Christ's institution of the Sacrament had turned the Mass into an abomination.[5]

Is it not a wonder that something so simple and so beautiful as Christ's gift of this Sacrament could be so abused and corrupted by those who wish to love and serve him? Protestants deny its beauty and

---

[4]Purgatory is that mythical place between heaven and hell where, according to Catholic teaching and without one word of support from the Scriptures, souls go to suffer for a time, to be purged of their remaining sinfulness or guilt until they are fit for heaven. The bizarre aspect of this teaching is that one should *want* to go to purgatory to be thus purged, while at the same time the church provides no end of ways for getting out of there early! Heresy is always contrary to the Scriptures and ultimately also contrary to reason, as this heresy demonstrates more dramatically than most.

[5]Cf. The Formula of Concord, SD VII, 109 p. 612.

its benefit altogether, and Roman Catholics turn it into an abomination. And then those who are lost in the confusion of errors about the Sacrament try to find a way out of their confusion by declaring, "Well, it's all really just a matter of interpretation. Protestants interpret it one way, Catholics another, and Lutherans in still a third way." But listen to what Jesus said, "Take eat . . . and take drink . . . my body and my blood for the forgiveness of sin." Confessional Lutherans teach that Christ's true body and blood (the doctrine of the real presence) are present with the bread and wine, given for us for the forgiveness of sins. Where is there an interpretation there? That is nothing but a virtual repetition of Christ's own words. There is only a trust that he meant what he said, that he can be present with his body and blood wherever he promises to be and that he can impart the benefit of his payment for our sins by his real presence in the Sacrament. Anything less or more than that is (mis)interpretation, a corruption of his Word, and faithless rejection of his promises.

Fellowship and the Sacrament

Precisely because of the importance of Christ's Word in the Sacrament, our churches have consistently practiced what is called close(d) Communion. That is, we offer the Sacrament to and receive it only with those who have the same confession of faith. For the Sacrament is indeed a "communion," a communion with Christ and also with one another. We do not want to encourage the false doctrine of those who hold to false doctrine by sharing this bond of faith, this communion, where there is not unity of confession. That does not mean, as some have charged, that we think everybody else is an unbeliever and going to hell. We do not judge anyone's faith, only the confession of faith. We cannot judge someone else's faith; for it is in the heart, and we cannot read hearts. But we can, indeed the Bible tells us often that we should judge what people say they believe, i.e., their confession of faith (Matthew 7:15; Romans 16:17).

Membership in a church body is a confession of faith. We may take it as a given that the individual accepts the teaching of the church he belongs to; if not, why does he belong to a church whose confession he does not share? Indeed St. Paul, when correcting the errors that had arisen already in his own day, urged that the Sacrament be given only to those who could examine themselves. Such examination, of course, was to be on the basis of the Word of God, an examination in which the one desiring the Sacrament could see his need for it, as well as Christ's supplying of his need in this precious means of grace (1 Corinthians

11:27,28). Where someone comes to us from another confession of faith, we are at a loss to know whether he can make such an examination or not.

Thus for his own sake we want to wait to offer the Sacrament until there is confession of faith that comes from the Scriptures and that includes separation from false doctrine. In our own churches too we would withhold the Sacrament if a person's words or life were a flat contradiction of the union that otherwise should be assumed by his membership in our church. Accordingly, if a member persisted in holding to false doctrine or if a member refused to repent of sin and insisted that he was free to continue in sin, we would refuse to give such a person the Sacrament. The Sacrament is intended to comfort the penitent, not to encourage the obstinate, be he a persistent heretic or an unrepentant sinner.

May Christ out of his abundant grace and mercy grant that we stick with his simple and beautiful Sacrament as he instituted it! We are happy to submit our reason and our emotions and our will to his Word. And all the more so we want to do that because of the rich blessings that he has promised to us in that Word. For what could be more beautiful and consoling than this: Christ, who has left behind the sorrows and the pain of his earthly life and has ascended to heaven, has not abandoned us; he stoops down from heaven and comes to us poor sinners again and again to give us himself and all that he gained for us by his holy cross and passion, by his glorious resurrection and ascension!

Therefore we go to receive the Sacrament where the words of institution are repeated as the elements are set aside and distributed for our reception. We prepare to receive the Sacrament, perhaps with fasting, as was often the custom, but certainly with repentant and believing hearts. For that is how the gospel is always to be received, no matter the dress that it wears. We remember Christ's sacrifice for our salvation on the altar of the cross. We most thankfully and gladly receive him and his saving benefit according to his promise. We leave his altar consoled that he is still the Christ who is for us and now in this special way also with and in us. Could there be a better reason to rejoice in him and to want to live with him and serve him until at last we see him face-to-face and serve him perfectly in heaven?

Summary

In sum, the means of grace is the gospel message that comes to us in the Word and in the sacraments. By that gospel the Holy Spirit creates and preserves in us the miracle of faith that trusts the promises of God in the message. We believe that Jesus is our Savior from sin because his Word has brought us to believe it. We believe that in the Sacrament of Baptism God promises to adopt us and offers us the forgiveness of sins; the gospel in Baptism has brought us to trust his promises in Baptism. We believe that Jesus' true body and blood are offered to us along with the elements of bread and wine and that we receive forgiveness of our sins in the Sacrament of the Altar; Jesus' gospel in the Sacrament has brought us to believe his promise in the Sacrament. So everything depends on the means of grace, and our faith happily looks outside of itself to its source in the gospel, most gladly receives Jesus again and again in that gospel, and delights to live with him through the gospel means of grace.

Finally, Jesus in John 15:15 calls his disciples, and by extension all believers, his friends. It is the essence of friendship that friends share with one another. Is it not an amazing thing? Jesus our Creator and Redeemer calls us friends. He proves it preeminently by his sacrifice for us on the cross. He chooses to share with us all the treasures of his grace. But what do we share with him? We share with him, yes, we give to him, all of our need for those treasures, our sin and guilt, our persistent weakness, and our remaining inclination to sin.

Friends also need one another. Our need for him is certainly obvious. But what does he need us for? He chooses to need us. For it is not to the angels that he entrusts the powerful, the saving, the precious means of grace. It is to us that he entrusts his precious gospel in the Word and the sacraments. What greater wealth is there than to have him in that gospel and then to be chosen to share the priceless treasure whenever and wherever the opportunity presents itself. The mother tells the stories of the gospel to children on her knee. The father strives to imitate the fatherhood of God in his dealings with his family—they should know from him what a beautiful thing it is to pray every day: "Our Father in heaven." The man finds a way to share his joy in Christ with his coworker or his golfing buddy. The woman talks to her friend about the wedding banquet of the Lamb. And on and on it goes, from one person to another, from this generation to the next. It's all about the means of grace. And it just doesn't get any better than that!

With the treasure of this gospel in Word and sacraments, not one of us need ever think or say, "God is far away and could not possibly be concerned with me. My sin is too great. God could not possibly love me. I am of no importance. God could not possibly want to bother with me." Just the reverse is true: With the gospel means of grace, no one is closer to you than God is, no one understands you better, and no one loves you more. There he is for you in the message of the cross. There he is for you in the water and the Word in Baptism. There he is for you, with you, and in you by his Word and the Sacrament of the Altar.

No, it just doesn't get any better than that!

Chapter 15
The Church

Inseparably connected to the doctrine of the means of grace considered in the last chapter is the Bible's teaching about the church. For it is to the church that the means of grace have been entrusted for use and for sharing. Yes, and it is through the means of grace alone that the Holy Spirit creates and sustains the church. What then is the church? We usually divide the subject into two main headings: the *invisible church* and the *visible church.*

The invisible church

The invisible church consists of all those who have saving faith, i.e., all those who believe that Jesus Christ, the virgin-born Son of God, who suffered and died in payment for our sins and who has risen from the dead and ascended into heaven, is their one and only Savior. The inseparable connection between the means of grace and the church should be immediately evident. For how do we know that Jesus Christ is the virgin-born Son of God? We know it only from the Bible, that primary treasure and storehouse of the gospel. And how do we come to trust that we neither can save ourselves nor need to save ourselves? That trust too comes only from the Bible and is both created and preserved by the gospel in the Bible. And how do we come then to trust that Jesus' perfect life and substitutionary death on the cross has paid for all our sins and that therefore he and he alone is our Savior? We come to know and continue to trust that truth only through the activity of the Holy Spirit; and his activity is always and alone in the gospel as it is applied to us in the Word and in the sacraments. By that gospel he brings us to and keeps us in such a faith so that we wait confidently for the day when, as he has promised, we will share in the glory of his resurrection and ascension. All those who have this faith are members of the invisible church in which alone forgiveness, life, and eternal salvation are to be found.

This one true Christian church is called the *invisible* church because its one defining characteristic is faith. And faith is invisible. Each of us knows if he has such a trust in Christ. But we cannot know in any absolute way if someone else has it. Others may say they have it and may confess such a faith, and normally we will trust their confession. However, we cannot see their faith inside of their hearts. It is as St. Paul said, "God's solid foundation stands firm, sealed with this inscription: 'The Lord knows those who are his'" (2 Timothy 2:19).

Jesus spoke of the invisible church often, usually referring to it in his parables as the kingdom of God. But why does he so often call the church a kingdom? Because in a kingdom there is a king who rules and subjects who are ruled. And that's the way it is with the church. *The kingdom of God by definition is the rule of Christ the King, indeed,* ***his ruling activity*** *wherever his kingdom is*. And where is this kingdom, this ruling activity of Jesus? It is in the hearts of believers; they are his subjects, whether considered individually or collectively. In Luke 17 we hear of the Pharisees who were looking for a visible earthly kingdom, with outward splendor and power, like the kingdom of David and Solomon. But Jesus told them plainly, "The kingdom of God does not come with your careful observation, nor will people say, 'Here it is,' or 'There it is,' because the kingdom of God is within you" (Luke 17:20,21).

Jesus tells us that the whole existence and activity of that kingdom is a secret, a mystery. That is, no one can find it for himself or figure it out from his own reasoning or feelings. The secret of this invisible kingdom and its entire existence and activity has to be revealed by Jesus. He shows how the secret is revealed and how that kingdom is established when in his parables he emphasizes the kingdom's intimate and inseparable connection to the gospel as its cause and sustaining power. He creates the kingdom through the seed of his Word as he sows it in the hearts of those who hear the gospel. He tells us that in the parable of the sower and the seed (Luke 8:4-15). The seed is the Word sown as that Word is proclaimed and heard. Some reject the Word and therefore Christ's rule, Christ's kingdom, outright. Some believe the Word and therefore receive the kingdom, but just for a time; then they fall away. Others believe for a longer time, but then because they remain wedded to wealth or pleasure or the desire to be safe from persecution, they too fall away. But some hear the Word in the soil of their hearts, hearts that are utterly unable apart from the seed to produce anything. They hear and receive and by the ability and power of that seed they remain alive with and through that life-giving Word. That's how the kingdom of God comes. That's how Christ establishes his throne and carries on his rule in hearts. That's how the invisible church is created, how it grows, and how it is sustained.

This is the way it is with those who are in the kingdom of God. They hear the Word; indeed, they keep on hearing it. The Word first produces faith that trusts the Word and the Savior who comes through it. And then it produces the results of faith, that is, good works that are motivated by the love of Christ in the gospel and commanded in the Word. What else is that but the ruling activity of Christ in the heart of each individual who trusts his gospel message?

The fruit may be much or little. It may be more now, less later, then more again still later on. But in its essence the fruit is the result of Jesus' rule in the heart. The heart and core of that rule is a trust that he is indeed the Savior, the one and only Savior. Thus one is a member of the invisible church from the moment the seed creates faith and as long as that faith remains. The fruit of good works follows the faith. The good works that come from faith do not create faith or membership in the invisible church—they demonstrate its presence. Apples don't make an apple tree; they demonstrate that the tree is an apple tree. Just so, the good works are the result of membership in the invisible church, not the cause of it. Jesus said exactly that: "My sheep listen to my voice; I know them, and they follow me. I give them eternal life, and they shall never perish; no one can snatch them out of my hand" (John 10:27,28). He likewise makes it plain in John 15:1-8. There he tells us that we are clean through his Word and that now as branches in him, the vine, we should bear the fruit of obedience to all of his Word; for through that Word he lives in us, and his life in us will bear fruit in our lives.

Jesus makes a similar point when he compares the kingdom of God to a tiny mustard seed sown in the garden and to yeast that a woman kneads into the dough (Luke 13:18-21). All of the potential of the tiny mustard seed to become a plant big enough to serve as a nest for the birds of the air rests in the seed. Likewise, the ability of the yeast to spread through the dough is in the yeast itself. So it is with the kingdom of God, with the ruling activity of Christ in the hearts of believers by means of the gospel. The whole credit for the ultimate ability of the believer to believe as well as the content of his faith is in the Word. Jesus plants the Word. Jesus causes it to become what the Word says it should become, namely, a living trust in him as Savior. That trust, that faith, then, like yeast may spread more and more through the dough of life. It goes from heart and head to hands and feet. It moves through attitudes and actions that are increasingly influenced and changed by the presence of Christ as Savior ruling in the heart.

In these and so many of Jesus' parables about the kingdom we are brought to marvel that Jesus makes the whole business of his kingdom, of his church, so intimate, so personal. His throne is to be sure high above the highest heavens. Look at the starry sky. Look at it through the most powerful telescope that you can find. He made it all, billions of stars and uncounted galaxies. Beyond all of it, unlimited by time or space, he dwells from eternity to eternity. And yet he descended to become man in the womb of the virgin and to be born in a manger. He humbled himself and became obedient to death, even death on the cross. After all that the sin of the whole human race did do to him, he ascended with his human nature inseparably joined to the divine beyond all space and time. And now that same Jesus does not despise the fallen he came to redeem.

Even to this very moment he is not ashamed to make one heart at a time, one heart after another, his throne room. There he dwells by means of the gospel of his saving work for us and for our salvation. There he lives and reigns, bringing us through each sowing of his Word to trust him and then to continue trusting him as the Savior who paid for our sins before we were ever born or had ever heard of him. There is nothing mechanical or coincidental about it. It is all so personal, all so connected, and connecting from the heart and mouth of Jesus to our hearts and lives, again, one at a time.

He expressed it all so beautifully shortly before he died and rose again to establish the kingdom. He said, "If anyone loves me, he will obey my teaching. My Father will love him, and we will come to him and make our home with him" (John 14:23). Where is that teaching? It is in the means of grace, in his Word and sacraments. Where does the requisite love come from? It comes from that very message of Jesus' love on the cross and at the empty tomb. Could he be more beautiful in his grace? Could his grace in the means of grace be more powerful—we actually believe all of this!?

The church then, again whether viewed from the perspective of the individual or collectively, has this glory: By means of the gospel, the church is the home of God with men, the temple and dwelling place of God our Father and Christ our Savior through the activity of the Holy Spirit working in us by means of the gospel (1 Corinthians 3:16; 2 Corinthians 6:16).

That too is what St. Paul is talking about when he reminds us, "You are all sons of God through faith in Christ Jesus, for all of you who were baptized into Christ have clothed yourselves [better translation: *have been clothed*] with Christ" (Galatians 3:26,27). Thus the church is not an abstraction or just an idea. It finds its reality and its existence in one heart after another, in one born again by water and the Word after another. In the church by means of the gospel, Christ draws near to us, comes to live with and in us, in each of us individually and then in all believers collectively. No one should consider himself alone in the church. No one should consider someone else or some group more the church than himself. The church is a person. The church is people. The church is each one and all who hear his voice and as a result trust him and him alone for salvation.

The point is emphasized to the highest degree when Christ is called not only the king of this spiritual and invisible kingdom but also the head of his mystical body on earth, the church. Could the connection be any closer? He dwells within us by faith. And we are related to him as members of a body are related to the body's head. His thoughts in his Word we want to have as our thoughts—thoughts that govern the activity of our mouths, our hands, and our feet. In sum, we want him to rule over everything that we are and have and hope to be. That's exactly how St. Paul puts it: "Speaking the truth in love, we will in all things grow up into him who is the Head, that is, Christ. From him the whole body, joined and held together by every supporting ligament, grows and builds itself up in love, as each part does its work" (Ephesians 4:15,16). That's the apostle's inspired description of the relationship of all believers to Christ and thus to one another; each believer is connected to every other believer by faith in Christ who is the head of each one and of all together.

As though Christ cannot find enough ways to express his love for and connection to the church, again whether we are speaking of it as individuals or collectively, he also calls the church his bride and himself the Bridegroom. Again, could there be a more beautiful way than that of describing his relationship with each of us? The picture is never one of a marriage that has grown old and tiresome or stale. It is always a picture of an engagement that waits eagerly for the wedding banquet to come in heaven when the church on earth *(the church militant)* will be joined there with him perfectly and forever *(the church triumphant).* The Old Testament frequently speaks of the people of God as the bride and God as the Bridegroom. Much of one whole book deals with the constant love of the Bridegroom even when the bride has shown herself unworthy and unfaithful—the book of Hosea. And both the gospels and the epistles in the New Testament repeat that imagery often (e.g., John 3:29; Matthew 25:1-13; 2 Corinthians 11:2; Revelation 19:7; 21:2,9,10; to mention just a few).

Among the most complete descriptions of the relationship of the church as bride and Christ as Bridegroom is that given by St. Paul in Ephesians 5:22-33. There Paul speaks of the way that marriage is supposed to be on earth by comparing it to the way that the perfect marriage is, the marriage between Christ and the church. Christ gives his all for his bride, does everything for her and in her interest. By all that he has done in his sacrifice of himself for her, he has purified the church, made her spotless and holy with his Word and in the Sacrament of Baptism. His bride, the church, in response gladly submits to him as her head as he speaks to her in his Word. Again, could there be a closer relationship even within an earthly marriage than that which is ours with Christ in the church?

The attributes of the church

And what can we say about that church, the kingdom of God, the body and the bride of Christ, in which Christ rules as Savior through his gospel message? What can we say of this mystical body of which he alone is the head? What are its attributes and characteristics?

The church is one. It is united as the one and only church because the faith in the Savior is one and the same. It doesn't matter where the individual lives or the ages of the many or their gender, their language, their wealth, or their intelligence. It is as St. Paul tells us, "You are . . . fellow citizens with God's people and members of God's household, built on the foundation of the apostles and prophets, with Christ Jesus himself as the chief cornerstone. In him the whole building is joined together and rises to become a holy temple in the Lord. And in him you too are being built together to become a dwelling in which God lives by his Spirit" (Ephesians 2:19-22).

Thus the unity of the church finds its center in Christ, and accordingly, *the church is Christian.* And where do we find Christ? Where does he find us? In the sacred Scriptures of the apostles and prophets of the Old and New Testaments—there and there alone Christ has promised that we will find him. And by means of the gospel in the same Scriptures he finds us. Where Christ is with his gospel, there the church is.

Accordingly, *the church is also apostolic,* since the content of the faith of the church as well as its cause is in the written Word of God, the Bible from the apostles and prophets. Paul emphasizes that unity of the church together with its Christian and apostolic essence when he says, "Make every effort to keep the unity of the Spirit through the bond of peace. There is one body and one Spirit—just as you were called to one hope when you were called—one Lord, one faith, one baptism; one God and Father of all, who is over all and through all and in all" (Ephesians 4:3-6). The essential unity of the church and its Christian and apostolic character are entirely gifts of God. These gifts come from his Spirit, who speaks to us and dwells with us in the Word and sacraments. Thus the faith of the church is not fickle, changing from year to year or generation to generation. The faith is firm and changeless in the deposit of faith handed down to us by Christ through his apostolic Word. It is fidelity to that changeless Word that makes the church *apostolic.*

This essential unity of the church is also expressed when we say that *the church is catholic,* that is, "universal." The church is *catholic,* universal, in the sense expressed by St. Paul. It is everywhere there are people who believe the apostolic message recorded in the Bible. So then the oneness, the essential unity, catholicity, and the apostolic nature of the church is not an organizational unity of a visible institution. It is an invisible unity of a common faith in Christ as Lord and Savior. The center of that creating and sustaining gospel is always in Christ and his work for us.[1]

The existence of the invisible church created and preserved by means of the gospel is really God's answer to Jesus' great High Priestly Prayer on the night before his suffering and death. He prayed: "Holy Father, protect them [i.e., those who would believe the message of the gospel] by the power of your name—the name you gave me [i.e., the name Jesus—the name which means "Savior"]—so that they may be one as we are one" (John 17:11). Again, the unity and the catholicity of the church is not organizational; it is an internal unity of faith in Christ.[2] Christ binds all who believe in him, no matter where they live, what their language is or their age or their gender, with this invisible bond of faith; he binds us to himself and to one another.

Accordingly, it is not up to each member or many members put together to decide what the church believes. Each and every one in the

---

[1]It is a gross misuse of the word *catholic* when the Roman church calls itself "Catholic"; for again, the catholicity of the church is not an organizational unity; even worse it is a misuse of the term since the Roman Catholic Church condemns the very faith in Christ *alone* as Savior, faith which is the very essence of the invisible church.

[2]We have considered it necessary to emphasize this point of internal rather than organizational unity because so many have falsely used this passage to assert that all outward church bodies should merge and become one big organization and so fulfill Jesus' prayer. But Jesus' unity with his Father is one of essence, not organization; so too the unity and oneness of the church is an essential unity of faith in Christ without reference to outward visible organizational form.

invisible church should be most gladly bound to the Word; for in Christ and in his Word alone is the faith and unity of church to be found. Indeed, it should be considered absurd for any member of the church or collection of members to want to come up with their own gospel, given the beauty and the perfection, the saving power and the life giving energy of the only true gospel. It was just with such a perverse absurdity in mind that St. Paul warned the Galatian Christians in the strongest possible terms against tampering with that gospel: "But even if we or an angel from heaven should preach a gospel other than the one we preached to you, let him be eternally condemned" (Galatians 1:8). Again we call to mind the name that Jesus gives to the church when he calls it a kingdom, the kingdom of God; it's not a constitutional monarchy and it's not a democracy; it's an absolute monarchy in which Christ is King and in which he rules by means of his changeless and unerring Word. And for our part, we would not want it any other way!

Because of Christ's redeeming work as its benefit is brought and given to us in the gospel, *the church is holy.* The church, each and every believer, is holy, a saint! Holiness is not something relative; that is, it is not a characteristic that perhaps some have more than others. No, not at all. Either a person is holy or not holy; there is nothing in between. To be holy is to be altogether free from the spot and stain of sin. It is to be rid entirely of guilt.

How can that be, that the church is holy? After all, each Christian must pray daily as Jesus himself taught us to pray: "Forgive us our sins." The church is holy not because her members on earth have gotten to the point where they no longer sin. The church, each believer, is holy because Christ has given us his own holiness in the gospel of full and free forgiveness in the Word and sacraments. As noted earlier, St. Paul sums it up perfectly: "Christ loved the church and gave himself up for her to make her holy, cleansing her by the washing with water through the word, and to present her to himself as a radiant church, without stain or wrinkle or any other blemish, but holy and blameless" (Ephesians 5:25-27). Notice how absolute, how complete the holiness of the church is as Paul describes it here. That church is not just a little bit washed with a slight glimmer. She does not have her stains and wrinkles covered by superficial makeup. No, she is already washed, radiant, wrinkle free, spotless, and holy! As we have noted so often before, Jesus did not just make our holiness possible or our redemption a work in progress. No, he completed our redemption. He accomplished it fully. He won our forgiveness for time and for eternity.

And he gives that forgiveness to us, to each believer, not in part but perfectly in his gospel, the gospel through the means of grace in the Word and the Sacrament of Baptism. Then he continues to confirm his promise and gift of holiness again and again as his gospel of forgiveness is preached and as he gives himself to us in the Sacrament of the Altar. So the entire holiness of the church is always perfect because it rests in Christ and his work, in Christ and his forgiveness, and in Christ and his grace.

Can we not also somehow share by our Christian lives the holiness that is ours perfectly by faith in Christ? Yes, in a certain sense we can. In the same chapter of Ephesians, Paul says, "Be imitators of God, therefore, as dearly loved children and live a life of love, just as Christ loved us and gave himself up for us as a fragrant offering and sacrifice to God" (5:1,2). With lives that submit to the rule of Christ in our hearts, we want to imitate his holiness. We want to live as he lived, a life that is an offering to God made in loving service to one another (Romans 12:1). The works that come from such a faith in life are indeed holy works. They are holy because they are done in imitation of Christ's own holiness. Yes, and chiefly they are holy because whatever fault or sin or stain may unintentionally be attached to those works has been forgiven. Thus, essentially, their holiness is the holiness of works washed just as we have been washed, washed in the blood of Christ, washed by forgiveness in the gospel, in the Word, and in Baptism. What an honor we have, that God should receive our works and declare them both acceptable and holy because they are done in Christ the Savior!

Jesus will show us the importance of those works and his delight in them on the Last Day. In the judgment he holds them up as results of faith, holy results that he treasured and wants the entire world to see. The works are held up as the results of our being the blessed of the Father who has made us holy, heirs of his kingdom, and heirs who then demonstrated that status with corresponding and appropriate works of love (Matthew 25:34-40). Thus the works don't make us holy; rather, we are already holy by virtue of the forgiveness of sins. As God's blessed, forgiven, and holy children we produce works that are holy.

The church is imperishable. It will endure forever. Here on earth and as long as the earth lasts, the church is called the *church militant*. That is, it is a church at war. The warfare is not a warfare like that between visible kingdoms. It is a spiritual warfare. St. Paul tells us that it is a battle against the devil (Ephesians 6:10,11; cf. also 1 Peter 5:8,9). St. John says that our battle is with the allure of the world and the gods of wealth and pleasure; these lie to us with false offers of peace and pleasure in this life. To see their lie, we need only look at the times in life when we have fallen for the lie and brought ourselves to sin by which we did damage to both ourselves and others. Thus, ultimately, the warfare is a battle against our own sinful self (Romans 7:14-16; Galatians 5:17-21).[3]

Jesus assures us that that battle, the battle of the church militant, our battle with the world, will often become violent on the part of the world. For the devil and the world will strive to exterminate the gospel and those who proclaim it (John 15:18-21; Revelation 6:9-11). That violence began shortly after the creation of the world, when Cain murdered Abel (Genesis 4), and has continued to this day. But all of the daunting power of the foes arrayed against us, against the rule of Christ in us, against faith in him and his redeeming work, do not drive us to despair and cannot destroy the church. The weapons at hand for opposing and defeating the powerful alliance of the devil, the world, and our own sinful flesh are greater than the weapons arrayed against us. St. John says that we overcome by faith (1 John 5:4); that is, our triumph, the triumph of the church, is in the continual trust that comes from the Word and sacraments, the trust in Jesus as Savior. The faith thus armed struggles, not alone but with Jesus himself and his Holy Spirit at our side (John 16:33; Romans 8:12-39).

Eventually the battle is over and done with for the individual Christian. Eventually the individual believer in the *church militant* becomes a member of the *church triumphant*. The church triumphant is the church in heaven, where there are no more battles to be fought but rather an unending enjoyment of the victory won for us by Christ in his resurrection from the dead. Jesus spoke of that ultimate and everlasting victory for each believer often in the parables about the kingdom of heaven. Always the picture in those parables is one of victory after struggle. The struggle is a life and death struggle; it is what life is all about for the believer while in this world. At the same time the victory is always and purely a gift of God that is received by all in the church triumphant as a gracious gift which no one could ever deserve, no matter how severe or difficult the struggle on earth (cf. especially each of the parables in Matthew 25 and the song of the saints in heaven in Revelation 19:1-19).

---

[3]For a more complete consideration of the dual nature of the Christian as both saint and sinner at the same time and the struggle between the two that goes on our whole life long, cf. chapters 8, 9.

So we have again the great paradox: Our salvation is altogether a gift of God, but those who refuse the struggle of faith in the church militant eventually cast aside that gift of salvation and lose the goal of eternal life in the church triumphant. However, for those engaged in the struggle, there is the assurance that on Jesus' side there is always the desire and the power to save us and bring us to that blessed and eternal goal (Luke 12:32; John 6:37-40). The confidence of the believer is a confidence in Christ who has already given us eternal life—that life is not a life yet to be won or earned by us but a life assured by Christ's victory for us.

As it is for the invisible church in the individual, so it is for the invisible church collectively. The church collectively also is the church militant on earth and becomes the church triumphant in heaven. The church collectively as the company of believers is *imperishable* and thus will never end. Jesus assures of that when he tells us, "Heaven and earth will pass away, but my words will never pass away" (Matthew 24:35). Already in the Old Testament he promised the same thing many times, most beautifully in Isaiah 55 and Ezekiel 37. To say that the Word will never pass away, that it will always remain and bring forth the fruit of faith, is the same thing as saying that the church on earth will never perish, so long as this world lasts. For that is what the Word does. It creates and sustains faith and it creates and sustains the church on earth, so that the devil, the world, and the flesh of the whole world can never destroy the church founded on Christ, the rock of Peter's confession (Matthew 16:18).

The battle and warfare of the church collectively is essentially no different from the battle and warfare of the church in the individual. It is a spiritual battle, not a battle for physical or worldly power. Indeed, when the church battles for worldly power, it does not act as church and is not the church. The weapons of the church on earth viewed collectively are no different than the weapons of the church on earth in the individual. Jesus said it all in the Great Commission to the church on earth in Matthew 28:18-20. It is the business of the church to preach and teach and administer the sacraments. It is the business of the church to expect opposition and persecution as it does so and as Jesus promised it would. But in it all it is the task of the church to remain faithful to Jesus and to the Word by which he has saved us (John 15). It is not the business of the church to grab for earthly power in order to force faith on people; forced faith is no faith. Only the gospel can create and preserve faith. It is by the preaching of the gospel that the church wages her spiritual war against the devil's attempts to destroy her. And it is with that sword of the gospel that the church remains *imperishable.*

So then, the invisible church is *one, holy, Christian, apostolic, catholic, and imperishable.* As such it is the only saving church. For apart from Christ and from faith in his saving work for us, there is no salvation, just as Jesus himself said (John 3:16-18) and as the church herself has repeated from her Lord down through the ages (Acts 4:12; Philippians 2:10,11; Galatians 1:8,9). The Christian church is accordingly not just one way to heaven among many. It is the only way, just as Jesus is the only Savior, the one true way, truth and life, as he himself testified (John 14:6). How ungrateful, yes how wicked and perverse it would be for those who know the greatness of Christ's love and the beauty with which he has adorned the church to think otherwise of him and his bride! May we never find ourselves in the number of those who abuse Christ and disgrace his bride by thinking or teaching otherwise about him and about her! Rather, may our love for Christ and our devotion to the church, his mystical body on earth and his bride, ever grow as we through Word and sacraments come to know him ever better and cherish his church and kingdom in us ever more faithfully!

The visible church

The invisible church thus defined and described is indeed a wonder, a beautiful miracle of God. Whether we consider it in the individual believer or as the collection of all believers, the church as described in the passages above and in so many others is the living dwelling place of God on earth. It is the beloved bride of Christ; as such it listens to his voice, loves to hear and follow him, and eagerly awaits the day when all believers in heaven will enjoy the never-ending wedding feast. Indeed, the world exists only for the sake of the church, only so long as believers are in it and are yet to be brought into it.

However, if the church is invisible, how can it be found, since we cannot see the faith hidden inside the believers? Though the faith of the church, of believers, cannot be seen, the cause of that faith can be seen. The gospel is preached and the sacraments are administered. That happens in a place, a place that can be seen. It is the use of the gospel means of grace that tells us where the church is to be found, just as Jesus said, "Where two or three come together in my name, there am I with them" (Matthew 18:20). Where is his name, his revelation of himself? Where else but in the means of grace! Thus the means of grace, the gospel in Word and sacraments, is also called the *mark(s) of the church.* As footprints in the sand are marks telling us that someone is nearby, so the presence of the gospel is the mark that tells us that the church is near at hand. Where the gospel is preached and the sacraments administered according to Christ's institution, that is where the church is. We cannot say in how many or in which ones assembled there because, again, faith is invisible. But among those hearing his Word and receiving his sacraments there will be those who hear and receive and believe. God has promised that in Isaiah 55:10-13. The preaching of the gospel is not done in vain; where it is preached in its truth and purity, there God's purpose with the gospel is accomplished, i.e., the church is created and sustained.

The book of Acts from beginning to end is a testimony to the power of the means of grace as the *mark of the church.* For, again, where that gospel was preached, there was Christ, there was the Holy Spirit, and there the church was created and preserved. All of the epistles as well make the same point. Paul so often begins his epistles with an address to the believers, to the saints, in such and such a place. Just exactly who those saints were could not be known by one and by all. But the presence of the gospel guaranteed that there were believers in that place.

Accordingly, *the visible church is the company of those who are gathered around the gospel.* Where the gospel is, there the visible church will also be. Those who are members of the invisible church by faith will almost always be members also of the visible church.[4] Again, that does not mean that all members of the visible church are likewise members of the invisible church. For it is faith in Christ as Savior that makes one a member of the invisible church. That's an important point to keep in mind, lest one falsely imagine, as indeed so many do, that their seat in heaven is secure simply because they belong to a visible church. They make faith in the church a substitute for faith in Christ.

Jesus warned against such a misplaced faith in the strongest possible terms. Consider the rich young man in Matthew 19:16-23. He was outwardly a member of the church, indeed a very good member. But inwardly he worshiped his wealth. Consider the two men who went up to the temple to pray in Luke 18:9-14. Both were members of the visible

---

[4]There may be rare exceptions to the rule that members of the invisible church will also be members of the visible church. It may be that at times some Christians may live isolated from other Christians either because of the outward persecution of the church or because an individual Christian can find no company of believers that holds to all of the truth of God's Word. In such circumstances one may not be able to join a visible church body. Such believers bear a heavy burden indeed when they are unable to encourage the faith of others and be encouraged by the joint use of the means of grace.

church. But one, for all of his outward virtue, did not long for and receive forgiveness. Rather, he trusted in his own merits for his salvation. In John 8:31-47 Jesus confronted those Jews who trusted that their physical descent from Abraham and their outward connection with the people of God made them automatically heirs of the kingdom of heaven.

In so many of his parables about the kingdom of God Jesus warns against a false trust in mere outward association with the gospel, as though just being around the Word of God made one a child of God (e.g., Matthew 21:28–22:14; all of chapter 23; 25:1-30). To put it another way, membership by faith in Christ in the invisible church is what makes us want to belong also to the visible church; it's not membership in the visible church that makes us members of the invisible church, but just the other way around.

It is sad but true that even among those who appear to be the best members of the church, even among pastors and teachers of the church, there are those who are not members of the invisible church. They either are hypocrites or teachers so false in their teaching that they deny the essential elements of the gospel by which alone faith is created and sustained. And so Jesus warns us all to be on our guard against both hypocrisy and faith-denying, faith-killing false doctrine. He could not have said it more clearly or more powerfully than he did in Matthew 7:21-23:

> "Not everyone who says to me, 'Lord, Lord,' will enter the kingdom of heaven, but only he who does the will of my Father who is in heaven. Many will say to me on that day, 'Lord, Lord, did we not prophesy in your name, and in your name drive out demons and perform many miracles?' Then I will tell them plainly, 'I never knew you. Away from me, you evildoers!' "

Precisely because it is possible for people to deceive themselves into thinking that they are members of the invisible church simply because of their outward connection to the visible church body, Peter joins in Jesus' warning against becoming mere mouth-Christians (German: *Maulchristen*) who are devoid of any of the fruits of faith. Such a one, Peter says, "is nearsighted and blind, and has forgotten that he has been cleansed from his past sins. Therefore, my brothers, be all the more eager to make your calling and election sure" (2 Peter 1:9,10). The only way to do that is to remain constant in repentance, which confesses our always-absolute need for our Savior and then in faith trusts in Jesus' perfect life and substitutionary death in payment for our sins. Such a faith will seek to give evidence of its presence in the exercise of a Christian life, in a struggle against sin, and in a devotion to sound doctrine drawn from the Word of God.

To put it another way, the invisible faith will have visible fruit. The appearance of fruit alone does not make one a member of the invisible church; that membership is by faith alone—visible fruit in the hypocrite or the self-deceived is rotten to the core, even though the core cannot be seen, no matter how good it looks on the outside. Nevertheless, it is at the same time true and important that true faith will produce true fruits of faith. As noted earlier, their quality and number may vary, but fruit there will always be.

The importance of the visible church

Thus while membership in the visible church does not make us members of the invisible church, nevertheless membership in the visible church is a matter of great importance to us. For it is in the fellowship of believers that the gospel is heard and that faith is created and preserved. It is in the fellowship of believers, in the visible church, that we share our faith for mutual encouragement and strengthening along life's way. It is in union with the visible church that we carry out the many aspects and facets of Christ's commission to preach the gospel and make disciples of all nations (Matthew 28:18-20).

But there is a problem. There are so many visible organizations and churches that call themselves Christian. How can I know which one to join and support? I can't tell by the faith of the members, because faith is invisible. I can't even tell by the outward holiness or the mere "nice and friendly nature" of the members. Though fruits of faith are always present, it is only faith that makes one a Christian. In Christians the fruit is genuine; in unbelievers it is fruit that only appears genuine.

How then can I decide which visible organization or church to join and support? The determining factor for joining and supporting a visible church is not invisible faith but the visible *confession of faith.* What the church teaches determines whether a church or organization is an orthodox/confessional church or a heterodox/heretical church. The word *orthodox* literally means "straight teaching." The word *heterodox* means "other [than straight] teaching."

It should be the concern of every Christian, indeed it is the obligation of every Christian, to seek a church that confesses only the orthodox/straight teaching taught by the Bible. Jesus tells us, "If you hold to my teaching, you are really my disciples" (John 8:31). And he warns us against having anything to do with false teachers, that is, with those whose teachings are not in accord with and drawn from his Word. He says, "Watch out for false prophets. They come to you in sheep's clothing, but inwardly they are ferocious wolves" (Matthew 7:15). Notice that Jesus' emphasis in this and related passages is on the teaching of the false prophets—not on their zeal or sincerity or even the outward holiness of their lives. The wolf is zealous and sincere in what it does; it does what wolves do. So too the false teacher; he may be very zealous and sincere. However, since he departs from the truth of God's Word, he is to that extent a wolf—he destroys.

St. Paul makes the same point in Romans 16:17,18: "I urge you, brothers, to watch out for those who cause divisions and put obstacles in your way that are contrary to the teaching you have learned. Keep away from them. For such people are not serving our Lord Christ, but their own appetites. By smooth talk and flattery they deceive the minds of naïve people." There is hardly a book in the whole of the Bible that does not make this same point. From beginning to end, the Bible warns us that the world will always be full of false teachers who will deceive the ignorant and the unwary and the doctrinally lazy and indifferent. And at the same time with each mention of false teaching and false teachers comes the earnest warning that St. Paul gives here: Have nothing to do with teachers and teachings that depart from the Word of God.

That the Bible warns so sternly and so often to avoid false doctrine and to cling alone to the true doctrine should surprise no one. After all, correct and pure doctrine is not merely a matter of personal choice or opinion. When it is drawn from God's Word, it comes from God. To contradict God from whatever motive is the highest possible insult to our Creator and our Redeemer. Surely the most basic instinct of the believer should be to shun such an insult to the One who made us and who has given himself on the cross for our redemption.

We are not saying that everyone who holds to a false teaching or even that every false teacher is an unbeliever. We cannot know that. That is for God to judge. For, again, faith is invisible. We are not considering here whether false teachers or their followers are members of the invisible church. We are considering only what we can know and consider; we are considering *the confession of faith,* not faith itself. We take people at their word. If they say that they believe that Christ is the virgin-born Son of God and their only Savior, we believe them. But if at the same time they deny any other doctrines clearly taught by the Word of God, we will warn against the error and do nothing to support them in their error.

Also, we will not want to do anything that might give the impression that denials of God's Word don't matter to God or to us. We will not worship with them nor will we join or support the organization or church that holds to any false doctrine. Jesus' words are plain and clear: "Watch out!" And Paul could not have said it any more sharply: "Keep away from them!" To be sure there may be times when we find ourselves in churches that we know teach false doctrine. We attend or are attendants at weddings in such churches and are present at funerals in them. But we are there as observers, not as worshipers; we do not join in the prayers and hymns but merely observe. We do not receive the sacraments there nor do we support them. With a little bit of thought, that can be done without becoming obnoxious or an arrogant nuisance, while at the same time making a clear confession of devotion to the whole of God's Word.

The Word of God itself forms this mind-set of avoiding heterodox churches and organizations. As well, it stems from our love for God and his Word by which we are saved. How ungrateful it would be of us to say, "Well, I know that such and such a church teaches contrary to the Bible, but that doesn't bother me; after all, it also teaches some things that are good. And besides that the people and preachers there are so nice and so sincere." Christ is the Bridegroom of the church; to be indifferent to false doctrine is to be unfaithful to your Bridegroom. Christ is King; to teach or tolerate false doctrine is in his mind and ought to be in ours an act of rebellion. Christ is the head of his mystical body, which is the church; to be careless about what we preach and teach is to have a spastic body uncontrolled by the head and therefore always dangerous and harmful.

It is not only love for Christ and his Word that compels us to avoid all false worship and joint church work with those who teach false doctrine. It is also an attitude of love to those who may be innocently in error. What would it say to someone in error if we pretended by our joint worship and church work that there really was nothing wrong with false doctrine? Wouldn't such a person in error have every right to conclude that we consider doctrine to be just a matter of personal opinion, that no one is right and no one is wrong? We would confirm the one in error in his error. By refusing to join in worship and church work with those in error we are saying in the most emphatic way we can: Doctrine is serious business; it's not just a matter of opinion or, as the saying goes these days, merely "the faith-tradition" that we prefer. We are not free nor do we want to be free to believe anything apart from God's Word.

Indeed, and to make matters worse, to deny one doctrine is to pave the way for denying every other doctrine, even the central and saving truth that Jesus alone is Savior. For once God's Word has been contradicted on one point there is really no barrier against denying his Word on still other points; indeed, such a growing denial is all but inevitable, as the history of the visible church amply demonstrates. Yes, and ultimately that is the aim of the devil with all false doctrine, to undermine and attack the faith-creating doctrine that Jesus alone is Savior.

Thus there really is no such thing as a little false doctrine any more than there is such a thing as a little bit of poison acceptable in the food we eat. Poison in the food might be just a trace, probably not enough to kill you; however, would you be indifferent to it or offer it to someone? If we are so fussy about poison offered in food for the body, which perishes, one would think that we should be at least as fussy about poison in doctrine that always harms the soul and faith even when it doesn't completely kill it. To be indifferent to false doctrine is like looking at someone blindly stumbling towards the edge of the cliff and remaining silent because he might not fall over it or because we don't want to hurt the blind man's feelings; that would be no act of love to the blind man. Just so, to know that someone—blindly or otherwise—is falling for false doctrine, which is always harmful to faith and may ultimately destroy it, and to pretend that there is no danger is not love. It's indifference. It's cowardice. It's loveless.

That such indifference to pure doctrine will always be a plague in the visible church and that such indifference only leads to ever-greater error and eventually to the loss of the gospel altogether is, as already noted, a truth emphasized often in the Bible and sadly demonstrated in the history of the church. Paul warns against this horrible plague that could be avoided if people would just stay zealous in their learning of and in their faithfulness to the Word of God. Not content with that Word, wanting to pick and choose in it what suits them and then to reject what doesn't suit them, many will have "itching ears," always after something new that they like better than the pure Word (2 Timothy 4:3,4). Peter warns us about that same thing (2 Peter 2). And among Jesus' final words to his church, echoing what he had said at the beginning (John 8:31,32), Jesus warns those who become careless and indifferent with respect to his Word that he will take it away from them if they continue in such indifference (Revelation 3:14-22).

The oft-repeated warnings that God gives us in his Word find an echo in our Lutheran Confessions. Just read the Preface to *The Book of Concord* (Kolb, pp. 1-15). You will see it again and again. There is, on the one hand, the recognition that many in other visible churches are still Christian, in spite of their perhaps innocent or naïve embrace of some false doctrine. But you will see as well, on the other hand, the earnest and zealous desire of the confessional Lutherans to have nothing to do with false doctrine and its supporters, to do everything permissible to warn against and to avoid all such teaching contrary to the pure Word of God.[5]

Yes, indifference to pure doctrine can finally get so bad that those who thought they were Christians, by their holding to false teaching, become what St. John calls "antichrists" (1 John 2:18-23). Compromising and giving up on one doctrine after another, they finally lose Christ himself. But St. John gives us the antidote for such a plague that ultimately kills faith: "See that what you have heard from the beginning remains in you" (v. 24).

The ultimate manifestation of this falling away from Christ that comes when people no longer cherish the Word of God is described for us by St. Paul in 2 Thessalonians 2:1-12. There Paul speaks of the emergence of the one particular Antichrist. He rises from within the visible church. He sets himself up as superior to the Word of God, with the authority to create doctrine opposed to the gospel and to present it as necessary even for salvation. He is splendid in outward forms and appearance, even sometimes able to produce what the apostle calls "counterfeit miracles, signs and wonders." Those will be deceived by the Antichrist who lose their love of the only infallible truth, that revealed in the Bible; those who lose that love will lose also and accordingly their zeal for its pure teaching. They will be dazzled and then blinded by what appears holy instead of by what is holy. Once the Antichrist emerges from within the church, Paul says that he will stay in the outward visible church until Christ himself comes at the end of the world and destroys him. Our Lutheran Confessions have correctly identified the Antichrist as the Roman papacy. For it is only in the Roman papacy that we see in the visible church a man who claims for himself the right to proclaim doctrine, even to condemn the gospel of salvation by grace alone through faith alone.[6]

---

[5]Cf. also, for example, AP XXVIII (pp. 293-294), FC SD XII (pp. 656-660).

[6]Among the most blatant claims of the popes to such authority are those found in the Canons and Decrees of the Council of Trent, the decrees of the First Vatican Council and reaffirmed at the Second Vatican Council. But the claims go back much further than these 16th, 19th, and 20th century councils; by the time of the Reformation it was already abundantly clear that the Roman papacy is the Antichrist spoken of in 2 Thessalonians 2. For confessional Lutherans, the doctrine of the Antichrist is not

It is a scandalous thing to see how careless and cavalier so many who consider themselves Christians are on this whole matter of remaining faithful to all that God has revealed to us in his Word. One sees Christians worshiping even with those who openly deny that Christ is God. There are "services" in which Christians, Muslims, Jews, Buddhists, and Hindus pray together. To whom are they praying? How is that even conceivable, that a Christian would worship with someone who rejects Jesus and his Word, Jesus and his work? Jesus' own words after all are so plain and emphatic and clear. He says, "I am the way and the truth and the life. No one comes to the Father except through me" (John 14:6) and, "If you hold to my teaching, you are really my disciples" (John 8:31) and, "He who does not honor the Son does not honor the Father, who sent him" (John 5:23). St. Paul is likewise emphatic in applying the point: "If anybody is preaching to you a gospel other than what you accepted, let him be eternally condemned!" (Galatians 1:9).

Again, just about every book of the Bible makes exactly the same point. It is no act of love to those whose teachings depart from the Word of God, be it by much or by little, to pretend that such teaching is not an offense to God and harmful to those in such error. Indeed, it would appear that most people are more worried about hurting someone else's feelings than they are about insulting and offending God; they are more concerned about being called narrow-minded than they are about damaging a soul by pretending that error doesn't matter or that ultimately there really is no such thing as error, just different opinions, different "faith traditions."

Again, we are not saying that all false teachers and all those who follow them are unbelievers. That is for God to judge. Even those who are blinded by the Antichrist may by some strange inconsistency still believe that Jesus is their only Savior—not because of but in spite of what the Antichrist teaches. And others otherwise misled likewise may hear the gospel and by its always-miraculous power come to saving faith. Salvation ultimately depends on that gospel message, even when it is proclaimed by those in error, yes, even when it is embraced by those who at the same time hold to teachings that contradict the clear Word of God. But their faith is never the result of false teaching; false teaching can only harm and threaten faith, even when it does not always

---

just historical judgment of the church, it is a doctrine revealed in the Scriptures (e.g., Apology of the Augsburg Confession, Art. XV; Smalcald Articles, the Second Article; Formula of Concord, Solid Declaration, Art. X).

destroy it altogether. Accordingly, St. Paul too rejoiced that even those with mixed motives sometimes managed still to proclaim enough of the gospel for the creation of faith (Philippians 1:15-18), without in the least accepting that it didn't matter what people taught or what they believed or with what motives they proclaimed the gospel.

Our concern, then, is not to judge someone else's faith or lack of faith. That is God's business. But the Scriptures clearly and repeatedly tell us that it is our business to judge doctrine, to judge the confession of faith. Thus, our refusal to engage in joint worship or church work with those in error proceeds from love to God and his Word and love as well for those in error (Ephesians 4:11-15).

While refusing to worship or do church work with those who teach false doctrine, we at the same time want to make a positive confession to the truth of God's Word, whether the false teachers and their adherents will receive it or not. We do that in the humble and sincere confession that we too are sinners and in constant and desperate need of God's mercy and forgiveness. We do it in the full awareness that the truth of God's Word is ours, not because we are better than anyone else; rather, it is precisely because of our always-absolute need of his grace that we cling so tenaciously to all of his Word. For it is by his Word that he shows us his grace in Christ and then through that precious message creates and sustains our faith. We desire nothing more than that we would be faithful to him in his Word and that we might share that Word in all its truth and purity with the whole world. We can imagine no greater hurt or damage to others than to confirm them in error, which is damaging to their soul, whether they recognize that damage or not.

Finally, we will want to join only with those who teach and confess God's Word in all of its truth and purity also out of love for our own souls. For false doctrine and a false fellowship with those who teach it, be it much or little, is always damaging to the soul. It always gets in the way of faith and therefore of our relationship with God. It is, as we have noted so often before, just as God says to us through Isaiah: "This is the one I esteem: he who is humble and contrite in spirit, and trembles at my word" (Isaiah 66:2). To imagine that joining in worship or in the administration of Word and sacraments with those who deny all or parts of God's Word is pleasing to God is a flat denial of all that God himself has to say on the subject. That God would be indifferent to our contradiction of his Word is beyond imagination. It is not a humble and contrite spirit that exalts itself above God's Word and considers itself free to ignore it by little or by much. It is not one who trembles at the Word that joins in worship with those who deny any portion of that holy, precious, and saving Word.

Thus, we will seek to join and associate ourselves only with an orthodox church or religious organization. Such associations may take many forms, but all of the forms will have this in common:

1. They teach and preach the Word of God in all of its truth and purity.
2. They are devoted to all of the doctrines taught in God's Word and confessed in the three creeds and in the six Lutheran Confessions and in such other doctrinal statements, as may be necessary, drawn from the Scriptures and in harmony with the confessions.[7] Such a church will be *orthodox,* that is, teaching only what the Scriptures teach; it will be *confessional,* that is, confessing that the Lutheran Confessions are a correct exposition of the chief doctrines of the Bible; and not least it will also and accordingly be *evangelical,* that is, eager to proclaim to all the world the supremacy of the gospel of forgiveness by grace alone through faith alone in Christ as the center, the heart and the core of the mission of the church. Indeed the greater the devotion to and understanding of the pure gospel, so much the greater should be the zeal to share it!
3. They exercise doctrinal discipline; that is, if a pastor or teacher in their midst is teaching false doctrine, they strive to correct that teacher; should the efforts at correction fail, then such a pastor or teacher must be removed from his office. Among members as well, every effort is made to maintain a correct confession of faith. If members fall into error, every effort is made with the Word of God to correct the error. Should a member refuse the correction of God's Word and continue to cling to and even propagate error, then the member too will lose fellowship with the orthodox church.
4. They exercise as well a godly discipline with respect to the public life of their members. For to openly live in defiance of the Word of God and to impenitently defend one's sins is evidence of unbelief. It is a visible, public denial of faith. If after all warning and urging, the individual continues in impenitence, continues to defend his sin, then excommunication is the only proper, indeed the only

---

[7]For a more thorough consideration of how one should know if his church teaches the Bible in all of its truth and purity, we refer the reader to chapters 3 and 4 of this work; in chapter 4 the role of the creeds and confessions is also considered.

loving thing that the church can do. Jesus says exactly that in Matthew 18:15-20. St. Paul urged the Corinthian Christians to take that responsibility seriously in 1 Corinthians 5. The goal of all such discipline is to show the impenitent how serious his condition is before God, with the prayer that the impenitent will be moved by the law to fear the wrath of God and to long for grace and pardon and renewed fellowship with the bride of Christ. The goal is that the sinner who again longs for forgiveness receives it anew in the proclamation of the gospel. Again it is not love to refuse to exercise such discipline; to ignore or condone an openly rebellious lifestyle is to confirm someone in his error and to share in the responsibility for his ultimate condemnation, as God warned through the prophet Ezekiel (chapter 33).

It should be the serious concern not just of pastors and teachers but of all Christians that they know what their church believes, teaches, and confesses. In the history of the visible church, indifference to sound doctrine and practice, that is to say, indifference to the Word of God itself, inevitably leads to the loss of that precious Word. For so precious to God is his own Word that he will not allow it to be forever taken for granted, then ignored, and ultimately despised. When that happens, sooner or later, he withdraws it—God takes his Word seriously, even when people refuse to! When the pure Word goes, its saving benefit of course will go also. Woe to those who are careless with his Word so precious and life giving! Woe to those through whose indifference faith is threatened and often destroyed! Woe to those who having the pure Word and sacraments consider them nevertheless optional and thereby guarantee their eventual loss! On the contrary, blessed are those who hear the Word of God and keep it (Luke 11:28). Blessed are those who with always repentant and still faithful hearts live to learn it, preserve its saving doctrine in our midst, and share it in its truth and purity with all the world just as Jesus commanded (Matthew 28:18-20).

But still some loudly protest: "We shouldn't be so narrow-minded, so bigoted. After all, look at all the damage that has been caused in the history of the world by religious intolerance! We should therefore let people believe whatever they want to believe, lest we reignite the bloodshed in our society and nation that we have seen so often elsewhere."

We should note in answer that nowhere have we said that people should be forced to believe something that they do not want to believe. A refusal of church fellowship is not a license for violence. Indeed, both the doctrine of the Lutheran church as well as its history make the point: Faith cannot be forced, and no one should ever attempt to force faith or pure doctrine on anyone. Only the gospel can create faith; the sword only creates hypocrites. It is a sad and tragic mark in history that others have tried to force a doctrinal position—invariably a wrong one!—by means of the sword of the state. Both Roman Catholic persecutions of those they considered heretics and equally zealous and often bloody Protestant efforts along the same lines were disgraceful, sinful, and utterly contrary to the Word of God.

But what about orthodox Lutherans when they were in the majority in parts of northern Europe? When they were in the majority, when the rulers themselves were Lutherans, they never started wars or put a knife to anyone's throat to force them to be Lutherans. And that was not because they were indifferent to false doctrine. It was rather because they took the doctrine of the means of grace seriously: Only the gospel can create and sustain faith, and God has given the work of preaching the gospel and preserving sound doctrine to the church—not to the state. A pure doctrinal standard can be gained only by the pure preaching and teaching of God's Word; expulsion from the fellowship of an orthodox, confessional, and evangelical visible church of those who reject the Word is not the same thing at all as launching a Roman inquisition or a Protestant heresy trial followed by a burning at the stake![8]

Indeed, it is evidence of the indifference of so many to the truth of God's Word and the perversity of others that they defend all manner of error and then try to wrap their defense in the mantel of love. Again, it's not love by any proper definition of that word to be indifferent to teachings contrary to the Word of God, teachings which always harm faith and often destroy it.

As for those outside of the church who point to examples of bigotry and persecution as their excuse for despising the visible church and ultimately the gospel itself, one might well point out that if they want examples of bloody persecution, they will find them more readily and abundantly among their fellow unbelievers: Stalin, Hitler, Mao, and

---

[8]Let the reader note again the above referenced Preface to *The Book of Concord*. While the lay authors of the Preface were princes, mayors, and members of city councils in territories that usually had a majority Lutheran population, the closest they came to any restriction on religious liberty was (*1*) the insistence that they would not allow or support false doctrine in their own churches, and (*2*) censorship of books that promoted false doctrine in their territories. While we might not agree with the latter, their position for its day was miles away from the persecutions launched by Catholics and Protestants. They acknowledge already in the Preface that only the Word of God, the means of grace, can convert and preserve the church.

Pol Pot, just to mention a few of the more recent examples, were all unbelievers who loathed the gospel. Each in his turn shed more blood than all of the badly mistaken people put together who called themselves Christians and persecuted those who disagreed with them.[9]

We make the point not to defend persecutions or persecutors but merely to note the intellectual dishonesty or ignorance of those who reject the gospel and a defense of sound doctrine because some abused the gospel and used it as an excuse for violence and bloodshed. The intellectually dishonest and the ignorant are happy to ignore the role of the church, of believers, in feeding the hungry, in building schools and hospitals, in tending to orphans and widows, in counseling the troubled, etc., all of which are consistent with Jesus' love and his assignment to us as Christians (Galatians 6:10). Such works are the constant occupation of those who strive to imitate in life the love of Christ in his life and death for us. But scoffers would much rather focus exclusively on the infrequent and unhappy errors of those who mistakenly thought that it was their assignment to bring by force the kingdom of heaven to earth. They are like the idol worshiper Ahab, who together with his wife, the wicked Jezebel, murdered the faithful prophets in Israel. Then, when the nation suffered the divine consequences of its sins and Ahab met the great prophet Elijah, Ahab greeted him with the words: "Is that you, you troubler of Israel?" (1 Kings 18:17)—as though it was Elijah's fault that God was angry with the nation!

So, then, we will not apologize for holding to the truth of God's Word. Nor will we be ashamed to say in love to God and in love to those in error: "This is what the Lord says!" That is exactly what God himself has called us to do (Ezekiel 2; Luke 9:26; Revelation 22:12-20).

Forms of the visible church

The visible church may take many different forms. There is no one divinely established form for it in the New Testament. *A form of the visible church is any group of Christians that is gathered around the Word of God for the purpose of carrying out one or more of the works enjoined by the Great Commission.* Jesus told his disciples of every age to preach and teach his Word in all of its truth and purity and to make

---

[9]In the interest of historical accuracy but without sufficient time to pursue the point here, we would note at least in passing that most of the so-called religious wars in Christian history had religion as the excuse for the war, not the real reason; religion was the mask behind which the power-hungry and greedy liked to hide.

disciples of all nations. And St. Paul reminds us that as part of that commission we should do good to all as we have opportunity (Galatians 6:10). But no one Christian can do all of that. Indeed, even groupings of Christians in one place at one time will be able to do only some of it. And so Christians gather in many different organizations to perform collectively Jesus' great assignment to his church of every age. To all such groupings of Christians gathered around his Word to carry out one or more aspects of his assignment, Jesus' words apply: "Where two or three come together in my name, there am I with them" (Matthew 18:20). Those who gather together in the name of Jesus are together to hear his Word and to share it. They are gathered together in one way or another to learn/teach his Word in its truth and purity and to carry out one or more of the assignments that Jesus has given to us in his Word.

The most common form for such a gathering in New Testament times has been a local parish or congregation. There God's Word is heard and taught regularly. There public worship services are conducted. There individual believers have the opportunity to confess their sins and receive in the proclamation of the gospel God's grace heaped upon grace. There the faithful encourage one another with their joint confession of faith. There the Sacrament of Baptism and the Sacrament of the Altar are regularly administered. There children are instructed. There the erring are corrected and the weak strengthened. There those firm in faith are encouraged to grow in love and grace. There the group shares the gospel with the community. There the sick are visited, the poor helped, the troubled counseled, and the aged prepared for their entry into heaven.

Even the most energetic of local parishes by itself will not be able to carry out all of the works assigned to the church. The church needs to train pastors and teachers. The church needs to carry the gospel to the far corners of the world where it has not been heard. The members in a local parish want to encourage their fellow believers around the world who may need their support with pastors and teachers trained here or with financial assistance in the training of their own pastors and teachers. Few parishes alone are able to aid as they might like those suffering from earthquakes and storms. Few are capable of helping to take care of the aged with homes designed especially for their needs.

To help one another in doing these things, local congregations join together around the gospel to form a synod. The synod isn't divinely instituted, any more than the local parish is. The invisible church is divinely instituted, but its visible forms are created by believers gathered around the Word and sacraments to do what Christ bids us do in his Word. And so parishes are formed and synods established. Through this banding together, groups of congregations "walk together" (the word *synod* in its Greek root means "a walking together") to build schools for the important work of training pastors and teachers and for sending out and supporting missionaries in our nation and around the world.

In a given region of the country, in addition to membership in the synod, individuals or congregations may join together to establish a grade school, an area Lutheran high school, or such other institutions of learning as the faithful in that area may consider useful. They may join together in associations for helping the aged and for counseling those whose needs are greater than can be supplied by the local congregation or the parish pastor.

In one way or another, all of these are striving directly or indirectly to carry the gospel to every creature. And to that extent each of them is a church, that is, a visible institution formed by Christians gathered around the Word of God to do what God's Word bids us do with his Word. Those supporting Christian schools and Christian social service organizations recognize that in the world there are many organizations that provide education to the young and help for the needy. But often such organizations do so with a decidedly un- or even anti-Christian worldview. So it is understandable that Christians would want to reflect their faith and their love for Christ and for one another by providing such services in a manner consistent with and reflecting the truths of the gospel.

It is because these various organizations and institutions are gathered about the Word of God for the purpose of sharing the gospel that they fit the definition of a visible church. That is so, even though the work of a school or of a social service organization is limited. Again, even the work of a local congregation is limited—no one congregation can do alone all that Christ has given us to do in the sharing of the gospel with the world and in demonstrating Christian love to the world and to one another.

It is a beautiful thing to see in the visible church that many people are devoted to the work of their local parish and then to that as well of the synod and other institutions that share with them an orthodox confession of faith. It is likewise a beautiful thing to see with what harmony all of these various organizations can work together. Each does what it has been established to do and that with respect for the work that other forms of the visible church have been established to do. The congregations and their pastors appreciate and support the work of their schools. The teachers in the schools carry out their specific and blessed assignment of teaching those entrusted to their care; however, they do not imagine that they are independent of their pastors' responsibilities and their need for the congregations' support. The social service agencies do not interfere or compete with the work of the congregation but understand that they supplement it. The missions of the church do not demand that education be neglected so that only missions are established. The schools do not insist that all resources be devoted to education. The missions of the church understand the need for trained pastors and teachers that the schools are best suited to provide. And those who prepare pastors and teachers prepare them for the whole mission of the church. Again, it is a beautiful thing and one for which we give thanks to God when it all comes together!

The universal priesthood of all believers

In the Old Testament, a sharp distinction was made between the priests and Levites, on the one hand, who served full time in the service of the church and everyone else on the other hand. The priests especially were to depict in their whole life and work the life and work of the Great High Priest to come, Jesus Christ.[10] But the visible church in the New Testament has no divinely instituted priestly caste. That is, Christians should not be separated into a ruling class of clergy and then a second rate class of laity or—which is just as bad—a ruling class of laity and an employee class of hireling clergy. St. Peter summed up best the way things should be in the church when he wrote the *sedes doctrinae* for *the doctrine of the universal priesthood of all believers.* Peter is addressing each and every Christian when he writes, "You are a chosen people, a royal priesthood, a holy nation, a people belonging to God, that you may declare the praises of him who called you out of darkness into his wonderful light" (1 Peter 2:9).

Each phrase in this beautiful passage is highly significant. In the Old Testament the chosen people were the descendants of Abraham, Isaac, and Jacob. The royal house was the family of King David, from the tribe of Judah. The priestly family was from the tribe of Levi and the priests from that tribe came only from the descendants of Aaron. The nation was holy because God had chosen to reveal to it his rich promises of the Savior who would be King over all the earth, descended

---

[10]For a consideration of the Old Testament priesthood and its function as a picture of Christ's Great High Priestly office, cf. chapter 11.

from royal David's line. He would be Priest as well, the one who would fulfill by his sacrifice of himself all of the sacrifices that foretold his one great sacrifice—a theme carried forward especially in the epistle to the Hebrews in the New Testament.

But now believers are the chosen people, called by the gospel and chosen from every nation on earth. Because of Christ the King, they are a nation of kings; that is, Christ rules all things in heaven and on earth for their benefit and in their interest (Ephesians 1:22). Each of these believer-kings in the New Testament church is also a priest before God. It is the work of priests to offer sacrifices and to intercede before the throne of God for others. Christ offered the sacrifice that redeemed them, and now as priests they offer the sacrifice of their bodies and of their prayers in praise and thanksgiving and intercession as a fitting response to his sacrifice for their redemption (Romans 12:1). The position of king and priest is no longer separated as it was in the Old Testament times. As royal priests, each and every one of them is equally a part of this holy nation, made holy by the message of forgiveness won by Christ on the cross. And each and every one as an equal member of this holy nation of believers shows forth the praises of God in word and work during his time of grace on earth.

What does it mean to show forth the praises of God? What else but to reflect in their lives their gratitude for the message of the gospel. As their lives reflect their devotion to the Word of God, Christians especially long to show forth God's praises as they share the good news of forgiveness and salvation with one another and with the world! For God is praised most fully and best when the work of his Son is shared again and again with one and all. Children do that when they forgive one another and even their parents. Women do it when they forgive their husbands and their children. Husbands do it when they forgive their wives and children. Each in his turn does it as each in turn shares the message of the gospel with those close at hand, with friends and relatives as opportunity presents itself, and with the world in union with the orthodox church.

It is that work of sharing the gospel with one another that Jesus gave to the church as a whole and to each member of it when he said to his disciples after his resurrection, "Receive the Holy Spirit. If you forgive anyone his sins, they are forgiven; if you do not forgive them, they are not forgiven" (John 20:22,23; cf. also Matthew 16:19). He had earlier explained whose sins should be forgiven and whose not forgiven. Those to be forgiven were those who confessed their sin and repented; those who refused to repent and who instead defended their sin should not be forgiven but should be counted as unbelievers (Matthew 18:15-22).

That all are priests and all should share this gospel of forgiveness, that this is not a work reserved for some priestly caste, Paul demonstrated in 1 and 2 Corinthians. In 1 Corinthians he complained that the members of the church there had neglected their priestly role by tolerating the open sins of an impenitent member (1 Corinthians 5). Then in 2 Corinthians 2:5-11 he urged the members to forgive this same person who had now come to repentance. Paul forgave the man too. But that was not just Paul's business alone. The forgiveness of the other priests, that is, of the members of that man's own church, was an important work that he urged the members to perform. Thus all Christians have this great priestly work to perform, to forgive sins and otherwise as well to share the gospel. Exactly that is what Jesus has told each of us already in the Lord's Prayer when he teaches us to pray: "Forgive us our sins, *for we also forgive* everyone who sins against us" (Luke 11:4). St. James considers it the constant work of Christians to confess and to forgive one another, to pray for one another, to help one another in time of need (James 5:16)—in a word, to live and act as priests.

For priests there is no assignment greater than that of imitating Christ, the Great High Priest, in granting forgiveness as freely as he has granted it to us in the gospel. And there is no greater honor than to serve in love those Christ gives kingly-priests the opportunity to serve, be they friends or those who count us as enemies (Matthew 5:43-48; Romans 12). Jesus shows us the nobility and the importance of just such an imitation of his own royal work in the parable of the king who forgave with the expectation that the one forgiven would also forgive. Indeed, he warns against any refusal on our part to act as royal priests (Matthew 18:23-35).

Let each then treasure his high and exalted position as a king and priest before God and exercise most gladly the greatest work that Christ has given him to do, namely, to act as a royal priest in sharing the gospel of forgiveness and then in living a life of service that reflects the love of Christ our Savior. Again, that is the role and the highest office of every Christian, man and woman, adult and child.

So then in sum, we see that the very title given to this doctrine virtually defines it. It is the doctrine of *the universal priesthood of all believers;* that is, each and every believer, young and old, men and women, all alike are kings and priests before God, entrusted with the keys of the kingdom of heaven (cf. Luther's Small Catechism, Fifth

Chief Part). They unlock heaven as they carry out their royal and priestly functions of forgiving one another and sharing the message of that forgiveness with one another and the world.

The holy office of the ministry

What then is the role of the pastors and teachers of the church if all are called to be and are actually royal priests before God and in the world? If each should share the gospel by teaching it to those who have and who have it not, and if all are to forgive regardless of their station in life, then what need is there for those designated as "called workers" in the church?

The doctrine of the universal priesthood of all believers has standing next to it the doctrine of *the holy office of the ministry.* This doctrine too is as self-defining in its title as is the doctrine of the universal priesthood of all believers. These two doctrines do not conflict with or contradict each other. Quite the contrary, each doctrine supports the other.

What then is the holy office of the ministry? It is first and foremost a *ministry.* The word means "service." St. Paul understood that so well and taught it by example in all of his work and in all of his epistles. Again and again he refers to himself as a servant of the gospel and as a servant with the gospel (e.g., 1 Corinthians 3:5; 2 Corinthians 4:5,6). Chiefly then, those called to the holy office of the ministry are the servants of Christ. They serve him when they serve the church with the gospel entrusted to them. For even though all are priests, not all are equally equipped for the work, the service, of thoroughly instructing their fellow priests and publicly administering Word and sacraments in the name of Christ and in behalf of fellow believers. Paul acknowledged that too (1 Corinthians 4; 12:29). Precisely for that reason Christ himself has given us the holy office of the ministry. The pastors and teachers of the church are God's gifts to us. They serve him by serving us with their teaching and public preaching of the Word of God and the administration of the sacraments. St. Paul said it most completely in Ephesians 4. The entire chapter is rich in instruction about this ministry and its connection to the whole of the church. We make special reference to verses 11-13 as the sum of it all. St. Paul, speaking of the ascended Christ, says:

> It was he who gave some to be apostles, some to be prophets, some to be evangelists, and some to be pastors and teachers, to prepare God's people for works of service, so that the body of Christ may be built up until we all reach unity in the faith and in the knowl-

edge of the Son of God and become mature, attaining to the whole measure of the fullness of Christ.

As noted earlier, there is no one divinely instituted form for the visible church. Likewise, we may conclude from Paul's words here that there is no one divinely instituted form for the ministry either. The important and necessary element of the ministry is that it deals with public preaching or teaching of the Word of God and often with that the public administration of the sacraments for the building up of the church. That takes place in the local congregation most commonly through the office of the parish pastor. The pastor conducts the regular worship services of the church. He teaches the Word of God to young and old. He administers publicly the sacraments of Baptism and Holy Communion. He hears as needed the private confessions of members needing special counsel from the Word of God for their lives and consciences. He visits the flock entrusted to his care and spiritual oversight, especially the sick and those preparing for death.

The holy office of the ministry, likewise, is found in schools established by the church for the sharing of the gospel with the young, for the training of still others for civil vocations, or for the advanced training of those who may become pastors and teachers of the church. In the schools and in other forms of the visible church, workers have been called to publicly carry out the work for which that particular institution was established.

Again, the ministers of the church serve. They belong to Christ and are given by Christ to the church to serve him by serving us with the Word. One of the best definitions of the ministers of the church and their relationship to the rest of the church is that *they are the servants of Christ in the midst of the people of God*. Thus, people are not free to tell them to teach or preach anything other than or contrary to the Word of God. Indeed, the reverse is true. Were they to preach or teach contrary to the Word of God, they would be rebellious servants; they would be acting as tyrants striving to impose their own will on God's royal priests. They should be removed by those they had been called to serve.

Therefore, at the public ordination or installation of the called servants of the church we expect them to take a solemn oath of loyalty to all of God's Word and to its correct understanding as we have it summarized in the Lutheran Confessions. And on our part when we issue the call to those who serve, we make it clear in the call that that is exactly what we expect of them—we will not require them to depart from that standard for their preaching or teaching or for the carrying out of any of the other responsibilities of their office.

Paul emphasized that role of the public ministers of the church as servants of Christ who belong to Christ and are sent by him to serve God's people with the pure Word. In his farewell address to the pastors and teachers of the church at Ephesus, he reminded them of how he had carried out the ministry entrusted to him and urged them to follow his example. He especially urged them to remember that they had their office from the Holy Spirit. He said:

> I have not hesitated to proclaim to you the whole will of God. Keep watch over yourselves and all the flock of which the Holy Spirit has made you overseers. Be shepherds of the church of God, which he bought with his own blood. I know that after I leave, savage wolves will come in among you and will not spare the flock. . . . So be on your guard! (Acts 20:27-31)

He urged these same things on the pastors that he had trained (cf. especially 1 and 2 Timothy and Titus).

St. Peter too reminds the public ministers of the church that their role is one of service to God in the service of his people. At the same time he sums up well the relationship between the public ministers of the church and those they serve. He tells them, "Be shepherds of God's flock that is under your care, serving as overseers—not because you must, but because you are willing, as God wants you to be; not greedy for money, but eager to serve; not lording it over those entrusted to you, but being examples to the flock" (1 Peter 5:2,3). Thus, just as the ministers of the church are not hired hands who have come to do the arbitrary bidding of members, so too they are not lords set over the church to dictate to its members as they see fit and apart from the Word of God. No, their service is patterned after the service of Christ himself. As he came to be the lowliest of the low, even to wash the feet of the disciples, so they too would be sent for service. The hallmark of that service is faithfulness to him and an eagerness to spend and be spent in the service of his people (Matthew 20:24-28; Mark 10:45; John 13:1-17).

The ministry is called an *office.* That word is to remind us that the public ministers of the church are not such simply because that's what they decided they wanted to be as the result of some sort of supposed "inner call." An office is a position into which one is placed by someone else. The public ministers of the church do not appoint themselves. As already noted, they are gifts of God to the church. They become his gifts and they enter into the office of the ministry by a *call.* When we speak of the call into the office of the ministry, we are not speaking of some fluttering in the heart of the individual by which he all by himself thinks that he is or should be a pastor or teacher of the church.

To be sure, the public servants of the church during their lives were moved by the gospel to desire such service. Paul says that that desire is a good work (1 Timothy 3:1). But the desire alone is not a call and does not make one a pastor or teacher of men and women in the church. Paul tells us that those who desire that noble task should have certain characteristics. They should be mature men, able to teach, of upright character and reputation, not new to the faith but experienced in Christian doctrine and life (1 Timothy 2,3; 5:22; Titus 1:5-9).

Who should decide when one has these characteristics sufficient to the task of being a pastor or teacher of the church if the decision is not just that of the individual through some sort of "inner call"? Already in Paul's day the church itself decided who should serve in the office of the ministry. Thus, the call comes *from Christ through the church.* The church has various ways of extending its call. Sometimes Paul himself chose workers to accompany him. But where the church was already established, such a decision was not without the mind and consent and will of the church itself. We see that already in Acts 6. When the church needed additional forms of the ministry to meet the needs of the church in Jerusalem, the church itself called those who would serve. We see it as well when Paul began his missionary journeys. He was sent out from the church at Antioch. The Holy Spirit worked directly but also through the members of the church (Acts 13:1-3). In Acts 14,15 we note a whole range of actions taken by Paul and by the church as a whole in selecting those who should serve publicly in one form or another of the ministry.

Thus no one becomes a public minister of the gospel apart from the call of Christ, which since the time of the apostles normally comes through the visible church. That call may be extended in various ways, as it was in the book of Acts. There is no divinely prescribed way of doing it. Because of that reason the church has a considerable range of freedom in setting up calling procedure. Whatever the procedure, due respect and reverence for both the universal priesthood of all believers and for the holy office of the ministry itself needs to be exercised. Among procedures common in our day, for example, is that of officials of the church taking responsibility for assigning candidates for the preaching and teaching ministry; they do that with the consent of the church and only after the candidates have been certified by the training system for pastors and teachers as fit for the ministry. Even then, the call is considered as coming primarily from Christ through those they are being called to serve.

After that initial call, pastors and teachers may move from one area of service to another. But that is always and alone by the call of the parish, the school, or the organization that they are to serve. It should never be through the ambition and the manipulation of a call by the servant—"campaigning for a call"—to another specific school or congregation that the servant thinks he deserves more than the field of service already entrusted to him. Such campaigning by the servant is sacrilege and a serious sin indeed. The call is to be considered a "divine call," because it comes from Christ through his church to do Christ's work in the midst of Christ's people.

It is this whole matter of the call that keeps us from speaking of called workers as employees. Again, they belong to and are sent to us by Christ and that through the church. So the church, God's royal priests, considers the needs of the church and formulates a call for a worker that can help satisfy those specific needs. Once a called worker receives and accepts the call, the worker will not be considered as "hired" but as called by Christ through the church.

The church receives called workers as gifts of the Savior. As such they deserve obedience to the Word of God, which they bring, as well respect and honor, as Jesus said in Luke 10:16 (cf. also Hebrews 13:17 and 1 Timothy 5:17). As the church does not hire the worker but calls Christ's servants, so too the church does not fire workers either. To be sure, a worker may be removed if guilty of teaching false doctrine or of leading a life that brings the gospel into disgrace. Such a removal would be a mark of faithfulness to the Word of God and to what God requires in his Word of his public servants.

Additionally, it may happen that a worker is asked to resign or a call is revoked if the worker clearly is no longer able because of age or illness or required ability to carry out the work needed. In some instances a call may be revoked if the needs of the church change—e.g., the school is closed or the parish no longer needs two pastors. But in all such cases, the greatest care needs to be taken that both the servants of the church and those they serve are respectful of the truth that the holy office of the ministry is not merely a human arrangement for the convenience of either the worker or those who called him. It is ungrateful sacrilege indeed to simply throw God's gifts to the curb, so to speak; to treat them with disrespect is to treat the one who gave and sent them with disrespect.

Likewise, the worker needs to remember that he exists for the call, not the call for him—as though he was entitled to it and could hang on to it forever even if his service was no longer needed or he was no longer able to provide the service required. Both the servant and those served need to remember that the work and the worker belong first to Christ. Both the worker and the church need to remember who really owns both the call and the worker.

God himself in his Word sets the qualifications for the public ministers of the church. Those who publicly and in the name of Christ and the church lead in worship and in teaching in the church need to meet those qualifications established particularly in the passages from 1, 2 Timothy and Titus cited previously.

If the call is for the parish pastorate or for the teaching of the church as a whole, the call is reserved for men. That is not because men are somehow better than women. Nor is it because there are not women who could perhaps do much of the work as well or in some cases even better than some men. It is because it is the will and the Word of God that has reserved the role of headship for men (1 Timothy 2:12). Where the role of headship over men is not at issue, there women also serve in the holy office of the ministry, as they do most blessedly in our school system or in positions where they serve other women. However, "women pastors" is a contradiction in terms; it is only possible where the Word of God has been deliberately set aside by women and by those who have asked for their service in a role that God has not assigned to them.

The practice that allows only men to serve in certain forms of the public ministry is certainly not popular in our day. But we are obliged to bring all into subjection to the Word of God (2 Corinthians 10:4,5). Again, God ordains the holy office of the ministry. It is a service that he has instituted and established, as Paul makes so clear in Ephesians 4 and elsewhere. As such God alone has the right to prescribe who should serve in it and under what conditions.

To be sure, there were rare occasions in the Bible when God himself chose a woman to be his special messenger (e.g., Exodus 15; Judges 4,5; 2 Kings 22; Luke 2:36-38). But it is worthy of note that in at least some of these instances, men had to a considerable extent become unfaithful to the Word of God. In the process, they had given up their responsibility to be leaders among God's people. That God picked these faithful women was a great honor to them, and just as much, it was a rebuke to the men. It is further worth noting that God can do just as he pleases in picking directly such individuals as he wants to serve him in some particular circumstance; but that doesn't mean that we can do just as we please. To put it another way: God is never bound, but we are bound to his revealed Word. Nor will we rebelliously grumble about it!

We can speak of two kinds of calls to the holy ministry. The one is an *immediate* call. An immediate call is one that comes directly from God without the activity of the church. Such were the calls of the apostles and prophets in the Bible. But even in biblical times such calls were rare and the exception. Since the time of the apostles we do not expect God to act apart from the church. That is so, both because he hasn't done so for a very long time nor did he ever promise that he would always do so. In fact, since the days of the apostles those who claimed to have an immediate call were most often, if not always, heretics. And, second, we do not expect it because the books of the Bible have been completed; immediate calls came at times when the revelation of God was not yet complete. Now that we have all that God has promised to reveal, we normally expect him to extend *mediate* calls; that is, the call comes through the church. Indeed, we have it as a principle that no one should serve in the public ministry of the church without a call from the church.[11]

Again, just as there is no one divinely instituted form of the visible church in the New Testament, so also there is no one divinely instituted form for the holy office of the ministry. Just as today the local congregation or parish may well carry out more functions of Christ's assignment to the church than any other form, so also the office of the parish pastor today may exercise more functions of the holy office of the ministry than any other form of the office does. But the schools of the church and such other organizations as have been established to carry out one or more aspects of Christ's assignment to the church are "church." So also are those who are called publicly to serve in these institutions in the holy office of the ministry.

The various forms of the visible church then with a careful mind and eye on the Word of God call servants of the church to represent themselves and most of all to represent Christ. Christ's people must see to it that the called workers have been properly trained for the work they seek to do with and through the called worker. They make sure that the worker has pledged faithfulness to the Scriptures and the confessions. They determine that the worker is of good public reputation and character. And then, asking the blessing of God on their deliberations, they extend a formal and public call to the worker. They will outline in the call the work they expect the servant of the church to carry out.

---

[11]Cf. especially the Augsburg Confession, Art. V (p. 40), XIV (p. 46), XVIII (p. 92); The Apology, Art. VII, VIII (p. 178), XIII (p. 220), XIV (pp. 222,223); Formula of Concord, SD, Art. II (p. 551).

When the servant of the church receives such a call, he receives it as *from Christ through the church.* With the receipt of the call, the one who is already serving the church as pastor or teacher or in some other capacity as a called worker must reckon with the fact that he now has two divine calls—the one to the place where he is already serving and the other to a new field of service. There is no divinely prescribed pattern that the worker must use in deciding between two calls, both of which have Christ as their ultimate source. Christ is giving the worker a choice to make. The worker will bow low in prayer and ask the Lord of the church to bless his consideration of the two calls. The called servant will seek the advice of other pastors or teachers or officials of the church. He will certainly look for counsel from both calling bodies. And then he will decide where he considers it in the best interest of the church that he serve.

It is not possible here to list all of the factors that may go into the consideration of a call. It is enough to say that it should all be done with prayer and with reverence for Christ and his Word and his church; it should all be done with as realistic as possible an appraisal of the servant's own gifts and abilities and how they match the needs of the calling bodies (an appraisal best done with the advice of coworkers who probably know him better than he thinks!). And as well it should be done with an awareness of his own legitimate needs and those of the family that the Lord has given him.

The one who has such a call is by virtue of that call in the *holy* office of the ministry. It is a holy office because the work is holy and because those the worker is called to serve are also holy—royal priests before God and in the world. The office is the high and noble one, and there can be no greater honor than to serve in it. Again, and it is worth emphasizing, those properly called and serving in the holy office of the ministry should be received with respect (1 Timothy 5:17; Hebrews 13:17). The Holy Spirit has sent them (Acts 20:28). And it is as Jesus said: When we receive those he has sent to serve us, we are receiving him (Matthew 10:40; John 13:20). They are his special gifts for the building up of our faith, given to assist us in drawing ever closer to Jesus and closer to his Word (Ephesians 4:11-13). Like the rest of us, they too are sinners always in desperate need of grace; indeed they should be more aware of that than anyone else precisely because of their constant occupation with the Word of God. And it should be their appreciation for grace and forgiveness given by Christ so freely to them that they serve with love and devotion both Christ and those who have called them.

As there is no higher office in the world, at the same time it is the lowliest office in the world. For those who occupy it have as their greatest ambition that they should be the servants of the servants of God. That's what Jesus gave them as their highest goal (Matthew 20:26; 23:11). Moreover, whatever gifts they possess that make them useful tools of the Holy Spirit are just that—gifts. They have their entire fitness for this holy office and whatever success they may find in it as a most generous gift from Christ their Savior, as St. Paul most beautifully describes in 2 Corinthians 3,4. Yes, and it is this very lowliness that is the servant's greatest joy, besides the joy that he has in his own salvation through the gospel. For the faithful servant is not responsible for creating either the message or its success. The message is entirely that of the master. And so too is the success. The joy of the servant is the glory of Christ and the honor that he has of proclaiming that glory in the gospel.

If the faithful messenger is rejected, it is because those rejecting the messenger despise the Savior who gave the message. Rejection there will often be (Matthew 10:24; John 13:16). That is, however, not a cause for despair, painful though it be; for just such rejection is what Christ promised and what his faithful servants have expected and often received (Acts 5:4-42; 7:54-60; 9:16).

The difficulties of the holy office of the ministry are more than compensated by its joys. The servant of the Word grows as he shares it and is assured that his faithfulness will bear most blessed fruit. God promised that and he does not lie. He has promised it over and over again since the days of the prophets (e.g., Isaiah 55:11). Even the prophets who had the most difficult ministry of all rejoiced in the mercy of God that they had received and that they had to share, even when it seemed that no one was listening (1 Kings 19:18; Lamentations 3:21-23). Indeed, when their master thinks they need it most, he will give them even outward evidence that their service has not been in vain. Paul with all his trials and tribulations, many of them caused by those he had served, also experienced the love and the devotion that so many had for him (e.g., Acts 20:36–21:16).

In sum, no one benefits more from service to the Savior and his people than the one whose life is devoted to the service of the Savior and his people. In difficult days the servant learns to trust the promises of the master. In days of success the servant gets to see the Savior glorified through work that God has deigned to give to the lowliest of the low.

So then, we receive with joy and thanksgiving the gifts of God to us all. Those gifts most precious are the gift of salvation, the gift of this exalted station that we are a chosen people, a royal priesthood, a holy nation chosen to show forth the praises of our Redeemer. And we as well receive with thanksgiving and honor those who he so generously gives to us for the building up of our most holy faith. It is a beautiful and wondrous thing: God gives the gospel means of grace; through the gospel means of grace he creates the church, this royal priesthood; through his church, his royal priests, he calls workers to the holy office of the ministry; through their service with the means of grace he continues to build his church, to call and build up other royal priests. It is one grand circle by which God is glorified in the world, souls are rescued from the jaws of the devil, and the church marches on from the church militant on earth to the church triumphant in heaven.

The church—how God, the means of grace, the doctrine of the universal priesthood of all believers, and the holy office of the ministry are connected.

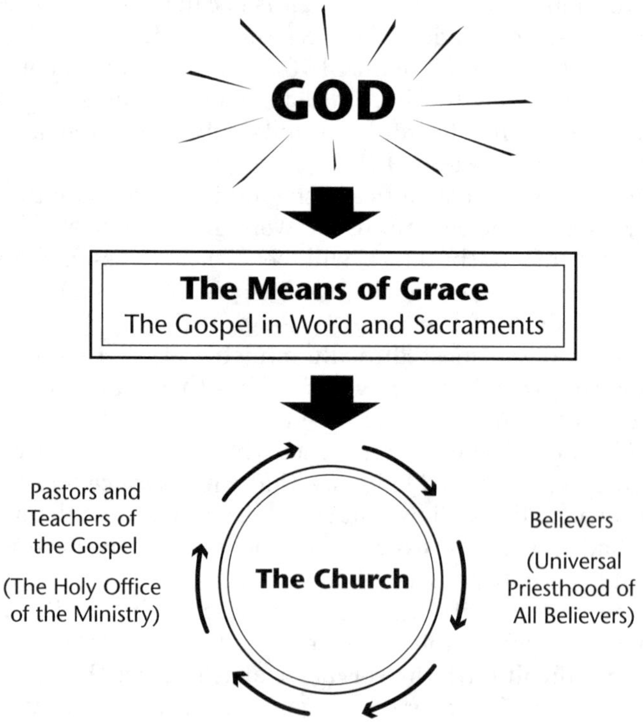

God, by means of the gospel in Word and Sacraments, creates the church in which all are priests and some are called ministers of the gospel; in the church the preaching and teaching of the gospel and the administration of the sacraments "creates" believers, i.e., more members of the universal priesthood of all believers; Christ through the believers calls pastors and teachers to proclaim the gospel; thus each is the cause of the other.

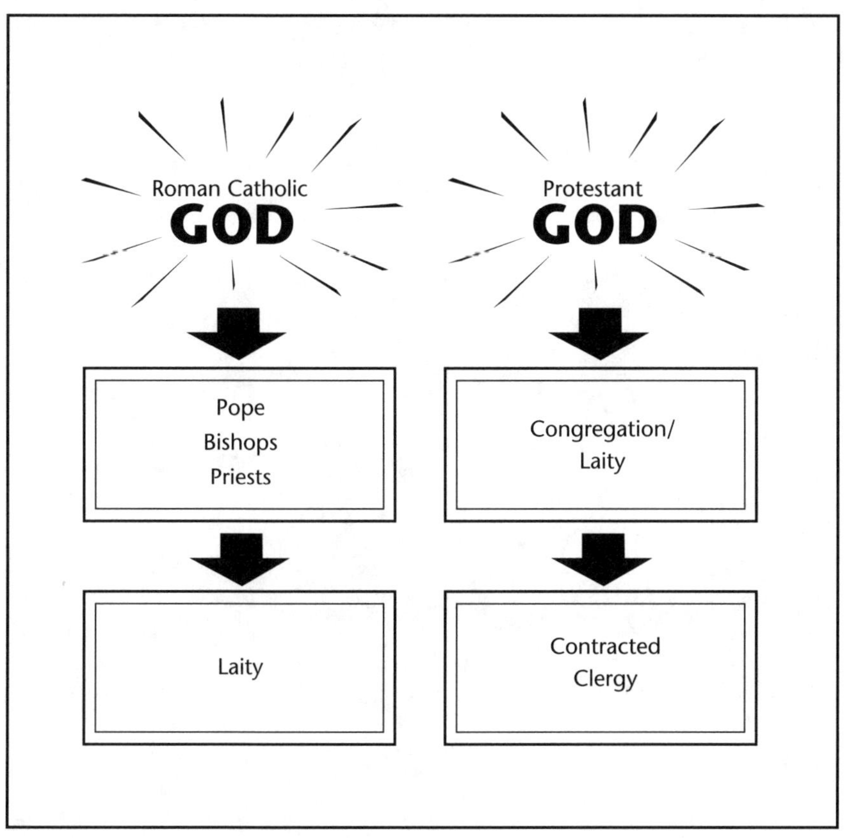
Roman Catholic
GOD
Pope
Bishops
Priests
Laity
Protestant
GOD
Congregation/
Laity
Contracted
Clergy

Chapter 16
The Christian Life

At the beginning of the last chapter we noted that the doctrine of the church and all that has to do with the church is inseparably connected to the doctrine of the means of grace. It is the gospel means of grace that creates the church and preserves it. And it is the one great purpose of the church thus created by the gospel to cherish that gospel and to teach and share it in all of its truth and purity. It is likewise the goal of the church in proclaiming God's Word to teach us how God wants us to live. For the Word of God is not just head teaching; it is teaching that informs and guides all of life. Indeed, St. Paul tells us that God's goal in redeeming us is that we should live lives filled with good works:

> [The grace of God] teaches us to say "No" to ungodliness and worldly passions, and to live self-controlled, upright and godly lives in this present age, while we wait for the blessed hope—the glorious appearing of our great God and Savior, Jesus Christ, who gave himself for us to redeem us from all wickedness and to purify for himself a people that are his very own, eager to do what is good. (Titus 2:12-14)

In this chapter we will focus our attention on the Christian life that follows and flows from our gospel-created faith. At once we see again the inseparable and intimate connection with the gospel. It is the gospel that creates faith, and from the gospel must flow all that is God-pleasing as a result of the faith created.

The doctrine of the Christian life is often referred to as *sanctification.* The word *sanctification* means "a holy life." The word is used in both a broad and narrow sense. In the broad sense, sanctification is everything that has to do with a holy life, from its creation at conversion up to the hour of death and the Christian's transfer from the church on earth to the church in heaven. In this chapter, however, we will be considering the doctrine of *sanctification in the narrow sense* of the word. In the narrow sense, sanctification is the Christian life that one leads as a result of conversion, as a fruit of faith.

At the very beginning it is important to note the significant differences between sanctification in the narrow sense on the one hand and *justification* on the other hand. In justification, in all that has to do with coming to faith and gaining heaven, people are passive. That is to say, we do not cooperate with God in our justification and coming to faith; that is entirely God's work in Christ and by means of the gospel (cf. chapter 13). In sanctification in the narrow sense, in the Christian life that follows faith, there is a certain cooperation between God and the Christian. In sum it works this way:

God	The Christian
1. At conversion God gives us a new will that wants to please him.	1. The Christian exercises his new will by looking to God for ways of pleasing him.
2. In his Word God shows us in the law what works he wants us to do and what works he wants us to shun.	2. The Christian struggles against sin and consciously cultivates obedience to God's Word and loving service to those around him.
3. In his rule over history, God sees to it that we have ample opportunities to show our love for his Word and for willing service to our neighbor.	3. The Christian uses the opportunities that God gives by struggling against sin and doing the works that please God.
4. In his Word he gives us the ability and the strength to take advantage of the opportunities he gives us to hear his Word and keep it.	

Clearly the Christian's life is always a work in progress. That is, unlike our salvation that is always complete and entirely God's gift, our Christian life from day to day is lived out under the cross. Jesus defines our life under the cross especially in Mark 8:34-38. There Jesus tells each and every one of his followers that just as he carried a cross of pain and of struggle and ultimately of death, so too will we. The essence of that cross is a life in which each of us strives to deny self out of love for Jesus, strives against "I want" and "I think" in favor of "What does God want?" and "What does his Word say?" It is a life devoted to the kind of loving service that Jesus lived for me—a life that puts him and his Word first, everyone else next, and me last.

That such a life is a struggle, difficult, and often painful should be immediately obvious. In our fallen nature each says, "Me first!" We manage to suppress that impulse to an exclusive self-service (which is really self-worship) only with difficulty. We still have our sinful nature inherited from Adam and Eve. That nature is never converted and only dies when we go from earth to heaven at the moment of death. For every impulse of the Christian nature created at conversion, that sinful nature has an opposing response.

We note that response in just about every good impulse that we have to live a life devoted to Christ. The Christian in me delights to hear God's Word and is eager to follow it. The sinful nature replies, "Not now; not so much; don't take it all that seriously!" The Christian in me is eager to serve and to help anyone and everyone I am able to help solely because it is pleasing to God and beneficial to those I serve. The sinful nature protests, "I help my neighbor in the expectation that he will help me; I give to the cancer fund in the hope that, should I get cancer, my gift will come back to me."[1] The Christian in me strives to live an outwardly *and* inwardly chaste and decent life simply because it wants to reflect gratitude for the purity God gives in Baptism. But the sinful nature is willing to behave decently—at least in public—only because it craves respect from those around me, especially those who can be useful to me or only because it does not want the painful consequences of getting caught in outward shame and disgrace. And as for those who do me wrong, the Christian in me is eager to forgive, just as God has so freely and willingly forgiven me. But the sinful nature says, "They had best watch out for the day when I will repay them with interest! At the very least they should expect nothing good from me."[2]

The words of St. Paul cited previously are in sharp contrast to what our sinful nature has in mind. So too are Jesus' words in the Sermon on the Mount in Matthew 5–7. Read the chapters with care and see if you can find a single verse that is easy, that doesn't go against the grain of our fallen nature! Being a Christian in head and heart requires

---

[1]Have you noticed that almost all public charities appeal for contributions with the expressed add on: Give and you will get a raffle ticket/door prize/ "free" tote bag/chicken dinner? The well-learned assumption behind all such appeals is that people, for the most part, do very little unless something is in it for them.

[2]For a more complete consideration of the struggle between the Christian in us and our still-remaining sinful nature, cf. chapter 8.

a miracle that only God can perform through the gospel. Being a Christian in life is no easier; it too requires a miracle inspired by the totally self-giving love of Christ for us, as St. John sums it up so well:

> We love because he first loved us. If anyone says, "I love God," yet hates his brother, he is a liar. For anyone who does not love his brother, whom he has seen, cannot love God, whom he has not seen. And he has given us this command: Whoever loves God must also love his brother. (1 John 4:19-21)

The word *brother* here, as so often in the Bible, refers to all those near or far who I can see are in need of help that I am able to provide. And the Greek word for *love* is that kind of love that seeks the ultimate good of those who are loved. It is not mere affection or liking; Greek has a different word for that. Love in this verse (as in that great love chapter, 1 Corinthians 13) is a love that is a choice made to seek the best interest of the one loved; it is a choice to serve, whether or not the service can be repaid or is even appreciated.[3]

Paul puts the sharpest possible point on that kind of love. He tells us, as Jesus does in the aforementioned Sermon on the Mount and as Solomon said as well (Proverbs 25:21), that such a love is to be active in service to all; it is to be active even in service to those who without cause from us are our enemies. He sums it all up so completely and so perfectly: "Do not be overcome by evil, but overcome evil with good" (Romans 12:21). Again, let the one who thinks the Christian life is an easy one read the whole of Romans 12 and see if there is anything in it that comes naturally or easily!

Accordingly, to God be all thanks and praise every moment of our lives that our salvation is not caused—no, not in the least part—by our good works! For if it were, every moment of our lives would carry over it the verdict of guilty and the sentence of death and hell. No, our salvation is—and we cannot say it too often or too emphatically—entirely the work of Christ on the cross, just as the faith that embraces Christ's work for us is a miracle created in us by God through the gospel.

Nevertheless, that doesn't mean that we have been saved to sin or that the struggle to live lives that flow from the love of Christ is optional. Good works are not necessary as a cause of salvation, but

---

[3]Thank God that the love called for is not mere affection, mere liking. I may find it quite impossible to like or have warm, fuzzy feelings toward those who hurt me or my loved ones or the church. But I can choose to love them in the sense that I seek their ultimate good, I pray for them, do not wish them ill, and even look for opportunities to repay their ill with good.

they are necessary. The good work of hearing God's Word commanded in the Third Commandment is so vital and necessary because our faith cannot survive without it. And good works that serve our neighbors (the Fourth through Tenth Commandments) are necessary because they need them and because God has commanded them.[4]

So it is just as Jesus said: Ours *must be* lives lived under the cross, not just lives that could be, should be, might be, or sometimes are under the cross. A life under the cross, a life of self-denial for the sake of Jesus and his Word, is a life in which

1. I struggle against the inborn and deeply rooted inclination of my sinful flesh to put self first;
2. I seek to put the Word of God and the best interest of those I am able to serve before my own wants and self-interest, whether that's convenient or not, easy or not;
3. I struggle against the tendency in my own heart to the self-righteous notion that I am good enough the way I am and need not struggle anymore against my favorite sins or *the* favorite sin of putting myself first;
4. I struggle even against the opposite tendency to despair when I discover how far away I still am from the kind of life God wants me to live. It is a life in which I battle against despair of his love and mercy when I suffer pain and loss in life, either because of my own sins or the sins of others. In such despair one turns his back on the Word of God and the saving merit of Christ just as much as that one does who trusts in whole or in part on his own works to gain salvation.

All of that is part and parcel of the Christian life, of living under the cross. And again, it is not optional. To refuse the cross is to refuse Christ, who both calls us to it and sends it in order to keep us ever mindful of the fundamental truth that he alone is Savior. For how can we look at even a moment of our lives and imagine that we have done it all and are already good enough to gain heaven? Paul, as his life was drawing to a close, confessed that he had not yet gotten to that point and knew he would not until he went from the cross to the crown in heaven (Philippians 3:12-14).

It is with this very difficulty and the pain of living under the cross in mind that Jesus calls us to himself to give us both comfort and aid as

---

[4]For a complete and excellent consideration of the necessity of good works in the Lutheran Confessions, cf. especially Art. IV, V, Epitome and Solid Declaration of the Formula of Concord (pp. 497-501; 574-586).

we follow after him under the cross. He speaks to us so tenderly: "Come to me, all you who are weary and burdened, and I will give you rest. Take my yoke upon you and learn from me, for I am gentle and humble in heart, and you will find rest for your souls. For my yoke is easy and my burden is light" (Matthew 11:28-30).

How well Jesus understands us! We focus on our pain and our difficulty. He brings us to focus on him and his Word. The sinful flesh will complain that it's all too hard and that it is about time that someone served *me.* However, Jesus gives the new man—the Christian nature that comes from gospel-created faith—strength and courage in his Word. The rest of which Jesus speaks is the rest that comes to the struggling soul aware of its imperfections and failures; it is the rest of forgiveness in the gospel. It is the rest that renews and reinvigorates us for renewed struggle. Likewise, it is the assurance from the gospel that one day the struggle will end in the victory that Christ has won for us by his struggle, his cross, his suffering and death for us and for our salvation. The assurance of both kinds of rest, the rest of forgiveness now and the rest assured at the end of this short life's battle, make his yoke easy for us and his burden light. After all, he has not left us alone. By his presence with us in his Word and sacrament he carries our cross with us. Indeed, he permits nothing heavier than what we can bear and nothing more than what is intended for our good and our strengthening. What athlete does not strain and sweat in order to gain strength and become better at his sport? Even a tree gains strength from being buffeted by the wind. Just so, Jesus assures us that the struggle is itself a blessing. For if we had no struggle we would quickly forget our need of his constant aid. Had we no regrets and nothing to repent of, we would soon forget the greatness of his love in bringing us salvation at so great a cost to himself, the cost of his own cross.

So then, in love to him, in response to his love for us, we strive to live lives that are pleasing to him, lives that are rich in good works.

What then is a good work? God does not leave us in doubt on the definition of works that are good in his eyes. As we shall see in all that follows in this chapter, for a work to be good in the eyes of God,

1. the work must first be done in accord with the law of God and not contrary to it.
2. it will be done in grateful thanksgiving to God for the gift of salvation—not to earn or merit that which only God can give as a gift of grace on account of the merit of Christ.
3. generally speaking, and this is most evident in the Second Table of the Law (the Fourth through Tenth Commandments), the work will be done for the benefit of others, not just for what I can get in return.

4. it will be done in the joyful expectation that God accepts it and is pleased with it. That expectation is justified even though none of our works are in themselves ever perfect, because they are done in connection with Christ; that is, whatever stains them—and us—is covered by the blood of our Savior who forgives even the unintentional stains on our good works.

The law of God is summarized in the Ten Commandments. The first three are called the *First Table of the Law* and they deal primarily with our duty to God. The last seven commandments, the *Second Table of the Law,* deal chiefly with our duty to our fellow man.

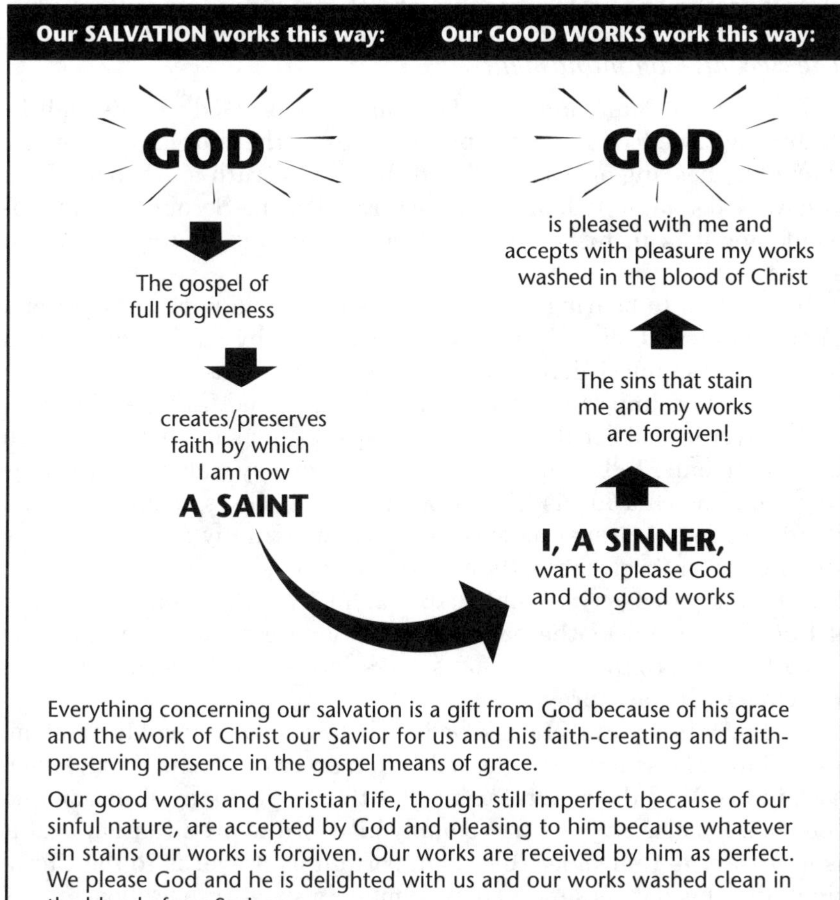

Everything concerning our salvation is a gift from God because of his grace and the work of Christ our Savior for us and his faith-creating and faith-preserving presence in the gospel means of grace.

Our good works and Christian life, though still imperfect because of our sinful nature, are accepted by God and pleasing to him because whatever sin stains our works is forgiven. Our works are received by him as perfect. We please God and he is delighted with us and our works washed clean in the blood of our Savior.

Good Works—The First Table of the Law

The First Commandment

Our duty to God is that we fear, love, and trust in him above all things; that is the sum and substance of the First Commandment (Matthew 10:37,38; 22:37). That means that we put God first in our lives. It means that his Word, not our own opinions or feelings, not the opinions or feelings of others either, is the guide and rule of our thoughts, words, and deeds. We fear nothing more than offending him. In love to him, we let no one turn us aside from devotion to him and to his Word. We look to no one for our ultimate happiness in this life or blessedness in the next but to him and to him alone.

The Second Commandment

The Second Commandment calls on us to use God's name rightly. Accordingly, we look for such opportunities as the church provides for the public hearing of his Word, and that in its truth and purity. That is how God's name is honored in accord with the Second Commandment. For it is in his Word that God reveals his saving name and saving work.

In addition to hearing his Word in its truth and purity, the Second Commandment bids us use his name rightly by calling on him in prayer. The simplest definition of prayer is that it is our speaking to God. That's an important definition to remember. Many people think that prayer is God speaking to us. God speaks to us in his Word and in the sacraments. To be sure, in our prayers we may call to mind things that God has said in his Word—but then it is God's speaking in the Word, not in the prayer as such. For example, in my sorrow over my sins I pray for forgiveness; then perhaps even as I pray I hear echoing in my mind passages like John 3:16; 1 John 1:7–2:2; or John 6:37. Even if I do not remember the passages word for word, their content may come to mind, content that God speaks in his Word and helps me to remember even as I pray.

Or, I may in my prayers ask God for help with a particular problem. I ask him to bless my struggle to do all in accord with his Word; I even seek in his Word the general principles that apply to my situation and then ask his blessing as I try to apply his Word to my situation. But it is necessary to remember that as important as prayer is to the Christian's life, it is not, as supposed by so many, a substitute for hearing his Word and applying it to life. Again, in prayer we speak to God; in his Word and sacraments God speaks to us. Prayer is, as the poet says, the

Christian's vital breath. But it is a breath that first has its impulse from the love and promises of God in the Word and sacraments.

We can better understand the nature of prayer if we consider prayer under these headings:

1. Prayers for spiritual blessings, such as prayers for forgiveness, strength to fight against temptation, or a better appreciation for and understanding of his Word and its application to my life. To these prayers God always says "Yes!" They are always according to his will. The answer to these prayers will be found in a faithful use of God's Word and sacraments. The one who asks for a stronger faith and then ignores the hearing of God's Word is not serious in his prayer; such a one is like the fool who prays that he will not starve to death and then refuses to eat. The whole of the gospel shows both God's answer to such prayers and his eagerness to answer them.
2. Prayers for temporal blessings, such as prayers for health, sufficient wealth, rescue in time of trouble or need, or guidance for life's work and in the perplexity of life's work. The Bible often encourages us to pray for such blessings. We should not think that God is indifferent to our earthly needs and cares only for our highest and greatest spiritual needs. God does not see us as having an unimportant earthly part and then an important spiritual part. He sees us in total as his creation and his dear children by faith in his Son's redeeming work. Therefore, there is no concern that is so little that we might think he doesn't want to be bothered with it. Jesus encourages us often in such prayers (e.g., Matthew 6:25-34; Luke 18:1-8), and the apostles echo that encouragement (e.g., 1 Thessalonians 5:17; 1 Peter 5:7). When we bring such prayers to God, we have the certainty of his promise that he will give us the best possible answer to our prayer. That may not always be exactly what we asked for; but when it is not, we have the certainty that what he sends is better. Paul discovered that and encourages us to remember it (2 Corinthians 12:7-10). Indeed, the patient Christian will often have occasion to call that truth to mind: God answered a prayer in a way far better than could even have been imagined. Interesting in this connection is the encouragement that Jesus gives us in our prayers in Matthew 7:7,8: "Ask and it will be given to you; seek and you will find; knock and the door will be opened to you. For everyone who asks receives; he who seeks finds; and to him who knocks, the door will be opened." Notice the progression and the unity of thought. Ulti-

mately there is giving, finding, opening. But it may not all happen at once. In the hour of great need, one asks, but the giving is delayed. So he seeks an answer from the God who seems to turn away from him. But still he does not find the help he sought. So he knocks, yes, pounds on the door of heaven with his prayer; he holds before God God's own promises, which cannot deceive or fail. And at length God gives the answer best suited to the real need of the one crying to him. The one praying finds mercy and acceptance at the foot of the cross. The door of heaven, of God's own heart, flings wide open and Jesus meets him with a warm welcome and a tender embrace in grace. We have beautiful examples of the point in the account of the Canaanite woman in Matthew 15:21-28 and, again, in St. Paul's prayer in 2 Corinthians 12:7-10. So to these prayers we always add in word or thought: May your will be done! For his will is always best. We offer these prayers in humble confidence, not on the basis of our merit or trusting in what we think we deserve; we offer them, trusting in the merit of his Son and confident that he always keeps his promises to hear and answer.

3. Intercessory prayers are prayers offered for others, for friends and family, for enemies (that their enmity may be turned), for the government, and for all sorts and conditions of men. Paul especially encourages us in such prayers (e.g., 1 Timothy 2:1-4; 2 Thessalonians 3:1,2). He provided as well an example of a life of prayer for others; his epistles regularly begin with prayers for those to whom he was writing. In these prayers too, we commend the answer to the mercy of God, trusting in his promise to hear and to bless in accord with what is in the best interest of those for whom we pray. One interesting aspect of such prayers is that we often can ourselves be part of God's answer to them: the one who prays for the state is part of God's blessing of the state when that one obeys the law; the one who prays for his neighbor and then does what he can to help his neighbor becomes part of God's answer to his own prayer. A day has been well spent when at its close I can call to mind ways in which God answered my prayers through me.
4. Praise and thanksgiving should be a part of every prayer. The very fact that God's ears are open to our prayers, that he invites and welcomes them, is already reason to begin with praise and thanksgiving. A good way to start each day is with a thanksgiving for God's blessings, calling to mind such blessings as are new every

morning in the gospel, in life, and in the opportunities God gives us to serve and be useful. The book of Psalms is filled with prayers of praise and adoration. Jesus gave thanks before the miracles of feeding the thousands (John 6:11; Matthew 15:36). Paul too gives us beautiful examples of such prayers in all of his letters; one of his most beautiful is his prayer in Romans 11:33-36.

Some might wonder why God so encourages us to pray when he always does what is best for us, and that even without our prayers—a point Luther also makes in his Small Catechism's explanation of the Lord's Prayer. The answer is simple: God bids us pray; God promises to hear us; God shows us in his Word how often prayer mattered and made a difference. We are content to trust God's commands and God's promises!

We can think of no better way to conclude our consideration of prayer than with the summary comments of one our greatest theologians from the 17th century. He writes:

> We may reasonably marvel over the great worthiness of prayer. The Father promises to listen, the Son prays for us, the Holy Spirit prays in us, the holy angels bring our prayer before God's throne. The Father is the truth; therefore we ought not doubt that we are heard. The Son is righteousness; therefore we ought not doubt the power of his intercession. The Holy Spirit is wisdom; therefore we ought not be afraid even if we do not know what we should pray for; for the Spirit intercedes for us. The holy angels are faithful messengers; therefore we ought not doubt that our prayers will come before God's throne.[5]

Rich and beautiful are the promises that God attaches to his invitation to us to pray. And still, given all the obstacles to prayer that the devil, the world, and our own sinful flesh throw up against it, do perhaps even the holy angels stop and take note of it when God's promises finally bring us to pray? Do they perhaps stoop down and marvel and say, "Behold, he prays!"?

The Third Commandment

The Third Commandment calls on us to take advantage of those opportunities that God gives us for the public hearing and sharing of

---

[5]From Johann Gerhard's sermon *Am Festtage der heiligen Pfingsten V, "Von der Einwohnung des Heiligen Geistes in den Herzen der Gläubigen—Rom. 8,14-16;"* Gerhard's *Postille*, B. I, S. 522,523.

his Word. The church exists to provide us with just such opportunities. It does that through the worship services arranged and conducted so that we may hear and receive from God what he longs to give us in his Word and sacraments. Then in union with the church, we also keep the Third Commandment when we publicly confess our loyalty to that Word in public worship. That public confession of loyalty should be joined to an eagerness and zeal to share his precious gift of the gospel with those who worship with us and with the entire world. The one who says that he can do that all by himself at home and alone hasn't paid attention to the Word he claims to hear at home. For the Third Commandment and all of the Old Testament—especially in the book of Psalms—as well as the example of Jesus and the apostles enjoin public worship on us as a happy privilege. Only where and when such public worship is impossible because of persecution or the lack of a church faithful to God's Word in its truth and purity is absence from public worship legitimate.

It would be good if on entering church, be it the smallest chapel or the most grand, we would see inscribed above the entry the happy exclamation of Jacob: "Surely the LORD is in this place. . . . This is none other than the house of God; this is the gate of heaven" (Genesis 28:16,17). For we have come at God's invitation to visit him where he especially dwells with all his grace and mercy, namely, where his Word is proclaimed and his sacraments administered. And then what better way to leave at the end of the service than with the words of the psalmist on our lips, even as we look forward to returning: "I rejoiced with those who said to me, 'Let us go to the house of the LORD'" (Psalm 122:1).

Attendance at and support of the public worship of the church, of course, does not mean that we ignore private worship. On the contrary, our private devotions are encouraged and inspired by and find their beginning and completion in the enjoyment of the Word and sacraments in church. The most important part of both our public and our private worship is the reading or hearing of God's Word. That is where it all begins. After we have listened to what God has to say, then life can become a response to his speaking to us of his love and grace in Christ.

Good Works—The Second Table of the Law

The last seven commandments tell us what works toward our neighbor are pleasing to God. It is interesting to note that none of those works do God any apparent good at all. He commands them because of his love for our neighbor, a love equal to his love for us; thus, if we harm our neighbor or fail to help him when we can, God takes it all personally as an affront to himself. Can we even bear to imagine it: passing by a hungry Christ, a naked Christ, a shivering Christ, a desolate and weeping Christ?

The Fourth Commandment

That the good works called for in the Second Table of the Law are intended for our blessing and benefit as well as the benefit of those around us is at once evident in the first commandment of the Second Table—the Fourth Commandment. Under the Fourth Commandment we consider especially the three estates that God himself has established for our blessing and benefit.

The three estates

The family

The family is the fundamental and the most important of the three estates. To the extent that the family succeeds, both the church and the state may prosper. To the extent that God's arrangement for family life is despised and set aside, to that extent both church and state are threatened and weakened. Indeed the destruction of the state and of civil society almost always has the decay of the family at its root and its primary cause.

The young especially need to be carefully instructed in God's intentions for our blessing through his institution and regulation of family life. That is so in order that they may give God's intentions for them careful thought as they set about forming families of their own. Such instruction is of vital importance especially because society and often its elders have made such a mess of family life that decent models of God-pleasing family life may be very hard to find.

What then does God's Word have to say about the family? First of all, we note already at the creation of Adam and Eve (Genesis 1,2) that God established three basic purposes for marriage and the family. He declared that it would not be good for Adam to remain alone and without human companionship. And so as his greatest gift to Adam, God created Eve and gave Adam and Eve to each other. Their *companionship* was a great gift and blessing indeed and a primary purpose of marriage; companionship remains a blessing and purpose that God still intends for marriage.

The second purpose that God gave for marriage in the Garden of Eden was the *bearing and rearing of children* (Genesis 1:28). Children are spoken of in the Bible as a blessing of the Lord (Psalm 127). It is from children that we gain a special insight into the grace and love of God. For just as children can neither earn nor repay their parents for their status as children and for the love and care lavished on them by their parents, so also we as children of God by faith in Christ Jesus. We too can neither earn nor deserve that status, nor ever repay God our Father for the love and care that he lavishes on us.

At the same time we imitate his love and grace in caring for the children that God entrusts to our care. Additionally, in the simplicity and trust of little children we see again the nature of that faith which we have in God as our Father; we get to understand just a little bit better and with greater appreciation what it means when we are called the children of God. Yes, and not least we have the honor of being missionaries as we give back to God at their baptisms the children he has given us. What an honor God has given to parents that parents should imitate God's love for them as they love and train their children with his Word!

To be sure, at times families may not experience the blessing and as well the special trials that children bring to marriage. But where husband and wife prevent children from entering into the family without a God-pleasing reason, there one of God's primary purposes for marriage is being frustrated and hindered. No couple should lightly plan such a course or expect God's blessing on their intention.

The third purpose of marriage came after the fall into sin. The third purpose is the *prevention of immorality* (1 Corinthians 7:2-5). The sexual urges that we have are not in themselves sinful. Indeed, were it not for such desires the human race would have died out long ago. God has established marriage as the means for blessing and regulating and satisfying those desires. In marriage the desire of a partner for the other is to be satisfied lovingly, not selfishly or violently. The standard of Ephesians 5:22-33 and the model of Christ and the church stands even over this aspect of marriage: Let each give to the other out of love and respect for the other, not using their bodies as a means of control or manipulation. That such a relationship is blessed is as obvious as it is sometimes difficult to achieve. But the blessing is worth the effort.

What is left of these three divinely established purposes for marriage in our world today? In courtship it is common and expected that the couple cannot get enough of each other's company. Sadly, after marriage it is just as common to find the two drifting ever further apart. The husband finds more companionship with his friends who enjoy the same hobbies or sports that he does. The wife whose husband no longer enjoys her company goes off to satisfy her loneliness either by means of her children or with other female friends. That friends outside of the marriage are important and can indeed be a great blessing no one should doubt, but when they become a substitute for the companionship of a spouse, the family will be undermined and God's intended blessing frustrated.

Given the different interests and inclinations of men and women, we should not expect that the blessing of companionship would happen automatically. Companionship in marriage needs cultivating and nourishing as the husband shares his concerns and joys with his wife and as the wife shares hers with her husband. As couples grow together and mature, they need to find interests that they can share. Clearly their interests will not always be the same, but the loving recognition of the needs of the other forms patience in each along with the desire to satisfy unselfishly the needs of the spouse.

As rare as it often is to see the blessings of companionship in many a marriage, even more rare may it be to note God's arrangement of the order that he established already at Eve's creation. But that order is part and parcel of the companionship that God intended in instituting marriage. It was God's intent that Adam should be the head of the family and Eve the helper suitable for his headship. St. Paul beautifully describes how that relationship should work in Ephesians 5:22-33. St. Peter makes many of the same points in 1 Peter 3:1-7. The relationship between Christ and the church is set as the model for the relationship between husband and wife.

Again, consider that divine pattern, as Paul does: Christ the Bridegroom of the church does everything for his bride—indeed still and always and that after two thousand years calls her his *bride;* nothing is too difficult for him as he seeks her best interest. He gives himself for her and even now acts as Lord of all, always with her best interests in mind. And his bride? She gladly submits to his headship, happily yields to his Word, and follows his lead in everything. For she knows that his headship is always exercised in her best interest, whether she sees that immediately or not.

What a beautiful model for marriage! How blessed that marriage where Christ's marriage with the church is the model! Correspondingly, the marriage and the companionship are weakened where the pattern is set aside or despised. God has created in men a desire for headship and in women the special ability to look to their husbands for leadership. Where those natural inclinations are snuffed out, their husbands are treated by their wives as if they were children who need to be managed and manipulated. And husbands, for their part, go back to acting like children who want freedom and escape both from the responsibility and from the companionship of marriage. Treated like children by their wives, they respond by ignoring, resenting, or leaving their spouses altogether. And a wife responds with still greater contempt for her husband, as the downward spiral continues apace.

The threat to marriage and the family that is posed by the upsetting of the order that God gave to it in the Garden of Eden is evident in the first sins in that same garden. Notice how God rebukes Adam in Genesis 3:17. Adam had abandoned his role of headship in the marriage when he followed the lead of his wife into sin. Eve, for her part, had rebelled not just against the Word of God when she fell but against the headship of her husband as well. So we notice already in Genesis 3 the beginning of the temptation wives have to rebel against their husbands even while at the same time wanting that headship (3:16b). So also in husbands there has been since the fall the two competing impulses: on the one hand, the husband wants respect for his headship; on the other, he too easily neglects the responsibility of exercising that headship and that in the best interest of his spouse—just as Adam did nothing to help Eve or to interrupt the beginning of her descent into sin.

To the extent that a marriage is guided by the Word of God, to the extent that couples strive to pattern their marriages after God's institution and the model of the marriage between Christ and the church, to that extent husband and wife will be aware of these competing tendencies within each and work to remedy them. The wife will remember that God wants her to submit to her husband's headship and will strive to subdue the temptation to rebel. Instead, she will encourage his headship. The husband will recognize that his headship is intended for the benefit of the family and especially of his wife; he will strive to overcome the temptation to ignore his wife's benefit and to abandon his headship in the interest of his own convenience or pleasure.

Each couple may find its own way of working out this divinely intended arrangement for their marriage. But that marriages in which each observes God's intention for marriage are rare these days needs no proof. When was the last time a movie or television sitcom portrayed a marriage in which the husband was respected as a head of the house and the wife was cherished as a gift of God for the sustaining of her husband and family?

Indeed, an opposite picture of marriage appears to be the norm these days. Wives want to be free of the "patriarchy." Husbands encouraged to abandon their headship have no difficulty in abandoning the marriage. And so what's left? Women who are "free" to raise children alone, deprived of the financial and moral support of faithful husbands. And husbands cut loose from the moral center of their lives in the family find themselves floundering in the search for a partner or a purpose in life that matters. Children bereft of godly patterns of behavior between the sexes are all but doomed to repeat in their own marriages the loveless selfishness that they have learned from society in general and often from their parents as well.

And so the second purpose of marriage, the bearing and the raising of children in the fear and admonition of the Lord, is left behind. Children there may be. But in so many families children raised in the fear and admonition of the Lord is a priority either altogether forgotten or lost in the disorder of disintegrating and loveless marriages.

As to the third purpose of marriage, the prevention of immorality, that too disappears as wives ignore their husbands' "needs" and husbands act crudely and selfishly towards their wives. Both contribute thereby to the further disintegration of what was to be a wonderful blessing of God for each of them and through each to the other.

But why belabor the point? Is it not obvious that God's arrangement for marriage is better? Is it not apparent that the wreckage of so many young people can be traced in no small part to the wreckage that they experienced in family life? To be sure, there are indeed times when marriages must dissolve (of which more below). To be sure, there are tragic circumstances in which one parent is better than the two or in which one parent is lost by serious illness or death. But it is beyond doubt that society and families and children would all be better off if the norm was the family as God established it and as St. Paul pictured it in Ephesians 5.

So twisted and distorted has the institution of marriage become in the popular mind that even "marriage" between those of the same sex is considered appropriate; those who think otherwise are dismissed as haters and bigots. But it is God who instituted marriage and expressed his will that marriage should be between one man and one woman (Genesis 2:24; Matthew 19:1-9). A "marriage" between members of the same sex is a contradiction in terms *(ein Unding)* as well as an abomination in the eyes of God (Romans 1:18-28).

But the cry and protest go up: "Don't people with homosexual desires have rights just like everyone else? Is it fair that they be discriminated against when God made them that way in the first place?" We are not interested in entering into a debate with anyone about how homosexual desires originate, whether such behavior is learned or in some way inherited. Ultimately, it doesn't really matter.

What does matter is that God's Word clearly labels such desires and behavior as sinful. What matters is that the one with such temptations seeks the mercy of God and strength from God in Word and sacraments to resist what may be very powerful temptations indeed. The struggle may be lifelong and difficult. It may be a struggle of great anguish in heart and soul. But so is the struggle of every Christian. Many a Christian has some tragic or potentially fatal flaw in his character that can bring about his own destruction if he gives himself over to it. Even in matters of sexual morality, the husband or wife whose spouse falls ill or dies is not thereby given a license to satisfy altogether "normal" desires outside of marriage. In every such case the Christian learns that we live under the cross; we are not in heaven yet. To make the Christian life easy and comfortable simply by declaring that every desire imaginable is normal and every behavior that follows from such desire is acceptable is to replace the Word of God with the fallen mind of man as the only guiding principle for life. Such is neither a Christian path nor the path to heaven.

As difficult and as painful as the struggles of the one wrestling with desires and urges that are contrary to the Word of God are, we dare not forget the alternative to such a struggle. Sadly, the culture of the day depicts most falls into sins against the Sixth Commandment as no fall at all. Absent from the picture of the adulterer or the one engaged in a homosexual lifestyle are the consequences that God sends to such flagrant and open despising of his Word. Even in this life those who flaunt his will can expect at some point to taste the bitter fruits of loneliness, the sense of guilt that cannot be wished away, often disease that mocks the supposed satisfaction sought, and finally death apart from the consolations of the gospel. And, of course, death is only the beginning of the eternal consequence of despising both the law and the gospel.

The warnings from God's Word serve as a hammer against the bold pursuit of a disordered life. The one tempted to such a life will do well to consider not the lies of the devil trumpeted so shamelessly these days but rather the seriousness of God in his Word. Such a one will do well to remember that God has given even the law for our benefit also in this life. Especially, we all do well to flee to the wounds of Christ and his suffering for our sins and for our salvation; there and there alone do we find the grace and strength to continue the struggle. Not freedom from temptation has he promised us but strength for the battle is what he grants. Not a conscience ever free from blame does he guarantee but the covering of the wounds received in battle with the fruits of his victory for us on the cross and at his empty tomb. But it is worth keeping in mind that the covering of the wounds and the fruits of victory come after battle—not after surrender!

God takes his Word seriously when it comes to matters of marriage and the family. Where his Word is the guide, there family life is truly a blessing and society is blessed as well by such stable marriages and families. On the other hand, where God's ordinances for family life and marriage are set aside, there one will see on every hand evidences of God's judgment. The judgment may be in quite natural consequences, but consequences that God sends and does not hinder or prevent. Look at the carnage in society where the family has disintegrated. Sons who have no strong father figure in their lives have difficulty learning self-discipline. Daughters with no godly father figure do not learn to look for a husband whose headship they can respect and follow. And so one generation passes on to the next patterns that tend towards disorder and ever increasing chaos in homes and in society. Wives who serve as both father and mother have a load that few are equipped to carry and that in normal circumstances God did not intend them to carry.

That at times children may grow up in single parent families through no fault of the parents and may nevertheless prosper is not at issue here. Even in such circumstances children will benefit when they absorb from examples among friends and relatives what the norm is. What is at issue is God's intention and the judgment of God on societies and families that willfully cast his design aside. The individuals in such instances thought that they would be happy if they followed their own inclinations and desires in opposition to God's intentions. They and society discover in physical and emotional and societal sickness the sad consequences of setting God's Word aside. It is just as God promised in Galatians 6:7,8: "Do not be deceived: God cannot be mocked. A man reaps what he sows. The one who sows to please his sinful nature, from that nature will reap destruction."

So, again, we need to do the best we can in instructing especially the young on God's will for this first and most important of the three estates. To the extent that they listen to and follow what God intends for marriage and family life, to that extent they will experience God's blessings even in this life on their marriage and family life. To be sure, even then there will be crosses enough; for the cross is what Jesus told us to expect in this life. But far better the cross of his sending, which cross he helps us carry and by which he promises to bless us, than the burden and the plague we bring on ourselves when we set aside his Word in favor of our own fallen opinions.

Marriage then, as God instituted it, *is established by a freely given and binding consent* between a man and a woman to live together as husband and wife for as long as they both live.

"Freely given" means that there is no force or coercion involved; it means that each is able to give such a consent (i.e., old enough and of sound, unimpaired mind); it means that each has no other binding consent which would prevent giving another consent—marriage to someone else removes the ability to give a new binding consent. In times past, people used to speak of "having to get married." That is, the girl became pregnant and now they had no choice but to get married. That in such cases the couple should give serious consideration to marriage may well be obvious. That in such cases we would seek to establish a freely given consent to marriage likewise should be obvious. But pregnancy in and of itself is not a reason to get married; couples in such circumstances need the careful guidance and instruction from God's Word to determine a God-pleasing course of action. Should they get married? Should the child be kept or adopted if marriage is not an option? Again, they need some careful counseling from someone guided by the Word of God.[6]

A freely given and binding consent is a consent that is unconditional. To say, "We will get married if we have enough money two years down the road" or "I'll marry you if you stop drinking/smoking/gambling/playing basketball every night with your friends" is not a binding consent. *Unconditional* means that the decision has already been made; we are committed to living together as husband and wife, so long as we both shall live. A "marriage" without such a commitment is no marriage at all. In fact, lacking the intent to remain with one another for a lifetime, the union is often doomed to failure even before it begins. For once the partners consider themselves always free to leave, they will be far less likely to put up with the difficulties that are part and parcel of any such close living arrangement. When couples remember that they have pledged loyalty to one another and to God, a loyalty that will last a lifetime, they will be much more inclined to look for and find solutions to the problems that befall all such relationships.

Finally, it is assumed in a binding consent that there is no deceit involved that would make it impossible to carry out the purposes God

---

[6]Abortion in such cases is not an option unless the life of the mother is clearly in danger.

has given to marriage. The innocent party is entitled under such a circumstance to an annulment of the marriage. An annulment, as distinguished from a divorce, declares that there really never was a marriage. Thus, for example, if one knew that he or she could not have children but hid that from the other, then the consent is invalid; if that impossibility was only discovered after the marriage, the consent would still be valid—the deceit has to be a conscious, an intentional deceit. Or, if one knew that he or she was a homosexual and did not really intend to carry out the purposes of marriage, that too would make the consent invalid.

It is the binding consent that establishes the marriage in the eyes of God *(Consensus facit matrimonium).* We see that in the Garden of Eden. God created Eve and gave her to Adam, and the two rejoiced in the gift of each to the other. We see it in the marriage of Isaac and Rebekah in Genesis 24. We see it in the marriage of Mary and Joseph in Matthew 1:18-24; they were pledged to one another. Once the Lord told Joseph that Mary's child was the Son of God, he kept his pledge and the marriage subsequently took place.

In times past, it was the custom that a couple declared their consent at the time of engagement. While engagement may well be a good time for a couple to announce a binding consent, it is no longer assumed that such is the case. Nevertheless, there is a time before the wedding when each gives to the other a binding consent. Clearly it is before the wedding. No one is free any longer at the wedding! No one plans or goes to a wedding to see if the couple will get married or not; that has been decided and settled some time earlier.

So it is not the wedding ceremony that makes the marriage; it is the freely given binding consent that establishes the marriage in the eyes of God. Does that mean that a marriage ceremony is unnecessary or that a couple is free to live together as husband and wife before or without such a ceremony? It is a pious and worthy custom that Christian couples publicly announce their consent and seek the blessing of God, of their parents, and of the church by means of a public wedding. Additionally, the Word of God urges us everywhere to be patterns of discipline and godliness. Accordingly, we do not want to live as do those who live together without any commitment beyond the moment and the convenience. To be sure, some have wedding ceremonies with nothing of commitment implied and only an extravagant display to show for it. But for the Christian couple, the marriage ceremony and its vows are serious. The whole manner of planning the ceremony and its conduct should be designed by the couple to show the desire of the couple to have Christ as the true head of their house and his Word as their guide in their lives together.

So while it is the consent that makes the marriage, the wedding ceremony in church, while not absolutely necessary, is not unimportant and should not be lightly discarded. It should be an occasion for celebrating God's gift of each to the other and of thanking him for the gift of marriage. It should be an opportunity for setting a Christian example for others. At the very least, the wedding keeps the couple from giving the offensive example that they think no differently than so many others about living together.

With these purposes in mind for the ceremony, most couples would do well to give more thought than is customary to keeping the wedding chaste and decent; that is, they should strive to keep out of their wedding ceremony the extravagance that will impoverish either them or their parents. As well they will shun any unchristian music or other displays that would contradict the real purpose of the ceremony. The ceremony is after all a worship service, not a carnival or a circus. In a worship service it is Christ who is the center and his Word the guide for what is done in his house. Accordingly, when they plan their wedding, the couple will want to make sure that they do it in consultation with their pastor.

Perhaps nowhere is it more obvious than in God's intentions for marriage and for family life that the Christian swims against the tide, against the culture and bias of the day. That is true when we speak of the divinely given purposes for marriage. It is true when we consider the roles that God has given to husbands and wives. It is true when we reject the assumed wisdom of the day about "marriage" between members of the same sex. And it is going to be true as well when we speak of the matter of divorce.

It might be obvious that where husband and wife each take seriously the purposes of marriage and the roles that God has given to each, the problem of divorce would never really arise. The prevalence of divorce in society and even among church members is noisy testimony to the degree to which God's plans for marriage have been set aside, ignored, and despised. Jesus too had to deal with the problem of divorce in his own day. But Jesus minced no words about God's intention for marriage and his verdict on those who set marriage aside with a divorce that had no legitimate grounds (Matthew 19:1-9; cf. also St. Paul's extensive discussion of marriage, divorce, and morality in 1 Corinthians 6:9–7:40).

It is clear from Jesus' words and from St. Paul's as well that there is no such thing as a sinless divorce. While it is rare that there is a truly innocent party in a divorce, nevertheless, there are two causes mentioned that give one party to the marriage a right to a divorce. Jesus says that adultery destroys the marriage bond. St. Paul tells us that if the unbeliever leaves the believer, the believer in the marriage is not obliged to consider him or herself still married. Whether the unbeliever was one before leaving or became one by leaving doesn't really make any difference as far as the dissolution of the marriage is concerned.[7] Essentially adultery and malicious desertion are the same thing: They are examples of the flagrant destruction of the binding consent that established the marriage in the first place.

Couples may at times need to be reminded so to live with one another that they do not provoke unfaithfulness or desertion. A wife, for example, by her coldness toward her husband can tempt him to unfaithfulness. A husband by his abuse of his wife can tempt her to desertion and, yes, toward the very coldness towards him that tempts him to unfaithfulness. How often one encounters just such a spiral downward, as each uses whatever weapon is at hand to punish the other. Having said that, it remains true that there are no acceptable excuses for adultery or desertion. Even in these tragic instances where the marriage bond has been broken by adultery or desertion, efforts may be made to repair the damage and restore the marriage.

Are adultery and desertion the only sins that destroy the binding consent in marriage and thus justify divorce? Or are they the two most flagrant destroyers of the marriage bond? A possible answer to these questions may be found by revisiting the purposes of marriage considered earlier. Those purposes are companionship, the bearing of children, and the prevention of immorality. Do adultery and desertion destroy those purposes? Clearly they do. Are there other sins that just as clearly threaten and destroy the fulfillment of those purposes? Spousal abuse, persistent drunkenness, or drug abuse come to mind as ways in which the purposes of marriage can be frustrated and the marriage bond thereby destroyed.

We must however avoid the temptation to create a long list or catalogue of offenses that are the equivalent of adultery or desertion; such a catalogue too easily degenerates into a grab bag of excuses in which some will search for an easy justification for a sinful divorce where no justification really exists. In the case of a troubled marriage where one

---

[7]Clearly if the one departing was a member of a Christian congregation and left the marriage without any scriptural grounds, such a one needs to be dealt with as Jesus tells us to deal with public sin and impenitence in Matthew 18:15-18.

or both partners to the marriage is considering divorce, the couple may find the counsel of a wise pastor or other Christian counselor indispensable in sorting out the issues at hand and dealing with them. It should be with fear and trembling that a couple considers the destruction of "what God has joined together" and what he clearly has intended to last a lifetime. Sadly, for many in our day the meaning of "until death do us part" in the marriage vows has come to mean "until we find an excuse to leave each other" or "until we decide that we don't love each other any longer." Those who have taken that attitude toward their marriage vows will have no difficulty in grabbing hold of one "cause" or another to justify their sinful divorce.

Given that divorce has to a considerable extent lost any stigma in our society, couples do well to pray each day that the Lord give them wisdom and strength to nurture in their marriage the divinely instituted purposes of marriage. That cannot be urged too strongly. For where husbands and wives are devoted to Christ as the ultimate head of their house and to his Word as the guide for their lives together, there the temptations to unfaithfulness and desertion will certainly be much easier to overcome. Yes, and if the couple discovers that one behavior or another is threatening the purposes of marriage, they will do well to deal with the threat early on; too often little problems left untended become the devil's wedge for separating husband and wife more and more until the blessings God intends for marriage are but a distant memory. Then husband and wife sink into a dull toleration of each other or even contemplate divorce. Is it not abundantly clear how vital a close connection to Jesus, to his Word and sacraments, is for a successful married life?

In such homes may husband and wife as well look to the proper training of their children. The Bible has much to say about the relationship between parents and their children. Parents should see their children as God's precious gifts to them, on loan for a day at a time (Psalm 127). They should strive to see their children as Jesus sees them; for Jesus took them in his arms and blessed them (Mark 10:13-16). In the Sacrament of Baptism he does the same with our children. Jesus stresses the importance of following his examples with our children by means of both a warning and a promise in Matthew 18:5,6. He promises that those who receive children in his name receive him; but he warns that for those who cause *his* children to sin, it would be better that they be thrown into the sea with a millstone tied around their necks. The promise should cheer and encourage a Christian parent; the warning should send a shudder down the spine of those tempted to indifference toward their children's Christian training.

And just how do we receive Jesus in receiving his gift of children? And how would we cause them to sin and call down so terrible a judgment from God on our necks? Again, God's Word is clear. We receive these gifts and Jesus in them when we raise children by word and example in the truths of the Scriptures. Paul says so much and so simply: "Fathers, do not exasperate your children; instead, bring them up in the training and instruction of the Lord" (Ephesians 6:4). Children in a family where the rule is "Do as I say, not as I do!" will certainly be exasperated; that is, they will be frustrated and put in an ill temper for doing what they should do in love and respect for the parents God has placed over them. How do children learn to treasure the Word of God and prayer where they see little evidence of either at home? How do children learn to address God with all boldness and confidence with the words "Our Father" when they see in their human father indifference or cruelty or arbitrariness or a lack of either discipline or forgiving tenderness? How do they learn to show compassion to the weak and to help those in need if their earthly mother is too busy to be bothered with tending to their weakness and seeing her goal in life as helping them in their need?

No greater blessing and no greater responsibility could God give to us than that of raising our children as we would have wanted to raise the Christ Child himself, were he entrusted to our care. That is exactly the case, however, as Jesus tells us when he reminds us that in receiving our children, we receive him! What an honor! What a blessing out of all proportion to the effort involved! It's hard to remember that blessing when we think of children as ours for 18 or so years; it's easier if we in prayer call to mind that they are ours just for today, one day at a time. It's easier to remember if we try to see in them the greatest missionary opportunity in the world—for that is in fact what they are.

The rule set down in Proverbs 22:6 generally holds true: "Train a child in the way he should go, and when he is old he will not turn from it." The rule holds whether a child is trained for good from the Word of God or trained to do evil by word and example from his or her parents! To be sure, with the best of intentions and efforts parents may experience frustration in their efforts—perhaps the holy writer had even that in mind when he said that the child will not depart from it "when he is old"! Nevertheless, it is a great blessing indeed when parents can see their children grow as God's children through their own efforts to raise them as such. No earthly wealth or honor can match such a blessing!

Blessed indeed are children with parents guided by the Word of God in the raising of their children. Parents would do well from time to time to read together the book of Proverbs; it was written by a father who was training his son.

Children for their part have the honor of respecting and obeying their parents as they would want to obey God. For parents stand in the place of God, and to disrespect, despise, and disobey them is to disrespect, despise, and disobey God (Proverbs 30:17; Ephesians 6:1-3). (Again, let parents carefully note that such is their role and behave accordingly!) Luther in his comments on the Fourth Commandment in his Large Catechism makes such an excellent point of the honor that children have in obeying and serving their parents. He points out that all the monks and nuns in the world with all of their self-imposed works cannot have the satisfaction that a child has in obeying his or her parents. For God has not commanded the self-imposed works, but he has promised his blessing on the works of obedience rendered by a child to his or her parents. And (as Luther says so often) God does not lie!

Can there be any doubt that what God has to say about this first estate needs ever-greater emphasis in our day? Can there be any question that the setting aside of God's Word for marriage and family life has been the primary cause for so much of the misery that we see in families and in society in general? Certainly the difficulty of life in a fallen world would be much easier to bear, even with a goodly measure of patience and courage, if the Word of God was restored as our guide. But it is a daunting task indeed for that to happen even in a Christian family when the public square no longer knows anything about either modesty or shame. Nevertheless, nowhere do Christians have a greater honor from God than in the honor he gives them through the blessing he intends for them in their families when they strive to live in accord with his Word. His intended blessings are hindered to the extent that his Word is set aside; they are advanced in no small measure when Christ is King and his Word the guide. What he says generally certainly applies to family life as well: "Blessed rather are those who hear the word of God and obey it" (Luke 11:28).

To be sure, God does not give everyone the blessings of a family. But even those who live alone and without a family of their own have contributions to make to family life. St. Paul was unmarried and without a family of his own, but no one would argue that he was therefore not blessed by God or that his life was a waste! He saw himself as a father to many children, namely, his children by virtue of the gospel he had brought to them (e.g., 1 Corinthians 4:15; Galatians 4:19). He lived to serve them. He lived to teach them by word and example. He lived to cherish his relationship with them and was in turn encouraged, nourished, and strengthened by their relationship with him. He speaks of that generally in all of his epistles; he speaks of it in very personal terms especially in 1 and 2 Timothy and Titus.

Those who live alone, of course, are not without their burdens and temptations, even though theirs may be very different from the burdens and temptations of those in families. But they will go a long way towards bearing their burdens and fighting against their temptations if they concentrate on ways of serving and being useful to others. That's what Paul did (1 Corinthians 7:32). Freed from the obligations of family life, he was free to serve in ways that people in families are often unable to serve. Their service at least is divided, distracted, and limited by the responsibilities of serving their own families.

As the goal within a family should be unselfish service, so no less the goal of those without a family should be selfless service. It takes a good measure of grace to be selfless in service within a family; it takes at least as much to be selfless in service without the hoped-for reciprocal warmth and support of a family. Nevertheless, God does not let those who serve him outside of a family life go without his grace and favor. They have more time to grow in knowledge from the study of his Word. They have more time to live in a world larger than that of one family. They have a greater variety of opportunities to serve as they both look for the special gifts God has given each as an individual and then identify where those gifts can best be employed. As members of a family are hurt by the self-centered life of any member in the family, so the one who is alone hurts himself most if he dwells on the gifts God did not give him instead of cherishing and using the gifts that God has given; and as well he hurts those around him who could be served and uniquely so by his selflessness.

Whether in families or alone, all will have temptations and frustrations that are part and parcel of their state in life. But all also will find strength for the struggle in the gospel and blessings greater than any frustration when they serve with the gifts that God has given them for service. So St. Paul encourages each of us to share one another's burdens while we carry uniquely the burdens that God gives us as individuals (Galatians 6:2-5). In carrying the burdens of one another we imitate the compassion of Christ; in carrying our own unique burdens, those which we can only carry alone, we learn to lean on the Savior and to draw ever closer to him and to his Word for strength sufficient for the day. In sum, that is our life here on earth: to strive to live for him who has lived and died to make us his own for time and for eternity.

The church

God has given no greater aid or support for the first estate than the blessings he wants to give through the second estate. The second estate, the church, also began in the Garden of Eden before the fall into sin. Adam as the head of his family was also its first pastor. After the fall and throughout the Old Testament, God provided for the teaching of his Word and for public worship. Already in Genesis 4 there was public worship as Cain and Abel brought sacrifices to the Lord. Noah was a prophet and preacher of repentance (Genesis 6; 8:20; Hebrews 11:7). Wherever he went, Abraham built an altar and "called on the name of the LORD" (e.g., Genesis 13:4). In the book of Judges God provided his people with one prophet after another to teach his Word. After the exodus from Egypt, God gave priests and also prophets for the public proclamation of his Word.

In the New Testament, Jesus promised his perpetual presence with the church that he has established with the gospel (Matthew 28:18-20). And St. Paul assures us that God will continue to provide for his church on earth by giving her such leaders as she needs for the accomplishment of the saving purposes outlined in Matthew 28 (Ephesians 4:10-13).

It is a great miracle and gift of God that he has wondrously kept his promise to preserve the church. In spite of persecution on the outside and the ever-present threats to the gospel by false teachers on the inside of the visible church, the church endures. Just as Jesus promised so often, in spite of all the obstacles, his Word and its proclamation will last until the end of time.

We have already considered at some length the work and nature of the church (chapter 15); therefore, here we will only summarize a few of the more important points that highlight the work of the church as an estate instituted by God for our blessing during this, our earthly pilgrimage on the way to heaven.

The church, that is, Christians individually and collectively, has the singular assignment of proclaiming the Word of God in all of its truth and purity and administering the sacraments according to Christ's institution. That's the assignment that Jesus gave to the church at his ascension. That's the work that was carried out by the apostles and those they trained to teach after they had finished their own pilgrimage. The church especially through the visible institutions of parishes and schools and workers called to serve in them carries out that assignment given by Christ to all believers. The church brings the gospel to those it baptizes. It proclaims the message of forgiveness to people near and far. The church trusts the promise of Christ to be always present with his Word and sacraments, the promise to call the elect to himself and to strengthen such as have already come to him.

Therefore, in spite of all the obstacles, in spite of the fact that the church in every age looks like it is about to perish—in spite of it all—the believers gather together to hear the Word and receive the sacraments. They publicly proclaim the gospel to those near and those far away, and they cling to the miraculous faith that Christ will keep his Word and that therefore their labors are not in vain.

Thus, the church does as an institution many of those things that the individual Christian cannot do alone. It trains pastors, teachers, missionaries, and other such workers as are needed for carrying out Christ's Great Commission in Matthew 28.

However, having said that, we always need to remember that the church as an institution is not a substitute for the Christian's individual responsibility. The church is there as an institution to help the Christian in carrying out his responsibility, not to take all responsibility away from the individual. The church through its pastors and teachers, for example, teaches the Word of God to our children, but it does that as an aid to parents, not as a substitute for the teaching that is primarily their responsibility. Luther's Small Catechism is taught in schools and confirmation classes, but it was written initially and primarily for fathers to teach their children. The church assists parents—it doesn't take their place.

Likewise, the church helps members with the teaching of the Word in public services and in Bible classes. By that teaching Christians are equipped to share that same Word in their homes, in private devotion, and in the personal sharing of the gospel where they have the opportunity to do that with friends and coworkers. Often the gospel shared by members of a congregation is more effective than the efforts of pastors to reach the lost; for people expect pastors to come with the gospel and often easily dismiss what they say with the thought, "Well, that's what they're paid to do." But when a member shares the gospel, even if it is nothing more than the "Come and see" of St. Philip (John 1:46), that can be a very effective beginning for the proclamation of the gospel more fully later on.

The church by the pure teaching of the Word helps members grow in their understanding of what it means to be a Christian and to live a Christian life. But the church cannot live that life for us; members who think that merely by their membership in the church they have done all that's needed in the living of a Christian life are not Christians but hypocrites.

Thus, the church has one and only one business in all that it does: the proclamation of the gospel and the administration of the sacraments. The forms that the church uses for that one occupation are many and varied to be sure. The church has parishes and schools. It has institutions for serving the troubled and the aged and the infirm with the message of the gospel and with help for them in their special needs. It has a publishing house for the printing and the dissemination of Christian literature. But all of these are legitimate institutions precisely because they advance that one single assignment that Christ has given to the church. As St. Paul reminds us, they serve that purpose because through them God uses his Word so that

> we will no longer be infants, tossed back and forth by the waves, and blown here and there by every wind of teaching and by the cunning and craftiness of men in their deceitful scheming. Instead, speaking the truth in love, we will in all things grow up into him who is the Head, that is, Christ. From him the whole body, joined and held together by every supporting ligament, grows and builds itself up in love, as each part does its work. (Ephesians 4:14-16)

Those words of the apostle sum up well what we do with and for one another in the second estate. Where that work is faithfully carried out, individuals and families will certainly be blessed. And again we note that to the extent that families are strong, to that extent the church will be strong. Strong in doing what? Strong in strengthening individuals and families as together we strive to live in Christ as Christ lives in his church through the preaching of the gospel. Certainly in this day and age we need all the mutual encouragement we can get as the individual Christian and the church swim against the godless tides that threaten to engulf us all!

When the church as an institution is busy with that work, it will have neither time nor inclination to mix in work that God never gave it to do in the first place. That is, the church is not where we collectively and as an institution seek to establish world peace, end world hunger, save the environment, get the government to . . . , and on and on. While such efforts may be noble in themselves, they are not the business of the church as such. To be sure, Christians as individuals, as citizens of the state, will want their faith to influence their life in the community, the state, and the world—who they vote for and the like. And Christians as citizens may well support such causes in society that they consider worthy of support for the best interests of the whole. To be sure, the church may support in a limited way her own institutions for helping the poor and giving counsel to the troubled and aid to the otherwise needy. But these must not become the central focus of the work of the church. The primary focus must remain preaching and teaching the gospel and administering the sacraments.

One cannot help but notice that churches often make a "social gospel" the center of attention after they have given up the focus on the pure teaching of God's Word. For teaching all that God has given us in his Word is bound to upset many; it is easier to leave doctrine to the individual and join in efforts that will offend no one. The church that makes its *primary function* the concerns of this world for health and welfare and good government and the like has lost its way. The church that uses its clergy to serve as a lobbying group before the government has lost its way; it seeks to accomplish what it considers the will of God for the world and has forgotten that only the Word of God can create faith and produce a Christian life. The government with its laws can enforce outward decency to some extent, but it cannot create a Christian society or nation. Only the Word of God can do that, the Word as it is shared by God's people and proclaimed by the church in her parishes and schools. To put it all another way: It is the business of the church to deal with souls, to deal with them one at a time, to heal them with the balm of forgiveness, to strengthen them for a life that leads to heaven, and to share those blessings with as many as possible.

Next to the family, the church with its gospel in Word and sacraments is indeed a great gift of God. With all the flaws of those who serve and those served, it nevertheless remains as God's temple and dwelling place on earth. Through its proclamation of the gospel God comes to dwell with us. Through its instruction from the Word of God it provides us with the guide for a life that pleases God here, and in the gospel it opens to us the gates of heaven in the hour of death.

The government

Government is the third estate through which God would bless our lives on earth. Unlike the family and the church, government was instituted after the fall into sin. The existence of government assumes that all are sinners and that most need an outward discipline to keep society from collapsing in chaos and violence, as each person seeks to get his own will done at the expense of all and any who get in the way.

While we easily see the connection between God and the institution of the family and the church, God's finger is a bit less obvious in the instituting of government. That is, we see his institution of government initially through his control and guiding hand over history and then later from what he has to say about government especially in the New Testament.

From the time of the building of the Tower of Babel, people have organized themselves into communities with goals for life in this world—whether those goals are for good or ill. By the time that we meet Abraham in the book of Genesis, governments of one sort or another had already existed in the world for a long time. At the time of Joseph, Egypt had a highly developed form of government.

It is in the law that God gave to the new nation of Israel after the exodus from Egypt that we begin to get a clearer view of God's institution and intentions for government. Especially in the book of Deuteronomy we see a fairly comprehensive law code that God himself gave for the nation.[8] While the political law of the Old Testament was intended for Israel and thus as such does not apply to us, nevertheless, we can draw a number of useful conclusions about God's intentions for government in general from that law:

1. The institution of government assumes that the law inscribed on the heart of man at creation has since the fall become clouded in the minds and hearts of men.
2. It assumes that even where that law, the natural law, is still active in people there are nevertheless many who ignore it and many who will not let that law and the voice of conscience direct their outward behavior.
3. Accordingly, some external regulation is necessary for the orderly functioning of society, for the protection of the weak, and for the general welfare.
4. The external regulation must be accompanied by external punishment for the breaking of the law.
5. Both the law and its threats are aimed not at the inside of man but at his outward behavior.

---

[8]For a further consideration of this topic, cf. chapter 9 for a discussion of the political law in the Old Testament under the heading "The three kinds of law in the Bible."

Accordingly, the work of government and the work of the church are very different. Governments deal primarily with outward behavior; the church deals primarily with the heart and soul. The government has laws and force to control behavior; the church has the gospel to create and preserve faith. The government is concerned with this life alone; the church is concerned with this life as the prelude and preparation for eternal life.

In the New Testament there is no political law as such. But, nevertheless, the New Testament is not silent about the Christian and his relationship to the state. Jesus tells us that we should pay our taxes (Luke 20:22-25). He said that in the context of a government that used the taxes for the maintaining of public order, the creation and support of a currency used in trade, and the building of roads and the like. The government of Jesus' day used the taxes as well for the support of violent and wicked officials and for cruel and violent treatment of the people. Consider the slaughter of the holy innocents and the necessary flight of the holy family (Matthew 2:1-18) that we remember every year on December 28. Consider especially Jesus' trials in the courts of Pontius Pilate and King Herod. Nevertheless, Jesus left no room for rebellion against the right of the government to tax, even though much of the government's revenue would be misused.

The apostles Peter and Paul have a good deal to say about government and the attitude that Christians should have toward it. It is important to remember that their words are part of the divinely inspired Word of God. It is important as well to keep in mind that when God gave those words through the inspired apostles, he was talking about government in general. That is, he was not speaking of a "Christian country" or of "Christian government and law." There was and is no such thing. Indeed the government under which the apostles lived had made Christianity an illegal religion. It was so hostile to the gospel that it arrested and martyred many Christians and most of the apostles.

Nevertheless, what do the apostles tell us about our relationship to the state? St. Peter sums it up:

> Submit yourselves for the Lord's sake to every authority instituted among men: whether to the king, as the supreme authority, or to governors, who are sent by him to punish those who do wrong and to commend those who do right. For it is God's will that by doing good you should silence the ignorant talk of foolish men. Live as free men, but do not use your freedom as a cover-up for evil; live as servants of God. Show proper respect to everyone:

> Love the brotherhood of believers, fear God, honor the king. (1 Peter 2:13-17)

Again it is worth noting that Peter is not naïve when he writes these words. He knows very well that many rulers are in their character and in their carrying out of their duties evil men. He knows as well that many whose duty it is to enforce the law are themselves chief among lawbreakers. But he takes no note of that. He says, "Submit," and adds the important phrase "for the Lord's sake." That is, submit because that is what the Lord wants. He doesn't say, "Submit when they do their duty; submit when it serves your own best purposes and intentions; submit when they themselves carefully follow the laws they are supposed to enforce on others." No, he tells us that we should submit because that's what God wants us to do.

St. Paul makes the same point in greater detail. He urges us to pray for the state and its officials and adds an important blessing that comes to us from God's answer to our prayers for the state. He says,

> I urge, then, first of all, that requests, prayers, intercession and thanksgiving be made for everyone—for kings and all those in authority, that we may live peaceful and quiet lives in all godliness and holiness. This is good, and pleases God our Savior, who wants all men to be saved and to come to a knowledge of the truth. (1 Timothy 2:1-4)

Certainly it is clear that we should obey the government for which we pray. It is equally clear that as we obey it and God preserves civil order in answer to our prayer, it will be easier for us to live peaceful and quiet lives in godliness and honesty. If you doubt that, just look at places on earth where there is no effective government; a quiet and peaceful life in godliness and honesty is in such places almost impossible.

The blessing this passage adds has to do with the proclamation of the gospel itself. Christ came to redeem us all and it is his good and gracious will that the proclamation go out into all the world. But where there is no effective government maintaining law and order, the proclamation of the gospel is hindered or even prevented. Therefore also for the sake of the great mission of the church we pray for the state. For though the government is not interested in maintaining law and order for the sake of the gospel, nevertheless, that is an important blessing that God gives through this third estate.

Paul is equally clear about our duties to the third estate in Romans 13:1-7. Let the reader of these verses note carefully what the apostle tells us, namely,

1. Each one of us is to submit to the governing authority.
2. God has established all authority.
3. The one who rebels, therefore, rebels against God and brings judgment on himself.
4. The government holds the sword to enforce its will and accordingly has the right even to take human life.[9]
5. The government is God's servant for the punishment of outward acts of evil and the protection and rewarding of those who do good.

Notice that the apostle does not say that the government is to be obeyed only when it carries out those functions properly. When it does, that is a great and special blessing of the Lord for which we certainly pray and give thanks. But again, Paul was not naïve. He knew full well and from personal experience that the government often did not carry out its God-given functions properly, that often it was even violently opposed to the preaching of the gospel. Nevertheless, he says, as does St. Peter in the previously cited passage: Submit, obey!

Accordingly, it is not up to the Christian to decide that it is time to be rid of a government that the Christian thinks is no longer doing its proper duty or carrying out even its own laws properly. When God considers it time to be rid of a government, he will find ways to do that. That's not up to us. To be sure, in those nations where there is a constitutional right to replace one set of rulers with another through a ballot box, there the citizen is not engaged in rebellion when he votes for new rulers; he is supporting the law of the state itself. But where the citizen uses bullets instead of ballots, there he should not imagine that he has the blessing of God for his actions. There is nothing in what Jesus said or what Peter and Paul wrote by inspiration that would allow for violence against the state.

But did not the apostles themselves disobey the government when they continued to preach the gospel, as in Acts 4 and 5? And what about the Christians in all those years up to the Edict of Milan by the

---

[9]Normally by the power of the sword we mean that the state has the right to execute a criminal and the right to wage what are called "just wars." Just which crimes merit the death penalty is for the state to decide; just what makes a war a "just war" is often difficult to say, given that the state controls the message when it goes to war; only much later may one discover that the reasons for a war were hidden and that perhaps the war was not "just" after all. To say more than that here goes beyond the scope of this book; about all that we can say is that we are largely left with the state's own verdict when it goes to war; we are obliged not to rebel against the authority placed over us and also to do our part in defending our nation.

Emperor Constantine in A.D. 313? For most of the time before A.D. 313, Christianity was an illegal religion; nevertheless, Christians even in the face of death at the hands of the state continued to believe and continued to share the gospel. Wasn't that disobedience to the state?

We notice two important things in answer to the question. The first is that the apostles themselves tell us what the exception is when it comes to obeying the government; when the government ordered them to cease sharing the gospel, they answered, "Judge for yourselves whether it is right in God's sight to obey you rather than God. For we cannot help speaking about what we have seen and heard" (Acts 4:19,20). Thus, if the government commands something that is clearly contrary to the Word of God, we have the right to refuse obedience. That's what the apostles did and what Christians have done down through the ages when the state has tried to forbid faith and the sharing of the gospel.

The second thing that we note is just as important: the right to refuse to obey when commanded by the state to do something contrary to the Word of God nowhere carries with it the right to seek the violent overthrow of the state. Even when Christians had sufficient numbers to launch a revolt against the state that was persecuting them, they did not thereby have a right to revolt. The apostles did not return to the Christians after they had suffered a beating at the hands of the Sanhedrin and say, "The government has totally abandoned its proper function; it's time to storm the temple and throw the rascals out!" Nor did the Christians in those years before A.D. 313 ever launch a revolution to topple the corrupt Roman government, even when they may have had sufficient numbers to succeed in doing it. Two options are open when the government persecutes, when it commands what God forbids or forbids what God commands. The two options are peaceful resistance or flight. Indeed, Jesus himself foretold the destruction of Jerusalem that would occur in the year A.D. 70. By that time the government of Jerusalem was utterly incapable of carrying out the proper functions of government. Even the temple precincts were filled with blood. But what does Jesus tell his followers to do when the day of destruction is clearly at hand? Does he tell them to storm the city and temple and set things right with a Christian government? Not at all! He tells them to flee (Matthew 24:15,16).

We see other examples of those options in both the Old Testament and in the New Testament. When David was being pursued by Saul, he resisted by taking flight and that even after Saul had begun to persecute the church (1 Samuel 22). But when he had the opportunity to violently revolt, to kill Saul, he refused to do it and spoke eloquently of his duty to await God's own dealing with Saul (1 Samuel 24:1-7). When remaining in Israel was too much, he left (1 Samuel 27). While David's behavior among the Philistines may be open to criticism, the important point for us here is that he never revolted against his own king nor sanctioned anyone else revolting. That was so even when he had the ability to hasten God's own promise to David that David should be king.

In the New Testament we have the example of the Christians in Acts 8. When a general persecution broke out in Jerusalem, they scattered throughout Judea and Samaria and "those who had been scattered preached the word wherever they went" (Acts 8:4). But never did they revolt or long for the day when they could succeed in launching a revolution. That behavior is consistent with the behavior of Christians through the ages when they were subject to governments that did not act as governments should in punishing the outward behavior of evildoers and in protecting those who do good. More than that, it is in accord with the apostle's divinely inspired injunction: "Therefore, it is necessary to submit to the authorities, not only because of possible punishment but also because of conscience" (Romans 13:5); and their conscience was formed in submission first and foremost to the Word of God.

Thus, the Christian is obliged to obey the law of the land insofar as it does not command something contrary to the Word of God. If it should so command, then the Christian has both the right and the duty to resist. If, for example, the state would require that a Christian doctor perform an abortion even if the life of the mother were not clearly threatened, the doctor would have to refuse. He could as a citizen with rights granted in the law of the land seek a change in what the government required of him, but he would not have the right to launch a rebellion or to encourage others to revolt. His options are peaceful resistance, even to the point of suffering the consequences of such a resistance, or flight (whether into a different occupation or a different territory). Or, if the government would require that the church cease its teaching that homosexual behavior is a sin and insist that the church sanction and even perform marriages between couples of the same sex, the church would have to refuse and resist. Its members could work for a change in the law through the courts and the ballot box, but the church could not urge them to a violent revolution. Resistance and even suffering the consequences of resistance is nothing new for Christians; however, revolution is not a legitimate solution to the problem.

The alternatives of resistance or flight may present the Christian with a heavy price to pay for loyalty to the Word of God. But as difficult and expensive as such loyalty may be, it is still as nothing compared to the price paid by God himself for our redemption. Indeed, the apostles rejoiced that they had the honor of suffering for the sake of the gospel (Acts 5:41).

So it is the primary business of the state as instituted by God to govern the outward behavior of people in the interest of maintaining an orderly society. It is to carry out that business by means of law and punishment for those who break the law. It has the tools of taxes and the sword for accomplishing its will. And the business of the Christian is to pray for the state and its rulers, to submit to its authority, and in general to further its proper function by obeying the law of the land and urging others to do the same.

Just as it is the duty of the state to deal with outward behavior, so it is not the duty of the state to deal with the faith of the soul. That is, the state should not interfere with the work of the church in its proclamation of the Word of God. What people believe is really none of the state's business; outward behavior is what should concern the state. We notice that already in the Old Testament; believing rulers understood that. Joseph, after he became the most powerful man in Egypt next to the pharaoh, did not force his faith on the nation. Likewise, the great prophet Daniel was a leading ruler in the governments of a number of kings; he, like Joseph before him, confessed his faith but did not use the power of the state to impose it on the nation.

Just as clearly, it is not the business of the church to tell the state what to do, to try to create a "Christian government." To be sure, Christians as citizens of the state may campaign and support such laws as they think best support public decency and order. But they do that as citizens—not as representatives of the church trying to force the Word of God on those who do not believe it and do not want it.

A Christian, for example, as a citizen may vote for candidates for public office that he thinks will act in harmony with the natural law and thus promote the general health and welfare of society. He may decide to run for public office as well. But it is not the business of the church or its pastors and teachers as representatives of the church to actively pursue a "Christian agenda" as lobbyists in the halls of the government.

Christians will recognize that they are really citizens of two kingdoms: the one of this world (the state in society) and the one that is eternal (the invisible church on earth leading to the church eternal in heaven). The two kingdoms have the same King: Christ. But the way Christ rules over the two and the way the Christian acts in each are distinct. In the earthly kingdom Christ rules by his control over history. The Christian citizen acts in obedience to Christ when he obeys the laws of the land that can be obeyed without violating the law of God. He uses as well such rights as the temporal kingdom gives him for the benefit and betterment of society. The state gives him, for example, the right to oppose or support zoning laws. The Christian may use that right to oppose the location, let us say, of a pornographic bookstore or an abortion clinic. He may rightly argue that such things are counter to the public good for a whole host of reasons. He may campaign against the local public school's social studies curriculum when he sees that it promotes or treats as an indifferent matter abortion, same sex marriage, and the view that all religions are alike and that there really is no such thing as absolute truth. The Word of God has formed his thinking. However, when he enters into a campaign in the earthly kingdom, he is obliged to use earthly tools; that is, he will argue with his voice and his vote, with reason and natural law. He will not run into the council chamber waving his Bible and the catechism. The state is not interested in those things and is not governed by them. That is not the language of the state. The state is and ought to be interested in outward behavior that promotes an orderly society, peace, and public decency as it (rightly or wrongly) understands those things. It is to those goals that the Christian as a citizen of the earthly kingdom will address himself, even though it is the Word of God that has formed his attitude and his faith.

Thus, the actions of the Christian as a citizen of the state are one thing; the behavior of the church as an institution is quite another thing. The church is concerned with not just this life but the next. It will use the tools that Christ has given to it for the goals and the work he has given to the church. It will use the Word of God to rebuke sin, even the sins of rulers. It will use the gospel to call all who will listen to the forgiveness that Christ has won for us all. It will warn of the judgment of God that falls on society, on nations, and states that despise even natural law. And it will warn especially of the eternal consequences of clinging in unbelief to sin. But as an institution it will not become a pressure or lobbying organization to try and control the state. To put it another way: Just as the state should stay out of the business of proclaiming the gospel, so the church as an institution should stay out of the business of government—even though the members of the church as individuals are active as citizens in society and have as citizens rights and obligations over and against the state.

The point can be made even on a very practical level. The church in its preaching and teaching opposes as it should abortion when the life of the mother is not clearly in danger. But what happens if the church as an organization enters the public square to campaign against abortion? What of the poor woman who had an abortion? Does she conclude, "This is a church that doesn't want me, that teaches that God hates me because I did this terrible thing!"? She may reasonably conclude exactly that and never come to hear the message of the gospel.

That is not to say that the Christian as an individual, as a citizen, may not enter into such a campaign. But the church as church hinders its own primary work of proclaiming the gospel to all when it drives people away from the gospel by public campaigning even against obvious evil. The same is true when the church allies itself with a political party for whatever reason. Those not of that political persuasion identify that church with all and sundry in that party—whether the church intends that or not. And thereby those who disagree consider themselves not welcome in that church. Again, we are not here considering the actions of the Christian as citizen but the actions of the church as church. The Christian as a citizen should be involved in the affairs of his nation and indeed has much to contribute to the welfare of the state. But the church as such is charged with the proclamation of the gospel, not the governing of the state.

The point is that as much as possible the church as church and the state as state should stay out of each other's business. They have different goals and different tools. Mixing them together invariably does damage to the goals and tools of both of them.

That is not to say that a complete separation is ever possible. To some extent the two kingdoms will inevitably intersect. Thus, for example, the church and its schools are obliged to obey the fire safety laws in their buildings. The workers of the church may be obliged to participate in governmentally sponsored and required pension plans. The church is not free from legal liability if its workers break the law. At the same time the church benefits from police and fire protection from the state. It even is helped to some extent in its work when the government for reasons of its own exempts both church property and contributions to charitable organizations from taxes. Students in parish and worker training schools may benefit from books that the state provides for schools that want them or from scholarships that the state may give to students, no matter where they go to school.

But when it comes to the core function of the church, the proclamation of the Word of God, the church in her parishes and schools should avoid entanglement as much as possible. Where the state directly supports a school, the state has purchased the right to dictate curriculum and policy. It may not do so today but eventually it will want to exercise that right. The state-supported school whose curriculum, enrollment, and employment policies run afoul of the current thinking of the government should not expect that the government will never interfere with its operation. What then will become of the church school that has come to depend on the state for subsidy, for its existence? Will it compromise the truth of God's Word to avoid closing? Or will it surrender its buildings and/or faculty because it can no longer afford them? Either choice would be avoided if the church had supported its own mission in the school. Indeed, why should the general public be expected in the first place to support that mission? And if it does, why should anyone be surprised if the general public through its governmental representatives considers that it has a right to impose its own priorities on the school it is paying for?

The same principle holds for the government's support of various chaplaincy programs. It is to the church that God has entrusted the gospel. And it is the church that should call and support those who publicly proclaim it. Moreover, if the government is hiring and paying for clergy, then the government has the right to determine what the clergy will preach and teach. In point of fact, when the government does engage in such hiring, it does so for reasons of its own, not for the proclamation of the pure gospel. Accordingly, chaplains should be the responsibility of the church. State-hired chaplains will find it difficult indeed to do mission work in their state-sponsored capacity. The state will certainly not look with favor on such a chaplain when he opposes false doctrine in defense of the true. In hospitals, prisons, and in the military, the church seeks to serve her own members and anyone else who will listen, to serve with the pure proclamation of the Word of God. That's the business of the church, not of the state.

We cannot here consider every possible way in which church and state may or may not interact. Hopefully, these few examples may suggest the general parameters of how the principle of separation of church and state, of the second and third estates, is applied.

As we can never sufficiently thank God for the blessings of the first two estates, so too we can never sufficiently thank him for the blessings of the third estate. That is especially the case where the state protects the rights of citizens to believe what they will and accordingly protects also our right to believe and teach the Word of God in all of its truth and purity.

The Fifth through Tenth Commandments

We have considered at some length the Fourth Commandment under the heading of the three estates. In what remains of this chapter we will briefly summarize the rest of the Second Table of the Law, while recognizing that much of it is also covered in our discussion of the three estates. These commandments are concerned with the loving service that we should give to our neighbor, and that out of love first and foremost to God himself. Accordingly, every failure to keep any of the commandments is at once failure to keep the First Commandment. For if we loved God above all things, we would not offend him by failing to love and serve our neighbor. Jesus says that such loving service of our neighbor is the second greatest commandment (Matthew 22:39).

In the Fifth Commandment God forbids murder and by implication calls on us to do all that we can to help our neighbor preserve his body and life. It is important to emphasize in this connection that such service to our neighbor must be in accord with the law of God. Someone, for example, may feel that it is an act of love to permit or conduct an abortion when the life of the mother is not in danger. But that is not what the Fifth Commandment says when it forbids murder, and it certainly is no act of love to the unborn child whose day of grace is thus violently snuffed out.[10] But it is service to God most pleasing when we do what we can to assist our neighbor in need. Jesus says that he treasures and counts such works as works done to him (Matthew 25:40). What an honor! When I see my neighbor in need, it is as though I see Jesus in need—and I have the opportunity of serving him—yes, what an honor!

The Sixth Commandment calls us to a chaste and decent life in thought, word, and deed. It exalts marriage as the divinely instituted means for a godly satisfaction of God-given sexual desires. In marriage the couple lives a chaste and decent life when each loves and honors the other. To forbid marriage or to treat it as something less noble than the single life is, as Paul says, a doctrine of the devils (1 Timothy 4:1-5). The

---

[10]Abortion can be justified only when the life of the mother is clearly in danger; in such cases the Christian has the painful task of choosing between a life and a life. Why God would inflict so gruesome and painful a choice on anyone is a mystery whose answer must wait until heaven. It is another one of those instances in which the Christian under the cross clings alone to the promise of God's love and mercy, a promise that cannot lie, no matter how painful the cross of the moment.

couple that has a sexual relationship outside of marriage may say that they are acting in love, but the Word of God in the Sixth Commandment and throughout the Bible says that such a relationship outside of marriage is not love but lust, fornication, or adultery. A man cannot turn his beloved away from Christ, the ultimate Bridegroom, and call it love; and a woman cannot turn the eyes of her beloved away from God to rebellion against him and call it love. No matter how the pair may feel, it is God's Word that governs, not our feelings, our reason, or the perverse notions of the day. It is a great and noble work pleasing to God when couples and individuals before marriage aim at and strive for hearts, minds, and bodies that honor God with, as Luther puts it, "a pure (chaste) and decent life." And no less it is an act of worship pleasing to God when in marriage each is faithful to and cares for the other out of love to God as well as out of love for the spouse.

In both the Fifth and Sixth Commandments the Christian may experience a struggle against his fallen nature that is difficult indeed! It is not easy to put others first, even a cherished spouse. It is not easy before marriage or even often in marriage to keep the mind and body free of lust for the forbidden. When the struggle is difficult, the Christian becomes more acutely aware of the fact that his life is lived under the cross. It is exactly at such times that we fly and flee to the gospel in Word and sacrament for comfort and for strength to endure and struggle against temptations that may seem almost impossible to bear. St. Paul gives us excellent advice for the struggle when he tells us,

> Whatever is true, whatever is noble, whatever is right, whatever is pure, whatever is lovely, whatever is admirable—if anything is excellent or praiseworthy—think about such things. Whatever you have learned or received or heard from me, or seen in me—put it into practice. And the God of peace will be with you. (Philippians 4:8,9)

Excellent advice indeed! To the extent that we fail to follow it, to that extent we will see again how much we need God's grace and the sacrifice of his Son on the cross to pay for our sins. To the extent that we heed his counsel, to that extent we will experience in life and in conscience the promise that Paul adds: "And the God of peace will be with you."

Things are no less a challenge for us in the Seventh Commandment. There God calls on us to live an honest life. How easy that sounds, but how difficult it often is to accomplish! An honest life means that we work diligently so that we can support ourselves, our family, and, as much as possible, help those who cannot support themselves (Ephesians 4:28; 2 Thessalonians 3:10-12; 1 Timothy 5:8;

6:1,2). It means that we refuse to steal from an employer by laziness or from the state by dishonest tax returns. It means that we see all our possessions as gifts given by God. He gave such gifts through the ability that he has given us to work with our hands and minds. We are accordingly his stewards, entrusted with a measure of time and ability. It is as well his gift that we have opportunities to work and serve with that time and that ability. At times he gives us gifts as well through gifts from others or through an inheritance. At still other times the gifts of God may come in part through the fruits of savings or through investment in useful business, like the investment of the wise wife in Proverbs 31.

Whether our possessions are the result of God's gift to us, the ability to work and earn, or the generosity of others in their gifts or in an inheritance, all that we are and have comes from his hand; all that we have is entrusted to us as stewards of his bounty. Does he want us to enjoy for ourselves the gifts he has given? Of course he does. And so we receive and enjoy his gifts with thanksgiving. But at the same time we are mindful of the needs of the family and the stranger, not least of the needs of the church at home and abroad. An extravagant or wasteful or lazy lifestyle that does not make those needs also a priority steals from God the return that he wants on his investment in us. God promises to provide for us when we do not rob him of his due but instead seek to serve him with the time and treasure that he has given us. Read Malachi 3:8-18 and see how God promises to bless those who serve him with the gifts he has given. The bottom line of the promise is that you cannot out-give God. He always repays and does so with abundant interest.

St. Paul summed up the matter so succinctly in Ephesians 4:28: "He who has been stealing must steal no longer, but must work, doing something useful with his own hands, that he may have something to share with those in need."

The prophet Joel in the Old Testament too put the matter so well. He was praying that God would end the famine in the land. But why should God do that? Was it so that the people would all again be fat and happy? No! The prophet called the nation to genuine and heartfelt repentance, a repentance that looks for a restoration of prosperity, with these words: "He may turn and have pity and leave behind a blessing—grain offerings and drink offerings for the LORD your God" (Joel 2:14). Isn't that interesting? Not to satisfy self, not to satisfy human greed, but for enough to give back to God, that is what the prophet prayed for! The joy that the individual would have from the return of God's blessing would certainly be great and real—but secondary to the opportunity God's blessings gave for grateful service to him.

Obviously, then, greed and envy, selfishness, and a lust to be wealthy so that I need never look again to God's hand for what I need in this life—all of that is contrary to the Seventh Commandment (1 Timothy 6:6-10; Matthew 6:25-34). One of the more popular ways of displaying greed in our day is the vice of gambling. By gambling one seeks wealth apart from work and at the same time sets at risk the wealth that God has given. Sadly, in all too many cases, so eager is the lust for unearned wealth that some end up losing everything it its pursuit. Even Christians sometimes lose self-control and become consumed with an overwhelming desire for more wealth. Marriage and family end up as casualties of such excessive gambling. The one who answers "But if I win, I'll be more generous to those in need!" seeks a pretty mask for an ugly vice. Even if he is serious—a doubtful proposition!—his argument is really this: "I will do evil in the hope that good may come of it." That is certainly not a God-pleasing motivation. If one with such an attitude wins, the devil tempts him to further greed; if he loses, he should see in the loss the judgment of God on his own perverse and greedy heart. God provides a clear reminder, "Godliness with contentment is great gain" and warns that "the love of money is the root of all kinds of evil" (1 Timothy 6:6,10).

Among the most difficult and, likewise, most easily ignored of the commandments is the Eighth Commandment. It bids us speak honestly in court and in legal documents (including our tax returns!). But beyond that it commands us to speak well of our neighbor, to neither gossip about him nor slander him, even when he is at fault. It calls us to defend him and as the catechism puts it "to put the best construction on everything." While the Bible often speaks of the sins of the tongue against our neighbor (e.g., Psalm 50:19-22; Zechariah 8:17; 1 Corinthians 13:7; James 4:11), Proverbs 31:8,9 puts the matter most graphically: "Speak up for those who cannot speak for themselves, for the rights of all who are destitute. Speak up and judge fairly; defend the rights of the poor and needy." Who are those who cannot speak for themselves? Who are the destitute, poor, and needy? Who more than those being gossiped about? They are absent and helpless before the daggers in the mouths of their attackers. And that is so even if what the gossip says is true.

To be sure, public sin and especially false doctrine must be publicly rebuked, as Jesus and the apostles and prophets show us repeatedly in the Bible. But loveless and malicious chatter about our neighbors' flaws, faults, and failings rarely have such high motives in mind. Luther speaks about that in his comments on the Eighth Commandment in the Large Catechism. He tells us that if we are so high-minded about our neighbors' sin, then we should speak to him or to the appropriate authorities. That's just what Jesus said (Matthew 18:15-17). But if we do not want to do that, Luther says, "Now you smell the roast! The speaking is coming not from a heart that loves and seeks improvement, but from loveless malice" (Large Catechism, Kolb, p. 422).

It is plain to see in these commandments that the Christian life that results from faith consists not just of outward behavior, as important as that is. The Christian's outward life has as its necessary prerequisite a Christian heart and mind-set. The Ten Commandments show that necessary prerequisite in the First Table of the Law and then again most explicitly in the Ninth and Tenth Commandments. The Ninth and Tenth Commandments deal with coveting.

Coveting is a wishing for or a wanting of things that God has withheld from me. It is pining for things that I cannot obtain by honest labor, savings, and investment or that I will never obtain through gift from another. That coveting may often end up in stealing or dishonorable use of the courts to get something by legal trickery is certainly true. But the coveting all by itself is already a sin. It is just as Jesus said so clearly: The heart is the root source of most of the evil that is done outwardly (Matthew 15:19). Thus, if we are to lead a Christian life, that life must start in the heart. The heart must first be made clean and pure by the grace of forgiveness. Then and only then can there follow a heart that strives to grow in a love and gratitude to Christ; then and only then will the heart begin to show love and gratitude in a life of obedience.

It should be obvious that so much of what we have considered under the heading of the Christian life runs against the inborn assumption that I will be happy if I just get my own way and "do my own thing." That's the way of the world and the dominant theme of our culture. In point of fact, the reverse is true. Our peace and happiness both here and hereafter consist of a life that is hidden with Christ in God. St. Paul calls us to such a life and expresses it beautifully:

> Since, then, you have been raised with Christ, set your hearts on things above, where Christ is seated at the right hand of God. Set your minds on things above, not on earthly things. For you died, and your life is hidden with Christ in God. When Christ, who is your life, appears, then you also will appear with him in glory. (Colossians 3:1-4)

In the rest of Colossians 3 the apostle sums up masterfully what that kind of a life is that is hidden with Christ in God. The chapter bears frequent reading and review!

To sum up then under the Ten Commandments and to repeat what is meant by good works, we may put it this way:

1. A good work is a work that is done in accord with and in obedience to the law of God.
2. A good work is a work that is done to the glory of God and not a work by which I hope to merit in some way or degree my own salvation.
3. A good work, especially those called for in the Second Table of the Law, is done for the benefit of my neighbor without a selfish motive that acts only when there is the possibility of return or reward.
4. A good work before God is a work done with the joyful expectation that God is pleased with it and will cleanse whatever is lacking in my motives or performance with the forgiving blood of Jesus.

It is of course simply impossible here to give a codebook or a canon law book that lists all that is involved in the leading of a Christian life. Here and in earlier chapters (cf. especially chapter 9) we have tried to express the principles that God gives us in his Word, principles that have endless application. It is the business of the Christian to examine his own heart and life in the light of God's Word and then to apply that Word as best he can in his day-to-day life. To that end he may often have occasion to ask his pastor or other Christian friends for advice and counsel. God has given us friends and counselors so that we can serve them in love and so that they can help guide us as well in our pilgrimage from here to our eternal home.

PART VI

ESCHATOLOGY

Chapter 17
Eschatology

Eschatology is the study of last things. Under that heading we consider what happens to us when we die and after we die, the existence of heaven and hell, the end of the world, and the return of Christ to judge the living and the dead.

Eschatology is a broad topic indeed. But we have to say at the outset that as we consider all of these things, we will often find that we have more questions than answers. There are a number of reasons why that is the case.

The first is the most obvious: In all of these things we are subject to the Word of God alone. We can know only what he has told us in his Word. Idle speculation apart from that Word invariably lands people in a swamp of confusion and contradiction.

Second, God has not chosen to answer all of the questions that we may have about life after death or about heaven and hell. We may reasonably assume that he has not answered all of our questions because we wouldn't understand the answers, even if he had given them. After all, once we leave this life and enter into eternity, we will be separated from our earthbound definitions of time and space. We will enter into an existence that has no more temptation, no more sin, and none of the consequences of sin; that is a condition impossible for us in the here and now to even begin to imagine—so bound are we by time and space, so beset by temptations, sins, and their consequences.

So in his Word about these last things God does what he always does in his Word: He speaks absolute and utterly reliable truth; he comforts the penitent sinner; he warns the impenitent; and he shows forth the glory of his grace in Christ our Savior. As we are content with and rejoice in all of his Word, so we will be content with and rejoice in what God has to tell us in the study of the last things.

Death

The Bible has a number of passages that sum up the whole matter of death for us in a way that is designed at once to take the sting out of our consideration of our own impending end. That we need such counsel from God should be evident to all. The fear of death is natural to us particularly since God at creation never intended that we should die. He built into us, so to speak, a longing for life and a dread of death. But whether we want to think about it or not, death is a reality that is inescapable. We need God's own Word to put it all into a proper perspective. Listen to the way he does that through the writer to the Hebrews: "Just as man is destined to die once, and after that to face judgment, so Christ was sacrificed once to take away the sins of many people; and he will appear a second time, not to bear sin, but to bring salvation to those who are waiting for him" (Hebrews 9:27,28).

Notice how the holy writer puts at once a positive spin on the whole matter. Yes, it is true; we must die. Yes, it is certain; at death we face the judgment of God. Ah, but that's not for the believer a terrible prospect at all. For in all that follows death we cling as we did in life to that one great joyful certainty: Christ bore our sins to bring salvation to those who wait for him, yes, and who long to see him in glory.

That's how St. Paul also wants us to think about our death. He puts it so succinctly: "The wages of sin is death, but the gift of God is eternal life in Christ Jesus our Lord" (Romans 6:23). He understands well that death is a horror to us by nature. Even the animals shrink from it and struggle to stay alive when death threatens. For as already noted, death is in a way unnatural; we were not created to die but to live forever. But the entry of sin into the world ended that golden aim that God had for us all at creation. God's promise already in Genesis 2:17 and 3:19 that the consequence of sin is death has come true in every generation since the time of Adam and Eve. So far only two people have been spared that dread consequence, Enoch (Genesis 5:24) and Elijah (2 Kings 2:1-12). Clearly anything that is a consequence of sin cannot be pleasant for us to contemplate, especially when what follows death lies so shrouded in mystery. But see how the apostle at once takes away our dread by focusing our attention on Christ and on his grace and on his work for our salvation! As filled with horror as the ultimate consequence of sin is, just so filled with hope and with joyous expectation is the gift of God that we have in Christ. His work for our salvation was perfect in every way. His gift of that salvation in the Word and sacraments is perfect in every way. His ultimate gift of eternal life after we have tasted the momentary consequences of sin in death will likewise be perfect in every way.

We see the pattern already in this life: We suffer loss, we get sick, and we experience tragedy. For the unbeliever all of these things are nothing but terrible, but for the Christian there is the recognition that it is through just such things that God draws us to himself. He weans us away from the impermanent, the unsteady, and the perishing things of this world so that we see more and more that he is our ultimate joy and our salvation. So it is with the whole matter of death. For the unbeliever it is something to be wished away, thought about as little as possible, and faced either with dread or with the impious and desperate hope that death will end everything. But for the Christian, as dread and as unnatural as it is, death has become the portal to eternal life and the entry gate to the bliss of paradise. After their fall, God blocked the way to the Garden of Eden so that Adam and Eve would not make a run to the tree of life, eat from it, and then be stuck in this world forever; they might in their fallen state have thought such a thing to be good for them. However, God in his infinite mercy kept them from the tree of life in the Garden of Eden so that they would finally die and enter by faith in the promised Savior into the real paradise of heaven.

So then what is death? As we experience it, it is the separation of the soul from the body. The body, as God promised in Genesis 3:19, returns to the dust from which Adam's body had originally been formed. But the soul lives on. Jesus said that in such a succinct way when the Sadducees, who denied the resurrection and life after death, quizzed him on the subject. Jesus, quoting from God's Word in the Old Testament (Exodus 3:6), said, "'I am the God of Abraham, the God of Isaac, and the God of Jacob'. . . . He is not the God of the dead but of the living" (Matthew 22:32).[1] The bodies of these men had been dead for over a thousand years. Yet, Jesus says that they are still alive.

St. Paul is again brief but clear in what we should expect at the time of this separation of the body and the soul. Speaking of his own approaching death, the apostle recognized that he would in death not only be separated from those he loved to serve but his body and soul—his physical earthly self and spiritual self—would also be separated. Moreover, that would be a good thing. He says,

> For to me, to live is Christ and to die is gain. If I am to go on living in the body, this will mean fruitful labor for me. Yet what shall

---

[1]As an interesting aside we may note that Jesus quotes from Exodus, not from other Old Testament books that more clearly speak of life after death. Why did he do that? It might be because the Sadducees accepted only the first five books of the Bible as authoritative; Jesus, of course, considered all of the books and each word in them God's own Word. But here he accommodated himself even to the unbelief of his enemies and used what they did accept to prove their error and to affirm what the rest of the Old Testament had to say on the subject.

> I choose? I do not know! I am torn between the two: I desire to depart and be with Christ, which is better by far; but it is more necessary for you that I remain in the body. (Philippians 1:21-24)

Notice again that there is no dread in Paul's voice. If he remains in this life, it is only so that he can be useful to those he served; but if he dies, he will still be with Christ. In fact, that was what he considered the core of his life here and now, to be with Christ. So, if after his body dies, he is still with Christ, what is there to fear? Quite the contrary, there is only reason to rejoice and even to look forward to the time when Christ will consider Paul's usefulness here at an end. When that time comes, Paul will still be with Christ. That's all that matters.

Yes, so "better by far" is it that when we consider our own death, Paul bids us think of it as he does and as it actually is:

> Now we know that if the earthly tent we live in is destroyed, we have a building from God, an eternal house in heaven, not built by human hands. Meanwhile we groan, longing to be clothed with our heavenly dwelling, because when we are clothed, we will not be found naked. For while we are in this tent, we groan and are burdened, because we do not wish to be unclothed but to be clothed with our heavenly dwelling, so that what is mortal may be swallowed up by life. Now it is God who has made us for this very purpose and has given us the Spirit as a deposit, guaranteeing what is to come. . . . We are confident, I say, and would prefer to be away from the body and at home with the Lord. So we make it our goal to please him, whether we are at home in the body or away from it. (2 Corinthians 5:1-9)

It is with the realization in mind that after death we will no longer be plagued with sin and all it consequences that we look forward to the day of our death, not as a day of gloom and defeat but as a day of victory. The Spirit assures us of that. He assures us of that in the very words that Paul writes as the verbally inspired Word of God. So certain is it, therefore, that the apostle invites us to sing with him his great hymn of praise and thanksgiving:

> When the perishable has been clothed with the imperishable, and the mortal with immortality, then the saying that is written will come true: "Death has been swallowed up in victory." "Where, O death, is your victory? Where, O death, is your sting?" The sting of death is sin, and the power of sin is the law. But thanks be to God! He gives us the victory through our Lord Jesus Christ. (1 Corinthians 15:54-57)

Do you notice in all of this the balance that the Scriptures strike for us? On the one hand, God's Word wants to remove from us all dread of death as we focus on Jesus and his gift of eternal life. On the other hand, however, the exact nature of that perfect life with Jesus in heaven is not described in very great detail. And why not? Were we to see perfectly even now into that perfect life, how could we be content with Paul to say, "For now it is fine for me to stay here so that I can be useful and serve"? So, with Paul we look forward to the day of victory, the day of our entering into the perfect bliss of heaven. But we do so without grumbling that we are still here. When the time comes, Jesus will call us to himself and we will be happy to hear his voice and follow him into the home he has prepared for us in heaven. For now we will be content to serve as he thinks it best for those around us, those that he loves and wants to love through our service still in this life.

So then, death is the separation of the soul from the body. The body returns to dust and the soul goes to be with Christ in perfect enjoyment. Here that enjoyment was always disturbed by our fallen condition, by temptations, and by sins and their consequences, but in heaven that is all past and gone. In heaven there is forever a perfect life with Christ. More than that we do not need to know. That's enough for us.

That takes care of all the questions we might want to ask, for example: How can the soul be happy without the body, since all the soul knows and experiences here it knows and experiences either through or in union with a body? How can we see him without eyes, hear his voice without ears or a physical brain? Indeed, how can we even think of joy or pleasure without physical senses? All of these are reduced to silly questions once we consider the facts presented to us in the Scriptures. God loved us enough to become man for us; Jesus loved us enough to suffer the torments of the damned on the cross for us. If God loved us that much already in eternity and then in the life and death of our Savior, is it possible to imagine that we will be disappointed in the ultimate realization and experience of his love in heaven? It is simply inconceivable that we will be disappointed. Rather, we will have eternity to appreciate what Paul meant when he wrote, "As it is written: 'No eye has seen, no ear has heard, no mind has conceived what God has prepared for those who love him'" (1 Corinthians 2:9). And so it is too that we listen in grateful thanksgiving to God for what he has told us about our death and its happy outcome: "'Blessed are the dead who die in the Lord from now on.' 'Yes,' says the Spirit, 'they will rest from their labor, for their deeds will follow them'" (Revelation 14:13).

Heaven

Just what is heaven like? We really would like to know. In its essence it is simply this: In heaven we will perfectly enjoy life with Christ and accordingly also with all the saints and angels who are there with us.

That life is eternal. In heaven we will never again experience death. It is important to remember the essential definition of death: Death is separation. In Genesis 3, when Adam and Eve sinned, they experienced the first kind of death, the death that is a separation from God in unbelief and rebellion. Horrible indeed was that separation. Just read the account again of their encounter with God after they had sinned. What do you see? You see fear as they hide from him, anger when he speaks to them, loathing of God and of each other as Adam seeks to pin the blame for his sin first on God, then on God's greatest gift to him, his wife.

Few indeed can say that they have never experienced in life this kind of death. Our sins too bring this kind of separation. In our guilt we hide from God and foolishly hope either that he did not see us or doesn't care enough to be bothered about our guilt. But then the sins come, as we say, home to roost. We suffer pain or loss. We get sick and lose loved ones. Conscience will not leave us alone. And so we get angry with God: "Why did you let this happen to me? It's all your fault! You could have prevented my folly! But now I suffer in shame! Yes, and it's also the fault of my parents/my spouse/my friends/society/my lousy job/demanding relatives!"

All of that is death, a separation from God brought about by our sin. But the whole purpose of the gospel from Genesis 3 to Revelation 22 is to show us the Savior who has removed that death, that separation, by his coming and by his death and resurrection for us and for our salvation. Often in this life that sweet message of the gospel has brought us to life, to real life, the life that trusts in the blood-bought forgiveness. We nevertheless prove our need for the gospel again and again when we return to death by further willful sin. But in it all Jesus keeps calling to us with life, just as he said, "I have come that they may have life, and have it to the full. I am the good shepherd. The good shepherd lays down his life for the sheep" (John 10:10,11).

In heaven, our life will never again experience this kind of death, this spiritual death of separation from God in rebellion and unbelief. That is no small blessing: Never again to be afraid of God or anything else; never again to feel the gnawing of conscience on the soul; never again to know the temptations that threaten to rip us away from the enjoyment of peace with God, peace with our own soul, and peace with those around us. So great will that blessing be that it is scarcely possible for us to imagine it in the here and now. St. Paul sums it up when he says shortly before his own death, "The Lord will rescue me from every evil attack and will bring me safely to his heavenly kingdom. To him be glory for ever and ever. Amen" (2 Timothy 4:18).

Just as heaven will be an eternal life without any more spiritual death, so it will also be eternal life without any physical death. For after all is said and done, physical death and all the sickness and pain that announce its advent are nothing more than the result of spiritual death. That's what God told Adam (Genesis 3:19). And that's what every cemetery witnesses to us each day. But with spiritual death gone, so too will physical death disappear together with all that announces its approach. Hunger and thirst, pain and sickness of every sort, these all are heralds of death; they announce its inevitability. While they may be satisfied or softened or put off for a while, they always return to declare, "You are fragile, you are frail, you are mortal; and the day is coming when need and pain will not be put off but will win the victory over the mortal body. As strong as you think you are and as wise, one day a tiny germ, a bit of cholesterol in the blood stream, or a microscopic virus will do you in." As that ancient gravestone put it so well: "Where you are, I once was; where I am, you too soon shall be!"

In heaven that is all past and gone, just as its causes of temptation and sin and guilt are gone. How tenderly, how beautifully, how perfectly that condition is described in the last book of the Bible:

> Never again will they hunger; never again will they thirst. The sun will not beat upon them, nor any scorching heat. For the Lamb at the center of the throne will be their shepherd; he will lead them to springs of living water. And God will wipe away every tear from their eyes. (Revelation 7:16,17)

The picture is perfect! Jesus is at its center. And we, each one of us, are the tender objects of the Father's love for the sake of the Lamb. His sacrifice has placed us, as it were, in the Father's lap as his dear children. Who would not long for such a blessed state! Who could keep from love unbounded for such a Savior, such a Father and, yes, such a Holy Spirit who has brought us even now to foretaste of that bliss in the enjoyment of his Word and sacraments!

That's what it means to have eternal life. It means the end of any spiritual or physical separation from God. It is the everlasting enjoyment of life as God intended it to be for us at creation and as Jesus perfectly restored it for us by all that he did in his work for our salvation. It's all there already in that beautiful summation of the gospel in John 3:16: "God so loved the world that he gave his one and only Son, that whoever believes in him shall not perish but have eternal life."

Anything else that we can say about heaven is really just another way of saying that it is eternal life with Jesus at its center. Thus, heaven is the everlasting experience of perfect joy. Jesus was fond of picturing that joy for us as the joy of a wedding banquet at which he is the Bridegroom and his church—each believer and all believers together—is the bride. He did that in some of his parables about heaven and about judgment day (e.g., Matthew 22:1-14; 25:1-13). In Revelation 21 John sees the church coming down out of heaven as a beautiful bride accompanied with shouts of joy and praise to God that the wedding banquet of the Lamb has begun and will never end.

Already in the Old Testament the theme of heaven as the experience of everlasting joy is expressed often, especially in the Psalms and in Isaiah. Psalm 16:11 tells us that even now we know such joy but that ultimately we will experience it fully and forever. David says, "You have made known to me the path of life; you will fill me with joy in your presence, with eternal pleasures at your right hand." The path of life is, of course, God's Word, in particular the message of the gospel. To the extent that we depart from it in this life, to that extent our experience of joy in God's presence is marred or lost. Ah, but in heaven such departures will be no more. And therefore the joy of heaven will be full, perfect in every way. Isaiah puts our entrance into heaven this way: "They will enter Zion with singing; everlasting joy will crown their heads. Gladness and joy will overtake them, and sorrow and sighing will flee away" (Isaiah 35:10).

To say much more about the nature of our joy in heaven is to attempt a description of the indescribable. For, again, how do we begin to imagine a condition in which all sin and temptation and guilt are forever vanquished together with their painful consequences? St. Paul bids us be content with the assurance that God has given us for that joyous and eternal life when he says,

> I consider that our present sufferings are not worth comparing with the glory that will be revealed in us. (Romans 8:18)

And,

> Though outwardly we are wasting away, yet inwardly we are being renewed day by day. For our light and momentary troubles

> are achieving for us an eternal glory that far outweighs them all. So we fix our eyes not on what is seen, but on what is unseen. For what is seen is temporary, but what is unseen is eternal. (2 Corinthians 4:16-18)

We of course would like to ask a thousand questions for which there can be only the most tentative of answers. Perhaps one of the most insistent is "Will we know one another in heaven?" Well, in heaven we will be in the company of all the saints and angels and together with them worship God in perfect harmony with God and with one another. So we certainly are not going to feel lonely there!

St. Paul may be giving us a bit of a clue for answering the question. In 1 Corinthians 13, when speaking of the Christian love that we should have and practice towards one another, he concludes by saying that the three greatest things in the Christian's life are faith, hope, and love. He says that the greatest of these is love. And why is that? Because faith in heaven is replaced with sight, and hope is replaced with the full and perfect experience of what we now hope for. However, love remains. Love always has an object, that is, someone who is loved. To be sure, in heaven the chief object of our love will be God himself. But it isn't love for God that Paul is talking about in this chapter; it is love for one another. That might bring us to conclude that we will know one another.

Or, we might think of it this way: The persons of the Holy Trinity perfectly and completely love one another, but that love that each has for the other overflows in a perfect love for us. That love is so abundant, so great, that the Trinity does not rest until it has worked out our salvation and that at great expense to God. If the love of God can so overflow to us, it is not a stretch to imagine that our perfected love for God in heaven will also overflow to one another. For after all, in heaven our love will no longer be marred by selfishness and stained by self-worship, jealousy, and envy. Together we will live and worship before the throne of the Lamb who will be all in all to us—and that love for him who is all in all need not be kept from extending out to those with whom we worship.

It is all the easier to think that way when we recall with what great emphasis Jesus called on us to love one another here on earth (e.g., John 15:9-17). That we should love one another is the second greatest commandment after the commandment to love God with all our heart and soul and mind and strength (Luke 10:25-37). Indeed, our love for one another is to be a reflection and a result of our love for God (1 John 3:11-24). There is no reason to imagine that God's pleasure in our love for one another would cease once our love for him is perfect in heaven.

Just how we will join with our loved ones there we cannot say, except to note that we will be perfectly happy with the arrangement. Jesus only tells us that our family relationships in heaven will be different (Matthew 22:30). But he doesn't spell out for us exactly what that means. Again, whatever those relationships are, they will be perfect and we will certainly not be disappointed.

Another question frequently asked is "Are their degrees of glory in heaven?" Why that question should bother people is something of a mystery. Given that we will be perfectly happy in heaven, one would think that that should be enough. Nevertheless, there are passages in the Bible that do speak of degrees of glory. Jesus, for example, tells the disciples that in heaven they will sit on thrones judging the twelve tribes of Israel (Matthew 19:28). And indeed the apostles and the patriarchs, or the prophets of the Old Testament, are pictured in the book of Revelation as seated on thrones around the throne of the Lamb (e.g., 4:10; 5:8).

St. Paul puts the matter into somewhat clearer perspective when he tell us that there will be differences in heaven, just as there are differences on earth; he points to the variety of planets and plants and animals. Then he concludes, "The sun has one kind of splendor, the moon another and the stars another; and star differs from star in splendor. So will it be with the resurrection of the dead" (1 Corinthians 15:41,42; cf. also Daniel 12:3). One star is capable of shining only as fully as it has the capacity to shine; so in heaven it may be that some are capable of a greater shining, so to speak, than others. A half gallon bucket of water can only hold a half gallon; when it is full, it is full—even if there is another bucket that can and does contain a whole gallon of water. The point is that whatever degrees of glory there are in heaven, no one is going to be jealous or envious of someone else; and no one is going to look down on another either.

The bottom line and the ultimate answer to all of our questions about heaven is simply this:

> How great is the love the Father has lavished on us, that we should be called children of God! And that is what we are! . . . Dear friends, now we are children of God, and what we will be has not yet been made known. But we know that when he appears, we shall be like him, for we shall see him as he is. Everyone who has this hope in him purifies himself, just as he is pure. (1 John 3:1-3)

If we are God's dear children, and if we shall indeed see Jesus as he is in all of his love and grace and mercy, then it is more sure and certain than life itself: We will not be disappointed! Let us then cling with ever-greater joy and delight to his precious Word and sacraments by which he will bring us to our blessed end and that glorious goal!

One might think of it this way: In his Word God lets us peek through a keyhole at things indescribable and eternal. We see Jesus, the almighty and eternal God veiled in flesh in the weakness of the manger and on the cross. We gaze up into heaven at his ascension, when he does not leave us but withdraws only from our sight. In it all we peek through the keyhole at God's essence as the God of perfect justice and ineffable grace and mercy. We do not see his essence fully but only so much of it as we can absorb in faith created by his Word. The same is true in God's description of heaven in his Word. We get a glimpse of eternity, of perfect harmony with our own souls, with him, and with one another. We get just a glimmer of a glance at joy that knows no end; we look through the keyhole provided by his Word. But that's enough. "Now we see but a poor reflection as in a mirror; then we shall see face to face. Now I know in part; then I shall know fully, even as I am fully known" (1 Corinthians 13:12).

Hell

Sadly, not everyone will end up experiencing that eternal joy with Christ and the saints and the angels. For as real as heaven is for those who die trusting in the victory Christ won over our sin and our death, just so real is the hell that Jesus said was "prepared for the devil and his angels" (Matthew 25:41). To that place/condition of eternal torment go all those who have not believed the message of the gospel.

What the Bible tells us about hell is just as serious as what it tells us about heaven. It is a favorite trick of the devil, one that he uses with great success, to seduce people into thinking that God would never send anyone into eternal torment. People like to think like that when they are looking for an easy escape from struggle against sin or against a condemning conscience.

One practice all too common these days that makes it easy for those living in their sins to dismiss thoughts of hell's reality is a church funeral for people who have openly lived contrary to God's law and apart from his gospel. What an insult to God and his Word! How will those who conduct such funerals ever answer on the day of judgment? For they have proclaimed to all attending that God is a joker whose Word means nothing. They have built iron doors on hearts where the

Holy Spirit would pound with the law to work a repentance that longs for forgiveness in the gospel. But why bother with repentance? Why bother with a Christian struggle in this life? Why bother with the gospel? If after death even those who despised the law and treated with contempt the great sacrifice of Christ end up in the lap of the Father and in the arms of the Son they despised, then the whole of God's Word is worthy of contempt!

No, it will not do to dismiss what God has to say about hell. Rather, the Christian should pay heed lest he too be deceived into thinking that God is not serious about his Word. He should pay heed lest he grow careless in his Christian struggle. He should pay heed lest he become indifferent to the mission of the church and, therefore, of each Christian to share the gospel at home and through all the world, that souls may be delivered from hell for heaven by its saving message. For just as the Christian struggle makes little sense if there is no hell (after all, the loss of heaven may not be all that bad if the alternative is nothingness), so the sharing of the gospel won't be all that urgent for those who imagine that there is no hell from which the gospel delivers us.

What then is hell? It is by definition eternal death, that is, an eternal separation from God's grace and mercy. As long as we are alive in this world we can never be completely separated from God's goodness. For, as Jesus said, God "causes his sun to rise on the evil and the good, and sends rain on the righteous and the unrighteous" (Matthew 5:45). Every breath we take is evidence of God's goodness to all. Indeed, each day of our lives is a gift of God intended to point us to the purpose of life, namely, that we should seek him and ultimately be found by him in his Word.

In hell all that is good about life is gone, gone forever, in the death that is not nonexistence but, rather, eternal separation from God's goodness and any possibility of grace. The Bible describes that separation in most graphic terms. Isaiah speaks of it as an eternal fire that is never quenched; that is, those there are never fully annihilated so that the fire would go out at the end of their suffering (Isaiah 66:24). Jesus tells us that those in hell are in a darkness in which they weep and gnash their teeth; people weep when they are in pain; they gnash their teeth when their pain knows no escape or when in rage and frustration they must realize that they have no one to blame for their inescapable agony but themselves (Matthew 8:12).

Like Isaiah, Jesus tells us that such torment is as eternal as heaven is for the blessed (Matthew 25:41,46; Mark 9:48). Most explicit is the description of hell and its misery in Revelation 14:10,11, where it is described as the experiencing of God's anger unmixed in a torment of fire and brimstone that allows for no rest day or night.

Writers and artists ever since have not been lacking in their depictions of that terror described in God's Word. Dante, for example, in *The Divine Comedy,* imagines that the inscription over the entry to hell reads, "Abandon hope all you who enter here." And in another place he calls hell that place where "there is no hope of hope." How graphic! To have no hope is quite bad enough; to have no hope of hope is hopelessness squared! He has captured well at least a part of hell's essence. Michelangelo and Rembrandt, to mention only two, have likewise graphically depicted in their paintings the seriousness of God in the last judgment, both in the exaltation of the saints and in the terror of the damned.

Let no one be deceived with the vain imagination that God is not serious about his Word. Let no one lull himself to sleep with the notion that because God is a loving God, he therefore could never send anyone into hell. Let no one foolishly think that after death impenitent sinners will still have a chance for repentance and entrance into heaven or at the worst will only experience annihilation. That's not what God's Word says, says repeatedly and emphatically. For the God of love is also a God of justice. His justice and his love were both fully satisfied on the cross where Jesus suffered the torments of the damned in our place and for the redemption of all. But those who reject that price so beyond measure and his suffering so horrible reject also its saving benefit. And why should that surprise anyone? So many of the teachings of the Bible require a miracle of the Holy Spirit for us to believe them, not least the heart of the gospel itself. But this teaching requires no such miracle. That God would not endure his Son's sacrifice so great and his own love so beyond measure to be spurned and treated with contempt should require no great brilliance to understand! The surprising thing is that the devil is so successful in getting people to think otherwise!

Not wishing to dwell too long on so tragic a subject, let the reader who wants more ponder the descriptions that Jesus himself gives of hell. Consider the torment of the man in hell that Jesus talks about in the account of the rich man and poor Lazarus (Luke 16:19-31). The rich man is in torment made worse by the sight of Lazarus in heaven; he is in hell because he showed his worship of his wealth instead of living a life of faith that would have shown compassion to poor Lazarus. Not even a drop of water will be given to relieve his torment. Consider Jesus' parables in Matthew 25. Each of them speaks of the certainty of hell for those who reject the gospel message. Read of the woe that Jesus speaks over those who had so many opportunities to hear his Word and repent but who rejected those opportunities so graciously and so often given (Matthew 23).

Again, we may have many questions that we cannot answer, questions that serve little purpose beyond diverting our attention from the chief point of all of the Bible's descriptions of the real and eternal torment that is hell. And what is that chief point? Two passages capture the essence best: Matthew 10:28 and Philippians 2:12,13. While encouraging his disciples not to lose heart when persecution comes and not to be afraid even of those who may kill them, Jesus says, "Do not be afraid of those who kill the body but cannot kill the soul. Rather, be afraid of the One who can destroy both soul and body in hell" (Matthew 10:28). Tremble, lest by ignoring and finally casting his Word aside you lose its saving benefit and end up in that torment intended originally only for the devil and his angels. What Jesus has to tell us about the reality and the horror of hell should serve as a warning not to treat lightly any of his Word. For God takes all of his Word seriously.

St. Paul makes the same point so briefly yet so emphatically when he tells us, "Continue to work out your salvation with fear and trembling, for it is God who works in you to will and to act according to his good purpose" (Philippians 2:12,13). Given the context of all that Paul says not only in this epistle but also in all of his writings, he is certainly not telling us here to earn our salvation. What he is telling us is that God has taken great care to "work in us" that faith which trusts his Word and he impels us to put it into practice in our lives. What he is telling us is that we should be very careful not to cast aside his work in us either by self-righteousness, which is trust in our own merits, or by imagining that since he has redeemed us we can now sin boldly. Both of those temptations are ever present and always threaten. And it is only by focusing always on what God says in his Word and sacraments that the Holy Spirit will give us the strength to resist and to overcome these deadly temptations. As soon as we lose that sense of dread, the dread of losing so great a salvation, just so soon do we begin to treat God and his Word carelessly and finally with the contempt even of unbelief.

Therefore, the bottom line for us in what God says to us about hell will always be a dread of going there and a corresponding love for our Savior and the desire to become ever more attached to his Word by which we are rescued from its eternal torment. Yes, and it will direct us as well to the great mission of the church, that of carrying into all the world the gospel by which souls are rescued from hell. Again, endless questions about details not provided in his Word only serve to distract us from the point made so powerfully in these two passages and so often elsewhere in his Word.

The Last Day and final judgment

Closely connected to all that God has to say to us about death and heaven and hell are his words to us about the end of the world, its Last Day and the final judgment. As certain as death and heaven and hell are, just so certain is it that one day the world as we know it will end. Jesus often promised it. Even as he ascended into heaven the angels sealed his visible departure from the disciples with the promise: "This same Jesus, who has been taken from you into heaven, will come back in the same way you have seen him go into heaven" (Acts 1:11). In so many of his parables Jesus spoke of his return on the Last Day, of the final judgment, and of its significance for the whole of our lives on earth. Read especially Matthew 22–25. So much of what Jesus tells us there is intended to prepare us for our end in death and our appearance on the Last Day before his throne of judgment.

Again, with this topic, as with the subjects of death and heaven and hell, we often have more questions than answers. For just as our death takes place in time but plunges us into eternity, so also the Last Day begins with a point in time but quickly passes all of humanity into eternity. In eternity, time and space either cease to be relevant or have different definitions than we can grasp in the here and now. So the Holy Spirit in his Word accommodates himself to our limitations. He gives us a number of pointers to the reality of the Last Day, to foretaste of it and of the certainty of its coming.

In the Old Testament, for example, there are the promises of the destruction of Jerusalem. Ezekiel foretold it often and graphically (e.g., Ezekiel 7). And the prophecies were fulfilled to the letter in 586 B.C. (cf. 2 Kings 25; 2 Chronicles 36; and Daniel's great prayer in Daniel 9). Likewise, Jesus foretold the destruction of Jerusalem again (e.g., Matthew 13:1,2; Luke 19:41-44). That prophecy too was fulfilled to the letter in the year A.D. 70 when Titus destroyed Jerusalem. The point is that just as those promises of God were fulfilled, so too will the promise be carried out that one day the world will end and all will be judged. Indeed, so often when Jesus speaks of the coming destruction of Jerusalem, he seamlessly mixes in elements of the destruction of the world on the Last Day: the destruction of Jerusalem in 586 B.C. and again in A.D. 70 and indeed all the other prophecies of the destruction of one kingdom and nation after another, all of these serve as a prelude and prefiguring of the destruction on the Last Day. What then can we say about that Last Day and last judgment?

First of all, a Last Day will most surely come, and on that day Christ will return visibly just as he promised (Matthew 26:64; Mark 13:26; Acts 1:11; 1 Thessalonians 4:16; Titus 2:13).

Second, when he returns, all the dead will rise and all will appear before his throne for judgment (John 5:28,29; Matthew 25:32; Acts 24:15; 2 Corinthians 5:10). On that day all will be seen with bodies and souls reunited. Is this judgment any different from the judgment of those who died before the Last Day? Is it somehow different from that judgment received in the hour of their death? It is certainly no different in the verdict; those who died in unbelief and went to hell will receive the same verdict on the Last Day. Likewise, those who died and went to heaven need not fear a reversal of the blessed verdict they received in the hour of death (Hebrews 9:27; Revelation 14:13).

If the verdict is the same, then what point is there in this judgment on the Last Day? The best that we can say is that the first judgment was an individual judgment. But the judgment on the Last Day is Christ's great triumph day when all will see him and worship him, even those who are doomed to eternal destruction (Philippians 2:10,11). The worship, of course, of those condemned will not be the joyful worship of the believers. Rather, it will be the worship of despair with the confession that God is just in their condemnation. But it is a day of great triumph and joy for both the saints in heaven and the believers who are still living on earth on that Last Day. For on that day all will see with their own eyes the final fulfillment of all that God has promised in his Word. That was the confidence of Job (Job 19:25,26). That was the expectation of Paul (1 Thessalonians 4:16; 2 Thessalonians 2:8-12). And that was the repeated promise of Jesus (e.g., John 6:40).

We may summarize the Last Day and the final judgment this way:

1. A day is certainly coming on which all human history will end, on which day Christ will return visibly and all the dead will rise with bodies and souls reunited to appear before him for judgment (John 5:22-29; 1 Corinthians 15:52).
2. At that judgment those who have believed the gospel will have their good works that they did as a result of faith put on display for all to see; those who rejected the gospel will be publicly con-

demned and their failure to produce fruits of faith will be presented as evidence of their unbelief (Matthew 25:31-46; John 5:28,29; 2 Corinthians 5:10; Revelation 20:12).

3. Then those thus judged will go to their reward, the believers to an eternal bliss in heaven and the unbelievers to an eternal torment with the devil and his angels in hell (Daniel 12:2; Matthew 25:31-46; Luke 9:26; John 3:16-36; 6:35-65; 2 Corinthians 5:10).

It is important to note that in so many of these passages, which speak of the judgment on the Last Day, our works in this life receive prominent mention. For that's the nature of a courtroom: not one's invisible faith is at issue but the visible works are the evidence introduced at trial. To be sure, hypocrites and unbelievers produced works too that on the outside looked very good. But the judge of the heart sees and knows if those works were the fruits and the results of faith in him or if they had some other motive. Only those visible works that are the results of invisible faith are praised.

We see that with special clarity in the great parable of the last judgment in Matthew 25:31-46. Notice how Jesus addresses those rewarded with heaven. He calls them to enter "the kingdom prepared for you since the creation of the world," that is, before they were ever born or had done anything to merit heaven. Unlike a human court in which the evidence is introduced and then the verdict pronounced, the reverse happens on the Last Day: first comes the verdict, then the evidence that demonstrates the justice of the verdict—in the heart was faith, in the life was the proof of it.

Then notice the verdict over those condemned. They are sentenced to eternal punishment "prepared for the devil and his angels." It was never God's good and gracious will that they go there; it was intended only for the devil and his angels. But the condemned go there—not because they never did anything that appeared good in the eyes of the world but because "you did not do [it] for me." That is, whatever visible works they may have had, they did not come about as a result of a relationship with Christ—as visible proofs of an invisible faith.

To underscore the point that it is not the works that save us but that they are introduced at the last judgment as visible proofs of an invisible faith, we note what Jesus says also in John 5:19-30. Read the entire section and you will see that eternal life is clearly the gift of God through faith that embraces the Savior. Then note especially verse 29 when he speaks of the resurrection and judgment on the Last Day. He says, "Those who have done good will rise to live, and those who have done evil will rise to be condemned."[2] This Jesus says *after* he has already made it clear that eternal life is a gift. However, in the judgment that gift received in faith is shown as having results in life, namely, the doing of good.

Notice too in all of these descriptions of the last judgment no mention is made of the sins of those entering heaven. Why not? They have all been forgiven! What point is there in mentioning them? They have been washed away in the blood of the Lamb, washing which the believers enjoyed day after day in this life and which they will enjoy fully and perfectly in heaven (Revelation 7:9-17). Thus, while the faithful mourn in repentance their whole life long over their sins and failures to perfectly reflect their faith, at the last judgment all such mourning will end. For there will be no more sins and no more temptations to sin in heaven but only perfect joy over the redemption won for them by Christ and received by them here in faith.

What a day that will be for each believer! Just think of it: All that was suffered silently and without any comfort save that of the gospel itself will be exposed to the light for praise from the Savior. All that was done without the slightest hint of gratitude in this life will hear the praise of God before the whole world. All that was done simply because it was in accord with God's Word but that at the time seemed so pointless and in vain, all of it will receive from him for whom it was done the highest acclamation. Oh to be sure, none of these things were ever done perfectly or even with a perfect motive, but at the last judgment that won't matter. The work will be held up as a perfect jewel, a diamond, and a sapphire, fit only for the praises of the Lamb who sits on the throne.

That's what St. Paul is talking about in 1 Corinthians 15, his great resurrection chapter. To mention just the point most pertinent here, the apostle speaks of the difference between our bodies now and our bodies at the resurrection and in heaven. He says,

> The body that is sown is perishable, it is raised imperishable; it is sown in dishonor, it is raised in glory; it is sown in weakness, it

---

[2]For those who can read Greek, their study of the language will be repaid in full with this verse alone, translated more literally: "those who were *doing* good things" as contrasted with "those who were *practicing* evil things." Those who were going into heaven did good things and they are mentioned, but those who *practiced* evil had that evil as their way of life. They worked at it, so to speak. They had something/someone other than Christ as the organizing and motivating principle of life. St. Paul in 2 Corinthians 5:10 uses this same verb of "practicing" for both those acquitted and those condemned (cf. also Galatians 5:21).

> is raised in power; it is sown a natural body, it is raised a spiritual body. . . . For the trumpet will sound, the dead will be raised imperishable, and we will be changed. For the perishable must clothe itself with the imperishable, and the mortal with immortality. When the perishable has been clothed with the imperishable, and the mortal with immortality, then the saying that is written will come true: "Death has been swallowed up in victory." (15:42-44,52-54)

So then, at the resurrection on the Last Day all that is wrong with our bodies and, yes, with our souls too will disappear. To put it another way, the body and soul will together forever be set free from the sinful nature that infected them from the moment of conception (original sin) and that showed that corruption throughout earthly life with sins of thought, word, and deed (actual sin). All that is wrong with us as a result of sin, including mortality, will disappear on the Last Day—the sin forgiven and its consequences forever destroyed. That's the difference between a "natural body" and a "spiritual body" in the resurrection: still a body, but minus its sins and limitations.

When will all of this happen? When will the Last Day finally come? We certainly reject all the foolish attempts that have been made to pinpoint an actual date for Jesus' return. Jesus himself warns against such folly and does so emphatically when he declares that even he (in the state of humiliation of his human nature) does not choose to know the exact date (Mark 13:32). It isn't difficult to conceive of reasons why God does not choose to tell us the exact date of Jesus' return. If he did, we can well imagine that people would put off repentance until that day promised—by which time, of course, the gospel would have disappeared together with any faith in it. It is for the same reason that he does not reveal to us the day of our death: we simply are too perverse in our nature to handle that knowledge with wisdom!

So instead of telling us the hour of our death or the date of the Last Day, he tells us instead always to be ready, to watch for his coming. He urges that repeatedly in almost every instance when he speaks of the Last Day (e.g., Matthew 24–25; Mark 13; Luke 12:40; 21:36). The apostles make the same plea: Watch (e.g., 1 Corinthians 15:52). St. Peter (2 Peter 3) is especially graphic in his call to us to watch and be prepared always for that day. For it will come so swiftly ("like a thief," i.e., without an announcement or warning) that there will then be no time to prepare, to repent, or to perform good works as fruits of faith. In an instant all that we know of time and space, of landscapes and geography will disappear and be destroyed or transformed.

Though we do not have an announced date for the Last Day, God in his Word has given us enough signs of its coming for us to know that it indeed is drawing near. Jesus tells us (Matthew 24:37-39) that in the days before his coming most people will behave just as they did before the coming of the flood in the days of Noah; that is, they will be busy with business, with enjoying themselves, with family and friends, giving no thought to the end of all things and the coming judgment. They will have their god: self and self-interest. In the midst of all their self-indulgence there will be what there always is when people live only for self: strife and wars, confusion in society and culture, betrayal of friends and family, and not least, opposition to and hatred of the gospel; there will be heresy even where the gospel is still heard (Mark 13:22; 1 Timothy 4:1; 1 John 2:18). Yes, some of the most horrible errors will appear inside of the church itself with the persistence of the Antichrist (2 Thessalonians 2:1-12) in leading people away from trust in Christ to trust in his own deceiving wonders and invented doctrines.[3]

To be sure, most of these things have been happening and that to an ever-greater degree since the days of Adam and Eve. Nevertheless, as they happen in our day they serve as a reminder that we will never have a heaven on earth as we know it now; they warn us against the folly of imagining that somehow the church can transform the world into an earthly paradise. Yes, and they warn us that the very effort is akin to the building of the Tower of Babel (Genesis 11), which also brought down the wrath of God on people who thought they could do without him.

There is, however, one promise of Christ about the timing of the end of the world that is all but unique to our time. Jesus said,

> This gospel of the kingdom will be preached in the whole world as a testimony to all nations, and then the end will come. I tell you the truth, this generation will certainly not pass away until all these things have happened. Heaven and earth will pass away, but my words will never pass away. (Matthew 24:14,34,35)

Jesus gives the assurance that even in the worst of times his gospel and the church will endure. However, the especially telling feature of the promise is that he will not return until that Word has been proclaimed in all the world. That promise has largely been fulfilled in our age; it would be difficult to find places on earth where the message has

---

[3]Cf. chapter 15, p. 463 and the footnote.

not penetrated at one time or another and to one degree or another. Then he adds that significant remark that the generation to which he addressed these words would not end until he returned. In Jesus' way of looking at time, there are but two generations: the generation of promise before his birth and the generation of fulfillment that ends with his coming again.

So what then is left to happen before all of his promises to this generation have been fulfilled? Nothing! It is for us as Jesus said: Watch! You do not know the day or the hour. Nor is it your business to know it. Your business is to be ready when he comes, be that in the hour of death or on the day of his second coming—the day of resurrection and judgment. That watching consists of a faithful hearing of his Word. It is a life of repentance that laments sin. It is a life that rejoices to hear the Savior's voice in the gospel of redemption and forgiveness. It is a life that as a result of the love of God, of his immeasurable grace and mercy in Christ, strives to live a life that loves God and his Word and serves our neighbor. It is a life that shuns, therefore, all that is contrary to that Word and lives to receive again and again the blood-bought grace and forgiveness of the Redeemer. Such a one can always pray with St. John the last words of the Bible: "Come, Lord Jesus" (Revelation 22:20).

So we look and long for his coming. For then it will finally all come together and Jesus will be seen for what he has always been: All in all! Then finally we will sing and say—and actually and fully mean it: "Behold, he has done all things well!" Then we will see Jesus! He found us naked and clothed us with his own righteousness. He found us dead and breathed life and life eternal into us. He saw us starving and fed us with himself. He came to us mortally wounded and poured healing salve into all our wounds. He looked on us weeping and in despair and that through our own fault and then spoke to us powerful words of comfort. He did it all. He did it all by his work and by his Word. Eternity will indeed have to last forever to give us sufficient time to thank and praise him for it all!

Millennialism

Together with the folly of trying to fix the day of Christ's return we must note as well the various false teachings of those who expect a glorious rule of Christ in an earthly kingdom either before his final coming or during an interim between his second coming and the Last Day. Those who teach these things are called *chiliasts* or *millennialists,* from words that mean one thousand years. Their teaching comes from an attempt to understand especially Revelation 20 in a literal manner. If it were to be understood in a literal manner, one might expect that all of the millennialists would teach the same thing, but such is by no means the case. We cannot here examine every millennial theory that has been proposed on the basis of Revelation 20. We can only sum them up.

Some teach that Jesus will return visibly before the end of the world and set up an earthly kingdom where he will rule together with the believers. After that period of time, that millennium, the world will end.

Some teach that there will be a millennium of peace and prosperity for the church on earth and at its end Christ will return.

Some teach that there will be a *rapture* before the end of the world, when all the believers will be taken up into heaven and the earth will be left to rot and ruin until Christ returns on the Last Day.

Each of these errors depends on a high degree of imagination in the reading of Revelation 20, an imagination that ignores or neglects all of the clear passages of the Bible that we have noted in this chapter which describe the final judgment and the Last Day. Revelation 20 needs to be read in the light of the clear passages of the Bible that speak of these things.[4]

If we keep in mind all of those clear passages, we will come to understand that Revelation 20, like so much of the book of Revelation, contains one picture after another of the end of the world and the return of Christ. The thousand years of Revelation 20 is really the entire New Testament period that ends on the Last Day. It is during this period of time from Christ's ascension until his return that the devil is bound, at least to this extent that he cannot prevent the preaching of the gospel and its saving work of creating faith. Then, as the end approaches, it will be as Peter and Paul prophesied in 2 Peter 2,3 and 2 Timothy 3:1-5. So wicked will people become and so corrupt will their teaching be that it will be all but impossible for the gospel to be proclaimed or for people to believe it. When that happens, then Christ will keep his promise that his Word will endure until the end—he will return for the vindication of his Word and the final rescue of his church!

The first resurrection spoken of in Revelation 20:4-6, likewise, must be understood in the light of the rest of what the Bible says on the subject of the resurrection. Jesus tells us about the first and second resurrection in John 5:19-29. The first resurrection is the one that takes place when through the message of the gospel we are

---

[4]For the "rules" that we use for the correct understanding of the Bible, cf. chapter 4 and the section on rules of interpretation, p. 69-83.

raised from the spiritual death of unbelief to the life of faith in Christ's redeeming work. As long as we continue in that faith, Christ rules as King and governs all things for our benefit (Romans 8:28-39; 1 Corinthians 15:20-27; Ephesians 1:3-14). Then, when he returns visibly on the Last Day, the second resurrection is made manifest—the resurrection of all the dead, the visible reuniting of the body and the soul at the great judgment day spoken of in Revelation 20:11-15.

If we read all that the Bible has to say about death and resurrection, about the return of Christ and the final judgment, there will be no need for fanciful interpretations of Revelation 20 or of anything else in the book of Revelation. The purpose of the book is not to give free rein to wild imagination. The purpose of the book is clearly stated in the first three chapters and again in the last chapter of the book. The purpose is the same as that of all of the descriptions of the Last Day—to urge us to be faithful to the Word of God, to cling to the gospel in the face of all that opposes it, and to strive to live in accord with the Word of God in spite of all the temptations to abandon the struggle before God himself brings our struggles to an end either through death or by his visible return on the Last Day.

Often those occupied with millennial teachings join with those teaching the notion that one of the signs that their imagined millennium is beginning will be the conversion of all Jewish people to Christianity. That false teaching too is based on a reading of one passage in the Bible that is ripped out of its context and out of the context of all the rest that the Bible teaches about conversion. The passage is Romans 11:26, in which Paul says that finally all Israel will be saved. But read the whole chapter, indeed the entire epistle to the Romans. It is clear that the Israel to be saved is the church, consisting of believing Jews and Gentiles. That's exactly the way that Jesus spoke of Israel in John 8:31-51, where he rejected the idea of his unbelieving Jewish hearers that their physical descent from Abraham is what made them heirs of heaven. St. Paul declares the same thing in all of Romans 9 (cf. especially vv. 6-8).

It is interesting to note that those occupied with assorted millennial teachings are rarely occupied with anything else in the Bible. If we listen to them, we will hear one word from the Bible and a hundred words spun from their own imaginations. Sadly they miss most of the point of all that the Bible in the many passages that we have noted above has to say. When the Bible speaks of the hour of our death and of the day of judgment, the emphasis is always onc and the same: Watch! Watch by being faithful to all of God's Word.

To put it most succinctly: What the Bible tells us about death, about heaven, about hell, and about the Last Day and Christ's return has no different purpose than all of the rest of God's Word. The purposes for which God gave us his Word are those we have repeated throughout this book.[5]

God gave us his Word to bring us to faith in Christ, a faith that leads us from spiritual death to spiritual life, from this life to eternal life.

God gave us his Word to show us how to live here in this world as a reflection of our gratitude to him for his gift of salvation through the gospel of forgiveness won for us by our only Savior, Jesus Christ.

God gave us his Word to show forth the glory of his own name, especially in the name and work of the Savior.

A departure from a clear focus on these purposes that God has given to his Word inevitably ends in false doctrine that harms faith, that deflects our attention away from the life that we should live in accord with his Word, and that detracts from God's name of Savior. That point too we have emphasized repeatedly in this work. All false doctrine in one way or another

- is contrary to the clear teaching of the Scriptures
- detracts from the glory of Christ as Savior
- fails to comfort the penitent or fails to warn the impenitent

And so we end this work and our consideration of eschatology, of the last things, as we began the work and have pursued it now to its conclusion:

May Jesus Christ be praised by the faithful teaching of his Word and by our faithful clinging to that Word.

May Jesus Christ, who loved us and gave himself for us, be praised.

May Jesus Christ—our God and Savior here, the content of our faith now, and the goal of our life with him forever in heaven—be praised!

---

[5]Cf. chapter 2 for a more complete consideration of the purposes of the Bible.

Scripture Index

Lutheran Confessions Index

Subject Index